INTERNATIONAL MIGRATION LAW

Revised Second Edition

by

Richard Plender

MARTINUS NIJHOFF PUBLISHERS
DORDRECHT / BOSTON / LONDON

Library of Congress Cataloging in Publication Data

Plender, Richard.
   International migration law.

   Includes index.
   1. Emigration and immigration law. I. Title.
K3275.P54 1987   341.4'84   87-22008
ISBN 90-247-3604-8

Published by Martinus Nijhoff Publishers,
P.O. Box 163, 3300 AD Dordrecht, The Netherlands

Sold and distributed in the U.S.A. and Canada
by Kluwer Academic Publishers,
101 Philip Drive, Norwell, MA 02061, U.S.A.

Sold in the U.K. and Ireland
by Kluwer Law, part of Kluwer Publishing Ltd.,
1 Harlequin Avenue, Brentford,
Middlesex TW 8 9EW, U.K.

In all other countries, sold and distributed
by Kluwer Academic Publishers Group,
P.O. Box 322, 3300 AH Dordrecht, The Netherlands

INTERNATIONAL MIGRATION LAW

To
Sophie Clare

Contents

Preface

Since the publications of the first edition of this book, significant changes have taken place in the rules of law affecting migration. The principles governing the right to leave any country including one's own have been profoundly influenced by the process initiated in the Final Act of the Helsinki Conference and by the work recently undertaken for the United Nations Economic and Social Council. A new Protocol on Multiple Nationality has been concluded. The International Labour Organization has promoted several new instruments, including the Migrant Workers (Supplementary Provisions) Convention and Recommendation of 1975, the Maintenance of Social Security Rights Convention of 1982 and the European Agreement on the Provision of Medical Care of 1980. At the same time it has ceased to urge its members to ratify one or two older agreements and it has taken a leading role in the movement to reduce the volume and alter the character of labour migration in Southern Afria. The Draft Convention on Territorial Asylum came to nothing; but the debates on the proposal yielded valuable material and the case-law on the Geneva Convention and New York Protocol has expanded rapidly, especially at the European level. A Protocol on Refugee Seamen has been adopted; and within the Council of Europe several Recommendations have been made, together with the Declaration on Territorial Asylum and the Agreement of 1980 on Transfer of Responsibility for Refugees.

The European Communities have doubled in size. The principles of Community law affecting migration have been given new immediacy as a result of the judgment of the European Court in *Van Duyn,* among other cases. Five new Directives have been issued and two new Regulations made, apart from the three Treaties and Acts of Accession. Within the Council of Europe, a new Convention on Social Security and one on Migrant Workers have entered into force, although the parties remain limited in number. In Africa, two new economic communities have been formed; and the Banjul Charter has been concluded, with provisions addressing the rights involved in migration. The Andean Pact has expanded its principles governing the movement of labour and the principles applicable in the Caribbean have been modernized, with the formation of the new Community.

The changes wrought by bilateral arrangements and national law during the last fifteen years have been so large as to defy synthesis: but two trends can be detected. The first is a pervasive 'restrictionism' in immigration control, which has entailed the modification or termination of numerous labour agreements and establishment conventions and the revision of the immigration laws of most of the jurisdictions here considered. The second is the increasing penetration of international law in this area, illustrated by the effect on British nationality law of the Joint Declaration on Hong Kong or the convergence of Colombian, Ecuadorian and Peruvian aliens laws in accordance with the Code of Practice drafted in pursuance of the Pact of Cartagena.

These changes are reflected in the structure of the new edition of this book. Less space is devoted to dispelling the notion that the control of nationality and migration falls within the reserved domain. The qualifications that need to be made to that assertion are now so clear that they speak for themselves. A chapter has been added on the Right to Leave any Country including One's Own; and there are fresh chapters on Freedom of Movement in the European Communities, on Council of Europe Conventions, and on Other Regional Arrangements (Benelux, the two West African Communities, the Central African Community, the Caribbean Community, the Andean Pact and the Nordic Community). There is also a new chapter on the Expulsion of Aliens. To make space for these, the chapters dealing with the territorial application of immigration laws, with prohibited immigrants and with naturalization have been omitted; but an attempt has been made to incorporate elsewhere some of the material contained in them. Of the chapters carried over from the first edition, all have been completely re-written apart from Chapters II (Historical Perspectives) and V (Exceptional Duties to Admit Aliens); and those two have been revised. In place of a single bibliography at the end of the book, there are now separate bibliographies at the end of each chapter; for the literature on the subject has become abundant. A new table of treaties and other instruments has been compiled and the more important instruments are printed in whole or in part in a companion volume, *Basic Documents on International Migration Law*. The latter are to be made available in a separate publication, for the convenience of students and practitioners.

Grateful acknowledgement is made of a grant from the Nuffield Foundation which made it possible to engate as research assistant for six months Mr Simon Ripley, LL.B., whose diligence, skill and irrepressible good humour are much appreciated by the author. Warm thanks are also given to Mrs Kathleen Fedouloff, who produced several drafts of the text and tables on her word processor, with her customary efficiency and care and with extraordinary forbearance.

The law is stated as at 31 December 1986, although it had been possible to take account of a few major developments during the course of production.

Abbreviations

A	Atlantic Reporter (United States)
A 2d.	Atlantic Reporter (second series) (United States)
A.B.	*Administratiefrechtelijke Beslissingen*
A.B.A.J.	American Bar Association Journal
A.C.	Appeals Cases (United Kingdom)
A.C.F.	*Arrêté du conseil fédéral suisse*
A.C.W.S.	All Canada Weekly Summaries
A.D.	Annual Digest of Public International Law Cases
Adm. Law Bull.	Administrative Law Bulletin
A.F.D.I.	*Annuaire français de droit interntional*
Aff. soc. int.	*Affaires de la société internationale*
AGPS	Australian Government Publishing Service
A.I.R.	All India Reports
Ann. A.A.A.	*Annuaire de l'association des anciens auditeurs de l'académie de droit international de la Haye*
Ann. dr.	*Annales de droit* (Belgium)
Ann. Eur.	*Annuaire Européen*
Ann. fac. giur.	*Annali della facolta giuridica*
Ann. I.D.I.	*Annuaire de l'institut de droit international*
A.J.C.L.	American Journal of Comparative Law
A.J.D.A.	*Actualité Juridique Droit Administratif*
A.J.I.L. (Supp.)	American Journal of International Law (Supplement)
A.L.J.	Australian Law Journal
A.L.J.R.	Australian Law Journal Reports
All E.R.	All England Reports
All Pak. S.C.R.	All Pakistan Supreme Court Reports
A.L.R.	Argus Law Reports (Australia)
ALR S.L.	African Law Reports (Sierra Leone)
Am. Jur.	American Jurisprudence
Am. Pol. Sci. Rev.	American Political Science Review
App. D.C.	Appeals Cases, District of Columbia (United States)
A.P.S.	Accounts and Papers Series (United Kingdom)
Ark.	Arkansas Reports (United States)
A.R.O.B.	*Administrative Rechtspraak Overheidsbeschikkingen*
Ar. V.	*Archiv des Völkerrechts*

ASILS Int.L.J.	American Society of International Law Students International Law Journal
AsylVfG	*Asyl Verfahrensgesetz*
A.T.F.S.	*Arrêts du tribunal fédéral suisse*
Aust. Y.I.L.	Australian Yearbook of International Law
A.V.	*Allgemeine Verfung*
A.W.R. Bull.	Association for the Study of the World Refugee Problem Bulletin
B.and A.	Barnewall and Alderson, King's Bench Reports (England)
B. and Ad.	Barnewall and Adolphus, King's Bench Reports (England)
B. and C.	Barnewall and Cressell, King's Bench Reports (England)
BAnz.	*Bundesanzeiger* (Federal Republic of Germany)
Basic Documents	R. Plender, *Basic Documents on International Migration Law*, 1988
BayVGH	*Bayern Verwaltungsgerichthof*
B.C.R.	British Columbia Reports (Canada)
B.C. Third World L.J.	Boston College Third World Law Journal
B.D.I.L.	British Digest of International Law
Bevans	Charles I. Bevans: Treaties and Other International Agreements of the United States of America 1789–1948
B.F.S.P.	British and Foreign State Papers
B.G.Bl.	*Bundesgesetzblatt* (Federal Republic of Germany)
B.I.A.	Board of Immigration Appeals (United States)
Bijl. Hand.	*Bijlagen bij het verslag der handelingen van de Eerste Kamer*
B.L.D.	*Bulletin législatif Dalloz* (France)
Bomb. L.R.	Bombay Law Reports
Bos. and Pul.	Bosanquet and Puller, Common Pleas Reports (England)
B.P.I.L.	British Practice in International Law (ed. Parry, Lauterpacht)
Brooklyn J.I.L.	Brooklyn Journal of International Law
B.S.B.D.I.	*Boletín da Sociedáde Brasiliera International*
B.S.P.	British State Papers
Buffalo L.R.	Buffalo Law Review
Bulletin	Bulletin of the International Commission of Jurists
Bull. Supp.	Supplement to the monthly Bulletin of the European Communities
B.U.L. Rev.	Boston University Law Review
Burr.	Burrow, King's Bench Reviews (England)
BVerfG (E)	*Bundesverfassungsgericht (Entscheidungen)* (Federal Republic of Germany)
BVerwG (E)	*Bundesverwaltungsgericht (Entscheidungen)* (Federal Republic of Germany)
B.Y.I.L.	British Yearbook of Internatioal Law
Cab. and E.	Cababe and Ellis, Queen's Bench Reports (England)
Cah.dr.eur.	*Cahiers de droit européen*
Cal.	California Reports (United States)
Cal. 2d.	California Reports (second series) (United States)
Cal. App.	California Appellate Reports (United States)
Cal. West. Int. L.J.	California Western International Law Journal
Can. B.R.	Canadian Bar Review
C. and J.	Crompton and Jervis, Exchequar Reports (England)

C. and P.	Carrington and Payne, Nisi Prius Reports (England)
Can Y.B.I.L.	Canadian Yearbook of International Law
Car. and Kir.	Carrington and Kirwan, Nisi Prius Reports (England)
Case W. Reserve J.I.L.	Case Western Reserve Journal of International Law
Cas. t. Talb.	Cases *tempore* Talbot (England)
Cath. L.	Catholic Lawyer
CCA	Circuit Court of Appeals
C.C.L.	*Collection complète des lois, décrets, ordonnances, règlements, avis du Conseil d'Etat* (France)
C.E.	Reports of the Committee of Experts established under the European Social Charter
CFR	Code of Federal Regulations (United States)
Ch.	Chancery Reports (England)
Ch.D.	Chancery Division Reports (England)
C.I.A.B.	Canadian Immigration Appeals Board, Selected Judgements
C.J.E.C.	Court of Justice of the European Communities
C.J.S.	*Corpus Juris Secundum*
Clark and F.	Clark and Finelly, House of Lords Reports (England)
C.L.I.C.	Canadian Law Information Council
C.L.J.	Cambridge Law Journal
C.L.P.	Current Legal Problems
C.L.R.	Commonwealth Law Report (Australia)
Clunet	Clunet, *Journal du droit international*
C.M.L.R.	Common Market Law Reports
C.M.L.Rev.	Common Market Law Review
Colo.	Colorado Reports (United States)
Colum. J. Trans. L.	Columbia Journal of Transnational Law
Colum. L.R.	Columbia Law Review
Com. Act.	Act of the Commonwealth of the Philippines
Comp. L. Ybk.	Comparative Law Yearbook
Conf. R.	Reports of the Conferences between the Senate and the House of Representatives of the United States
Cong. Rec.	Congressional Record (United States)
Conn.	Connecticut Reports
Co. Rep.	Coke's Reports (England)
Cornell Int.L.J.	Cornell International Law Journal
Cornell L.Q	Cornell Law Quarterly
Cranch	Cranch's Supreme Court Reports (United States)
Crim. App. Rep.	Criminal Appeals Reports (England)
Crim. L.R.	Criminal Law Review
Cro. Car.	Croke's Reports, *tempore* Charles I (England)
Czechoslovak Y.I.L.	Czechoslovak Yearbook of International Law
D. and R.	Dowling and Ryland, King's Bench Reports (England)
D.A.R.D.D.R.	*Dokumente der Auslandischen Regierung der Deutschen Democratiken Republik*
Denver J.Int.L. and Pol.	Denver Journal of International Law and Policy
Dept. Reg.	Department of Regulations issued by the U.S. Immigration and Naturalisation Service

XX

Dept. State. Bull.	Department of State Bulletin
Detroit Coll.	
of L. Rev.	Detroit College of Law Review
D. (L)	*Recueil Dalloz de doctrine de jurisprudence et de législation* (France) (Legislation)
D.L.R.	Dominion Law Reports (Canada)
Doc. dir. comp.	*Documentacao e direito comparado*
D.R.	District Registry
Droit. soc.	*Droit social*
Duvergier Rep.	Duvergier Reports of debates in the French National Assembly
DVBl	*Deutsches Verwaltungsblatt*
D.Z.	*Dokumentation der Zeit* (German Democratic Republic)
E. and Ir. App.	English and Irish Appeals Reports
East P.C.	East, Pleas of the Crown (England)
E.B.	*Entscheidungen des Bundesverwaltungsgerichts* (Federal Republic of Germany)
ECO	Entry Clearance Officer
E.C.R.	European Court Reports
E.D.	*Enciclopedia del Diretto* (Italy)
Edw.	Edwards, Admiralty Reports (England)
EHRR	European Human Rights Reports
E.L.Rev.	European Law Review
Encyclopédie	*Encyclopédie Juridique, répertoire de droit public et administratif,* 1959 ed., with 1970 supplement (France)
E.S.B.	*Entscheidungen des Schweizerisches Bundesgerichts*
E.T.S.	European Treaty Series
Ex.	Exchequer Reports (England)
Ex. D.	Exchequer Division Reports (England)
F.	Federal Reporter (United States)
F. 2d.	Federal Reporter (second series) (United States)
Fallos	Fallos Argentinian Reports
Fam.	Family Law Cases
F.C.	Federal Cases (Canada)
F.C.A.	Federal Code Annotated (United State)
F. (Ct. of Sess.)	Fraser, Court of Sessions Cases (Scotland)
F.I.	*Foro Italiano*
F.L.R.	Federal Law Reports (Australia)
F.O.R.	Foreign Office Reports (England)
For. Aff.	Foreign Affairs
Fordham L. Rev.	Fordham Law Review
For. Rel.	Foreign Relations
F.R.	Federal Register (United States)
Friedenswarte	*Die Friedenswarte, Zeitschrift für Zwischenstaatliche Organisation* (later *Blatter für Internazionale Verständigung und Zwischenstaatliche Organisation*)
F.S.M.	Foreign Service Manual (United States)
F. Supp.	Federal Supplement (United States)

G. de los T.	*Gracéta de los Tribunales* (Guatemala)
G. du P.	*Gazette du palais* (France)
Geo. L.J.	Georgetown Law Journal
Giur.it.	*Giurisprudenza italiana*
G.R.	General Reports (Philippines)
Gray	Gray's Law Reports (Massachusetts, United States)
G.S.R.	General Statutory Rules and Orders (India)
G.U.	*Gazetta Ufficiale* (Italy)
Guar.Gaz.	Guardian Gazette
G.V.	*Gids Vreemdelingenrecht*
Hale P.C.	Hale, Pleas of the Crown (England)
Hague *Recueil*	*Académie de droit international: Recueil des cours*
Harv. Civ.R. – Civ. Lib.L.Rev.	Harvard Civil Rights – Civil Liberties Law Review
Harv. I.L.J.	Harvard International Law Journal
Harv. L.J.	Harvard Law Journal
Harv. L.R.	Harvard Law Review
H.C. Deb.	Reports of debates in the House of Commons (England)
H.C.	House of Commons (paper number)
H.L. Deb.	Reports of debates in the House of Lords (England)
H.L. Jo.	House of Lords Journal
H. of R.	Reports of debates in the House of Representatives (Australia)
How.	Howard's Supreme Court Reports (United States)
H.R.	House of Representatives Reports (United States)
Human Rights J.	Human Rights Journal
I.A.B.	Immigration Appeal Board (Canada)
I.A.J.Y.	Inter-America Judicial Yearbook
I. & N. Dec.	Immigration and Nationality Decisions
I.C.J. Rep.	International Court of Justice Reports
I.C.L.Q.	International and Comparative Law Quarterly
I.D.	Interim Decisions of the Board of Immigration Appeals (United States)
I.L.C. Ybk.	United Nations, International Law Commision, Yearbook
I.L.R.	International Law Reports
I.L.M.	International Legal Materials
I.L.O.	International Labour Organization
Imm.A.R.	Immigration Appeals Reports
I.N.	Administrative Decisions made under the Immigration and Nationally Act (United States)
Ind. J.I.L.	Indian Journal of International Law
Ind. Rel. L.J.	Industrial Relations Law Journal
InfAusIR	*Information zum Auslandischen Recht*
INS	Immigration and Naturalisation Service
Int. Aff.	International Affairs
Int. Lab. Rev.	International Labour Review
Int. Law.	International Lawyer
Int. Mig.	International Migration
Int. Rel.	International Relations
I.R.	Irish Reports

I.R.C.	Inland Revenue Commisioners (United Kingdom)
Israel Ybk.H.R.	Israel Yearbook of Human Rights
Jac. & W.	Jacob and Walters Chancery Reports
J.C.P.	*Juris classeur périodique (semaine juridique)* (France)
J. Crim. L.	Journal of Criminal Law
J.D.I.	*Journal du droit international*
J.E.L.	Journal of Ethiophian Law
J.Ind.L.Inst.	Journal of the Indian Law Institute
J.N.	*Journal Notorial*
Jo des trib	*Journal de Tribunaux*
Jo.Int.Comm.Jur.	Journal of the International Commission of Jurists
Jo.Int.L. and Econ.	Journal of International Law and Economics
Jo.L.Soc.Scot.	Journal of the Law Society of Scotland
J.O.	*Journal officiel des Communautés européennes*
J.O.R.F.	*Journal officiel de la République Française*
J.T.	*Journal des tribunaux* (Belgium)
J.W.	*Juristische Wochenschrift* (Federal Republic of Germany)
J.Y.I.L.	Jewish Yearbook of International Law
J.Z.	*Juristische Zeitung* (Federal Republic of Germany)
K.B.	King's Bench Law Reports (England)
K.L.R.	Kenya Law Reports
Knapp	Knapp's Privy Council Reports
L. and Contemp. Prob.	Law and Contemporary Problems
L.Ed.	Lawyers Edition
L.I.	Legislative Instrument (Ghana)
LIEI	Legal Issues in European Integration
Lit. Ass.	Littleton's Reports of English Assize Cases
Lit. Rep.	Littleton's Reports of Common Pleas (England)
L.J.K.B.	Law Journal King's Bench Reports (England)
L.J.K.B.O.S.	Law Journal King's Bench Reports Old Series (England)
L.J.Newsp.	Law Journal Newspaper
L.J.Q.B.	Law Journal Queen's Bench Reports
L.N.	Legal Notice (Malaysia)
L.N. Doc.	League of Nations Documents
L.N. Off. Jo.	League of Nations Official Journal
L.N.T.S.	League of Nations Treaty Series
Lofft.	Lofft, King's Bench Reports (England)
L.Q.R.	Law Quarterly Review
L.R. Ch.	Law Reports, Chancery Appeals Cases (England)
L.R.C.P.	Law Reports, Common Pleas (England)
L.R. Ex. C.R.	Law Reports Exchequer Cases Preserved
L.R.Q.B.	Law Reports, Queen's Bench (England)
L.Soc.Gaz	The Law Society Gazette
L.T.	Law Times Reports (England)
L.W.	United States Law Week

M.b.	*Moniteur belge*
M.E.I.	Minister of Employment and Immigration
Mich.Ybk. I.L.S.	Michigan Yearbook of International Legal Studies
M.L.R.	Modern Law Review
MNRS	*Nouveau recueil générale des traîtés* (Ed. by M. de Martens and Successors)
Moo. P.C.	Moore, Privy Council Reports
Mysore L.J.	Mysore Law Journal
Neths. I.L.R.	Netherlands International Law Review
Neths.Ybk.Int.L.	Netherlands Yearbook of International Law
New L.J.	New Law Journal
N. Ir.	Northern Irish Reports
N.J.	*Neue Justiz*
N.J.W.	*Neue Juristische Wochenschrift* (Federal Republic of Germany)
N.R.	National Reporter
N.R.C.D.	National Redemption Council Decree (Ghana)
NVwZ	*Neue Verwaltungsrechts Zeitschrift*
Nw. U.L. Rev.	Northwestern University Law Review
N.Y.	New York Reports (United States)
N.Y. 2d.	New York Reports (second series) (United States)
NVL Sch.J.Int. &Comp. L.	New York Law School Journal of International and Comparative Law
N.Y.S.	New York Supplement (United States)
N.Y.S. 2d.	New York Supplement (second series) (United States)
N.Y.U.L. Rev.	New York University Law Review
N.Z.L.R.	New Zealand Law Reports
O.J.	Official Journal of the European Communities
O.J. Sp.Ed.	Official Journal of the European Communities, Special Edition (English language)
Okl.	Oklahoma Reports
OLG	*Oberlandesgericht*
Op. A.G.	Opinions of the Attorney General
O.R.	Ontario Reports
O.W.N.	Ontario Weekly Notes
P.	Probate Reports (England)
Pa.	Pennsylvania Supreme Court Reports
P. and D.	Probate and Divorce Reports (England)
P.A.U.T.S.	Pan American Union Treaty Series
P.B.	*Pandectas Brasileiras*
P.b.	*Pasicrisie belge*
P.C.I.J.	Permanent Court of International Justice Reports
P.D.	Probate Division Law Reports (England)
P.D.A.	Probate, Divorce and Admiralty Division Reports
Pe. M.	Pesakim Mehozim Reports (Israel)
Pet.	Peters' Supreme Court Reports (United States)
Philippine L.J.	Philippine Law Journal
P.I.	Philippines Islands Reports

Pis D.	Piskei Din Reports (Israel)
P.L.	Public Law (United States)
P.L.R.	Palestine Law Reports
P.N.D.C.L.	Provisional National Defence Council Law
Pol. Sci. Q.	Political Science Quarterly
P.R.	Patent Rolls (England)
Proc. A.S.I.L.	Proceedings of the American Society of International Law
P. Rp.	Philippines Reports
Pub. L.	Public Law (United Kingdom)
Q.B.	Queen's Bench Law Reports (England)
Que. P.R.	Quebec Practice Reports
Quest. Soc.	*Questions Sociales*
R.D.	*Revista de Direito* (Brazil)
R.D.I.	*Revista di Diretto internazionale* (Italy)
R.D.I./R.D.I.L.C.	*Revue de droit international et de législation comparée* (formerly *Revue de droit international*)
R.D.I.P.	*Revue de droit international privé*
Rec. Cons. d'Et.	*Recueil des décisions du Conseil d'Etat* (France)
Rechts	*Rechtsherstel* (Netherlands)
R.E.D.I.	*Revue égyptienne de droit international*
Rep. Act.	Act of the Republic of the Philippines
Rep. U.N.P.	Repertory of the United Nations Practice
Rev.admin.	*La Revue administrative* (France)
Rev.crit.dr.int.priv.	*Revue critique de droit international privé*
Rev. D.I.C.D.	*Revista de Derecho International y de Ciencias Diplomaticas* (Argentine Republic)
Rev.dir.econ.	*Revista de direito e economia*
Rev.dr.de l'homme	*Revue des droits de l'homme*
Rev.dr.int.priv.	*Revue de droit international privé*
Rev.hell.dr.int.	*Revue hellenique de droit international*
Rev.inst.eur.	*Revista de instituciones europeas*
Rev. Int. Comm. Jur.	Review of the International Commission of Jurists
Rev.int.eur.	*Revue de l'intégration européenne*
Rev.jur. et pol., indép. et coop.	*Revue juridique et politique, indépendance et coopération*
Rev.trim.dr.belge	*Revue trimestrielle de droit belge*
Rev.trim.dr.eur.	*Revue trimestrielle de droit européen*
RFL	Review of Federal Law
R.G. Bl.	*Reichsgesetzblatt* (Germany)
R.G.D.I.	*Recueil général du droit international*
R.G.D.I.P.	*Revue générale de droit international public*
R.G. St.	*Entscheidungen des Reichsgerichts in Strafsachen* (Germany)
Riv.dir.eur.	*Rivista di diritto europeo*
Riv.dir.del lav.	*Rivista di diritto del lavoro*
Riv.dir.int.	*Rivista di diritto internazionale*
Riv.dir.int. e comp. del lav.	*Rivista di diritto internazionale e comparato del lavoro*

R.M.C.	*Revue du Marché Commun*
RO	*Recueil officiel des lois et ordonnances de la Confédération Suisse*
R.P.D.I.	*Revista Peruana de Derecho Internacional*
Rot. Parl.	*Rotulae Parliamentarum* (England)
R.S.	Revised Statutes of Canada, 1952
R. St.	Revised Statutes of Canada, 1906
R.V.	*Rechtspraak Vreemdelingenrecht*
S.	Senate Bill No. (United States)
S.A.	South Africa Law Reports
Sandf. Ch.	Sandford Chancery Reports (New York)
San Diego L.Rev.	San Diego Law Review
S.A.T.S.	South African Treaty Series
Scand. Stud. in L.	Scandinavian Studies in Law
S.C.L.R.	Southern California Law Review
S.C.R.	Supreme Court Reports (Canada)
S.C.R. (Ind.)	Supreme Court Reports (India)
Schw. Jb. Int. R.	*Schweizerische Jahrbuch für Internationales Recht*
S.E.O.V.	*Sammlung der Erkenntnisse des Osterrischen Verfassungsgerichtshofes* (Austria)
Sess. Pap.	Sessions Papers (United Kingdom)
S.I.	Statutory Instrument
Sirey	Sirey: *Recueil général des lois et des arrêts* (France)
S.L.J.	Seoul Law Journal
S.L.T.	Scotts Law Times
Sol. Jo.	Solicitors Journal
SOR	Statutory Orders and Regulations (Canada)
Sov. Jew. Aff.	Soviet Jewish Affairs
S.R. and O.	Statutory Rules and Orders (United Kingdom)
S. Rept.	Senate Report (United States)
Stan. L. Rev.	Stanford Law Review
Stat.	Statutes at Large (United States)
Stb.	*Staatsblad* (Netherlands Offical Bulletin)
Str.	Strange, King's Bench Reports (England)
St Rspr Vgl	*Standige Rechtsprechung Vergleiche*
St. Tr.	State Trials (England)
S.W.	Southwestern Reporter (United States)
Sw. Tr.	Swabey and Tristam, Probate and Divorce Reports (England)
Syd. L.R.	Sydney Law Review
Taunt.	Taunton, Common Pleas Report (England)
TB/S	*Ten Berge/Stroink*
T.C.	Tax Cases
Temple L.Q.	Temple Law Quarterly
Texas Int. L.J.	Texas International Law Journal
Tex. Civ. App.	Texal Civil Appeals Reports
TH	Thanet House (location of immigration adjudicators and Immigration Appeal Tribunal, United Kingdom)
The Times	*The Times* newspaper of London
The Times L.R.	*The Times* Law Reports (England)

Third World Q.	Third World Quarterly
T.I.A.S.	Treaties and other international Agreements Series (United States)
T.G.S.	Transactions of the Grotius Society
T.L.R.	Times Law Reports (England)
UBCL Rev.	University of British Columbia Law Review
U.N.Doc.	United Nations Document (number)
U.N.G.A. (O.R.)	United Nations General Assembly (Official Record)
U.N.R.I.A.A.	United Nations Reports of International Arbitral Awards
U.N.S.C. (O.R.)	United Nations Security Council (Official Record)
U.K.T.S.	United Kingdom Treaty Series
U. Miami. L.Rev.	University of Miami Law Review
U.N.T.S/	United Nations Treaty Series
U. Pa. L. Rev.	University of Pennsylvania Law Review
U. Pitts. L.R.	University of Pittsburgh Law Review
U.S.	United States Supreme Court Reports
U.S. App. D.C.	Reports of the United States Court of Appeals for the District of Columbia
U.S.C.S.	United States Code Service
U.S.C.A.	United States Code Annotated
U.S. Cong. and Ad. News	United States Congressional and Administrative News
U.S.T.	United States Treaty Series
Va. J.I.L.	Virginia Journal of International Law
Vand. J. Jrans.L.	Vanderbilt Journal of Transnational Law
Vaughan	Vaughan, King's Bench Reports (England)
V.D. (N.S.)	Valyo's Digest (New Series) (Philippines)
Vedomosti SSR	*Vedomosti Verkhovnogo Soveta Rosiiskoi Sovetskoi Federativnoi Sotsialisticheskoi Respubliki*
Ven.	Ventris, King's Bench Reports (England)
Ves. Senr.	Vesey Senior, Chancery Reports (England)
Ves. Supp.	Vesey, Chancery Reports, Supplement (England)
V.L.R.	Virginia Law Review
V.R.	Victoria Reports (Australia)
Vt.	Vermont Reports
VwGH	*Verwaltungsgerichthof*
W.A.C.A.	West African Court of Appeals Reports
Wall.	Wallace's Supreme Court Reports
Wash.	Washington (State) Reports
West Indian L.J.	West Indian Law Journal
Wheat.	Wheaton's Supreme Court Reports (United States)
Wirt. und Recht	*Wirtschaft und Recht*
W.I.R.	West Indies Reports
W.L.R.	Weekly Law Reports (England)
Wm. & Ma. L. Rev.	William and Mary Law Review
W.N.	Weekly Notes (Australia)
W.W.R.	Western Weekly Reporter (Canada)
W. Virg. L.R.	West Virginia Law Review

Yale L.J.	Yale Law Journal
Ybk.	Yearbook of the European Convention on Human Rights and Fundamental Freedoms
Ybk. E.L.	Yearbook of European Law
Ybk. I.L.S.	Yearbook of International Legal Studies
Z.A.o.R.V.	*Zeitschrift für Auslandisches und offentliches Recht und Völkerrecht*
Z.O.	*Zeitschrift für Ostrecht*
Z.o.R.	*Zeitschrift für offentliches Recht*
Zb.O.S.N.	*Zbiór Orzeczen Sadu Najwyzszego* (Poland)
Z.S.R. (N.F.)	*Zeitschrift für Schweizerisches Recht* (Neue Folge)
Z.V.	*Zeitschrift für Völkerrecht*
Z.W.N.T.A.	*Zbiór Wyrokow Najwyzszego Trybunalu Administracyjnego* (Poland)

Introduction

Among the principles commonly advanced in the older textbooks on international law is the rule that States are free to control at will the entry and residence of aliens. Fenwick[1] claimed that by inference from the sovereignty of States, it was a well established general principle that a State might forbid the entrance of aliens into its territory or admit them only in such cases as might commend themselves to its judgment. That sentence was quoted with approval by Pitt Cobbett.[2] Hyde[3] and Jessup[4] are among those who wrote in expansive terms of the State's discretion in the control of aliens. Hackworth[5] asserted that in the absence of treaty obligations, a State might admit aliens on such terms and conditions as it might deem to be consonant with national interests and deport from its territory those whose presence it might regard as undesirable. Kelsen[6] stated that it was an accepted maxim of international law that every sovereign nation had the power to admit aliens only in such cases and upon such conditions as it might see fit to prescribe and to expel them at any time and for any reason.

Expressions of opinions as categorical as those found in the older textbooks have occasionally been expressed by representatives or legal advisers of States. The Law Officers, when asked to advise about a Louisiana statute designed 'to prohibit free persons of color from entering the State of Louisiana by sea' and to punish offenders with great severity, ventured the opinion that the enactment was exceedingly illiberal but concluded that every independent State is entitled to exclude from its territory the subjects of foreign States, unless it has entered into a treaty on the subject.[7]

The emphasis on States' freedom of action, which is found in the older textbooks, appears misplaced in the conditions of contemporary international relations. In this book an account is given of the modern rules of international law which limit the freedom of States to control immigration and emigration. In part, those rules are to be found in a network of treaties, bilateral and multilateral, regional and universal. In part they are to be found in principles of general international law. Both these treaties and these general rules have grown in their number and sophistication during the last quarter of a century. Their proliferation is largely (but not exclusively) a consequence of growth of the general international law of human rights and the development of regional rules governing economic integration.

The argument advanced in the older textbooks does not have an ancient pedigree. Certain of the classical theorists, as we shall see, defended the proposition that international law protected a right to travel. Thus, for Francesco de Vitoria, 'It was permissible from the beginning of the world, when everything was in common, for anyone to set forth and travel wheresoever he would'.[8] Grotius,[9] Pufendorf[10] and Wolff[11] recognised a State's duty to permit the transit of aliens for innocent purposes and, in certain cases, to permit their residence. Even Vattel[12] argued that no nation can, without good reason, refuse perpetual residence to a fugitive.

As recently as at the end of the nineteenth century there continued to be support for the view that the power to control the ingress and egress of aliens was circumscribed by international law. At the meetings of the Institute of International Law in Hamburg in 1891, Geneva in 1892 and Lausanne in 1898 the view was expressed that the first of the restrictions imposed on States by international law is that it cannot isolate itself form foreign States or their subjects.[13]

The view that the reception and treatment of aliens is a matter of extensive discretion appears to have arisen in consequence of a series of judicial decisions reached at the end of the nineteenth century in response to a westward migration of Chinese labourers. These decisions are cited in most of the older textbooks to which reference has been made.[14] Not all of these judicial decisions are expressed in language as broad as that of the textbooks.[15] At least one is based partly on doubtful reasoning.[16] In others, the extensive language employed in the domestic courts may be contrasted with the measured tones used in the corresponding international engagements. Thus, in the *Chinese Exclusion case,* Justice Field concluded that the power of exclusion of foreigners was an incident of sovereignty of the United States, which could not be granted away by treaty or otherwise.[17] Yet the Treaty between the United States and China dated 17 November 1890 set out in Article I the terms on which the United States could restrict the admission of Chinese labourers.[18] It is not entirely clear whether that Article purported to declare the current state of customary international law or to amount to a concession from the Empire of China. In either event, it provides impressive evidence of the existence, at that time, of the view that the right to control immigration was neither absolute nor unqualified.

Whenever in the opinion of the government of the United States the coming of Chinese labourers to the United States, or their residence therein, threatens to affect the interests of that country, or to endanger the good order of that country, or of any locality within the territory thereof, the government of China agrees that the government of the United States may regulate, limit or suspend such coming into residence but may not absolutely prohibit it. The limitation or suspension shall be reasonable ... and immigrants shall not be subject to personal maltreatment or abuse.

It is therefore appropriate to exercise restraint in treating these well-known decisions of domestic courts as evidence of rules of modern international law. Moreover, the view that international law imposes significant restrictions in the power of the States to control immigration and emigration is supported by several writers of repute.

Writing during the First World War, when the practice of imposing restrictions on foreigners had become widespread, Edwin Borchard argued that the alien occupies a position between two extremes, the one a barbaric exclusion of all aliens, the other a complete equality of aliens and nationals. In phraseology reminiscent of Mr Rolin-Jacquemyn's submission to the Institute of International Law, Mr Borchard maintained that the first extreme, complete exclusion, was not compatible with the existence of the State as a member of the society of nations. Qualifications of the alien's right of admission and sojourn were permissible only if based on reasonable grounds.[19]

Eleven years later, J.L. Brierly made a plea for the use of international law for the purpose of controlling the dangerous tendency towards assertions of untramelled sovereign powers. 'The problem of immigration', he wrote, 'will not be dealt with in the "international mind" until nations have begun to realize that the same economic facts which create a problem of immigration for one may create a problem of emigration for another.'[20] Even at this date, and indeed during the Second World War, the view that States enjoy an absolute discretion was by no means universally accepted. At least one Latin American writer found it possible to approach the problem from the opposite angle. For him the question was whether the alien had an absolute right of free entry. He answered the question in the negative, maintaining that there was a power to exclude aliens or to expel them for specific good reasons, including the defence of the State, social tranquillity, individual security and public order.[21]

In response to Oppenheim's argument that a State has the power under international law to expel aliens at pleasure, Sir Hersch Lauterpacht replied that it would be difficult to find confirmation of this view in the practice of international tribunals. These (he said) have consistently stressed the limitations upon the power of expulsion.[22] Judge Read acknowledged in the *Nottebohm* case that by admitting an alien, the State brings into being a series of legal relationships with his State of nationality;[23] and earlier, in the case concerning *Treatment of Polish Nationals in Danzig,* the Permanant Court deliberately refused to endorse the proposition that a State can exclude *all* aliens.[24] Some of the more authoritative modern Francophone writers have added their voices to those of the champions of interdependence.[25] Rousseau advanced a carefully balanced conclusion on the subject.[26] In his view, aliens do not have an absolute right to enter the territory of foreign States; and although custom and international law recognize the practice of asylum, States have some important discretionary powers with respect to expulsion. De Visscher[27] wrote of *'l'influence dangereuse des practiques restrictives de l'immigration sur les tensions internationales'*.

In 1978 Dr Goodwin-Gill published a monograph supporting the argument that the rules of customary international law governing the control of migration are now sufficiently developed to dispense with any claim to absolute State sovereignty in this area of activity.[28] He argued that issues arising from the exercise of powers of exclusion and expulsion are commonly affected by matters such as nationality and fundamental rights. For this reason, any claimed presumption that such powers are sealed within the reserved domain requires close scrutiny. A similar argument has been advanced on the basis of ample research by J. Nafziger.[29] The contention, thus far advanced as a legal proposition, has received a diplomatic endorsement from the Secretary-General of the Commonwealth, who has given practical rather than theoretical reasons for resort to international law as a means of solving some of the problems created by international migration.[30]

THE RELEVANCE OF NATIONALITY

The rules of international law limiting the competence of States in matters of migration are inextricably tied to the international rules governing the opposability of nationality. This must be so, since even the most basic rules of customary international law governing migration are based upon the distinction between nationals and aliens or between different classes of aliens. The proposition that a State must admit its own nationals to its territory is, by now, sufficiently well established but one of the crucial issues arising in the analysis of the proposition is the identification of a State's nationals. The problem arises particularly in the event of the collective denaturalization of an expelled minority and in the event of the maintenance of tiered or structured systems of nationality.

Treaty obligations in respect of migration are commonly, if not normally, concluded on the basis of nationality. The Treaty establishing the European Economic Community[31] is exceptional only in the sense that it provides for the free movement of 'workers' without specifying explicitly that they must be nationals of the Member States.[32] It is clear from Community legislation that in order to benefit from the freedom of movement for workers, a person must be a national of a Member State.[33] Hence there arises the necessity of determining whether a person is a 'national' for the purposes of that Treaty. The definition of nationality used for those purposes may but need not conform with the definition used for other purposes.[34]

Even in the absence of treaty obligation, States which are bound together by political, historical or geographical ties commonly seal their cordial relationship by extending privileges to one another's nationals. Thus the United Kingdom imposed no significant controls upon the admission to its territory of Commonwealth citizens prior to 1962; and visas were never required for the admission of such citizens to the United Kingdom before May 1985,[35] when a requirement of this nature was imposed on citizens of Sri Lanka. A Libyan Decree of 1970 declared that nationals of other Arab countries would not be considered as aliens in Libya. A subsequent law conferred specific migratory rights in Libya to Egyptian nationals.[36] Likewise the German Democratic Republic continues to permit the admission of nationals of certain Socialist countries, without visas, and expects to receive a similar facility from those countries in return. In consequence of practices of this kind, questions of international law may arise which cannot be answered other than on the assumption that the *propositus* possesses an identified nationality, which must be recognized by the State against which a claim is advanced.

Even where the receiving State draws no material distinction between nationals of different foreign States, a migrant who complains of a breach by that State of its international obligations must in principle address his complaint to his own State, which alone is capable of espousing his claim at the international level.[37] This is so whether the individual's complaint is of a breach of a convention or a breach of a customary rule. It seems doubtful that a complaint of a breach of the Havana Convention concerning the Status of Aliens[38] could be made other than by the State whose national appears to have suffered in consequence of the breach; and this is so even if the substance of the complaint is that there has been a failure to treat the nationals of any foreign State equally with nationals of the host State in respect of the matters governed by the treaty.[39]

Some grasp of the principles of nationality is also a necessary preliminary to a comparative study of immigration laws. States which make legislative provision for the control of immigration into their territories commonly provide that the prospective immigrant's admission shall be determined partially or in certain cases by reference to his national status.[40] Only in the most exceptional of occasions is a right of entry conferred by national law on a group defined by reference to a criterion other than nationality. Under the Law of the Return, 5710–1950, Israel permits Jews of all nationalities to enter and settle in Israel as *olehs* by a process of *aliyah*.[41] Even in this case, however, although the entrant's national status does not determine his eligibility for admission, his

6

admission affects his nationality, for an *oleh* on completing his *aliyah* acquires the nationality of Israel.

For these reasons, Chapter I offers an account of some principles of nationality law at the domestic and at the international level.

1. C. Fenwick, *Cases on International Law,* 1951, p. 205.
2. P. Cobbett, *Cases on International Law,* ed. F. Grey, 1930, p. 302.
3. C. Hyde, *International Law,* 1945, Vol. II, pp. 871–1012.
4. P. Jessup, *A Modern Law of Nations,* 1964, pp. 78–84.
5. G. Hackworth, *Digest of International Law,* Vol. III, p. 717.
6. H. Kelsen, *Principles of International Law,* 1966, p. 366.
7. Lord McNair, *International Law Opinions,* 1956, Vol. II, p. 105.
8. F. de Vitoria, *De Indis et de Jure Belli Reflections,* section III, trans. J. Scott.
9. H. Grotius, *De Jure Belli ac Pacis,* Vol. II, Chap. II, paras. 15(1) and (2).
10. S. Pufendorf, *De Jure Naturae et Gentium, Libri Octo,* Book III, para. 5, trans. C. Oldfather, 1934, p. 354.
11. C. Wolff, *Institutiones Juris Naturae et Gentium,* Vol. IV, Chap. IV see A. Verdross, '*Les règles internationales concernant le trâitement des étrangers*', 37 Hague *Recueil* (1931-III) 322 at 339.
12. E. De Vattel, *Le droit des gens,* Book I, sections 124, 230.
13. *Infra* Chapter II, page 72, note 91 and sources cited there.
14. *Musgrove v.Chun Teeong Toy,* [1891] A.C.272 at 283; *Attorney-General for Canada v. Cain,* [1906] A.C.542 at 546; *Nishumura Ekiu v. U.S.,* 142 U.S. 651 at 659 (1892); *Fong Yue Ting v. U.S.,* 149 U.S. 698 (1893); *Chae Chan Ping v. U.S. (Chinese Exclusion case),* 130 U.S. 581 (1899).
15. In *Musgrove v. Chun Teeong Toy (supra* note 14) the Privy Council appears to have confined its advice to the observation that an alien had no absolute and unqualified right of action if excluded from British territory.
16. In *Attorney General for Canada v. Cain, (supra* note 14) the Privy Council relied upon Vattel's writings as authority for the view that the supreme power of any State has the right to refuse to permit any alien to enter, or to attach whatever conditions it sees fit on a grant of admission, or to deport at will even a friendly alien. The confidence thus placed in Vattel's writing is misplaced: *supra* note 12.
17. *Supra* note 14.
18. I. Moore 252. The Convention paved the way for the Chinese Exclusion Act, 6 May 1882, 22 Stat. 58.
19. E. Borchard, *The Diplomatic Protection of Citizens Abroad,* 1915, p. 36.
20. J. Brierly, 'The Draft Code of American International Law', 7 B.Y.I.L. (1926) 14, 23.
21. J. Irazamy y Puente, 'Exclusion and Expulsion of Aliens in Latin America', 36 A.J.I.L. (1942) 252.
22. *The Function of Law in the International Community,* 1933, p. 289 cf. L. Oppenheim. *International Law,* 1955, Vol. I, p. 675.
23. He felt able to assert, however, that when an alien comes to the frontier seeking admission the State has an unfettered right to refuse it: (1955) I.C.J. Rep. 34 at 46. A similar view was expressed by Judge Chagla in *Rights of Passage over Indian Territory (Merits),* (1960) I.C.J. Rep. 6 at 119.

24. P.C.I.J. Ser A/B No. 44 (1932) at p. 41. See also the views of Umpire Ralston in the *Boffolo Case, Venezuelan Arbitraions of 1903*, p. 696.

25. C. Delessert, *L'établissement et le séjour des étrangers au point de vue juridique et politique*, 1924; S. Basdevant, *'Théorie générale de la condition de l'étranger'*, 8 R.D.I. (1930) 1.

26. C. Rousseau, *Droit international public*, 1977, Vol. III, p. 31.

27. P. de Visscher, *Théories et réalités en droit international public*, 1953, p. 219.

28. G. Goodwin-Gill, *International Law and the Movement of Persons between States*, 1978. See esp. p. 57.

29. 'The General Admission of Aliens under International Law', 77 A.J.I.L. (1983) 804.

30. S. Ramphal, *One World to Share*, 1979, p. 54.

31. Rome, 25 March 1957, 298 U.N.T.S. 11; *Basic Documents* VI 1.

32. See W. Bohning, *The Migration of Workers in the United Kingdom and the European Community*, 1972, p. 136ff; T. Hartley, 'The Internal Personal Scope of the EEC Immigration Provisions', 3 E.L. Rev. (1978) 191 at 193; D. Loschak, *'Les ressortissants de la CEE'*, 5 Droit Soc. (1976) 83; R. Plender, 'An Incipient Form of European Citizenship' in F. Jacobs (ed.), *European Law and the Individual*, 1976, p. 39ff.

33. Council Directive 64/221 of 25 February 1964, O.J. Sp.Ed. 1963–4, p. 117, Article 1, *Basic Documents* VI 3; Council Regulation 1612/68 of 15 October 1968, O.J. Sp.Ed. 1968, p. 475, Article 1, *Basic Documents* VI 4; Council Directive 68/360 of 15 October 1968, O.J. Sp.Ed. 1968, p. 485, Article 1, *Basic Documents VI 5;* Council Directive 72/194 of 18 May 1972, O.J. Sp.Ed. 1972, p. 474, Article 1, *Basic Documents* VI 7; Council Directive 75/34 of 17 December 1974, O.J. 1975 L 14/10, Article 1, *Basic Documents* VI 9.

34. For the United Kingdom's definition for Community purposes see Declaration dated 31 December 1982, U.K.T.S. 67 (1983), O.J. C23/1.

35. Cmnd. 9539. Later visas were demanded of nationals of India, Ghana, Nigeria and Bengla Desh, as well as Pakistan: HC 584 of 21 October 1986.

36. Revolutionary Decree of 26 March 1970; Law No 113 of 28 August 1972.

37. H. Lauterpacht, *International Law and Human Rights*, 1950, p. 347; C. Hurst, 'Nationality of Claims', 7 B.Y.I.L. (1926) 163; I. Sinclair, 'Nationality of Claims: British Practice', 27 B.Y.I.L. (1950) 125. The basis of this rule is explained, not without circularity, in the *Panevezys-Saldutiskis Railway Company Case*, P.C.I.J. Ser. A/B No. 76 (1939) at p. 16.

38. 20 February 1928, 132 L.N.T.S. 301; 22 A.J.I.L. (1930) Supp. 136.

39. There are in the field of migration law some important exceptions to this general rule, most notably in the case of obligations imposed by I.L.O. Conventions, where an attempt has been made to 'denationalise' the obligations. See I.L.O. *'L'application des conventions internationales du travail aux travailleurs étrangers'*, 46 Rev. crit. dr. int. priv. (1957) 23. Professor Riphagen has proposed that any State party to a multilateral treaty should be considered an injured State, capable of obtaining redress for the breach of an obligation stipulated for the protection of individual persons irrespective of their nationality. Draft article 5(d)(iv), I.L.C. Ybk. (1984-II) 100. See S. Rosenne, *Breach of Treaty*, 1985, p. 133.

40. For example, in the United States, it is provided that no person shall receive preference or priority in the issuance of an immigrant visa by reason of his nationality, save as provided by sections 101(a)(27), 201(b) and 203 of the Immigration and Nationality Act 1952, provided that the number of immigrant visas and conditional entries granted to nationals of one State shall not exceed 20,000 in any fiscal year. (Immigration and Nationality Act 1952, section 202). Section 101(a)(27) makes special provision for the admission of natives of western Hemisphere countries and the Canal Zone; section 201(b) makes provision for the admission of spouses of United States nationals; section 203 makes provision for the admission of children of United States nationals and others. In Ireland, the Aliens (Amendment) Order 1962 as amended by the Aliens (Amendment) Order 1975 provides in effect that persons born

8

in Great Britain or Northern Ireland are exempted from the general legal provisions concerning aliens. In the Netherlands, the Act concerning the Status of Moluccans 1976 provides that those who were transferred as a group when Indonesia become independent should be treated as if they were Dutch nationals for immigration purposes.

41. P. Weis, *Nationality and Stratelessness in International Law*, 1979, pp. 114–5; N. Bar-Yaacov, *Dual Nationality*, 1961, p. 243; S. Rosenne, *'La loi israëlienne sur la nationalité'*, 81 J.D.I. (1954)4.

CHAPTER 1

Immigration Law and Nationality Law

As a description of a legal status, the word 'nationality' is modern. The origin of this use of the word coincides with the origin of the nation-state. Koessler observes that the matrix of the word 'nationality' is the French term *'nation-alité'*,[1] and Makarov adds that our modern legal concept of nationality was fashioned by the French Revolution.[2] Article 25 of the French Constitution of 1793 proclaimed *'la souveraineté réside dans le peuple';* the significance of that article is apparent as soon as it is compared with the following extract from the writings of a modern French jurist, Boulbès:

> *Dans l'Ancien Droit la nationalité française était strictement l'allégeance envers le roi de France. La volonté du roi était donc la source de l'allégeance française et il pouvait par une simple manifestation de cette volonté conférer à tel ou tel la nationalité française . . . Une collation de cette nature n'est plus possible aujourd'hui où la souveraineté est passée du roi à la nation . . .*[3]

The foregoing might lead us to draw the tentative conclusion that the modern application of the word 'nationality' marks the prevalence (at least locally) of the idea that the individual may owe allegiance to the metaphysical concept of the nation, rather than the sovereign in person. However, an examination of the etymological history of the term is unlikely to elucidate the concept embodied in it, since jurists have tended to be indiscriminate in their use of the captions 'national', 'citizen' and 'subject', and this tendency is particularly marked in the late eighteenth century. Even Vattel, who preferred to use the term *'citoyen'*, occasionally, confused it with the word *'sujet'*.[4] The articles of Confederation of the United States (1777)[5] spoke of 'citizens', but it was not until the enactment of the Federal Constitution (1787) that the term 'subject' ceased to be synonymous with the term 'citizen' in the law of the U.S.A. In 1870 the Governments of the United Kingdom and the United States conclud-ed a treaty 'to regulate the *citizenship* of the British *subjects* who have emigrat-ed . . . to the United States of America'.[6] The treaty provided that certain of these subjects 'shall be at liberty to resume their British *nationality'*.[7] Citizenship, subjecthood and nationality are all descriptions of the status of a legal person *vis-à-vis* a political environment. So it is not surprising that all three concepts have been profoundly influenced by political theory.

THE DEVELOPMENT OF NATIONALITY

A form of citizenship was, of course, well-known in the Greek city-states, where Athenians in the fourth century B.C. distinguished between citizens (ἀστοι, πολιται) metics (μετοικοι) and mere strangers of travellers (ζεῳ νοτ). Until the introduction of primitive forms of naturalization,[8] citizenship was essentially a hereditary status, obtained only when both parents of the *de cujus* held Athenian citizenship themselves. Every freeman whose parents satisfied this test was enrolled in his deme at the age of eighteen, and remained a member of it for life. Tenure of Athenian citizenship was the prerequisite for the enjoyment of certain political rights,[9] and since the metic occupied an intermediate position between the citizen and the stranger[10] it is tempting to draw close analogies between Athenian citizenship and modern nationalities. Such comparisons should not be made unless it is stressed that fourth-century Attica knew no clear distinction between law, justice, morality and religion.[11] Professor Sabine argues that the Attican tended to think of citizenship not as a possession but as something shared, like membership in a family.[12] Furthermore, the distinction between citizen and metic diminished under the influence of Themistocles, and as a result of the admission into the community of large numbers of metics, after the decimation of the citizen population at the battles of Syracuse and Chaeronaea. Some of the Greek city-states (such as Delphi) granted to the entire populations of their allies extensive citizenship rights; these rights seem to have included everything other than the right to become archon, and possibly, the right to vote. Such rights were enjoyed by residents and non-residents alike,[13] and since the enjoyment of these privileges was separated from tenure of citizenship (or membership of the deme) the latter ceased to retain not only its original exclusiveness, but also its original significance and its similarity to nationality in the modern sense.

It is not uncommon to find some modern jurists comparing present-day nationality laws with the citizenship laws of 'ancient' Rome.[14] Such comparisons may be justifiable, for Roman citizenship, at certain times was viewed as an exact legal status, more or less defined, and conferring ascertainable privileges. Thus, a Republican *Lex Minicia,* probably passed in the sixth century of the city, appears to have been designed to preserve the purity of Roman citizenship.[15] It provided that if a Roman woman married a *peregrinus* and had *connubium,* the children should no longer be Roman citizens, but should take their father's status. Thus, too, we find that only Roman citizens were subject to *jus civile,* and consequently, only these citizens could obtain *dominium.* However, those who draw comparisons between Roman concepts of citizenship and modern concepts of nationality are not always careful to specify the period of Roman legal history to which they mean to refer. Moreover, the absence, during the third pre-Christian century, of a firm distinction between the Roman legal status of *a civis* and that of a *peregrinus* frustrates any attempt to equate the former of those conditions with modern alienage and the latter with modern nationality. Finally, tenure of Roman citizenship did not invariably confer unmitigated privileges. Indeed, a *civis sine suffragio* had relatively few privileges, and it may even be said that his status had a penal character – as is evidenced by the fact that it was often accompanied by forfeiture of his land.[16]

During the latter part of the third century B.C. Roman law took cognizance of four main groups of persons. The first group consisted of enfranchised Roman citizens (*cives Romani*); into this category fell not only the more established inhabitants of Rome but also citizens of certain incorporated communities and colonies. The second group consisted of disenfranchised citizens (*cives sine suffragio*); that is, members of communities too dangerous to be left independent, even under a treaty of alliance. The third group consisted of Latins, and the fourth consisted of *socii,* citizens of allied states who occupied an intermediate legal position between that of the Latins and that of the *cives sine suffragio.*

Towards the close of the Republic and during the early Imperial period the Roman possessions were fragmented into numerous autonomous communities. By the end of the second century A.D. almost every free subject of Rome was connected with such a community by citizenship. The latter status was acquired by birth, adoption, manumission or by gift of the magistrates. Legitimate children normally acquired the citizenship of their fathers, whereas illegitimate ones took the citizenship of their mothers' native communities.[17] In this system it was possible to encounter statelessness (as when a slave was freed without manumission) and plural citizenship (as when a person acquired one citizenship by birth and another by adoption).

However, as the Roman Empire grew towards universality, and as Roman citizenship came to be extended to the vast majority of the free subjects of Rome, the practical utility of that status diminished.[18] Thus, Roman citizenship became replaced by a new system of subdivision of citizenships, based on the nexus between the *de cujus* and his local community (*municipium*).

It seems that during this later Roman period the acquisition of local or municipal citizenship tended to be governed by the principle of *jus soli* rather than the principle of *jus sanguinis.* If this is correct, then from the sixth century to the ninth the tendency must have been reversed. There are at least two reasons why the *jus sanguinis* principle may have come to prevail over the *jus soli*. Firstly, the conquering tribes refrained from systematic destruction of Roman institutions and were content to live according to their own laws while permitting the subdued people and their descendants to enjoy their own. Secondly, the successors to the Roman empire shared a tribal heritage, and tribalism may be defined as a system of communal government in which the composition of the political unit and the enjoyment of political rights by individuals are governed by descent alone.[19]

The German tribes, while eroding the distinctions between the *municipia,* welded the Roman mass into a non-political whole. At the same time they permitted the preservation of Roman law. From the tenth century onwards the growth of cities such as Florence and of the industries and trades to which these cities owed their prosperity called for the existence, within each area, of a commercio-legal system founded on the enjoyment of a common legal status by the inhabitants of each territorial unit. These social and economic conditions seem to have been largely responsible for the renaissance of Roman law, and, both as a result of the revival of Roman law and as a result of the need to replace the *jus sanguinis* principle by one providing for greater local uniformity, the use of the *jus soli* principle increased. North of the Alps there was a similar development, due not to the growth of cities but to the rise of feudalism, for it was unthinkable that a member of a tribe should be able to invoke his tribal law against his feudal overlord, particularly if the latter was a member of a different tribe.[20]

A comparable process took place in England. Alfred's success in stemming the advance of the Danes, and the successes of his son and grandson in merging the Danelaw with the rest of their territories heralded not only the creation of the kingdom of England, but also the growth of the *jus soli* principle.[21] By the early tenth century a system of allegiances based on the *jus soli* principle had become pervasive: one statute of Aethelstan manifests the fact that the lordless man was regarded with very great suspicion.[22] Nevertheless, a radical distinction between the free man and the slave continued to exist until well after the Norman Conquest and even among free men there were varying degrees of independence and various kinds of allegiance. The most powerful nobles owed allegiance to the King alone, but the vast majority of freemen owed their first allegiance to their local lord and owed ultimate (almost notional) allegiance to the King as overlord.

Moreover, kinship remained a very important social and legal link in the early Saxon period.[23] There was a 'constant tendency to conflict between old customs of the family and newer laws of the State',[24] and as the unity and power of the State grew, the legal significance of kinship diminished. However, this latter development was gradual in the extreme, and in view of the relative rarity of travel it can scarcely have been perceptible. The development was not complete by 1066, for long after the Conquest, Englishmen in search of protection or vengeance frequently resorted to kin rather than King, and the laws of the early Normans condoned this procedure. [25]

During the Norman feudal period the *jus soli* principle was reinforced. William and his immediate successors ruled a kingdom peopled by several separate races, but unified by the facts of geography and military power, and by the systems and theories of feudalism which related the political hierarchy to land tenure. It was thus natural that the basis of allegiance should continue to be found in the *jus soli* principle. In *Elyas de Rabeyn's Case* (1290) a foreign-born man successfully claimed a portion of an English estate (as he could normally do only if he were a liege of the King). However, in reaching their conclusion, the judges expressly stated that their action was not to constitute a precedent, and so, paradoxically, the case illustrates that a person born abroad was not normally of fealty to the King of England.[26] This presupposes acceptance of the territorial principle.[27]

Conflicts between the *jus soli* principle and the *jus sanguinis* principle are, of course, particularly likely to occur in connection with the status and rights of foreign-born children of parents native to England. In an attempt to resolve some such conflicts, Parliament passed in 1351 the statute *De Natis Ultra Mare*.[28] The first item of that statute declared that children of the Kings of England, wherever born, may inherit the Crown. The second item provided that various named persons born abroad might take their inheritance on the death of the English-born ancestors. The third item dealt with foreign-born children whose parents at the time of the children's births owed allegiance to the King of England. It stated that such children might take their inheritance if, at the time of their births, their mothers had been absent from England with the husbands' consent.[29]

Although the *jus soli* principle was thus attenuated and modified, its application could produce bizarre results. Bracton pointed out that there were some Frenchmen in England who owed allegiance to the Kings of both England and France, and might be obliged to perform personal service to the King in whose realm they resided, and to send troops to the other monarch.[30] Moreover, a person born out of England or France could nevertheless come to owe allegiance to the Kings of either of those countries, for in the thirteenth and fourteenth centuries primitive forms of endenization were developed on both sides of the English Channel.[31]

Instructive, though it is, to regard feudal rules of obligation as progenitors of modern nationality laws, feudal concepts of fealty are not strictly comparable with nationality in the modern sense.[32] In Norman society the King was remote from his subjects in the sense that he dealt with them at second hand as regards all three arms of political power – the army, the revenue and the courts.

With the advent of the Renaissance English nationality law came to be influenced by a conflict between the view that allegiance is owed to the King and the view that it is owed to the kingdom. The re-birth of the classics, the growth of nationalism, the increase in international trade and the related temporary alliance between merchants and monarchs, the Reformation and the secularization of political theory combined to strengthen the idea of a State as a unified force, supreme in its own territory, but dependent for its moral welfare and military strength on the skill of the sovereign. In *Cobledike's Case*[33] a court sitting during the reign of Edward I had impliedly rejected the theory that allegiance is owed to the kingdom rather than the King; although this rejection was cited by Coke in *Calvin's Case* (1608), its influence on English and European political theory seems to have been negligible. In the words of J. Mervyn Jones, 'the pure milk of the common law doctrine of allegiance to the Crown is to be found in *Calvin's Case.*[34]

This was a fictitious action, set on foot in the High Court of England in the name of *Calvin v. Smith.*[35] The object of this action was to resolve difficulties in determining the status in English law of persons born in Scotland before the accession of James to the English throne (*the antenati*) and those born there after his accession (*the postnati*). A joint session of the Commissioners of England and Scotland proposed that the *postnati,* at least, should be declared naturalized in both England and Scotland, but this was unacceptable to certain 'professors of the common law' who declared that 'no man can be . . . natural of two distinct kingdoms'. The judges present at the discussion disagreed with this reasoning, on the ground that allegiance followed the natural person of the King and not his 'body politic'.

Calvin was a *postnatus* who sought to recover English lands of which he claimed to have been disseised by Smith, whose reply was that Calvin was incapable of holding land in England because he had been born out of the allegiance. The Lord Chancellor and twelve judges declare that Calvin was a subject and not an alien in English law. Coke defined his terms:

> They that are born under the obedience, power, faith, ligeality or legiance of the King are natural subjects and not aliens.

Coke added that subjecthood was acquired at birth and thereafter it could not be changed. Thus, although the *postnati* were subjects in England, the *antenati* remained Scottish (aliens).

Although *Calvin's Case* involved examination of the theory that allegiance is owed to the body politic rather than the natural person of the King, and although that case constitutes a powerful precedent on both sides of the Atlantic,[36] it provides no direct authority on the question of the nationality of foreign-born children of English parents. In *Bacon v. Bacon* it was held that the foreign-born daughter of an English merchant could inherit English property even though her mother was an alien; for the mother was 'sub potestate viri and *quasi* under Allegiance of our King'.[37] That case was applied in *Collingwood v. Pace*[38] three years later. Dealing with the Statute *De Natis Ultra Mare,* Lord Hale observed that construction had been such that if an English merchant married an alien and had foreign-born children, they would be natural-born subjects. He then drew a distinction between persons specially licensed to travel abroad, and persons not so licensed. In such cases, he held, 'if an Englishman not licensed or qualified by law as a merchant, go beyond the sea and live there, not for the cause of religion, and there marry a *feme* alien, and hath issue, that issue is an alien'.[39]

Professor Parry's study of the development of English nationality law in the seventeenth century renders otiose any detailed examination of that subject in the present context.[40] However, it should be observed that the seventeenth century was crowded with events significant for the development of British nationality law. The Civil War, *The Leviathan,* the propagation of Locke's thesis that the supreme power resides in the people and the resurgement[41] of the view that the Original Contract is the basis of sovereignty all seem to have combined to weaken the theory that allegiance is owed to the King in person rather than the body politic represented in him. It is clear that such a weakening took place. When William of Holland acceded to the English throne, the theory that allegiance is owed to the King in person apparently did not render the *postnati* British subjects in English law.[42]

A similar process occurred during the period of the union with Hanover. Hanovarian *postnati* were generally accorded the privileges of British subjects, but in *Isaacson v. Durant* (1886) Lord Coleridge, C.J. confirmed that these *postnati* were not British subjects. In doing so, he was forced to disagree with the assertion made by Coke in *Calvin's Case* to the effect that allegiance is owed to the King personally rather than to his body politic. 'Our minds clearly recognise that to the King in his politic, and not his personal capacity, is the allegiance of his subjects due'.[43]

By the time when the status of the Hanovarian *postnati* was ascertained three unions of the Crown had been accomplished, one empire had been won and lost, and another had been constructed in its place.[44] In this period more than one of the principles of *Calvin's Case* were put to the test. Coke had inclined to the view that the people of a conquered territory automatically became subjects of the conqueror, whereas Bacon argued that conquest had no automatic effect on the subjecthood of the subjugated population unless the sovereign expressly conferred that status by statute or treaty.[45] As the empire grew, Bacon's view gradually prevailed. Natives of the new dominions did not acquire British subjecthood by the mere act of conquest. Rather, subjecthood was usually conferred as a result of a deliberate decision enshrined in the appropriate treaty of capitulation or in a statute passed by

Parliament in London. Thus, in 1724 the Law Officers inclined to the view that in the absence of specific provision to the contrary, Jamaica was merely a conquered country, and not a colony of British subjects.[46] When Canada was retained after the Seven Years' War and its French inhabitants came under British rule, they acquired British subjecthood through the Treaty of Paris.[47] A similar method was employed in the case of Colombo in 1776.[48] The case of India is of particular interest in this respect. In 1773 it was declared that the Sepoy officers of Calcutta were 'not ... subjects of Britain but aliens and natives of Hindustan'.[49] It was not until a statute of 1813 asserted the 'undoubted sovereignty of the Crown of the United Kingdom' in India[50] and treaties of 1814 ensured recognition of this sovereignty by France and Holland[51] that the general common law rules of British nationality were extended to India.

Once the extension of British subjecthood to the inhabitants of the new territory was accepted in principle, the common-law rules – including some of those enunciated by Coke – came into play. The foremost source of allegiance remained *jus soli,* but subjecthood could still be acquired *jure sanguinis,* and for two centuries attempts were made to extend the hereditary principle. In the early seventeenth century, the foreign-born child of English parents was a British subject, but he could not transmit that subjecthood to his own children born abroad. In the eighteenth century this situation was amended by statute[52] but the statutes were construed restrictively[53] and were finally repealed.[54] When the *jus sanguinis* principle was extended, the extensions were made in addition to, and not in derogation of, the *jus soli* principle. Thus, a person born in India at a time when India was claimed as a dominion of the Crown under effective British occupation[55] was a British subject. Moreover, in accordance with the principle of indelibility of allegiance, he held that status for life.

The principle of indelibility of allegiance was challenged by the American Revolution, not only as a result of the political problems which the revolution presented, but also as a result of the politico-legal theories which it accompanied. Indeed, the refutation of the principle that a subject cannot divest himself of his allegiance to the sovereign lies at the heart of the Declaration of Independence.[56] On the outbreak of the Revolution, each inhabitant of the American states was given the opportunity to choose to remain a British subject or to take citizenship of the United States of America. The test for the maintenance or acquisition of citizenship by these former colonists was not *jus sanguinis* or *jus soli* but adherence: those who adhered to Britain remained British subjects; those who adhered to the independence party became citizens of the United States.[57]

In *Shanks v. DuPont,* Ann Shanks had claimed a portion of the property of her grandfather. In accordance with Article 7 of the Treaty of Paris, 1783, it was necessary to determine the claimant's national status before it was possible to decide whether she had a legal interest in the land. Justice Story made this determination on a purely factual basis, and thus succeeded in reconciling two apparently inconsistent statements, namely that the *de cujus* had a right of election, and that the Governments settled her national character:

> It cannot, we think, be doubted that Mrs. Shanks being then voluntarily under British protection, and adhering to the British side, by her removal with her husband, was deemed by the British Government to retain her allegiance, and to be, to all intents and purposes, a British subject . . . But it must be considered that it was . . . a mere election of allegiance between two nations, each of which claimed her allegiance. *The Governments, and not herself finally settled her national character. They did not treat her as capable by herself of changing or absolving her allegiance; but they virtually allowed her the benefit of her choice, by fixing her allegiance finally on the side of that party to whom she then adhered.*[58]

This test of adherence was applied only in determining the national status, in the eyes of U.S. law, of persons who had been subjects of European countries prior to the Declaration of Independence. The common law continued to apply in the thirteen states to govern the national status of the American *postnati*, and, in accordance with that law, persons born in any of the states after the Declaration of Independence acquired U.S. citizenship *jure soli*. Thus, delegates at the 1787 Convention did not find it necessary to include in the Constitution a definition of U.S. citizenship.[59] The decision in the *Dred Scott Case*[60] made such a constitutional definition a necessity.

Scott was a slave who had belonged to Dr. Emerson, an army surgeon living in Missouri (a 'slave state'). In 1834 Dr. Emerson and his wife took Scott to Illinois (a 'free state') and two years later they took him to a military post at Fort Snelling (then in Wisconsin Territory, which had been a slave state until the passing of the Missouri Compromise, which purported to turn it into a free state). In 1838 Dr. Emerson and his family returned to Missouri, taking with them Dred Scott and his wife and children. Dr. Emerson then died, and left a will whereby he bequeathed his estate to his wife in trust for his daughter, with Mrs. Emerson named executrix. She did not wish to own any slaves, but could not liberate them becaue she held them only in trust. So, in an attempt to secure Scott's release, it was agreed that Scott would file a suit against Mrs. Emerson, alleging that he had been liberated by being taken to the free states of Illinois and Wisconsin. The Supreme Court of Missouri held that since Scott and his family had returned to Missouri, they had retained their character as slaves. Scott then sought to take the case to the federal courts and to this end he sougth to establish diversity of jurisdiction. Since it was Scott's contention that he was a citizen of Missouri, and since Mrs. Emerson held Missouri citizenship, the woman 'sold' the man to her brother, who was a citizen of New York

State. In 1856 the U.S. Supreme Court decided by a majority that it was without jurisdiction since Scott, being a slave, was not a citizen of any state.

The *Scott Case* became the subject of famous debates between Abraham Lincoln and Stephen Douglas during their senatorial campaign in Illinois in 1858.[61] After his success in the election for presidency, Lincoln issued the Emancipation Proclamation, which declared that former slaves should be freed, but did not declare that they should become citizens. Following the war, the Republicans introduced in Congress the Civil Rights Bill, which became an Act in 1866.[62] The first section of that Act contained the first statutory description of a citizen of the United States; it provided

that all persons born in the United States and not subject to any foreign power, excluding Indians not taxed, are hereby declared to be citizens of the United States

and that such citizens of every race and colour, without regard to any previous condition of slavery, should have the same right in every state or territory of the U.S.A. to full and equal benefit of all laws. The *Dred Scott Case* continued to be the source of doubts, however, since it gave rise to the view that a free black man could not become a citizen of the United States. It was in order to resolve this remaining doubt that the Fourteenth Amendment to the U.S. Constitution was adopted in 1868. That amendment begins with these words:

All persons born or naturalized in the United States, and subject to the jurisdiction thereof are citizens of the United States and of the state wherein they reside.

An attempt to build on that Amendment, by applying the doctrine of adherence to *a postnatus,* was made without success. In *Elk v. Wilkins* a member of one of the indian tribes left his tribe and lived among the white people in Omaha, where he sought to vote. The registrar refused to allow the indian to vote, arguing that the indian was not a citizen of the United States. The latter based his claim to citizenship on the Fourteenth Amendment; to sustain this argument he had to demonstrate that he was subject to the jurisdiction of the United States, and to show that he was subject to U.S. jurisdiction, he argued that he had manifested his adherence to the U.S. The Supreme Court held that Elk had been born subject to the jurisdiction of the tribe and not the United States, and that in consequence he was not a citizen.[63] Fifteen years later, in *U.S. v. Wong Kim Ark,* the Supreme Court interpreted the Fourteenth Amendment in accordance with the principle of *jus soli* and in the light of *Calvin's Case,* and held that the U.S.-born child of Chinese parents was a citizen of the U.S.A., and was consequently free to enter the United States, notwithstanding the Chinese Exclusion Act.[64]

The use of adherence to determine the national status of the American *antenati* had grown contemporaneously with various political theories based on concepts of social contract. (This fact helps to explain why Condorcet and Lafayette endorsed the Declaration of Independence with such enthusiasm).[65] Seen in this light, the politico-legal theories which accompanied the American Revolution must have presented a challenge to the doctrine of indelibility of allegiance. The effects, on this doctrine, of the practical problems raised by the Revolution were no less significant.

In *Doe d. Thomas v. Acklam,* a certain Elizabeth Harrison, a natural-born British subject, died intestate, seised of the fee simple estate of some valuable lands. Her next of kin, Mary Thomas, had been born in the United States after the recognition of their independence, of parents born there before that time. The English court held that Mary Thomas was an alien, incapable of inheriting lands in England. Tindal, counsel for the plaintiff, argued that

> the nation could only be separated from this country by one of three modes, by cession, by conquest, or by voluntary separation acknowledged and sanctioned by the Legislature ... they cannot of their own accord put off their own allegiance.

In contrast, Parke (for the defendant) paid great attention to those passages in *Calvin's Case* which mention the reciprocal nature of allegiance. The implication of his argument was that the social compact between subject and King could be broken by mutual agreement, and that the compact between the King and his former subjects in America had been broken in this way. Parke conceded that the bond of allegiance 'cannot be dissolved by either party without the concurrence of the other' and added that

> that may be done by the mutual consent of both parties, and here the act of the Sovereign was authorised by Act of Parliament, 22 G. III, c. 46

(the Act by which the King was authorised to conclude a peace with the colonies). However, Abbott, C.J. based his decision firmly on the ground of practicality, stressing that very great inconvenience would result if the great mass of the inhabitants of the United States were treated as subjects of the two distinct countries.[66]

The Chief Justice expressed his satisfaction at discovering that his decision conformed with American case-law, and his judgment was, in fact, cited with approval by the U.S. Supreme Court in *Inglis v. Trustees of the Sailor's Snug Harbour.*[67] In that case the Supreme Court held that a person born before the outbreak of the American Revolution, being incapacitated by his infancy from making a choice of allegiance, inherited the national status of his father, subject to the right to renounce that status on reaching majority. Thus the Court concluded that such a person, having failed to renounce his inherited national status, was a British subject, and was incapable of owning land in New York.

The decision in the *Inglis Case* was expressly compatible with English law, since it concerned the status of an *antenatus*. However, the English judiciary had demonstrated in *Acklam's Case* its reluctance to attenuate the doctrine of indelibility of allegiance in the case of *postnati*. Not until the passage of the Naturalization Act of 1870 was that doctrine ended, in accordance with the Anglo-American Bancroft Convention of 1868.[68]

During the nineteenth century it became customary for European powers in Oriental countries to extend their protection to persons other than their own subjects. In conformity with this pattern, Britain extended protection to the descendants of British subjects in whose favour the *jus sanguinis* principle no longer ran, *protégés* within organized native States and the inhabitants of territories ruled by Britain but not claimed as British possessions. Such persons were known as British protected persons. The fact that it was considered necessary to confer on them a specific title indicates that they occupied a somewhat unusual position. Until 1949 they had no more rights than aliens for the purposes of immigration law (though from 1949 onwards they were subject to the same immigration laws as British subjects).[69] The legal rights and duties of British protected persons also came to be shared by immigrants to self-governing dominions under the British Crown, when they had become naturalized in the relevant dominion but had not been recognized as subjects under British nationality law.[70]

Meanwhile, the older dominions began to clamour for a system of imperial naturalization which would enable them to confer full British subjecthood on alien immigrants. The 1870 Naturalization Act had conferred on colonial legislatures the power to provide for naturalization to be effective only within the limits of the colony. In 1901 a Departmental Committee of the Home Office recommended that colonies and possessions overseas should be able to confer immigrants a British subjecthood which would become a 'common status', recognized throughout the Empire.[71] Clearly, it was desirable to have such a status conferred in accordance with a 'common code' whereby each competent legislature would grant subjecthood in accordance with the same principles. At the Imperial Conferences of 1902 and 1907 agreement on certain basic principles was reached.[72] These principles became the foundation of the British Nationality and Status of Aliens Act, 1914. As its title implies, that Act formed a new code for nationality in general. It did not turn nationality into a statutory concept, but tended to confirm the view that the source of subjecthood was allegiance.

The Act fell into three parts. The first redefined the means of acquiring original nationality – *jure sanguinis* and *jure soli* (a person acquired British subjecthood *jure soli* if he was born 'within His Majesty's dominions and allegiance')[73] At first the Act restricted the acquisition of original nationality *jure sanguinis* to the first overseas-born generation[74] but after the war this was amended in favour of children of British subjects by annexation and in Crown service[75] and thereafter subjecthood was transmissible *jure sanguinis* indefinitely, subject to satisfaction of certain formal requirements.[76] The need to satisfy these formal requirements disappeared in 1943.[77] The second part of the Act provided for a new naturalization scheme, whereby each governing dominion determined the conditions under which it would confer British subjecthood, subject to some general principles, such as a universal five years' residence requirement:[78] The third part dealt with the status of aliens, and with married women and miscellaneous supplementary issues.[79] This part was intended to come into operation in each part of the Empire on its adoption by the Imperial Parliament, but some of the dominions proceeded to debate and enact it in their own legislatures, with the result that several disparities arose. Thus, the 1914 Act ensured that throughout the Empire there was a 'common code' of nationality, with minor differences from one part to the other. This system worked imperfectly. Some of the dominions adopted racially discriminatory immigration legislation, which tended to vitiate the benefits of the common status. For example, a British subject from Ceylon might well find it more difficult to immigrate into Canada[80] or Australia[81] than would an alien from the U.S.A. On the whole, however, it seems that Harvey is correct in asserting that Commonwealth cooperation was successful in ensuring the preservation of the code and of the economic, political and legal advantages which accrued from British subjecthood.[82] It was not until after the Second World War that this situation came to an end.

During the first half of this century the Commonwealth overseas (as the Empire came to be called) fell into two parts. The first was composed of trusts, colonies and protectorates – where the acquisition of subjecthood depended on legislation passed in the U.K. The second part consisted of the self-governing territories. A committee of the 1926 Imperial Conference described the latter as 'equal in status, in no way subordinate to one another in any aspect of their domestic or external affairs, though united by a common allegiance to the Crown.[83] The preamble to the Statute of Westminster reaffirmed this principle.[84] Accordingly, it was natural that the Statute of Westminster should be followed by the creation of a separate citizenship for each independent Commonwealth country. In 1946, Canada, after consulting her fellow members of the Commonwealth, passed the Canadian Citizenship Act, which provided that British subjects by connection with Canada should be known as 'Canadian citizens'.[85] That Act determined the conditions under which Canadian citizenship would be conferred in future. It provided that everyone who was a Canadian citizen should, by virtue of his tenure of that status, become a British subject.

There were obvious political and administrative advantages in the Canadian system. In 1947 a conference of experts met in London to discuss the possibility of extending it to the rest of the Commonwealth. It was agreed that each country would have its own citizenship and would determine the conditions under which that citizenship would be granted (thus, each country within the Commonwealth would determine the criteria for naturalization of aliens as citizens of that country). For these purposes the United Kingdom and its remaining colonies would be treated as a unit. Those who acquired local citizenship in this way would automatically acquire a second status known as British subjecthood or Commonwealth citizenship (those two terms to be interchangeable). Each Commonwealth country would recognize the citizens of every other Commonwealth country as British subjects or Commonwealth citizens, not as aliens. Each Commonwealth country would make it easier for citizens of other Commonwealth countries to obtain its citizenship than for aliens to do so. The essence of this scheme was that local citizenship would be the gateway to British subjecthood (Commonwealth citizenship) and that citizenship would be a creature of statute, rather than a consequence of allegiance.[86] This system was adopted as the basis of the British Nationality Act, 1948 and the corresponding enactments in other Commonwealth countries. Under that scheme there were four main national groups; British subjects (or Commonwealth citizens), citizens of the Republic or Ireland, British protected persons and aliens.

Although the British Nationality Act of 1948 may have appeared novel to lawyers trained strictly in the previous English tradition, from a comparative perspective it appears far from radical. Multiple or tiered systems of nationality had been used before, not only in ancient times, but also in modern ones, and there was a precedent for a structured system of this kind in the French legal distinction between *citoyens français, sujets français* and *étrangers*. Even in British nationality law prior to 1949 distinctions had been drawn between British subjects by connection with different territories within the Commonwealth. Sometimes (as in the case of the immigration laws of West Indian territories) it was thought covenient to distinguish between British subjects who 'belonged' to a particular island and British subjects who did not 'belong' to it. The criteria for determining whether a person belonged to a particular island were reminiscent of nationality laws *stricto sensu.*[87] The 1920 Protocol Relating to Military Obligations in Certain Cases of Double Nationality recognized, by clear implication, a distinct 'nationality' possessed by subjects of the Union of South Africa.[88] In 1929 Sir Cecil Hurst observed that certain British subjects regularly possess two nationalities – the common status enjoyed by all subjects of the British Empire, and also the nationality of the particular autonomous part of the Empire to which they belong.[89]

The 1948 Act, and the corresponding legislation adopted throughout the Commomwealth, aimed at preserving the 'common status' of British subjects.[90] Those Acts did not preserve the 'common code', and the laws governing the acquisition of local citizenship varied widely from one part of the Commonwealth to another. The United Kingdom and its colonies retained a sort of 'common status' of their own. A single citizenship was enjoyed by individuals who had associations with the United Kingdom, and persons connected with colonies. Beause of the difficulties, in the field of immigration law, resulting from the maintenance of a composite status of citizenship of the United Kingdom and Colonies, the Parliamentary Committee on U.K. Citizenship[91] and the authors of the 'Rose' survey, *Colour and Citizenship,*[92] recommended that the composite status should be abandoned in favour of separate citizenship for the United Kingdom and each of its colonies.[93]

The scheme established by the British Nationality Act of 1948 was complicated by three factors in particular: transitional arrangements, British protected persons and the Republic of Ireland. The framers of the 1948 Act, determined to ensure that no subject should lose his status as a result of that statute, incorporated into it provisions to stipulate that while an independent Commonwealth country remained without a comprehensive citizenship law, certain groups of persons would be known as 'potential citizens' of that country, and such persons would become, in the law of the United Kingdom, 'British subjects without citizenship', and would remain such until the adoption of the citizenship law in the relevant Commonwealth country.[94] The British Nationality Act, 1948 was the first Act of Parliament[95] to define the conditions for the acquisition of the status of a British protected person. The cumulative effect of the Act and of the Order in Council which followed it was to confine the term to persons who had specified connections with specified protectorates and trust territories and those who, by virtue of local law, were subjects of named protectorates and protected states.[96] For most purposes of U.K. domestic law, British protected persons continued to be treated in much the same way as aliens, but the British Nationality Act, 1948 expressly exempted them from the restrictions which applied to aliens seeking to enter the United Kingdom and the same Act originally ensured that British protected persons would have a few privileges in regard to naturalization.[97] In 1948 the position of the Irish was disputed and obscure: under English law, a person born in the south of Ireland was a British subject, but under Irish law such a person was a citizen of Eire.[98] So far as the Irish are concerned, the chief effect of the 1948 Act was to ensure that they occupied a position mid-way between British subjects and aliens, yet distinct from British protected persons: in general, they had the privileges, but not the status, of subjects.[99]

These terminological difficulties were increased by the interchangeability of the expressions 'British subject' and 'Commonwealth citizen'. For a quarter of a century United Kingdom statutes tended to select one or other of these expressions for political reasons, according to the overtones which each expression contains.[100] Thus, the Commonwealth Immigrants Acts, 1962 and 1968 restricted the right of 'Commonwealth citizens' to enter the United Kingdom, whereas the Representation of the People Acts, 1949–1969 extended the franchise to defined groups of 'British subjects'. The new Commonwealth countries immediately eschewed the term 'British subject', and that term was thereafter employed only in the United Kingdom and in Canada,[101] Australia[102] and New Zealand[103] (in addition to Southern Rhodesia).[104] Even in those countries there were objections to the use of the term.[105]

One of the intentions of the framers of the 1948 legislation was to erect a 'common status' of British subjects, founded on 'common clauses' to be inserted into the nationality laws of each Commonwealth country. This aspiration did not materialize in detail. The Indian Citizenship Act, 1955 provided that citizens of Commonwealth countries other than India should be known as 'Commonwealth citizens', but it did not provide that Indian citizens should be known by the same title.[106] Conversely, the Pakistan Citizenship Act, 1951 (as amended) conferred Commonwealth citizenship on citizens of Pakistan, but faied to provide expressly that Commonwealth citizenship shall be shared equally by citizens of all other Commonwealth countries.[107] Ceylon had no 'common clause' at all.[108] The Cyprus Citizenship Law of 1967 provided that anyone who was not a citizen of Cyprus should be known as an alien.[109]

Even where mutual recognition of the status of Commonwealth citizens was assured, mutual recognition of the rights accruing from that status was often absent. Introducing the British Nationality Bill to Parliament, the Lord Chancellor expressed himself as follows:

> Let it be plainly understood that common nationality does not necessarily confer rights in other member states ... All we can say is that, although there is no special treatment which necessarily follows throughout the Commonwealth, we hope and believe that, other things being equal, the fact that a man possesses British nationality will stand him in good stead in his application, whatever that application may be.[110]

In particular, a British subject did not enjoy, by virtue of his status, the right to enter the territory of a Commonwealth country of which he is not a citizen. Indeed, long before the adoption of the British Nationality Act, 1948 certain Commonwealth legislatures chose to restrict the immigration rights of British subjects from other Commonwealth countries. In *In Re Munshi Singh*[111] the Chief Justice of Canada held that tenure of British subjecthood did not constitute a full qualification for entry to Canadian territory. The Chief Justice even went so far, in that case, as to say that the status of a British subject is not superior to that of an alien, so far as immigration is concerned. In *De Marigny v. Langlais*,[112] Casey, J. said that it was 'firmly established' that the status of a British subject did not carry with it the right of free entry into any Commonwealth country. Robert R. Wilson observed that

> almost all Commonwealth countries have in some form or other imposed restrictions on the immigration of British subjects or Commonwealth citizens. This is particularly true in the case of the 'old' Commonwealth countries which have long discriminated against so-called 'non-white' immigrants'.[113]

In 1962 the Privy Council upheld the judgment of the Fijian Judge Hammett, in *Thornton v. Police*. In that case the appellant argued that he was immune from deportation from Fiji since he was a British subject within the meaning of the British Nationality Act of 1948. Viscount Simon observed that the 1948 Act dealt with the status of British subjects, not with the incidents of that status; thus he and his fellow members of the Committee dismissed the appeal.[114]

In the year in which the British Nationality Act became law, J. Mervyn Jones wrote that in U.K. law three main rights flowed from British subjecthood, namely the right to vote in Parliamentary and local government elections, the right to enter the United Kingdom and the right to be considered as a candidate for appointments in the foreign and civil service.[115] In 1962 the right of British subjects to enter the United Kingdom was severely curtailed, and in 1968 some citizens of the United Kingdom and Colonies became subject to immigration control.

BRITISH NATIONALITY LAW

Whereas in other countries nationality law commonly forms the basis for the imposition of immigration control, in the United Kingdom the immigration law provided the inspiration for the British Nationality Act 1981. By the end of the preceding decade, the imposition of immigration controls on certain citizens of the United Kingdom and Colonies had become well established. For the purposes of immigration a distinction was drawn between citizens of the United Kingdom and Colonies who derived that status by association with the United Kingdom and those who derived it by association with existing or former dependencies. The former were known as patrials. They alone enjoyed the right of abode, while other citizens were subject to immigration control.[116]

One of the principal purposes of the British Nationality Act 1981 was to distinguish for the purposes of nationality law, rather than immigration law, between those whose status was acquired by association with the United Kingdom and those whose status was acquired by association with dependencies. The former were to be known as 'British citizens'. The latter were to be known as 'British Dependent Territories citizens' or as 'British Overseas citizens', those two titles reflecting a distinction between associations with existing and former dependencies.

The second main object of the Act of 1981 was to apply the principle of sexual equality in the regulation of nationality. Thus, citizenship was to be transmissible on marriage to husbands as well as to wives; and citizenship was to be transmissible to children in the female as well as the male line. It followed that it was necessary to impose new restrictions on the transmission of citizenship *jure sanguinis* to second and subsequent generations born overseas; for otherwise the application of the principle of sexual equality would have led to a multiplication of overseas-born British nationals.

The third principal purpose of the British Nationality Act 1981 was to restrict the acquisition of British citizenship *jure soli* in the interests of immigration control. That citizenship was not to be acquired by the children, born in the United Kingdom, of parents who had no right at the time of the birth to remain indefinitely in the kingdom. The Government judged that where such a child acquired that citizenship, and with it the right of abode, it might not be consonant with the child's rights to require the departure of the parents. In this sense the former rule applying in the law of nationality could, in the Government's assessment, create an impediment to immigration control.

Under the new scheme[117] a person born in the United Kingdom acquires British citizenship at birth only if either parent had that status at that time and was then 'settled' in the United Kingdom.[118] The parent is considered to have been settled in the United Kingdom if he or she was ordinarily resident there at the time of the birth, without being subject under the immigration laws to any restriction on the period during which he or she may remain.[119] In the event of the adoption in the United Kingdom of a minor, the latter acquires British citizenship if the adoptor (or either of two adoptors) has that status at the date of the adoption.[120] If the adoptive parents are merely settled in the United Kingdom, however, the child does not acquire British citizenship by law on adoption.

British citizenship by descent is now acquired by children born overseas to any person, irrespective of sex, who was at the time of the birth a British citizen other than by descent. Hence, the transmission of British citizenship *jure sanguinis* is limited in principle to the first generation born overseas. There are however two exceptions to this principle. Firstly, where a person was recruited in the United Kingdom to serve in Crown service under the government of the

United Kingdom, and is serving overseas, that person's child born abroad will acquire British citizenship automatically. Secondly, a child born abroad will acquire British citizenship by descent if either parent is at the time of the birth a British citizen serving one of the institutions of the European Communities, having been recruited for that service in a country which was a member of the Communities at the time of the recruitment.[121]

The second generation born overseas benefits from advantageous rules governing registration. A person born outside the United Kingdom is entitled to be registered as a British citizen, on application made within twelve months of the birth, provided that three conditions are met. The first is that either parent was a British citizen at the time of the registrant's birth. The second is that the parent obtained that status by descent form a person born, adopted, registered or naturalized in the United Kingdom. The third is that the parent in question lived in the United Kingdom for a period of three years (excluding absences not anounting in aggregate to 270 days) at any time prior to the birth. Where the first two of these conditions are met, but the third is not met, the child is entitled to be registered as a British citizen if he would otherwise be stateless. In any event, the Secretary of State has a power to register any minor as a British citizen.[122]

Under the new scheme, the term 'British protected person' continues to be used to describe those having specified connections with protectorates, protected States or United Kingdom trust territories.[123] Those who were formerly known as British subjects without citizenship[124] are now known as British subjects.[125] British protected persons and British subjects are entitled to be registered as British citizens on advantageous terms. The same facility is extended to British Dependent Territories citizens and British Overseas citizens.[125] Such applicants are entitled to acquire British citizenship by registration after five-years' residence in the United Kingdom, provided that during the twelve months preceding the application they were not subject to any restriction on the period during which they might remain in the kingdom. In computing those five years, absences are disregarded if they do not amount in aggregate to more than 450 days or to more than 90 days in the year preceding the application. An applicant is disqualified, however, if he was in breach of the immigration laws at any time in that five-year period.[127]

There are four special cases in which a person is entitled under distinctly transitional provisions to be registered as a British citizen. During the five years after the entry into force of the Act, a person is entitled to be registered as a British citizen by virtue of residence in the United Kingdom or Crown employment, on much the same terms as under the preceding law.[128] Secondly, a woman who was a citizen of the United Kingdom and Colonies on the eve of the commencement of the Act of 1981 is entitled to be registered as a British citizen within five years thereafter if on that date she was entitled to be registered as a citizen of the United Kingdom and Colonies by reason of her marriage.[129] Thirdly, a person born in a foreign country[130] is entitled to be registered as a British citizen, on application made within five years after the entry into force of the Act, if he had acquired citizenship of the United Kingdom and Colonies by descent from a father having specified connections with the United Kingdom and if he had a right of abode.[131] Finally, there is a provision for the registration of a person as a British citizen when he has renounced citizenship of the United Kingdom and Colonies and had been entitled under the previous law to reacquire that status.[132] In each of these four cases, the draftsman has created a facility of registration in order to preserve legitimate expections developed under the antecedent legislation.

These cases apart, British citizenship which is not acquired at birth may be acquired only by naturalization. This is a matter of discretion rather than entitlement.[133] The Act of 1981 makes provision for two species of naturalization: the one in consequence of residence or Crown service and the other in consequence of marriage. In the former case, the residence qualification is identical with that required of British subjects, British protected persons, British Overseas citizens and British Dependent Territories citizens, in the event of their registration.[134] Five years' service abroad for the government of the United Kingdom will be treated equally with five years' residence.[135] In addition to the requirements of residence or Crown service, the applicant must fulfill conditions respecting his character, linguistic ability and intentions. He must satisfy the Secretary of State that he is of good character; that he has a sufficient knowledge of the English, Welsh or Scottish Gaelic language; and that he intends to make his home in the United Kigdom or to enter or continue in Crown service or in the service of an international organization to which the United Kingdom belongs, or in the employment of a company or association established in the United Kingdom.[136]

The conditions governing the acquisition of British Dependent Territories citizenship reflect in many respects those which govern the acquisition of British citizenship. In particular, British Dependent Territories citizenship is acquired *jure soli* only if at the time of the birth either parent is a British Dependent Territories citizen or is settled in a dependent territory.[187] As in the case of British citizenship, British Dependent Territories citizenship is normally transmitted only to the first generation born overseas, but passes in the female as well as the male line.[138] Provision is made for registration as British Dependent Territories citizens of certain minor children of those who acquired that citizenship by descent.[139] In special cases of a transitional nature, British Dependent Territories citizenship is available by registration to those who have been resident in dependent territories, or have married citizens of the United Kingdom and Colonies who enjoyed that status by association with dependent territories.[140] There is also provision for a right to registration by virtue of the applicant's father's citizenship[141] and those who formerly had the right to resume citizenship of the United Kingdom and Colonies enjoy, in appropriate cases, the right to register as British Dependent Territories citizens.[142]

In the case of the British Overseas citizenship, there is, of course, no cause for the enactment of provisions governing the acquisition of the status *jure soli*. The policy of the Act of 1981 is to avoid the transmission of the status *jure sanguinis*. The new statutory provisions governing the registration of minors as British Overseas citizens are, however, consonant with the corresponding provisions governing the registration of minors as British citizens or British Dependent Territories citizens.[143] The same comment applies *mutatis mutandis* in the case of the provisions governing the registration of persons as British Overseas citizens by virtue of marriage.[144]

Under section 37 of the 1981 Act, the status of a Commonwealth citizen is conferred on every British citizen, British Dependent Territories citizen, British Overseas citizen and British subject. Likewise, it is conferred on every person who is a citizen of a Commonwealth country under any enactment in force in that country.

The symmetry of the new British Nationality Act has now been disturbed by two developments. First, the Act of 1981 envisaged that those whose national status was acquired solely by reason of their association with the Falkland Islands and Dependencies should be British Dependent Territories citizens. (Formerly they had been known as citizens of the United Kingdom and Colonies.) Following the hostilities between the United Kingdom and Argentina in 1982 the decision was taken to confer British citizenship upon Falkland Islanders who had previously been British Dependent Territories citizens.[145] Secondly, following the Joint Declaration between the Government of the United Kingdom and the Government of China on the legal status of Hong Kong,[146] the British Government proposed that a special status should be available for those who acquired their status by association with that dependency. On 1 July 1997, British Dependent Territories citizens, who held that status only by reason of a connection with Hong Kong, would lose that status. On or after 1 July 1987, British Dependent Territories citizens having a connection with Hong Kong would be eligible to acquire a new status: British National (Overseas).[147]

UNITED STATES NATIONALITY LAW

The Immigration and Nationality law of the United States continues to be regulated by the Walter McCarren Act or Immigration and Nationality Act of 27 June 1952, as amended.[148] For all practical purposes, the Nationality Act of

1940[149] is repealed and its remaining provisions transferred to the Act of 1952. Although the system of national statuses created by the Walter McCarren Act is very much simpler than that created by the British Nationality Act 1981, it does entail a distinction between United States nationals and United States citizens. Every citizen is a national; but in three instances persons become United States nationals without being United States citizens at birth.

The first is the case of a person born in an outlying possession of the United States on or after the date of formal acquisition of such possession. The second is the case of a person born outside the United States and its outlying possessions of parents both of whom are nationals but not citizens of the United States and who have had a residence in the United States or its outlying possessions prior to the birth of such person. The third case is that of a person of unknown parentage, found in an outlying possession of the United States while under the age of five years, until shown prior to his attaining the age of 21 not to have been born in such outlying possession.[150] For these purposes the outlying possessions of the United States are defined to mean American Samoa and Swains Island.

Puerto Rico, Guam and the United States Virgin Islands (together with Alaska and Hawaii) are treated as parts of the continental United States for the purpose of applying the principle of *jus soli*. A person born in the United States and subject to its jurisdiction is a United States citizen and national at birth.[151]

The acquisition of citizenship of the United States is governed solely by the constitution and enactment of Congress.[152] The Fourteenth Amendment to the Constitution of the United States indicates two methods by which a person may become a citizen: by birth in the United States and by naturalization.[153] Section 301 of the Walter McCarren Act as amended[154] continues to provide that a person shall be a national and citizen of the United States at birth if 'born in the United States and subject to the jurisdiction thereof'.[155] To be subject to the jurisdiction of the United States, a person must be born within its power and obedience.[156] Children of foreign sovereigns and ambassadors and ministers and in the case of enemy aliens are not born 'subject to the jurisdiction' of the United States.[157] With these exceptions, the principle of *jus soli* continues to apply. Indeed, in the case of Indian, Eskimo, Aleutian and other aboriginal tribes, there is now statutory provision[158] to the effect that a child born in the United States is a citizen at birth, notwithstanding the fact that his parents may owe direct tribal allegiance.

A person is a citizen if born outside the United States and its outlying possessions of parents both of whom are citizens of the United States, provided that at least one parent has a residence in the United States and its outlying possessions prior to the birth.[159] A person born outside the United States and its outlying possessions obtains United States citizenship and nationality *jure sanguinis* if at the time of the birth one parent is a citizen of the United States who has been physically present there, or in one of its outlying possessions, for a continuous period of one year prior to the birth, provided that the other parent is a national but not a citizen of the United States.[160]

A native of an outlying possession of the United States acquires United States citizenship and nationality if one of his parents was at the time of the birth a citizen of the United States who has been physically present there for a continuous period of one year prior to the birth.[161]

Those born outside the United States and its outlying possessions of parents one of whom is an alien and the other of whom is a citizen of the United States, become citizens and nationals of that country at birth if the parent having United States citizenship was physically present in the United States for not less than ten years, including at least five years since attaining the age of fourteen. Periods of honourable service with United States armed forces or with international organizations to which the United States belongs are treated as periods of physical presence in the United States for this purpose.[162] This rule has been subject to two revisions, one in 1972 and the other in 1975.

In *Rogers* v *Bellei*[163] the Supreme Court considered a challenge to the former rule governing the transmission of United States citizenship to the child of a United States citizen and an alien. The former rule provided that the child would lose his citizenship unless he came to the United States and was physically present there for five years between the ages of 14 and 28. Absences of less than twelve months in aggregate did not break the continuity of that physical presence.[164] The Supreme Court upheld the constitutionality of that rule, finding that it was neither arbitrary nor unreasonable. Nevertheless, the case drew to the attention of Congress the increasing frequency of marriages between United States citizens and aliens and the increasing frequency of births abroad in consequence of these marriages. Congress considered that the intent of the law could be met by a lesser period of residence and accordingly it reduced the statutory period from five years to two.[165] In 1978, Congress examined the question again and revoked the residence requirement altogether.[166] In recommending this course of action to Congress, the Judiciary Committee expressed the view that the residence requirement, even if limited to two years, created an inequity which should be removed. At the same time, the Committee sought to allay the fears of those who maintained that the proposed action would result in generations of citizens residing abroad with little connection with the United States. That concern was met by the rule which provides that in order for a U.S. citizen to transmit his citizenship to a child born abroad of one alien parent, the U.S. citizen must have resided in the United States for ten years.

Naturalization in the United States is conducted by specified federal courts.[167] The tradition has been unbroken since the first Naturalization Act in

1790.[168] The statutory requirements for naturalization are comparatively limited; but no alien has a right to naturalization without satisfying those requirements.[169] An applicant must demonstrate a knowledge and understanding of fundamentals of the history of the United States and of its principles and form of government.[170] Further, he must in principle demonstrate an understanding of the English language, including an ability to read, write and speak words in ordinary usage.[171] This requirement does not apply, however, to anyone physically aged fifty or over who has been living in the United States for periods amounting in aggregate to twenty years.[172] The requirement relating to ability to read and write is met if the applicant can read or write simple words and phrases.[173]

The Immigration and Nationality Act specifically prohibits the naturalization of persons opposed to government or law, or who favour totalitarian forms of government.[174] Deserters from the armed forces are ineligible for naturalization as are those who have been relieved of service in the armed forces because of alienage.[175]

Save in the case of spouses of United States citizens, applicants for naturalization must have resided in the United States for five years continuously, after being lawfully admitted for permanent residence. During that period applicants must have been continuously present for at least half of that time.[176] Spouses of United States citizens are eligible for naturalization after three years' residence.[177] In either event, applicants must demonstrate that throughout the statutory period they were, and at the date of naturalization they are, 'of good moral character.'[178]

SOVIET NATIONALITY LAW

Formerly the basic principles of Soviet nationality and citizenship law were found in the 1936 Constitution and in the Soviet Citizenship Act of 1938.[179] That Act has been described as representative of a 'drastic change' in Soviet law.[180] It initiated the third stage in the process of centralizing Soviet citizenship law. In the first stage, the central Government had little control over matters of citizenship, except that it governed the naturalization of aliens abroad. Effectively, jurisdiction in most citizenship matters remained within the competence of the local authorities. In the second stage, the various Republics of the Soviet Union, having established better control over their populations, assumed primary jurisdiction in most matters of citizenship. The 1938 Act marked the advent of federal primacy in citizenship matters, in accordance with Article 14(v) of the Constitution of 1936.[181] It is true that Article 21 of that Constitution provided that

Uniform Union citizenship is established for citizens of the U.S.S.R. Every citizen of a Union Republic is a citizen of the U.S.S.R.

This, however, should not be taken to imply that citizenship of the U.S.S.R. was a composite status, in any significant way analogous with Commonwealth citizenship. As George Ginsburg has written:

> permanent residency in a Union Republic and possession of that Republic's citizenship are almost synonymous expressions in contemporary Soviet jurisprudence. Besides, all local legislation defining the conditions for the acquisition and loss of republican citizenship lapsed pursuant to the directive contained in the federal decree of June 2, 1939, leaving domicile as the sole objective for deciding the question of which Republic's citizenship an individual is vested with.[182]

Thus, citizenship of a Union Republic may legitimately be regarded as a secondary (almost vestigial) status.[183]

The Soviet Citizenship Act of 1938 was, however, a very brief instrument, which left much to administrative discretion and did not contain detailed rules about the acquisition of original citizenship of the U.S.S.R.[184] Traditionally, Soviet practice has given pre-eminence to the *jus sanguinis* principle, and the authorities seem to be unanimous in asserting that the same principle was in fact applied under the 1938 code.[185] In particular, the 1938 Act seems to have perpetuated, by its silence on the point, the rule established in 1931, that 'a person is recognized as a citizen of the U.S.S.R. by virtue of birth, when both parents, or one of them at the time of his birth were citizens of the U.S.S.R.[186]

With the entry into force of the new Soviet Constitution on 7 October 1977, there came a reiteration of the principle formerly set out in Article 14(v) of the Constitution of 1946. The new Constitution declares that a single Union citizenship has been established in the U.S.S.R. Each citizen of a Union republic shall be a citizen of the U.S.S.R.[187] The new Constitution adds, however, that the bases and procedure for the acquisition and loss of Soviet citizenship shall be determined by a Law on Citizenship of the U.S.S.R. The Law so envisaged was adopted by the U.S.S.R. Supreme Soviet on 1 December 1978.[188] It entered into force on 1 July 1979, whereupon the Law of 1938 ceased to have effect.[189]

Jus sanguinis continues to be the basic principle governing the acquisition of citizenship of the U.S.S.R. By Article 11 of the Law of December 1978, a child acquires Soviet citizenship at birth if at that time both of his parents hold that citizenship. Where one parent is a citizen of the U.S.S.R. and the other is not, the child acquires that citizenship if he is born on the territory of the U.S.S.R. or if at least one parent has a permanent place of residence in the U.S.S.R. at the time of the birth. When that last condition is not fulfilled, the nationality of the child is determined by agreement of the parents. The child of a Soviet and of a stateless parent acquires citizenship of the U.S.S.R., irrespective of his place of birth.[190]

In its provisions governing the acquisition of citizenship by the children of stateless persons, the new Soviet law approaches the provisions of the New York Convention on the Reduction of Statelessness (to which the Soviet Union is not a party). A child of stateless persons who have a permanent residence in the U.S.S.R. becomes a citizen of that country if born on its territory. A child found on Soviet territory becomes a citizen of the U.S.S.R. if both his parents are unknown.[191] Others, however, who are residing in the territory of the U.S.S.R. and who are not citizens of the U.S.S.R., are considered as stateless persons if they have no evidence of belonging to the citizenship of a foreign State.[192]

The acquisition of Soviet citizenship by naturalization is determined by the Praesidium of the U.S.S.R. Supreme Soviet. The Law of 1 December 1978 does not specify the criteria to be applied by the Supreme Soviet on such applications: although it does contemplate that applications may be made even by persons residing abroad.[193]

By Article 29, if other rules than those which are contained in the Law of 1 December 1978 are established by an international treaty in which the U.S.S.R. participates, then the rules of the international treaty are to be applied.

FRENCH NATIONALITY LAW

The French law of nationality has been profoundly affected by demographic factors, and, in particular, by the need to facilitate the assimilation of immigrants to metropolitan France.[194] The same law has equally been affected by the colonial history of France, and, in particular, by the distinction drawn between *citoyens français* and *sujets français*. The latter derived their status from their associations with the French colonies, but in law they were no less a part of the French nation than were the former. This was made manifest in a Law of 1946 which provided that all nationals of the overseas territories of France (including Algeria) should have the status of citizens.[195]

With the abolition of the distinction between *sujets* and *citoyens* and the enactment of the 1946 Constitution came the institution of the status of '*citoyen de l'union française*'. That status was shared by persons who had the requisite associations with France (including its non-metropolitan territories) and with the protectorates, colonies, associated states and territories 'administered' by France (formerly under mandate).[196] However, the 1958 Constitution affirmed that there is only citizenship in the French community.[197] It is true that certain persons from non-French territories continued to be known as French nationals (for example, Tunisians and Moroccans were known as French *ressortissants* even though the countries from which they came were not under French sovereignty). Such exceptions, however, were mere usages, fortified by the fact that persons from such territories might be protected, on the international plane, by the Government of France.[198]

The relinquishment by France of her sovereignty or control over non-metropolitan territories has not been followed by the creation of an *entente* usefully comparable with the Commonwealth. Consequently, on the achievement of independence by a territory formerly under French jurisdiction, French nationality is seldom enjoyed by former French nationals whose previous status derived only from the nexus between them and the once dependent territory. Rather, the statement that *'il n'existe qu'une citoyenneté de la Communauté'* remains accurate, and as the frontiers of the French empire recede, the territorial applicability of French nationality law withdraws.[199] By the same process, the unilateral regime of nationality law tends to be replaced by a conventional regime, whenever there comes into being a new entity with international personality sufficient to conclude the treaty in question.[200] These treaties generally confirm the abrogation of the delegated legislation by which French nationality law was made applicable in the territories concerned, and the basis of French nationality law in these non-metropolitan territories is thereby removed.[201]

French citizenship may be acquired at birth *jure sanguinis* or *jure soli,* Aymond has described the *jus sanguinis* principle as *'la source principale de la nationalité d'origine'*.[202] Formerly, French citizenship was transmitted through the father, but it might be transmitted through the mother, notably when the *de cujus* was a native of a foreign country, and did not elect to take his father's status, nor to take citizenship in his country of birth.[203] In addition, French citizenship might be acquired by filiation (legitimation, adoptive legitimation or adoption) or by marriage, declaration, redintegration or naturalization.[204]

The French system of nationality was subjected to a thorough revision in 1973.[205] That Law dispensed with most of the distinctions formerly drawn between the nationality regime in metropolitan France and in its possessions abroad.[206] The remaining distinctions are predominantly procedural in character.

Under the new system, the principal basis for the acquisition of French nationality at birth continues to be *jus sanguinis*. A person acquires French nationality if he has at least one French parent; but where only one of the parents is French, a child born abroad may renounce his French nationality within the six months preceding his attainment of majority.[207] Nationality is transmissible irrespective of the legitimacy of the child's birth.[208] In conformity with Articles 1 and 2 of the New York Convention on the Status of Stateless Persons[209] the French Law of 1973 extends French nationality to persons born in France (including its Overseas Departments and Territories) where those persons' parents are stateless or are nationals of foreign States which fail to provide for the transmission of the parents' nationality to the child. The Law further provides that a foundling discovered in France is presumed to have been born there, and the same rule applies in respect of the Overseas Departments and Territories.[210]

A person who fails to acquire French nationality at birth may acquire it thereafter by any of five means: filiation, marriage, birth and residence in France, declaration and naturalization. The role of filiation in French nationality law has been reduced by the abolition of a distinction between legitimate and illegitimate children. A child who acquires French nationality thereby is presumed to have been French from birth; and a similar rule applies in the case of adoption.[211] Marriage alone has no effect upon the nationality of the spouse; but in the event of marriage to a French national an alien or stateless person of either sex becomes eligible to obtain French nationality by declaration.[212]

Under the former law a French native of foreign extraction acquired French nationality on attaining the age of majority if he had been habitually resident in France since attaining the age of sixteen or had completed his national service in French forces. The Law of 1973 modified this rule in two respects. First, it provided that a minor born in France of foreign parents should acquire French nationality on being conscripted into the French armed forces with a view to undergoing military service.[213] Secondly, under the old law a French native of foreign extraction could disclaim French nationality within the six months preceding the attainment of the age of majority. That period was extended in 1973 to one year.[214]

The right to acquire French nationality by declaration is extended to French natives of foreign extraction who have been habitually resident in France throughout the five years ending with the date of declaration.[215] It is also extended to children who have been informally adopted by French nationals, together with certain other children who have been housed and brought up in France.[216]

In the case of naturalization, it is always necessary that the applicant be resident in France at the date of the signature of the naturalization decree; and it is normally required that the applicant should have been habitually resident in France for the five preceding years. In two instances the residential period is reduced to two years. The first of these cases is of aliens who have completed at least two years of higher studies with a view to obtaining a degree or diploma from a French university and the second is of aliens who have rendered important services to France, or can do so.[217] The residential requirement is relaxed altogether in the case of parents with a least three minor children;

aliens who have rendered important services to France; persons who belong to the French cultural and linguistic community; spouses and adult children of persons who acquire French nationality; aliens who have completed a term of military service in French forces; and nationals of territories in which France exercised sovereignty or powers of protection.[218]

NATIONALITY LAW IN THE PEOPLE'S REPUBLIC OF CHINA

Nationality in the People's Republic of China is now governed by the Nationality Law of 1980, the first legislation on the subject since the Kuomintang's enactment of 1929.[219] The Law of 1980 draws no distinction between the diverse nationalities (or ethnic groups) that make up the population of the People's Republic. On the contrary, it provides expressly that persons belonging to any of the nationalities of China have Chinese nationality.[220] Thereby it complements the Law of National Autonomous Regions, which contains special protective provisions for ethnic minorities in frontier regions.[221] The Law of 1980 applies the principle of unity of nationality at the international as well as the domestic level. Article 3 provides that the People's Republic will not recognize dual nationality for any Chinese national. China applies this policy notwithstanding its (apparent) continued adherence to the Hague Convention on Certain Questions Relating to the Conflict of Nationality Laws, 1930. The latter provides in Article 3 that a person having two or more nationalities may be regarded as its national by *each* of the States whose nationality he possesses.[222]

It is the Chinese tradition to apply the principle of *jus sanguinis* as the primary rule governing the acquisition of nationality at birth. The Law of 1980 adheres to the tradition but modifies it by use of the principle *jus soli* so as to reduce the size of the overseas born population of Chinese nationals. It remains the case, however, that a native of China does not necessarily obtain Chinese nationality *jure soli* even if he would otherwise be stateless. A person born in China whose parents are Chinese nationals, or one of whose parents is a Chinese national, has Chinese nationality.[223] A child born abroad whose parents are Chinese nationals acquires Chinese nationality at birth unless the parents are settled abroad at the time of the birth and the child then obtains foreign nationality.[224] A person born in China whose parents are stateless or of uncertain nationality but are settled in China has Chinese nationality.[225]

Article 7 of the Nationality Law provides that aliens or stateless persons who are willing to abide by China's Constitution and laws may acquire Chinese nationality upon approval of their applications, provided that they are close relatives of Chinese nationals or they have settled in China or they have other 'legitimate reasons'. A person whose application for naturalization is approved must forfeit his other national status.[226] No period of residence is specified as a condition of naturalization. The naturalization of a married person does not bring about a sympathetic naturalization of the spouse; nor does the naturalization of a parent bring about a sympathetic naturalization of the child. A parent may, however, apply for the naturalization of a child, and the latter forfeits his Chinese nationality on reaching adulthood, if he is then settled abroad and acquires a foreign nationality of choice.[227]

The conditions of renunciation of Chinese nationality reflect the conditions for its acquisition by naturalization. A Chinese national may renounce that status, upon approval of his application, if he is a close relative of an alien or has settled abroad or has other 'legitimate reasons'.[228] State functionaries and members of the armed forces on active service cannot renounce Chinese nationality.[229] Applications for naturalization and for renunciation of Chinese nationality are subject to examination and approval by the Ministry of Public Security.[230]

The Nationality Law of 1980 has immediate practical significance for the ethnic Chinese populations of Hong Kong and Macau.[231] Article 4 and 5 of that Law by implication confirm that natives of Hong Kong of Chinese extraction are Chinese nationals; and Article 3 implies that such persons will be regarded in China as having Chinese nationality only. The Joint Declaration on the Status of Hong Kong[232] specifies those who will have the right to live in the Hong Kong Special Administrative Region after 1997. They will be: Chinese nationals born in Hong Kong; anyone who has been ordinarily resident in Hong Kong for at least seven years; and anyone else who had the right of .bode only in Hong Kong before it returned to China. The question of nationality was governed in an Exchange of Memoranda accompanying the Joint Declaration. The British Memorandum committed the United Kingdom to abolishing British Dependent Territories citizenship for people deriving that status from connections with Hong Kong and replacing it with an appropriate status: that of British National (Overseas) which cannot be transmitted to children born after 1997. The Chinese Memorandum declares that 'all Hong Kong Chinese compatriots, whether they are holders of British Dependent Territories citizens' passports or not, are Chinese nationals'. Taking account of the historical background of Hong Kong and its realities, such compatriots will be permitted to use travel documents issued by the Government of the United Kingdom for the purpose of travelling to other States and regions.

The Joint Declaration requires no legal provisions for its implementation in China (saving China's abstention from offering objection to the use by Chinese nationals of travel documents issued by the United Kingdom's authorities). On the British side, its implementation has entailed the enactment and preparation of legislation which provides, *inter alia,* for the right of British Dependent Territories citizens from Hong Kong to register as British Nationals (Overseas) between 1 July 1987 and 1 July 1997; and for the automatic acquisition of British Overseas Citizenship by those who fail to register.[233]

In the case of Macau, the position of Chinese law is at present identical with the Chinese legal rule applying to Hong Kong. Ethnic Chinese 'compatriots' are Chinese nationals. Portuguese nationality law provides that those born in Macau prior to 1980 are Portuguese nationals as well as those born after 1980 who can demonstrate familiarity with Portuguese customs or who have Portuguese parents.[234] That nationality is not recognized in China, when advanced by a person having Chinese nationality under Chinese law. It seems not unlikely that an arrangement similar to the Joint Declaration of 1985 will be required in order to resolve the difficulties arising from this conflict of laws.

NATIONALITY IN GENERAL INTERNATIONAL LAW

Vattel's description of nationality as the bond which ties a State to each of its members has had a profound effect on the development of concepts of nationality in international law. Oppenheim[235] and Lauterpacht[236] adopt Vattel's definition with hardly an amendment, and Batiffol defines nationality as *'l'appartenance juridique d'une personne à la population constitutive d'un Etat'*.[237] However, even though Batiffol's definition bears an obvious resemblance to Vattel's, it is characterised by some significant differences. It not only dispenses with the bond metaphor, but also implies that the nexus between the individual and the State is the sociological fact that the former belongs to the latter, an implication which is clearly consistent with the judgment of the International Court in the *Nottebohm Case*.[238] Batiffol's definition is for similar reasons consistent with the decision in *Messih v. Minister of the Interior*, in which the Egyptian Conseil d'Etat concluded that

nationality is the juridical and political link which unites an individual with a State. Now, a State is composed of subjects, and nationality being the link which unites them to it, the rules of nationality form part of public law and do not concern personal status.[239]

According to article 1 of the Harvard Draft, nationality is the status of a natural person who is attached to the State by the tie of allegiance.[240]. One knows that in the United States, and formerly in the United Kingdom, nationality is or was acquired only by one born within the sovereign's allegiance. As an expression of an international concept, however, a definition of nationality which depends on the establishment of allegiance is liable to lead to circularity, inaccuracy and incompleteness: circularity, because in many systems allegiance is now the consequence rather than the source of citizenship; inaccuracy, because a person may owe allegiance to the sovereign of a State in which he is not a national; incompleteness, because to omit any mention of the sociological basis of nationality is to describe that status insufficiently. Indeed, modern international legal concepts of nationality tend to show more similarities with the former United States criterion of adherence than with its modern criterion of allegiance. In the *Flegenheimer Claim* the United States Immigration Service refused to register the *de cujus* because he had manifested his 'adherence to German nationality' by the overt acts which connected him with the Reich. The Italian-United States Claims Commission took cognizance of these acts.[241] If international concepts of nationality may be derived from domestic law, the converse is equally true. When a State has no legislation or *jurisprudence constante* on the subject of nationality, international concepts may be invoked with particular utility. Some writers maintain that in such a situation the State in question has no nationals[242] but this view has been vigorously attacked by Van Panhuys,[243] who points out that it fails to take account of the fact that international law may be invoked when the *lex causae* is unreliable.[244]

In *A.B. v. M.B.*[245] the District Court of Tel-Aviv held that the *de cujus* was a national of Israel at a time after the repeal of the Palestine Citizenship Orders in Council, 1925–39,[246] but before the adoption of the Israel Nationality Law. It observed that the point of view according to which there might be no Israel nationals was not consistent with public international law. The judge continued:

> So long as no law has been enacted providing otherwise, my view is that every individual who, on the date of the establishment of the State of Israel was resident in the territory which to-day constitutes the State of Israel is also a national of Israel. Any other view would lead to the absurd result of a state without nationals – a phenomenon the existence of which has not yet been observed.

It appears that Dr. Weis is correct in interpreting this case as an example of the adoption of international law into domestic law (rather than as an example of a positive international law of nationality).[247] In the view of the present writer, Dr. Weis's interpretation of *A.B. v. M.B.* is wholly consistent with the judgment of the Austro-Roumanian mixed arbitral tribunal in *Kahane (Successor) v. Parisi and the Austrian State*[248] in which the tribunal upheld the Roumanian nationality of the Jews in question, even though Roumanian legislation on the subject was conspicuously absent. His interpretation is also consistent with the advisory opinion of the Permanent Court of International Justice in *Nationality Decrees in Tunis and Morocco*.[249]

This is not to imply that the international concepts of nationality may be invoked as a source of positive nationality law only when domestic law is rudimentary or silent. In the United States, the courts have not been reluctant to construe nationality statutes in accordance with international principles[250] and in the United Kingdom there is no lack of authority for the proposition that international law may be invoked to assist the courts in interpreting domestic nationality statutes; indeed, such invocations have been made on several occasions.[251]

Hitherto we have been concerned with the application of international law to domestic nationality laws in situations in which the latter are construed so as to be consistent with the former. Separate considerations arise when it is alleged that the two are inconsistent. It is now trite to observe that the rule enunciated by the Permanent Court in its advisory opinion in the dispute concerning the *Nationality Decrees in Tunis and Morocco* admits numerous exceptions.[252] Professor Verzijl, acting as Commissioner in the *Georges Pinson Case* expressed himself as follows:

> *s'il est vrai que, en règle générale, tout Etat est souverain pour déterminer quelles personnes il considéra comme ses ressortissants, il n'en est moins vrai que, ainsi que l'a constaté la Cour permanente de justice internationale dans son avis consultatif concernant les décrets de nationalité promulgués au Maroc et en Tunisie, que cette souveraineté peut être limitée par des règles du droit de gens.*[253]

Van Panhuys observes that the right in question derives from international law[254] and it follows that such a right may be limited by the law to which it owes its origin. In the *Flegenheimer Claim* the Italian-United States Conciliation Commission referred to the 'unquestionable principle of international law' whereby each State is deemed to have the sovereign right to determine who its nationals shall be.[255] Yet in the same case it is agreed that 'the Commission will have to admit or reject, at an international level, a nationality the existence or inexistence of which shall be established . . . at a national level'. Remarks to a similar effect were made in *In Re Rau*,[256] the *Buzzi Case*[257] and in *Messih v. Minister of the Interior*.[258] In *U.S. ex rel. Schwarzkopf v. Uhl*,[259] Swan, J. observed that

> each country determines for itself who are its nationals, *subject to certain limitations on expansive claims to nationality imposed by international law.*

Further confirmation of the accuracy of those propositions can be found in numerous other primary sources[260] as well as in secondary sources[261] including the Harvard Draft.[262]

There continues to be some dispute about the effects and nature of the limitations with international law imposes on the right of each State to legislate with respect to nationality. International tribunals have tended to restrict their remarks to the opposability of nationality, and to avoid enquiring into the other consequences of a finding that the domestic nationality law of a State fails to conform with the international standard. It is thought that such non-conformity may, in certain cases, constitute a delict *per se,* and that in such cases the failure to satisfy the international standard may justify a claim for reparation.[263] Be that as it may, it is clear that one of the consequences of the failure of domestic nationality law to accord with the international standard is the fact that the former ceases to be opposable *vis-à-vis* another State. The question of opposability arises most frequently in connection with the nationality of claims principle. For it is an elementary principle of international law that, in the absence of treaty terms or other special provisions to the contrary, a State may not make specific representation to another State concerning an individual who is not a national of the complainant State.[264] The principle remains basic to the international diplomatic and legal system, even though it has been somewhat attenuated as a result of the development of rules of international law governing human rights.

For this reason, a description of the international legal concept of nationality involves a description of the main principles which govern a State's right to exercise, on behalf of an individual, diplomatic protection *vis-à-vis* another State. These principles may be summarized in six propositions, as follows:

(1) If no State by its domestic nationality law claims the *de cujus* as its national, none may exercise diplomatic protection on his behalf, except that a native of a protectorate or a mandated or trust territory may be protected by the State or international organization which is responsible for the international affairs of that protectorate or mandated or trust territory.[265]

(2) If only one State by its domestic nationality law claims the *de cujus* as its national, that State may exercise diplomatic protection on his behalf, and it is not open to the respondent State to allege that, in the absence of a real and substantial connection between the *de cujus* and the claimant State, the former is not to be regarded as a national or *ressortissant* of the latter. However, as an exception to this rule, one State may exercise diplomatic protection on behalf of a national of another, if the protecting State and the State of nationality have come to an agreement to this effect; in such a case the *de cujus* is known as a *protégé,* and he is protected as a *protégé* rather than as a national.

(3) If two or more States, by their domestic nationality laws, claim the *de cujus* as their national, and each such State recognizes the *de cujus* as a national of the other State(s), each such State must refrain from exercising, on behalf of the *de cujus* diplomatic protection *vis-à-vis* the other State(s).[266]

(4) If one State, by its domestic nationality law, claims the *de cujus* as its national exclusively, and another state, by its domestic nationality law, claims the *de cujus* as its national, and the former State seeks to exercise on behalf of the *de cujus* diplomatic protection *vis-à-vis* the latter State, the *de cujus* must

be regarded as a national of the State with which he has the most real and substantial connection.[267]

(5) If two or more States, by their domestic nationality laws, claim the *de cujus* as their national, but not as their national exclusively, and if one of his States of nationality seeks to exercise on his behalf diplomatic protection *vis-à-vis* a State which does not claim him as its national, the respondent state is not obliged to recognize the *de cujus* as a national of the claimant State, in the absence of a real and substantial connection between the claimant State and the *de cujus*.[268] However, once it is established that this connection exists, the respondent State may not invoke against the claimant State the argument that the connections between the *de cujus* and the claimant are less real and substantial than the connections between him and the other State(s) which claim(s) him as a national.[269]

(6) If two or more States claim the *de cujus* as their national, and at least one of those States claims him as its national exclusively, and that State seeks to exercise on his behalf diplomatic protection *vis-à-vis* a State which does not claim him as its national, the respondent State is not obliged to treat the *de cujus* as a national of the claimant State unless there is a real and substantial connection between him and the claimant State. It is believed that this sixth rule is the point firmly decided by the International Court of Justice in the *Nottebohm Case*.[270]

NATIONALITY IN THE CURRENT INTERNATIONAL RELATIONS OF COMMONWEALTH COUNTRIES

For the purposes of the international relations of Commonwealth countries, the common status of Commonwealth citizens is generally irrelevant. Diplomatic practice makes it clear that the nationality of the *de cujus* is normally his primary citizenship (that is, his quality of being a citizen of a particular Commonwealth country or unit, e.g., his citizenship of India). A clear example of the operation of that principle is given in the Treaty of Commerce, Establishment and Navigation between the United Kingdom and Japan, 1962. The parties to that treaty agreed to confer certain privileges on one another's nationals. Article 2(a) provided that the term 'nationals' in relation to the United Kingdom means:

> all citizens of the United Kingdom and Colonies, all citizens of any territory for the international relations of which the United Kingdom is responsible and all British protected persons; except in each case those who *belong* to any territory to which the present Treaty may be extended under the provisions of article 32 but has not been so extended.[271]

44

Commonly, the term 'national' is used in international treaties between Commonwealth countries and foreign States, and the treaty fails to give a definition of the term, but uses it in such a way as to make it clear that it does not refer to Commonwealth citizens as a whole. For example, the Agreement between Canada and Italy for the Settlement of Certain Canadian War Claims and the Release of Italian Assets in Canada, 1951 provided *inter alia* that the Italian Government should pay an indemnity to the Canadian Government, and that this indemnity should 'free the Italian Government of any responsibility towards the Government of Canada and Canadian nationals (individuals, corporations and associations) as regards the above mentioned claims.'[272]

The applicability of principles of general international law to the relations of Commonwealth countries *inter se* has for long been modified by the *inter se* doctrine and by the common status of Commonwealth citizens. It is possible to over-estimate the effect of these two factors, and to ignore the fact that the *inter se,* doctrine, by stressing that relations between Commonwealth countries were *sui generis,* not only removed those relations from some of the methods of scrutiny and evaluation available in general international law, but also subjected them to some special methods of examination available only in Commonwealth practice.[273] These special methods of examination inevitably involved the use of concepts akin to primary citizenship long before the formal creation of such citizenships from 1946 onwards. At the Imperial Conference of 1911 the India Office presented a memorandum on the position of British Indians (*sic*) in the Dominions.[274] The memorandum drew attention to the disabilities suffered by 'His Majesty's Indian subjects' in respect of the right to enter South Africa, Australia, New Zealand and Canada.

Dr. Cuthbert Joseph's careful analysis of nationality law and diplomatic protection in the Commonwealth demonstrates that the common status of Commonwealth citizens now has relatively little impact on the diplomatic settlement of intra-Commonwealth disputes.[275] One of the clearest indications of this point is to be found in the Minorities Treaty between India and Pakistan, solemnised in 1950. That treaty, which deals with the position of migrants from East Bengal, West Bengal, Assam and Tripura, records the desire of both Governments to emphasize 'that the allegiance and loyalty of the minorities is to the State of which they are citizens, and that it is to the Government of that State that they should look for redress of their grievances.[276] The fact that a citizen of an independent Commonwealth country also possesses Commonwealth citizenship does not lead to the conclusion that his protection may properly be undertaken by the Government of the United Kingdom, nor does it imply that one Commonwealth country cannot defend his interests in a dispute with another country in the Commonwealth. It follows *a fortiori* that an independent Commonwealth country may espouse the claims of its *protégés,* including those on whom it may have conferred the title 'British protected person'. Such an espousal may be made not only in disputes with foreign States, but also in disputes with Commonwealth countries. Before Samoan independence, citizens of the Trust Territory of Western Samoa were considered as *protégés* in the practice of New Zealand. Even after the achievement of independence by Western Samoa, New Zealand agreed by treaty to continue undertaking the diplomatic protection of nationals of Western Samoa, both in Commonwealth countries and in foreign States.[277]

British subjects (without citizenship) are eligible for protection against foreign States. It is usual for the United Kingdom to exercise diplomatic protection on their behalf when it is alleged that they have suffered injury as a result of action taken in contravention of international law by such a State and increasingly by Commonwealth countries. In 1954 the Governments of Poland and the United Kingdom concluded an agreement to govern the compensation to be paid to U.K. nationals for the expropriation of their property in Poland. Within the terms of the agreement, the enjoyment of U.K. nationality was extended to citizens of the United Kingdom and Colonies, British protected persons *and* British subjects without citizenship.[278] Nowadays, it is common to define nationals of the United Kingdom as individuals having the status of a U.K. national (or that of a British citizen or British subject) under United Kingdom law and having in either event the right of abode in the United Kingdom. However, practice is inconsistent and varies according to the context, which could in appropriate cases require a definition broad enough to encompass all British citizens, British Overseas citizens, British Dependent Territories citizens, British protected persons and British subjects.[279]

THE REGULATION OF NATIONALITY BY MULTILATERAL TREATIES

The rapid development of customary rules governing the opposability of nationality, in this century, has been accompanied by a simultaneous development of treaty law. Such treaties now serve the purposes of reducing statelessness, regulating multiple nationality and establishing standards to govern the conflict of nationality laws and the nationality of married women. Further, the number of bilateral treaties governing nationality questions has multiplied, chiefly but by no means exclusively in consequence of the process of decolonization.[280] Consequently, both the conditions for the acquisition, retention and loss of nationality and the incidents of a given national status are now regulated in the case of very many States by international conventions.

It is to the League of Nations that we owe the origin of this development. In September 1925 the Council of the League created the Preparatory Committee for the International Codification Conference and charged it with the task of preparing for the codification of three areas of international concern. Of these three, the regulation of nationality was one.[281] For the purpose of assisting the Committee in its work the Harvard Law School prepared its Draft Code, which began with the statement of principle that each State shall determine by law who are its nationals, subject to the provisions of any special treaty to which that State is a party and subject to the general principles of international law. The Draft envisaged that States would be under an obligation in certain cases to confer their nationality. In particular, a person who would otherwise be stateless would be entitled to obtain the nationality of his State of birth. Equally, the Draft envisaged cases in which States would be forbidden to extend their nationality. With specified exceptions, the naturalization of an alien would prohibited if he had his habitual residence abroad.[282]

The Conference was not prepared to adopt rules of so progressive a nature as had been proposed by the Harvard Law School. In 1930 the Conference drew up the Hague Convention on Certain Questions relating to the Conflict of Nationality Laws[283] together with three Protocols, one relating to Military Obligations in Certain Cases of Double Nationality;[284] one relating to a Certain Case of Statelessness;[285] and a third governing Statelessness.[286] The Convention of 1930, which entered into force in 1937, began by drawing a distinction between the grant and the opposability of nationality:

> It is for each State to determine under its own laws who are its nationals. This law shall be recognized by other States in so far as it is consistent with international conventions, international custom, and the principles of international law generally recognised with regard to nationality.[287]

The convention recognized both *jus soli* and *jus sanguinis* as acceptable bases for the conferment of nationality and therefore acknowledged the inevitability of cases of multiple nationality. For the purpose of avoiding the difficulties arising in such cases, the Convention provided for the right of expatriation to be extended to dual nationals who have acquired their national statuses without voluntary act. A State was not to refuse authorisation for the renunciation of a nationality by such a person, if he had his habitual and principal residence abroad and had satisfied 'the conditions laid down in the law of the State whose nationality he desires to surrender.[288]

The Protocol relating to Military Obligations in Certain Cases of Double Nationality provided, in Article 1, that a person possessing two or more nationalities should be exempted from all military obligations in one of his States of nationality if he habitually resides in the other and is in fact more closely connected with that other.

The impetus given by the League Council to the development of international rules governing nationality was retarded by the advent of the Second World War. In the years immediately preceding the outbreak of the War,

priority was given to the necessity of devising treaties to facilitate the resettlement of refugees from Germany.[289] In the years immediately following the
war, the resettlement of refugees again took priority over problems of nationality.[290] A series of peace treaties and other bilateral agreements addressed
some of the problems arising in the field of nationality from the territorial
adjustments made at the end of the War.[291] In 1950, however, the Economic
and Social Council of the United Nations turned its attention to the question of
nationality. It urged the International Law Commission to draft an international convention on the elimination of statelessness.[292]

The first product of this revival of interest in nationality law was the
Convention relating to the Status of Stateless Persons, 1954.[293] It was not until
June 1960 that this relatively modest measure entered into force; and by that
date the International Law Commission had embarked upon the preparation
of a more ambitious instrument which was later to become the Convention on
the Reduction of Statelessness, 1961.[294] Whereas the Convention of 1930 had
sought to avoid the occurrence of statelessness in consequence of the conflict
of nationality laws, the Convention of 1961 imposes on contracting States a
positive duty to confer their nationality upon those who have specified connections with such States and would otherwise be stateless.[295] The draftsmen of
the Convention of 1961 appear to have been inspired by the judgment in the
Nottebohm case.[296] Whereas in the *Nottebohm* case the link between in individual and a State is applied as a test of opposability of nationality, in the
Convention of 1961 certain links between an individual and a State are used for
the purpose of establishing an entitlement to a national status.

At the same time a different United Nations agency directed its attention to
a particularly troublesome aspect of nationality law. The Commission on the
Status of Women urged the conclusion of a treaty to govern the nationality of
married women. The resulting agreement was the Convention on the Nationality of Married Women.[297] The basic principle established thereby is that
neither the celebration nor the dissolution of a marriage nor the husband's
change of nationality during the subsistence of a marriage shall automatically
affect the nationality of the wife. Rather, the wife's acquisition or loss of
nationality shall be determined by her consent.[298]

In more recent years the development of international rules governing
nationality has been achieved more by regional than by universal arrangements. The Council of Europe sponsored the conclusion in 1963 of a Convention on Reduction of Cases of Multiple Nationality.[299] This provides *inter alia*
that a national of a Contracting State who acquires of his own free will the
nationality of another Contracting State by means of naturalization, option or
recovery should lose his former nationality. A person possessing the nationality of two or more Contracting States may renounce one such nationality with
the consent of the State whose nationality he desires to renounce. By a

48

Protocol dated 1977[300] it is agreed that such consent shall not be withheld by the Contracting State whose nationality a person of full age possesses *ipso jure* provided that the person has his ordinary residence outside the territory of that State. Further, the Convention of 1963 and the Protocol of 1977 make detailed provision for the avoidance of duplication of military obligations in cases of plural nationality.

The development of rules of international law governing nationality has been so impressive, during the present century, that it may cause us to qualify the famous statement made by the Permanent Court of International Justice in the case concerning *Nationality Decrees in Tunis and Morocco*.[301] In that case the Court maintained that 'in the present state of international law, questions of nationality are ... in principle, within the reserved domain'. It is to be emphasised, however, that the Court qualified that famous statement by an equally significant assertion: 'the question whether a certain matter is or is not solely within the jurisdiction of a State is an essentially relative question; it depends upon the development of international relations'. The materials assembled in this chapter may serve to demonstrate that international relations have so developed, in the course of the present century, that very many aspects of the law of nationality are now removed from the reserved domain of domestic jurisdiction.

NOTES

1. " 'Subject', 'Citizen', 'National' and 'Permanent Allegiance' ", 56 Yale L.J. (1946–7) 58, 61.
2. A. Makarov, *Allgemeine Lehren des Staatsangehörigkeitsrechts*, 1962, pp. 103 *et seq*. However, as early as 1758 Vattel wrote that *'Les nations ou Etats sont des corps politiques, des sociétés d'hommes, unis ensemble pour procurer leur salut et leur avantage à forces réunies'*. Consequently, he defined nationality as 'the bond which ties a state to each of its members': *Droit de gens*, 1758, *Préliminaires*, para. 1. On the other hand, the French Constitutions of 1791, 1793, 1795 and 1799 employed the term *'citoyen'*, and it was not until 1835 that the modern use of the word *'nationalité'* was accepted in the *Dictionnaire de l'académie française*. See G. Cogordan, *Droit des gens: La nationalité au point de vue des rapports internationaux*, 1871, p. 2, n. 1; M. Duverger, *Constitutions et documents politiques*, 1968, pp. 4, 29, 39, 70.
3. P. Boulbès, *Droit français de la nationalité*, 1955, p. 12. C.f. P. Aymond's observation that *'La notion de nationalité, lien de droit public qui assujettit un individu à un Etat, a succédé à la vieille idée féodale d'allégeance, lien personnel unissant le souverain à son sujet': La nationalité française*, 1947, p. 16; see also J. Brissaud, *A History of French Public Law*, trans. J. Garner, 1915, pp. 210–214.
4. E. de Vattel, *Le droit des gens*, Book I, s. 52.
5. Article 4.
6. 60 B.S.P. (1869–70) 36 (italics added). For a criticism of the passage, see J. Jones, *British Nationality Law*, 1956, p. 76 n. 1.
7. Article 2 (italics added).

8. See generally C. Ténékidès, 90 Hague *Recueil* (1956-II) 469 at 535–542; C. Larsen, *Greek Federal States, their Institutions and History,* 1968; H. Daly, *Naturalization,* 1860, p. 10; H. Batiffol, *Droit international privé,* 1974–1976, Vol. I, pp. 129–130.
9. For example, the deme nominated the jurymen, whose office and functions tended to be more legislative than judicial, and hence Aristotle regarded eligibility for jury-service as a hallmark of citizenship. The deme also presented by election candidates for the ballot from which all major political offices (except generals) were selected.
10. For example, the metic could not hold land and was compelled to choose a mediator between himself and the state, but he was obliged to serve in the army, and enjoyed certain civic rights. See P. Van Panhuys, *The Role of Nationality in International Law,* 1959, p. 32.
11. J. Starke, *An Introduction to International Law,* 1967, p. 6.
12. G. Sabine, *A History of Political Theory,* 1937, p. 5.
13. C. Daly, *supra,* note 8 at p. 10.
14. H. Van Panhuys, *supra,* note 10, p. 32; W. Buckland and A. McNair, *Roman Law and Common Law,* 1965, p. 23; J. Brissaud, *supra* note 3, p. 41; Sir David Maxwell-Fyfe (later Lord Kilmuir, L.C.) 453 H.C. Deb., col. 402 (7th July, 1948).
15. F. Walton, *Historical Introduction to Roman Law,,* 1923, p. 165.
16. H. Jolowicz, *Historical Introduction to the Study of Roman Law,* 1952, p. 356.
17. F. Savigny, *Private International Law,* 1880, p. 90.
18. 'The Roman Empire had no true concept of nationality . . . The development of a concept of nationality presupposes both a plurality of states and a system of international relations': C. Parry, *Nationality and Citizenship Laws of Commonwealth and the Republic of Ireland,* 1957–1960, Vol. I, p. 3. See also Jolowicz, *supra,* note 16, p. 357.
19. See generally, J. Bryce, *The Ancient Roman Empire and the British Empire of India,* 1914; J. Vinogradoff, *Roman Law in Medieval Europe,* 1929, pp. 43 *et seq.*
20. G. Cheshire, *Private International Law,* 1965, pp. 18–19.
21. A. Cockburn, *Nationality,* 1869, p. 7.
22. Aethelstan II, 2; reproduced in F. Attenborough, *The Laws of the Earliest English Kings,* 1922, p. 129.
23. See the list of names to support the action against Wulfbold: Robertson, *Anglo-Saxon Charters,* 1922, p. 131.
24. F. Pollock and F. Maitland, *The History of English Law,* 1968, Vol. I, p. 31.
25. Sabine, *supra,* note 12, pp. 213–214.
26. *Rot. Parl.* I, 44.
27. Parry observes that is not a necessary corollary of this case that a person born in England is a subject: *supra,* note 18, Vol. I, p. 31.
28. 25 Ed. III, st. 1. This followed Parliamentary resolutions of 1343 and 1350. See Parry, *supra,* note 18, Vol. I, p. 32 and Pollock and Maitland, *supra,* note 24, Vol. I, p. 31.
29. This item was cited by Bacon in *Calvin's Case,* (1608) 7 Co. Rep. Ia; 2 St. Tr. 559. It was applied in *R.* v. *Eaton,* (1627) Lit. Rep. 23.
30. *De Legibus Angliae,* 1883 ed. Vol. VI, chap. 24, pp. 375–6.
31. In England, the earliest extant endenization recorded on the Parliamentary rolls is that of Elyas Daubnay in 1295: *Rot. Parl.* I, 135(a). In France, *lettres de bourgeoisie* had been issued from the thirteenth century. See Batiffol, *supra,* note 8, p. 126, P. Viollet, *'Histoire de droit civil français,'* 1905, p. 409.
32. Parry, *supra,* note 18, Vol. I, p. 29. Reference to feudal and pre-feudal concepts is, however, instructive in elucidating the origins of naturalization. In the course of his judgment in *Calvin's Case,* (1608) 2 St. Tr. 559, 639, Coke observed that 'it appeareth out of the laws of King W(illiam) I of what antiquity the making of denizens by the King of England hath been'. This seems to be a reference to the fourth of the Ten Articles of William I, 1066–1089.

33. References at 7 Co. Rep. 9b and 2 St. Tr. 688. See also the *Prior of Chelsea's Case,* (1353) Lit. Ass. 27, pl. 48.
34. Jones, *supra,* note 6, p. 51.
35. 2 St. Tr. 559.
36. See *U.S.* v. *Wong Kim Ark,* 169 U.S. 649 (1897); *U.S. ex rel. Lacas* v. *Curran,* 297 F. 219 (1924); *Cabebe* v. *Acheson,* 183 F. 2d. 795, 797 (1950).
37. (1641) Cro. Car. 601.
38. (1664) 1 Vent. 413, 434.
39. See 7 Ann., c. 5 (1708); 10 Ann., c. 5 (1711); 4 Geo. II, c. 21 (1730).
40. Parry, *supra,* note 18, Vol. I, pp. 40–57.
41. Hooker's *Ecclesiastical Polity,* which exerted such a powerful influence on Locke, may be the origin of the theory.
42. Evidence in support of this theory can be found in the Act of Anne, 7 Ann., c. 5 (1708) which made an incidental distinction between the sovereign's Scottish and English subjects.
43. 17 Q.B.D. 54, 65.
44. Parry, *supra,* note 18, Vol.I, pp. 72–77.
45. 7 Co. Rep. 17a.
46. G. Chalmers, *Opinions of Eminent Lawyers on Various Points of Jurisprudence,* 1814, p. 204. Jamaica seems to have been a conquest from Spain (1655) recognized by the Treaty of Madrid (1679). See the judgment of Lord Mansfield, C. J. in *R.* v. *Vaughan,* (1769) 4 Burr. 2494.
47. Article 4.
48. Capitulation of Colombo, articles 16 and 19.
49. Parry, *supra,* note 18, Vol. I, p. 788.
50. East India Company Act, 1813.
51. Peace of Paris, 1814; treaty with France, article 12; treaty with the Netherlands, article 4.
52. British Nationality Act, 1730 (4 Geo. II, c. 21) section 1; British Nationality Act, 1772 (13 Geo. III, c. 21) section 1.
53. *De Geer* v. *Stone,* (1882) 22 Ch. D. 243.
54. British Nationality and Status of Aliens Act, 1914, section 28 and third schedule. See Jones, *supra,* note 6, appendix 4.
55. I.e. after 1813. It was established in *Calvin's Case,* if not before, that unless the *de cujus* was born in territory under the actual occupation of the King, he is not a subject. Thus, the implication of *Calvin's Case* was that native inhabitants of the lost French provinces were not subjects.
56. The same declaration charged that George III had attempted to establish tyranny over the colonies by obstructing laws for the naturalization of aliens. Sutherland, *Constitutionalism in America: Origin and Evolution of its Fundamental Ideas,* 1942, pp. 243–279. The latter charge seems unfounded. The Act for the Naturalization of Foreign Protestants Settled in the Colonies of America, 1740 (13 Geo. II, c. 7) imposed stringent requirements for naturalization, but the Naturalization Act of 1773 (14 Geo. III, c. 14) provided that conditions for naturalization of aliens in England should be similar to those specified for the colonies. Some American states adopted their own naturalization laws. See Naturalization Acts of Maryland (1666), Virginia (1671), New York (1683 and 1715), South Carolina (1693), Delaware (1700) and Pennsylvania (1700).
57. Tenure of citizenship of the United States of America, at this time, flowed from tenure of citizenship of one of the states of the Union, the latter status being a prerequisite for the former. In this respect, there is an analogy between early American and modern British law. See J. Cable, *Decisive Decisions of United States Citizenship,* 1967, p. 6. In *Boyd* v. *Nebraska ex ret. Thayer,* 143 U.S. 135, 163, 1892 the U.S. Supreme Court observed: 'The right of

election must necessarily exist in all revolutions such as ours, as is well established by adjudged cases'. The Federal Constitution conferred on Congress a power to establish a uniform code of naturalization. Accordingly, Congress adopted the Naturalization Acts of March 26th, 1790, 1 Stat. 103; January 29th, 1795, 1 Stat. 414; June 18th, 1798, 1 Stat. 566; and April 14th, 1802, 2 Stat. 153. The view that state legislatures had a concurrent jurisdiction to enact naturalization laws was upheld in *Collet* v. *Collet,* 2 U.S. 294 (1792), doubted in *U.S.* v. *Villato,* 2 U.S. 370 (1797) and finally rejected in *Chirac* v. *Chriac,* 12 U.S. 259 (1817).

58. 28 U.S. 241, 247 (1830); italics added.
59. Cable, *supra,* note 57, p. 6.
60. *Scott* v. *Sandford,* 60 U.S. 393 (1857).
61. Cable, *supra,* note 51, pp. 29–30.
62. 14 Stat. 27; 39th Cong., Sess. I, Chap. 31, April 9th, 1866.
63. 112 U.S. 94 (1884).
64. 169 U.S. 649 (1898).
65. See M. Condorcet, *Sur la Constitution, Lettres d'un citoyen des Etats-Unis . . .,* in *Oeuvres Complètes,* 1804; G. Chinard, *The Letters of Lafayette and Jefferson,* 1929.
66. 4 D. and R. 394; 2 B. and C. 778, 786, 792, 798 (1824).
67. 28 U.S. 99, 126 (1880).
68. It is possible that some judicial attenuation of the doctrine of indellibility of allegiance was made in *Doe d. Millar* v. *Rogers,* (1844) 1 Car. and Kir. 390, but that case related only to the case of a woman British subject who married an alien. The Bancroft Conventions between the United States and migrant-exporting states sought to ensure those states' recognition of the principle of expatriation, recognised by Congress in the Act of July 17th, 1868 (15 Stat. 223). In anticipation of the Convention of 1868, the U.K. Government established a Royal Commission on Naturalization, 25 A.P.S. 607.
69. British Nationality Act, 1948, section 3 (3).
70. The Canadian interest in encouraging immigration by enacting such laws is evident in the Naturalization Acts of 1828 (Upper Canada), 9 Geo. IV, c. 21; 1831 (Lower Canada) 1 Will. IV, c. 53; 1841, 4 and 5 Vict., c. 7; 1849, 12 Vict., c. 197; 1854, 18 Vict., c. 6; 1858, 22 Vict., c. 1.
71. Cmd. 723, paragraph, 31.
72. See Parry, *supra,* note 18, Vol. I, p. 448, *Précis of the Proeedings,* Cd. 5741; *Minutes of Proceedings,* Cd. 5745; *Papers Laid Before the Conference,* Cd. 5746-1.
73. Section 1(1)(a).
74. Section 1(1)(b); interpreted in *Abraham* v. *A. G.,* [1934] P. 17, *Markwald* v. *A. G.* [1920] 1 Ch. 348.
75. British Nationality and Status of Aliens Act, 1918, section 2.
76. British Nationality and Status of Aliens Act, 1922, section 1, adding paragraph (*v*) to section 1 (1) (b) of the principal Act.
77. British Nationality and Status of Aliens Act, 1943, sections 1 (2) and 9.
78. Sections 2–9.
79. Sections 10 (national status of married women), 11 (status of widows), 12 (status of children), 13 (loss of British nationality on foreign naturalization) . . . 17 (capacity of alien as to property), 19–24 (procedure and evidence), 25–28 (supplemental).
80. By an Order in Council of 1930 (P.C. 2115) the Governor-General of Canada prohibited the landing in Canada of any immigrants of the Asiatic race (subject to exceptions).
81. The so-called 'white Australia' policy was made possible by the Immigration Restriction Act, 1901, the Immigration Restriction (Amendment) Act, 1905, the Immigration Restriction Acts, 1905, 1908, 1910 and the Immigration Acts of 1920, 1924, 1925, 1930, 1932, 1933, 1935, 1940, 1948 and 1949.

82. C.O.I., *Consultation and Cooperation in the Commonwealth*, 1952, p. 57.
83. Cmd. 2768. This was not strictly correct: some Canadian legislation still required formal assent in London; the British North America Act, 1867 could not be amended without such formal assent.
84. Statute of Westminster, 1931, 22 and 23 Geo. V, c. 4; but see S. De Smith, *The New Commonwealth and its Constitutions*, 1964, pp. 3, 10.
85. See C. Joseph, *Nationality and Diplomatic Protection: the Commonwealth of Nations*, 1970, p. 100.
86. White Paper, *The British Nationality Bill*, Cmd. 7326.
87. K. Patchett, 'English Law in the West Indies: A Conference Report', 12 I.C.L.Q. (1963) 922, 956.
88. 178 L.N.T.S. 277.
89. British Representative to the Committee of Jurists, *Société des Nations, Questions Juridiques*, Vol. V, *Procès-Verbal, Session du 11 au 19 mars, 1929*, p. 70.
90. Natives of the Channel Islands might, if they chose, be called 'Citizens of the United Kingdom, Islands and Colonies'. The change in title did not imply any difference in status.
91. Committee on United Kingdom Citizenship, *Commonwealth Co-operation: Fantasy or Reality?* 1969, p. 8.
92. E. Rose, *Colour and Citizenship*, 1969, p. 751.
93. However, it is thought that these arguments were misconceived. In the first place, they failed to deal with the objection that it would be impossible for citizens of colonies to be protected on the international plane by the Governments of the relevant colonies, since those colonies lack international personality, Withdrawal of citizenship of the U.K. and Colonies from such persons, in advance of the advent of independence by the colonies, might, therefore, render the persons stateless. This would be out of harmony with article 8 of the New York Convention on the Reduction of Statelessness, 10 August 1961, Cmd. 1825. *Basic Documents* II 6, ratified by the U.K. in 1966. In the second place, the arguments in question failed to deal with the objection that from the point of view of immigration law the greatest problem arose in relation to persons who were citizens of the U.K. and Colonies by association with *former* colonies.
94. Section 13 and third schedule.
95. However, it was not the first statute to do so; see the British Protected Persons Order in Council (1934/499).
96. British Protectorates, Protected States and Protected Persons Order, 1949 (1949/140). British Nationality Act, 1948, section 30; Parry, *supra*, note 18, Vol I, pp. 352–363; Jones, 'Who Are British Protected Persons?' 22 B.Y.I.L. (1945) 122–129.
97. Sections 3(3), 10.
98. Constitution of the Irish Free State, 1922, article 3; *Murray* v. *Parkes*, [1942] 2 K.B. 123.
99. Sir David Maxwell-Fyfe, later Viscount Kilmuir, L.C., 453 H.C. Deb., cols. 412–3 (7th July, 1948).
100. During the debate on the British Nationality Bill in 1948, Rf. Hon. Chuter Ede explained that the term 'British subject' had to be avoided for the benefit of Boers and Quebequois as well as Indians: 453 H.C. Deb., col. 392 (July 7th, 1948).
101. Canadian Citizenship Act, 1946, section 26, renumbered as section 21 by 14 Geo. VI., c. 29 (1950) section 9.
102. Citizenship Act, 1948–1969, section 7. This Act consists of the Nationality and Citizenship Acts of 1948 (No. 83), 1950 (No. 58), 1952 (No. 70), 1953 (No. 85), 1955 (No. 1), 1958 (No. 63), 1959 (No. 79), 1960 (No. 82), 1966 (No. 11), 1967 (No. 11) and 1969 (No. 22).
103. British Nationality and New Zealand Citizenship Act, 1948 (No. 15) section 3.
104. Although the term 'British subject' was employed in the Southern Rhodesia Citizenship

Act, 1949 and in the Citizenship of Southern Rhodesia and British Nationality Act, 1963, it is not employed in the Citizenship of Rhodesia Act, 1970.

105. See De Smith, *supra,* note 84, p. 16. In Australia the Government has found it necessary to cease to issue Australian passports with the words 'British Subject' prominently displayed on the cover, since that practice gave the misleading impression that the bearers had the right to enter the United Kingdom, See Rt. Hon. Billy Snedden's statement, *Canberra Evening News,* February 14th, 1967.

106. Indian Citizenship Act, 1955, section 11.

107. However, by section 2 of the Pakistan Citizenship Act, 1951 (as amended) it was provided that the term 'Commonwealth citizen' should have the same meaning as in the British Nationality Act, 1948.

108. Citizenship Act, 1948.

109. Republic of Cyprus Citizenship Law, 1967, section 2(1).

110. 155 H.L. Deb., col. 757 (May 11th, 1948).

111. [1914] B.C.R. 243.

112. [1947] K.B. 741.

113. *The International Standard and Commonwealth Developments,* 1968, p. 284.

114. [1962] A.C. 339, 343. A similar argument had been raised in *Musson* v. *Rodrigues,* [1935] A.C. 580, but in that case the Committee was able to give judgment for the appellant on other grounds. *The Court of Appeal of West Indian States* decided in 1968 that Antiguan Constitutional principles did not confer on Commonwealth citizens from Montserrat the right to take up residence in Antigua: *Margetson* v. *Attorney-General,* 12 W.I.R. (1968) 469. In *R.* v. *Chief Immigration Officer, gatwich Airport, ex parte Harjender Singh, The Times* L.R. 26 February 1987, Nolan, J. noted that a British protected person is not a beneficiary of the right of abode in the United Kingdom and dediced that such a person is not a 'British National' for the purposes of the Geneva Convention on the Status of Refugees, 28 July 1951, 189 U.N.T.S. 150. *sed quaere.*

115. 'The British Nationality Act, 1948', 25 B.Y.I.L. (1948) 158, 161. The Act became law in 1948 on receiving the royal assent, although it did not come into force until January 1st, 1949, in accordance with section 34(2).

116. For present purposes no account is taken of those Commonwealth citizens having the right of abode who were not citizens of the United Kingdom and Colonies. For the latter, see the Immigration Act 1971, section 2(1)(d) and 2(2)(a) and (b).

117. So far as is material, the British Nationality Act 1981 entered into force on 1 January 1983: see section 53 thereof.

118. Section 1(1).

119. Section 52(2). See further Immigration Act 1971, section 8(5A) inserted by British Nationality Act 1981, section 39(4).

120. Section 1(4).

121. Section 2.

122. Section 3(1)–(3).

123. Section 38; Solomon Islands Act 1978.

124. British Nationality Act 1948, sections 13 & 16; British Nationality Act 1965, section 1.

125. British Nationality Act 1981, section 30.

126. Section 4(1).

127. Section 4(1)–(2).

128. Section 7. Further conditions are required but not set out fully at this point.

129. Section 8. Further conditions are required but not set out fully at this point.

130. I.e., a country other than a Commonwealth country or territory or the Republic of Ireland: section 52.

131. Section 9.
132. Section 10.
133. Section 6.
134. Schedule 1, paragraph 1(2); *supra,* note 177.
135. Schedule 1, paragraph 1(3).
136. Schedule 1, paragraph 1(1).
137. Section 15(1).
138. Section 16(1).
139. Section 17(2)–(3).
140. Sections 19 & 20.
141. Section 21.
142. Section 22.
143. Section 27.
144. Section 28.
145. British Nationality (Falkland Islands) Act 1983, section 1.
146. Beijing, 19 December 1985, UKTS No 26 (1985), *Basic Documents* II. 9.
147. Hong Kong (British Nationals) Order 1986, S.I. 948.
148. 66 Stat. 163, 8 U.S.C.S. nos. 1101–1503.
149. Act of 14 October 1940, 54 Stat. 1137, 8 U.S.C.S. no. 451.
150. Immigration & Nationality Act 1952, section 308(1). See *Cababe* v. *Acheson,* 84 F. Supp. 639 (1949), aff'd. 183 F. 2d. 795.
151. Section 301(1).
152. *Ex Parte Ng Fung Sing,* 6 F. 2d. 670 (1925), *Junso Fujii* v. *Dulles,* 122 F. Supp. 260 (1954).
153. *Elk* v *Wilkins,* 112 U.S. 94, 28 L.Ed. 643 (1884).
154. Amended by P.L. 92-584 of 27 October 1972, sections 1&3, 86 Stat. 1289 and by P.L. 95-432 of 10 October 1978, sections 1&3, 92 Stat. 1046.
155. This provision reflects the Fourteenth Amendment and Congress is without power to restrict the effect of birth in the United States in this regard: U.S. v. *Wong Kim Ark,* 169 U.S. 649, 42 L.Ed. 890 (1897); *Kiyokuro Okimura* v. *Acheson,* 99 F. Supp. 587 (1951) 14 C.J.S. 1132.
156. *Caolo* v. *Dulles,* 115 F. Supp. 125 (1953).
157. *U.S.* v. *Wong Kim Ark, supra,* note 205.
158. Immigration & Nationality Act 1952, as amended, section 301(b).
159. Section 301(c).
160. Section 301(d).
161. Section 301(e).
162. Immigration & Nationality Act 1952, section 301(g).
163. 401 U.S. 815 at 831 (1971).
164. Act of 11 September 1957, P.L. 85-316, 71 Stat. 639.
165. See P.L. 92-584, 92 U.S. Cong. & Ad. News (1972) 4826.
166. See P.L. 95-432, 95 U.S. Cong & Ad. News (1978) 2521.
167. Immigration & Nationality Act 1952, section 310; amended by P.L. 85-508 of 7 July 1958, section 25, 72 Stat. 351; P.L. 86-3 of 18 March 1959, section 20(c), 73 Stat. 13; P.L. 87-3p1 of 26 September 1961, section 17, 75 Stat. 656.
168. See *In Re Clark,* 301 Pa. 321 (1930).
169. *Petition of Di Franco,* 339 F. Supp. 414 (1963).
170. *Trujillo-Hernandez* v. *Farrell,* 503 F. 2d. 954 (1974).
171. *In re Blasko,* 446 F. 2d. 1340 (1972).
172. Qualification added by P.L. 95-579 of 2 November 1978, section 3, 92 Stat. 2474. See 95 U.S. Cong. and Ad. News (1978) 5549.
173. Immigration and Nationality Act 1952, as amended, section 312. *Petition of Di Censo,* 218

N.Y.S. 2d. 418 (1961) (word 'arrest' is word in ordinary usage).

174. Section 313.

175. Sections 314 & 315.

176. Section 316.

177. Section 319.

178. A homosexual man was of 'good moral character' where his sexual relations were with consenting adults in private: *In re Brodie,* 394 F. Supp. 1208 (1975). Conversely, an alien who admitted homosexual relations in private in a State in which sodomy is an offence involving moral turpitude was not of good moral character: *Petition of Nemetz,* 485 F. Supp. 47 (1980).

179. Soviet Citizenship Act, No. 198, of 19th August, 1938, *Vedomosti SSSR* (1938) No. 11.

180. T. Taracouzio, 'The Soviet Citizenship Law of 1938', 33 A.J.I.L. (1939) 157.

181. V. Grzybowski, *Soviet Private International Law,* 1970, p. 257.

182. *Soviet Citizenship Law,* 1968, p. 20.

183. However, Republican citizenship had practical significance in determining the laws applicable to Soviet citizens abroad, particularly in matters of family law: Ginsburg *supra,* note 2, p. 22. In this respect it performs a function often served in common law jurisdictions by domicile.

184. Taracusio, *supra,* note 180.

185. Ginsburg *supra,* note 182, pp. 24–27; and 'Soviet Citizenship Legislation and Statelessness as a Consequence of the Conflict of Nationality Laws', 15 I.C.L.Q. (1966) 1, 9–12; Taracouzio, 33 A.J.I.L. (1939) 157, 158.

186. Soviet Citizenship Act, No. 22, of 22nd April, 1931.

187. Article 33.

188. *Vedomosti SSSR* (1978) No. 49, item 816. See C. Osakwe, 'Recent Soviet Citizenship Legislation', 28 A.J. Comp. L. (1980) 625; and G. Ginsburg, *The Citizenship Law of the USSR,* 1983.

189. *Vedomosti SSSR* (1978) No. 49, Item 817 (Decree of Supreme Soviet).

190. Article 12.

191. Law on Citizenship of the USSR, 1 December 1978, Articles 13, 14.

192. Article 9.

193. Article 26.

194. R. David, *Le droit français,* 1960, Vol. I, p. 262.

195. Law of May 7th, 1946.

196. J. Niboyet, *Traité de droit international privé français,* 1947–50, p. 158; A. Weiss, *Traité théorique et pratique de droit international privé,* 1907–1913, Vol. I, p. 433.

197. Article 77.

198. J. Valery, *Manuel de droit international privé,* 1914, pp. 124, 127.

199. R. Boulbès, *supra,* note 3, p. 45.

200. E.g, treaties with Tunisia (June 3rd, 1955) and Vietnam (August 16th, 1955).

201. See Ordinance of 19th October, 1945, Articles 11–14.

202. *Supra,* note 3, p. 46.

203. Formerly, Articles 17, 19, 95.

204. Formely, Articles 34–43, 52–77.

205. Law No. 73–42 of 9 January 1973, J.O. Jan 10, 1973. See R. Plender, 'The New French Nationality Law', 23 I.C.L.Q. (1974) 709.

206. Law No. 73–42 of 9 January 1973, Article 6. See D. Le Vert, 'Vers un aménagement du code française de la nationalité', 25 Rev. Jur. et Pol. (1971) 717.

207. Articles 17 & 19.

208. The reform is in conformity with the Law of Parental Responsibility, Law of June 4, 1970, 1970 D. 138.

56

209. 28 September 1954, 360 U.N.T.S. 117; *Basic Documents* II. 4.
210. Article 22.
211. Article 24.
212. Article 37.
213. The change was designed to bring nationality law into conformity with a change in electoral law dated 1970, permitting those undergoing military service to vote irrespective of their age: Law No. 70-589 of 9 July 1970, D 1970 (L) 178.
214. Article 48.
215. Article 52.
216. Article 53.
217. Article 63.
218. Article 64.
219. Reprinted in China Official Annual Report (1981) 297. For previous legislation, see Law on the Acquisition and Loss of Chinese Nationality, 1909, 4 A.J.I.L. (1910) Supp. 160; Nationality Law, 1912 and Amended Nationality Law, 1914; Law of Nationality, 1929, 4 China L. Rev. (1930) 39.
220. Article 1.
221. Law of National Autonomous Regions, 1984.
222. 12 April 1930, 179 L.N.T.S. 89; U.K.T.S. 33 (1937); *Basic Documents*. II. 1.
223. Nationality Law, 1980, Article 4.
224. Article 5.
225. Article 6.
226. Article 8.
227. Article 9.
228. Article 10.
229. Article 12.
230. Article 16.
231. See T. Chen, 'The Nationality Law of the People's Republic of China and the Overseas Chinese in Hong Kong, Macau and South East Asia', 5 N.Y.L. Sch. J. Int'l. & Comp. L. (1984) 281.
232. Beijing, 19 December 1985, Cmnd. 9543, U.K.T.S. No. 26 (1985); *Basic Documents* II. 9.
233. Hong Kong Act 1985; Draft Order in Council of 17 October 1985, Cmnd. 9637.
234. Law No. 37/81 of 3 October 1981 (Law of Nationality), Article 1.
235. *International Law*, 1952, Vol. I, p. 508.
236. *International Law and Human Rights*, 1950, p. 347.
237. *Supra,* note 8, pp. 66.
238. (1955) I.C.J.Rep. 4.
239. 28 I.L.R.(1950) 291, 292.
240. Cited with approval by M. Hudson, I.L.C. Rapporteur, I.L.C. Ybk, (1952-II) 3, 6.
241. 25 I.L.R. (1958-I) 91, 93.
242. R. Quadri, *La Sudditanza nel Diritto Internazionale*, 1936, p. 294.
243. Van Panhuys, *supra,* note 10, p. 29.
244. The view attacked by Van Panhuys is probably inconsistent with the traditional view, enshrined in the Montevideo Convention on the Rights and Duties of States, that a *defined* populace is an essential ingredient of statehood. See Article 1 of the Convention, 26th December, 1933, 49 Stat., 3097; R. Higgins, *The Development of International Law through the Political Organs of the United Nations*, 1961, p. 13.
245. 3 Pe. M. (1950–51) 263, 272, 17 I.L.R. (1950) 110; but see *Re Goods of Shiphris*, 3 Pe. M. (1950–1951) 222, 17 I.L.R. (1950) 110.
246. Palestine Citizenship Order, 1925/777); Palestine Citizenship (Amendment) Order, 1931

(1931/671); Palestine Citizenship (Amendment) Order 1939 (1939/363); repealed, Palestine Act, 1948, section 3(2). Prior to the entry into force of the Law of 1952, Palestinian citizenship had ceased to exist. See *Hussein* v. *Governor of Acre Prison*, 6 Pis. D. (1952) 897, 17 I.L.R. (1950) 112; *Oseri* v. *Oseri*, 8 Pe. M. (1953) 76, 17 I.L.R. (1950) 111 and Israel Transition (Temporary Provisions) (No. 2) Amendment Law, 5708–1948

247. See Van Panhuys, *supra*, note 10, p. 30.

248. V.Z.O. (1931) 222, 5 A.D. (1929–30) 213 (No. 131).

249. P.C.I.J. Ser. B. no. 4 (1923) at p. 24; c.f. *Panevezys-Saldutiskis Railway Company Case*, P.C.I.J. Ser. A/B No. 76 (1939) at p. 16.

250. *U.S.* v. *Wong Kim Ark*, 169 U.S. 649 (1897); *U.S. ex. rel. Lacas* v. *Curran*, 297 F. 219, 220 (1924); *Cabebe* v. *Acheson*, 183 F. 2d. 795, 797 (1950).

251. C. Morgenstern, 'Judicial Practice and the Supremacy of International Law', 27 B.Y.I.L. (1950) 42; H. Lauterpacht, 'Is International Law Part of the Law of England?' 25 T.G.S. (1939) 51; A. McNair, 'When do British Treaties involve Legislation?' 9 B.Y.I.L. (1928) 59; *R.* v. *Keyn*, (1876), 2 Ex. D. 63; *Isaacson* v. *Durant* (1870) L.R. 6 Q.B. 31; *Sutton* v. *Sutton* (1830) 1 R. and M. 663; *Doe d. Thomas* v. *Acklam*, (1824) 2 B. and C. 779; *Re Bruce*, (1832) 2 C. and J. 436; *Stansbury* v. *Arkwright*, (1833) 5 C. and P. 575; *Co-operative Committee* v. *Attorney-General for Canada*, [1947] A.C. 87; *R.* v. *Commanding Officer, 30th. Batt. Middlesex Regiment*, [1917] 2 K.B. 129; *R.* v. *Lynch*, [1903] 1 K.B. 444; *Re P. (G.E.) (An Infant)*, [1965] Ch. 568, 585.

252. See in particular, I. Brownlie, 39 B.Y.I.L. (1963) 284. See also the spate of writing which followed the decision in the *Nottebohm Case (Second Phase)*, including J. Jones, 'The Nottebohm Case', 5 I.C.L.Q. (1956) 230; J. Kunz, 'The Nottebohm Judgment (Second Phase)', 54 A.J.I.L. (1960) 343; H. Waldock, 'Decline of the Optional Clause', 32 B.Y.I.L. (1955–6) 244, 261–263; J. Glazer, '*Affaire Nottebohm* (Liechtenstein v. Guatamala) A Critique' 44 Geo. L.J. (1955–6) 313 and editorial in 31 N.Y.U.L. Rev. 1135.

253. V U.N.R.I.A.A. 326 (1928).

254. *Supra*, note 10, p. 153.

255. 25 I.L.R. (1958-II) 91 at 97, 98.

256. 6 A.D. (1931–2) 251 (No. 124) (German-Mexican Mixed Claims Commission).

257. 3 Moore 508 (§ 423).

258. 28 I.L.R. 291.

259. 137 F. 2d. 898; 12 A.D. (1943–5) 188 (No. 54) (emphasis added).

260. *Salem Case* 6 A.D. (1931–2) 188 (No. 98); *Lempert* v. *Bonfol*, 60 E.S.B. 67, 7 A.D. (1933–4) 290 (No. 115); *Perkins* v. *Elg.* 307 U.S. 325 (1939); *Ullman* v. *Ministère Public* (1915–6) R.D.I.P. 67; *Perez* v. *Brownell*, 356 U.S. 44 (1956), 26 I.L.R (1958-II) 404; *Rajdberg* v. *Lewi*, (1927) Zb. O.S.N. No. 107, 4 A.D. (1927–8) 314 (No. 209); *American Insurance Co.* v. *356 Bales of Cotton*, 1 Pet. 511 (1828).

261. D. Sandifer, *Evidence Before International Tribunals*, 1939, pp. 149 *et seq.;* Makarov, *supra*, note 2, p. 329; E. Borchard (rapporteur) 36 A.I.D.I. (1931-I) 277–278.

262. I.L.C. Ybk. (1952-II) 3, 6 (Article I).

263. This conclusion is in conformity with that of Van Panhuys, *supra*, note 10, pp. 157–158. See also Lauterpacht, *supra*, note 236, p. 27; G. Schwarzenberger, *Manual of International Law*, 1960, Vol. I, p. 56; P. Weis, *Nationality and Statelessness in International Law*, 1979, pp. 88–91. The view here expressed is fortified by the traditional statement that a state, by taking up the case of one of its nationals is in reality asserting its own right: *Mavrommatis Palestine Concessions Case*, P.C.I.J. Ser. A. No. 2 (1924) at p. 12; *Panevezys-Saldutskis Railway Co. Case*, P.C.I.J. Ser. A/B No. 76 (1939) at p. 16.

264. D. Greig, *International Law*, 1970, p. 493.

265. *Flegenheimer Claim*, 25 I.L.R. (1958-I) 91 at 150, 153.

266. *Georges Pinson Case,* V.U.N.R.I.A.A. (1928) 327; *Canevaro Case,* XI U.N.R.I.A.A. (1916) 397; *Mergé Claim,* 20 I.L.R. (1955) 443.
267. *Barthez de Montfort* v. *Treuhander Hauptverwaltung,* 3 A.D. (1925–6) 279 (No. 206).
268. *Baron de Born* v. *Yugoslav State,* 3 A.D. (1925–6) 277, 278 (No. 205).
269. *Salem Case,* II U.N.R.I.A.A. 1188 (1931); 6 A.D. (1931–2) 188, 192–3 (No. 98).
270. (1955) I.C.J. Rep. 4.
271. 478 U.N.T.S. 86 (italics added).
272. 236 U.N.T.S. 252; Article 1.
273. J. Fawcett, *The British Commonwealth in International Law,* 1963, p. 203; Joseph, *supra,* note 85, p. 44; R. Jennings, 30 B.Y.I.L. (1953) 320.
274. Cd. 5746-1, p. 272.
275. Joseph, *supra,* note 85, pp. 221–238.
276. 131 U.N.T.S. 4.
277. 453 U.N.T.S. 3 (1962), Article V(d), Joseph, *supra,* note 85, pp. 173, 203.
278. Cmnd. 9343; Foreign Compensation (Poland) (Nationalisation Claims) Order, 1956 (1956/618) Article 7(b).
279. See the Promotion of Investment Agreements with the Yemen, Sana'a, 25 February 1982, Cmnd. 9096, Article 1(c)(i); St. Lucia, Castries, 18 January 1983, Cmnd. 8872, Article 1(c); Panama, Panama City, 7 October 1983, Cmnd. 9736, Article 1(c)(ii). See also the Double Taxation Agreements with Tunisia, London, 15 December 1982, Cmnd. 9345, Article 3(1)(i); Togo, London, 9 February 1984, Cmnd. 9229, Article 3(c)(i); Sweden, Stockholm, 30 August 1983, Cmnd. 9330, Article 3(c)(i); New Zealand, London, 22 December 1983, Cmnd. 9264, Article 3(c)(i); China, Beijing, 26 July 1984, Cmnd. 9439, Article 3(d)(i); Norway, Oslo, 3 October 1985, Cmnd. 9730, Article 3(c).
280. See the list of bilateral treaties in R. Donner, *The Regulation of Nationality in International Law,* 1983, 286–87. See further K. Zemanek, 'State Succession after Decolonization', 116 Hague *Recueil* (1965-III) 187.
281. See League of Nations Official Journal (1925) 143. The other two topics were territorial waters and State responsibility for injuries to aliens.
282. 23 A.J.I.L. (1929) Spec. Supp. 1.
283. 12 April 1930, 179 L.N.T.S. 89; *Basic Documents* II.1.
284. 178 L.N.T.S. 227.
285. 179 L.N.T.S. 116; *Basic Documents* II.2.
286. U.K.T.S. No. 112; Cmnd. 5447, *Basic Documents* II.3 (in force 1973).
287. Article 1.
288. Article 6. The development of international rules governing nationality was further advanced at this period by the Pan-American Convention on Nationality of 26 December 1933, 28 A.J.I.L. Supp. 63 and the Inter-American Convention on the Nationality of Women of the same date, 28 A.J.I.L. Supp. 61.
289. Convention relating to the Status of Refugees, 28 October 1933, 159 L.N.T.S. No. 3663; Convention concerning the Status of Refugees coming from Germany, 14 July 1938, 192 L.N.T.S. 59.
290. Convention relating to the Status of Refugees, 28 July 1951, 189 U.N.T.S. 137, *Basic Documents* III.2; First Protocol to the Universal Copywright Convention concerning the Application of that Convention to the Works of Stateless Persons and Refugees, 6 September 1952, 216 U.N.T.S. 176.
291. See Treaty of Peace between Allied and Associated Powers and Italy, 10 February 1947, 49 U.N.T.S. 3; Treaty between Poland and the Soviet Union, 15 Feruary 1951, 432 U.N.T.S. 210; Accord between Italy and Yugoslavia, 18 December 1954, 284 U.N.T.S. 239.
292. Res. 319 B III (XI) of 11 August 1950.

293. 28 September 1954, 360 U.N.T.S. 117; *Basic Documents* II.6.
294. *Supra,* note 93.
295. Donner, *supra,* note 280 at p. 151.
296. *Supra,* note 320.
297. 20 February 1957, 309 U.N.T.S. 65.
298. See Case 21/74, *Airola* v. *Commission,* [1975] ECR 221.
299. 6 May 1963 E.T.S. No. 88 (1971), Cmnd. 4802, 634 U.N.T.S. 221; *Basic Documents* II.7.
300. *Basic Documents* II.8. By the Convention on the Exchange of Information regarding the Acquisition of Nationality, 10 September 1964, 932 U.N.T.S. certain European States undertook to provide each other with information concerning changes of nationality from that of one party to that of another. By an additional Protocol to the Convention of 1963, 24 November 1977, E.T.S. 96, the parties undertook to communicate to each other certain further information.
301. P.C.I.J. Rep. Ser. B. No. 4, p. 24 (1923).

BIBLIOGRAPHY

N. Bar-Yaacov, *Dual Nationality,* 1961.
J. Basdevant, 'Conflits de nationalité dans les arbitrages vénézuéliens de 1903–1905', 5 Rev. dr. int. priv. (1909) 41.
C. Blake, 'Legislation, Citizenship and the State: the British Nationality Act 1981', 45 M.L.R. (1982) 179.
P. Blaser, *La nationalité et la protection juridique de l'individu,* (thesis, Neuchatel) 1962.
E. Borchard, 'Decadence of the American Doctrine of Voluntary Expatriation', 25 A.J.I.L. (1931) 312.
M. Bos, 'Surinam's Road from Self-Government to Sovereignty', 7 N.Y.I.L. (1976) 131.
H. Briggs, 'Barcelona Traction: the *Jus Standi* of Belgium', 6 A.J.I.L. (1971) 327.
M. Cogordan, *La nationalité au point de vue des rapports internationaux,* 1879.
E. Cotran, 'Some Legal Aspects of the Formation of the United Arab Republic and the United Arab States', 8 I.C.L.Q. (1959) 346.
R. Donner, *The Regulation of Nationality in International Law,* 1983.
R. Flournoy, 'Observations on the New German Law of Nationality', 8 A.J.I.L. (1914) 477.
W. Griffin, 'The Right to a Single Nationality' 40 Temple L.Q. (1966) 57.
J. Jones, *British Nationality Law,* 1956.
J. Jones, 'The Nottebohm Case', 5 I.C.L.Q. (1956) 230.
C. Joseph, *Nationality and Diplomatic Protection: the Commonwealth of Nations,* 1970.
P. Koenig, *'La nationalité en allemagne',* 24 A.F.D.I. (1978) 237.
A. Makarov, *'La nationalité de la femme mariée',* 60 Hague *Recueil* (1937-II) 115.
A. Makarov, *Allgemeine Lehren des Staatsangehörigkeitsrecht,* 1962.
F. Mann, 'The Present Validity of Nazi Nationality Laws', 89 L.Q.R. (1973) 194.
P. Mutharika, *The Regulation of Statelessness under International Law and National Law,* 1977.
C. Parry, *Nationality and Citizenship Laws of the Commonwealth and the Republic of Ireland,* 1957.
C. Parry, 'The Duty to Recognize Foreign Nationality Laws', 19 ZaöRV (1958) 337.
B. Peselj, 'The Rule of the Nationality of Claimant: Due Process of Law and the United States Congress', 53 A.J.I.L. (1959) 144.
R. Plender, 'The New French Nationality Law', 23 I.C.L.Q. (1974) 709.
W. Pollack, 'The Eligibility of British Subjects as Judges of the Permanent Court of International Justice', 20 A.J.I.L. (1926) 714.

Z. Rode, 'Dual Nationals and the Doctrine of Dominant Nationality', 53 A.J.I.L. (1959) 139.

D. Sandifer, 'A Comparative Study of the Laws relating to Nationality at Birth and to Loss of Nationality', 29 A.J.I.L. (1935) 248.

C. Seckler-Hudson, *Statelessness, with Special Reference to the United States*, 1934.

P. Van Panhuys, *The Role of Nationality in International Law*, 1959.

A. Verdross, *'Les règles internationales concernant le traitement des étrangers'*, 37 Hague *Recueil* (1931-III) 322.

P. Weis, *Nationality and Statelessness in International Law*, 1979; 'The United Nations Convention on the Reduction of Statelessness 1961', 11 I.C.L.Q. (1962) 1073.

R. White and F. Hampson, 'What is my Nation? Who Talks of my Nation? British Nationality Act 1981', 31 I.C.L.Q. (1982) 849.

E. Zeballos, *La nationalité au point de vue de la législation comparée et au droit privé humain*, 1914–19.

CHAPTER 2

Historical Perspectives

For many years there has been a sporadic debate about the existence or nonexistence of a rule permitting each State to impose direct[1] controls on alien immigration. This debate has often centred around the supposed conflict between two principles, Sibert asks whether any rule of international law requires a State to admit aliens to its territory, and replies to his question in the following words:

> *pour résoudre cette question il a été fait appel à deux principes différents: 1° au principe de la souveraineté des états, envisagé d'une manière absolue, ou bien 2° au principe de leur interdépendance.*[2]

The former of those principles is championed by Oppenheim[3] and Robert C. de Ward[4] and has the support of the majority of the Anglo-Saxon theorists of the early twentieth century. The latter (in Sibert's analysis) lies at the root of article 13 (2) of the Universal Declaration of Human Rights[5] and is supported not only by numerous European continental jurists, but also by several prominent members of the Latin American school. A. H. Roth argues that the truth lies somewhere between the two postulated extremes, and believes, that although the weight of *theory* tends to support the champions of state sovereignty the facts of international life demonstrate the *reality* of State interdependence.[6] Roth's conclusion is akin to that of Fauchille who observed that both champions of the sovereignty school, and adherents of the interdependence school admitted that there were exceptions to the principles which they upheld.[7] Thus, by adopting either of the two principles it was possible to achieve a similar result; but the result was never identical, for in the one case the admission of foreigners was thought to be demanded by legal obligation, and in the other it was thought to be demanded by mere comity or expediency.

It will be the object of this chapter to describe the historical context of the conflict between the sovereignty theory and the interdependence theory, and also some of the antecedents of that controversy. It is thought that the following pages will demonstrate that the right to exclude aliens has not always been regarded as an essential attribute of a State's sovereignty. On the other hand, States have rarely accepted (other than by treaties of limited participation) that their interdependence obliges them to admit aliens. In modern times, the most significant limitations on a State's right to exclude aliens are based not on a principle of interdependence, but on extant and nascent rules designed to protect human rights.

THE ORIGINS OF EXCLUSIONARY POWER

Even a cursory examination of feudal documents reveals numerous examples of the lord's power to exclude from his domain named individuals or defined groups of foreigners.[8] However, the exercise of this power was exceptional. The regular maintenance of immigration control made its debut in the western world at a remarkably recent date.

In England, the royal practice of issuing travel documents to foreigners[9] became customary in the late Norman period. In Angevin times these documents became formalised and several distinct classes emerged.[10] Nevertheless, this practice was developed for the itinerant's benefit; it certainly does not constitute evidence of any rule whereby strangers were forbidden to enter the country other than with the King's permission.[11] Indeed, clause 41 of the Magna Carta of 1215 expressly guaranteed that merchants who had not previously been forbidden to enter England should remain free to travel into and through the kingdom 'in accordance with ancient and lawful customs'.[12]

After an examination of that item, and of contextual sources, W. F. Craies concluded as follows:

> Except with reference to foreign sovereigns, their ambassadors and their forces . . . there seems to be no prerogative of the Crown either to exclude or expel aliens.[13]

That conclusion appears to be somewhat extravagant. Although for long periods successive English monarchs permitted alien merchants to 'go and come with their merchandises after the manner of the Great Charter'[14] the same sovereigns occasionally invoked an exceptional power to expel or exclude defined groups of aliens.[15] That power was later invoked by the Tudors when the Flemish, Irish and Huguenot influxes prompted demands for a reduction in the overall rate of immigration.[16] Thus, it was established at common law that an alien committed no offence if he entered England without the sovereign's permission, although he was liable to be denied admission if the King saw fit to exclude him.[17] In this respect English common law reflected both the principle of sovereignty (whereby the King could exclude named individuals) and the principle of free movement (whereby aliens enjoyed *prima facie* the right to enter the kingdom).[18]

Each of these principles attracted the comments of Gentilis. As Spanish Advocate, he espoused the case of members of the Spanish force, defeated by the Dutch, who had taken refuge in England. He readily conceded that King James had the sovereign power to send these Spaniards whither he wished.[19] However, elsewhere in his work, Gentilis referred to the principle of free movement, and, in particular, to freedom of maritime travel. He argued that a captor does not have the right to conduct his captives through the territory of a third State, but in reaching this conclusion he did not maintain that the sovereign has an absolute right to decide whom he will admit to his territory. Instead he based his conclusion on the narrower ground that the ruler of a third country has an interest in avoiding the inspiration of fear there by outsiders.[20]

Grotius appears to have given rather more weight to the principle of sovereignty. One of the two legitimate causes for which a sovereign might, in accordance with Grotian theory, engage in war was the defence of the persons or properties of the sovereign's own subjects. It followed *a fortiori* that a sovereign might exclude foreigners from his kingdom in defence of the personal or proprietary rights of his people. Nevertheless, Grotius drew a sharp distinction between the exclusion and the expulsion of aliens. He declared that expulsion without due cause was barbarous, and contrary to the law of civilized nations. Moreover, he cited the writings of St. Ambrose to demonstrate that even famine does not justify such an expulsion.[21]

With the publication of Pufendorf's *De Jure Naturae et Gentium* came a reinforcement of some limitations on a sovereign's power to refuse to admit aliens to his territory. Among the duties of humanity catalogued by Pufendorf was the sovereign's obligation to admit to his territory aliens having lawful reasons for demanding admittance. Pufendorf clearly considered that commercial motives might constitute, 'lawful reasons' for an alien's admittance, and he further maintained that a sovereign who admits foreigners to his territory must ensure that they are treated properly – that is, in accordance with their station.[22] Paradoxically, Francisco de Vitoria proved the inspiration for Pufendorf at this point. The former had attempted to justify the Spanish seizure of South American territories by reference to a principle of free movement, whereby each man had the right to travel abroad if he did not harm the natives of the countries to which he went; the latter replied that the owner of a territory had the right to decide whom he would admit to it, provided that he took into consideration the alien's reason for travelling. The former had argued that the right to travel was a corollary of the right to trade; the latter asserted that the sovereign had, in certain circumstances, the power to curtail even trading.[23] Eventually Pufendorf sought to achieve a synthesis of the principles of sovereignty and free movement by formulating the following rule: 'every State may reach a decision according to its own usage on admission of foreigners who come to it for reasons other than are necessary and deserving of sympathy; only no-one can question the barbarity of showing indiscriminate hostility to those who come on peaceful missions'.

Pufendorf's modification of Vitoria's thesis gained support from Kant, who, in his *Perpetual Peace* defined hospitality as the *right* of a foreigner not to be treated with hostility merely by reason of his arrival on foreign soil. However, Kant conceded that a foreigner cannot normally claim the right to be a guest, but only the right to be an ordinary visitor, since a special benevolent treaty would be required to give him the 'freedom of the house'.[24] In accordance with this concession, Vattel stated that a sovereign might prohibit the entrance to his territory either of foreigners in general, or of certain persons, or in certain cases, as the welfare of the State might require.[25]

In the mid-eighteenth century, Blackstone summarised the current state of international law and common law on the subject:

> by the law of nations no member of one society has the right to intrude into another . . . [Nevertheless] great tenderness is shown by our laws . . . with regard to the admission of strangers who come spontaneously. For so long as a nation continues at peace with ours, and they themselves behave peaceably, they are under the King's protection.[26]

THE BEGINNINGS OF PERMANENT IMMIGRATION CONTROL

Within a few years after the publication of that statement, the situation was changed. The immediate cause of the enactment of the first statute dealing with immigration into England was the flight there of a small number of refugees from the French revolution. In the three years from 1789 these refugees numbered about eight thousand, but their arrival coincided with the popular Francophobia which accompanied the deterioration in relations between Britain and France, and with fears that Jacobin emissaries had infiltrated the ranks of the refugees. Accordingly, in 1792, the Government prepared the Alien Bill, which began with a questionable preamble recording that 'a great and unusual number of aliens have lately resorted to the kingdom'. The Bill was entered on the statute book in 1793.

The new Act provided that masters of vessels arriving in the kingdom should give customs officers details of any foreigners transported by them, on pain of a fine of £ 10 per alien or detention of the vessel; that any alien arriving after January 1st, 1793 should give to the customs officer an account of his personal history and status, on pain of deportation or even transportation; that any arms belonging to an alien might be seized; that the King in Council might direct that aliens of any description might not land, or might land only in certain places; that the King might order any alien who had arrived after the beginning of 1792 to live in any specified district; that any alien who had arrived after the beginning of 1792 should register his name and address if he were in the kingdom on January 10th, 1793; that any alien who had been imprisoned might be deported; that any alien who had been sentenced to transportation and had subsequently been found in the kingdom might be put to death, and that the exercise of these and other powers might not be challenged by *certiorari*. It is not difficult to see why a commentator as sober as Erskine May followed the Marquis of Landsdown in describing the Act as 'equivalent to the suspension of . . . Habeas Corpus'.[27] The Act was phrased to operate 'until the first day of January, 1794 and from that time to the end of the next session of Parliament and no longer'. It was accompanied by other restrictions on traditional freedoms, for the national emergency preceding the outbreak of the Napoleonic Wars saw the passage of the Traiterous Correspondence Bill and Fox's Libel Bill.[28]

The impending war brought about similar developments on the other side of the English Channel. By a decree of 1795 the French Government provided:

Tout étranger, à son arriveé dans un port de mer ou dans une commune frontière de la République, se présentera à la municipalité; il déposera son passeport, qui sera renvoyé de suite au comité de sûreté générale pour y être visé . . .[29]

That decree was strengthened by the Order of the Executive Directorate, 1796.[30] In 1797 France adopted its Passports Law – a comprehensive statute, described by Grahl-Madsen as the starting-point for modern aliens legislation.[31]

Meanwhile, fears that Jacobin emissaries had infiltrated immigrant groups spread in America and in Switzerland, with the result that legislatures in each of these federations approved Bills providing for the control of immigration.[32] The American statute bore remarkable similarity to the English statute approved five years earlier. In particular, the President received authority to order the deportation of any alien whose presence he deemed to be dangerous to the national security. However, this presidential power, in particular, attracted resentment, and the Alien Act, which had been phrased to apply for only two years, was not renewed at the expiration of that peroiod.

In Canada, also, the authorities took measures to counteract the danger of an influx of revolutionaries. From 1794 onwards those authorities considered it necessary to maintain permanent administrative machinery to scrutinize aliens entering the territory (notably under the Nova Scotian Act, 38 Geo. III, c. 1).

It is noteworthy that the British enactment differed from Canadian practice in that it was designed to apply to aliens even after their admission to the territory of their new domicile, and it differed from the United States legislation in permanence. Although some of the provisions of the Alien Act were relaxed in 1802[33] and 1814,[34] the original Act was renewed at intervals, and was substantially intact in 1815. In 1816 Addington moved a new Bill, designed to authorize the continuation for a further two years of most of the provisions of the extant legislation. Despite the opposition of Brougham and of Sir Samuel Romilly, Lord Hamilton and Dudley North, the Bill was passed.[35] By Section 24 the new Act continued to have effect until 1818 when it was superseded by a similar statute, whereby the restrictions on alien immigration continued to be applied for a further two years.[36] In 1818 Castlereagh moved the renewal of the Alien Act, arguing that it caused little inconvenience by comparison with the Act of 1793 and that it was necessary in view of the presence in England of 20,000 aliens.[37] The Bill became an Act, and the restrictions on alien immigration continued to be applied until 1822, when Peel moved a further Bill to extend the restrictions for another two-year period. The opposition was quick to observe that this was the eighth year of peace, and that the Bill before the House was based on a wartime Act.[38] At the third reading of the Bill, the future Lord Denman stressed the novelty of the 1793 Act, and thus the relative novelty of the provisions of the Bill. [39] The Bill was carried.

In 1824 the restrictions on aliens arriving or resident in the kingdom were renewed for a further two years, but this time it was provided that the restrictions should not apply to aliens who had been resident in the kingdom for seven years.[40] Not until 1826 did the Crown surrender its statutory power to order the deportation of an alien domiciled in England, even when the latter had committed no offence, had received no proper trial and did not know the nature of the allegations against him.[41]

THE DECLINE OF THE PRINCIPLE OF FREE MOVEMENT

The prevailing political instability in Euope in 1848 had some results similar to the French Revolution: it led to an exodus of political refugees, whose presence in England led to fears of disturbances there. In 1848 Parliament approved the Aliens Removal Act (11 and 12 Vict., c. 20) which provided, in section 1, that powers should be conferred on the Home Secretary and the Lord Lieutenant of Ireland to order the removal of any alien against whom written allegations had been made if the Home Secretary or Lord Lieutenant deemed it 'expedient' to do so. Although the 1848 Act provided, in section 3, that an alien might appeal to the Privy Council if he believed that he had good reason for failing to comply with a removal order made in respect of him, the appellate procedure was primitive. By section 5 an alien who had been committed under the Act, and within one month of his committal had not been sent out of the realm, might appeal to a court for his discharge, but the court had an absolute discretion in deciding such cases. By section 7, the Act was to remain in force for one year and from then to the end of the next session of Parliament, and no longer. The Act was not, in fact, renewed at this time, but on the outbreak of the disturbances in Ireland it was reintroduced in a schedule to the Prevention of Crime (Ireland) Act, 1882.

However, the 1848 Act was exceptional. In general, the mid-nineteenth century witnessed the application by the Government of Great Britain of markedly liberal policies towards aliens. By an Act of 1826 (7 Geo. IV, C. 54) the more onerous restrictions on alien immigration were repealed and re-placed by a system of alien registration. This system was re-drafted in 1836 by an Act which provided for full reports to be made on aliens landing in the kingdom, for declarations and registrations to be made or undertaken by alien immigrants and for information about these aliens to be transmitted to the Home Secretary.[42] These provisions remained in force until their repeal in 1905, in accordance with the introduction of a new and more restrictive code of alien immigration control.[43] The 1905 Act, however, did not reinstate the old system of aliens registration; this system was not reintroduced other than in modified form in 1914. Moreover, prior to 1914 alien registration was an alternative, not a supplement, to alien immigration control. In 1872 Lord Granville stated in a letter to Mr. Layard that 'by the existing law of Great Britain all foreigners have the unrestricted right of entrance into and residence in this country'.[44]

The temporary predominance of liberal immigration policies in England in the mid-nineteenth century was reflected in similar policies on the other side of the Atlantic. Until the end of the Napoleonic Wars the rate of emigration from England to Canada was low, and the majority of the migrants from the British Isles to that Dominion were of Irish or Scottish origins. In addition, there was considerable movement to Canada of British subjects from other British possessions in the Western Hemisphere, but this movement was not always accomplished without friction. In 1815 the Nova Scotia Assembly addressed a protest to the British Government against the introduction of negroes from Bermuda.[45] All this time the United Kingdom Government was opposed to the emigration of Britons from the British Isles to Canada. The reversal of this policy in 1827 was determined by the desire of H. M. Government in the United Kingdom to encourage members of the Irish and other poor communi-

68

ties of urban England to seek opportunities for selfimprovement in North America: it was in 1827 that the British authorities established Canada's first immigration service, charged with the task of caring for destitute migrants to Canada. The legislatures of several of the Canadian provinces reacted unfavourably to the adoption of this new policy. In 1828 the Nova Scotia Assembly adopted legislation to provide that no immigrant passenger might land in the province until the master of the vessel on which he arrived had entered a bond of £ 10, which would be refunded only if the immigrant did not, within one year, become a public charge by reason of sickness, old age, poverty, or inability to support himself because of his immaturity of years.[46] Later, the same Assembly substituted for this bond system a system in which a head tax was applied uniformly for all immigrants.[47]

The head tax system was also employed in New York, where the legislature conceded that the exclusion of foreigners was an international matter (and therefore within the exclusive competence of the federal Congress) but attempted to require a specified sum to be paid for each alien passenger landed.[48] The validity of this statute was challenged before the Supreme Court in the *Passenger Cases,* in particular, in *Smith v. Turner,*[49] a case which arose out of an action in debt brought by the health officer of the City of New York against the master of a British ship, which arrived in New York with 295 steerage passengers in respect of whom the head tax had not been paid. The federal Supreme Court held that the imposition of the head tax was unconstitutional, as a regulation of commerce. Similar judgments were given in respect of legislation purporting to provide for the collection of head taxes in New York[50] and other states of the U.S.A.[51] and in respect of similar legislation subsequently adopted in New York in an attempt to overcome the decision in *Smith v. Turner.*[52] The repeated (though unsuccessful) attempts of the State legislatures to control indirectly the volume of immigration into their territories provided an impetus to the federal Government. In 1875 Congress prohibited the entry to any part of the United States of alien prostitutes and convicts and of certain aliens with mental or physical incapacities.[53] By a federal statute of 1882 a duty of fifty cents was imposed for every alien passenger transhipped to the United States from foreign countries.[54] In 1891 the federal Government of the United States increased the qualitative controls over the immigration of aliens by excluding persons suffering from certain contagious diseases and by authorizing the deportation of those who had evaded the controls established by the previous two enactments.[55]

At the same time the volume of emigration from China rose significantly. Oriental migrants, characteristically willing to work for rewards lower than those which would have been acceptable to Europeans, encountered severe opposition from those who considered that their presence tended to depress the labour markets of their new domiciles. The federal Government of the

United States adopted in 1882 the Chinese Exclusion Act.[56] In *Lau Ow Bew v. U.S.*[57] the federal Supreme Court held that the Chinese Exclusion Act did not apply to those Chinese who had already entered and established a domicile in the U.S.A., since such immigrants enjoyed the rights of egress and regress by virtue of a most-favoured-nation clause in a treaty between the United States and China. However, in three other cases decided in the same year, the same court upheld as constitutional those parts of the Chinese Exclusion Act which provided for a system of registration of Chinese labourers and authorized their deportation if after one year they did not produce certificates of registration.[58] The 1882 Act was amended in 1884,[59] and then, in 1888, a new statute imposed further restrictions on the immigration of Chinese labourers to the United States.[60]

In the case of Australia, the likelihood of a very large Chinese influx prompted all political parties to unite in supporting the Immigration Restriction Bill, which became an Act in 1901. On this statute successive Australian Governments constructed that Commonwealth's immigration policies for half a century.[61] The Act effectively reduced immigration from South-East Asia by means of a dictation test,[62] but it was less successful in halting the introduction of workers from the Indian subcontinent, particularly in view of the fact that Australian employers had been among the chief supporters of the Kanaka labour-traffic. That traffic attracted widespread humanitarian objections, and from 1904 onwards, the Australian Government resisted the traffic simply by refusing to issue the appropriate entry-permits. The so-called 'White Australia Policy' can be said to have begun in earnest at this point, for henceforth the immigration of Asian and (to a much lesser extent) African labourers was discouraged by the non-issuance of entry documents. Apart from a few minor changes, some of them made in accordance with agreements between Australia and India, China and Japan, this situation remained unaltered until after the Second World War.[63]

In the case of Canada there is greater evidence of the impact of United States immigration policies. When States on the western seaboard began to restrict immigration into their territories, Canada was caught by the backwash. Two years after the passage of the British North America Act, the Canadian legislature adopted an Immigration Act, which provided that the master of every immigrant ship should list any disabled passengers carried, and that no indigent might land without depositing a bond. The same Act limited the number of passengers who might be carried per square foot of superficial deck space or per tonnage displacement of each immigrant ship.[64] Three years later this Act was amended by further legislation which was primarily designed to protect migrants by proscribing such injurious conduct as the sale of passage tickets at exorbitant prices, but which conferred on the Government the power to prohibit the immigration of paupers and 'vicious' persons.[65]

Thereafter, the passage of the Homestead Exemption Act[66] and the Dominion Lands Act[67] attracted more pioneers, and the development of the railways had a similar effect.[68] From 1891 onwards the Canadian government took action by statute to prevent the immigration of paupers; but the most significant of the restrictive measures taken at this time was probably the Chinese Immigration, Act 1885 – an Act passed to protect Canada against the backwash effect of the U.S. legislation of 1882.[69] By this Act, most persons of Chinese origin became ineligible to enter the U.S. other than by paying a head tax of fifty dollars.

The enactment of racially and culturally exclusive immigration laws in Canada continued until well after the First World War. Immediately after that war the immigration of Mennonites, Doukhbours and Hutterites was prohibited by Order in Council.[70] In 1923 a similar Order excluded most east Indian immigrants, and in 1930 the immigration of Asiatics was forbidden (subject to very few exceptions).[71]

The absence of similar legislation in the United Kingdom in the second half of the nineteenth century was conspicuous.[72] Ever since the passage of the Lascars Act of 1823 seamen of Indian origin had been subjected to certain disabilities in respect of employment in British ships, and the landing of destitute Lascars in Britain had been prohibited.[73] However, the number of Lascar seamen settling in England was always small, and was negligible other than in certain ports (such as Cardiff). Certain restrictions on the migratory rights of non-European seamen enjoying British subjecthood were imposed, even as late as 1925, when the Special Restrictions (Coloured Alien Seamen) Order was promulgated,[74] but such restrictions were rare.[75]

JUDICIAL DECISIONS AT THE TURN OF THE CENTURY

In *Nishimura Ekiu v. U.S.* Mr. Justice Gray said that

> it is an accepted maxim of international law, that every sovereign nation has the power, as inherent in sovereignty, and essential to its self-preservation, to forbid the entrance of foreigners within its dominions, or to admit them only in such cases and upon such conditions as it may see fit to prescribe.[76]

He based this assertion on the proposition put forward by Vattel. Almost contemporaneously with Mr. Justice Gray's decision came that of the Privy Council in *Musgrove v. Chun Teeong Toy*.[77] The factual similarity between these two cases is considerable. The latter case concerned the Victorian Chinese Act, 1881;[78] the former concerned the Immigration Act of 1891, which supplemented the Chinese Exclusion Act.[79] In both cases the immigration authorities had denied admission to an Oriental migrant and the migrant sought to establish the unconstitutionality of the legislation whereby the authorities purported to act.[80]

In *Musgrove v. Chun Teeong Toy* the Lord Chancellor pointed out that the plaintiff's case depended on the alleged legal right, enforceable by action of an alien to enter British territory. He continued:

No authority exists for the proposition that an alien has any such right. Circumstances may occur in which the refusal to permit an alien to land might be such an interference with international comity as would properly give rise to diplomatic remonstrance from the country of which he was a native, but it is quite another thing to assert that an alien excluded from any part of Her Majesty's dominions by the executive government there, can maintain an action in a British Court and raise such questions as were argued before their Lordships in the present appeal.[81]

In *Attorney-General for Canada v. Cain, Gilhula* the Privy Council did not suggest that the exclusion of an alien might involve even a breach of comity. This case concerned the constitutionality of Canada's Alien Labour Act, 1897, which prohibited action to assist the immigration of foreigners under contract to perform unskilled labour in Canada, and provided for the return of aliens who had immigrated to Canada unlawfully.[82] The Committee stated that

by the law of nations the supreme power in every State has the right to make laws for the exclusion ... of aliens.[83]

These words followed the phraseology exployed by Sir Thomas Erskine in *In Re Adam*[84] but the main authority on which the Privy Council relied, and the main authority invoked by Erskine seventy years earlier, was Vattel.

The maintenance of Canada's racially-exclusive immigration legislation required acceptance of a wider principle, namely that the legislature of the Dominion was competent to pass effective legislation for the exclusion of certain British subjects from overseas. Accordingly, in *In Re Munshi Singh* the Chief Justice of British Columbia stated that a British subject has, by virtue of his status as such, no right to enter the territory of a British Dominion to which he is not attached.[85] The Chief Justice added that:

in my opinion the British subject has no higher right than an alien in coming to the shores of Canada.

There is evidence to show that English legal opinion in the late nineteenth century reflected these several judgments. As early as 1892 Montague Crackenthorpe, Q.C. wrote that it can hardly be disputed that every civilized State is entitled to make what regulations it pleases both as to emigration from, and immigration into its territory.[86]

Crackenthorpe's view was reiterated by several of his contemporaries. Heilborn drew a close analogy between the proprietory rights of individuals and the territorial sovereignty of States; one of the clear implications of his observations was that a State might prevent persons who did not belong to it from 'trespassing' on its property.[87] De Martens was more explicit:

> *Chaque état, en vertu de son omnipotence à l'intérieur, a le droit indubitable de fixer les conditions auxquelles il les admet sur son territoire.*

He did add that certain international law rules limited State competence in this regard, but the limitations which he envisaged related to the treatment of aliens after their admission.[88] Hall wrote that in strict law a country can refuse the hospitality of its soil to any, or to all, foreigners, but he did add that to exclude all foreigners would be to withdraw from the brotherhood of civilized peoples.[89] By 1906 Anzilotti stated the principle of free movement with considerable diffidence.

> *On ne saurait affirmer d'une manière certaine,*
> he said,
> *qu'aujourd'hui, sauf les cas très nombreux où des traités (traités d'établissement, etc.) sont intervenus, il existe pour les états une obligation juridique d'admettre les étrangers sur leur territoire.*[90]

The Institute of International Law expressed some highly progressive ideas about the limitation of national sovereignty in relation to immigration. According to article 6 of the Institute's proposals of 1892, the free entrance of aliens into the territory of a civilized State should not be curtailed in a general and permanent manner other than in the interest of public welfare (*l'intérêt public*) and for the most serious of reasons. Article 7 of those proposals added that the protection of the national labour force does not, by itself, constitute a justification for non-admission of foreigners.[91] The principles underlying these proposals were reflected in the writings of several leading contemporary jurists. Bluntschli stated that no country may prohibit all foreigners from entering its territory, that the State may for reasons of public welfare expel certain named foreigners and that public welfare alone entitles a State to prohibit foreigners from entering its territory.[92] Nys wrote in 1905

Que l'Etat puisse réglementer l'immigration, le point n'est pas douteux, mais il n'a pas le droit de la prohiber.[93]

A similar opinion was given by Suárez.[94] The enunciation of this view by Suárez is particularly comprehensible in the light of the self-interest of Latin American States in seeking to attract migrants, at that time. Article 72 (10) of the Brazilian Constitution of 1891 provided that in times of peace every person might enter Brazilian territory whenever he chose to do so. Similar provisions appeared in the constitutions of Bolivia and Nicaragua. Lapradelle and Niboyet refer to a decision of the Supreme Court of Brazil in 1910, in which the court proclaimed the right of aliens to enter Brazilian territory.[95]

However, even in Latin America numerous legislatures took action to guard against an influx of Orientals and other 'non-Europeans'. A law passed in Haiti in 1903 imposed numerous restrictions on Syrian immigrants.[96] A Costa Rican decree of 1914 provided that Arabs, Armenians, Syrians and gipsies of any nationality should be ineligible to enter the country.[97] In Panama, a series of Laws and Decrees adopted between 1909 and 1917 applied to persons of Turkish, Syrian and North African race the same restrictions as had been applied to persons of Chinese race.[98] A Venezuelan Law of 1919 prohibited the immigration of any person not of European race (or of yellow race in the case of islanders native to the northern hemisphere).[99] Thus, even Suárez conceded that an alien may be denied admission to a country on the ground that he belongs (for example) to the yellow or African race.[100]

In 1909 the Solicitor for the U.S. State Department was required to deal with the refusal of the Ecuadorian authorities to admit a Chinese labourer of U.S. nationality. Referring to 'the undoubted right of a sovereign nation to exclude foreigners classified as undesirable by local law, the Solicitor opined that no justifiable objection could be made against Ecuador's decision to exclude the labourer.[101]

Similarly, in the first edition of his treatise, Oppenheim concluded that a State, although incapable of excluding all aliens from its territory without violating the *spirit* of the law of nations, is under no obligation to admit all objectionable aliens to its territory.[102] Apart from a few minor changes, these passages remained unaltered in the next six editions of Oppenheim's work. The fifth edition of Hall's treatise on international law contained an argument to the effect that the right of intercourse was probably a fiction, and that even if it existed, it must have been limited by the qualification that a State may take what measures it considers necessary to prevent the right of access or the right of intercourse from being used to its injury. It added that recent legislation adopted in the United States was a 'somewhat excessive' instance of the use of a State's right to exclude aliens, but that the most limited view of State sovereignty must accept that this right exist.[103]

RESTRICTIVE LEGISLATION EARLY IN THE PRESENT CENTURY

The wave of Oriental migrants reaching the western shores of the United States and Canada had not yet subsided when another wave of migrants began to reach the eastern shores of those countries. This second wave consisted of emigrés from central and eastern Europe, including large numbers of Jews escaping from the pogroms (or the consequences of the pogroms) in Roumania and the contiguous States. Between 1905 and 1914 more than ten million migrants arrived in the United States alone; thus, between 1851 and 1914 the United States received about thirty million immigrants.[104] During the same period the level of migration of east and central European Jews to the United Kingdom also rose: between 1987 and 1914 about 120,000 such Jews settled in the U.K. In Canada, too, the rate of immigration seems to have been inflated by the Jewish exodus from parts of Europe; in 1913 well over 400,000 migrants arrived.

In the United States the sheer size of the influx resulted in the voicing of calls for stricter immigration control. These demands became more vociferous after the assassination of President McKinley in 1901, and they were heeded by Congress, which adopted in 1903 the General Immigration Law.[105] This Act not only provided for the imposition of a head tax on most immigrants but also added epileptics, the insane, professional beggars and anarchists to the list of categories of prohibited immigrants. It introduced into United States immigration law the concept of moral turpitude, by providing that an alien should be ineligible to enter the territory of the U.S.A. if he had been convicted of a 'felony or other crime or misdemeanour involving moral turpitude'. Congress still refrained from imposing immigration controls whereby each migrant might be required to obtain specific permission to enter and settle in the United States, but instead in 1907 it commissioned the Dillingham Report, which appeared in 1911.[106] Many of the recommendations of that significant document were embodied in a new Act,[107] which codified the extant legislation and added four major new provisions. The first was the imposition of a literacy requirement. The second was the introduction of a power to deport aliens convicted of certain specified offences. The third was the prohibition (subject to a very few exceptions) of immigration from an enlarged Asian geographical area. The fourth was the bestowal on the Secretary of Labor of an extraordinary power to admit applicants who would otherwise be subject to automatic exclusion.

As the United States of America began to introduce qualitative tests, the Canadian Government felt constrained to do likewise. In 1902, 1905, 1906, 1907, 1908, 1910 and 1911 the Canadian Parliament adopted legislation to restrict the immigration of indigent or diseased persons, and to augment the facilities available for the assistance of such diseased or indigent persons as might in exceptional cases gain admittance.[108] By an Order in Council of 1910 paupers were virtually prohibited from entering Canada for permanent settlement.[109]

The westward movement of refugees from eastern and central Europe also had a profound effect on the development of immigration law in the United Kingdom. The Jewish influx led to a series of demends for more restrictive immigration policies.[110] Twice in four years the House of Lords approved Bills to restrict alien immigration, but neither of these Bills was passed by the Commons.[11] In 1902 the Unionist Government established a Royal Commission on alien immigration. Having received that Commission's report the Government decided to legislate.[112] After one false start[113] the Government secured the passage of the Aliens Act, 1905.[114] In defence of that Act, Prime Minister Balfour declared that the right to deny admission to aliens was 'the final and indestructible right of every free community . . . amply justified by every principle of law.'[115]

The Aliens Act provided that no 'immigrant' should land from any 'immigrant ship' other than with the permission of an immigration officer. An 'immigrant' was an alien steerage passenger who landed in the kingdom and did not demonstrate that he would remain in the kingdom only for a limited period. An 'immigrant ship' was defined as a vessel carrying at least twenty steerage passengers to be landed in the kingdom. Within a few years the Act was widely condemned as inefficient. In 1906 it was estimated that 28 per cent of alien immigrants had evaded control by travelling in boats too small to be classed as 'immigrant ships'; by 1910 that proportion had risen to over 42 per cent.[116] Furthermore, there was no general power to remove any alien considered to have become a security risk since his admission to the kingdom; and this lacuna was potentially inconvenient in view of the deteriorating relations between the United Kingdom and Germany. In 1911 the Home Secretary (Winston Churchill) announced that the Government was considering the possibility of fortifying the controls established by the Act of 1905.[117]

THE FIRST WORLD WAR

On the morning of August 4th, 1914, war broke out between the United Kingdom and Germany. The House of Commons was apprised of these facts on the following day and at once it adopted a series of wartime enactments. Among these was the Aliens Restriction Bill, which was introduced by the Home Secretary, who explained that its main object was to secure the detention or removal of spies. The Bill passed all of its stages in a matter of hours and received the royal assent later in the day.[118]

Just as the Alien Act of 1793 was passed as a temporary measure to deal with an emergency, and was subsequently amended to apply in a period of peace, so the Act of 1914 was phrased to operate only in a time of war or imminent national danger or grave emergency, but at the end of the war it was amended, so as to ensure its continuance in time of peace.[119] In the *Soblen Case*[120] the Court of Appeal emphatically rejected the argument that the wartime provisions of the 1914 Act no longer had force of law in 1963.

The Act enabled the King in Council to make Orders to prohibit or restrict the landing or embarkation of aliens, Orders to deport aliens, to require them to live in specified areas, to make them comply with any provisions as to registration, to prohibit or require them to change their abode, or to restrict their travel. It also conferred on the King in Council the power to make Orders 'for any other matters which may appear necessary or expedient with a view to the safety of the realm'. Immediately after the passage of the Act the King in Council adopted an Order to impose on aliens restrictions which, by peacetime standards, would have been considered severe.[121] On the passage of the Aliens Restriction (Amendment) Act, 1919 a new Aliens Order was promulgated.[122] That Order continued to be the main instrument governing the admission of aliens until well after the conclusion of the Second World War.[123] In 1953 a new Aliens Order was made; it remained in force, subject to very few amendments, until 1972.[124]

The effects of the First World War on domestic immigration laws were marked throughout Europe and beyond. That war followed a period in which there had been a world-wide movement towards restrictive immigration policies. As De Visscher observed:

> La première guerre mondiale précipita le mouvement. Successivement atteints par les crises économiques et sociales, les Etats crurent y parer en appliquant une politique étroitement nationaliste et protectionniste.[125]

France, the greatest country of immigration in Europe, went so far as to permit immigration only within the limits of quotas, and even Switzerland embarked on an exceptional policy of restriction.[126]

On July 9th, 1914 the Colombian minister declared formally that his country had found it necessary to prevent the immigration of dangerous aliens. He justified this curtailment of free movement by stating that the restriction was imposed in the exercise of the State's rights of self-preservation and defence – rights which appertained to every sovereign State.[127] In the United States two Immigration Acts were passed as war measures. The Act of May 22nd, 1918 authorized the President to control the ingress and egress in time of war or national emergency of any persons whose presence was deemed contrary to public safety; the Act of October 16th, 1918 related to the exclusion and expulsion of anarchists and other radical aliens.[128] In addition, some minor changes in immigration law in the United States were made in connection with the First World War, but in 1920.[129]

The First World War was also instrumental in securing the establishment of a passport system for transnational travel, first in Europe and later beyond the confines of that continent. Such a system had indeed been applied to a limited extent before the War, even in South America[130] and Southern Africa,[131] but until 1914 the use of passports was far from general, and those European countries which had previously adopted legislation to ensure the maintenance of a passport system had in many cases allowed that legislation to pass into desuetude.[132] In the United Kingdom, an Order of 1914 made the use of passports compulsory for aliens entering the kingdom and this system was maintained after the conclusion of the war.[133] In the United States, an Act of 1918 provided that it should be unlawful for any U.S. citizen to attempt to enter or depart from any part of U.S. territory unless he bore a valid passport.[134]

Shortly after the First World War two immigration Bills were introduced, without success, in the Congress of the United States. A third Bill was introduced, and was approved on May 19th, 1921.[135] This law provided that the number of immigrants of any one nationality who might enter the United States in any year should not exceed three per cent of the number of foreign-born persons of that nationality resident in the United States in 1910. Under that law about 350,000 aliens were permitted to enter the United States annually, and most of them came from northern and western Europe. The law was due to expire on June 30th, 1922, but was extended for two years by the Act of May 11th, 1922.[136]

On February 9th, 1924 the House Committee on Immigration and Naturalization, viewing with trepidation the scheduled expiration of the Three Per Cent law at the end of the following June, reported that 'there is an immediate and urgent need for the enactment of immigration legislation'. A new Bill was introduced, and, after amendments, it was adopted on May 26th, 1924.[137] The new Act altered quota allocations in such a way as to favour yet further those migrants who came from the north and west of Europe. It also provided that admission would normally be denied to persons ineligible for naturalization as U.S. citizens. The main effect of that last provision was to exclude Oriental migrants – particularly those from Japan.

The Japanese Government protested that the Act conflicted with the 'gentlemen's agreement' concluded between Japan and the United States in 1908. The same Government alleged that the Act contravened the Treaty of Commerce and Navigation, signed by the two countries in 1911. The Japanese note observed that distinctions based on race are particularly unwelcome. It recognized the federal Government's right to control immigration, but added:

78

when in the exercise of such right, an evident injustice is done to a foreign nation in disregard of its proper self-respect, of international understanding or of ordinary rules of comity, the question ... justifies diplomatic ... adjustment.[138]

This was not the first time that the Japanese Government had campaigned against racially discriminatory immigration laws. During the negotiations on the League Covenant, that Government proposed adding a clause which would have endorsed the principles of equality of nations and just treatment for nationals of all States. Canadian concern over this proposal was expressed in a cable from the Canadian Privy Council to Sir Robert Borden, asking that all signatories to the Covenant recognize that the right of each State to control the character of its own population by restriction of immigration is maintained without impairment. At one point Canada seemed willing to compromise with Japan on this point but the Australian delegate would accept no such compromise unless it were balanced by specific protection of national control over immigration and naturalization.[139]

The British Commonwealth, like the League of Nations, provided a forum for the debate on racially discriminatory immigration laws. A memorandum prepared by the India Office, and presented to the Imperial Conference of 1911, urged that British Indians in the Dominions should be accorded 'generous treatment'.[140] At the Imperial War Conference in 1917 the India Office urged that 'Asiatics of British nationality' and other Asiatics should be treated equally with respect to immigration control.[141] Eventually, at the Imperial War Conference of 1918, the Indian delegate presented the following resolution, which was adopted unanimously:

The right of the Government of India is recognized to enact laws which shall have the effect of subjecting British citizens [sic] domiciled in any other British country to the same conditions in visiting India as those imposed on Indians desiring to visit such country ...[142]

Such protests had a limited effect.[143] In 1922 Fauchille suggested that international law restricted the right of a State to forbid the immigration of aliens, on the ground of their race. However, the limitations which he envisaged were minimal:

pour que se produisent de pareilles conséquences qui justifieraient l'exclusion, il faudra qu'il s'agisse d'hommes appartenant à une civilisation absolument différente et venant sur le territoire en quantité considérable.[144]

Long before the First World War, States commonly excluded indigent aliens from their territories. This practice applied even in Latin America. A Costa Rican law of 1914 provided for the exclusion of indigent aliens, adding that 'the current economic situatoin of the country ... makes it necessary to look in immigrants for ... a secure financial status, enabling them to contribute in the highest degree to the development of the public wealth.'[145]

However, Fauchille was prepared to draw a distinction between the refusal of admission to indigents, and the enactment of immigration laws based on the motive of protecting the national labour force. The former was permissible and sanctioned by State practice; the latter was permissible only if undertaken in defence of the interests of a particular class of citizens, or in time of widespread unemployment.[146] Borchard, on the other hand, tended to favour the State's sovereign right to exclude aliens from its territory for any reasons (although he did add that exclusion was generally applied for political, social or economic reasons, and that the network of treaties by which certain States were bound together had practically established the freedom of international intercourse).[147]

Although Fauchille's formulation allowed States a great deal of latitude in times of economic crisis, the advent of the depression evoked further support for the 'sovereign right' school. The 'sovereignty' thesis was endorsed in a series of judicial proceedings,[148] and it gained further authority from the Convention on the Status of Aliens, adopted at the Sixth International Conference of American States,[149] and from the Draft Convertion adopted at the International Conference on the Treatment of Foreigners, held under the auspices of the League of Nations in Paris.[150] The same thesis gained support from the Permanent Court of International Justice in the case of the *Treatment of Polish Nationals or Other Persons of Polish Origins or Speech in the Danzig Territory*.[151] Most significant of all was the implicit endorsement of the 'sovereignty' thesis given in State practice. More than twenty States of immigration adopted legislation to restrict and reduce the immigration of foreigners.[152]

Nevertheless, even through the depression a minority of States continued not only to admit foreigners freely, but also to defend the principle of free migration as a rule which should (perhaps only ideally) be universally accepted in normal circumstances. Commenting on this principle, Redslob wrote:

> '*Personne n'est étranger dans l'Amérique espagnole*', disent telles chartes d'outre-mer.[153]

THE SECOND WORLD WAR

The outbreak of the Second World War was marked by a strengthening of immigration controls in the laws of all the major belligerents. In the United Kingdom no new Act of Parliament was needed, but in 1939 a series of Aliens Orders was promulgated.[154] In the United States, Congress adopted the Alien Registration Act of 1940, which provided for the registration and fingerprinting of all aliens, and prescribed additional deportable classes.[155] In France, a Decree of 1939 provided that no alien might be admitted to French territory without appropriate documentation;[156] a series of further Decrees restricted the liberties of aliens in France.[157] In Germany, the Reichstag adopted on May 11th, 1937, a major new Act governing the admission and supervision of aliens.[158] That Act was supplemented, on August 22nd, 1938, by a Decree which dealt with the powers of the Reich in respect of the supervision of aliens, and which continued to have effect in the German Federal Republic until 1965.[159] This wave of emergency legislation seems to have attracted no diplomatic protest against the principle of imposing such severe restrictions, but some diplomatic notes expressed disquiet about certain immigration restrictions allegedly imposed in violation of treaty obligations.[160]

The progress of the Second World War was contemporaneous with the development, in the United States and other allied powers, of a movement towards emphatic reiteration of the moral principle described in the phrase 'equality of mankind'. One of the early consequences of this movement, in the United States, was a strengthening of the opposition to the racially exclusive provisions in U.S. immigration law. After the much-publicised visit of Mme. Chaing Kai-Shek to the United States in 1943 Congress repealed the Chinese Exclusion Act.[161] In 1946 Filipinos and persons belonging to races native to India were granted the privilege of admission to the United States, and were declared eligible for naturalization there.[162] Some *de facto* discrimination against members of races indigenous to the Far East remained since the quota system was unfavourable to Orientals, but the reduction of racial discrimination *eo nomine* proved to be influential.

In Australia in 1947 the first small post-war concession was made in the direction of a more liberal policy towards the admission of non-European migrants. The Government announced that non-Europeans who had been admitted to the territory of the Australian Commonwealth for business reasons, and had resided there for fifteen years, would be permitted to remain there without renewal of their permits. In 1952 the same Government made a second concession: Japanese wives of Australian servicemen would be permitted to enter Australia on permits valid, in the first instance, for five years. In Canada, four post-war developments were instrumental in shaping a revision of the former immigration policy. First, the post-war boom and the effects of the low birth-rate in the 1930s combined to produce a labour shortage which demanded a high rate of settlement. Secondly, Canada's need for immigrants was coincidental in time with the needs of hundreds of thousands of refugees to discover new domiciles: under special refugee schemes, Canada accepted 300,000 immigrants after the war. Thirdly, the complexities of Canada's piecemeal immigration legislation in force at the end of the war justified the introduction of a new Bill to govern the whole subject of immigration law, and that in turn provided an opportunity for wholesale re-examination of former policies. Finally, the world-wide movement towards adoption of more liberal policies in respect of the admission of members of non-European ethnic groups had its effect in Canada. Four years after the repeal of the Chinese Exclusion Act in the United States, the Canadian Parliament repealed its Chinese Immigration Act.[163] Under Canada's Immigration Act of 1952 the Governor-General retained the power to make regulations prohibiting or limiting the admission of persons by reason of ethnic group, geographical area of origin, peculiar customs, habits, modes of life or methods of holding property and probable inability to become assimilated.[164] As a matter of policy this power was not long exercised, and there was by 1966 'no discrimination by reason of race, colour or religion'.[165]

In the United Kingdom, the post-war labour shortage and the humanitarian desire to accommodate refugees were both instrumental in ensuring the settlement of 200,000 immigrants, about half of whom were former members of the Polish armed forces. The Polish Resettlement Act, 1947 made provision for the Assistance Board to provide accommodation for members of these forces and members of various other groups of Polish refugees.

However, in numerous instances, the effects of the Second World War were comparable with the effects of the First, in that emergency legislation was not always repealed on the achievement of peace. In Several West Indian territories a series of wartime enactments was passed, and immigration law continued to be governed by those enactments (subject to more recent amendments). Throughout the British West Indies, these statutes tended to show considerable uniformity. Control of immigration tended to be governed by three statutes: the Aliens (or Immigration) Law, the Deportation of British Subjects Law and the Expulsion of Undesirables Law. Jamaica and Barbados both fit this pattern. In the former, alien control was primarily governed by a statute which was passed at the end of the Second World War and contained some recognizably wartime characteristics.[166] Most aliens were required to submit to registration in accordance with a regulation of 1940.[167] The immigration of Commonwealth citizens of Jamaica was governed by a statute passed at the end of the Second World War.[168] In Barbados, the immigration of aliens was governed by the Aliens Restriction Act of 1939, although the other two Barbadian immigration enactments were not of Second World War vintage.[169]

The world-wide increase in transnational migration following the Second World War had a particularly marked effect on the legislation of the United States. The first major influx into the territory of that federation consisted of the 96,000 persons who entered under the War Brides Act of 1945.[170] A further 5000 immigrants entered under the G.I. Fiancées Act of 1946.[171] The Displaced Persons Act, 1948 made possible the admission to the U.S.A. over a period of two years of 205,000 refugees, in addition to 27,000 persons of German ethnic origin expelled from their European domiciles.[172] This Act was amended in 1950 to facilitate the admission of a further 136,000 refugees and nearly 28,000 more German expellees.[173]

From 1949 onwards the Senate Committee on the Judiciary (later joined by the House Committee on the Judiciary) examined the immigration and nationality laws of the United States. A voluminous report of both committees was published and in accordance with that report, a Bill was introduced before the Senate by Senator McCarran.[174] The Bill was examined by numerous governmental and nongovernmental agencies. Further Bills were then introduced in the Senate (by Senator McCarran) and the House (by Mr. Walter, among others).[175] Eventually, two modified versions of these Bills were introduced by Senator McCarran and Mr. Walter.[176] Each chamber of Congress approved its respective Bill, and a new Immigration and Nationality Act – popularly known as the Walter-McCarran Act – came into force in 1952.[177]

The Walter-McCarran Act finally eliminated the use of race as a bar to immigration and naturalization. At the same time, it introduced a more selective system of immigration control, designed to give preference to aliens with skills or qualifications demanded in the United States, and it contained provisions designed to ensure thorough screening of immigrants, to guard against the admission of persons who might prove to be security risks. It followed the national origin formula of the Quota Act of 1924 in allocating quotas among the independent countries of the world.

The revision of immigration law in the United States was closely followed by revisions of policy, and later law, in Australia. In 1956 the Australian Government provided that non-Europeans who had already settled in that Commonwealth in accordance with the extant laws should be eligible for naturalization. At the same time the Government changed its policy so as to enable non-European immediate relatives of Australian citizens to be admitted for permanent settlement, and provided that highly-qualified non-Europeans would be allowed to enter on temporary permits for indefinite periods. In 1957 naturalization became available to those who had entered on temporary permits, but Europeans and non-Europeans were not treated alike in this respect, since the former could be naturalized after five years' residence, and the latter only after a period of fifteen years. In the following year the Commonwealth Parliament adopted the Migration Act, which dealt with immigration, emigration and deportation. This Act cleared away the tangle of amendments which had been made to the 1901 Act, and abolished the English-language dictation-test. It also dispensed with the arbitrary power of the Minister to order the deportation of any person within five years of the latter's arrival in Australia. However, since the 'White Australia Policy' remained a mere policy, not formally incorporated into a statute, it remained unaffected by the 1958 Act, which made no attempt to place the policy on a statutory basis, nor to curtail substantially the discretionary delegated powers whereby the policy was operated. On March 9th, 1966 a major review of policy was undertaken. The Minister for Immigration announced two alterations in the Government's policy. Firstly, naturalization would be granted to non-Europeans on the same basis as to Europeans – that is, after five years' residence. Secondly, specially-qualified non-Europeans would be permitted to immigrate not merely as dependants, but as breadwinners in their own right.[178]

RECENT TRENDS

In 1965 the United States Congress made a further amendment to the Walter-McCarran Act, though the most important sections of the amending Act did not come into effect until 1968.[179] The 1965 amendement dispensed with the system whereby the national quotas for immigrants to the United States were determined by reference to the number of persons of that nationality lawfully resident in the U.S. in a base year. That system had tended to fossilise the national composition of migrants to the United States, and, in particular, to favour migrants from western Europe. The new selection system is based on the principle 'first come, first served',[180] subject to the limitation that not more than 20,000 natives of any single foreign State may be admitted in any one fiscal year. In addition, the 1965 Act attempts to protect American workers by providing that an unskilled worker may normally be admitted only if the Secretary of State has certified to the Attorney-General that there are insufficient workers in the United States to take the employment in question, and that the alien's admission will not adversely affect the conditions of similarly employed workers in the United States.[181] In 1967 the Canadian Government revised its Immigration Regulations in such a way as to permit immigration officers to apply the same standards to prospective immigrants from all areas of the world.

While the United States, Canada and (to a lesser extent) Australia were taking measures to relax those immigration controls which tended to discriminate against non-white migrants, Parliament in London was occupied in the imposition of new immigration controls, noteworthy for their effect on immigrants from the Caribbean and the Indian subcontinent. The origins of the migration of West Indians to England may be traced to the Second World War itself, when significant numbers of Commonwealth workers moved to Britain to take employment in factories, or to serve in the armed forces (notably the Royal Air Force). At the conclusion of the war, many of these migrants returned to the Caribbean, but, by virtue of their status, as British subjects, they retained their right to enter the United Kingdom, as one of the three major privileges which accrued from that status.[182]

In 1961 the Government of the United Kingdom concluded that the volume of net immigration had reached such a level as to justify the imposition, for the first time, of statutory control on the immigration of British subjects into the United Kingdom. After a certain amount of consultation with Commonwealth Governments[183], the United Kingdom's Government introduced the Commonwealth Immigrants Bill, which became an Act in 1962. That Act was amended in 1968, amidst heated controversy over the so-called 'Kenyan Asians'. In 1969 and 1970 further legislative changes were introduced, to provide for certain rights of appeal against decisions made by persons administering the United Kingdom's immigration laws.[184] In 1971 the new (Conservative) Government of the U.K. sponsored a further Bill, designed to ensure that the admission of Commonwealth citizens would be governed by laws more closely resembling those which had hitherto governed that admission of aliens. The Bill passed its final parliamentary stages on October 28th, 1971 and entered into force on 1 January 1973.

During the last two decades three migratory trends have manifested themselves in a wide variety of industrialised and industrialising States. The first trend is the imposition of new restrictions upon primary immigration, in consequence of the international recession. Such restrictions have been imposed especially, but by no means exclusively, in west European States.[185] The second trend is connected to the first: indications are strong that there has been a marked increase in clandestine immigration, to which the response of the international community has been mixed. While in some countries there has been a policy of intermittent amnesty[186] in others efforts have been redoubled to prevent further clandestine migration and to that end new controls have been imposed.[187] The third trend, which may also be connected with the first, is a rise in the number of applications for asylum, particularly on the part of fugitives from third world countries.[188] In many instances this tendency has led to a more rigorous application of the criteria for eligibility set out in the Geneva Convention and New York Protocol on the Status of Refugees.

NOTES

1. C.f. 'indirect' immigration controls; i.e. measures designed to affect the rate or composition of migrant flows by altering the conditions under which migrants will live, once they have been admitted to their new domiciles. Such 'indirect' controls were employed from an early date. See for example 1 R. III,c. 9 (1376).
2. M. Sibert, *Traité de droit international public*, 1951, p. 571.
3. L. Oppenheim, *International Law*, 1955. Vol. I pp. 488, 490.
4. 'Our New Immigration Policy', 3 For. Aff. (1924–5) 99–110.
5. 'Everyone has the right . . . to return to his country', *Basic Documents* I. 1.
6. *The Minimum Standard of International Law Applied to Aliens*, 1949. p. 44.
7. P. Fauchille, *Traité de droit international public*, 1921, Vol. I, p. 890. The bibliography of the controversy is surveyed by A. Macheret, in *L'immigration étrangère en Suisse à l'heure de l'intégration européenne*, 1969 at p. 15.
8. E.g., exclusion of Geoffrey Plantagenet: T. Roche, *The Key in the Lock*, 1969, pp. 15–16; expulsion of the Jews in 1290. H. Richardson, *English Jewry under Angevin Kings*, 1960, pp. 178–180; C. Roth, *A History of the Jews in England*, 1964, p. 33.
9. Sometimes such documents were issued to subjects: P.R. 9 Hen. III (1224) 161, 275.
10. E.g. P.R. 9 Hen. III (1245) p. 454.
11. There is little evidence of the issuance of travel documents to the numerous *Francigenae* migrants who entered after 1066: *Chronicon of Henry of Knighton*, ed. J. Lumby, 1889, Vol. I, p. 58; C. Petit-Dutaillis, *The French Monarchy in France* and England, trans. Hunt, 1966, p. 60; *Cambridge Medieval History*, 1926, Vol. V, p. 508; A. Poole, *From Domesday Book to Magna Carta*, 1954, pp. 135, 140, 154, 336, 363 and 467; R. Davis, *King Stephen*, 1967, p. 21. Similarly, there are few records of documentation issued by King John to Flemish migrants; J. Holt, *Magna Carta*, 1965, pp. 149, 260 (but see P.R. 26 Hen. III (1241) p. 304). Documents issued to Jewish immigrants after the massacre of Rouen (1096) are less scarce: P.R. 4 Hen. III (1219) p. 95. Even so, it is clear that most such immigrants bore no permits. The author's conclusion is fortified by the fact that examination has revealed no record of an alien's conviction for landing in England at this time without the King's assent, although an entry in the exchequer accounts records the seizure of a ship for putting in at a place not designated as a port: R. Madox, *History and Antiquities of the Exchequer of the Kings of England*, 1711, p. 530.
12. The item was not formally repealed until 1969: Statute Law (Repeals) Act, 1969, section 1, schedule 1, part 1. For conflicting opinions as to the interpretation of the item, see Lord Grenville in the debate on the Aliens Bill, 1792. W. Cobbett's *Parliamentary History*, Vol. XXX, col. 146; H. Blackstone, *Commentaries on the Law of England*, 1765, Vol. I, p. 259; J. Chitty, *Prerogativa Regis*, 1968 ed., p. 49; D. Stenton, *After Runneymede*, 1965, p. 20; R. Thomson, *An Historical Essay on the Magna Carta of King John*, 1829, p. 233. By 5 R. II, stat. 1, c. 2 (1381) section 7, it became an offence for any person other than a peer, a notable merchant or a soldier to depart from the kingdom without a licence. However, this seems to have been designed to prevent the export of certain valuable commodities. C.f. 13 R. II, stat. 1, c. 20 (1389); 2 Hen. V, c. 6 (1415); 15 Hen. VI, c. 7 (1436).
13. 'The Right of Aliens to Enter British Territory', 6 L.Q.R. (1890) 27, 29.
14. See 11 R. II, c. 7 (1387); c.f. 9 Ed. III, stat. 1, c. 1 (1335); 6 R. II, c. 8 (1382); 14 R II, c. 1 (1390), confirmed, 3 Hen. VIII, c. 8 (1486) section 7; 14 R. II, c. 6 (1390); 16 R. II, c. 3 (1391); 5 Hen. IV, c. 9 (1483).
15. *Rot. Parl.* Vol. II, p. 162, No. 36 (1346).
16. Elizabeth, in particular, tended to rely on her prerogative, acting through the Privy Council rather than through Parliament. E.g., *Acts of the Privy Council, 1571–1575*, pp. 50, 135, 306, 336, 345.

17. Blackstone, *supra,* note 12, Vol.I, pp. 260–261.
18. In this detail, English common law was typical of several of the legal systems of north-west Europe. See J. Stiernhook, *De Jure Sveonum et Gothorum,* 1672, Vol. II, pp. 229 *et seq.*
19. A. Gentilis, *Hispanicae Advocationis,* 1661, Vol. I, p. 25.
20. *Ibid.,* Vol. I, pp. 21, 103, 162; see also *ibid.,* Vol. I, p. 25.
21. H. Grotius, *De Jure Belli Ac Pacis,* 1702 ed., Vol. II, Chap. II, para 15.
22. S. Puferdorf, *De Jure Naturae et Gentium, Libri Octo,* Book III para 5, trans. c. Oldfatter, 1934, p. 354.
23. F. De Vitoria, *De Indis et de Jure Belli Reflectiones,* and his *Law of Nations, 1934. Appendix p. xxxvi.* Trans. J. Scott.
24. E. Kant, *Perpetual Peace,* 1795, p.33.
25. E. de Vattel, *Le Droit des Gens,* Book I, s. 231.
26. *Ibid.,* Book II, s. 125.
27. *The Constitutional History of England since the Accession of George III,* 1901, Vol. III, p. 51.
28. Sir W. Holdsworth, *History of English Law,* 1938, Vol. X, pp. 679, 688.
29. Decree of 23 messidor, year 3 (11th July, 1795) article 9; 8. C.C.L. 185.
30. Order of 4 nivose, year 5 (24th December, 1796); 9 C.C.L. 250. See also the Order of 12 germinal, year 5 (1st April, 1797); 9 C.C.L. 337.
31. Passports Law of 28 vendemiare, year 6 (19th October, 1797); 10 C.C.L. 79; A. Grahl-Madsen, *The Status of Refugees in International Law,* 1966, Vol. I, p. 11.
32. For the U.S., see the Act of June 25th, 1798, 1 Stat. 570; for Switzerland, see the Laws of 25th July, 1798 and 13th February, 1799 on the Rights of Citizenship and Freedom of Establishment.
33. 42 Geo III, c. 92 (1802) repealed and superseded by 43 Geo. III, c. 155 (1802).
34. 54 Geo III, c. 155.
35. 34 H.C. Deb. (first series) cols. 436 *et seq.*
36. 58 Geo. III, c. 96 (1818) renewed the aliens restriction laws for a further two years; 58 Geo. III, c. 97 (1818) restricted for two years the eligibility of aliens to registration and endenization.
37. It appears that little attention was paid to Sir Samuel Romilly's observation that the Bill perpetuated a system in which an alien could be refused political asylum, even though he were a refugee: 34 H.C. Deb. (first series) col. 471. The French demands that the Alien Act should be used to frustrate political asylum demonstrated that Sir Samuel's fears were not groundless. See the letter from M. Otto to Lord Hawkesbury, August 17th, 1802.
38. June 5th, 1822, *Hansard Parliamentary Debates* (new series) vol. VII, pp. 1723–1724.
39. Sir J. Arnoud, *Memoir of Lord Denman,* 1873, Vol. I, p.220.
40. Aliens Act, 5 Geo. IV, c. 37, section 2.
41. Aliens Act, 1816 (56 Geo. III, c. 86) section 1; repealed, Aliens Registration Act, 1826 (7 Geo. IV, c. 54) section 1. See further *Mure* v *Kay,* (1811) 4 Taunt. 34, 43–44.
42. Aliens Restriction Act, 1836 (6 and 7 Will. IV, c. 11).
43. Aliens Act, 1905, section 10 (2).
44. March 8th, 1872; Fontes Ser. B. section 1, Vol. II (i) passage 807, cited by Roth, *supra,* note 6, p. 40.
45. J. Martell, *Immigration and Emigration from Nova Scotia, 1815–1888,* 1943, p.141.
46. 9 Geo. IV, c. 25, re-enacting the Act respecting Aliens, 1793 (38 Geo. III, c. 1).
47. Aliens Act, 1851, Nova Scotia Statutes Revised, Title XVII, Chapter 59; Aliens Act. 1864, Nova Scotia Statutes Revised, Title VIII, Chapter 38.
48. New York 2 Revised Statutes 430.
49. 48 U.S. 282; 7 How. 283, 289 (1849); 4 U.S.S.C. Digest Annotated 598.
50. *City of New York v. Miln,* 11 Pet. 102 (1837).

51. In particular: *Norris v. City of Boston,* 7 How. 283 (1849).
52. *People v. Compagnie Générale Transatlantique,* 107 U.S. 59 (1882). Note that these cases were distinguished in dissenting opinion in *Pabst Brewing Co. v. Crenshaw,* 198 U.S. 18 at 41 (1905); *Gilman v. Philadelphia,* 3 Wall. 714 (1909) see also *Doyle v. Continental Insurance Co.,* 94 U.S. 535 at 542 (1877.
53. Immigration Act of 1875, March, 18 Stat. 477.
54. Immigration Act of 1882, August, 22 Stat. 214.
55. Immigration Act of March 3rd, 1891, 26 Stat. 1084.
56. Act of May 6th,f 1882, 22 Stat. 58.
57. 141 U.S. 34, 36 (1892).
58. *Fong Yue Ting v. U.S., Wong Quan v. Same, Lee Joe v. Same,* 149 U.S. 698 (1892). However, once admitted to the U.S., a Chinese or other alien enjoyed the benefits of the Fourteenth Amendment: *Yick Wo v. Hopkins,* 118 U.S. 356 (1885). The constitutionality of the Chinese Exclusion Act was further confirmed in *Nishimura Ekiu v. U.S.,* 142 U.S. 651 (1892). In *Lees v. U.S.,* 150 U.S. 476 (1893) the federal Supreme Court upheld the constitutionality of the Contract Employment Act, 1885 (23 Stat. 332) which further restricted the introduction of foreign labour to the United States. The same Court held that statute inapplicable when a religious society in New York recruited a pastor from England: *Church of Holy Trinity v. U.S.,* 143 U.S. 457 (1891).
59. Chinese Exclusion Amendment Act of July 5th, 1884, 23 Stat. 115; upheld, *Chae Chan Ping v. U.S.,* 130 U.S. 581 (1889).
60. Act of October 1st, 1888, 25 Stat. 504.
61. Immigration Restriction Act, 1901 (No. 17); Immigration Restriction Amendment) Act, 1905 (No. 17); Immigration Restriction Acts, 1908 (No. 25) and 1910 (No. 10); Immigration Acts, 1912 (No. 38), 1920 (No. 51), 1924 (No. 47), 1925 (No. 7), 1930 (No. 56), 1932 (No. 26), 1933 No. 37), 1935 (No. 13), 1940 (No. 36), 1948 (No. 86) and 1949 (No. 31).
62. Section 3; test abolished, 1958. See also Pacific Island Labourers Act, 1901 (No. 16).
63. There was a corresponding development in New Zealand: Immigration Restriction Act 1908 (No. 78) Part III, sections 29–42, repealed, Finance Act, 1944 (No. 3), section 10 (1) (a) and Immigration Restriction Amendment Act, 1920 (No. 23) section 4 (1).
64. Immigration Act, 1869, 32–33, Vict., c. 10, sections 4, 9.
65. Immigration Act, 1872, 35 Vict., c. 28, sections 7, 23, 24.
66. (1878) 41 Vict., c. 15.
67. (1872), 35 Vict., c. 23; amended, 37 Vict., c. 19 (1874); re-enacted, Dominion Lands Act, 1883, 46 Vict., c. 17.
68. The development of the Canadian Pacific Railway was of supreme importance in this respect. In 1885 the railway reached Vancouver. The construction of the railway resulted in an influx of Chinese labourers, and its completion facilitated the migration of Orientals to eastern Canada.
69. 48–49 Vict., c. 71; the Act was later amended by sections 1 and 2 of the Chinese Immigration Amendment Act, 1892 – a statute designed to have the same effect on Canadian law as the decision in *Lau Ow Bew v. U.S.*
70. P.C. 1204 of June 9th, 1919.
71. P.C. 182 of January 31st, 1923; P.C. 1966 of August 14th, 1930, superseded by P.C. 2115 of September 16th, 1930, enacted by virtue of the Immigration Act of 1927, 18–19 Geo. V, c. 29.
72. In 1872 Erskine May wrote as follows: 'Nothing has served so much to raise, in other states, the estimation of British liberty, as the protection which our laws afford to foreigners' *supra,* note 27, Vol. III, p. 49. For similar a statement see C. Thornberry, 'Dr. Soblen and the Aliens Law of the United Kingdom', 12 I.C.L.Q. (1963) 414, 415.
73. By virtue of this Act, a Lascar was to be regardded, for certain purposes, as an alien, and

consequently he could not be discharged in the United Kingdom. Despite the repeal of the Lascars Act by the Statute Law Revision Act, 1963, certain forms of statutory discrimination against Lascars remained sanctioned by law until 1970, notably by virtue of the Merchant Shipping Act, 1894, section 125 (interpreted in the light of section 18 (1) and of the Indian Independence Act, 1947). However, section 125 of the 1894 Act was eventually repealed by the Merchant Shipping Act, 1970, section 100 and schedule 5.

74. S.I. 290. This compelled coloured seamen to register as aliens unless they could produce proof of their British subjecthood. Once registered, they lost preference in employment: British Shipping (Assistance) Act, 1935, section 1.

75. In 1925 a Lascar Welfare Council was established: *The Times*, June 28th, 1925, p. 20.

76. 142 U.S. 651, 659 (1892).

77. [1891] A.C. 272; but see *R. v. Carter*, 52 C.L.R. (1934) 221 (Evatt, J.).

78. Laws of Victoria, Chinese Act, 1881, section 3.

79. 26 Stat. (1889–1891), 51st. Cong., Sess. 1–2) 1084, cap. 551, March 3rd, 1891.

80. In neither case was there prolonged discussion about the principle of free movement. Thus, Sir W. Phillimore, Q.C. and J.W. McCarthy, for Chun Teeong Toy, conceded that 'every State may by international law exclude aliens' but it was argued that the Crown had so preogative right to exclude aliens. [1891] A.C. 272, 276. In *Nishimura Ekiu v. U.S.*, Mr. Lyman I. Mowry, for the appellant, merely referred to international law to support his assertion that the powers conferred by the Act were of such an extraordinary nature that it was the evident intention of Congress that a record of the proceedings should be kept: 142 U.S. 651, 658.

81. [1891] A.C. 272, 282. See also *Raner v. Colonial Secretary*, (1904) 21 S.A. 143.

82. Contrary to the Alien Labour Act, 1897, 60–61 Vict., c. 11, section 6.

83. [1906] A.C. 542, 546.

84. 1 Moo. P.C. 460 (1837). The case is best regarded as an example of 'voluntary deportation', as to which, see P. O'Higgins, (1963) Crim. L.R. 680, 681–2; *R. v. Assa Singh*, [1965]2 Q.B. 312, 320; Criminal Justice Act, 1967, section 103 (2) and schedule 7, part I; R. Heuston, *Essays in Constitutional Law*, 1961, pp. 67–68; *R. v. Flaherty, The Times* L.R., June 24th, 1958; *R. v. McCartan*, [1958] 3 All E.R. 140, 142; *R. v. Ayu*, [1958] 3 All E.R. 636; *R. v. East Grinstead Justices, ex parte Doeve*, [1968] 3 W.L.R. 920; *R. v. Brixton Prison (Governor) ex parte Havlide*, [1969] 1 W.L.R. 42; D. McClean and J. Wood, *Criminal Justice and the Treatment of Offenders*, 1969, pp. 152 *et seq.*,; *R. v. Edgehill*, [1963] 2 W.L.R. 170; *Yager v. Musa, The Times* L.R., January 31st, 1962.

85. 20 B.C. (1912–1914) 243. Presumably attachment to Canada would be demonstrated by birth there: *R. v. Soon Gin An*, [1941]3 D.L.R. 125.

86. *The Destitute Alien*, ed. White, 1892, p. 50.

87. P. Heilborn, *Das System des Völkerrechts*, 1896, p. 22.

88. F. De Martens, *Traité de droit international*, 1883, Vol. I, p. 443.

89. W. Hall, *A Treatise on International Law*, 1895, p. 223.

90. D. Anzilotti, 13 R.G.D.I.P. (1906) 17–18. A striking example of the conventional exceptions to which Anzilotti refers is the Treaty of 30 January, 1907, between Japan and Canada, which provided that subjects of each State should have full liberty to enter, travel and reside in any part of the dominions of the other. The treaty was examined in *In Re Nakane and Okazake*, 13 B.C.R. (1908) 370.

91. 12 A.I.D.I. (1892–1894) 220.

92. J. Bluntschli, *Das Moderne Völkerrecht der Civilisirten Staten*, 1878, p. 233.

93. E. Nijs, *Le droit international*, 1905, Vol. II, p. 233.

94. F. Suárez, *Tratado de derecho internacional público*, 1916, Vol. 1, pp. 319–320.

95. P. Lapradelle and J. Niboyet, *Répertoire de droit international*, 1929–31, Vol. VIII, pp. 19–20.

96. Immigration Law of August 13th, 1903, replacing Immigration Law of September 21st, 1864; noted by Zeballos, 12 R.G.D.I.P. (1905) 441.

97. Decree of June 10th, 1914; c.f. Decree of August 31st, 1914, made under the General Immigration Law of July 20th, 1896; see also Decree No. 59 of July 29th, 1896.

98. Law of 11th March, 1909; Decree of 15th April, 1909; Laws of 24th March, 1913; 19th December, 1914 and 3rd February 1917.

99. Law of June 24th, 1919, article 9 (1).

100. *Supra,* note 94, Vol. I, p. 320, and *'De la condition juridique des étrangers au Venezuela',* 48 J.D.I. (1921) 37, 39.

101. G. Hackworth, *Digest of International Law,* 1940–1944, Vol. III, p. 727.

102. *Supra,* note 3, paragraph 314.

103. Hall, *supra,* note 89, p.56.

104. Statistics presented in 20 Senate Documents, 61st Cong., 3rd Sess., 1910–1911 (Dillingham Commission, document 756).

105. March 3rd, 1903, 32 Stat. 1213. C. Seckler-Hudson, *Statelessness with Special Reference to the United States,* 1934, p. 229.

106. United States Immigration Commission, 1907–1910, 61st Cong., 3rd Sess., Senate Document 662, printed in 1910–1911 Senate Documents, Vols. 7–11 and independently in 42 volumes. The Commission was established by section 39 of the Immigration Act of February 20th, 1907 (34 Stat. 898). See J. Senner, 'The Immigration Question', X (1) *Annals of the American Academy of Political and Social Science* (1897) 1–19; P. Peirce, 'Control of Immigration as an Administrative Problem', 4 Am. Pol. Sci. Rev. (1910) 374; R. Ferrari, 'The Immigrant in the New York County Criminal Courts', 3 J. Crim. L. (1912) 194; I. Hourwich, 'The Economic Aspects of Immigration', 26 Pol. Q. Sci. (1911) 615, 626; T. Powell, 'Judicial Review of Administrative Action in Immigration Proceedings', 22 Harv. L.R. (1908–9) 360; S. Kansas, *United States Immigration, Exclusion and Deportation, and Citizenship of the United States,* 1940, pp. 9–10.

107. Immigration Act of February 5th, 1917, 39 Stat. 874; P.L. 301.

108. Immigration Acts, 2 Ed. VII, c. 14; 4–5 Ed. VII, c. 14; 6 Ed. VII, c. 19; 6–7 Ed. VII, c. 19; 7–8 Ed. VII, c. 33; 9–10 Ed. VII, c. 17; 1–2 Geo. v, c.2.

109. P.C. 458 of March 15th, 1910, replacing P.C. 2037 of September 11th, 1908.

110. In 1889 a Select Committee of the House of Commons 'contemplated the possibility' of introducing further immigration control: (1889) X Sess. Pap. 265. Three years later the Conservatives announced immigration control to be an element of the party's official policy.

111. The Bills were introduced by Lords Salisbury and Hardwicke respectively: 26 Parl. Deb. col., 1047 (July 6th, 1894); 27 Parl. Deb., col. 117 (July 17th, 1894); 28Prl. Deb., col. 889 (August 14th, 1894); 55 Parl. Deb., col. 713 (March 23rd, 1898); 61 Parl. Deb., col. 314 (July 8th, 1898).

112. Cd. 1741; 132 Parl. Deb., col. 987 (March 29th, 1904); R. Falkner, 'The Immigration Problem', 19 Pol. Sci. Q. (1904) 32; Conservative Party, *Campaign Guide,* 1904, p. 702.

113. A Bill introduced in 1904 made slow progress before the Standing Committee and was withdrawn: 132 Parl. Deb., col. 996 (March 29th, 1904); 133 Parl. deb., col. 1062; 139 Parl. deb., cols. 548, 571, 581 (August 2nd, 1904).

114. 145 Parl. Deb., cols. 473, 687 (April 18th and May 2nd, 1905); 148 Parl. deb., cols. 268–326, 345–352, 390–474, 794–876 (June 27th and 28th and July 3rd, 1905); 149 Parl. Dab., cols.110, 289, 375, 903, 1137, 1257, and 1299 (July 10th, 11th, 17th, 18th, 19th and 20th, 1905); 151 Parl. Deb., cols. 4, 547, 989 (August 3rd, 8th and 11th, 1905). By section 10 (1) the Act came into force at the beginning of 1906.

115. 145 Parl. Deb., col. 796 (May 2nd, 1905).

116. Roche, *supra,* note 8, pp. 65, 98.

117. 21 H.C. Deb., col. 443 (February 9th, 1911).
118. Mr. Ronald McNeill observed that he and his colleagues did 'not really know the terms of the various clauses': 65 H.C. Deb., col. 1990. For royal assent, see 65 H.C. Deb., col. 2041.
119. Aliens Restriction (Amendment) Act, 1919, section 1.
120. *R. v. Brixton Prison (Governor) ex parte Soblen,* [1963] 2 Q.B. 243, 297. The Aliens Act, 1905 was not repealed until after the War, and thus the two enactments worked concurrently from 1914 until 1919, when the 1905 Act was repealed by section 16 (2) of the Aliens Restriction (Amendment) Act 1919.
121. Aliens Restriction (Consolidation) Order, 1914 (1914/1374). See also Aliens Restriction (Belgian Refugees) Order, 1914 (1914/1478).
122. Aliens Order, 1920 (1920/448).
123. Aliens Order, 1920, amended by Aliens Orders, 1920/2262, 1923/326, 1925/760, 1931/715, 1939/994, 1940/782, 1940/890, 1940/1900, 1941/1043, 1941/1902, 1942/95, 1942/1575, 1943/1378, 1944/465, 1944/1315, 1945/1209, 1945/1535, 1946/380 and 1947/2117.
124. Aliens Order, 1953 (1953/1671) amended, Aliens Orders 1957/597, 1960/2214, 1964/2034, 1967/1282, 1968/1649 and 1969/737, and Aliens (Appeals) Order, 1970 (1970/151); repealed, Immigration Act, 1971, section 34 and schedule 6.
125. p. 220.
126. Macheret, *supra,* note 7, p. 20.
127. Fauchille, *supra,* note 7, Vol. I, p. 898.
128. 40 Stat. 559; 40 Stat. 1012.
129. An Act of May 10th, 1920 (41 Stat. 593) dealt with the deportation of allien enemies, etc. An Act of June 5th, 1920 (41 Stat. 981) dealt with the admission of certain illiterates on the request of citizens having served in U.S. during the War. See U.S. Cong. and Ad. News (1952) 1666.
130. E.g., the Haitian Law of September 21st, 1864.
131. E.g., the Transvaal Law of December 25th, 1896.
132. This was the case in the United Kingdom, where the Aliens Restriction Act of 1836 (6 and 7 Will. IV, c. 11) had lapsed and been replaced by the Act of 1905. In France the passports system established under the Passports Law of 28 vendemiaire, year 6, had been allowed to lapse.
133. Aliens Restriction (Consolidation) Order, 1914 (1914/1374) articles 1, 10; Aliens Order, 1919 (1919/1077) article 15.
134. Act of May, 22nd, 1918, 40 Stat. 559, section 2.
135. 42 Stat. 5; U.S. Cong. and Ad. News (1952) 1666; *Supra,* note 105, Seckler-Hudson, pp. 94, 123, 211–212, 283–284.
136. 42 Stat. 540.
137. H.R. 7995; Conf. R. 716; U.S. Cong. and Ad. News (1952) 1669; 43 Stat. 153.
138. A. Konvitz, *The Alien and the Asiatic in American Law,* 1946, pp. 24–25.
139. R. Wilson, *The International Law Standard and Commonwealth Developments,* 1966, p. 139.
140. Cd. 5746, p. 272; C. Joseph, *Nationality and Diplomatic Protection,* 1970, p.222.
141. Cd. 8566, pp. 159–162.
142. Cd. 9177, p. 195. At first the Government of India was reluctant to invoke the principle of reciprocity in this way. The Indian Naturalization Act of 1926 contemplated the exclusion of Europeans and Americans from naturalization and the treatment of other applicants on a strictly reciprocal basis, but under the Government of India Act, 1935, naturalization became a matter for the discretion of the Central Government; consequently, the 1926 provision was not applied. However, in 1939 the Asiatic (Transvaal Land and Trading) Act imposed serious commercial and proprietary disabilities on British subjects from India living

in the Transvaal. In combination with other measures, that Act induced the Indian Government to adopt the Reciprocity Act, 1943. Under that Act, the Central Government may impose reciprocal disabilities on persons domiciled in any British possession where persons of Indian origin are subjected to disabilities in respect of 'entry, travel, residence, the acquisition, holding or disposal of property, the enjoyment of educational facilities, the holding of public office, the carrying of any occupation, trade, business or profession or the exercise of the franchise'. The Act was invoked against South Africa in 1944, by the Reciprocity (South Africa) Rules, the Reciprocity (Natal and the Transvaal) Rules and the Reciprocity (South Africa) (Local Franchise) Rules.

143. C. De Visscher, *Théories et réalités en droit international public,* 1970, p. 221.
144. Fauchille, *supra,* note 7 at p. 895.
145. Decree of August 31st, 1914, *Leyes de Costa Rica,* II, p. 199.
146. *Supra,* note 7 at pp. 894–5.
147. E. Borchard, 1915, *The Diplomatic Protection of Citizens Abroad,* pp. 46–47. The 'continental' theory (that there is a *right* to international intercourse) has been expressly rejected by the Administrative Court of Appeal of Munster in the *Residence of the Alien Trader (Germany) case,* 21 I.L.R. (1954) 208, 210.
148. In *Soltanow v. Ministry of Foreign Affairs,* Z.W.N.T.A. V (1927) No. 1183, 4 A.D. (1927–8) 328 (No. 221) the Supreme Administrative Court of Poland held that at the moment of the decision there was no rule which would give to every foreigner the right to enter Poland. A similar decision was reached in the *Admission of Aliens (Austria) Case,* 1 A.D. (1919–22)231 (No. 160), S.E.O.V. II (1922) 57 (No. 120) despite the fact that articles 62 and 63 of the Austrian Constitution conferred on aliens equal rights with nationals in respect of the protection of life and property. The Federal Supreme Court of the Argentine Republic referred in *In Re Blas Hernández* to the 'unquestionable right of the nation to prevent the entry of aliens or to put conditions on their admission', 173 *Fallos* 179, citing 151 *Fallos* 24 (1935). Similar remarks were made by the U.S. Supreme Court in *U.S. ex rel. Polymeris v. Trudell,* 284 U.S. 279 (1931).
149. 12 A.J.I.L. (1928) Off. Doc. 137. This provided in article 1 that 'States have the right to establish by means of laws the conditions under which foreigners may enter or reside in their territory'.
150. 5 March 1929, L.N. Doc. C. 36 M. 21 (1929-II) 421. This provided that High Contracting Powers remained free to regulate the admission of aliens to their territories and to subordinate those aliens to such conditions as they should deem necessary.
151. P.C.I.J. Ser. A/B No. 44 (1932) at p. 41. Here the Court expressly refrained from dealing with the question whether a State may legitimately exclude all aliens, but reiterated that each state may determine under what conditions it will admit foreigners to its territory.
152. Australia: Immigration Restriction Act (No. 17) of 1901, amended, *supra,* note 61; Austria: Law of December 19th, 1925, B.G.Bl. No. 457; Belgium: Royal Order of December 15th, 1930; Canada: P.C. 1206 of June 7th, 1922; Costa Rica: Decree of August 31st, 1914; Cuba: Presidential Decree of April 19th, 1932; Czechoslovakia: Law No. 39 of March 13th, 1928; Denmark: Law of March 31st, 1926; Finland: Law of February 7th, 1930; France: Decree of 10th July, 1929, 29 C.C.L. 504; Greece: Royal Decrees of March 10th, 1926 and June 17th, 1927, reproduced (in French) in Carabiber, *Conflicts de lois et conditions des étrangers en droit international privé grec,* 1930, 131–133; Haiti: Immigration Law of 13th August 1903; Holland: Act of 4th June, 1858, Royal Decrees of 27th July, 1887, 11th August 1920, 31st March, 1922, 12th December, 1922, Criminal Code, article 438, and Regulations regarding Foreigners, article 27, amended by Royal Decree of 31st March, 1922; Honduras: Decree No. 181 of 1929; Hungary: Law 1929/IV and Decree No. 100,000/1930; Irish Free State: Aliens Order (No. 2) of 1925; Latvia: Regulation of 15th April, 1929; Lithuania: Lithuanian

Citizenship Law of January 9th, 1919, Regulations for Residence of Aliens in Lithuania of 15th February, 1924, Law of 27th February, 1925, Law of 25th June, 1929, Employment Law of 14th June, 1930, Emigration Law of 1st January, 1931; Mexico: Decree of 13th August, 1931; Norway: Act of 22nd April, 1927; Poland: Basic Executive Decree of June 4th, 1927, Ministerial Decree of February 20th, 1931; Portugal: Decree No. 18415 of June 3rd, 1930; Roumania: Royal Decree No. 118 of April 1st, 1930; Spain: Law of April 5th, 1930, Law of January 16th, 1931, Royal Decree of 6th July, 1923; Sweden: Law of August 6th, 1894, Law of August 2nd, 1927; Switzerland: Federal Law on the Sojourn and Establisment of Aliens of March 26th, 1931. See H. Fields, 'Closing Immigration throughout the World', 26 A.J.I.L. (1932) 671, 698.

153. R. Redslob, *Les principes du droit des gens moderne*, 1937, p. 184.

154. Aliens Order, 1939 (1939/994); Aliens (Approved Ports) Order, 1939 (1939/1057); Aliens (Landing and Embarkation Cards) Order, 1939 (1939/1124); see also Exemption Directions (1939/1056) and (1939/1448); Registration Directions (1939/1058), (1939/1059) and (1939/1060); Aliens (Employment) Order, 1939 (1939/1660). Note further the amendment of section 7 of the Aliens Restriction (Amendment) Act, 1919 by article 7 of the Defence (General) Regulations, 1939 (1939/1681), and see article 2 of the Defence (Armed Forces) Regulations, 1939 (1939/1304).

155. Act of June 28th, 54 Stat. 670.

156. Decree of 19th September, 1939, 22 B.L.D. (1939-II) 1152, modifying the Decree of 14th May, 1938, articles 1 and 5 (b), 38 C.C.L. 344.

157. Decrees of 23rd December, 1939, 22 B.L.D. (1939-II) 1580; 6th February 1935, 35 C.C.L. 53; 18th November, 1939, 22 B.L.D. (1939-II) 1408.

158. *Gesetz über das Pass-, das Ausländerpolizei-, und das Meldewesen sowie über das Ausweis-wesen*, 11 May, 1937, R.G.Bl. 1937, I 589.

159. *Ausländerpolizeiverordnung* (Aliens Control Decree of 22 August, 1938, R.G.Bl. 1938 I 1053, repealed and replaced by *Ausländergezetz* (Aliens Law) of 28 April, 1965, B.G.Bl.I 353.

160. See, for example, the exchange of letters between Egypt and the United States, reproduced in Hackworth, *supra*, note 101, Vol. III, pp. 729–730.

161. Act of December 17th, 57 Stat. 600; Konvitz, *supra*, note 138, p. 26.

162. Act of July 2nd, 1946 and Presidential Proclamation of July 4th, 1946, 60 Stat. 416, 1353.

163. Immigration Act, 1947, 11 Geo. VI, c. 19, section 4.

164. 1 Eliz. II, c. 42, section 61 (g).

165. *Canadian Immigration Policy*, White Paper, October, 1966.

166. Aliens Law, cap. 9 of Laws of Jamaica, Revised edition, 1953, consisting of Nos. 34 of 1945 and 14 of 1948. Section 9 (7) governs the disclosure of plans and printed matter, and section 14 deals with the importation of firearms, explosives and the like.

167. Aliens Restriction (Defence) Regulations, 1940.

168. Immigration Restriction (Commonwealth Citizens) Law, 1945 (No. 33) amended, Jamaican Nationality Act, 1962 (No. 8) schedule 4, and Foreign Nationals and Commonwealth Citizens (Employment) Act, 1964 (No. 48) section 1.

169. Expulsion of Undesirables Act, 1927 and Immigration Act, 1952.

170. Act of December 28th, 59 Stat. 659.

171. Act of June 29th, 60 Stat. 339.

172. Act of June 25th, 62 Stat. 1009; U.S. Cong. and Ad. News (1952) 1674.

173. Act of June 16th, 64 Stat. 219. For the relationship between postwar migrations, and law in general, see F. Kulischer, *Europe on the move: Law and Population Changes 1917–47*, 1948; J. Schechtman, *European Population Tranfers, 1939–45*, 1946.

174. S. Rept. 1515, 81st Cong., 2nd sess; S. 3455.

93

175. S. 716 and H.R. 2379 respectively.
176. S. 2055 and H.R. 5678 respectively.
177. Act of June 27th, 66 Stat. 163. Forseeing that the Quota system would be discriminatory in effect, President Truman vetoed the Bill, which was then passed over the veto: House Doc. U.S. 11614.
178. Statement by Hon. Hubert Opperman, 50 H. of R. 68, 69. See also the speech of Mr. Gough Whitlam, Deputy Leader of the Opposition, at the sixteenth Australian Citizenship Convention, 1966, *The Australian,* January 19th, 1966.
179. P.L. 89–236 of October 3rd, 1965, section 2 (a), amending the Immigration and Nationality Act of 1952, section 201. See J. McCarthy, 'The New Immigration Law', 11 Cath. L. (1965) 313.
180. Committee Print, Summary of Public Law 89–236, October 1965, p. 1.
181. Section 212 (a) as amended by Act of October 3rd, 1965, 79 Stat. 911–912; for a full discussion of this Act, see Kansas, *New Immigration Law effective July 1, 1968, Simplified,* 1967.
182. J. Jones, 'British Nationality Act, 1948', 25 B.Y.I.L. (1948) 158, 161.
183. The U.K. Government stated that consultation of this kind had been unsuccessful, but Rt. Hon. Grantly Adams and other Commonwealth leaders protested at the lack of consultation: 649 H.C. Deb., col. 707 (speech of Rt. Hon. Patrick Gordon-Walker, November 16th, 1961).
184. Immigration Appeals Act, 1969; Aliens (Appeals) Order, 1970 (1970/151); Immigration Appeals Act, 1969 (Commencement No. 1) Order, 1970, (1970/118); Immigration Appeals Act, 1969 (Commencement No. 2) Order, 1970 (1970/791); Aliens (Appeals) (Commencement No. 1) Order, 1970 (1970/792); Immigration Appeals (Notices) Regulations, 1970 (1970/793); Immigration Appeals (Procedure) Rules, 1970, (1970/794). The appeals system established by this legislation is perpetuated by sections 12–23 of the Immigration Act, 1971.
185. France: 'Loi Bonnet', Law 80–9 of 10 January 1980, J.O.R.F. 11 January 1980 p. 71, D 1980 (L) 79 (largely repealed by Law 81–973 of 29 October 1981, J.O.R.F. 30 October 1981 p. 2970, D 1981 (L) 361. United Kingdom: Statement of Changes in Immigration Rules, 9 February 1983, H.C. 169; Netherlands: Act of 9 November 1978, Stb. 1978, No. 737 & Royal Decree of 26 October 1979, Stb. 1979, No. 567; FRG: Work Promotion Amendment Law of 3 August 1981, BGBl I 802, 1042; Belgium: Royal Decree of 5 October 1979, M.B. 15 December 1982; Austria: Frendenpolizeigesetz of 17 March 1954, BGBl 1954/75, Amendment of 11 July 1974, BGBl 1974/422; Switzerland: Ordinance of 20 April 1983, S.R. 142, 202; Sweden: Aliens Act 1980 and Aliens Order 1980, No. 377.
186. See 'Rights and Obligations of Unauthorised Immigrants in Receiving Countries', No. 4, 6th I.C.M. Seminar, 11–14 April 1983, MC/SA1/VI/4.
187. E.g. Belgium: Law of 30 June 1971 & Law of 22 July 1976; France: *Code du Travail,* Article L-341, (2); see M. Batiffol and P. Lagarde, *Droit international privé,* 1983, Vol. I, p. 173; F.R.G.: *Auslandergesetz,* 28 April 1985; United Kingdom: *R.* v. *Home Secretary, ex parte Magbool Hussain,* [1976] 1 W.L.R. 97; *R.* v. *Bangoo and Others,* [1976] Crim. L.R. 246; *R.* v. *Home Secretary, ex parte Safdar Hussein,* [1978] 1 W.L.R. 700; *Zamir* v. *Home Secretary* [1980] 2 All E.R. 768; *Khawaja* v. *Home Secretary,* [1983], 1 All E.R. 765.
188. See U.N.H.C.R. Executive Committee, *Report on International Protection, 1982,* U.N. Doc. A/AC 96/609/Rev. 1.

BIBLIOGRAPHY

C. Bouvé, *Exclusion and Expulsion of Aliens in the United States*, 1912;

J. Brissaud, *A History of French Public Law*, trans. J. Garner, 1912;

J. Cable, *Decisive Decisions of United States Citizenship*, 1967;

Sir A. Cockburn, *Nationality or the Law relating to Subjects and Aliens*, 1869;

W. Diplock, 'Passports and Protection in International Law', 32 Tr. Grot. Soc. (1947) 42;

A. Feller and M. Hudson, *A Collection of Diplomatic and Consular Laws and Regulations of Various Countries*, 1933;

H. Fields, 'Closing Immigration throughout the World', 26 A.J.I.L. (1932) 671;

C. Fraser, *Control of Aliens in the British Commonwealth of Nations*, 1940;

M. Konvitz, *The Alien and Asiatic in American Law*, 1947;

E. Kulischer, *Europe on the Move: War and Population Changes, 1917–47*, 1948;

T. Lie, *Report on the Allocation of Functions among the Various Organs Concerned in the Field of Migration*, U.N. Doc. E/CN. 5/40, 1948;

R. Plender, 'British Subjects', Encyclopedia of Public International Law, 1986;

R. Plender, 'Protection of Immigrant and Racial Minorities', 13 Wm. and Ma. L. Rev. (1971) 338;

R. Plender, 'Recent Trends in National Immigration Control', 35 I.C.L.Q. (1986) 531;

P. Richardson, *International Labour Migration: Historical Perspectives*, 1984; N. Sibley and A Elias, *The Aliens Act and the Right of Asylum*, 1906;

L. Varlez, *'Les migrations internationales et leur reglementation'*, 5 Hague *Recueil* (1927) 169.

CHAPTER 3

The Right to Leave Any Country Including
One's Own

Few liberties are more generally proclaimed or more widely abridged than the right to leave any country, including one's own. At the international level, that right finds expression (in somewhat similar language) in Article 13(2) of the Universal Declaration of Human Rights,[1] Article 12(2) of the International Covenant on Civil and Political Rights[2] and Article 5(d)(ii) of the International Convention on the Elimination of All Forms of Racial Discrimination.[3] The Final Act of the Conference on Security and Cooperation in Europe records in 'Basket III' that the participating States will consider favourably applications for travel, with the purpose of allowing persons to leave their territory temporarily, and will deal in a positive and humanitarian spirit with applications for exit permits with the object of achieving family reunification, particularly in the event of marriages between citizens of different States.[4]

Article 2(1) of the Fourth Protocol to the European Convention on Human Rights declares that 'Everyone shall be free to leave any country, including his own'.[5] Article 22(2) of the American Convention on Human Rights[6] and Article 12(2) of the African Charter of Human and Peoples' Rights[7] contain similar stipulations. Several international instruments concerned with migration for employment have provisions designed to guarantee for the worker and his family the right to leave his own country and his country of employment. Among the instruments in this category are the European Social Charter,[8] Directive 68/360 of the Council of the European Economic Community[9] and I.L.O. Convention No. 97 concerning Migration for Employment.[10]

The right to depart from a State's territory for temporary purposes or permanently is recognized expressly in the constitutions of numerous States, diverse in their geographical locations, legal traditions and political inspirations. Among the national constitutions and bills of rights which recognise that right are those of Algeria,[11] Antigua and Barbuda,[12] Argentina,[13] Austria,[14] the Bahamas,[15] Barbados,[16] Belize,[17] Bolivia,[18] Brazil,[19] Canada,[20] Chile,[21] the Congo,[22] Costa Rica,[23] Cyprus,[24] Guatemala,[25] Guyana,[26] Iraq,[27] Italy,[28] Japan,[29] Jordan,[30] Kenya,[31] Kiribati,[32] the Republic of Korea,[33] Kuwait,[34] Liberia,[35] Malta,[36] Mauritius,[37] Nicaragua,[38] Nigeria,[39] Paraguay,[40] the Philippines,[41] Portugal,[42] Rwanda,[43] Saint Christopher and Nevis,[44] Saint Lucia,[45] Saint Vincent,[46] Sierra Leone,[47] Spain,[48] Trinidad and Tobago,[49] Tunisia,[50] Turkey,[51] Tuvalu,[52] Venezuela[53] and Zimbabwe.[54] In several other States the right to depart appears capable of being protected obliquely by means of a constitutional affirmation of the Universal Declaration of Human Rights.[55] In yet others, the relevant constitutional provisions are inexplicit but recognition is accorded to the right to choose one's residence.[56]

In England, the right to depart was guaranteed in the Magna Carta of 1215, which spoke of the right of 'safe and secure exit' for foreign merchants and of the right of others 'to go out of our Kingdom ... safely and securely'.[57] In France, Title 1 of the Constitution of 1791 spoke of the 'freedom of everyone to go'.[58] In the United States a Congressional enactment dated 1868 declared that 'the right of expatriation is a natural and inherent right of all people.[59] It seems to follow *a fortiori* that Congress considered that the right of departure was natural and inherent.

There is ample support in the writings of the most highly qualified publicists for the proposition that there is a right to leave any country. Francesco de Vitoria[60] asserted that 'It was permissible from the beginning of the world for anyone to travel wheresoever he would'. Grotius[61] characterised the right to depart as the 'most specific and unimpeachable axiom of the law of nations'. Vattel[62] defined the right in equally forthright terms.

In the present century, Lauterpacht[63] has argued that the unqualified recognition of the right of expatriation is desirable for the purpose of avoiding international friction and essential for the assertion of the dignity of man; and that the right of emigration is of similar significance. He contended that there is no compelling reason militating against recognition of the right of emigration in international law. Higgins[64] asserts that the rights of entry, sojourn and exist are indivisible and that international law recognises a right to emigrate.

Nevertheless, the obstinate fact remains that some restrictions upon the right of emigration are imposed in most States, while in a few there is in practice no more than a facility to depart at the discretion of national authorities. This circumstance led José D. Ingles, the special Rapporteur of the United Nations Sub-Commission on Human Rights, to complain that more people are effectively confined behind their national boundaries today than in previous periods of history.[65] One author writing recently has been led to advance the proposition that 'State practice in the municipal sphere tends to reflect a claim of absolute discretion, rather than any restrictive rule of general international law. Indeed, it may be that the provisions in question are not even potentially of a norm-creating character'.[66]

It is thought, however, that modern State practice does not compel us to reach so pessimistic a conclusion. If in many States some restrictions are imposed upon the departure of nationals and of aliens, this may lead us to be cautious in defining the right of emigration, but not to deny the existence of the right, which finds its expression in so many solemn pacts, constitutional provisions and authoritative writings. If in some States the opportunity to depart is severely curtailed, this need not lead us to infer that there is no right of emigration. On the contrary, the diplomatic reaction to the restriction of emigration may serve to reinforce the view that a right to depart does indeed exist in modern international law. Such is the case with the famous debate in the General Assembly of the United Nations in 1948 on the measures taken by the Soviet Union to prevent Soviet wives of foreign husbands from leaving Soviet territory. The Assembly concluded that the measures in question violated the provisions in the Charter governing respect for human rights.[67]

SUCCESSIVE STUDIES

During the last thirty years, the right to depart has been the subject of several successive studies conducted by international commissions, with the object of defining that right and of devising an effective mechanism for its enforcement. Among the earliest of these studies, yet still the most authoritative, was that of Judge Ingles in 1963.[68] That study finds its basis in the wording of Article 12 of the Covenant on Civil and Political Rights but since it is Ingles' thesis that the Covenant reflects the Universal Declaration of Human Rights and that the Declaration reflects customary law, the study has implications for the law at large.

   The wording of the Universal Declaration of Human Rights is similar to that of the International Covenant on Civil and Political Rights, but not identical. The former envisages 'such limitations as are determined by law, solely for the purpose of securing due recognition and respect for the rights and freedoms of others and of meeting the just requirements of morality, public order and general welfare in a democratic society'.[69] The latter authorises restrictions on the right of departure which are provided by law and 'are necessary to protect national security, public order (*ordre public*), public health or morals or the rights and freedoms of others'. Judge Ingles contends that the expression' general welfare' appearing in the Universal Declaration must be equated with the expressions 'national security', '*ordre public*' and 'public health' in the Covenant.[70] His argument is persuasive. It is inconceivable that the parties to the International Covenant intended to authorise action inconsistent with the Universal Declaration. The language in the Covenant gives substance and meaning to the relatively imprecise formula in the Declaration.

   Judge Ingles next argues that one is bound to stand by the original English meaning of 'public order' in the Declaration and to reject the mischievous

98

implications of qualifying its meaning in accordance with the French *ordre public*. If it is not easy to accept that argument in its entirety[71] it is nevertheless possible to assent to the substance or main part of it. The expression 'public order (*ordre public*)' appearing in the Covenant cannot be wider than the term 'public order' in the Declaration and neither can be equated with the laws generally of the State in question. In the drafting of both instruments the committees had come to reject Soviet proposals which would have qualified the right of departure by the words 'in accordance with the procedure laid down in the laws of that country' or an equivalent expression.[72]

Thus, Judge Ingles' study leads to the conclusion that the right to depart may be qualified only be limitations provided by law and necessary to protect public security, public order, health or morals, or the rights and freedoms of others. Restrictions based on public security may legitimately be imposed by Governments (according to Ingles) only within the framework of a general policy permitting everyone to leave the country and for specific reasons presenting a real danger to the security of the State. Restrictions based on public order or morals could be justified only in the event of previous conviction of a crime, or if there is a grave danger to the life, liberty or property of the applicant. International standards, particularly those set by the World Health Organization, are appropriate for the purpose of determining whether a restriction on departure is justified in the interests of public health. Restrictions imposed in the interests of 'the rights and freedoms of others' are defensible only when necessary for the protection of the prospective travellers' dependents or in order to enforce legal obligations (including tax debts) or exceptionally, on the ground that the applicant has a special knowledge or skill. That last ground is 'understandable in the case of developing countries' but could not be justified in normal times in any highly industrialised country save in the case of persons possessing military or State secrets.[72]

Judge Ingles asserted that the availability of an effective remedy against abuse of discretion by government officials is of the greatest importance. He presented to the Sub-Commission his Draft Principles on Freedom and Non-Discrimination in respect of the Right of Everyone to Leave any Country, which included a Draft Article to guarantee a right to a fair hearing and recourse to an independent tribunal in the event of a denial of a travel document or permission to leave the country.[73] The judge left open the question whether his draft principles could best be incorporated in a Convention or in a Declaration or Resolution. His report was, however, received less warmly in Socialist than in western States, particularly in view of his comments on the Berlin Wall.[74] No instrument of the kind envisaged by Judge Ingles was completed together with the human rights Covenants of 1966.

In 1968, the year designated by the United Nations as the 'International Year of Human Rights', an attempt was made to revive Judge Ingles' initiative. At the meeting in Bangalore of the International Commission of Jurists, the Indian Commission of Jurists and the Mysore State Commission of Jurists, the subject of the colloquium was the Right to Freedom of Movement.[75] The delegates concluded that 'there is, in the first place, a right to freedom of movement' which should be accepted by all States, subject to established limitations.[76] A distinction was to be drawn between a right to leave a foreign country and a right to leave one's own country; for Judge Ingles' study had shown that the former was respected more widely and with fewer exceptions than the latter. According to the delegates, there were only three instances in which limitations could be imposed on a right to leave a foreign country.

Firstly, that right could be restricted for such period as is necessary for reasons of public health. Secondly, restrictions were permissible if there were reasons for believing that the applicant had committed an offence in the foreign country (but in the event of the applicant's acquittal or release after imprisonment and in the event of a failure to prefer charges against him within a reasonable period, he must be permitted to depart). Thirdly, an alien could be prevented from leaving until he had met his fiscal obligations.[77] The right to leave one's own country was, in the delegates' opinion, a right expressed in Article 12(2) of the International Covenant on Civil and Political Rights[78] and for this reason any derogations must be construed very strictly. Any such restrictions must be declared by Law, reasonable in operation and necessary for public purposes, Moreover, the exercise of a power given for these purposes must not amount to an abuse of authority.[79]

Four years later a Colloquium on the Right to Leave and to Return was convened in Uppsala.[80] Sponsored jointly by the International Institute of Human Rights, the Blaustein Institute for the Advancement of Human Rights and the University of Uppsala, the Colloquium counted among its participants René Cassin and Bertram Gold. The Colloquium drafted and adopted a Declaration, in a form similar to that used by the General Assembly of the United Nations.

Article 1 of the Declaration states simply that 'Everyone has the right to leave any country, including his own'. Article 2 provides that every State shall recognise, implement and enforce the right of any person to leave its territory, temporarily or permanently. Subsequent Articles amplify the right of departure, stating in particular that no person shall be required to renounce his nationality as a condition of the exercise of the right to leave a country; that no State shall subject a person or his family to sanctions, penalties or harassment for seeking to exercise or for exercising the right to depart; and that any person who wishes to leave a country is entitled to take specified items of property with him. Article 6 reads a follows:

A person's right to leave a country shall be subject only to such reasonable limitations as are necessary to prevent a clear and present danger to the national security or public order, or to comply with international health regulations; and only if such limitations are provided for by law, are clear and specific, are not subject to arbitrary application and do not destroy the substance of the rights.

There follow draft provisions dealing with travel documents, the abolition of discrimination and the right to have prompt and effective recourse to a national tribunal.

The aspirations of the draftsmen of the Uppsala Declaration were not promptly realised. At the Conference on Security and Cooperation in Europe, held in Helsinki in 1975, delegates agreed upon a guarded form of words to facilitate the right to leave a State's territory, particularly for the purpose of family reunion.[81] The diplomatic significance of those words is not to be underestimated, for despite their reserved terms, they apply to cases commanding widespread public sympathy and appear in a document designed to confer reciprocal advantage upon the participating States, in particular the United States and the Soviet Union. The fact remains, in the words of Secretary- General Waldheim, 'that the Final Act is not a document which is legally binding on governments; that it provides for no enforcement mechanism'.[82]

The Helsinki Conference appears, however, to have provided a stimulus for re-examination of the right to depart. By Resolution 8(xxiv) of 9 September 1981 the United Nations' Sub-Commission on Prevention of Discrimination and Protection of Minorities requested the Secretary General to submit a concise note of the consideration given by the Economic and Social Council and by the Commission on Human Rights to Judge Ingles' study which had been published some eighteen years earlier. On receiving the Secretary-General's note, the Sub-Commission requested a distinguished Zambian jurist, Mr. Mubanga-Chipoya, to prepare an analysis of current trends and development.[83]

In 1984 the Sub-Commission received and considered a preliminary report by Mr. Mubanga-Chipoya. It charged him with the task of submitting a progress report in time for the next session of the Sub-Commission in 1985 and a final report in time for the following session.[84]

On 10 July 1985 Mr. Mubanga-Chipoya published his progress report.[85] For present purposes, the main issue is the identification and definition of the right to leave any country. Of this the report states as follows:

Despite this apparent world-wide acknowledgement of this right, the question might be asked whether it has become a right which has been and can be enforced, or is rather a mere human attribute without any reliable legal means of enforcement so far, as is exemplified in particular by the human rights of the black population in South Africa. From the replies received so far[86] the answer would appear to depend on whether, in a particular country, the supremacy of the law, as expressed by the courts, exists and, even more important, on whether and when the relevant municipal law prohibits denial of the right to leave and return.[87]

The report examines in some detail the phenomenon of the 'brain drain'. It suggests that a community has some legal claim on the skills and talents developed by members of that community and that 'an outflow of trained personnel should take place on an exchange basis, like any other exchange of goods or services in a given market'.[88] The proposal, albeit in embryonic form, seems to be that developing countries of emigration are entitled to be paid by developed countries of immigration for skilled labour. Such a proposal would not be unprecedented. The problem of securing adequate recompense for the loss by developing countries of skilled manpower was the subject of discussion at the Bellagio Conference in 1975 and at a conference convened by UNCTAD in Geneva in 1978.[89] There are, however, formidable objections to any scheme which equates men and women with goods and services, for the purposes of monetary exchange. For this reason, Professor Bhagwati[90] has proposed that developing countries should levy a tax on the earnings of professional, technical and kindred persons who emigrate from less developed to developed countries. The practical implementation of that proposal presents difficulties; but it avoids the unseemly and potentially abusive practice of exchanging men and women for hard currency. Moreover, the enactment, as distinct from the implementation, of Professor Bhagwati's proposal requires no international agreement, since it is consistent with existing concepts of tax jurisdiction to assert jurisdiction over the worldwide income of an individual abroad, provided that a sufficient connection exists between the taxing State and the individual or income.[91]

While the progress report gives some basis for disquiet, it contains a promise that a draft Declaration on the Right of Everyone to Leave any Country will be presented shortly to the Commission on Human Rights.[92] Furthermore, it strengthens Judge Ingles' proposal that a distinction is to be drawn between developing countries and others when assessing the legitimacy of any restrictions imposed for the purpose of reducing the outflow of trained personnel.[93]

An examination of the laws of some strategic countries will assist in assessing the prospects of drafting an effective declaration on the right to depart. The same exercise will help in defining the current state of customary international law.

The right to travel abroad is protected under the Fifth Amendment to the Constitution of the United States as an aspect of the 'liberty' of which an individual cannot be deprived save by due process of law.[94] In *Schachtman v. Dulles*[95] the Court of Appeals for the District of Columbia justified the placing of this construction on the word 'liberty' by asserting that the right to travel is a *natural* right. Indeed, there is a *prima facie* breach of the Fifth Amendment not only when a person is restrained from leaving the territory of the United States, but also when he is restrained by an officer of the United States from leaving a foreign country or place.[96]

In a powerful dissenting opinion in *Zemel v. Rusk*[97] Justice Douglas, joined by Justice Goldberg, expressed the view that the right to travel is at the periphery of the First Amendment, which provides a guarantee of freedom of expression. It now seems to be settled, however, that it is the Fifth and not the First Amendement which applies to the right to travel.[98] It follows that the rights is subject to 'reasonable' governmental restraint, in common with other aspects of the liberty protected by the Fifth Amendment.[99] It also follows that any statutory restrictions upon the right to travel must be construed narrowly, as derogations from a constitutional libery.[100]

The cases providing examples and amplifications of the right under the United States Constitution to travel abroad are concerned primarily with the right to travel to particular foreign countries. Restraints upon the bare exercise of right of exit are comparatively rare.

Under the former provisions of the Passport Act 1926[101] the Secretary of State was authorised to issue passports under such rules as the President should designate. In accordance with such rules, the State Department in 1964 refused to validate the passport of a United States citizen for travel to Cuba. The Supreme Court concluded that the restriction so imposed was a reasonable governmental restraint. The Court placed reliance on the Secretary of State's conclusion that the travel to Cuba by American citizens might involve the nation in dangerous international incidents, particularly in the event of the imprisonment of such citizens in Cuba without charges.[102] The terms of the Passport Act were amended in 1978. They now read as follows:

> Unless authorised by law, a passport may not be designated as restricted for travel to or for use in any country other than a country with which the United States is at war, where armed hostilities are in progress, or where there is imminent danger to the public health or physical safety of United States travellers.

Restrictions upon the issuance of passports to supporters of organizations considered by the Government to be subversive have been struck down repeatedly. In the leading case of *Kent v. Dulles*[103] the Supreme Court held that the Secretary of State was not authorised to withhold passports from members or supporters of the Communist Party. In *Aptheker v. Secretary of State*[104] the same Court held that section 6 of the Subversive Activities Control Act, 1950[105] was unconstitutional, since it restricted too broadly and indiscriminately the right to travel abroad. The action of the Secretary of State in declining to issue a passport to the Chairman of the Independent Socialist League was held to be unconstitutional in 1955.[106]

On the other hand, it has been held that a federal statute providing for the forfeiture of Social Security benefits in the event of prolonged absence from the United States did not amount to a deprivation of the liberty guaranteed by the First Amendment.[107] A federal statute requiring violators of narcotics law to register with customs officials when crossing the border was held to be valid.[108] Equally it has been held that the constitutionally-guaranteed right to travel is not infringed when a passenger is required to submit to a routine airport search before boarding an aircraft bound for foreign parts.[109] Nor is it infringed when a social club, whose real business is selling tours on chartered flights, is treated as an indirect air carrier.[110]

The Internal Revenue Code provides that subject to exceptions prescribed by the Secretary of State

> No alien shall depart from the United States unless he first procures from the Secretary or his delegate a certificate that he has complied with all the obligations imposed upon him by the income tax laws.[111]

The Immigration and Nationality Act[112] authorises the President of the United States to make a proclamation, for the purpose of imposing additional restrictions upon departure of citizens and aliens from the United States, when that country is at war or during a national emergency or (in the case of aliens) when there is a war between two or more foreign States. The restrictions so imposed may include a prohibition upon the departure of aliens except in accordance with reasonable rules prescribed by the President.[113]

Further, it is unlawful for any citizen of the United States to depart or to attempt to depart from that country unless he bears a valid passport.[114]

THE LAW OF THE UNITED KINGDOM

The right to depart from the United Kingdom 'without let or hindrance' is among the rights expressly conferred on persons having the right of abode.[115] The Immigration Act envisages the possibility that those without the right of abode might be subjected to controls on their departure[116] but neither that Act nor the rules adopted thereunder currently make provision for the imposition of such controls. In practice, all those wishing to embark from the United Kingdom are required to produce passports or national identity cards as evidence that they are eligible to be admitted at their destination. That requirement is imposed equally on those with and those without a right of abode.

Travellers who are ineligible to receive British passports are unlikely to be inconvenienced by that requirement. This is so since a passenger arriving in the United Kingdom must on request produce a valid national passport or other document satisfactorily establishing his identity and if such a passenger is subject to immigration control, he will be admitted for a period expiring before the expiry of the travel document.[117] Where, exceptionally, a person is found to have remained in the United Kingdom beyond the period of validity of the travel document and the authorities of the State which issued that document are unable or unwilling to supply him with a replacement in the United Kingdom, he may be issued with a 'Home Office Travel Document', valid for a single journey to his country of origin or any other specified country.

A traveller embarking in the United Kingdom is under a statutory obligation to submit to examination by an immigration officer at the port of departure. He is obliged to produce to the officer 'a valid passport with photograph or other document satisfactorily establishing [his] identity and nationality'.[118] This wording reflects that of the old Aliens Order, which it replaces.[119] For the purpose of testing the right to leave the United Kingdom without a passport, at the time when the Aliens Order was in force, one Ian Colvin sought to embark bearing a birth certificate and other documentary evidence of his identity. He was refused leave to embark[120] on the ground that the immigration officer was not satisfied of Mr. Colvin's identity and nationality. It is thought, however, that even as the law stood at that time, Mr. Colvin would have been entitled to an order of *mandamus* to compel the officer to permit him to embark, provided that his documentary evidence was such as to satisfy any reasonable officer of the bearer's identity and nationality.[121]

If this view is correct, it follows that a person who is eligible to receive a British passport may, with some difficulty and with alternative documentary evidence, secure the right to depart from the realm. The practical difficulties of travelling without a passport are, however, so evident that the right to obtain a passport is almost equated with the right to leave the kingdom.

In English law a passport is defined as 'a document issued in the name of the Sovereign on the responsibility of a Minister of the Crown to a named individual, intended to be presented to the Governments of foreign nations and to be used for that individual's protection as a British subject in foreign countries'.[122] The traditional view, certainly, is that a passport is issued by virtue of the royal prerogative so that no citizen can enforce in the courts a right to receive a passport.[123] Indeed, as recently as in 1968 the Government felt able to withdraw or refuse to renew the passports of certain citizens who had engaged in certain activities abroad of which the Government disapproved. Such was the case with Sir Frederick Crawford, whose passport was impounded when he came to England from Southern Rhodesia, where he had associations with the regime under Mr. Ian Smith.[124] Such was the case also with Mr. Alan Winnington who applied unsuccessfully for the renewal of his passport after he had visited North Korea and interviewed British soldiers held as prisoners there.[125]

It is thought, however, that it is no longer tenable to maintain the proposition that a citizen is unable to enforce in the courts a right to receive a passport. Such a proposition is certainly untenable in any case in which a United Kingdom national wishes to travel between Member States of the European Economic Community for the purposes envisaged in the founding treaty. In such a case, the United Kingdom is under an obligation to issue a passport to its national, subject only to derogations in the interests of public policy, public security and public health.[126] These derogations are strictly construed.[127]

A traveller is unable to invoke Community law if, although eligible to receive a British passport, he is not a 'United Kingdom national' for the purposes of Community law.[128] Nor can he invoke that law if he is not travelling for the purposes intended by the founding treaty.[129] Such a person is not unprotected against any abuse which may result in the withholding of his passport. The Parliamentary Commissioner for Administration (the Ombudsman) has the power to examine allegations of maladministration by the Passport Office, other than deliberate political decisions.[130]

What is more, the House of Lords has now decided that it has the power and duty to review not only the existence or extent of a royal prerogative but also the manner of its exercise, saving only those cases in which the prerogative was invoked for the purposes of protecting national security.[131] This decision implies that the courts will now review the manner of exercise of the prerogative power to issue, withhold, renew or revoke passports. In particular, a decision to revoke or withhold a passport will be quashed if it was made arbitrarily or in bad faith or if it was vitiated by a procedural defect such as a failure to afford to the applicant a proper opportunity of being heard or if the decision was one which no reasonable officer could make.[132]

In practice, the Passport Office follows well-established but informal rules in determining whether to withhold a passport. A British citizen, British subject (without citizenship) or British protected person will not be issued with a passport by the Passport Office in London and a British Overseas citizen or British Dependent Territories citizen will not be issued with such a document by or on behalf of a corresponding office overseas when he falls within any of three categories. The first consists of children who may not be removed from the jurisdiction without the consent of a Court or nominated person. The second consists of the mentally sick who cannot be removed without similar permission. The third comprises those very exceptional cases, such as that of Sir Frederick Crawford in 1968, in which a decision has been made at ministerial level that a passport is to be withheld on personal grounds.

Since the power to withhold or revoke passports now seems to be closely circumscribed, it is once again a matter of some importance to determine whether there exists an alternative means by which the Government may restrain a subject from leaving the kingdom. The common law certainly recognized the existence of the writ *ne exeat regno* to serve that end; but it has seldom been used in recent years. Indeed, it seems that writ has been invoked only three times in the present century and all three have failed.[133]

The origin of the writ *ne exeat regno* is obscure.[134] By the time of Fitzherbert and Coke, however, there were two known forms of the writ, one applicable to clerics and one to laymen.[135] Both forms were designed for high political purposes; and neither form of writ was traversable (or challengeable) by the person named in it. By the nineteenth century, however, the writ came to be used by private individuals for the purpose of preventing the exit of their debtors. Of this development Lord Eldon said,

> How it happened that this great prerogative writ, intended by the laws for great political purposes and the safety of the country, came to be applied between subject and subject, I cannot conjecture.[136]

The writ is no longer used for the purposes of debt collection. As will be shown,[137] the law affords a more expedient remedy to the creditor.

Some writers have maintained that the writ *ne exeat regno* can be used only in time of war or grave national emergency[138] but there seems nothing in the origin or subsequent use of the writ to confine it to such cases. It is unlikely that the writ simply disappeared as being obsolete, for English law has no doctrine of desuetude in relation to prerogative powers[139] and the Supreme Court of New Zealand did not find that the writ was obsolete in 1971.[140] It appears strongly arguable, however, that the Immigration Act 1971 has wholly replaced the writ. Section 1 of the Immigration Act confers on certain persons a statutory right to depart 'without let or hindrance'. The Act itself authorises certain restrictions on the exercise of that right but by necessary implication abolishes any other restrictions including those that might be imposed by the writ *ne exeat regno*. In the case of persons without the right of abode, there applies the principle that a prerogative power cannot be employed for the purpose of achieving a purpose for which a statutory power has been created expressly.[141] On that principle, it could be argued that the writ *ne exeat regno* cannot now be invoked even in relation to those who do not have the statutory right of abode.

The point remains moot, for in 1986 the Court of Appeal refered with approval to counsel's concession that the case before the Court 'was not one in which a writ *ne exeat regno* would be applicable'.[142] That phraseology might be taken to suggest that the writ has survived the entry into force of the Immigration Act. In the same case the Court of Appeal claimed and exercised a jurisdiction to issue an injuction restraining the defendent in a civil action from leaving the country and requiring him to deliver up his passport. The jurisdiction on which the Court relied was conferred by section 37(1) of the Supreme Court Act 1981. This provides that 'the High Court may be order . . . grant an injunction . . . in all cases in which it appears to the Court to be just and convenient so to do.' In the exercise of that provision the Court has a discretion to do what appears just and reasonable in the circumstances of the case.[143] The statute is broad enough to authorise the making of an injunction restraining a defendant from leaving the country, where there is a risk that in the absence of such an order, the plaintiff might not obtain information that the defendant has been ordered to disclose.[144] On similar principles, it seems clear that the Court could make such an injunction where there is a risk that in its absence the plaintiff might be unable to enforce a judgment that he has obtained against the defendant. In each case the hardship or inconvenience caused to the defendant must be measured against the hardship or inconvenience with which the plaintiff is threatened. The Court will grant the injunction only if satisfied that the balance of convenience justifies this action.

THE LAW OF THE SOVIET UNION

The Constitution of the Soviet Union is silent on the question of the right to depart from Soviet territory. Indeed, the Statute on the Passport System in the U.S.S.R. mentions the subject only briefly. It provides in Article 33 that a person wishing to depart from Soviet territory must complete a written application on a form distributed by the Ministry of Internal Affairs.[145] Prior to 1 January 1987, the subject was covered in only brief and inexplicit terms in the Statute on Entry into the U.S.S.R. and Exit from the U.S.S.R.[146] By Article 7 of the latter:

> Permission of the Praesidium for exit visas is granted by the U.S.S.R. Ministry of Foreign Affairs, diplomatic agencies of the U.S.S.R. Ministry of Foreign Affairs and the U.S.S.R. Ministry of Internal Affairs.

With effect from the beginning of 1987, however, there entered into force new Regulations on Entry into the U.S.S.R. and Exit from the U.S.S.R.

The new Regulations (made in 1986) govern both entry and departure, in the case of aliens as well as Soviet citizens.[147] Their principal interest, however, lies in the provisions governing departure, for temporary purposes or for permanent settlement. These provisions may be translated as follows:

23. An application for temporary departure from the U.S.S.R. on private affairs shall be considered on the presentation of appropriate documents.

    The period of temporary residence in the U.S.S.R. and abroad on private affairs shall be determined by taking into account the purpose of the journey. This period may be extended by organs of internal affairs of the U.S.S.R. and diplomatic representatives or consular establishments of the U.S.S.R. with the agreement of the authorities of the host country, as appropriate.

24. An application for departure from the U.S.S.R. abroad for reunification with members of one's family shall be considered on presentation of an invitation by a husband, wife, father, mother, son, daughter, own brother and own sister witnessed by the competent authorities of the respective foreign State, and notarially certified statements by family members remaining in the U.S.S.R., and also by a former spouse (if there are minor children of the marriage) [confirming] that the departing person has no unfulfilled obligations towards them which are stipulated by Soviet legislation.

    The joint departure from the U.S.S.R. of other relatives and dependants unfit for work, provided they live together and have a common household, shall be considered on the basis of the application of the departing individual.

    If the individual who applied for departure has no family members in the U.S.S.R., an application may be accepted for consideration on the presentation of an invitation also from another relative.

25. Departure from the U.S.S.R. on private affairs shall not be permitted to a citizen of the U.S.S.R.
    (a) if he is privy to State secrets or there exist other grounds affecting State security – until the circumstances hindering departure cease to operate;
    (b) if it results in the infringement of essential rights and legitimate interests of other Soviet citizens;
    (c) if he has unfulfilled obligations to the State or financial responsibilities which involve economic or legal interests of State, co-operative and other public organizations – until these obligations and responsibilities are discharged;
    (d) if there are legal grounds to make him criminally answerable – until the end of the proceedings in the concrete case;
    (e) if he is convicted for having committed an offence – until he has served his sentence or has been discharged from his sentence.

Departure from the U.S.S.R. on private affairs can be refused to a citizen of the U.S.S.R.:

(a) in order to secure the protection of public order, the health or morality of the population – until the circumstances hindering the departure cease to operate;

(b) if during his earlier stay abroad he committed deeds infringing the interests of the State, or infringements of customs or currency legislation were established;

(c) if on submitting his application for departure he gave false information about himself.

The same Regulations provide that applications for temporary entry and temporary departure shall be considered as rapidly as possible and as a rule within one month. In the event of an application for departure made by a person wishing to visit a relative who is seriously ill or has died, an answer is to be given in three days. Applications for departure for permanent settlement are to be considered within one month; but should further investigations be necessary the period may be extended to no more than six months. The results of the consideration of the application must be made known to the applicant, and in the event of a refusal reasons must be given. Where an application to depart from the Soviet Union on private affairs has been refused, a new application may be made six months after the date of the refusal. It is reported that it is generally very much easier in practice for a Soviet citizen to obtain a visa for departure to a Socialist than to a non-Socialist State.[148]

Since the former rules governing the issuance of exit permits were not published, it is not easy to assess the degree to which the new Regulations restate the former practice. Prior to 1987 it was possible to make some deductions as to Soviet practice in this area from the list of documents required of applicants for exit permits. Such a list was displayed in the hall of the Department of Visas and Registration of the M.V.D.[149] The documents required included a reference from the applicant's place of work, signed by the director of the establishment, the secretary of the local Party organization and the secretary of the applicant's labour union. Since the new Regulations make no mention of these documents, they appear designed to provide for a relaxation of controls on departure, at least for the purposes of family reunion.

Departure from the Soviet Union without observance of the statutory formalities is a State crime, punishable with imprisonment for up to three years. It is also an imprisonable offence to attempt so to depart or to conspire in or aid and abet an attempt by another to depart without observing these formalities.[150]

Soviet law makes no provision for an oral hearing of an application for a exit visa.[151] There is, apparently a right of appeal by reason of Article 23 of the Constitution of the U.S.S.R. This provides that

> Citizens of the U.S.S.R. shall have the right to lodge a complaint against the actions of officials, State bodies and public bodies ... Actions by officials that contravene the law may be appealed against in a court in the manner prescribed in the law.[152]

Prior to 1987 it was reported that Soviet citizens making applications for exit visas for permanent settlement abroad were a matter of routine subjected to several penalties, including loss of employment pending consideration of the application, which might last for several years.[153] For some years exit visas were not issued for the purpose of emigration save on payment of a capital sum representing the Soviet Union's investment in the training of the emigrant. In August 1972 there was a sharp increase in the scale of fees charged to prospective emigrants with higher education. The new fees ranged from $5,000 for a teacher to $25,000 for a prospective emigrant with a doctorate.[154] The scale of fees was the subject of vociferous protest and the Soviet Union subsequently reversed its practice in the matter. Fees are no longer demanded. The effect of the new Regulations upon the rate of emigration has yet to be gauged.

At least one Soviet expatriate has argued in favour of an extension of the right to emigrate well beyond the categories envisaged in the new Regulations. His argument was, however, addressed to the rights of a curiously-defined group of persons: convicted citizens, in particular homosexuals, polygamists and draft evaders.[155] His argument was rigorously opposed by Western writers, both on practical grounds and on the principle that the right of emigration ought not to be restricted to a category of citizens, however defined.[156]

If the present Soviet law falls far short of evidence in favour of an unqualified right of emigration, it is also far short of evidence in favour of an absolute discretion.[157] Indeed, the new Regulations were apparently adopted as part of the process of international cooperation initiated in Helsinki. Even in the period prior to 1987, Soviet practice in relation to *foreign* ethnic minorities yielded more support for the existence than for the absence of a right to depart, even for permanent resettlement. Several of the treaties concluded after the Second World War by the Russian Soviet Federated Socialist Republic provided for the repatriation of foreign nationals in Russia.[158] During the inter-war period, treaties were concluded for the purpose of securing the repatriation of Swedes and Germans. An agreement with Mongolia dated 3 November 1924 authorised the emigration of the Buriet tribe and (significantly) relieved members of that tribe of their Soviet nationality. In 1956–57, more than two thousand Spaniards were permitted to return to Spain. An agreement with Poland dated 25 March 1957[159] set out the time limits and procedure for the repatriation of Polish nationals from Soviet territory. In 1971 the Soviet authorities permitted more than 1200 ethnic Germans to be repatriated to West Germany.

While it is true that no arrangements have been made to authorise the emigration to the Republic of Korea of the Korean population of Sakhalin, the Soviet Union's failure to make such arrangements is not to be explained as evidence of a failure to recognize a right to repatriation. The Soviet Union does not recognize the Republic of Korea and proclaims itself prepared to permit the emigration to the Korean Democratic People's Republic of persons having the nationality of that State. Indeed, it seems that the Soviet Union is also prepared to countenance the emigration to Japan of those having Japanese nationality, in consequence of the Japanese 'occupation'.

In the case of Soviet nationals, evidence is strong that there are substantial numbers wishing to emigrate but denied the opportunity to do so.[160] The principal group of Soviet nationals who are adversely affected by present policy are the Jews, to whom exit visas are currently issued in substantially smaller numbers than previously. From a high point of 51,000 in 1979, the number of visas issued annually for the emigration of Jews fell to under 900 in 1984. The former Soviet representative on the United Nations Human Rights Committee reported in November 1984 that the number of applications for exit visas during the preceding five years exceeded by a rate of approximately two to one the number of visas issued.[161]

Nevertheless, representatives of the Soviet Union have defended Soviet policy on the grounds that almost all those wishing to leave had already done so; alternatively on the ground that there are compelling reasons of State, including considerations of national security, which justify a denial of an exit permit in each case in which this policy has been followed. Such statements are not consonant with a denial of the existence of a right, protected by international law, to depart from one's country. On the contrary, they appear to contain an acknowledgement of the existence of that right as a general rule, coupled with an assertion of the existence of established exceptions. The relaxation of the Soviet Regulations is consistent with the existence of such a right.

THE LAW OF THE NETHERLANDS

The right to leave is not expressly incorporated into Dutch law. Nevertheless, Article 65 of the Constitution provides that 'the provisions of aggreements the contents of which are binding on any one shall have this binding effect as from the time of publication'. Since the Netherlands is now a party to the International Covenant on Civil and Political Rights[163] it seems highly probable that any person subject to Dutch jurisdiction may invoke the right to leave any country, in accordance with Article 12(2) of that instrument.[164] The Dutch Government itself has given support to this view by casting doubt upon the converse (that is, the proposition that the rights guaranteed by Part III of the Covenant are not 'binding on anyone'.[165]

Indeed, one Dutch writer has expressed the view that the reason why the Constitution of the Netherlands fails to guarantee a right to depart is that this right is considered as natural and therefore pre-constitutional.[166] Before the Dutch ratification of the International Covenant on Civil and Political Rights, the Court of Appeal of Arnhem referred to the 'established principle that nationals may leave . . . the territory of their State'.[167]

Under the present Dutch law,[168] the underlying philosophy is 'that Netherlanders should, in principle, only be subject to special obligations relating to frontier control insofar as this is indispensable for the control of aliens.'[169] Dutch nationals are therefore free to cross the border at will; but they may be required to prove their Dutch nationality by producing travel documents or in some other satisfactory manner.[170] Dutch nationality may be proved by the use of the Dutch language, by statements of reliable third persons or by information obtained by telephone from the population registry in the municipality in which the traveller lives.[171]

The Dutch Minister of Foreign Affairs has in a statement elaborated on the right of a Netherlander to leave the territory of his own country.

> Not being in possession of a passport does not mean that a person cannot leave the country. Every *Nederlander* is free to leave the Netherlands without a passport. At the airports the officers do check whether one is in possession of a valid travel document, including a passport, but this is done only on behalf of the authorities of the country to which the person in question wishes to travel and of the airline with which he has booked.[172]

In the case of aliens, the right to depart has always been recognized in fact. The alien is, however, under an obligation not imposed on a Dutch national to present himself at a frontier control officer and a produce a travel document.[173] Exit visas are not required.

THE LAW OF JAPAN

Japanese law contains no legislative provisions placing restrictions upon the right of a national or of an alien to leave the territory of that country; nor is there any Japanese practice of placing such restrictions other than those set out below.

Any person leaving Japan is required to submit to examination of his travel documents at the point of departure. A Japanese national (other than a crewman) who wishes to depart from Japan in order to proceed to another place must carry with him a valid passport. Further he may not depart until he has received 'confirmation of departure from Japan', given in accordance with statutory procedures[174] by an Immigration Inspector.[175] An alien (other than a crewman) who desires to depart from Japan with the intention of proceeding to an area outside Japan is also under a duty to undergo confirmation of departure by the Immigration Inspector and may not leave Japan until such confirmation has been obtained.[176]

For the purpose of securing the effective functioning of criminal justice, Japan has since 1982 maintained a provision whereby confirmation of departure may be withheld from an alien when notification has been received that the alien falls within any of three categories.[177] The first consists of aliens subject to legal process for a crime punishable by death or penal servitude or imprisonment for three years or more and aliens against whom a warrant of arrest or a warrant of legal consultation has been issued. The second consists of aliens who have been sentenced to a period of penal servitude or (whether or not the period is suspended) and who have not yet served that term. The third group consists of aliens against whom a warrant for provisional confinement has been issued in accordance with Japanese extradition law.[178]

In the case of Japanese nationals, there is no power to delay confirmation of departure. Under Article 13 of the Passport Law[179] however, a passport may be withheld from a Japanese national if he is subject to prosecution for a crime punishable with the death penalty or with a penalty for a life term or a limited term of penal servitude for which the prescribed for a life term or a limited term of penal servitude for which the prescribed maximum period is not less than two years; or if a warrant of arrest has been issued in respect of him on suspicion of his having committed such an offence.

THE LAWS OF THE TWO GERMANIES

The Basic Law of the Federal Republic of Germany does not state expressly that all persons shall have the right to leave German territory. That right appears to follow, however, as a necessary consequence of Article 2(1) of the Basic Law, which provides that everyone shall have the right to the free development of his personality.[180] Moreover, the right to leave federal territory without let or hindrance is guaranteed implicitly in the Emigration Protection Law of 26 March 1975.[181] This Act regulates emigration advice services. Commercial emigration advice services require licences, which are issued only to applicants who demonstrate specialised knowledge and reliability.[182] Section 2 of the Emigration Protection Act prohibits the encouragement of emigration through advertising or through the payment of premiums to emigrants.

For the purpose of departing from federal territory a German national requires a passport or federal identity card. An applicant may be denied a passport only if one of five conditions is fullfilled:

i)   if the applicant would, as a passport-holder, endanger the internal or external security or other vital interests of the Federal Republic or of a Federal Land;

ii) if the applicant seeks to escape prosecution for a sentence pending against him in the Federal Republic;

iii) if the applicant seeks to evade his fiscal responsibilities or to infringe or circumvent customs and currency regulations.

iv) if the applicant seeks to evade his legal liability to provide maintenance; or

v)   if the applicant seeks to perform unauthorised service in a foreign army.[183]

The possibility of restraining a German national from leaving federal territory by refusing to issue a passport is even more limited than might at first sight appear. All German nationals over 16 years of age are issued with identity cards and are free to travel with an identity card alone to States members of the Organization for Economic Cooperation and Development.[184]

Particular exit restrictions are, however, imposed pursuant to the Conscription Act[185] and the Civilian Service Act[186]. Under the former[187] men of conscriptionable age who are liable to military service and are resident in the Federal Republic may not leave the area of application of the Act[188] for a period exceeding three months without first obtaining permission from the competent district recruiting office. The same restriction applies *mutatis mutandis* to men performing civilian service and to recognized conscientious objectors.[189] If the Federal Republic is in a state of alert, or under attack, the provisions of the Conscription Act are tightened to the effect that no man liable to military service may leave the area of application of the Act at any time without authorization.[190]

A foreign national is not required to possess a passport or identity card when leaving the territory of the Federal Republic. He may, however, be prevented from leaving that territory in any of five circumstances:

i)   if he endangers the security of the Federal Republic;

ii) if he seeks to evade prosecution for an offence or a sentence or collection of a fine imposed on him:

iii) if he infringes a provision of fiscal law, including customs, import, export or transit of goods or their introduction into federal territory;

iv) if he seeks to evade his legal liability to provide maintenance; or

v)   if he seeks to evade performance of compulsory public service.[191]

In the case of the German Democratic Republic, there is no constitutional guarantee of the right to depart; and while legislation on the subject of travel is ample[192] the right to leave the territory of the Republic receives only fleeting mention. The Ordinance on Matters of Family Reunification and Marriage between Citizens of the German Democratic Republic and Aliens sets out the legal conditions and procedures for citizens of the German Democratic Republic who wish to transfer their permanent residence to another State. This Ordinance and the accompanying Regulation for its implementation[193] have been drafted in the light of the Final Act of the Conference on Security and Cooperation in Europe and the recommendations made at the subsequent meeting of that Conference in Madrid.

In particular the Ordinance and accompanying Regulation make provision for decisions to be taken within six months of the receipt of any application for permission to depart for the purposes of family reunification. An applicant has no absolute right to receive such permission; for the latter may be refused on any of the grounds set out in Article 12 paragraph (3) of the International Covenant on Civil and Political Rights.[194] There is, however, provision for appeal in the event of refusal. Moreover, a fresh application may be made if the reasons for denying the application have ceased to exist.

Where the family connections are not sufficient to satisfy the authorities that permission should be given, or the applicant seeks to depart for reasons other than family reunification, there is no statutory right to leave German territory and in particular no right to receive a passport for the purpose. Provision is made for the ready issuance of passports for visits to certain Socialist countries. In consequence of bilateral arrangements, visits for the purpose of official business may be made without visas by citizens of the German Democratic Republic bearing official or diplomatic passports, when travelling to Algeria, Austria, Cyprus, Kampuchea, Laos, Nicaragua, Tunisia, the People's Democratic Republic of Yemen and Yugoslavia.

Applicants who are unable to satisfy the authorities that it would be right to permit them to leave for reasons of family reunification have no statutory claim to receive permission to depart from the territory of the German Democratic Republic. Their principal legal obstacle is the absence of a statutory entitlement to a passport, without which it is not lawful to cross the frontier.[195] The physical obstacles are, perhaps, sufficiently well known. Even so, the practice of the German Democratic Republic does not provide evidence of the absence of any right under international law to depart from one's own country. The Democratic Republic is a party to the International Covenant on Civil and Political Rights[196] and proclaims its policy to be fully in accordance with that Covenant, including Article 12(2) thereof. In particular it maintains that the restrictions imposed in the Democratic Republic 'are necessary to protect national security' within the meaning of Article 12(3).

The right to leave one's country assumes at present particular significance for the developing countries of Africa in view of the emigration from those countries of skilled personnel. Several such States, particularly in Franco-phone Africa, maintain legal provisions designed to restrict that emigration, although such provisions are by no means universally enforced.

In the case of Chad, nationals are required to possess an identity card or passport together with an exit permit (*'autorisation de voyage'*) in order to cross the frontier. Exit permits are issued by the Ministry of the Interior. Although not a party to the International Covenant on Civil and Political Rights, Chad has ratified to the International Convention on the Elimination of All Forms of Racial Discrimination and recognizes expressly the right to leave one's own country. In a Communication from the Chadian Minister of Foreign Affairs to the United Nations' Under Secretary-General for Human Rights, dated 27 July 1985, the former wrote as follows:

> *En dépit de l'article 13 de la Declaration Universelle des droits de l'homme et de l'article 12 du Pacte international relatif aux droits à toute personne de quitter tout pays y compris le sien, et de revenir dans son pays, it n'en demeure pas moins que de nombreuses personnes restent toujours privées du droit de quitter leur pays ou d'y revenir, notamment nos frères noirs d'Afrique du sud ...*

> *Si le droit à toute personne de quitter tout pays, y compris le sien, et de revenir dans son pays a eté consecré par la Declaration Universelle des Droits de l'Homme, au niveau des legislations nationales, des limites s'imposent. C'est ainsi qu' au Tchad les personnes condamnés ou poursuivies ne peuvent pas quitter le pays ...*[197]

It appears, therefore, that the issuance of passports and exit permits to Chadian nationals desirous of travelling abroad is or should be governed by the principles described in that letter. In particular, an exit permit may be refused to a person convicted or prosecuted in accordance with Articles 23 and 24 of the Civil Code.

The conditions of admission of Chadian students to national colleges make provision for the State to require each student to accept a contract of employment in the public sector, valid for ten years from the date of completion of study. The Chadian authorities therefore reserve the right to refuse an exit permit to any Chadian national who has graduated from a national college and failed to complete his contract of employment. In practice, however, ten-year contracts are not at present required and the Chadian authorities rely upon exhortation to persuade highly qualified emigrants to return.

Foreign nationals are also required to obtain exit visas for the purpose of leaving Chadian territory.[198] Such visas may be refused in the event of conviction of an offence or in the event of prosecution.[199]

In Burkina Faso a recent Presidential Order[200] governs the conditions of entry into the territory of the State, residence there and departure therefrom, in the case of both nationals and aliens. The Order provides that a Burkinan national seeking to depart must be in possession of an identity card and exit visa; but in practice the latter is required only in the event of travel by air.

A foreign national may be prevented from departing from Burkina Faso only in the event of his being charged with an offence against Burkinan law or convicted of such an offence.

In Burkina Faso, as in Chad, those nationals undergoing education in national colleges may be required to perform a contract of service in the public sector. Public employees may be required to complete their agreed period of service but no corresponding obligation is imposed on employees in the private sector.

THE LAW OF INDIA

Although the Constitution of India is not among those which guarantees expressly the right to depart, it contains in Article 21 the stipulation that no restraint may be placed upon an individual's person without the authority of the law. In the leading case of *Satwant Singh Sawhney v. Assistant Passport Officer, New Delhi*[201] the Chief Justice of India, giving the judgment of the Court, said that the real question for determination was 'whether a person living in India has a fundamental right to travel abroad.'[202] This question arose, in the Supreme Court's assessment, whenever an Indian citizen was denied a passport; for if the right to travel was part of personal liberty, a person could not be deprived of it save in accordance with a procedure established by law, which means 'enacted law'.[203]

Relying upon English and American precedent, the Supreme Court concluded that the right to travel was indeed part of 'personal liberty' and was protected by Article 21 of the Constitution.[204] It followed that the petitioner was entitled to a writ of *mandamus* compelling the respondent to issue a passport. The decision is particularly impressive in view of the facts giving rise to the dispute. The petitioner was said to have defrauded the import control authorities. His business activities in Kuwait were under investigation and it was alleged that if he were issued with a passport he might tamper with the evidence in that country.[205]

The decision of the Supreme Court has been subjected to criticism by one eminent author[206] on the ground that 'there can be no right to travel abroad' because 'the right to travel to foreign countries does not exist as a matter of international law' and 'in England no one can claim a passport as of right'. The comment about English law is clearly based upon superseded authority.[207] It fails to take account of the right created by Community law and enforceable in English courts[208] and the courts' recently declared power to review the manner of exercise of perogative power. The comment about international law is based upon the assertion that the Universal Declaration of Human Rights does not constitute a binding source of obligations and upon the observation that the admission of aliens is in principle a matter of discretion. It is suggested, with respect, that the right to leave any country, including one's own is distinct from the claim to enter any particular foreign State. In the sense that the right to leave one's country is recognized in a series of multilateral conventions[210] and in widespread State practice, international law does recognize the one aspect of the right to travel that was material for the purposes of *Satwant Singh Sawhney*.

The right to a passport under Indian law no longer derives from that decision alone but from the Passport Act 1967, which was passed in the wake of the Supreme Court's judgment. This provides (in summary) that a passport authority shall upon application from any Indian citizen, issue him with a passport valid for any country specified in the application unless any of four conditions are fulfilled.[211] Firstly, if the applicant is likely to engage in activities prejudicial to the sovereignity and integrity of India or if his presence abroad is likely to be detrimental to the security of India, the authority may refuse to issue a passport or to endorse it as valid for a particular foreign country. Secondly, the authority may refuse to issue a passport or to endorse it as valid for a particular foreign country if in the opinion of the Central Government the issuance of that document or the making of that endorsement would not be in the public interest or if the applicant's absence from India or his presence in a particular foreign country is likely to prejudice India's good relations with that or any other country. Thirdly, a passport may be refused where the applicant has been convicted of a crime involving moral turpitude[212] or if proceedings in respect of an offence alleged to have been committed by the applicant are pending before a criminal court in India or if a warrant for the applicant's arrest or a summons for his appearance has been issued by a court or if a court has enjoined the applicant not to leave India. Finally the authority may refuse to issue the passport if the applicant has been repatriated at public expense and failed to reimburse the expenditure incurred in his repatriation.

The terms of that Act were considered in 1987 in *Maneka Gandhi v. Union*.[213] In that case the Supreme Court held that the statutory power to withhold a passport or an endorsement in the 'public interest' did not violate Article 14 of the Constitution. The phrase 'public interest' was not unconstitutionally vague and indefinite since it was taken from Article 19 and must be construed accordingly. The result is that no person can be prevented from leaving India except under the authority of a law which is valid both substantively and procedurally. The procedure employed must be reasonable, fair and just; the applicant must be informed of the grounds on which the action is taken and must be given an opportunity to make representations against that decision. In short, the principles of natural justice must be observed.

CONCLUSION

The right to leave any country, including one's own, is guaranteed expressly in a series of multilateral treaties ratified by the greater part of the international community.[214] It is therefore beyond dispute that the right exists in international law, at least in the contractual sense and for the majority of States. Indeed, since adherence to those international instruments is very widespread indeed, since the right to leave is proclaimed in the constitutions of very many States and in the Universal Declaration of Human Rights, since States which are not parties to the International Covenant on Civil and Political Rights have been known to complain of the breach by other non-parties of the right of exit guaranteed by Article 12 of that Covenant, it may be argued that a State no longer has an unqualified entitlement under general international law to prevent its own and foreign nationals from leaving its territory.

Although the human rights covenants draw no distinction between the right of exit for nationals and that for foreigners, international practice distinguishes between the two. Even those States which confer no general right of departure upon their own citizens seldom claim the right to restrain foreign nationals from leaving their territory, save for specific reasons. Dr Weis appears broadly correct in asserting that 'the emigration of aliens can hardly be prevented under international law, except for reasons of national security or public order, criminal prosecutions, outstanding obligations *vis-à-vis* the State or maintenance obligations and, in the case of enemy aliens, in time of war'.[215]

A State's action in restraining a foreign national from leaving its territory, other than upon any of the grounds set out it Article 12(3) of the International Covenant on Civil and Political Rights, would normally warrant a strong diplomatic remonstrance. It is true that no such remonstrance was made in response to Libya's action in refusing to permit a British national, Malcolm Pike, to leave Libyan territory, on the ground that Mr. Pike's employers had failed to meet their fiscal obligations. In that case, Mr. Timothy Eggar, Parliamentary Private Secretary to the Foreign Secretary, stated in Parliament that

Local law there, as in many other Arab countries, provides that an employee may be held responsible for his firm's debts and should not be allowed to leave the country until the debts are settled. The Government cannot interfere in the process of law in Libya any more than we would accept attempts by Libya to interfere in our law.[216]

The statement appears surprisingly mild, in view of the fact that Libya is a party to the Covenant on Civil and Political Rights as well as the International Convention on the Elimination of All Forms of Racial Discrimination; and Libya neither imputed any impropriety to Mr. Pike nor maintained that it was within the power of the United Kingdom to secure compliance with the alleged obligations of his employer, a foreign company having no assets within British jurisdiction. At least the case appears to raise the question whether the restriction imposed by Libyan law was 'necessary to protect the rights and freedom of others'. Indeed, the Parliamentary Secretary's assertion that each State must accept without challenge each other State's local law on these matters is flatly inconsistent with the wording of the international covenants. The United Kingdom's reticence in this case can probably be explained on diplomatic rather than legal grounds. The case arose at a time when the United Kingdom had broken off diplomatic relations with Libya and appears to have been anxious not to prejudice the possibility of improving its exchanges with that country. In March 1986 Libya altered its law on this matter and Mr. Pike was permitted to return to the United Kingdom.

While States commonly impose more onerous and numerous restrictions upon the emigration of their own nationals than upon that of foreigners, those restrictions are not so various as to be incapable of classification nor are they so widely accepted as to escape international scrutiny. The United States, in particular, has complained of the Soviet Union's refusal to permit its citizens to depart more freely and maintained that the Soviet action amounts to a breach of the Helsinki Final Act.[217] International practice appears to indicate that restrictions upon the departure of a State's nationals will not elicit protest from other States if they are imposed on any of seven grounds. All seven may be subsumed within the grounds set out in Article 12(3) of the International Covenant on Civil and Political Rights.

Firstly, prohibitions or restrictions are unobjectionable if justified in the interests of national security. In particular, restrictions are unobjectionable where the national appears likely to engage in actions abroad contrary to the security of his own State. Restrictions are equally permissible under this heading when imposed for the purpose of compelling performance of an obligation to perform military or civilian service. The justification of any such restriction is of course a matter of assessment upon which States may differ; but unsubstantiated assertions of 'national security' will not suffice to shield a

State from remonstrance, as is demonstrated in the case of the Soviet refusal to permit Dr. Alexei Sakharov to depart.[218]

Secondly, restrictions imposed in the interests of public order are acceptable, particularly in the event of the issuance of a warrant for an individual's arrest to face charges of a serious crime, or in the event of his conviction.

Where an individual has failed to reimburse to his State the cost incurred by that State in repatriating him, his national authorities may well consider themselves justified in refusing to issue him with a passport for further travel. Such a restriction, which is liable to be relaxed on the reimbursement of the sums due, will hardly attract protest.

Restrictions upon the departure of nationals (or foreigners) are entirely consonant with accepted international usage when imposed for the purpose of collecting taxes, including customs duties, due from such persons. It seems that restrictions imposed on the travel of an individual will be treated as acceptable when imposed for the purpose of collecting taxes or duties owed by others under that individual's control, including companies owned by the individual or in which he has a substantial share.

Fifthly, international practice does not regard with disfavour prohibitions upon an individual's departure when such action may be justified in the interests of the protection of members of that individual's family for whose welfare he is responsible. Thus, the removal of a child from a jurisdiction without the consent of both parents or guardians is commonly prohibited as is the departure of a parent who proposes to leave in the State of origin a child for whose maintenance he is responsible.

Restrictions will attract no protest when imposed for the purpose of preventing the evasion of a civil liability, including a debt, or for the purpose of evading an obligation to appear before a civil court, as witness or defendant.

Finally, there is growing acceptance of the proposition that a developing country may properly require skilled or highly trained personnel to repay to the community in which they were trained the cost of their education. To this end, such persons are not infrequently required to serve their State of origin for a period, the length of which may be determined in accordance with the needs of the State and the degree of training.

It seems that restriction upon departure imposed other than on any of those seven grounds is incompatible with the International Covenant on Civil and Political Rights. The Human Rights Committee, in its views issued on individual communications received under the Optional Protocol to the Covenant, found violations of Article 12(2) when the government of Uruguay, without giving reasons, revoked or refused to issue passports to certain of its citizens residing abroad.[219] Indeed, there is some authority for the view that the right to depart may not be qualified even by the seven restrictions described in this chapter. The Inter-American Commission on Human Rights has declared that 'no state has the right to prevent an individual from leaving the country, except when that individual is accused of a common law crime.'[220]

NOTES

1. 10 December 1948; 42 A.J.I.L. (1949) Supp. 127; Cmnd. 7662; 131 B.F.S.P. 604, 'Everyone has the right to leave any country, including his own . . .'; *Basic Documents* I.1.
2. 16 December 1966; U.N.G.A. Res. 2200 (XXI), G.A.O.R. 21st Sess., Supp. 16; U.K.T.S. 6 (1977); *Basic Documents* I.2.
3. 7 March 1966; 60 U.N.T.S. 115; U.K.T.S. 77 (1969) *Basic Documents* I.3.
4. 1 August 1975; 14 I.L.M. (1975) 1293; 73 Dept. State Bull. (1973) 373, elaborated in the Concluding Document of the Madrid Session of the Conference on Security and Cooperation in Europe, Madrid, 9 September 1983, 22 I.L.M. (1983) 1395. See H. Russell, 'The Helsinki Declaration: Brobdignag or Lilliput?' 70 A.J.I.L. (1976) 242.
5. 16 September 1963; 58 A.J.I.L. (1964) 334; E.T.S. 46; Cmnd. 2309; *Basic Documents* V.2.
6. 22 November 1969; 65 A.J.I.L. (1971) 679; 9 I.L.M. (1970) 673; *Basic Documents* IX.4.
7. 7.26 June 1981; 21 I.L.M. (1982) 59; *Basic Documents* IX.5.
8. Article 2; 18 October 1961; 529 U.N.T.S. 89; E.T.S. 35: *Basic Documents* V.5.
9. O.J. L257/13 of 15 October 1968, *Basic Documents* VI.5.
10. Article 4; 1 July 1949; 120 U.N.T.S. 71; Cmnd. 7852; *Basic Documents* VII.2. See Chicago Convention on Civil Aviation 1944, 15 U.N.T.S. 295, Articles 13 and 22 and Annex 9 (International Standards and Recommended Practices Facilitation). By Article 3(5)(2): 'Contracting States should provide facilities which would enable their nationals to obtain passports without delay'. See also European Convention on the Legal Status of Migrant Workers. 1977. E.T.S. 93. *Basic Documents* V.7. Article 4(1).
11. Constitution of 9 November 1976, Article 57(2) ('within the framework of the law').
12. Constitution of 31 October 1981, Article 8(1).
13. Constitution of 1853 as amended, Article 14.
14. Basic Law of State of 21 December 1867, R.G.Bl. No 142, amended 1 January 1975, Article 4(2) (freedom of emigration restricted only on specified grounds including military service).
15. Constitution of 10 July 1973, Article 25.
16. Constitution of 30 November 1966, Article 22(1).
17. Constitution of 28 July 1981, Article 19.
18. Constitution of 2 February 1967, Article 7(g).
19. Constitution of 17 October 1969, Article 153 (in time of peace, respecting national law).
20. Canadian Charter of Rights and Freedoms, section 6(1), in Constitution Act 1982 (Canadian citizens).
21. Constitution of 8 August 1980, Article 19(7)(a) (respecting norms established by law, provided rights of third parties not infringed).
22. Constitution of 9 July 1979, Article 10.
23. Constitution of 1949 (as amended), Article 22.
24. Constitution of 1960, Article 13(2).
25. Decree-Law No 36/82, Article 23(2).
26. Constitution of 20 February 1980, Article 148.
27. Interim Constitution of 16 July 1970, Article 24 (except as provided by law).
28. Constitution of 22 December 1947, Article 16 (subject to legal restraints in interests of tax collection and military service).
29. Constitution of 3 May 1947, Article 22.

30. Constitution of 1 January 1952, Article 9(2) (except as provided by law).
31. Constitution of Kenya Act, No. 5 of 1969, Article 81.
32. Constitution of 12 July 1969, Article 14.
33. Constitution of Fifth Republic, Article 13.
34. Constitution of 11 November 1969, Article 31 (save in accordance with law).
35. Draft Constitution of 28 January 1983, Article 13(b).
36. Constitution of 21 September 1964 (as amended) Article 45(1).
37. Constitution of 4 March 1968, Article 15(1).
38. Statute on the Rights and Guarantees of the Nicaraguan People, (Decree No 52) of 21 August 1979, Article 15 (for Nicaraguan citizens).
39. Constitution of October 1979, Article 38.
40. Constitution of 25 August 1967, Article 56.
41. Constitution of 10 January 1973, Article 4(5).
42. Constitution of 2 April 1976 (as amended) Article 44(2).
43. Constitution of 20 December 1978, Article 21.
44. Constitution of 23 June 1983, Article 14.
45. Constitution of 22 February 1979, Article 12.
46. Constitution of 27 October 1979, Article 12.
47. Constitution of 1978 (Act No 12) Article 8.
48. Constitution of 29 December 1978, Article 19(2) (under conditions established by law).
49. Constitution of 22 January 1974, Article 8.
50. Constitution of 1 June 1959 (as amended), Article 10.
51. Constitution of 9 November 1982, No. 17863, Article 23 (restrictions permitted on grounds of national economic situation, civic obligations or criminal investigation and prosecution).
52. Constitution of 25 July 1978, Article 14.
53. Constitution of 23 January 1961 (as amended) Article 64.
54. Constitution of 7 December 1979, Article 22(1).
55. Eg: Constitution of France, 1958 (preamble) Constitution of Ivory Coast (preamble): Constitution of Senegal (preamble).
56. Eg: Constitution of Bahrain of June 1973, Article 19(b); Constitution of Benin of 1979, Article 137; Constitution of Vietnam of 18 December 1980, Article 71 proclaims 'freedom of movement' generally. Cf. Constitution of Burundi of 20 November 1981, Article 15 (freedom of movement within the territory of the Republic). Constitution of Botswana of 30 September 1966, Article 14 (similar); Constitution of the German Democratic Republic, Article 32 (freedom of movement within the State territory subject to national law); Constitution of Jamaica of 1962, Article 16 (freedom of movement within the territory of the Republic); Constitution of Zambia of 25 August 1973, Article 24 (similar).
57. Articles 41 and 42.
58. Constitution of 3–14 September, 3 C.C.L. 239.
59. Act of 17 July 1868, 15 Stat. 223.
60. *Reflecciones sobre Indios y el Derecho de Guerra*, sect. III p. 386 (trans. John Pawley Bate).
61. *Mare Liberum*, 1604–5, chap. 1 (trans. R. van Deman Magoffin).
62. *Le Droit des Gens*, 1757, Book I, chap. XIX, section 221 (trans. C.G. Fenwick).
63. Sir Hersch Lauterpacht, *Invternational Law and Human Rights*, 1950 at pp. 349–50.
64. R. Higgins, 'The Right in International Law of an Individual to Enter, Stay in and Leave a Country', 49 Int. Aff. (1973) 341 at p. 342 and 'Human Rights of Soviet Jews to Leave: Violations and Obstacles', 4 Israel Ybk. Human Rights (1974) 295 at p. 280.
65. *Study of Discrimination in respect of the Right of Everyone to Leave any Country including his Own and to Return to his Country*, 1963, U.N.DOC. E/CN. 4/Sub. 2/229/Rev. 1 p. 58. The conclusion in this respect appears to have been much influenced by the erection of the

Berlin Wall on 13 August 1961. At p. 60 Judge Ingles states that 'comparatively few countries appear to recognize, either in their constitutions, laws or administrative regulations, the right of a national to leave the country'. If this was correct in 1963, it appears less than correct today, for the reasons given in notes 10–58, *supra*. Indeed, in the Progress Report of Mr Mubanga-Chipoya, U.N.DOC. E/CN/Sub. 2/1985/9 paragraph 15 we read that 'In nearly all replies that address the question of the right to leave, it has been stated that this right is guaranteed by constitutional provisions or . . . statutes'.

66. I.e., Article 13(2) of the Universal Declaration of Human Rights, Article 12(2) of the International Covenant on Civil and Political Rights, Article 5(d) of the International Convention on the Elimination of All Forms of Racial Discrimination and Article 2(2) of the Fourth Protocol to the European Convention on Human Rights, *supra*, notes 1, 2, 3 and 5. G. Goodwin-Gill, *International Law and the Movement of Persons between States*, 1978, p. 29.

67. See D. O'Connell, *International Law*, 1970, Vol. I p. 312; L. Sohn and T. Buergenthal, *International Protection of Human Rights*, 1973, pp. 597–617.

68. *Supra*, note 65. Efforts to devise an international instrument on important aspects of the subject were made in advance of the Second World War, notably at the International Conference on the Treatment of Foreigners, 1929. Moreover, the Asian-African Legal Consultative Committee prepared draft Principles concerning Admission and Treatment of Aliens, including the right to depart, in Tokyo, 1961. Higgins describes Ingles' study as 'the best work on common interpretations of [Articles 12(3) of the Covenant on Civil and Political Rights]', see 'Human Right of Soviet Jews to Leave: Violations and Obstacles', *supra* note 63 at p. 279.

69. *Supra*, note 1, Article 29(2).

70. *Supra*, note 65 at p. 36.

71. It seems difficult to make sense of the use of the French expression *ordre public* in the English version of the Covenant if, as Dr Ingles proposes, the English meaning is to be given to the term 'public order'. Moreover, in the Universal Declaration the English 'public order' is rendered by the French '*ordre public*'. Even in its French sense, however, *ordre public* is not of limitless significance.

72. *Supra*, note 65 at pp. 40–46.

73. *Ibid*, Art. V, p. 67.

74. See S. Liskovsky, 'The Contribution of Jose D. Ingles' in K. Vasak and S. Liskovsky (eds), *The Right to Leave and to Return*, American Jewish Committee (New York) 1976, p. 487. See further R. Torovsky, 'Freedom of Movement: Right of Exit', 4 Jo. Int. Comm. Jur. (1962). Nevertheless, in 1963 the United Nations Conference on International Trade and Tourism, attended by 87 States and various international and non-governmental organizations, declared in Rome that 'freedom of travel from country to country should be the inalienable right of all'.

75. 10–14 January 1968.

76. Report of the Colloquium, p. 85.

77. *Ibid.*, p. 88.

78. *Supra*, note 2.

79. *Supra*, note 76 at p. 91.

80. 21 June 1972. See A. Cassese, 'International Protection of the Right to Leave and to Return', in *Studi in orore di Manlio Udina*, 1975. Vol. I, p. 219; R. James, 'Right to Travel Abroad', 42 Fordham L. Rev. (1974) 838.

81. *Supra*, note 4. See D. Turack, 'Freedom of Transnational Movement: the Helsinki Accord and Beyond', 11 Vand. J. Trans. L. (1978) 585; S. Roth, 'The Conference on Security and Cooperation in Europe and Soviet Jewry', (1974–I) *Soviet Jewish Affairs*.

82. Quoted in Russell, *supra*, note 4 at p. 244.
83. Resolution 1982/23 of 9 September 1982, following Secretary General's report E/CN. 4/Sub. 2/1982/27.
84. Resolution 1984/21 of 29 August 1984, following preliminary report E/CN. 4/Sub. 2/1984/10.
85. E/CN. 4/Sub. 2/1985/9; *supra*, note 65.
86. It is apparent from Annex II to the progress report that at the date of its publication communications had been received from only 23 States, approximately one fifth of the membership of the United Nations. Neither the United States nor the Soviet Union had by that date submitted a reply, nor had China, France or India.
87. *Ibid.*, para. 16.
88. *Ibid.*, paras. 35, 37.
89. See R. Pomp and O. Oldman, 'Tax Measures in Response to the Brain Drain', 20 Harv. Int. L. J. (1979) 1.
90. Prof. J. Bhagwati, ed. in *Taxing the Brain Drain: A Proposal* (Vol. I) and *The Brain Drain and Taxation*, (Vol II) 1976 and 'International Migration and the Highly Skilled: Economics, Ethics and Taxes', 1 Third World Q. (1979) 17 at pp. 22–23.
91. Pomp and Oldman, *supra*, note 88 at p. 43.
92. This was requested by the Commission in Resolution 1985/22.
93. *Supra*, text at note 72.
94. *Kent v. Dulles*, (1958) 357 U.S. 116, 2 L. Ed. 2d. 1204; *Aptheker v Secretary of State*, (1964) 378 U.S. 500, 12 L. Ed. 2d. 992; *Zemel v Rusk*, (1965) 381, U.S. 1, 14 L. Ed. 2d. 179; *United States v Lamb*, (1967) 385 U.S. 475, 17L. Ed. 2d. 526; *Califano v Aznavorian*, (1978) 439 U.S. 170, 58L. Ed. 2d. 435.
95. (1955) 96 App. D.C. 287, 225 F. 2d. 938.
96. *Walker v. Chief Quarantine Officer*, (1943) 69 F. Supp. 980 (Panama Canal Zone).
97. *Supra*, note 94.
98. *Califano v. Aznavorian, supra* note 94; *MacEwan v. Rusk*, (1964) 228 F. Supp. 306; *Reyes v United States*, (1958 258 F. 2d. 774; *Berrigan v. Sigler*, (1974) 162 App. D.C. 378, 499 F. 2d. 514.
99. See 'Supreme Court's Views as to the Concept of 'Liberty' under Due Process Clauses of the Fifth and Fourteenth Amendments', 47 L. Ed. 2d. 975 para. 5.
100. *Woodward v. Rogers*, (1972) 344 F. Supp. 974.
101. 22 U.S.C.S. para. 211(a).
102. *Zemel v. Rusk, supra*, note 94. The restriction was also authorised by section 215 of the Immigration and Nationality Act of 1952 ('the Walter-McCarren Act'), 8 U.S.C.S. para. 1185; *MacEwan v. Rusk, supra*, note 98. See further *United States v Travis*, (1963) 241 F. Supp. 468.
103. *Supra*, note 94.
104. *Supra*, note 94.
105. 50 U.S.C.S. para. 785.
106. *Schachtman v. Dulles*, (1955) 96 App. D.C. 287.
107. *Califano v. Aznavorian, supra* note 94.
108. *Reyes v. United States, supra* note 98, *United States v Eramdjian*, (1957) 155 F. Supp. 914.
109. *United States v. Davis*, (1973) 482 E. 2d. 893 (the search in this case resulted in the discovery of a loaded revolver).
110. *Monarch Travel Services Inc. v. Associated Cultural Clubs Inc.* 446 F. 2d. 552 (1972).
111. Internal Revenue Code 1954, section 6851; 26 U.S.C.A. Section 6851(d)(i). See *Klaas v. C.I.R.*, 36 T.C. (1961) 239.
112. Act of 27 June 1952, c. 477, 66 Stat. 166 ('The Walter McCarran Act').
113. *Ibid*, section 215; 8 U.S.C.A. section 1185; 40 Am. Jur. 523 para. 1. See D. Turack, 'Selected

Aspects of International and Municipal Law Concerning Passports', 12 Wm. and Ma. L. Rev. (1971) 805, 814–17; Parker, 'The Right to Go Abroad', 40 V.L.R. (1954) 853.

114. *Ibid*, as amended by Public Law 95–426 of 7 October 1978, 92 Stat. 992, section 707(a).

115. Immigration Act 1971, section 1(1).

116. A person has under section 2 of the Immigration Act 1971, as amended by section 39 of the British Nationality Act 1981, the right of abode if he is (a) a British citizen or (b) a Commonwealth citizen who, on the eve of the entry into force of the Act of 1981, was a Commonwealth citizen with a right of abode in the United Kingdom by virtue of sections 2(1)(d) or section 2(2) of the 1971 Act and who has not ceased to be a Commonwealth citizen in the meantime.

117. Immigration Rules, H.C. 169 paras. 3 and 15.

118. Immigration Act 1971, section 4 and schedule 2 paras. 2 and 3.

119. Aliens Order 1953, S.I. No. 1671, Para. 7.

120. Under the Aliens Order 1953, article 1. See 657 H.C. Deb. Col. 119 (23 May, 1969).

121. This is so despite the fact that section 1(4) of the Aliens Restriction Act 1914 provided that a person was presumed an alien until he proved the contrary (a provision reflected today in section 3(8) of the Immigration Act 1971). See *Kopelowitz v. McLaughlan*, (1916) 83 L.J.K.B. 1700; *Simon v. Phillips*, (1916) 85 L.J.K.B. 656; cf. *R v Beadon*, (1933) 24 Cr. App. Rep. 39. The view here expressed is shared by H. Street, *Freedom, the Individual and the Law*, 3rd ed. p. 281 and D. Williams, 'British Passports and the Right to Travel', 23 I.C.L.Q. (1974) 642.

122. *Per* Lord Alverstone, C.J. in *R v. Brailsford*. [1905] 2 K.B. 730, 745, quoted with approval by Ashworth. J in *R v. Home Secretary, ex parte Shadeo Bhurosah*, [1968] 1 QB. 266, 274.

123. The view is based on *R v. Brailsford, R v. Home Secretary, ex parte Shadeo Bhurosah, supra*, note 122, and *Public Prosecutor v. Koi*, [1968] 1 All E.R. 419. See Lord Diplock, 'Passports and Protection in International Law', 32 T.G.S. (1942) 42 at 44; C. Parry, *Nationality and Citizenship Laws of the Commonwealth and the Republic of Ireland*, 1961, Vol. I. p 13; J. Jones, *British Nationality Law*, 1956, pp. 291–292; H. Wade, *The Times* 7 August 1968.

124. *The Times*, 9 May 1968, page 1 col. f. For Parliamentary question and statement, see 764 H.C.Deb. Cols. 232–33, 270 (Written Answers, 9 May 1968), 623 (Oral Answers, 9 May 1968); for Parliamentary debate see 764 H.C.Deb. Cols 1041–1116 (14 May 1968).

125. *The Times*, 9 July 1968, page 1 col. b. and 15 July 1968, page 2 col. h.

126. Council Directive 68/360/EEC of 15 October 1968, O.J. 1968, O.J. Sp. Ed. 1968, 485, Article 2(2); *Basic Documents* VI.2.

127. Case 30/77, *R v. Bouchereau*, [1977] E.C.R. 1999.

128. For the definition of a 'United Kingdom national' see Note dated 31 December 1982 from H.M. Ambassador, Rome to Italian Foreign Minister, UKTS (1983) 67; O.J. 1983 C 23/1.

129. The EEC Treaty in Article 48 speaks of travel for the purpose of accepting an offer of employment actually made. The European Court, however, has spoken of travel for 'the purposes intended by the Treaty, *to look for* or pursue a gainful activity': see Case 48/75, *Royer*, [1976] E.C.R. 497 at 512; Case 118/75, *Watson and Belmann*, [1976] E.C.R. 1185 at 1204.

130. Parliamentary Commissioner Act 1967, section 4 and schedule 2 amended by the Secretary of State for Foreign and Commonwealth Affairs Order, 1968, S.I. No. 1657, Article 4. In at least one case the Ombudsman has found that there was maladministration resulting in the issuance of a passport in the wrong form. See *Second Report of the Parliamentary Commissioner for Administration*, 1968–69, 29 at 30, Case No. C831/67.

131. *Council of Civil Service Unions v. Minister of the Civil Service*, [1984] 3 All E.R. 935.

132. See *Secretary of State for Education and Science v. Tameside Metropolitan Borough Council*, [1977] A.C. 1014; *Congreve v. Home Office*, [1976] Q.B. 629; *Nakkuda Ali v. Jayaratne*, [1951] A.C. 66 at 76–77.

133. *White v. Milburn*, 107 L.J. Newsp. (1957) 401; *Fenton v. Callis*, [1969] 1 Q.B. 200; *Parsons v. Burk*, [1971] N.Z.L.R. 171.
134. Sir A. Fitzherbert considered that at common law there was a right to depart the realm without the King's permission: *New Natura Brevium*, 1794, *passim*. That view was shared by Sir W. Blackstone, *Commentaries*, Vol. I, p. 265 and by J. Beames, *Brief View of the Writ Exeat Regno*, 1824. See J. Bridge, 'The Case of the Rugby Football Team and the High Prerogative Writ', 88 L.Q.R. (1972) 83.
135. Fitzherbert, *loc. cit.*; Coke, *Institutes*, Vol. II, para. 34 and Vol. III, para 179.
136. *Flack v Holm*, (1820), 1 Jac. and W. 405 and 413. See further Holdsworth, *History of English Law*, Vol. I, p. 230.
137. *Infra*, text at note 143.
138. See Bridge, *supra*, note 134 at pp. 86–88 and sources cited there.
139. Sir F. Maitland, *Constitutional History of England*, p. 418.
140. *Parsons v Burk, supra*, note 134.
141. *Attorney General v De Keyser's Royal Hotels Ltd.*, [1920] A.C. 508.
142. *Bayer, A.G. v Winter and Others*, The Times L.R., 15 February 1986.
143. *Smith v Peters*, (1875) L.R. 20 Eq 511 at 512–513; *Astro Exito S.A. v Southland Enterprise Co Ltd.*, [1982] Q.B. 1248.
144. Such were the facts of *Bayer, A.G. v Winter, supra*, note 142.
145. Statute on the Passport System in the U.S.S.R., confirmed by Decree of the U.S.S.R. Council of Ministers, 28 August 1974, *Sobranie Postanovlenii Pravitel'stva SSSR* (1974) No. 19, item 109, reprinted in W. Butler, *The Soviet Legal System*, 1978, p. 557. See also principles of Civil Legislation of the U.S.S.R. and Union Republics, Article 9, as amended by Ordinance of the Council of Ministers No. 660 of 19 June 1969.
146. Confirmed by Decree of the U.S.S.R. Council of Ministers, 22 September 1970, *Sobranie Postanovlenii Pravitel'stva SSSR* (1970) No. 18, item 139, Butler, *supra*, note 145 at 553.
147. Made by the Council of Ministers, 23 August 1986 (not yet published).
148. M. Robin, 'Soviet Emigration Law and International Obligations under United Nations Instruments', 13 Jo. Int. L. and Econ. (1979) 403.
149. V. Chalidze, 'The Right of a Convicted Citizen to Leave his Country', 8 Harv. Civ. R. – Civ. Lib. Rev. (1973) 1.
150. Criminal Code of the R.S.F.S.R., Article 83. By Article 64 'Flight abroad or refusal to return from abroad to the U.S.S.R.' is punishable by deprivation of freedom for 10–15 years.
151. Statute on the Ministry of Justice of the U.S.S.R. confirmed by Decree of the U.S.S.R. Council of Ministers, 21 March 1972, No. 194, *Sobranie Postanovlenii Pravitel'stva SSSR* (1972), No. 6, item 32, as amended, 28 April 1976, *Sobranie Postanovlenii Pravitel'stva SSSR* (1976) No. 7, item 38; reprinted. Butler, *supra*, note 145 at pp. 235–51.
152. On the procedure for considering Proposals, Applications and Appeals of Citizens, Edict of the Praesidium of the U.S.S.R. Supreme Soviet, 12 April 1968, *Vedomosti SSSR* (1968) No. 17, item 44, superseding Decree on Considering the Appeals of Working People and Taking the Necessary Measures in Regard to Them, 14 December 1933, *Vedomosti SSSR, 1933, no. 26, item 153*.
153. See in particular M. Guggenheim, 'Of the Right to Emigrate and Other Freedoms: the Feldman Case', 5 Human Rights (1975) 75; R. Higgings, 'Human Right of Soviet Jews to Leave', 4 Israel Ybk. H.R. (1974) 275; W. Korey, 'The Right to Leave for Soviet Jews: Legal and Moral Aspects', 1 Sov. Jew. Aff. (1971) 5.
154. Laws 572 and 573, 3 August 1972.
155. Chalidze, *supra*, note 149, at 7.
156. H. Berman, 'Rights of Convicted Citizens to Emigrate', 8 Harv. Civ. R. – Civ. Lib. L. Rev. (1973) 15; W. Bennett, 'Terrifying Remedy: A Response to V.N. Chalidze's "Right of a

128

Convicted Citizen to Leave his Country"', 8 Harv. Civ. R. – Civ. Lib. L. Rev. (1973) 536.

157. See Goodwin-Gill, *supra*, note 66.

158. Supplement to Treaty of Peace between Germany and R.S.F.S.R., 27 August 1918, Article 10, reprinted in I. Shapiro, *Soviet Treaty Series 1917–28* (1950) at 23. For this and other examples, see M. Knisbacher, 'Aliyah of Soviet Jews: Protection of the Right to Emigration under International Law', 14 Harv. I.L.J. (1973) 89 at 92.

159. 281 U.N.T.S. 121.

160. See *The Position of Soviet Jewry*, 1980 and 1985 (World Conference on Soviet Jewry, London).

161. See the speech of W. Dam, Acting Secretary of State, before the Senate Judiciary Committee on 29 September 1982, 2069 Dept. State Bull. (1982) p. 58. See further, International Council of the World Conference on Soviet Jewry, *The Position of Soviet Jewry: Their Rights and the Helsinki Accords*, 1985 at 6.

162. See generally Y. Dinstein, 'Freedom of Emigration and Soviet Jewry', 4 Israel Ybk. H.R. (1974) 266.

163. Ratified 11 December 1978.

164. *Supra*, note 2.

165. Bijl. Hand. II (1975–6) 13 932, no. 3, p. 13.

166. See Partsch, 'The Right to Leave and Return in Western Europe and other Non-Communist States', in Vasak and Likovsky, *supra*, note 74 at 80–81.

167. 8 August 1977, N.J. (1977) No. 567.

168. Aliens Act (*Vreemdelingenwet* of 13 January 1965, Stb. No. 40; Aliens Decree (*Vreemdelingenbesluit*) of 19 September 1966, Stb. No. 387 and Aliens Regulation (*Voorschrift Vreemdelingen*) of 22 September 1966.

169. Explanatory Memorandum to the Aliens Decree, pp. 916–17, cited by A. de Rouw, 'Some Aspects of the Right to Leave and to Return with Special Reference to Dutch Law and Practice', 12 Neths Ybk I.L. (1981) 45 at 60.

170. Aliens Decree, Article 25.

171. De Rouw, *supra*, note 169.

172. Hand. II (1978–9) p. 2143, quoted by de Rouw, *supra* note 169 at 61.

173. Aliens Decree, Articles 22 and 23.

174. Ministry of Justice Ordinance.

175. Immigration Control and Refugees Recognition Act, No 319 of 1951, Article 60.

176. *Ibid.*, Article 25.

177. *Ibid.*, Article 25-2.

178. I.e., Surrender of a Fugitive from Justice Law, No 68 of 1953.

179. See Buraku Kaiho Kenkyusho, *Human Rights in Japan*, 1984.

180. *Ibid.*

181. *Gesetz zum Schutze der Auswanderer* of 26 March 1975, B.G.Bl. 1975 I, 774.

182. No licence is required, however, for advisory centres run by public corporations or by charities nor for organizations charged to recruit staff for employment abroad in accordance with the *Arbeitsforderungsgesetz* (Work Promotion Law) of 25 June 1969, B.G.Bl. 1969 I, 582.

183. *Gesetz uber das Passwesen* (Passport Law) of 4 March 1952, B.G.Bl. 1952 I, 290, section 7 (1).

184. *Verordung zur Durchfuhrung das Gesetzes uber das Passwesen* (Supplementary Decree on Passport Law) of 12 June 1967, B.G.Bl. 1967 I, 598.

185. *Wehrpflichtgesetz* (Conscription Law) of 6 May 1983, B.G.Bl. 1983, 529 and *Wehrpflichtgesetz* (Conscription Law) of 13 June 1986, B.G.Bl. 1986 I, 879.

186. *Gesetz uber der Zivildienst* of 29 September 1983, B.G.Bl. 1983 I, 1221; amended B.G.Bl. 1984 I, 1954.

187. Section 3(2).
188. I.e., the Federal Republic of Germany.
189. *Gesetz uber der Zivildienst, supra* note 186, section 23(4).
190. *Wehrpflichtgesetz, supra* note 185, section 48(1)(5)(b) and 48(2).
191. *Auslandergestz* (Aliens Law) of 28 April 1965, B.G.Bl. 1965 I, 353, section 19(2).
192. Passport Act, 28 June 1979, *Gesetzblatt der DDR*, Teil I, No 17, p. 148; Decree on Passport and Visa Matters of 28 June 1979, *Gesetzblatt der DDR*, Teil I, No 17, p. 151; Aliens Act of 28 June 1979, *Gesetzblatt der DDR*, Teil I, No 17, p. 154; Order Governing Travel of Citizens of the DDR of 15 February 1982, *Gesetzblatt der DDR*, Teil I, No 9, p. 187; Ordinance on Matters of Family Reunification of 15 September 1983, *Gesetzblatt der DDR*. Teil I, No 26, p. 254; First Regulation for the Implementation or Ordinance of Matters of Family Reunification of 15 September 1983, *Gesetzblatt der DDR*, Teil I, No 26 p. 255.
193. *Supra*, note 192.
194. *Supra*, note 2. See also text at notes 69–70.
195. Individuals who apply unsuccessfully for permission to leave and try to persuade the authorities to change their decision have been prosecuted under Articles 99, 100, 214 and 219 of the Penal Code. See generally J. Toman, 'The Right to Leave and to Return to Eastern Europe', 5 Israel Ybk. H.R. (1975) 215.
196. Ratified, 17 December 1973.
197. Disclosed and reproduced with consent of Chadian Embassy, Brussels. By South African law, no person may leave the territory of the State unless he is in possession of a passport or permit to leave: Departure from the Union Regulation Act No 34 of 1955, sections 2 and 5. (A statement made by an attorney by way of plea of mitigation does not constitute evidence of guilt in the event of a charge of breach of those sections! See *S* v. *Makhubo*, (1968) 2 SA 646.) The Secretary of State for the Interior is, however, under a duty to issue a permit to any person who satisfies him that he wishes to leave the territory of the State permanently: ibid., section 5.
198. See Decrees Nos 110/PG of 2 June, 1961, 211/INT-SUR of 4 December 1961 and Order (*Arrêté*) No 3109/INT-SUR of 4 December 1961.
199. Penal Code, Article 23 and 24.
200. *Ordonnance* No 84-049/CNR/Pres of 4 August 1984.
201. [1967] A.I.R. (S.C.) 1836. The decision has been subjected to criticism on unusual procedural grounds. Subba Rao, C.J., who presided, announced shortly after the hearing that he proposed to resign his office as Chief Justice in order to offer himself for election as President. He therefore gave his judgment (that of the majority) promptly, before having an opportunity of perusing the dissenting judgment. For criticism of this course of action and attendant case-law, see H.M. Seervai, *Constitutional Law of India: A Critical Commentary*, 3rd. ed., 1984, Vol II, p. 2081.
202. *Supra*, note 201 at 1841. See further K. Nambiar, 'Right to a Passport', 7 Ind. J.I.L. (1967) 526; M. Ghouse, 'The Vicissitudes of Freedom of Exit in India', 17 A.J. Comp. L. (1969) 559.
203. *A.K. Gopalan v. The State*, [1950] A.I.R. (S.C.) 27.
204. See further *Fateh Mahammed v. Delhi Administration*, [1963] A.I.R. 1035; *Andhra Pradesh v. Abdul Khader*, [1961] A.I.R. 1467; *Union of India v. Ghaus Mohammed*, [1961] A.I.R. 1526; *Sadashiva Rao v. Union of India*, [1965] 2 Mys. L.J. 605; *Choitiram Verhomal Jethwani v. A.G. Kazi*, [1967] Bomb. L.R. 544.
205. Further, the judgment is impressive in view of the fact that the right of internal free movement is guaranteed by Article 19 of the Constitution, which might have been taken to imply that freedom of movement is not covered by Artied 21. See *Kharak Singh v. Uttar Pradesh*. [1964] 1 S.C.R. 332 at 345.

130

206. H.M. Seervai, *supra*, note 201 at 2080 and 2087.
207. *R. v. Brailsford, supra*, note 122.
208. Council Directive 68/360/EEC, *supra*, note 126.
209. *Council of Civil Service, supra* note 131.
210. *Supra*, notes 1–9.
211. Passport Act 1967 (No. 15) section 5(2).
212. The expression is adopted into Indian law from section 212(a) of the United States' Immigra-
     tion and Nationality Act, 66 Stat. 404; 8 U.S.C.A. para. 1182(9). See *Ramirez v. U.S.
     Immigration and Naturalization Service*, (App. D.C.) 413 F 2d. 405 (1969).
213. [1978] A.I.R. (S.C.) 597.
214. The International Covenant on Civil and Political Rights had in 1985 been ratified by 83
     States; the Convention on the Elimination of All Forms of Racial Discrimination by 124; and
     35 States participated in the Conference on Security and Cooperation in Europe.
215. *Supra*, note 66.
216. 88 H.C. Deb. (N.S.) col. 528 (5 December 1985).
217. 2091 Dept. of State Bull. (1984) 36.
218. *Ibid.* See also speech of U.K. Representative to C.S.C.E., Mr Philip Hurr, dated 20
     November 1986 (distributed by Foreign Office).
219. *Sophie Videl Martins v. Uruguay* (No 57/1979) U.N.G.A.O.R. 37th Sess. Supp. No. 40
     (A/37/80) 1982, Annex XIV, para. 9; *Samuel Lichtensztejn v. Uruguay* (No. 108/1981) *ibid*,
     Annex XVII, para 10; *Carlos Varela Nunez v. Uruguay* (No 108/1981) *ibid* Annex XXIII,
     para 10.
220. Inter-American Commission on Human Rights, *Sixth Report on the Situation of Political
     Prisoners in Cuba* (1979) O.A.S. Doc. No OEA/Ser. L/V/II 48; doc. 7 p. 9.

BIBLIOGRAPHY

R. Aybay, 'The Right to Leave and the Right to Return', 1 Comp. L. Ybk. (1977) 121.
W. Bennett, 'Terrifying Remedy: A Response to V.N. Chalidze's Right of a Convicted Citizen to
  Leave His Country', 8 Harv. Civ. R.-Civ. Lib. L. Rev. (1973) 536.
H. Berman, 'Right of Convicted Citizens to Emigrate', 8 Harv. Civ. R.-Civ. Lib. L. Rev. (1973)
  15.
P. Boldex, 'The Right to Travel and Passport Revocation', 8 Brooklyn J. Int. L. (1982) 391.
L. Boudin, 'The Constitutional Right to Travel', 56 Col. L. R. (1956) 47.
J. Bridge, 'The Case of the Rugby Football Team and the High Perogative Writ', 88 L.Q.R. (1972)
  83.
A. Cassese, 'International Protection of the Right to Leave and to Return', *Studi in onore di
  Manlio Udina*, 1975 Vol. I, 219.
V. Chalidze, 'Right of a Convicted Citizen to Leave his Country', 8 Harv. Civ. R.-Civ. Lib. L.
  Rev. (1973) 1.
Y. Dinstein, 'Freedom of Emigration and Soviet Jewry', 4 Israel Ybk. H.R. (1974) 266.
A. Dowty, *The New Serfdom: Control of International Movement*, 1986.
M. Ghouse, 'The Vicissitudes of Freedom of Exit in India', 17 A.J. Comp. L. (1969) 559.
M. Guggenheim, 'Of the Right to Emigrate and Other Freedoms in the Feldman Case', 5 Human
  Rights (1975) 75.
H. Hannum, *The Right of Leave and Return in International Law and Practice*, 1985.
R. Higgins, 'Human Right of Soviet Jews to Leave', 4 Israel Ybk. H.R. (1974) 275.
J. Ingles, *Study of Discrimination in respect of the Right of Everyone to Leave any Country
  including his Own and to Return to his Country*, United Nations, E/CN. 4/Sub. 2/229/Rev. 1,
  1963.

S. Jagerskjold, 'Freedom of Movement', L. Henkin (ed) *The International Bill of Rights*, 1981, 166.

R. James, 'Right to Travel Abroad', 42 Fordham L. Rev. (1974) 838.

M. Knisbacher, 'Aliyah of Soviet Jews: Protection of the Right of Emigration under International Law', 14 Harv. Int. L.J. (1973) 89.

W. Korey, 'The Right to Leave for Soviet Jews: Legal and Moral Aspects', 1 Soviet Jewish Affairs (1971) 5.

S. Liskovsky, 'The Contribution of Jose D. Ingles', K. Vasak and S. Liskovsky (eds), *The Right to Leave and to Return*, American Jewish Committee (New York) 1976, 487.

V. Nanda, 'The Right to Movement and Travel Abroad', 1 Denver J.I.L. and Pol. (1971) 109.

N. Onuoha Chukunta, 'Human Rights and the Brain Drain', 15 Int. Mig. (1977) 281.

R. Pomp and O. Oldman, 'Tax Measures in Response to the Brain Drain', 20 Harv. Int. L.J. (1979) 1.

M. Robin, 'Soviet Emigration Law and International Obligations under United Nations Instruments', 13 Jo. Int. L. and Econ. (1978–9) 403.

A. de Rouw, 'Some Aspects of the Right to Leave and Return with Special Reference to Dutch Law and Practice', 12 Neths, Ybk Int. L. (1975) 215.

J. Toman, 'The Right to Leave and Return to Eastern Europe', 3 Israel Ybk. H.R. (1975) 215.

R. Torovsky, 'Freedom of Movement: Right of Exit', 4 Jo. Int. Comm. Jur. (1962).

D. Turack, *The Passport in International Law*, 1972. 'Freedom of Transnational Movement: the Helsinki Accord and Beyond', 11 Vand. J. Trans. L. (1978) 585.

United Nations Economic and Social Committee' Analysis of Current Trends and Developments regarding the Right to Leave any Country including One's Own: Progress Report by Mr. Mubanga-Chipoya, 10 July 1985, E/CN. 4/Sub. 2/1985/9.

P. Weis, 'The Right to Leave and to Return in the Middle East', 5 Israel Ybk. H.R. (1975) 322.

D. Williams, 'British Passports and the Right to Travel', 23 I.C.L.Q. (1974) 642.

CHAPTER 4

The Right to Return to One's Country

The principle that every State must admit its own nationals to its territory is accepted so widely that its existence as a rule of law is virtually beyond dispute. The principle is often implied by those who assert that each State has the right to deny admission to aliens.[1] Among the more specialised writers, those who defend the existence of the principle include François,[2] Weis,[3] Goodwin-Gill,[4] and Van Panhuys. The latter states that the 'duty to admit nationals is considered so important a consequence of nationality that it is almost equated with it'.[5] The Court of Justice of the European Communities acknowledged the rule in Case 41/74, *Van Duyn* v *Home Office,* holding that 'it is a principle of international law . . . that a State is precluded from refusing its own nationals the right of entry or residence'.[6]

Nevertheless, the precise meaning of the principle is disputed and in some respects obscure. The first problem is that of identifying the quality of the obligation; for it remains to be determined whether the duty of admission is merely the corollary of a second State's right to expel aliens, or the product of an internationally protected right to return to one's own country. The second difficulty is that of determining whether a State is under any duty to permit nationals from outlying territories or dependencies to enter the metropolitan territory. The third problem is posed by the denaturalization of an individual or minority, followed by expulsion. In such cases, the question arises whether a foreign State has any duty to recognize the efficacy of the denaturalization.

THE QUALITY OF THE OBLIGATION

It is clear that each State owes to each other State a duty to refrain from frustrating the latter's right to expel aliens from its territory. From this it then follows that when a State exercises its right to expel aliens, their State of nationality must admit them if no other country will do so.[7] In this sense, the duty to admit nationals is clearly a corollary of the right of expulsion. The question remains whether the duty is owed to the expelling State exclusively. This issue is of practical significance; for if the duty is owed only to an expelling State, it can arise only in the event of the lawful exercise of that State's rights. In the event of an unlawful expulsion, the State of nationality would be under no obligation to admits its nationals, at least in relation to the expelling State and possibly in relation to other States. Furthermore, if the obligation were merely the corollary of a right of expulsion, it would arise only in those cases in which no foreign State is prepared to permit the expelled individual or minority to settle in its territory.

The view that the duty is owed only to the expelling State derives support from authoritative writers who addressed the question a generation ago. Thus, Van Panhuys wrote that:

> This duty corresponds to the right of expulsion of the State of residence ... According to international law, the duty of admission only applies towards foreign States and not towards the national.[8]

A similar view was expressed by Leibholz.[9] Lord Denning gave further support to that view in *Thakrar v Secretary of State*.[10] In that case it was argued that a British protected person expelled from Uganda was entitled to be admitted to the United Kingdom notwithstanding the terms of the Immigration Act 1971. To that end his counsel relied upon the duty of admission under international law. The Master of the Rolls concluded that the rule of international law is a rule between two States only. It is not a rule between an individual and a State. The expelling State might call on the home State to receive the person whom it expelled; but the individual could not pray the rule in aid for his own benefit.

In these passages Van Panhuys and Lord Denning were concerned to dispel the notion that international law confers a right directly upon an individual which the latter can enforce against his own State. However, to acknowledge that the duty of admission is the corollary of the individual's right to return to his own country is not to assert that the right is enforceable by the individual; still less that it is enforceable in a domestic court, in a State of the dualist tradition, in the face of inconsistent national legislation. The duty of admission might reflect the individual's right to return to his country, even if that right is enforceable only by inter-State action or by some special procedure created by treaty. The modern international law of human rights affords several similar examples of individuals' rights enforceable by States.[11]

The right to return to one's own country is now acknowledged as a *human* right in a series of international conventions. In particular, it is expressed in the Universal Declaration of Human Rights,[12] the International Covenant on Civil and Political Rights,[13] the International Covention on the Elimination of All

Forms of Racial Discrimination,[14] the American Convention on Human Rights,[15] the African Charter on Human Rights,[16] and the Fourth Protocol to the European Convention on Human Rights.[17] These modern instruments may be contrasted with the Havana Convention on the Status of Aliens of 20 February 1925, which set out the principle formerly advanced in traditional international law: 'States are required to receive their nationals expelled from foreign soil . . .'[18]

A significant number of modern national constitutions characterise the right to enter one's own country as a fundamental or human right. Among those constitutions are those of Antigua and Barbuda,[19] the Bahamas,[20] Burma,[21] Cape Verde,[22] the Central African Republic,[23] Chile,[24] Dominica,[25] Egypt,[26] El Salvador,[27] Equatorial Guinea,[28] Fiji,[29] the Gambia,[30] Greece,[31] Guatemala,[32] Iraq,[33] Jamaica,[34] Jordan,[35] Kiribati,[36] Korea,[37] Kuwait,[38] Liberia,[39] Liechtenstein,[40] Malaysia,[41] Malta,[42] Mauritania,[43] Mauritius,[44] Nepal,[45] Nicaragua,[46] Nigeria,[47] Pakistan,[48] Papua New Guinea,[49] Portugal,[50] Rwanda,[51] Saint Christopher and Nevis,[52] Saint Lucia,[53] Saint Vincent,[54] Sierra Leone,[55] Singapore,[56] Solomon Islands,[57] Spain,[58] Sudan,[59] Sweden,[60] Thailand,[61] Tunisia,[62] Turkey,[63] Tuvalu,[64] Uganda,[65] the United Arab Emirates,[66] Venezuela,[67] Zaire,[68] Zambia,[69] and Zimbabwe.[70] In States in which no such constitutional rule exists, the national's right to enter his own country is occasionally proclaimed in domestic legislation.[71] In domestic judicial proceedings in Canada[72] and the United States[73] it has been held or implied that the citizen enjoys the constitutional right to enter his own country even in the absence of an express provision to that effect in the written constitutions of the countries concerned. In *Gonzales* v *Williams*,[74] *U.S.* v. *Williams*,[75] and *U.S.* v *Tod*[76] it was implied, held and affirmed that the immigration laws of the United States relate only to persons owing allegiance to foreign Governments.

The practice of India and of the United Kingdom in making provision for the resettlement of Asians from East Africa yields support for the view that the duty of admission is a reflection of the individual's right to reside in his country of nationality. The question of resettlement first arose in connection with the British protected persons and citizens of the United Kingdom and Colonies who departed from Kenya and other East African territories in the face of immigration and trades licensing legislation that imposed disabilities and restrictions upon them but did not make provision for their expulsion.[77] The immediate response of the Government of the United Kingdom was to secure passage of the Commonwealth Immigrants Act 1968, which for the first time imposed immigration control upon certain citizens of the United Kingdom and Colonies bearing United Kingdom passports.[78] The Government argued that its legislation was not inconsistent with the principle of international law whereby a State must admit its own nationals to its territory. The Solicitor General approved of the following reformulation of the principle, made by his colleague R.T. Paget:

... where one nation-State *expels* the citizens of another, and the citizen presents himself at the frontiers of his own State, that State is bound *by obligation to the expelling State* to accept him.[79]

Even at that stage, however, the Solicitor General and Mr Paget admitted that the principle was open to a less restrictive interpretation. Within a few months the Government admitted an obligation to resettle United Kingdom nationals in the United Kingdom, even in the absence of an expulsion and at the instance of a State outside East Africa.

The initiative on this matter came from India, which responded to the United Kingdom's action by imposing restrictions upon the admission to India of British nationals from East Africa.[80] The Indian Minister for Home Affairs explained in Lok Sabha that the measures were taken

... not by way of retaliation but the emphasize [to the U.K. Government] the urgent necessity of allowing persons their rights of citizenship irrespective of the country of origin.[81]

On 25 July 1968 the British Minister of State at the Foreign and Commonwealth Office informed Parliament that negotiations were continuing with India over the question and six days later Lord Shepherd announced the results of those negotiations. The arrangements provided that where British nationals were induced to leave Kenya through the withdrawal of residence or trading permits, their passports would be endorsed with a statement to the effect that they have a right of entry to the United Kingdom. Holders of such passports would be eligible for admission to India. Thus, even in the absence of an expulsion and at the instance of an interested State other than the State of former residence of the persons concerned, the United Kingdom formally acknowledged their right to reside in the country of their nationality.

That acknowledgement now finds expression in the special scheme for the admission to the United Kingdom of nationals other than British citizens, who are issued with special vouchers for the purpose. Such vouchers are granted to British Overseas Citizens, British Subjects (without citizenship) and British protected persons who are not dual nationals and are heads of household and are in Kenya or Uganda and regarded as being under pressure to leave; or who have left and are resident in India; or in the case of British Overseas Citizens, who are in other countries. Special vouchers are made available in allocations determined annually by the Secretary of State. Each voucher provides for the admission of the holder together with the holder's spouse[84] and dependent children. The scheme is designed to provide for the orderly resettlement in the United Kingdom of its nationals who have not been formally expelled.[85]

In the case of Uganda an act of expulsion was committed in 1972, the victims being members of the Asian community, many of whom were citizens of the United Kingdom and Colonies or British protected persons.[86] The Government of the United Kingdom appears to have taken the view that the expulsion was unlawful; and it would be difficult to dissent from that view, in the light of the frankly discriminatory and punitive terms of the Ugandan legislation. From this the United Kingdom's Government might have drawn the conclusion that it was under no legal duty to admit the Asians so expelled, any imaginable duty of admission being owed only to an expelling State exercising its lawful rights. Nevertheless, the Foreign Secretary (Sir Alec Douglas-Home) and the Home Secretary (Mr Robert Carr) informed Parliament that there was a legal duty on the United Kingdom to admit those expellees who are British passport holders.[87] When challenged on the point of international law, the Home Secretary reported that the Government had reached its conclusion on the advice of the Law Officers.

These considerations suggest that a State's duty to admits its nationals to its territory is not merely the corollary of each other State's right to expel aliens (a right which is subject to important limitations imposed by international law). The duty of admission is also a reflection of the individual's right to return to his own country and reside there. In order to identify the person who may vindicate that right by means of legal process, it is necessary to distinguish between proceedings in domestic and international courts and between the duty imposed by international conventions and the duty imposed by customary law. The question whether an individual may invoke before a domestic court a principle of international law is itself a question of domestic constitutional law. It is elementary that in a State following the dualist tradition, an individual may not rely upon an unadopted or unincorporated principle of international law in the face of an inconsistent domestic statute. It is on the basis of that principle that the Court of Appeal's decision in *Thakrar* v *Secretary of State*[88] finds its *ratio decidendi*. It is also in this sense (but in this sense alone) that we must understand Dr Weis' assertion[89] that between the individual and his State the right of entry is not a question of international law.

When the State's duty under international law to admit its own nationals to its territory is raised in an international forum, other than at the instance of an expelling State, the court or tribunal in which the question arises must satisfy itself of the claimant State's legal interest. If the claimant and respondent State are parties to an international convention governing the duty of admission[90] it is a matter of interpretation of each convention to determine whether the claimant State has a sufficient standing. The International Law Commission's Draft Articles on the Law of State Responsibility, prepared by Professor Riphagen, suggest that the onus lying on the claimant State will not normally be difficult to discharge. Under those Draft Articles, any State party to a multilateral treaty will be considered an 'injured State' in the event of a breach thereof, where the obligation was stipulated for the protection of individual persons, irrespective of their nationality.[91] An injured State is entitled to require the State which has committed an internationally wrongful act to dicontinue that act (i.e. to cease from excluding a national or minority from its territory).

The situation is less certain in cases in which one State seeks to enforce another's duty under general or customary international law to admits its nationals to its territory. It is thought, however, that a solution to the problem so arising may be afforded by a passage from the judgment of the International Court of Justice in the *Barcelona Traction Case (New Application)*.[92] Dealing with the duty of a State to observe the principles of international law governing the treatment of foreign nationals on its territory, the Court there spoke of 'the obligations of a State towards the international community as a whole'. The Court said of these obligations:

By their very nature [they] are the concern of all States. In view of the importance of the rights involved, all States can be held to have a legal interest in their protection: they are obligations *erga omnes*.

MIGRATION BETWEEN METROPOLITAN AND DEPENDENT TERRITORIES

The main multilateral instruments governing human rights, which speak of the right to return to one's own country, also proclaim the right to freedom of movement and residence within the borders of each State.[93] That right is further endorsed in certain economically motivated international instruments, including Article 48(3)(b) of the Treaty establishing the European Economic Community. The latter guarantees the right to move freely within the territory of Member States for the purposes intended by the Treaty.[94] When, therefore, an Italian national living in France was directed to reside in a particular *Département*, the European Court indicated that the direction amounted to a derogation from a fundamental principle of the Treaty. It could be maintained only if 'justified' on grounds of public policy and any such justification must be strictly proved.[95]

Thus there arises the question whether the national's right to enter the territory of his own State embraces the right to enter any part of that territory; and in particular to migrate from a dependency to the metropolitan territory. Despite some suggestion to the contrary in early American practice, it seems clear that customary international law does not protect the right to enter or live in any particular part of a State's territory.

The suggestion to the contrary is found in certain of the American materials relating to the admission of Filipinos prior to the independence of the Philippine islands. At the material time natives of the Philippines shared a common nationality, but not a common citizenship, with natives of the United States.[96]. In *De Lima* v *Bidwell* (1901)[97] it was held that Puerto Rico was no longer a foreign country within the meaning of the tariff laws, and in the same year, in *Fourteen Diamond Rings* v *U.S.*[98] a similar principle was applied to the Philippines. Two years later, in *Gonzales* v *Williams*,[99] the United States Supreme Court decided that a Puerto Rican woman was not liable to be denied admission to the continental United States under its immigration laws. Relying on this decision, the court held in *Roa* v *Collector of Customs*[100] that Filipinos were not to be regarded as aliens for customs purposes. Thereafter, in a series of opinions, the Attorney General of the United States affirmed and reaffirmed that in a international sense Filipinos in foreign countries are entitled to the rights and privileges of United States nationals; but a distinction was not firmly drawn between entitlement by reason of international law or usage and entitlement by virtue of the Constitution.[101] In 1917 a statute declared the immigration laws of the United States inapplicable to persons subject to the permanent jurisdiction of the United States.[102]

In 1917 Act was followed by a provision in the Act of 1924 which stated that the term 'alien' did not include citizens of islands under United States jurisdiction. In the years 1928 to 1930, Bills supported by the American Federation of Labor were introduced in Congress to bar the admission of Filipinos to the United States. It was argued that the Bills were probably unconstitutional; and one opponent of the Bills contended that 'a similar course has not been adopted by any civilized nation in the world'.[103] The opponents of the Bills were successful. Filipinos remained free to enter the continental United States until the passage of the Philippines Independence Act in 1936. Indeed, President Taft even observed that Philippine independence was born of a desire to restrict Filipino migration to the United States.[104]

Section 8(a) of the Philippines Independence Act[105] provided that for the purposes of U.S. immigration laws citizens of the Philippine Islands who were not also citizens of the United States should be considered as aliens. The Philippine Islands were to be treated as a separate country with an annual immigration quota of fifty. Section 14 of the same Act provided that upon the final withdrawal of American sovereignty of the Philippines Islands, the immigration laws of the United States should apply to persons who were born in the Philippine Islands to the same extent as in the case of other foreign countries. During the transitional period preceding the advent of full independence, Section 8(a), but not Section 14, took effect. At that time the Federal Government continued to issue passports to Filipinos, but these bore cautionary notes to the effect that they did not entitle their bearers to be admitted to the continental United States. Finally, in *Rebang* v *Boyd* (1957), the Supreme Court confirmed that on the independence of the Philippines, those Filipinos who had not acquired U.S. citizenship had, in conformity with the Constitution, become aliens subject to the immigration laws.[106].

On the other hand, the imposition of controls on migration from dependencies to metropolitan territories has been a widespread practice and one which has in most parts of the world escaped protest. When New Zealand, being entrusted with the territory of Western Samoa, extended to natives of that territory the status of New Zealand protected persons, New Zealand's legislature did not alter the provision whereby such persons were subject to immigration control in New Zealand unless domiciled there.[107] On the achievement of independence by Western Samoa, citizens of the new sovereign State were granted the privileges of Commonwealth citizens in New Zealand; in particular they were exempted from registration as aliens.[108] They remained, however, liable to be denied admission to New Zealand. Conversely, the Cook Islands, Nieue, Tokelau and the Ross Dependency from part of New Zealand for the purposes of the Citizenship law.[109] With minor exceptions, any person born in New Zealand (including those dependencies) is a New Zealand citizen and as such is exempted from the principal provisions of the Immigration Act.[110]

Indeed, even States which lack dependencies in the ordinary sense of that expression often impose restrictions on the migration of their nationals from one part of the national territory to another. The Soviet Union's internal passport system is, perhaps, sufficiently well documented.[111] Less familiar are the legal provisions on this subject applicable in the Federation of Malaysia. Freedom of movement is guaranteed in outline in Article 9(2) of the Malaysian Constitution but this freedom may be arrested in the interests of security, public health or punishment of offenders; and a law is not deemed unconstitutional if it incidentally imposes restrictions upon freedom of movement or residence.[112] The present Immigration Act[113] provides in section 7 that 'a citizen shall be entitled to enter Malaysia without having obtained a permit or pass'.[114] The same Act makes special provision for admission to East Malaysian States (that is, Sabah and Sarawak). In general, a citizen is not entitled to enter a East Malaysian State unless he 'belongs' to that State. (Exceptions are made in the case of those occupying certain federal offices of State and those travelling in order to exercise political rights or in order to discharge duties of the federal or State governments.) A citizen is regarded as belonging to an East Malaysian State if he is or has within the preceding two years been permanently resident in that State or became a citizen by reason of specified connections with that State, including ordinary residence there on independence.[115] For the purposes of the administration of these rules, the Immigration Act makes provision for the issuance of 'internal travel documents'.[116]

The distinction drawn by modern Malaysian law between citizens 'belonging' to separate States within the Federation owes its origin to a similar distinction formerly drawn in the laws of the United Kingdom's dependencies between British subjects who 'belonged' to particular territories or possessions.[117] The concept of 'belonging' was developed in the Caribbean territories particularly; and the some such territories it has survived the advent of independence and the corresponding enactment of separate citizenships.

The former British territories in the Caribbean have seldom retained static populations.[118] In the present century they have generally had a surplus of manpower and have therefore been inclined to restrict the settlement of outsiders, including those from propinquent territories.[119] Since the desire to impose such restrictions preceded the creation of independent citizenships for the several Caribbean territories, exoneration from immigration control was accorded only to those 'belonging' to each territory. In Jamaica, the admission of Commonwealth citizens is, even today, governed by the Immigration Restriction (Commonwealth Citizens) Act 1945 (as amended). A Commonwealth citizen is not to be a prohibited immigrant for the purposes of that Act if he 'belongs' to the island; and such a citizen belongs to Jamaica if he was born there of parents who at the time of his birth were domiciled or ordinarily resident there; or if he is domiciled in the island or has been ordinarily resident there for at least seven years or became a Jamaican citizen by registration or naturalization or is a dependent of any person who has satisfied any of the foregoing conditions.[120] The Act of 1945 must be read subject to Article 16(3)(b) of the Constitution of Jamaica[121] which guarantees to every citizen of Jamaica the right to enter Jamaican territory. Thus, every Jamaican citizen retains a constitutional right of entry, but every person who is not a Jamaican citizen but belongs to the island is free from the disabilities and restrictions imposed on prohibited immigrants. The non-citizen who 'belongs' to the island may, however, be deterred from entering it by the Foreign Nationals and Commonwealth Citizens (Employment) Act 1964, which is designed to protect local workers from competition with immigrants.[122] Under that Act (which extends to aliens as well as Commonwealth citizens) anyone other than a Jamaican citizen is required to obtain a work permit before undertaking employment in the island.[123]

In short, the practice of imposing controls on migration between dependencies, or between dependencies and metropolitan territories, was so widespread in the first half of the present century and is still so common today that it is quite impossible to maintain that it is in contravention of general or customary law. A prohibition upon the maintenance of these controls is conspicuous in its absence from Part IV of I.L.O. Convention No. 82 on Social Policy in Non-Metropolitan Territories, which deals specifically with the question of migrant workers.[124]

Different considerations are presented, however, by the provisions of the modern international conventions governing freedom of movement within the borders of each State, and in particular Article 12 of the International Covenant on Civil and Political Rights.[125] The latter provides that 'Everyone lawfully within the territory of a State shall, within that territory, have the right to liberty of movement and freedom to choose his residence'. Thus there arises the necessity of interpreting the phrase'within the territory of a State'. The point of departure in this exercise is that, in the sense in which it is most commonly used in international law, the term 'State' denotes an entity having the capacity to enter into diplomatic relations. In this sense, a dependent territory is not a State but is subsumed within the statehood of its parent.[126]

The ambiguity in this expression appears to have been overlooked during the course of the negotiations over the text.[127] In this respect the Covenant on Civil and Political Rights is to be contrasted with the Fourth Protocol to the European Convention on Human Rights, which also contains a guarantee of the right to move freely throughout the territory of the State. In the latter case, Article 5(4) provides that 'the territory of any State to which this Protocol applies by virtue of ratification or acceptance by that State, and each territory to which this Protocol is applied by virtue of a declaration by that State under this Article, shall be treated as separate territories for the purpose of the references in Article 2 or 3 to the territory of the State'.

The absence of such a qualification from the International Covenant on Civil and Political Rights may be taken as an indication (albeit faint and inconclusive) that the expression 'within the territory of a State' is a reference to the territory of a State in the international sense, including any dependency. A stronger indication to similar effect is given in the language of the reservations made by the United Kingdom and the Netherlands on ratifying the Convention. The former reserved the right to interpret the provisions of Article 12(1) relating to the territory of a State as applying separately to each of the territories comprising the United Kingdom and its dependencies. The latter made a similar reservation, declaring that it regards the Netherlands and the Dutch Antilles as separate countries for the purposes of Article 12(1). Neither the practice of France nor that of Malaysia affords a basis for doubting that the International Convention of 1966 guarantees freedom of movement throughout the territory of a 'State' in the international sense of the word. For in the former case, the Overseas Departments are treated as part of France for the purposes of aliens control and in the latter case, Malaysia has failed altogether to ratify the Convention.

The significance of the United Kingdom's reservation lies not only in the fact that it protects the right to maintain controls on migration from the dependencies to the metropolitan territory but also in the fact that it preserves the power to control immigration into dependencies from the United Kingdom and from other territories for whose international relations the United Kingdom is responsible. Without exception, the remaining dependencies of the

United Kingdom impose systems of immigration control applicable to British citizens coming from the United Kingdom and to those from other dependencies. In two very exceptional cases, immigration control is applied to all persons whatever.[128] Elsewhere, a distinction is drawn between those who belong to the territory and are accordingly immune from immigration control and those who do not belong. In several instances, the statute uses the very word 'belonger'. Thus, a person has the right to land in Hong Kong if he is a 'Hong Kong belonger'.[129] In general, a 'Hong Kong belonger' is a person who falls into any of four categories. The first consists of those who immediately before 1 January 1983 were British subjects by birth, naturalization or registration in Hong Kong or spouses or children of such persons. The second comprises British Dependent Territory citizens who obtained that status by birth, naturalization or registration in Hong Kong. The third group is made up of British Dependent Territory citizens who acquired that status by adoption in Hong Kong or by association with a British dependency other than Hong Kong, provided in either case that one parent has an 'appropriate qualifying connection with Hong Kong' by reason of that parent's birth, adoption, naturalization or registration. The fourth category consists of women who became British Dependent Territories citizens by marriage to persons having 'appropriate qualifying connections'.[130] The laws of Anguilla,[131] the British Virgin Islands[132] and Montserrat[133] also provide that those who 'belong' to the appropriate territory shall be immune from immigration control. In these cases the definition of the belonger coincides *mutatis mutandis* with that used in the case of Hong Kong.

A similar pattern is to be found in the laws of Saint Helena and in Tristan da Cunha, but with substitution of the terms 'islander' for 'belonger' and with a certain simplification of the definition.[134] In the Caymans, Vanuatu and Gibraltar, the 'belonger' has been transformed into the 'Caymanian',[135] the 'New Hebridean',[136] and the 'Gibraltarian'.[137] The 'Gibraltarian' was formerly defined as a person registered as such in a register kept for the purpose;[138] but the present definition has been amended in order to take account of the effects of the British Nationality Act 1981.[139] It is only in the Falkland Islands that the term 'belonger' is neither used nor translated into some local equivalent. Even in that case, however, immigration control is applied to British nationals other than those from the islands and their dependencies. With exceptions immaterial for present purposes, entry permits are required for all persons other than 'permanent residents.[140] A permanent resident is defined as a person born in the Falklands or its dependencies of parents who were then ordinarily resident there; or a person who has been ordinarily resident in the colony or its dependencies for a continuous period of seven years without being ordinarily resident for a similar period in any other country or territory; or a dependent of anyone in either of these two categories; or a person naturalized by the grant of a certificate of naturalization by the Governor General of the Falkland Islands.

In several of the foregoing cases, the 'belonger' or his local equivalent is not the only person immune from immigration control. Local circumstances commonly demand that certain other categories shall also be exempted. In the case of Hong Kong, resident British subjects and 'Chinese residents' share most of the privileges of Hong Kong belongers, as do persons who were resident United Kingdom belongers prior to 1 January 1983.[141] A 'Chinese resident' is defined as a person wholly or partly of Chinese race who has at any time been ordinarily resident in Hong Kong for a continuous period of not less than seven years. In Gibraltar, detailed legislative provision has been made to accommodate within the local legal system the rules of European Community law governing freedom of movement for workers and the freedom of establishment and the right to supply and receive services.[142] In the case of Vanuatu, the entry of French and British nationals is governed by their respective legal systems and controlled by the Resident Commissioner or Principal Immigration Officer of the power concerned.[143] The Falkland Islands[144] and the Turks and Caicos Islands[145] exonerate from control certain categories of entrants which the local authorities desire to attract for commercial reasons.

THE INTERNATIONAL EFFICACY OF DENATURALIZATION

A State's obligation to admit its own nationals to its territory could easily be circumvented if it were always open to the State to withdraw its nationality from those whom it wished to exclude. During the present century the practice of withdrawing nationality from dissident individuals or groups has become increasingly widespread. In the 1920s, between one and two million people were deprived of their Soviet citizenship by the Bolsheviks. The German Reich followed a similar policy in respect of Jews in the 1930s. Measures of a comparable character (although on a smaller scale) were adopted during the same decade by the Italian and Turkish authorities.[146] The Ugandan authorities under Life President Field Marshal Idi Amin Dada did not purport to withdraw Ugandan citizenship from the Asian community in 1972 but declared a policy of scrutinising the claim to Ugandan citizenship of each Asian resident and of imprisoning those residents whose claims to citizenship were found to be false. The effect on the departure of the Asian community was much the same as it would have been in the event of a candid act of denaturalization.[147]

It is unlikely that the Soviet, German, Italian and Turkish authorities would have pursued their policies of denaturalization had they not been persuaded that the decrees would be effective to relieve those States of their obligations in respect of the individuals or groups concerned. The traditional view, certainly, is that it is for each State to secure to the individual the *Voelkerrechtsindigenat*. In general, an individual will not be regarded as a national of any State which disowns him.

In the middle of the last century, the central European powers concluded a series of conventions governing the duty to repatriate former nationals.[148] As Dr Weis observes, the existence of these conventions yields support for the view that there is in general no duty to admit former nationals. If any such duty had existed, the conventions would have been unnecessary.[149] A similar inference can, perhaps, be drawn from the history of Roumania's treatment of its Jewish community at the turn of the century. By the Congress of Berlin 1878, the East European States were urged to treat their subjects equally, without discrimination on ground of race or religion. Roumania contrived to evade this obligation by denying her citizenship to Jews. Article 7 of the Treaty of Paris of 9 December 1919 addressed this problem. By that provision, Roumania undertook 'to recognize as Roumanian nationals Jews inhabiting any Roumanian territory who do not possess another nationality'.[150] The minority treaties concluded with Armenia, Austria, Bulgaria, Czechoslovakia, Greece, Hungary, Roumania and Yugoslavia conferred several specific rights upon members of the minorities in those countries, including the right to retain their nationality, on condition of maintaining their habitual residence there.[151]

For the purposes of the Hague Codification Conference 1930, the Preparatory Committee drew up a Basis of Discussion which envisaged that a person who loses his nationality without acquiring another, after entering a foreign country, would be assured of readmission to his country of former nationality, at the request of the State where he is residing. The Soviet observer argued, however, that this was wholly a political question[152] which several other States argued that the question fell outside the scope of the proposed Convention. The Soviet objection was not surprising. An Ordinance of December 1924 followed by a Decree of November 1926 provided for the denaturalization of several specific groups, including those who had left the territories of the Soviet Union, with or without the permission of the organs of the USSR, and had failed to return at the demand of the proper authorities.[153] It proved impossible to reach sufficient agreement to include in the Hague Convention of 1930 a provision of the kind envisaged by the Preparatory Committee. Instead, the Preparatory Committee's proposal was incorporated within a Special Protocol concerning statelessness. This Protocol envisaged that a State which had withdrawn its nationality from a former subject, after his entry into a foreign country, would be obliged to readmit him only if he had become permanently indigent or if he had been sentenced to not less than one month's imprisonment.[154] Moreover, the Special Protocol failed to obtain the ten ratifications required to bring it into force.[155] It would be difficult to find more convincing evidence of the proposition that there existed in 1930 no general duty to readmit individuals or groups whose nationality has been withdrawn.

That conclusion is reinforced by the decision of the Supreme Court of Poland in its decision in 1927 in *Rajberg* v *Lewi*.[156] There the Court held that the plaintiff, who had been deprived under Soviet law of Soviet nationality, could not be considered a Soviet national by other States, least of all by States like Poland, which had recognized the Soviet Republic *de jure*. There is more than an echo of this judgment in the relatively recent decision of the United States Circuit Court of Appeals in *U.S. ex rel. Steinworth* v *Watkins* (1947).[157] The point at issue there was whether the American courts would recognize the efficacy of a Costa Rican decree of 1944, declaring that the appellant had forfeited Costa Rican nationality. It was held that the denaturalization was effective. In the court's words, 'we must accept it as a lawful cancellation of the appellant's Costa Rican citizenship because done by a foreign sovereign within its own country'. The principle applied in these two cases was also applied in *Lempert* v *Bonfol*,[158] notwithstanding the non-recognition at that time of the Soviet government by the government of Switzerland, where the point arose. The Swiss Federal Tribunal held that it was bound to consider as stateless a person denaturalized by a Soviet decree, even if the latter was contrary to the international obligations of Soviet Russia.[159]

Since the Second World War, however, the international community has adopted a series of multilateral instruments aimed at reducing the effects of arbitrary or discriminatory denaturalization. Article 15(2) of the Universal Declaration of Human Rights proclaims that no one shall be arbitrarily deprived of his nationality.[160] On the basis of that Article, the Convention on the Reduction of Statelessness provides that no contracting State shall deprive a person of his nationality if such deprivation would render him stateless; nor may such a State deprive any person or group of nationality on racial, ethnic, religious or political grounds. Of these provisions, Dr Weis has written that

> It is a rule based on the principle of non-discrimination pervading the Charter of the United Nations in all its references to human rights and may well be on the way to becoming a general principle of international law.[162]

Article 5 of the International Convention on the Elimination of All Forms of Racial Discrimination lists among other civil rights the right to return to one's own country and the right to a nationality.[163] Commenting on this provision, Dr Donner states as follows:

> The right to a nationality is in this way linked to the right to equal treatment for all persons and the prohibition of discrimination. It would seem to be correct, therefore, to read this article as containing the inclusion of Article 9 of the Reduction of Statelessness Convention, 1961, with its prohibition of deprivation of nationality.[164]

Most significant of all is Article 12(4) of the International Covenant on Civil and Political Rights.[165] This provides that no one shall be arbitrarily deprived of the right to enter his own country. An examination of the *travaux préparatoires* makes clear that this provision is so framed as to exclude the permissibility of an act of denaturalization directed against an ethnic group or dissident individual or minority, with the object of depriving such persons of the right to return to their country of origin. During the course of the 954th meeting of the Third Committee, the Canadian delegate proposed the replacement of the words 'his own country' by the words 'country of which he is a citizen'. The amendment was opposed by the Italian delegate, on the ground that the Canadian amendment, if adopted, would enable a State to evade its obligations by means of denaturalization. The Italian argument prevailed; and it is in the light of the prevalence of that argument that the Article must now be read.[166]

These international conventions, ratified (in some cases) by the great majority of the States in the international community, have had a profound effect on the development of international law.[167] A relatively early indication of a change in the direction of international law on this point is given in the decision of the Swiss Federal Tribunal in *Levita-Muhlstein* v *Département Fédérale de Justice et Police*:[168] a decision which may be contrasted with that of the same tribunal thirteen years earlier in *Lempert* v *Bonfol*.[169] The applicant in the *Levita-Muhlstein* case was a Swiss national who had married a Jewish refugee from Germany, resident in France. A Decree pursuant to the *Reichsburgergesetz* purported to render him stateless; but the Federal Tribunal declined to recognize the decree in Switzerland on the ground that is was inimical to public policy. This was so even though the French authorities had recognized the decree, at least so far as necessary to hold that the refugee was liable to be conscripted into the French armed forces. The Tribunal based its conclusion on Swiss public policy rather than on international law. Moreover, the Tribunal supported its conclusion by an entirely separate argument based upon an interpretation of the legislation of the Allied Military Government, repealing the discriminatory decrees of the Reich. That interpretation appears highly questionable.[170] Nevertheless, the decision illustrates with sufficient clarity that the Swiss courts do not consider themselves bound to recognize the efficacy of a denaturalization decree which is of a discriminatory nature.

The case of the victims of German denaturalization decrees was taken a step further in 1949, when the German Basic Law was adopted. Article 116(2) provides that former German nationals who, between 30 January 1933 and 8 May 1945, were deprived of their citizenship on political, racial or religious grounds, and their descendants, shall be regranted German citizenship on application. They were to be considered as not having been deprived of their German citizenship if they had established their domicile in Germany after 8

May 1945 and had not expressed a contrary intention. In 1968 the Federal Constitutional Court held that the decree of 1941 violated fundamental principles, was intolerable to a degree irreconcilable with justice and must be considered to be null and void *ex tunc*.[171] This did not mean that German nationality was imposed on every person who believed that he had lost it. For Article 116(2) of the Basic Law secured a right of option for those who had survived.[172]

Finally, in a decision of the House of Lords in *Oppenheimer* v *Cattermole*[173] it was held that on a true construction of Articles 116(2) of the Basic Law the appellants had *on the enactment of the Basic Law* ceased to be German nationals, unless and until they applied to be such. Lord Hailsham of St Marylebone, Lord Hodson, Lord Cross of Chelsea and Lord Salmon added that the 1941 decree would, having regard to its nature, not have been recognized by the courts of this country as effective to deprive the appellants of their German nationality. Lord Justice Buckley, in the Court of Appeal, had taken the view that it is for the putative national law to determine whether a person is a national of that country; and that the English courts must apply that law however inequitable, oppressive or objectionable it may be. The House of Lords took a different view on this issue; and in several instances based their view on current public international law. Thus, Lord Hodson[174] stated Lord Justice Buckley's argument and added:

I do not agree that this is a correct view of the relevant international law . . . The courts of this country are not obliged to shut their eyes to the shocking nature of such legislation as the 1941 decree . . .

Lord Cross of Chelsea[175] reasoned as follows:

It may be said, perhaps, that though international law sets limits to the jurisdiction of sovereign states so far as concerns the granting of nationality, it sets no limits whatever to their power to withdraw it. I am not prepared to accept that this is so. I think, for example, that Martin Wolff, *Private International Law*, 2nd ed., p. 129, may well be right in saying that, if a State withdraws its citizenship from some class of its citizens living within its borders to which it has taken a dislike and of whom it would be glad to be rid, other States are not obliged to to regard such people as 'stateless'.

Lord Salmon of Sandwich[176] stated as follows:

I recognize that it is particularly within the province of any State to decide who are and who are not its nationals . . . [But] circumstances could arise in which a man might be treated as a national of a foreign State for the purpose of English law although he was not a national of that State according to its own municipal law ... I do not understand how ... it could be regarded as ... contrary to international comity or to any legal principles hitherto enunciated for our courts to decide that the 1941 decree was so great an offence against human rights that they would have nothing to do with it.

Modern State practice provides some support for the proposition that a decree of denaturalization may be ineffective to relieve the State of its duty to admit a person covered by such a decree. In March 1982 the Swedish Foreign Minister summoned the Polish Ambassador in Stockholm to receive a strong protest against the expulsion of 45 Poles to Sweden. Half of them were deprived of their Polish nationality and the others put on a ferry with documents precluding their return to Poland. The Foreign Minister maintained that the Polish action conflicted with all rules of international relations.[177]

This evidence suggests that in current international law a State cannot always release itself of its obligation to admit certain of its own nationals to its territory by promulgating a decree which deprives such persons of their nationality. A decree which discriminates on racial grounds, or is in any other sense 'arbitrary', need not be recognized by other States as effective to deprive of their nationality those to whom it purports to apply.[178] Where the element of arbitrariness is absent, the denaturalization decree may nevertheless be ineffective to relieve the former State of nationality of its obligation to readmit the individual. This will be the case if the decree deprives of nationality a person who has already gained admission to another State, on the understanding that he will be readmitted to his country of origin, and who has not obtained any other national status.[179] This conclusion may be defended on the traditional principle of good faith, coupled with the well-established rule[180] that each State owes to each other State a duty to refrain from frustrating the latter's right to expel aliens. An additional reason has recently been advanced for arriving at the same conclusion; 'where the purpose or primary effect of denationalization is to prevent a former citizen from returning to his country, a strong argument can be made that such action violates the common provision in most human rights treaties that prohibits the State from engaging in any act 'aimed at the destruction of any of the rights and freedoms recognized' therein.'[181]

PROOF OF NATIONALITY

An individual who claims that his nationality entitles him to enter a State commonly bears the burden of proving his national status. He will often discharge this burden by producing a passport. On several occasions international tribunals have taken cognizance of a claimant's passport in order to determine his national status.[182]

State practice in the issuance of passports is so varied, however, that it is impossible to establish a connection in international law between the issuance of a passport and the acquisition or tenure of nationality. The problem is not merely that very many States issue travel documents of various kinds to travellers of foreign nationality but that some States issue passports, in the strict sense of the term, to aliens of defined classes. In the case of Costa Rica, for example, Law No. 4812 of 28 July 1971[183] is designed to encourage aliens to settle in that country as resident pensioners or annuitants. The intention of the law is that the alien will take up Costa Rican nationality in due course. In the meanwhile, the Government of Costa Rica issues provisional passports to those who have entered the country in accordance with the Law. The regulations accompanying Law No. 4812[184] state that the resident pensioner or annuitant should reside in Costa Rica for six months our of every year. In practice, however, this provision has not been strictly interpreted and many provisional passport holders do not live in Costa Rica.[185] It seems unlikely that the issuance of a passport in accordance with Law No. 4812 relieves the bearer's national State of its duty to admit him, at the request of a third State or even at the request of Costa Rica. Circumstances might arise, however, in which a third State could properly demand that Costa Rica admit the bearer to its territory, in default of his admission to his country of nationality. For in an appropriate case it might be shown that in issuing the passport the Costa Rican authorities impliedly warranted to a third State that the bearer would be admitted to Costa Rica, if for any reason the State of nationality declined to fulfill its obligation towards him.

NOTES

1. *Supra*, Introduction, notes 1–10.
2. J. François, *Grondlijnen van het Volkenrecht*, 1967, pp. 242, 233–34.
3. P. Weis, *The Role of Nationality in International Law*, p. 45.
4. G. Goodwin-Gill, *International Law and the Movement of Persons between States*, 1978, p. 136.
5. P. Van Panhuys, *The Role of Nationality in International Law*, 1959, p. 56.
6. [1974] ECR 1337 at 1351.
7. G. Schwarzenberger, *International Law*, 1957, Vol. I, p. 361. The Inter-American Commission on Human Rights referred to this principle in observing that the expulsion of nationals without the consent of the State of destination violates international law: *Annual Report* (1980–81) 119.
8. *Supra*, note 5 at 55–6.
9. G. Leibholz, 'Verbot der Willkuer und der Ermessenmissbrauches im Völkerrecht', 1 Z.a.ö. R.V. (1929) 77 at 95.

10. [1974] 2 All ER 261 at 266. The precedent was followed by Nolan, J. in *R.v. Chief Immigration Officer, Gatwick Airport, exparte Harjandar Singh, The Times* L.R. 26 October 1987.
11. See M. Janie, 'Individuals as Subjects of International Law', 17 Cornell Int. L.J. (1984) 61. Notwithstanding its reference to the traditional principle (*supra* note 7) the Inter-American Commission of Human Rights has maintained that the liberty of the person includes the freedom to remain in his country of citizenship: OEA/Ser. L/V/II. 40, p. 45.
12. Article 13(2); U.N. Doc. A/811, *Basic Documents* I.1.
13. Article 12(3) (No one shall be arbitrarily deprived of the right to enter his own country'); Cmnd. 6702; *Basic Documents* I.2.
14. Article 5(d)(ii); Cmnd. 4108, *Basic Documents* I.3.
15. Article 22(5); 9 I.L.M. 673, *Basic Documents* IX.4. Hence the Inter-American Commission on Human Rights has deplored the imposition of limitations on the right of persons to return to their country of residence after voluntary or involuntary departure: *Annual Report* (1980–81) 121.
16. Article 12(2); 21 I.L.M. 59, *Basic Documents* IX.5.
17. Article 3(2); Cmnd. 2309, *Basic Documents* V.2.
18. 4 U.S.T.S. 4722.
19. Constitution of 31 October 1981, Article 8(1), (3)(g).
20. Constitution of 10 July 1973, Article 25(1), (2)(d).
21. Constitution of 3 January 1974, Article 148(c).
22. Constitution of 7 October 1980, Article 33.
23. Constitution of 1 February 1981, Article 2.
24. Constitution of 8 August 1980, Article 19(7)(a).
25. Constitution of 25 July 1978, Article 25(c) with 12(2)(d).
26. Constitution of 22 May 1980, Articles 49–52.
27. Constitution of 15 December 1983, Article 5.
28. Constitution of 15 August 1982, Article 9.
29. Constitution of 30 September 1970, Article 14(c) with 14(3)(d).
30. Constitution of 24 April 1970, Article 24(1) with 24(3)(d).
31. Constitution of 7 June 1975, Article 5(4).
32. Decree-Law No. 36/82, Article 14.
33. Interim Constitution of 16 July 1970, Article 24.
34. Constitution of 24 July 1962, Article 16(1) with 16(3)(b).
35. Constitution of 1 January 1952 (as amended), Article 9(1).
36. Constitution of 12 July 1979, Article 14(1) with 14(3)(c).
37. Constitution of Fifth Republic, Article 13.
38. Constitution of 11 November 1969, Article 28.
39. Constitution of 3 July 1984, Article 13(b).
40. Constitution of 5 October 1921 (as amended), Article 28.
41. Constitution of 31 August 1957 (as amended), Article 9.
42. Constitution of 21 September 1964, (as amended), Article 45(1).
43. Constitution of 10 July 1978, Article 11.
44. Constitution of 4 March 1968, Article 15(1) with 15(3)(d).
45. Constitution of 16 December 1962 (as amended), Article 12.
46. Statute on the Rights and Guarantees of the Nicaraguan People (Decree No. 52 of 21 August 1979), Article 15.
47. Constitution of October 1979, Article 38.
48. Constitution of 12 April 1973, Article 15.
49. Constitution of 15 August 1975, Article 52.

50. Constitution of 2 April 1. ʿ(as amended), Article 44(1).
51. Constitution of 20 December 1978, Article 21.
52. Constitution of 23 June 1983, Article 14(1) with 14(3)(d).
53. Constitution of 22 February 1979, Article 12(1) with 12(3)(d).
54. Constitution of 27 October 1979, Article 12(1) with 12(3)(d).
55. Constitution of 14 June 1978, Article 8(1) with 8(3)(b).
56. Constitution of 5 September 1963 (as amended), Article 13.
57. Constitution of 7 July 1978, Article 14(1) with 14(3)(c).
58. Constitution of 29 December 1978, Article 19.
59. Constitution of 8 May 1973, Articles 40–41.
60. Instrument of Government 1974, Chapter 2, Article 7.
61. Constitution of 22 December 1978, section 40.
62. Constitution of 1 June 1959 (as amended), Article 11.
63. Constitution of 9 November 1982, Article 23.
64. Constitution of 25 July 1962, Article 14(1) with 14(3)(c).
65. Constitution of 8 September 1967 (as amended), Article 19(c) with 19(3)(d).
66. Provisional Constitution of 18 July 1971, Article 37.
67. Constitution of 23 January 1961 (as amended) Article 64.
68. Constitution of 25 June 1967 (as amended), Article 25.
69. Constitution of 25 August 1973, Article 24(1) with 24(3)(b).
70. Constitution of 6 December 1979, Article 22(1) with 22(3)(d).
71. The United Kingdom's Immigration Act 1971, section 1(1) declares that all those having the right of abode 'shall be free to live in and to come into and from the United Kingdom without let or hindrance . . .'
72. *R v Soon Gin An*, (1941) 3 D.L.R. 125.
73. *The Martonelli Case*, 63 F. 437 (1894).
74. 192 U.S. 1 (1903).
75. 184 F. 322 (1911); 106 C.C.A. 464 (1911).
76. 285 F. 523 (1922); 26 A.L.R. 1316 (1922).
77. *Kenya*: Immigration Act, 1967 (No. 25); Immigration Regulations, 1967; Immigration Amendment Regulations 1968 and 1969; Trade Licensing Act, 1967 (No. 33); Trade Licensing (General Business Areas) Order, 1968; Trade Licensing (Specified Goods) Order, 1968; Trade Licensing (Amendment) Act 1969 (No. 17). See also Constitution of Kenya (Amendment) Act 1965 (No. 14).
    Uganda: Immigration Act (No. 19); Immigration Regulations, 1969; Trade (Licensing) Act, 1969; Trade (Licensing) (Amendment of Schedule) Instrument, 1969; Trade (Licensing) (Prescription of Forms) Regulation, 1969; Trade (Licensing) (Appointment of Licensing Authority) Instrument, 1969.
    Zambia: Immigration and Deportation Act, 1965 (No. 29); Immigration and Deportation Regulations, 1965; Immigration and Deportation (Amendment) Act, 1967 (No. 20; Immigration and Deportation (Amendment) Regulations, 1967; Immigration and Deportation Regulations (Commencement) Order, 1967; Immigration and Deportation Amendment (No. 3) Regulations, 1967; Trades Licensing Act 1968 (No. 41); Trades Licensing (Amendment) Act 1969 (No. 41).
78. See R. Plender, 'The Exodus of Asians from East and Central Africa: Some Comparative and International Law Aspects', 19 A.J. Comp. L. (1971) 287; B. Hepple, 'The Commonwealth Immigrants Act 1968', 31 M.L.R. (1968) 424; K. Nambiar, 'The Commonwealth Immigrants Act 1968 – Effect on Asians in Kenya', 8 Ind. J.I.L. (1968) 56.
79. 759 H.C. Deb. col. 1581 (emphasis added).
80. Passport (Entry into India) Amendment Rules, 1968, G.S.R. 476.

81. *The Times of India*, 7 March 1968, p. 1.

82. 769 H.C. Deb. col. 185.

83. 296 H.C. Deb. col. 391–92.

84. A woman is regarded as head of household only if single, widowed or divorced, or if her husband has a serious disability.

85. 759 H.C. Deb. col. 1256; 818 H.C. Deb. col. 380; 849 H.C. Deb. col. 656; 890 H.C. Deb. col. 23; H.C. (1981–2) No. 90–I, paras. 68–132. There is no right of appeal against refusal of a special voucher: *Shah v Home Secretary*, [1972] Imm. A.R. 56 (I.A.T.).

86. Immigration (Cancellation of Entry Permits and Certificates of Residence) Decree 1972 (No. 17); Declaration of Assets (Non-citizen Asians) Decree 1972 (No. 27).

87. 7 August 1972, 842 H.C. Deb. col. 1261–63 (Sir Alec Douglas-Home); 18 October 1972, 843 H.C. Deb. col. 262–270 (Mr Robert Carr).

88. *Supra*, note 10.

89. *Supra*, note 3.

90. *Supra*, notes 12–17.

91. Article 5(d)(iv); I.L.C. Ybk. (1984–II) 100; S. Rosenne, *Termination of Treaties*, 1985, p. 133. The view expressed by Professor Riphagen derives further support from the decision of the United Nations Human Rights Committee in *López v Uruguay*, 68 I.L.R. (1981) 29.

92. I.C.J. Rep. (1970) 4 at 33.

93. Universal Declaration of Human Rights, 10 December 1948, 42 A.J.I.L. (1949) Supp. 127, Cmnd. 7662 (Article 13(1) (*Basic Documents* I.1); International Covenant on Civil and Political Rights, New York, 16 December 1966, 6 I.L.M. (1967) 368, Article 12(1) (*Basic Documents* I.2); International Covention on the Elimination of All Forms of Racial Discrimination, New York, 7 March 1966, 660 U.N.T.S. 195, Article 5(d)(i) (*Basic Documents* I.3); Fourth Protocol to the European Convention on Human Rights, Strassbourg, 16 September 1963, 58 A.J.I.L. (1964) 334, Article 2 (1) (*Basic Documents* V.2); American Convention on Human Rights, San José, 22 November 1969, 9 I.L.M. (1970) 673, Article 22(1) (*Basic Documents* IX.4); African Charter on Human and People's Rights, Banjul, 26 June 1981, 21 I.L.M. (1982) 58, Article 12(1) (*Basic Documents* IX.5).

94. Rome, 25 March 1957, 298 U.N.T.S. 11 (*Basic Documents* VI.1).

95. Case 39/75, *Roland Rutili v Minister of the Interior*, [1975] ECR 1219.

96. Note, 'Status of Filipinos for Purposes of Immigration and Naturalization', 32 Harv. L.R. (1928–9) 809. For an account of the distinction between U.S. nationality and U.S. citizenship at this period see A. Kidd and M. Radin, *Legal Essays in Tribute to Orrin Kip McMurray*, 1935.

97. 182 U.S. 1 (1900).

98. 183 U.S. 176 (1901).

99. 192 U.S. 1, 5, 13 (1903).

100. 23 P. Rp. 315 (1912).

101. 24 Op. A.G. (1902); see also 32 Op. A.G. P.1 (1909) 144.

102. 39 Stat. 874, 897.

103. Senator Hawes, 72 Cong. Rec. 7526 (1930).

104. H. Taft, *Human Migration*, 1936, p. 370.

105. 48 Stat. 456, 462.

106. 353 U.S. 427 (1957).

107. British Nationality and New Zealand Citizenship Act, 1948, section 2(1); Western Samoa New Zealand Protected Persons Order, 1950; Immigration Restriction Act, 1908, section 12, amended by Immigration Restriction Act 1910, section 2.

108. Western Samoa Act, 1961, sections 5 and 6. See further Commonwealth Countries Act, 1977; Citizenship Act 1977; Foreign Affairs and Overseas Service Act, 1983.

154

109. Citizenship act 1977, sections 2 and 6.
110. Immigration Act, 1964, amended by Immigration (Amendment) Acts, 1965, 1968, 1969, 1976, 1977, 1978, (No. 2) 1978, 1979, 1980, Passports Act 1980; Undesirable Immigrants Exclusion Act 1919, amended by Immigration Restriction (Amendment) Act 1923).
111. See A. Picciarelli, 'The Soviet Internal Passport System', 19 Int. Law (1985) 915.
112. Federal Constitution of 11 December 1957, Article 4(2)(a) amended by Constitution (Amendment) Act 1964; Constitution and Malaysia (Singapore Amendment) Act 1965.
113. Immigration Act 1959–63 (Consolidating Ordinance No. 12 of 1959, Act No. 27 of 1963 and the Immigration (Transitional Provisions) Order 1963, F.L.N. 226.
114. See Federal Constitution of 11 December 1957, Articles 14–31 and Citizenship Rules 1964, L.N. 82/64.
115. *Ibid.*, sections 62–71.
116. *Ibid.*, sections 73–74.
117. See generally Sir K. Roberts-Wray, *Commonwealth and Colonial Law,* 1966, pp. 95–96; Sir W. Dale, *The Modern Commonwealth,* 1983, pp. 187–189.
118. R. Glass, *The Times,* 22 November 1961.
119. R. Mordecai, *The West Indies: the Federal Negotiations,* 1968, pp. 283–85.
120. Section 2(2).
121. Jamaica Constitution Order in Council, 1962/1550, second schedule, section 16(3)(b) (Constitution of 25 July 1962).
122. Section 1: Foreign Nationals and Commonwealth Citizens (Employment) Act 1964 (Appointed Day) Notice, Jamaica Gazette Supplement Vol. LXXXVII, 26 November 1964, No. 368.
123. Sections 2, 3(1). There are certain exemptions, irrelevant to the present discussion.
124. Geneva, 11 July 1947, 218 U.N.T.S. 345; 148 B.F.S.P. 619: *Basic Documents* VII.1.
125. *Supra,* notes 12–17.
126. Montevideo Convention on the Rights and Duties of States, 26 December 1933, 165 L.N.T.S. 19, Article 1(d). See J. Fawcett, *The British Commonwealth in International Law,* 1963, pp. 92–143.
127. See in particular the Secretary General's note, A/2929, 1 July 1955.
128. I.e., Ascension Island and the British Indian Ocean Territory. See the Entry Control (Ascension) Ordinance 1967, No. 1, amended by the Entry Control (Ascension) (Amendment) Ordinance 1979, No. 1; and in the case of the British Indian Ocean Territory, see the Immigration Ordinance 1971, No. 1, amended by the Law Revision (Miscellaneous Amendments) Ordinance 1981.
129. Immigration Ordinance No., 55 of 1971 amended by Ordinances Nos. 57 of 1972, 52 of 1976, 47 of 1977, 3 of 1979, 42 of 1979, 61 of 1979, 15 of 1980, 62 of 1980, 35 of 1981, 64 of 1981, 66 of 1981, 75 of 1981, 42 of 1982, 78 of 1982, 79 of 1982, 55 of 1983, 24 of 1984, 31 of 1984 and 40 of 1985 and by Legal Notices Nos. 183/72, 302/80/315/80, 373/81, 346/82, 392/82, 87/83 and 382/84. See also the legislation of the Turks and Caicos Islands: Immigration Ordinance No. 4 of 1971, amended by Ordinances Nos. 7 of 1974, 8 of 1975 and 9 of 1979.
130. Sections 2 and 8(1).
131. Anguilla: Immigration and Passport Ordinance, No. 14 of 1980, section 2, read with the Anguilla Constitution order 1982, S.I. No. 334, Articles 18(5). For the purposes of the Ordinance of 1980, a person not 'belonging' to the island is an alien. Immunity or exemption from control is extended to certain other categories, including Government servants, members of H.M. forces, representatives of the U.N. and of organizations to which Anguilla belongs and dependents of these. cf. the State of Saint Christopher, Nevis and Anguilla Immigration and Passport (Amendment) Act 1968, No. 20, section 2.
132. Immigration and Passport Ordinance 1977, No. 9, sections 3 and 5.

133. Immigration and Passport Ordinance, 1945, no. 7; amended by Immigration and Passport (Amendment) Ordinances, 1954, no. 13; 1956, No. 15; 1959, No. 10 section 2(2)(b); 1970, No. 18; 1973, no. 3; 1975, No. 25; 1975, No. 29; 1979, No. 21 and (especially) 1982), No. 24 and 1984, No. 6.

134. For Tristan da Cunha see the Entry Control (Tristan da Cunha) Ordinance, No. 1 of 1967, section 3. For Saint Helena, see the Immigrants Land-holding (Restriction) Ordinance, No. 8 of 1969, section 2, and the Immigration Ordinance, No. 6 of 1972, amended by the Immigration (Amendment) Ordinance, No. 13 of 1985.

135. Caymanian Protection Law, No. 23 of 1971, section 14 and 24 amended by Caymanian Protection (Amendment) Laws No. 7 of 1977, No. 22 of 1977 (No. 2), No. 32 of 1977 (No. 3), No. 13 of 1979, No. 3 of 1979, No. 3 of 1982, No. 13 of 1983 and No. 24 of 1984. See further the Cayman Islands (Constitution) (Amendment) Order 1984, S.I. No. 126.

136. Immigration Regulation No. 18 of 1971; Anglo-French Protocol of 6 August 1914, 10 L.N.T.S. 334, Article 8.

137. Immigration Control Ordinance, No. 12 of 1962, amended by Immigration Control (Amendment) Ordinances No. 19 of 1962, No. 20 of 1963, No. 11 of 1967, No. 19 of 1972, No. 17 of 1976 (No. 2) and No.7 of 1983 together with the Administration of Justice Ordinance, No. 12 of 1983.

138. Gibraltarian Status Ordinance, No. 13 of 1962, amended by Gibraltarian Status (Amendment) Ordinance, No. 13 of 1963.

139. Immigration Control (Amendment) Ordinance, No. 7 of 1983.

140. Immigration Ordinance, No. 10 of 1965, section 10; amended by Immigration (Amendment) Ordinances No. 12 of 1967, No. 10 of 1968 and No. 10 of 1974.

141. The only difference between persons in these three categories and 'Hong Kong belongers' is that unlike belongers they are liable to deportation under sections 20(6) of the Immigration Ordinance 1971, as amended.

142. Immigration Control (Amendment) Ordinances No. 19 of 1972 and No. 7 of 1983; European Communities (Amendment) Ordinance, No. 2 of 1985; European Communities (Spanish and Portuguese Accession) Ordinance, No. 21 of 1985.

143. Immigration Regulation No. 18 of 1971, amended by Joint Regulation 21 of 1980 and Immigration Regulation (Amendment) Act, No. 8 of 1984, Reg. 2(2).

144. I.e., persons, other than prohibited immigrants, who intend to engage on their own account in agriculture, animal husbandry, prospecting for minerals or in a trade, business or profession, for which they are qualified and have sufficient capital: Immigration Ordinance, No. 10 of 1965, section 10.

145. I.e., those entering under the Banking (Special Provisions) Ordinance, No. 4 of 1979 for the purpose of conducting business in accordance with that Ordinance and departing immediately thereafter.

146. A. Mutharika, *The Regulation of Statelessness under International Law*, 1977, 8–13.

147. R. Plender, 'The Expulsion of Asians from Uganda: Legal Aspects' 9 Rev. Int. Comm. Jur. (1972) 19.

148. See exchange of Notes between Austria and Prussia, 2–30 September 1849, Martens, *Recueil des traités*, Part XIV, p. 600; Treaty of Goetha, between Austria, Holstein-Lauenburg, the German Bund and Liechtenstein, 15 July 1851, Lessing, *Staatsangehörigkeit*, p. 132.

149. *Supra*, note 3 at 57.

150. See R. Donner, *The Regulation of Nationality in International Law,* 1983, 121 and sources cited there.

151. See R. Flournoy and M. Hudson, *Nationality Laws*, 1929 (e.g. for Poland, p. 646).

152. *Minutes of Conference*, p. 38.

153. See Donner, *supra* note 150 at 122.

156

154. The Hague, 12 April 1930; U.K.T.S. 112 (1973); *Basic Documents* II.3.
155. Article 9.
156. 4 A.D. (1927–28) 314, No. 209.
157. 14 A.D. (1947) 107, No. 41.
158. 7 A.D. (1933) 290, No. 115.
159. See Sir H. Lauterpacht, 'The Nationality of Denationalised Persons' in *Collected Papers,* ed. E. Lauterpacht, 1977, Vol. III, p. 383 at 399.
160. *Basic Documents* I.1.
161. New York, 30 August 1961; U.K.T.S. 158 (1975); *Basic Documents* II.6; Articles 8 and 9.
162. P. Weis, 'The United Nations Convention on the Reduction of Statelessness 1961', 11 I.C.L.Q. (1962) 1073 at 1087.
163. New York, 7 March 1966; 660 U.N.T.S. 195; *Basic Documents* I.3.
164. *Supra*, note 150 at p. 153.
165. New York, 16 December 1966, 6 I.L.M. (1967) 368; U.K.T.S. 6 (1977); *Basic Documents* I.2.
166. 14 U.N.G.A.O.R. 3rd Committee, 954th meeting, p. 232 (12 November 1959).
167. It is suggested, with respect, that it is only by ignoring the effect of these conventions and concentrating upon pre-war sources that Dr Weis is able to reach his conclusion 'that customary international law does not normally impose on the State of former nationality a duty of readmission': *supra* note 3, p. 57.
168. 13 A.D. (1946) 133 (No. 58).
169. *Supra*, note 158. For the *Reichsburgergesetz* of 9 May 1935, see BGBl. 1935 I, 593.
170. The French *Cour d'Appel* reached an opposite view on the interpretations of the Allied legislation in *Terhoch* v *Daudin et Assistance Publique,* 14 A.D. (1947) 121, No. 54. That decision was in turn followed in *Gungéré* v Falk, 16 A.D. (1949) 224, No. 68; 39 Rev. crit. dr. int. priv. (1950) 580.
171. *Frau Till G ... and Others* v *Verfungung des Amtsgerichts Wiesbaden*, Decision of 14 February 1968, B. Verf. G. 23, 98.
172. F. Mann, 'The Present Validity of Nazi Nationality Laws', 89 L.Q.R. (1973) 194.
173. [1975] 2 W.L.R. 347.
174. *Ibid*. at p. 357.
175. *Ibid*. at p. 368.
176. *Ibid*. at pp. 372–74.
177. *Hufrudstadsbladet,* 19 and 27 March 1982, cited by Donner, *supra* note 150 at 125.
178. This conclusion is suggested by the American Law Institute, 2 *Foreign Relations Law of the United States* (Revised) Tentative Draft No. 6 (1985) at para. 702.
179. Van Panhuys, *supra*, note 5 at 57.
180. *Supra*, text at note 7.
181. H. Hannum, *The Right to Leave and Return in International Law and Practice*, 1985, 75.
182. *Kahane (Successor)* v *Parisi and the Austrian State,* V Z.O. (1930) 222; 5 A.D. (1929–30) 213, No. 131; *Spaulding Claim*, 24 I.L.R. (1956) 452; *Zangrilli Claim*, 24 I.L.R. (9156) 459; *Mergé Claim*, 22 I.L.R. (1955) 443. See D. Turack, 'Selected Aspects of International and Municipal Law Concerning Passports', 12 Wm. and Ma. L. Rev. (1971) 805, 814–17.
183. *La Gazeta*, No. 188 of 4 October 1972 (Law on Retirement).
184. Amended Regulations of 18 December 1981.
185. T. Tyrell, *Costa Rica: A Brief Summary of the Retirement Law*, 1980, 4.

BIBLIOGRAPHY

V. Cable, *Whither Kenyan Emigrants?* Fabian Society (London) 1969.

J. Crouzetier, 'D'Helsinki à Madrid: la circulation des personnes et des informations en Europe', 84 RGDIP (1980) 752.

A. de Rouw, 'Some Aspects of the Right to Leave and to Return', 12 Neths, Ybk. Int. L. (1981 42.

Y. Ghai and Others. 'Expulsion and Expatriation in International Law: the Right to Leave, to Stay and to Return', 67 AJIL (1973) 122.

R. Higgins, 'The Right in International Law of an Individual to Enter, Stay in and Leave a Coutry', 49 Int. Aff. (1973) 341.

M. Janie, 'Individuals as Subjects of International Law', 17 Cornell Int. L. J. (1984) 61.

R. Lapidoth, 'The Right of Return in International Law, with Special Reference to the Palestinian Refugees', 16 Israel Ybk. H.R. (1986) 103.

R. Plender, 'The Exodus of Asians from East and Central Africa: Some Comparative and International Law Aspects', 14 A.J. Comp. L. (1971) 287.

K. Rabl (ed.), *Das Recht auf die Heimat: Vorträge, Thesen, Kritik, Rerche (Munich) 1965.*

V. Sharma and F. Wooldridge, 'Some Legal Questions Arising from the Expulsion of the Ugandan Asians', 23 ICLQ (1974) 397.

D. Turack, 'Freedom of Movement and the Travel Document', 4 Cal. West. Int. L. J. (1973) 8.

F. Wooldridge and V. Sharma, 'International Law and the Expulsion of Ugandan Asians', 9 Int. Lawyer (1975) 30.

CHAPTER 5

Exceptional Duties to Admit Aliens

Apart from those cases in which an obligation to admit an alien arises by reason of a treaty, there are a few instances in which general international law imposes on States special obligations in respect of the admission of defined categories of foreigners.

ACQUIRED RIGHTS

Aliens who have satisfied a residential qualification, determined by the law of the State in which they have established domiciles, commonly receive by operation of that law, or by formal administrative act, an indefinite right of residence, or are relieved (partially or wholly) from liability to deportation. An examination of national laws on this point reveals a certain congruence of practice. Indeed, it would be difficult to find a State in which the power to curtail the alien's right to remain may be exercised without regard to the length of his or her lawful residence.

In Argentina, the general rule is that an alien who has been admitted as a permanent resident may have his leave to remain in the country curtailed only in the event of specified breaches of the law (including immigration law), and only if the decision is taken by the administrative authorities within two years of the grant of the leave. Thereafter, the permanent resident obtains a qualified status of irremovability.[1]

In Austria, an alien who presents specified documents attesting to the lawfulness of his residence is eligible to be given unlimited leave to remain, with a corresponding exemption from deportation save in the event of grave violations of the law, after a period of four years' continuous residence. In practice, such leave is usually granted after a period of six to ten years' residence.[2] In Denmark, the power to expel an alien for supporting himself by unlawful means may be exercised only in relation to those who have been present on Danish soil for less than two years. In all cases of deportation, regard must be paid to the relationship between the alien and the Danish community.[3] In the Netherlands, an alien is eligible to receive an establishment permit (*'Vestigingsvergunning'*) after five years' residence, provided that he has a stable income and has not been sentenced to imprisonment for a period exceeding one month. Aliens who have resided in the Netherlands for over ten years are not required to prove that they have a stable income in order to receive an establishment permit.[4] In France, an alien is eligible to be issued with a *carte de résident* of ten years' validity, after three years' residence in the Republic, provided that the alien has sufficient funds for the maintenance of himself and any dependents and provided further that he has not been sentenced during those five years to a period of imprisonment of one year or more.[5] In the Federal Republic of Germany, an alien is eligible to receive resident status (*'umbefristete Aufenthalterlaubnis'*) after five years' residence, but eight years is normally required in practice. To obtain this status, the alien must have a special work permit and sufficient income and must be able to communicate in the German language and have housing of at least the standard considered as normal in the place of residence. To qualify for permanent resident status (*'Aufenthaltsberechtigung'*) the alien must meet all of the foregoing conditions and have eight years' legal and uninterrupted residence in the Federal Republic and have adapted to German conditions.[6]

In the Council of Europe countries as a whole, a right of permanent residence is accorded by national law or practice after periods of residence, varying from place to place but not exceeding ten years (the Swiss requirement).[7] Indeed, the European Assembly has therefore contemplated in 1987 the adoption of a Recommendation on the Right of Permanent Residence, to be followed by a Convention. It may well proceed to do so in 1988.

In the United Kingdom the right of abode is extended not only to British citizens but also to certain Commonwealth citizens who had a similar right on the eve of the entry into force of the British Nationality Act 1981 by reason of their connections with patrials by birth, adoption or marriage. Further, a non-citizen who is settled in the United Kingdom is liable to be deported only in the event of a recommendation of a court following conviction of an offence or (exceptionally) on the ground that deportation would be conducive to the public good or in the event of the deportation of a member of his family.[8] For this purpose, a person is 'settled' in the United Kingdom if he is ordinarily resident there without being subject under the immigration laws to any restriction on the period for which he may remain. It is the duty of an immigration officer, when exercising his discretion as to whether to admit as a returning resident a person who has been away from the United Kingdom for more than two years, to consider the length of the applicant's earlier stay in the United Kingdom, his purpose in returning and the nature of his ties with the United Kingdom by family connections, maintenance of a home or otherwise.[9]

In the case of Canada a distinction is drawn between permanent residents and others. A permanent resident may be removed only in pursuance of section 27 (1) of the Immigration Act. This provides for the deportation of a person who would have been inadmissible on specified grounds[10] on his entry to Canada; or who knowingly contravened terms and conditions of landing; or is engaged in subversion by force of any government; or has been convicted of an offence for which five years' imprisonment could have been imposed or for which at least six months' imprisonment was imposed; or who was landed on the basis of false documents or representations or wilfully failed to support himself in Canada.[11] By contrast, a person who has not attained permanent resident status may be removed on several other grounds and, moreover, on grounds less restrictive in nature. Thus, one who is not a permanent resident may be deported following his conviction of any indictable federal offence or if he works in Canada contrary to the Immigration Act or Regulations.[12]

Likewise, in the case of Australia, permanent residents are more favourably treated than others in this regard. The deportation of a permanent resident from Australia may be ordered only on his conviction of specified immigration offences, once the resident has remained in Australia lawfully for ten years.[13]

The current law of the United States makes special provision for the readmission of returning residents but does not expressly provide that such aliens shall have the right to re-enter. American courts have, however, construed the Immigration and Nationality Act somewhat liberally in order to facilitate the readmission of aliens who have resided in the country for substantial periods.[14] A returning resident is not liable to be excluded and may be dealt with only in deportation proceedings.[15] The courts of Brazil[16] and South Africa[17] have also construed immigration legislation liberally, in order to ensure that immigrants who have resided in those countries for substantial periods may continue to do so and may be assured of readmission after short absences abroad.

In view of this congruence of State practice, some have argued that there exists a principle of acquired rights which may be applied in the case of residence. Describing the initiative taken by the Democratic Party in the Canton of Zurich to secure the imposition of further restrictions on the employment and residence in Switzerland of aliens who have been present in the federation for five years, Macheret argues that the proposal was

> juridiquement inadmissible, car il conduirait à remettre en cause des droits acquis.[18]

Dr Goodwin-Gill reached the conclusion that the alien's interests will not all come within the limited doctrine of acquired rights 'but overall he has what may be loosely termed "legitimate expectations"'.[19]

While the identification of the elements in 'acquired rights' remains a matter of controversy[20] and 'there is no adequate measure of certainty with regard to [the application of the doctrine of acquired rights] to the various categories of private rights',[21] the existing authorities enable us to offer a definition. The expression may be taken to signify any rights, corporeal or incorporeal, properly vested under municipal law in a natural or juristic person and of an assessable monetary value. A right is not protected as an acquired right unless it is vested, in the sense that the State against which the right is asserted can be said to have taken some unequivocal step to invest the alien with an entitlement.[22] From this it follows that prolonged lawful residence by itself cannot give rise to an acquired right. The possibility could arise (if at all) only in a case in which a State has granted to an alien by some express act the right to reside indefinitely or for a certain period, without reserving the possibility of curtailing the alien's stay.

Even in this case, serious difficulties are presented. It seems that an acquired right denotes a proprietary right. Originally, the expression was confined to the protection of interests in land, although more recently it has been applied to the protection of interests in personalty[23] and interests in a contractual right were protected by the doctrine of acquired rights in the *Forests of Central Rhodopia Arbitration*.[24] It seems, however, that the doctrine has not yet been applied to the protection of a bare right of residence. It would, indeed, be difficult to apply it to such a right, since the licence to live in a certain territory can scarcely be assessed in monetary terms, and it is established that an international tribunal will not grant relief where the '*lucrum cessans*' is 'too remote or speculative'.[25] In the *Oscar Chinn Case* the Permanent Court concluded that Chinn never enjoyed an acquired right because the value of the commercial freedoms extended to him had no ascertainable worth: their value fluctuated in accordance with the vicissitudes of commercial life.[26]

From the sparse materials available, it seems that the right of residence lacks the proprietary element or the capability of being assessed in monetary terms that is indispensable for the protection of acquired rights. It is thought, however, that circumstances may occur in which an alien acquires a right, protected by international law, to conduct a trade, profession or other profitable activity in the territory of a foreign State. In such an event, the right is liable to be disturbed in the event of the alien's deportation or in the event of the withdrawal of the right of residence.

In 1932, Sir Hersch Lauterpacht thought it probable that 'the licence to exercise a profession is no less an acquired right than possession of a concession'.[27] The Upper Silesian tribunal neither vindicated nor challenged that view in its decision in *Kugele* v *Polish State*.[28] In that case a German businessman argued that the tax system introduced in Poland in territory formerly under German jurisdiction had the effect of depriving him of an acquired right. The tribunal based its conclusion on the ground that the remunerativeness of the business did not constitute any part of an acquired right. Thus it avoided the necessity of determining whether the right was vested. In *Jablonsky* v *German Reich,* however, a Jewish advocate from Kreutzberg alleged that his practice had been destroyed as a result of a German boycott, and that he had been forced to emigrate with his family to Palestine. Rejecting his claim, the tribunal stated:

> as a rule, the freedom to use one's working capacity and to exercise a profitable activity which rests on the general principle of industrial liberty does not constitute a subjective vested right. For such a right to exist there must be some title of acquisition and the recognition by the law of some concrete power.[29]

Those words seem to imply that if the advocate's right to practise had been recognized by the law, and if it had been assessable in monetary terms, his freedom to conduct his professional activities might well have become an 'acquired right', and even *de facto* expulsion to Palestine might have constituted a violation of that right.[30]

DIPLOMATS AND CONSULS

Diplomatic and consular immunities from domestic jurisdiction are traditionally explained and defended on three different grounds: extraterritoriality, the representative character of envoys and functional necessity.[31] It is thought that recent practice favours the last of these three bases.[32]

It is elementary that a foreign diplomat who arrives at the frontier of the State to which he has been accredited should be admitted to the territory of that State without unreasonable impediment. A breach of this principle will justify the accrediting State's formal protest. While no State is obliged to receive as envoy a person nominated by the sending State, it is relatively rare for the receiving State to raise objection to the sending State's choice; and when such objections are raised, this is invariably done well in advance of the nominee's proposed arrival. Other than in these cases, receiving States customarily grant to the envoys certain privileges and immunities, at least in so far as this is essential for the performance of their functions. One privilege which is manifestly necessary for the performance of those functions is the assurance of admission to the receiving State's territory. The point is reflected in domestic law, ancient and modern.

The former provision of the Panamanian Administrative Code which forbade the immigration of Chinese, Turks, Syrians and North Africans of the Turkish race did not apply to 'diplomatic and consular agents of the races whose immigration is forbidden'.[33] A Roumanian law of 1904 provided, on the basis of reciprocity, that diplomatic and consular representatives and certain other members of the personnel of foreign missions to Roumania should be admitted to Roumania without the necessity of having a visa on their passports or travel documents.[34] In the United Kingdom, section 8 (3) of the Immigration Act of 1971 provides that the stipulations in the Act:

> relating to those who are not British citizens shall not apply to any person so long as he is a member of a mission (within the meaning of the Diplomatic Privileges Act 1964), a person who is a member of the family and forms part of the household of such a member, or a person otherwise entitled to the like immunity from jurisdiction as is conferred by that Act on a diplomatic agent.

In principle, the diplomat's family includes the mother and sister of a bachelor or widower.[35] A member of the family of a diplomat may cease to form part of his household and so become subject to immigration control.[36]

Under the United States' former Immigration Rules of 1 January 1930,[37] a head tax was levied on certain alien immigrants, but not on 'diplomatic and consular officers and other accredited officials of foreign Governments, their suites, families and guests, for whatsoever purpose they come'. Under the current law of the United States, the term 'immigrant' does not embrace any alien who is:

(i)   an ambassador, public minister, or career diplomatic or consular officer who has been accredited by a foreign government recognized *de jure* by the United States and who is accepted by the President or by the Secretary of State, and the members of the alien's immediate family; and

(ii) upon a basis of reciprocity, other officials and employees who have been accredited by a foreign government recognised *de jure* by the United States who are accepted by the Secretary of State, and the members of their immediate families; and

(iii) upon a basis of reciprocity, attendants, servants, personal employees, and members of their immediate families, of the officials and employees who have a non-immigrant status under (i) and (ii) above.[38]

An alien who falls into any of those categories is exempt from certain grounds of inadmissibility. Such a person is freed from certain documentary requirements, but must in some instances meet the qualitative tests required of all aliens seeking to enter the United States. In the case of 'A-1' aliens (ambassadors, public ministers, career diplomatic or consular officers, etc.) none of the grounds of inadmissibility applies, except those provisions relating to reasonable requirements of passport and visa as a means of identification, unless the President so directs and specific instructions are issued by the Department of State. No visa may be issued in the 'A-1' category to an alien who is considered by the Department of State to be *persona non grata*.[39]

American influence on the development of immigration law in the Philippines has been profound.[40] Section 48 of the Philippine Immigration Act of 1940 provides for exemption from control to be extended to:

> an official of a recognized foreign government who is coming on the business of his government ... his family, attendants, servants, and employees, except that they shall be in possession of passports, or other credentials showing their official status, duly visaed by Philippine diplomatic officials abroad, unless the President orders otherwise, and that their names shall appear on the passenger lists of transporting vessels ...

American influence in this respect has also had its impact on Canadian law, which provides that diplomatic and (in some cases) consular representatives enjoy 'non-immigrant' status, and exemption from certain grounds of inadmissibility and deportation.[41] Elsewhere in the Commonwealth, British legislative influence is more in evidence, and immigration statutes tend to contain sections which specifically provide that the relevant sections of the appropriate enactments 'shall not apply' to persons enjoying diplomatic immunity from civil or criminal process.[42]

In order to identify persons enjoying those immunities, receiving States frequently arrange for the diplomats in question to receive distinctive visas, and sending States frequently grant to them special passports. The types of passport available vary from one country to another, but distinction is commonly drawn between regular, official and diplomatic passports. The United States Manual lists the following categories of United States passports in general use: dependants' passports, special passports, service passports and diplomatic passports. In the words of Mr Lee:

> While a diplomatic passport is *prima facie* evidence that the bearer is a foreign service officer of the issuing State and should therefore be treated with due respect and courtesy by all concerned, his legal status in the receiving State is ultimately determined more by the type of visa granted him than by the type of passport he possesses.[43]

Indeed, even the granting of a diplomatic visa by the receiving State does not necessarily guarantee the bearer's right to diplomatic privileges and immunities in that State, still less in third States.[44] The issuance of such a visa will normally be regarded by the immigration authorities of the receiving State (and commonly by those of third States) as evidence that the bearer is entitled to enter the territory of the State which issued the visa. If any dispute should arise as to the bearer's tenure of diplomatic status, that dispute may be settled by the executive authorities of the receiving State, and such a decision may be communicated by way of a Foreign Office Certificate or its equivalent.[45]

When such an individual has been admitted to the territory of the State to which he is accredited, he is customarily exempted from provisions dealing with aliens registration, the requirements of laws dealing with the issuance of work permits or their equivalents, and certain restrictions on freedom of movement within the territory of the receiving State. These supplementary privileges and immunities may be regarded as consequences of diplomats' immunities from the exercise of some forms of criminal jurisdiction, or as corollaries of diplomats' freedom of communication.

Under the Jamaican Aliens Restriction (Defence) Regulations of 1940 certain aliens were required to submit to registration, but exemption from these requirements was extended to duly accredited members of foreign and overseas diplomat corps and their families.[46] In the United States, each alien who applies for a visa must be registered and fingerprinted in connection with his application, and must provide signed copies of his photograph. Those requirements:

> may be waived in the discretion of the Secretary of State in the case of any alien who is within that class of non-immigrants enumerated in sections 101 (a) (15) (A) . . . or in the case of any alien who is granted a diplomatic visa on a diplomatic passport, or the equivalent thereof.[47]

(This exemption from registration and fingerprinting is no longer wholly exceptional, since an Act of 1957 authorizes the Secretary of State and the Attorney-General to waive the requirement of fingerprinting in the case of most non-immigrant aliens.[48]) As a consequence of his exemption from registration, a holder of a diplomatic visa issued by the United States Government is immune from the requirements relating to annual address reporting.[49] Under French law, members of diplomatic and consular missions accredited in France, together with their wives, ancestors and minor or unmarried children living with them, are exempt from aliens registration.[50] Such persons enter France bearing diplomatic or service passports. They are exempted from the requirement of obtaining residence permits and from the regulations governing reporting change of address.

In the United Kingdom, diplomats' immunities from the requirements relating to work permits and labour vouchers are consequences of the general exempting provisions of the Immigration Act.[51] In the United States, corresponding immunities are consequences of the non-immigrant classification of diplomats and their families. In the case of Jamaica the Foreign Nationals and Commonwealth Citizens (Employment) Act of 1964 deals with the grant of employment permits, but the Foreign Nationals and Commonwealth Citizens

(Employment) Exemptions Regulations of 1964 provide that the Act shall not apply to accredited members of foreign or Commonwealth diplomatic missions, nor to specified members of the households of such persons.[52] In the Philippines, the Alien Registration Act of 1950 provides in section 1 that:

> no accredited official of a foreign government recognized by the Republic of the Philippines, or member of his official staff and family, shall be required to be registered.[53]

That section should be read in conjunction with section 1 of the Act to Require the Registration and Fingerprinting of Aliens, which contains terms identical (*mutatis mutandis*) with those of the 1950 Act. Indeed, the Regulations governing the Registration of Aliens in accordance with the Alien Registration Act[54] provide that 'accredited officials of a foreign Government' shall be exempt from the provisions relating to fingerprinting. An official who falls into that category is also exempt from the Philippine law governing issuance of certificates of residence, but that exemption is a consequence of the official's 'non-immigrant' classification.[55]

The proposition that accredited members of foreign diplomatic missions should enjoy freedom of movement within the borders of the receiving State has derived more support from writers than from recent State practice. Sen argues that the right of an envoy to move about freely in the territory of the receiving State is one of the essentials of the proper functioning of a mission.[56] Nevertheless, several receiving States restrict the movement of diplomats within their territories and the tendency to do so appears to be increasing. Such restrictive policies – and, indeed, other policies involving the harassment of diplomats – have occasionally provoked retaliation in kind. In 1967 the United Kingdom's embassy in Beijing was set on fire, and a British envoy there imprisoned. After these events, two Orders in Council[57] were made by the executive authorities of the United Kingdom, forbidding nationals of the People's Republic of China to embark in the United Kingdom for any port outside the Common Travel Area. In view of the Diplomatic Privileges Act, 1964, these Orders in Council did not apply to members of the Chinese diplomatic mission in London. Nevertheless, in August 1967 the United Kingdom's Foreign Secretary issued instructions forbidding Chinese envoys to travel beyond any point further than five miles from Marble Arch (in the centre of London). The Chinese envoys were given two days' notice in advance of the imposition of these restrictions. There appears to have been no provision of English law conferring on the Foreign Secretary the power to impose the latter restriction, and therefore the only punitive sanction which might have been invoked to deal with a person who contravened his instructions would have been to declare the offender *persona non grata*. No

Chinese diplomat was declared *persona non grata* for this reason. No diplomatic protest from the Government of the People's Republic of China was received by the Foreign Office.

While the restrictions imposed on the liberty of a diplomatic envoy to travel freely throughout the territory of the receiving State commonly exceed the restrictions imposed on the alien's liberty to travel internally, certain States accord to diplomats exemption from the restrictions imposed on the internal movement of aliens. In French law, aliens have the right in principle to travel freely throughout metropolitan France but must, if requested to do so by a competent public official, present the documentary authority by which they are permitted to reside in France.[58] In particular, aliens who remain in France in excess of three months are obliged to obtain residence permits (*cartes de séjour*), and must declare any changes of habitual and permanent 'effective residence', even if the move is merely within a community if the latter consists of more than 10,000 inhabitants. Since they are exempted from the requirements relating to residence permits, foreign diplomatic officials and their families are exempted from these requirements relating to reporting changes of address.[59]

The exoneration of the diplomatic envoy from restrictions on travel within the borders of the receiving State remains an occurrence insufficiently general to amount to evidence of customary law. The International Law Commission recommended that 'subject to its laws and regulations concerning zones, entry into which is prohibited or regulated for reasons of national security, the receiving State shall ensure to all members of the [foreign or overseas] mission freedom of movement and travel in its territory'.[60] Article 26 of the Vienna Convention on Diplomatic Relations, 1961 is based on that Recommendation, but neither the generality of its acceptance nor the liberality of its construction is such as to support the existence of a customary rule.

Modern State practice suggests that the receiving State has an unqualified power to declare a foreign envoy *persona non grata*. Hall expressed the view that a country need not recall its agent unless it is satisfied that the reasons for which his recall is demanded, or for which he is declared *persona non grata*, are sufficient.[61] There appears to be no convincing and authenticated example of the testing of that thesis by the sending State's insistence on the presence of its nominee. During the Crimean War the President of the United States revoked the exequaturs of three British consuls, on the ground that the consuls had violated the United States' laws and neutrality obligations by recruiting in the United States men to serve in the British army. Lord Clarendon strongly denied that the consuls had been engaged in any such recruiting, but recognized the right of the Government of the United States to form their own judgment on the matter.[62] Indeed, Article 8 of the Pan American Convention on Diplomatic Officers provides that a State having already accepted a diplomatic officer may request his recall without being obliged to state the reasons for such a decision. An envoy declared *persona non grata* continues to enjoy his immunity from immigration and deportation controls until his departure from the territory of the receiving State; but, no doubt, if such an envoy refused to leave the territory of the receiving State, the latter might legitimately expel him.[63]

Just as each sovereign State is competent to refuse to receive as ambassador or diplomatic agent a person nominated for such a position by a sending State, so each sovereign country may decline to 'admit' (that is, accept) a person nominated by a sending State as one of its consuls. The right to refuse to 'admit' consuls in this sense is generally accepted in international practice, and in theory.[64] The Harvard Research Draft provides that a State shall permit any other State with which it maintains diplomatic relations to have consuls at any port, city or place within its territory where any other State is permitted to have consuls, but otherwise a State may refuse to admit a person to the exercise of consular functions to its territory without even assigning reasons.[65]

It is not uncommon for States to 'admit' as consuls their own nationals, or other persons previously resident in their territories. For this reason few questions are likely to arise as to a person's right to enter the territory of a State which has 'admitted' him as a consul of another State. There is an abundance of authority to support the proposition that no State may, in conformity with international law, exercise criminal jurisdication over a foreign State's consul in respect of actions taken by him in the pursuit of his official functions. That authority can be found in particular in international conventions[66] and in domestic legislation.[67] Since a consul can scarcely exercise his official functions if he is denied admission to the territory of the State in which he is to serve, it follows that he cannot, in conformity with international law, be prevented from entering it.

It is also frequent for consuls to enjoy in the territories in which they serve certain exemptions from restrictions applicable to other aliens there. Article 43 of the International Law Commission's Draft Articles on Consular Intercourse and Immunities recommended that:

> Members of the consulate, members of their families, and their private staff, shall be exempt from all obligations under local jurisdiction in the matter of the registration of aliens, residence permits and work permits.[68]

Article 46 of the Vienna Convention on Consular Relations[69] provided likewise, but added that the exemption should not extend to any consular employee who is not a permanent employee of the sending State or who carries on any private gainful occupation in the receiving State, or to any member of the family of such an employee. Commenting on the substance of this article, the

International Law Commission referred to the 'practice of numerous countries' which made it necessary to exempt consular officers and their families from the obligation to register as aliens and apply for residence permits.[70]

Whereas there is a substantial degree of uniformity of State practice in relation to consular exemption from aliens registration, there is no such degree of uniformity in relation to consular freedom of movement.[71] The Vienna Convention applied the principle of free internal movement subject to limitations justified on grounds of national security. Barely a year after its conclusion, however, the Soviet Union and the United States concluded a consular convention which allows a consul to travel freely only 'within the limits of his consular district to carry out his official duties'.[72]

The United States and the United Kingdom accept in practice the proposition that diplomatic agents of one State accredited to another are entitled to certain immunities while they are in transit through a third State to their post or to their own countries.[73] In both countries the local authorities assert the power to determine whether the individual is to be recognized as a diplomat, and whether his presence in the country is required for the purposes of his official duties. So in *U.S.* v *Rosal* a New York district court held that the former Guatemalan Ambassador in Belgium and the Netherlands was not entitled to immunity for after his dismissal as ambassador he was in the United States on purely private business, and was not in transit between the sending State and the receiving State.[74] Equally, in *R* v *Pentonville Governor, ex parte Teja,* the Court of Queen's Bench held that Costa Rica's unilateral action in appointing the applicant as its representative did not confer diplomatic immunity on him and so concluded that the applicant was liable to be sent from the kingdom as a fugitive offender.[75]

Nevertheless, it is thought that even in this respect Anglo-American practice exceeds the demands of positive international law. It is true that Wharton expressed the view that a diplomatic agent travelling to the country to which he has been accredited, through a third State, pursuing for this purpose a natural and proper route, is entitled to the same privilege as when travelling through the country to which he is accredited;[76] but recent practice scarcely demonstrates uniform acceptance of that proposition. Indeed, current U.S. law is far from unambiguous on the point, although it seems to imply that a diplomatic agent accredited to a third State does not enjoy the right to travel through the United States for that purpose.[77] Article 40 of the Vienna Convention of 1961 provides that a diplomatic agent passing through the territory of a third State *which has granted him a passport visa if such visa was necessary,* while proceeding to take up or return to his post, or when returning to his own country, shall be accorded inviolability and such other immunities as may be required to ensure his transit or return. This seems to imply that the third State is not under any positive obligation to grant the requisite documents to the diplomat.

REPRESENTATIVES OF AND TO INTERNATIONAL ORGANIZATIONS

Article 105 of the Charter of the United Nations provides that representatives of members of the Organization, together with the Organization's officials, shall enjoy such privileges and immunities as are necessary for the independent exercise of their functions. That Article has been supplemented by the Convention on Privileges and Immunities of the United Nations, to which the vast majority of U.N. members have acceded.[78] The Convention provides that members' representatives to the United Nations shall, while exercising their functions and during their journeys to and from the place of meeting, enjoy exemption in respect of themselves and their spouses from immigration restrictions and aliens registration.[79] The same Convention provides that officials of the United Nations shall enjoy similar immunities.[80] Corresponding provisions are to be found in the constitutional documents of numerous other international organizations.[81] In particular, such provisions may be found in the constitutions of various specialized agencies of the United Nations, supplemented by the Convention on the Privileges and Immunities of Specialized Agencies.[82]

The Convention on Privileges and Immunities of the United Nations and the Convention relating to Specialized Agencies formed the models for subsequent agreements made by other organizations, including the Council of Europe, the Organization of American States, the Organization of African Unity and, to a far lesser extent, the three European communities (European Coal and Steel Community, European Economic Community and Euratom).[83] These multilateral agreements have normally been supplemented by bilateral arrangements with States in which the organizations maintain their offices.[84] States which engage in such arrangements frequently implement them by adopting municipal legislation, such as the United States' International Organizations Immunities Act of 1945[85] and the United Kingdom's International Organizations (Immunities and Privileges) Act, 1950.[86]

The privileges and immunities of judges and counsel of international tribunals are the subject of special considerations. Holders of international judicial offices commonly receive diplomatic immunities by treaty. This solution is the basis of sections 19 and 20 of the Statute of the International Court of Justice and the agreement of 1946 between the Netherlands and the Court. General Assembly Resolution 90 (I) of 1946 specifically recommended that States should secure for the judges transit facilities and an extension of diplomatic privileges in any country in which they reside for the purpose of holding themselves permanently at the disposal of the Court. The same Resolution contained recommendations that States should secure for agents, counsel and advocates before the Court corresponding transit facilities and the immunities provided in the General Convention for representatives of members. In

Zoernsch v *Waldock* Lord Diplock observed that the immunities of persons holding international judicial offices arose 'from duties owed by States to one another in international law'.[87]

Commenting on the United States' law on immigration, Gordon and Rosenfield made a similar observation:

> Because of the necessities of foreign intercourse, *the precepts of international law,* and the consistent practice of this country, persons coming to the United Statesin diplomatic or quasi-diplomatic status have been accorded wide exemptions from immigration restrictions.[88]

In considering the nature of these precepts of international law, it is necessary to bear in mind the distinction between State representatives to international organizations, and representatives of international organizations who are visiting foreign States. The precept whereby the former are granted certain exemptions from immigration laws applicable in the States in which international organizations hold meetings may be regarded as a corollary of each Member State's right to be represented at such meetings. As Goy has written,

> *il existe un droit des Etats à se faire représenter aux réunions, qu'ils soient Membres de l'Organisation, invités par elle, ou même désireux d'être représentés.*[89]

The precept whereby representatives of such organizations are accorded exemptions from immigration controls of the countries to which they are required to travel, may be founded on the doctrine of implied powers.[90]

There remains some dispute as to whether a State must allow representatives of a Government which it does not recognize to enter its territory in order to attend an international conference or the offices of an international organization situated there. State practice suggests that the host State must do so. Switzerland always allowed free access to the offices of the League of Nations for representatives of all member States, including the Soviet Union, with which Switzerland then maintained no diplomatic relations.[91] The United States has consistently allowed representatives of States and Governments unrecognized by the State Department to enter U.S. territory for the purpose of attending meetings of the United Nations, at the request of the latter. Section 15 of the Headquarters Agreement between the United Nations and the United States provides that principal permanent representatives of States, or permanent representatives with the rank of minister plenipotentiary, shall be ensured free access to the United Nations premises in New York City. Similar facilities are extended to other members of the staff of any given mission by agreement between the host State, the sending State and the

Secretary-General. Aliens entering the territory of the United States to participate in the affairs of organizations with premises or holding conferences there enjoy certain immunities in accordance with the International Organisations Immunities Act of 29 December 1945.[92] Under the Immigration and Nationality Act, non-immigrant status is extended to aliens who fall within any of the following categories:

1. Accredited representatives of foreign governments (*whether or not recognized de jure by the United States*) to certain designated organizations;
2. Officers or employees of such organizations;
3. Attendants, servants and personal employees of such representatives, officers and employees; and
4. The immediate families of the above.[93]

However, many Islamic countries have consistently refused to admit to their territories representatives sent by Israel to meetings of international organizations: this despite the former countries' accessions to the General Convention on Privileges and Immunities.[94] Explaining her refusal to admit Israeli representatives to Alexandria, the situs of the Permanent Headquarters of the East Mediterranean Regional Committee of the World Health Organization, Egypt stated:

Le Gouvernment égyptien pourra prendre, à l'égard des ressortissants des pays dont les relations avec l'Egypte ne sont pas normales, toutes précautions nécessaires à la sécurité du pays.

The World Health Assembly asked the Egyptian Government to reconsider its position. In 1960 the Government of Pakistan refused admission to Israeli observers at the conference of the Economic Commission for Asia and the Far East; the chairman modified the schedule so as to ensure that the conference began in Thailand, where the Israeli representatives were readily admitted.

A separate, if less vexatious, problem arises from the fact that delegations to international organizations do not always consist exclusively of representatives of States or governments. In the case of the International Labour Organization, employers' and workers' delegates receive, under Article 40 of the Constitution, the right to enter the territories in which conferences are scheduled. In the interparliamentary assemblies of the Council of Europe and the European Community, immunities are to a large extent based on parliamentary immunities in municipal law.[95] In the United States, delegates to meetings of international organizations do not, unless they are representatives of governments, benefit from classification as non-immigrants under section 101(a)(15)(G) of the Immigration and Nationality Act, 1952. By contrast, the New Zealand provision ensures that appropriate immunities may be extended to representatives to international organizations 'whether [they are representatives] of Governments or not'.[96] It is thought that as a general rule States acting as hosts to meetings of international organizations which seat non-governmental representatives are no less obliged to admit those representatives than to admit the delegates of States. This obligation, which cannot have as its corollary the right protected by international law of a private person to attend meetings of the organization, is best seen as a prerequisite to the proper performance of the organization's functions: it is therefore a duty expressly or impliedly undertaken by the host State as a member.

The question of expulsion of such representatives is not mentioned in the General Convention on Privileges and Immunities, but the Specialized Agencies Convention permits expulsion for activities outside the representatives' official functions. Under the law of the United States, 'international organization aliens' (as such representatives are called) are permitted to remain on U.S. territory for as long as the Secretary of State continues to recognize them as such.[97] The only exceptions to this rule arise in the case of attendants, servants and personal employees; such persons are normally admitted initially for a period of one year, but even they may apply without fee for an extension of their stay. Termination of the principal alien's status likewise terminates the status of his family, attendants and personal employees. Principal resident representatives of foreign governments to international organizations, as well as staff and families, are given similar protection against deportation by section 102 of the Immigration and Nationality Act. The same section extends similar benefits to officers and employees of international organizations.

As a general proposition, and in the absence of treaty obligations, no State is obliged to admit to its territory representatives of an international organization; but special considerations apply to U.N. forces, and an organization may have the implied power which its members must respect, to send its representatives abroad. In the case of the Congo, the United Nations placed a force on its territory before the Republic became a member of the Organization. *A propos* of this episode, Professor Bowett has written:

it may well be that once a State has consented to the presence of the United Nations on its territory for a particular purpose, it is bound, by the principle of good faith, to extend all such privileges and immunities as are necessary for the proper functioning of the U.N. and the achievement of that purpose. *The same argument would be valid for any international organization.*[98]

In practice, most States exempt from immigration control representatives only of those organizations to which the States in question belong, or with which they have particularly cordial relations.

In the case of the United States, the organizations in question are those designated by executive order of the President as entitled to benefits under the

International Organisations Immunities Act.[99] Similar entry privileges are recognized for aliens entering under international agreements relating to the North Atlantic Treaty Organizations (designated 'NATO aliens').[100] In the United Kingdom (it will be recalled) the Immigration Act of 1971 contains exemptions in favour of any person entitled to the like immunity from jurisdiction as is conferred by that Act on a diplomatic agent.[101] This group must be said to include not only officials of foreign governments accredited to international organizations in the United Kingdom, but also officials of the organizations themselves. Further privileges and immunities may be conferred by Order in Council, particularly on groups of persons enumerated in the International Organizations Act, 1968,[102] namely:

1. representatives to organizations specified by Order in Council to be among those to which the U.K. or its government, together with one or more foreign governments, belongs, or the Commission of the European Communities or the Council of the Association, or representatives on or member of an organ, committee or other subordinate body of the organization, Commission or Council;
2. holders of high offices specified by Order in Council in the organization, Commission or Council;
3. persons employed by or serving under the organization, Commission or Council as experts or as persons engaged on missions for the organization, Commission or Council; and
4. representatives specified by Order in Council of any foreign sovereign power or government at a conference held in the United Kingdom attended by representatives of the United Kingdom or its government, and one or more sovereign power or government.

Chiefly, the immunities include the same immunity from suit and legal process as is accorded to head of diplomatic missions. In addition, a member of the official staff of a representative who is recognized as holding a rank equivalent to that of a diplomatic agent may, in certain circumstances, be entitled to the same immunities as the representative.[103]

Since it is usual for junior officials to enjoy immunities in respect only of acts done in the course of their official business, it is important to identify the person or body with the power to determine whether the act in question was done in the course of official business. In relation to immigration law, the problem is likely to arise (if at all) in a situation in which there is some dispute as to whether the official is attempting to enter a particular country on official business. No clear decision on such a point has been made, but it appears that in the absence of treaty provisions to the contrary, the matter might well be settled by the domestic courts without the intervention of the organization concerned.[104]

Articles 11 and 13 of the U.N.-U.S. Headquarters Agreement provide that the federal, state or local authorities of the United States shall not impede the transit to or from the Headquarters District of:

1. representatives of members or officials of the United Nations, or of specialized agencies, or the families of such representatives or officials;
2. experts performing missions for the United Nations or for such specialized agencies;
3. representatives of information agencies who have been accredited by the United Nations or a specialized agency in its discretion after consultation with the United States;
4. representatives of non-governmental organizations recognized by the United Nations for the purpose of consultation under Article 71 of the Charter; or
5. other persons invited to the Headquarters District by the United Nations or by such specialized agency, on official business.[105]

This agreement forms, of course, part of the domestic law of the United States. Aliens in transit to the United Nations Headquarters District are subject to exclusion from the United States only if they belong to certain proscribed subversive organizations, or it is determined that they seek to enter the United States to engage in activities prejudicial to the public interest or dangerous to national security.[106]

Section 24 of the General Convention on Privileges and Immunities of the United Nations provides that the *laissez-passer* (a document designed to secure the privilege of free transit) should be recognized and accepted as valid for the purposes of travel into the territories of members.[107] This imprecisely-worded section has not been interpreted, by all Member States, as a mandatory provision requiring them to permit holders of *laissez-passers* to travel without national passports and visas.[108] The *laissez-passer* may at least be useful in securing speedy issuance of visas, and in obtaining other special travel facilities.[109]

ARMED FORCES

Not infrequently, States find it necessary or appropriate to exempt from the main or substantial provisions of their immigration laws members of the armed forces of other countries, or of international organizations. A legal obligation to exempt members of those forces from certain provisions of immigration control may derive from an agreement between the receiving State and the sending State; or, in the case of an international organization, such an obligation may derive from the organization's powers, expressed or implied in its charter. It appears convenient to deal first with the armed forces of foreign States, and to turn later to armed forces of international organizations.

By custom, members of the armed forces of one State, entering the territory of another, with the latter's consent, enjoy certain privileges. The nature and scope of these privileges, and their legal character, have, however, been the subject of considerable controversy.[110] According to Oppenheim, crimes committed by the members of the armed forces of one country on the territory of another cannot be punished by the local authorities. They may be punished only by the commanding officer of the forces or by other authorities of the home State, at least where the crime is committed within the place where the force is stationed or in some place where the offender was on duty.[111] Chief Justice Marshall's judgement in *The Schooner Exchange* v *McFaddon*[112] lends credence to Oppenheim's view, and that judgment has been reinforced by the decision of the Brazilian Supreme Court in *Re Gilbert*.[113] Conversely, the courts of some States appear unwilling to accept so broad a proposition.[114] Frequently receiving States are prepared, in the absence of special agreements, to allow only disciplinary matters to fall within the exclusive jurisdiction of the sending States. In conformity with this practice, States which receive on their territories members of the armed forces of friendly powers normally require the entrants to comply with their immigration laws. Special exceptions and dispensations are commonly created in favour of members of the armed forces of nations with which they maintain particularly cordial relations, or with which they have entered into treaties.

In this context it is pertinent to refer to the treaty establishing the North Atlantic Treaty Organization,[115] and its three supplementary agreements; the N.A.T.O. Status of Forces Agreement, 1952,[116] the Agreement on the Status of N.A.T.O. National Representatives and International Staff,[117] and the Protocol on the Status of the International Military Headquarters.[118] Article III of the Status of Forces Agreement provides that members of the forces shall be exempt from passport and visa regulations and immigration inspection on entering or leaving the territory of receiving States. It also provides that they shall be exempt from aliens registration. The United States Senate, in expressing its approval for this item, added that it understood that acceptance of the article did not imply relinquishment by the United States of its power to ensure the dispatch of aliens whose presence in the United States would be dangerous to its well-being or security.[119]

Indeed, under the express terms of Article III, members of the forces are to acquire no right to permanent residence or domicile in the receiving State, and must present, on demand, their personal identity cards, issued by the sending States, and must also be prepared to present, on demand, their individual or collective movement orders.[120] Members of the forces are exempt from passport and visa requirements,[121] but a similar exemption is not extended to dependants, who, in United States law, remain subject to the grounds of inadmissibility contained in the Immigration and Nationality Act, 1952.[122]

Members of the civilian components of the forces, and their dependants, are subject to passport and visa requirements and to the grounds of inadmissibility contained in section 212(a)(27), (29) of the Immigration and Nationality Act.

In the United Kingdom, the N.A.T.O. Status of Forces Agreement is implemented through the Visiting Forces legislation,[123] which applies also to the forces of several Commonwealth countries, and to those of other States which may be specified by Order in Council. The principal legislation lays down the maximum degree of immunity which may be extended thereby to members of the visiting forces. The immunity which is, in fact, extended to members of those forces is specified by subsidiary Orders. Members of certain armed forces, designated under the Visiting Forces legislation, are exempted from the immigration controls established by the Immigration Act of 1971.[124] Similar exemptions are conferred on members of Commonwealth forces undergoing training in the United Kingdom.

In the case of the United Nations' forces a distinction must be drawn between the freedom to enter a State's territory and the freedom to move throughout it. The latter freedom may exist in a restricted or unrestricted form, according to the terms of the relevant agreements. For example, the United Nations Emergency Force (U.N.E.F.) in Egypt did not enjoy the freedom to move throughout Egyptian territory, but the United Nations Force in Cyprus (U.N.F.I.CYP.) was permitted to move freely throughout the island. In the case of the United Nations Operations in the Congo (O.N.U.C.), the force was guaranteed the right to move freely throughout the territory of the Republic, including the 'Province of Katanga'.[125]

Others have examined in detail whether members of United Nations forces may enter the territory of States other than with their explicit consent.[126] It is abundantly clear that members of a United Nations force established by the Security Council under Chapter 7 of the Charter, or by the General Assembly under the Uniting for Peace Resolution, may enter the territory of an aggressor State without first obtaining the latter's consent, provided, of course, that they enter that territory in accordance with their orders and in order to accomplish their functions. This principle was amply demonstrated by the entry of the United Nations Force into Korea, north of the 38th parallel, and by the continued presence of the O.N.U.C. force in the Congo after the purported withdrawal of consent by the heads of the regimes concerned.[127] Less tractable considerations are involved in the cases of the stationing of United Nations troops on the territories of non-aggressive States.

It appears that a Member State which is the victim of an act of aggression is bound by Articles 2(5), 25 and 49 of the United Nations Charter to admit to its territory members of United Nations forces established by decisions of the Security Council acting under Chapter 7. In other cases, the consent of the host State is a prerequisite to the legal admission of the force. The International

Court of Justice stressed this in its *Advisory Opinion on Certain Expenses of the United Nations.*[128] Such consent is normally conveyed by express agreement, and such agreements generally guarantee the exemption of members of the forces from domestic immigration controls, insofar as that exemption is required to ensure that the United Nations, rather than the host State, determines the composition of the force. It is unlikely that the United Nations or the contributing States would be willing to send a United Nations force to the territory of any State which refused to relieve members of that force from the main or substantive provisions of its immigration controls.

Paragraph 7 of the U.N.E.F. Status of Force Agreement read as follows:

Members of the force shall be exempt from passport and visa regulations and immigration inspection and restrictions on entering or departing from Egyptian territory. They shall also be exempt from any regulations governing the residence of aliens in Egypt, including registration, but shall not be considered as acquiring any right to permanent residence or domicile in the territory of Egypt. For the purpose of such entry or departure members of the force will be required to have only (1) an individual or collective movement order issued by the commander or an appropriate authority of the participating State; and (2) a personal identity card issued by the commander under the authority of the Secretary-General except in the case of first entry when the personal military identity card issued by the appropriate authorities of the participating State will be accepted in light of the said force identity card.[129]

That paragraph bears a resemblance to Article III(1) and (2) of the North Atlantic Treaty Organization Status of Forces Agreement, on which it is presumed to have been based.[130]

Paragraphs 4 and 5 of the Agreement between the United Nations and the Republic of the Congo on the O.N.U.C. force was based on paragraph 7 of the U.N.E.F. Status of Forces Agreement, and likewise ensured that members of the force should enjoy exemption from domestic immigration control and aliens registration and regulation, but should obtain no right to acquire or maintain Congolese domicile.[131] The basic agreement between the Government of Cyprus and the United Nations on U.N.F.I.CYP. invoked the General Convention on Privileges and Immunities of the United Nations.[132] This was supplemented by the Status of Forces Agreement, which contained a provision based on paragraph 7 of the U.N.E.F. Status of Forces Agreement.[133] Professor Bowett, interpreting that paragraph, wrote that force identity cards and, in the case of Secretariat officials, United Nations *laissez-passers,* would be accepted as sufficient entry documents; any other regulation of entry would give the host State unilateral control over the composition and functioning of the force.[134]

Indeed, the proper functioning of a United Nations force might be imperilled if the host State were to insist on its right to deny admission to any member of the force on whom it refused to confer a visa. It is to avoid such a situation that provisions such as those contained in paragraph 7 of the U.N.E.F. Status of Forces Agreement have been composed. Even in the absence of such a provision in the agreement between the United Nations and a host State, the latter's insistence on the right to deny visas (and hence admission) to certain members of the force should be regarded with the greatest suspicion. Proper observance of the principle of good faith will normally preclude any such insistence.

The United Nations may require transit facilities or bases in territories of States which have not been victims of acts of aggression, and which will not be hosts to peace-keeping forces. In practice, such transit rights have always been acquired under specific agreements, but it is probable that the Security Council has the power under Chapter 6 of the Charter to compel the grant of transit facilities when they are necessary for action taken under that Chapter.

Article 43 of the Charter embodies an obligation to provide assistance and facilities, including rights of passage, in accordance with special agreements. Members of the United Nations, at least, seem to have assumed the duty to provide transit facilities, in appropriate circumstances. While it is clear that 'special agreements' will continue to govern numerous details connected with the grant of such facilities, it is no less clear that such agreements have always included provisions to ensure that members of the force will enjoy exemptions from immigration control. For example, by Article III of the *Agreement . . . regarding the Status of the United Nations Forces in Japan* the Government of Japan undertook to ensure for members of the force under the United Nations Commission on Korea (U.N.C.O.K.) exemptions from immigration control and aliens regulation.[135]

In general, observer groups formed under Article 34 of Chapter 6 have no right to enter the territory of a State other than by the latter's consent. However, Member States have usually accepted observer groups when requested to do so, and have accorded them freedom of movement. In the case of the military observer group in Palestine, the Security Council passed a series of resolutions to stress that freedom of movement in the area was essential to the performance of the group's functions. Eventually, the armistice agreement between Israel and Egypt provided that members of the Mixed Armistice Commission and its observers should be accorded such freedom of movement as the Commission might deem necessary, provided that when such decisions were reached by a majority vote, only United Nations observers should be employed.[136]

For two centuries the principal writers have tended to accept that States are obliged by international law to extend certain immunities to the property and personnel of foreign vessels which are shipwrecked or forced by evident distress to take refuge on land or in territorial or inland water. This principle was mentioned by Vattel[137] and has been followed, in more recent times, by Hyde,[138] Hackworth,[139] Jessup[140] and O'Connell.[141] It was embodied in the judgment of Chief Justice Marshall in *Hallet and Browne v Jenks*[142] and in subsequent judgments delivered on both sides of the Atlantic.[143] In the *North Atlantic Coast Fisheries Arbitration* the Permanent Court of Arbitration observed that a provision in a treaty operating between the United States and the United Kingdom, providing that fishermen of the former might enter the bays of the latter for repairs, amounted to little more than an embodiment of an obligation accepted by all civilized nations.[144] The same principle seems to apply to aircraft. In *The Eleanor*[145] Sir William Scott qualified it as follows:

> It must be urgent distress, it must be something of grave necessity . . . the danger must be such as to cause apprehension in the mind of an honest and fair man. I do not mean to say that there must be an actual physical necessity existing at the moment, a moral authority would justify the act, where, for instance, the ship had sustained previous damage, so as to render it dangerous to the lives of the persons on board to prosecute the voyage.

In the event of a shipwreck, air-crash or severe storm forcing a vessel to land on foreign territory, the craft and its passengers and crew are not, of course, guaranteed immunity from all laws applicable in the local State.[146] Practice seems to indicate, however that the passengers and crew cannot be prosecuted for breach of immigration laws. In many countries there is express statutory provision to this effect. In the case of South Korea, Articles 20 and 21 of the Law (No. 1900) on Control of Exit and Entry of 3 March 1967, provide for the issuance of Emergency Landing Permits, and Landing Permits on the Occasion of a Disaster.

In the United Kingdom no such express statutory provision exists but section 24(1) of the Immigration Act of 1971 provides that it shall be an offence for a non-citizen 'knowingly' to enter the United Kingdom without permission. In *Re Lannoy*,[147] Lord Greene held that Article 1(1)(a) of the Aliens Order, 1920, which provided that aliens might not land in the Kingdom other than with the consent of an immigration officer, and Article 3(4) of that Order, which dealt with the powers of immigration officers to refuse to admit aliens, were both applicable to a case in which the alien did not wish to land in the United Kingdom, but had been forced to do so not by a storm but by the British armed forces. In the *Soblen Case*[148] Lord Parker relied on *Re Lannoy* to support his proposition that contravention of Article 1(1) of the Aliens Order, 1953, is an 'absolute' offence. It is thought that these cases should not lead to the conclusion that a person commits an offence against section 24(1) of the new Act if, without permission, he enters the United Kingdom 'knowingly', in the sense that he is aware of what he is doing, but involuntarily. The earlier cases turned upon different statutory provisions. In any case, the situation in which an alien is compelled by *force majeure* to land in the kingdom is to be distinguished from the situation in which he is conducted there by military force (as in *Re Lannoy*) or by self-inflicted wounds (as in the *Soblen Case*). In the event of *force majeure,* the alien cannot be said to be responsible for the events leading to his being conducted to the Kingdom. Moreover, it may be contended that Parliament did not intend to abrogate the facility customarily extended to victims of emergency.[149]

Similarly, in the United States, the Immigration and Nationality Act of 1952 fails to make special provision for victims of *force majeure*[150] but the consistent practice of the law-enforcement agencies has been to waive any fine which might have become due as a result of the failure to furnish a proper manifest of alien seamen and passengers, provided that the vessel had no orders to enter the United States port at the time of its last departure from a foreign port. In the United States, as in the United Kingdom, distressed passengers and crew have been admitted, even without documentation, for a limited period, pending their repatriation.[151]

In 1979 a Philippine Court of first instance addressed itself to the relationship between *force majeure,* international law and domestic immigration laws.[152] In this case the captain of a cargo vessel, the *M.V. Tung-An,* was forced at gunpoint to take on board 2,300 Vietnamese refugees, during a voyage from Bangkok to Hong Kong. The vessel changed course in the face of bad weather and was denied landing in Brunei. After 24 days at sea, the captain took his vessel into Philippine waters. He did not submit a crew list or passenger manifest, nor did he give his estimated time of arrival, as required by the Philippine Immigration Act 1940 and the General Port Regulations. On his prosecution for offences against that Act and those Regulations, the Court held that he could not be convicted. The vessel had entered Philippine waters as a result of proven necessity and accordingly there was an 'easement of involuntary entry' conferred on the captain by generally accepted principles of customary international law. Those principles would be recognized by a Philippine court even in the face of inconsistent domestic legislation.[153] In the event, all of the refugees were admitted to the Philippines and were later resettled elsewhere.

Relatively few conventions have been concluded to govern the immunities to be extended to victims of *force majeure* in time of peace. This, however, is probably an indication of the absence of serious disparities of State practice. Professor Cheng has expressed the view that international legal principles of *force majeure* are based on the concept of inevitability, found in the domestic laws of most civilized States.[154] Elsewhere, the same writer argues that a State can no more deny an aircraft in distress permission to land in its territory than it can refuse a maritime vessel permission to take refuge in its port.[155] He observes that pre-war agreements commonly contained the provisions to ensure the right to make emergency landings in the territories of other contracting parties, but that such provisions are not often incorporated in post-war air transport agreements. The International Convention for the Safety of Life at Sea does not contain any express provision whereby the parties agree to admit to their territories persons from vessels in distress.[156] The Convention on International Civil Aviation[157] specifically provides that parties must grant assistance to aircraft in distress in their territories. Neither of these conventions mentions immigration laws as such[158] but both appear to presuppose that the contracting States will exempt the distressed passengers from any penalty which might normally be imposed for unauthorized entry. The same comment applies with greater emphasis to Article 5 of the Treaty on Principles governing the Activities of States in the Exploration and Use of Outer Space.[159] In time of war the admission of shipwrecked servicemen is governed by the second Geneva Convention of 1949[160] and in the corresponding domestic legislation (if any) of the parties.[161]

NOTES

1. Law on Migration and the Encouragement of Immigration, 1981, No. 22439, section 16. By section 96(b) special consideration is given to aliens who have lived in the country for at least ten years.
2. *Fremdenpolizeigezetz*, BGBl. 1954/75; *Deportation of Resident (Austria) Case, Verwaltungsgerichthof* (VwGH) of 19 January 1983, Zl 82/01/0243.
3. Aliens Act, No. 226 of 8 June 1983, sections 25 and 26.
4. Aliens Act 1965, section 14.
5. *Ordonnance* No. 45-2658 of 2 November 1945, J.O.R.F. 11 January 1945 p. 71, D1946(L)24, Articles 23 and 24, amended by *Loi* No. 80–9 of 10 January 1980, J.O.R.F. 11 January 1980, p. 71, D1980(L)79, and *Lois* Nos. 84–622 of 17 July 1984, D1984(L)458; and 86–1025 of 9 September 1986, D1986(L)474.
6. *Auslandergezetz* (Aliens Law) of 28 April 1965, BGBl, 1965 I, 353, sections 2 and 8.
7. Belgium: Law of 15 December 1980, Article 13; Royal Decree of 8 October 1981, Chap. IV, Title I; Cyprus: Aliens and Immigration Regulations, 1952–87, Reg. 3; Iceland: Law No. 39 of 15 March 1951 and Law No. 100 of 23 December 1952; Luxemburg: Law of 28 March 1972, esp. Art. 9; Norway: Aliens Act 1956, sections 5 and 6; Aliens Regulations, 1957, reg. 31(4); Portugal: Decree-Law 264-B/81, Article 34; Switzerland: Federal Law on the Sojourn and Establishment of Aliens, 26 March 1931, S.R. 142.20, Article 6.
8. Immigration Act 1971, section 2(1)(d): a Commonwealth citizen had the right of abode if

born to or legally adopted by a parent who at the time of the birth or adoption had citizenship of the United Kingdom and Colonies by his birth in the United Kingdom or in any of the islands. Immigration Act 1971 section 2(2): a woman had the right of abode if she was the wife of a man who had the right of abode, or had at any time been the wife of a man who then had that right. See now British Nationality Act 1981, section 39(1), and see further I. MacDonald, *Immigration Law and Practice*, 1983, p. 36; Immigration Act 1971, section 2(1)(c).

9. Immigration Act 1971, section 33(2A), inserted by British Nationality Act 1981, schedule 4, paragraph 7(b). In *R v Barnet London Borough Council, ex parte Shah*, [1983] 2 A.C. 309 at 346 Lord Scarman, giving the conclusion of the House of Lords on this point, stated that immigration control may give rise to relevant facts, but no more, in determining whether a person is 'ordinarily resident' for purposes other than immigration. Ordinary residence for the purposes of the Immigration Act will not be negated by overstaying, although it may be negated by other breaches of the Immigration Act; *In Re Abdul Manan*, [1971] 1 W.L.R. 859; *R v Bangoo*, [1976] Crim. L.R. 746; *Immigration Appeal Tribunal v Maheswary Chelliah*, [1985] Imm. A.R. 192. For the meaning of 'ordinary residence' for immigration purposes, see *R v Immigration Appeal Tribunal, ex parte Ng*, [1986] Imm. A.R. 23. See further Immigration Rules, H.C. 169, paragraph 57; *R v Home Secretary ex parte Dominic Omosanya Adenuyiwa*, [1986] Imm. A.R. 1.

10. Immigration Act, S.C. 1976–77, Cap. 52, section 19(1)(c), (d), (e), (g) or 19(2)(a).

11. Under the antecedent legislation, a person who had been domiciled in Canada for at least five years was permitted to re-enter Canada unless he forfeited that privilege by some act of disloyalty. By section 3 of the Immigration Act of 1952, Canadian domicile could be acquired only by a person who has been 'landed' in Canada and after five years' residence. In *Re Leong Ba Chai*, [1953] 2 D.L.R. 766 it was held that a person might have Canadian domicile for the purposes of the Act even though he remained domiciled for the purposes of private international law in another country. See also *Re Murphy*, (1910) 15 B.C.R. 401; *Re Chin Chee*, (1905) 11 B.C.R. 400; *R v Mikka Singh*, (1931) 44 B.C.R. 278.

12. Section 27(2).

13. Migration Act 1958 (No. 62) – 1983 (No. 117), section 14. Section 51(xxvii) of the Australian Constitution confers on the Commonwealth Parliament the power to 'make laws . . . with respect to . . . immigration'. There has been some dispute as to the meaning of 'immigration' in that context, but it now appears that once the alien has been assimilated to the community the power no longer applies to him. In *R v MacFarland, ex parte O'Flanaghan and Kelly*, (1923) 32 C.L.R. 518, 555 Isaacs, J. took the view that section 51(xxvii) extends even to persons who have established a home in Australia: 'once an immigrant, always an immigrant'. The contrary view was taken in *R v Governor, Metropolitan Gaol, ex parte Molinari* [1962] V.R. 156 and in *R v Green, ex parte Cheung Cheuk To*, [1965] A.L.R. 1153. In *Ex parte Walsh and Johnson*, (1925) 37 C.L.R. 36, Higgins, J. observed that the power relates to immigration, not immigrants.

14. Immigration and Nationality Act, 1952, section 212(c), 101(a)(27) (B). See *Carmichael v Delaney*, 170 F. 2d. 239 (1948); *Roggenbihl v Lusby et al (The Malden)*, 116 F. Supp. 315 (1953); *Shaughnessy v U.S. ex rel. Menzel*, 345 U.S. 206 (1953).

15. *Chew v Colding*, 344 U.S. 590 (1953); *Stacher v Rosenberg*, 216 F. Supp. 511 (1963); *Rosenberg v Fleuti*, 374 U.S. 499 (1963).

16. *In re Alexandre Selim*, 88 R.D. 320, 4 P.B. 289 (1929).

17. *Van Rensburg v Ballinger*, [1950] 4 S.A. 427.

18. A. Macheret, *L'immigration étrangère en suisse à l'heure de l'intégration européenne*, 1969, p. 42. A Decree of 26 March 1969, amending Article 3 of the Decree dated 28 February 1968, imposed numerical restrictions on the employment of aliens in Switzerland but provided that

in computing those limitations no account should be taken of aliens who have satisfied a five-year residence requirement.

19. G. Goodwin-Gill, *International Law and the Movement of Persons between States*, 1978, p. 258.
20. M. Planiol, *Traité élémentaire de droit civil*, 1947, Vol. I, p. 96.
21. A/CN. 4/1 Rev. 1 (International Law Commission).
22. D. O'Connell, *International Law*, 1970, Vol. II, p. 763; and see also his *State Succession in Municipal Law and International Law*, 1967, Vol. II pp. 245–263; *Delassus* v *U.S.*, 9 Pet. 117 (1835); *Carino* v *Government of the Philippines*, 212 U.S. 449 (1908); G. Kaeckenbeeck, 'Protection of Vested Rights in International Law', 17 B.Y.I.L. (1936) 1 at 2.
23. *Mutual Assurance Society* v *Watts*, 1 Wheat. 279 (1816); *Society for the Propagation of the Gospel in Foreign Parts* v *New Haven*, 8 Wheat. 464 (1823); *U.S.* v *Arredondo*, 6 Pet. 691 (1832); *Delassus* v *U.S.*, 9 Pet. 117 (1835); *Mitchel* v *U.S.*, 9 Pet. 711 (1835); *U.S.* v *Clarke's Heirs*, 16 Pet. 228 (1842); *Doe* v *Eslava*, 9 How. 42 (1850); *Townsend* v *Greely*, 5 Wall. 326 (1866); *Cessna* v *U.S.*, 169 U.S. 165 (1897); *Municipality of Ponce* v *Roman Catholic Apostolic Church in Puerto Rico*, 210 U.S. 296 (1907). See R. Jennings, 'State Contracts in International Law', 37 B.Y.I.L. (1961) 156, 173.
24. 7 A.D. (1933–4) No. 39, p. 91.
25. *Schufeldt Arbitration*, U.S. – Guatemala Arbitral Tribunal, 24 A.J.I.L. (1930) 799.
26. P.C.I.J. Ser. A/B No. 63 at p. 88 (1934).
27. Commenting on *Niederstrasser* v *Polish State*, 6 A.D. (1931–2) No. 33, 66 at pp. 68–69.
28. 6 A.D. (1931–2) No. 34 at p. 69.
29. 8. A.D. (1935–7) 138 at 140 (No. 42).
30. In a case involving State succession, it will not necessarily be clear that the successor State is bound to respect the rights acquired previously. The traditional view as to the effect of State succession on acquired rights was summed up by Marshall, C.J. in *U.S.* v *Percheman*, 7 Pet. 51, 87 (1833): 'the people change their allegiance, their relation to the ancient sovereign is dissolved, but their relations to each other and their rights of property remain undisturbed'. The modern view seems to be that when State succession occurs the new sovereign may divest individuals of rights previously acquired, provided that the divestment is not arbitrary: *Chicago Railway Co.* v *McGlinn*, 114 U.S. 542 (1885).
31. P. Wilson, *Diplomatic Privileges and Immunities*, 1967, pp. 26–45; J. Brierly, *The Law of Nations*, 1963, p. 256; F. Deak, 'Classification, Immunities and Privileges of Diplomatic Agents', I S.C.L.R. (1928) 209–252; H. Briggs, *The Law of Nations*, 1952, p. 748; L. Lee, *Consular Law and Practice*, 1961, pp. 223–290.
32. The extraterritoriality thesis was favoured by H. Grotius, *De Jure Belli ac Pacis*, 1702, Book II, Vol. II, Chap. VII, and by C. Bynkershoek, *De Foro Legatorum*, trans. Laing, 1946. It is criticised by Brierly, *supra* note 31, p. 222; J. Moore, *Digest of International Law*, 1906, Vol. II, p. 775 and J. Fort-Dumanoir, '*De l'étendue de l'immunité de juridiction des agents diplomatiques*', (1921) J.D.I.P. 831. The same thesis met with disapproval from the Privy Council in *Chung Chi Cheung* v *R*, [1939] A.C. 160, 175, and from Lord Brett in The *Parlement Belge*, [1881] 5 P.D.A. 207. The thesis that diplomatic immunities should be based on the representative character of the agents was propounded by Marshall, C.J. in *The Schooner Exchange* v *MacFaddon*, 7 Cranch 116 (1812) and by Lord Chancellor Talbot in *Barbuit's Case*, (1737) Cas. t. Talb. 281. The theory itself found an adherent in E. de Vattel, *Le droit des gens*, Livre IV, chap. VII, para. 92. The functional necessity theory formed the basis for the work of the International Law Commission in its draft articles: *Report of the Tenth Session of the International Law Commission*, 47. The Vienna Convention on Diplomatic Relations, 1961, seems to have proceeded on this basis, for its preamble states that: the purpose of such privileges and immunities is not to benefit individuals but to ensure

efficient performance of functions of diplomatic missions as representing States.

33. Article 1853, as amended by Act No. 6 of 1928.
34. Regulations of 1 April 1904 concerning Police Service at Points on the Frontier, in Ports and Railway Stations, Article 10.
35. *Gupta* v *Home Secretary,* [1979–80] Imm. A.R. 52.
36. *Wijesutinya,* TH 52961/79 (1685), unreported. See further *Home Secretary* v *Qazi,* [1982] Imm. A.R. 121.
37. A. Feller and M. Hudson, *A Collection of the Diplomatic and Consular Laws and Regulations of Various Countries,* Vol. II, pp. 1347–1348.
38. Immigration and Nationality Act, section 101(a)(15)(A); F. Auerbach, *Immigration Laws of the United States,* 1961, pp. 346–352.
39. Immigration and Nationality Act, section 102; 22 CFR 41.91(e)(2)(i); 22 CFR 41.91(e)(1); Auerbach, *supra,* note 38 at 347.
40. *Borovsky* v *Commissioner of Immigration,* (1951) G.R. No. L-4342; Central Book Supply Co., Inc., *Citizenship, Naturalization, Immigration and Alien Restriction Laws,* 1966, p. 227.
41. Immigration Act, S.C. 1976–77, Cap. 52, section 7(1).
42. See, for example, Australia: Migration Act, 1958 (No. 62), section 8(1)(b) as amended by Migration Act 1966 (No. 10); Jamaica: Aliens Law, 1945–1948, section 17; Kenya: Immigration Act, 1967, section 2; Malaysia: Immigration Exemption Order, 1963; New Zealand: Immigration Act 1964 (No. 43), sections 3, 12 and 19.
43. *Supra,* note 31, p. 176.
44. In *U.S.* v *Coplon and Gubitchev,* 88 F. Supp. 915 (1950) a U.S. District Court denied diplomatic immunity to Valentin A. Gubitchev, even though he possessed a diplomatic passport and had been issued with a diplomatic visa.
45. See, for example, *Engelke* v *Musmann,* [1928] A.C. 433 and the United Kingdom's Diplomatic Privileges Act, 1964, section 4.
46. Aliens Law, section 11(5).
47. Immigration and Nationality Act, sections 221(b), 261, 262.
48. Act of 11 September 1957, 71 Stat. 641, section 8.
49. Immigration and Nationality Act 1952, section 265.
50. *Ordonnance* of 2 November 1945, *supra,* note 5, Article 4; Decree of 30 June 1946, Article 6, CCL385.
51. Section 8(3). Formerly the immunity was governed by the Aliens Restriction (Amendment) Act, 1919, section 14(1); Aliens Order, 1953, Article 24(1); Diplomatic Privileges Act, 1964, section 2 and Schedule 1, Article 1(b); and Commonwealth Immigrants Act, 1962, section 17(1).
52. Jamaica Gazette Supplement, Vol. LXXXVIII, No. 149, Thursday 26 November 1964, No. 369.
53. Rep. Act No. 562, amended.
54. 21 June 1950.
55. Rules and Regulations governing Issuance of Certificates of Residence, 13 January 1950.
56. B. Sen, *A Diplomat's Handbook of International Law and Practice,* 1965, pp. 100–101. Wilson's arguments seem to be based on a similar premise: *supra,* note 31.
57. Aliens Order, 1967 S.I. 1282 and Aliens (Embarkation) (Restriction) Order, 1967 S.I. 1288.
58. Decree of 18 March 1946, D1946(L)148.
59. Decree of 31 December 1947, D1948(L)21, Article 1.
60. Article 24 of the Draft Articles adopted by the Commission at its tenth session, I.L.C. Ybk. (1958-II) at 96.
61. W. Hall, *A Treatise on International Law,* 1924, p. 359.
62. 48 B.F.S.P. 298–300.

63. Havana, 20 February 1928, 155 L.N.T.S. 259.
64. The Bolivian Consular Regulations of July 4, 1887, provided, in Articles 92 and 93, that the Government of Bolivia did not consider itself obliged to receive the person sent to it, if it had sufficient reasons, which should be communicated to the Government which appointed him. In Ecuador, the Presidential Decree of 27 October 1916, provided in Article 1 that the admission of consuls-general, consuls, vice-consuls and consular agents to the Republic was subject to the provisions of treaties, or, in the absence of treaties, to the general rules of international law and the principle of reciprocity.
65. Articles 2 and 7; the text of the Harvard Research Draft Convention on the Legal Position and Functions of Consuls appears in 26 A.J.I.L. (Supp.) (1932)189.
66. Convention on Consular Agents, *supra*, note 63, Article 16; Sino-Soviet Consular Agreement, Beijing, 23 June 1959, 356 U.N.T.S. 83, Article 6; Harvard Research Draft Convention on the Legal Position and Functions of Consuls, *supra,* note 65, Article 21; Draft Provisional Articles on Consular Intercourse and Immunities; Report by Jaroslav Zourek, Special Rapporteur, United Nations International Law Commission, U.N. Doc. A/CN. 4/108, I.L.C. Ybk. (1957-II) 71–103, Article 27.
67. Feller and Hudson, *supra,* note 37, pp. 51–54, 284, 347–348, 375–376, 407–414, 460–461, 485–486, 491, 563, 212–213, 600, 628, 646, 654–655, 661, 676, 709, 714, 729, 755–756, 814, 942–944, 956, 1018–1019, 1085, 1093, 1263–1264, 1340, 1218, 1221, 1404. See in particular the United Kingdom's Aliens (Foreign Representatives) Direction, 1963, S.I. No. 2133 paragraph 2; and Commonwealth Immigrants (Control of Immigration) Exemption Order, 1962, S.I. No. 1316, Article 1(d) read with Diplomatic Immunities (Commonwealth Countries and Republic of Ireland) Act, 1952.
68. U.N. Doc. A/CONF. 25, 23 April 1963 and G.A.O.R. 16 Sess., Supp. No. 9 (A/4843).
69. Vienna, 24 April 1963, 596 U.N.T.S. 261, Cmnd. 2113. See Lee, *supra* note 31, pp. 79–106. See generally G. Do Nascimento e Silva, 'The Vienna Conference on Consular Relations', 13 I.C.L.Q. (1964)1214 and H. Blix, 'The Rights of Diplomatic Missions and Consulates to Communicate with Authorities of the Host State', 8 Scand. Stud. in L. (1964)9.
70. G.A.O.R. 16 Sess., Supp. No. 9 (A/4843).
71. Lee, *supra* note 31, pp. 103–106.
72. Vienna Convention, *supra,* note 69, Article 27; Consular Convention between the U.S.S.R. and the U.S.A., Moscow, 1 June 1964, 655 U.N.T.S. 213, Article 27.
73. *Bergman* v *De Sieyes,* 170 F. 2d. 360 (1947). In *New Chile Gold Mining Co* v *Blanco,* (1888)4 T.L.R. 346, the immunity was recognized in favour of a Venezuelar ambassador while resident in France.
74. 191 F. Supp. 663 (1960).
75. [1971] 2 W.L.R. 816, 823.
76. *Commentaries on American Law,* 1846, paragraph 168.
77. Immigration and Nationality Act, sections 101(a)(15)(A) and 212(d)(8).
78. New York, 13 February 1946, 1 U.N.T.S. 15. See W. Sharp, *Field Administration in the United Nations System,* 1961, p. 109.
79. Article IV, section 11(d).
80. Article V, section 18(c).
81. E.g. Constitution of the Food and Agriculture Organization, Quebec, 16 October 1945, 40 A.J.I.L. (1946) Supp. 76, Article XV, section 2; Constitution of the United Nations Educational, Scientific and Cultural Organization, London, 16 November 1945, 4 U.N.T.S. 275, Article XII; Articles of Agreement of the International Monetary Fund, Washington, 27 December 1945, 1 U.N.T.S. 39, Article IX, section 8; Convention on International Civil Aviation, Chicago, 7 December 1944, 15 U.N.T.S. 295 (Part II: The International Civil Aviation Organization), Article 60; Agreement Concerning the Establishment of the Eu-

ropean Central Inland Transport Organization, London, 27 September 1945, 5 U.N.T.S. 327, Article VIII, sections 16 and 17.
82. 21 November 1947, 33 U.N.T.S. 261.
83. D. Bowett, *The Law of International Institutions*, 1982, pp. 346–47; General Agreement on Privilèges and Immunities of the Council of Europe, Paris, 2 September 1949, 250 U.N.T.S. 14; Agreement on Privileges and Immunities of the Organisation of American States, Washington, 15 May 1949, P.A.U.T.S. 22; General Convention on the Privileges and Immunities of the O.A.U., Accra, 25 October 1965, 1 Sohn 117; Protocol on the Privileges and Immunities of the European Communities, Brussels, 8 April 1965, I Ybk. (1965)429.
84. See, for example, agreements between: United States and United Nations, Washington, 14 August 1946, 1 U.N.T.S. 11; Council of Europe and France, Paris, 2 September 1949, 249 U.N.T.S. 207; the United Nations and Switzerland, Bern and New York, 11 June and 1 July 1946, 1 U.N.T.S. 163; the International Labour Organization and Mexico, Mexico City, 5 January 1955, 208 U.N.T.S. 225. See also the Exchange of Letters constituting an Agreement between the United Nations and Egypt, in respect of the United Nations Expeditionary Force, New York, 8 February 1957, 260 U.N.T.S. 61.
85. Act of 29 December 1945, 59 Stat. 669.
86. Now replaced by the International Organisations Act, 1968.
87. [1962] 2 All. E.R. 256, 265.
88. C. Gordon and H. Rosenfield, *Immigration Law and Procedure*, 1959, pp. 108–109; see also Auerbach, *supra*, note 38, pp. 177–180.
89. 'Le droit d'accès au sièges des organisations internationales', 66 R.G.D.I.P. (1962)357, 359.
90. Y.L. Liang, I.L.C. Ybk. (1957-II)5.
91. J. Perrenoud, *Régime des privilèges et immunités des missions diplomatiques étrangères et des organisations internationales en Suisse*, thesis, Geneva, 1949, p. 79, note 2.
92. 59. Stat. 669.
93. Section 101(a)(15)(G). 'Immediate family' means aliens who are closely related to the principal alien by blood, marriage or adoption, and reside regularly in his household: 22 CFR 41.1.
94. E.g., Iran, 6 May 1947; Iraq, 15 September 1947; Egypt, 19 September 1948; Pakistan, 22 September 1948; Libya, 10 March 1949.
95. See Council of Europe Agreement, *supra*, note 84, Articles 13–15; European Economic Community Protocol, *supra*, note 83, Articles 7–9.
96. Immigration Act, 1964 (No. 43) section 3(h), amended, Immigration Amendment Act, 1969 (No. 83) section 2; Diplomatic Privileges and Immunities Act, 1968 (No. 36) section 9(2)(b); cf. Diplomatic Immunities and Privileges Act, 1957 (No. 21) section 11(2)(b).
97. 8 CFR 214.2 (g).
98. *Supra*, note 83, at p. 348 (emphasis added). For futher materials on this episode see F. Riad, 'The United Nations Action in the Congo and its Legal Basis', 17 R. Egypt Dr. Int. (1961)1; O. Schachter, 'Legal Aspects of the United Nations Action in the Congo', 55 A.J.I.L. (1961) and Q. Wright, 'The United Nations and the Congo Crisis', 2 VA J.I.L. (1961)41.
99. 59 Stat. 669; Immigration and Nationality Act, section 101(a)(15)(6)(i), (iv).
100. Auerbach, *supra*, note 38, pp. 182 *et seq.*
101. Section 8(3) (emphasis added); the section is derived from the Aliens Order 1953, S.I. 1671, Article 24(1), amended, Aliens Order 1964, S.I. 2034.
102. Sections 1, 3, 6, 10.
103. Schedule 1, part II, and part IV, paragraph 20(4).
104. Analogy may be drawn with *U.S. v Rosal*, 191 F. Supp. 663 (1960) and *R v Pentonville Prison Governor, ex parte Teja*, [1971] 2 W.L.R. 816.
105. Accepted, 4 August 1947; 61 Stat. 756.

106. 22 CFR 41.31; Departmental Regulation 108.411, 24 F.R. 6682 of 18 August 1959.

107. See M. Brandon, 'The United Nations Laissez-Passer', 27 B.Y.I.L. (1950)448, 449–450.

108. See, for example, the position in the United States: 8 CFR 2(c)(2).

109. Bowett, *supra*, note 83, p. 358.

110. D. Greig, *International Law*, 1970, pp. 171, 191, 212–216; G. Draper, *Civilians and the N.A.T.O. Status of Forces Agreement*, 1966; D. Wijewardane, 'Criminal Jurisdiction over Visiting Forces with special reference to International Forces', 4 B.Y.I.L. (1965–1966)122; G. Barton, 'Foreign Armed Forces, Immunity from Supervisory Jurisdiction', 26 B.Y.I.L. (1949)380; E. Re, 'The N.A.T.O. Status of Forces Agreement and International Law', 50 Nw. U.L. Rev. (1956)349; E. Schwelb, 'Jurisdiction over the Members of the Allied Forces in Great Britain', Czechoslovak Y.I.L., (1942)147; M. Bathurst, 'Jurisdiction over Friendly Armed Forces – the American Law', 23 B.Y.I.L. (1946)338.

111. L. Oppenheim, *International Law*, 1955, Vol. I, pp. 847–848.

112. (1812)7 Cranch, 116, 3 L. Ed. 287. The Chief Justice asserted that there is a class of cases in which *every* sovereign is understood to waive the exercise of exclusive territorial jurisdiction. Such a case arises when the sovereign allows the troops of a foreign power to pass through his dominions. The Panamanian Supreme Court in *Panama* v *Schwarzfiger*, 24 Official Judicial Register of Panama (1925)772 went further: 'It is a principle of international law that the armed forces of one State, when crossing the territory of another friendly country, with the acquiescence of the latter, are subject, not to the jurisdiction of the territorial sovereign, but to that of the officers . . .'.

113. 13 A.D. (1946)86 (No. 37).

114. See, for example, the decision of the Egyptian *Conseil d'Etat* in *Ministère Public* v *Triandafilou*, 11 A.D. (Supplementary Volume, 1919–1942)165 (No. 86).

115. 63 Stat. 2241.

116. London, 19 June 1951, 199 U.N.T.S. 67; 4 U.S.T. 1792.

117. Ottawa, 12 December 1951, 5 U.S.T. 1087.

118. Paris, 28 August 1952, 5 U.S.T. 870.

119. Auerbach, *supra*, note 38, at p. 185.

120. Agreement between the Parties to the North Atlantic Treaty regarding the Status of their Forces, Washington, 4 April 1949, 4 U.S.T. 1792.

121. 22 CFR 41.70(a)(2) and 41.5(d).

122. Section 212(a)(27), (29).

123. Visiting Forces Act, 1952; International Headquarters and Defence Organizations Act, 1964.

124. Section 8(4). Formerly: Aliens Order, 1953, Articles 23, 24(3); Aliens (Persons on Military Courses) Direction, 1958 (1958/1554); Commonwealth Immigrants Act, 1962, section 1(2); Commonwealth Immigrants (Control of Immigration) Exemption Order, 1965 (1965/153).

125. Basic Agreement of 29 July 1961, S/4389/Add. 5, paragraph 1; S.C.O.R. 15th year, 877th meeting, paragraph 15.

126. D. Bowett, *United Nations Forces: A Legal Study*, 1964, pp. 412, 427 and sources cited there; R. Falk and S. Mendlovitz, *The United Nations*, 1966, *passim*.

127. Bowett, *supra*, note 126, pp. 43, 156–204, 412. It appears that by the crucial date the O.N.U.C. force had matured into a force under Chapter 7 of the Charter.

128. (1962) I.C.J. Rep. p. 151 at 170–171, 175.

129. *Supra*, note 84.

130. *Supra*, note 120.

131. Agreement relating to the legal status, facilities, privileges and immunities of the United Nations Operations in the Congo, New York, 27 November 1961, 414 U.N.T.S. 229.

132. Article 7.

133. Exchange of Letters constituting an Agreement concerning the Status of the United Nations Peacekeeping Force in Cyprus, New York, 31 March 1964, 492 U.N.T.S. 57, Articles 7, 8.
134. *Supra,* note 126, at p. 435.
135. Tokyo, 19 February 1954; 214 U.N.T.S. 51, 52.
136. Rhodes, 24 February 1949, 42 U.N.T.S. 251, 268.
137. E. de Vattel, *Le droit des gens,* Book II, chap. VII, s. 94.
138. C. Hyde, *International Law, Chiefly as Interpreted and Applied by the United States,* 1945, Vol. I, p. 399.
139. G. Hackworth, *Digest of International Law,* 1940–1944, Vol. II, p. 277.
140. P. Jessup, *The Law of Territorial Waters and Maritime Jurisdiction,* 1927, p. 194.
141. D. O'Connell, *International Law,* 1970, Vol. II, pp. 627–629.
142. (1805)3 Cranch 210, 219.
143. *The Eleanor,* (1809) Edw. 135, 161; *The New York,* (1818)3 Wheat, 59. See the decision of Umpire Bates in *The Creole,* 2 Moore 358 (1853).
144. XI U.N.R.I.A.A. (1910)174.
145. *Supra,* note 143.
146. *Cushin and Lewis* v *R,* [1935] L.R. Ex. C.R. 103.
147. [1942] 2 All E.R. 232, 236–237.
148. *R* v *Home Secretary, ex parte Soblen,* [1962] 3 All E.R. 373, 378.
149. Naturally, English courts might nevertheless be bound by the principle of *Mortensen* v *Peters,* (1906)8F. (Ct. of Sess.) 93 to apply an unambiguous statute even though it might be in contravention of a rule of international law. A similar principle applies in the United States: see Marshall, C.J. in *Foster* v *Neilsen,* (1829)2 Pet. 253, 307, 7 L. Ed. 415; *Jones* v *U.S.,* (1890)137 U.S. 202; *In Re Cooper,* (1891)143 U.S. 472, 502; *Pearcy* v *Stranahan,* (1906)205 U.S. 257.
150. See, however, the United States' Tariff Act of 1922 (42 Stat. 858, 952) which provided that vessels arriving in ports in distress or for the purpose of taking on stores would not be required to make any customs entry if they departed within 24 hours. This provision was based on a well-established principle: see *The Brig Concord,* (1815)9 Cranch 387.
151. Hackworth, *supra,* note 139, Vol. II, p. 278.
152. *The M.V. Tung-An, People of the Philippines* v *Dah Shing Shen and Others,* Manila, 6th Judicial District, 14 September 1979, Case No. 46549, before Judge B. Relova.
153. The Constitution of the Philippines, Article 11(3) states that the Republic of the Philippines applies generally accepted principles of international law as part of the law of the land.
154. *General Principles of Law as applied by International Courts and Tribunals,* 1953, pp. 75, 77.
155. *The Law of International Air Transport,* 1962, p. 349.
156. London, 31 May 1929; 136 L.N.T.S. 81; see Article 3.
157. Chicago, 7 December 1944; 15 U.N.T.S. 295.
158. C.f. Article 17 of the Statute on the International Regime of Maritime Ports, annexed to the Convention on the International Regime of Maritime Ports, Geneva, 9 December 1923, 58 L.N.T.S. 285, which provides that no State party is thereby bound to permit the admission of passengers whose entry to national territory is prohibited by domestic laws.
159. London, Moscow and Washington, 27 January 1967, U.K.T.S. 10 (1968); 61 A.J.I.L. (1967)644, 645. That Article provides that contracting States will regard astronauts as 'envoys of mankind in outer space' and will render to them all possible assistance in the event of accident, distress or emergency landing on the territory of another State party or on the high seas. When astronauts make such landings they are to be safely and promptly returned to the State of registry of their space vehicle.
160. Geneva, 12 August 1949, 75 U.N.T.S. 3, 31.
161. E.g., the United Kingdom's Geneva Conventions Act 1957.

BIBLIOGRAPHY

E. Denza, *Diplomatic Law*, 1976.

L. Lee, *Consular Law and Practice*, 1961.

L. Lee, *The Vienna Convention on Consular Relations*, 1966.

R. Lillich, 'Duties of States regarding the Civil Rights of Aliens', Hague *Recueil* (1978)329.

G. Witzsch, 'Human Rights of Aliens under the NATO Status of Forces Agreement', 11 Col. Jo. Trans. L. (1972)267.

CHAPTER 6

Freedom of Movement in the European Communities

Preeminent among the modern regional arrangement for freedom of movement is the system established by the European Economic Community. It is
true that other regional arrangements are in some respects more advanced.
Such is the case, for example, with the system established between the Benelux States.[1] It is also true that the European Economic Community's arrangements are made subject to important qualifications under transitional arrangements applicable to Greece[2], Portugal and Spain.[3] Moreover, a common policy
governing immigration of nationals of third States into the Community has yet
to be achieved.[4] The fact remains, however, that the rules governing freedom
of movement within the European Economic Community together with certain ancillary rules applicable to the sectors of coal and steel and atomic
energy,[5] have been applied, expanded and developed for more than a quarter
of a century. Moreover they extend, wholly or subject to transitional arrangements, to a Community whose population already exceeds 300 million and
may expand further. Indeed, the Communities' arrangements have a significance extending well beyond the territory of the Member States. This is so not
least because provisions based on the EEC Treaty[6] have been incorporated in
conventions concluded between the Community and third States, including
Turkey[7] and the 65 African, Caribbean and Pacific States associated with the
Community under the third Treaty of Lomé, concluded on 8 December 1984.[8]

There is little reason to believe that the European Communities' régime will
diminish in significance in the immediate future. Although migration for
employment within the Community is currently in decline[9] the present recession has promoted its own legal problems, including those of determining
whether, and to what extent, freedom of movement is extended to part-time
employees or the unemployed.[10] Moreover the enlargement of the Community
has presented to the European Court certain peculiar difficulties arising from
the transitional provisions, and promises to continue to do so.[11] In particular,
there is reason to believe that certain of the principles currently applied to the
movement between Community States of nationals of those States may be

applied in due course to the movement between those States of nationals of third countries. In a judgment dated 9 July 1987 the European Court held that migration policy is capable of taking within the social field within the meaning of Article 118 of the Treaty to the extent to which it concerns the situation of workers from third countries 'as regards their impact upon the Community employment market and on working conditions'. Although that judgment appears to exclude the cultural integration of third counrty migrants from the Community's competence, it opens the door to a Community régime for migrants from beyond the Community's external borders.

THE TERM 'WORKER'

Article 48 of the EEC Treaty sets out to secure, by the end of the transitional period, 'freedom of movement for workers'.

Article 52 provides for the abolition in the course of the transitional period of restrictions on the 'freedom of establishment of nationals of a Member State in the territory of another Member State'. Article 59 speaks of the 'freedom to provide services . . . in respect of nationals of Member States who are established in a State of the Community other than that of the person for whom the services are intended'. The broad outlines of the distinctions so drawn are sufficiently clear: Article 48, and the remaining Articles in Chapter I of Title III, are concerned with those engaged, actually or potentially, under contracts of employment. Article 52, and the remaining articles in Chapter 2, are concerned with the self-employed who set up in business in a Member State other than their own. Chapter 3, including Article 59, is concerned with those who remain in one Member State while providing services to persons in another Member State.[13]

If the use of the word 'worker' in the English text of Article 48, or of the word 'travailleur' in the French text does not indicate with sufficient precision that it denotes an employee, any doubts upon that matter are resolved by the other texts, particularly the Dutch and German versions, which use the words 'werknemers' and 'Arbeitnehmer'; and by the context, including Article 48(3) (a), which speaks of the right 'to accept offers of employment actually made'. This reading is confirmed by the origins of Article 48, for it is based in part on the wording used in Article 69 of the European Coal and Steel Community Treaty, which embodies the Member States' undertaking to remove certain restrictions 'upon the employment in the coal and steel industries of workers . . .'.[13] The impression thus given is reinforced in the principal implementing legislation, most particularly by Council Regulation 1612/68 of 15 October 1968 and Directive 68/360 of the same date, which speak of 'the right to take up an activity as an employed person'.[14]

The more precise demarcation between the three chapters in Title III remains uncertain. It is, perhaps, the distinction between the 'worker' and the recipient of the 'freedom of establishment' that is likely to give rise to the greatest difficulty. The distinction is to be drawn in accordance with a common Community criterion and not in accordance with the national rules applicable in the particular Member States in which the alleged worker is to be engaged; for adoption of the second of those rules would tend to produce distortions in the labour market of the very kind that the Treaty and its implementing legislation seek to eradicate. Support for this view may be found in an early social security case, *Hoekstra (nee Unger) v. Bestuur der Bedrijfsvereniging voor Detailhandel en Ambachten*[15] where the Court stated that 'Articles 48 to 51 of the Treaty, by the very fact of establishing freedom of movement for 'workers', have given a Community scope to this term'.

In 1986 the European Court was finally called upon to rule on the issue; and held that the essential characteristic of the employment is the fact that, during a given time, one person provides services for and under the direction of another in return for remuneration. Hence, a student teacher qualified as a worker, for she satisfied all three elements in the employment relationship.[16] In identifying those three characteristics as essential elements in employment, the European Court applied the comparative method.[17]

In a series of decisions of inferior national courts, the question has been raised whether a person qualifies as a worker when the activities in which he was engaged, although constituting 'employment' were intermittent or desulatory.[18] Given the conflicting nature of those judgments, and in some instances their unsatisfactory reasoning, it may be judged fortunate that the matter has now been brought to the European Court.

In *Donà v Mantero*,[19] the Court ruled that 'the practice of sport is subject to Community law only in so far as it constitutes an economic activity'. More recently in *Levin*, it was asked whether the term 'worker' embraced a person employed part-time for a salary lower than that considered necessary in the country of employment to meet the cost of subsistence; and if so, whether the worker can rely upon the freedom of movement if it is shown that his chief motive for residing in that Member State is for a purpose other than the taking of limited employment.

The dispute arose from the claim of a British woman to reside in the Netherlands, where she had obtained part-time employment as a chambermaid, after the rejection by the Dutch authorities of a previous application made by her South African husband for permission to remain in the Netherlands with his wife as a person of independent means. The Court ruled that the term 'worker' does indeed cover a part-time employee, whose salary is below the level considered necessary for subsistence, provided that he or she occupies real and effective paid employment; the worker's intentions in seeking the employment are to be disregarded. The result is subtly different to the one proposed by the Advocate General, Sir Gordon Slynn, who answered the first question in the affirmative, without adding a qualification as to the reality and effectiveness of the employment; but stated in reply to the second question that the worker's right of entry is dependent upon its being shown that the employment is a genuine and substantial purpose of the worker. The solution proposed by the Advocate General would have had the advantage of close adherence to the text: since the Treaty speaks of the right to enter 'for the purpose' of accepting an offer of employment; and the legislation speaks of the right to stay or leave 'in order to' take up activities as employed persons.[20] Moreover, it would have had the advantage of ensuring that a national of one Member State engaged in work on the territory of another would be protected against discrimination on grounds of nationality, even if employment were less than 'real and effective'. It appears, however that the European Court was impressed by the difficulties which would confront national administrations or courts in assessing the purposes or intentions of particular migrants; and by the danger of differing interpretations or applications, in the several Member States, of the rule proposed by the Advocate General.

Subsequently the Court expanded in its judgement in the *Levin* case. It held that a national of a Member State who pursues within another Member State activities by way of employment which may be regarded as effective and genuine work benefits from the provisions of Community law relating to the free movement of labour even if he supplements his income by financial assistance provided from the public funds of the State in which he is employed.[21]

The Court's decision in the *Levin* case leaves open the question whether a person may qualify as a 'worker' when he has not yet been engaged under a contract of employment but is merely seeking work. There is some suggestion in that judgment that an unemployed person may benefit from freedom of movement, since the Court stated that the freedom may be invoked 'only by persons actually *engaged or seriously wishing* to be engaged in employment.' This passage contains an echo of the Court's words in Case 48/75, *Jean Noël Royer*[22] where it spoke of 'the right of nationals of a Member State to enter the territory of another Member State and reside there for the purposes intended by the Treaty – in particular *to look for* or pursue an occupation or activities as employed or self-employed persons'. Moreover, in *Watson and Belmann*[23] Mr Advocate General Trabucchi concluded that there was an implication, in Article 1 of Regulation 1612/68, of a right to enter a Member State's territory in search of employment. The minutes of the Council meeting at which Directive 68/360 was adopted clearly imply that Article 48 applies to a person in search of employment: according to those minutes, such a person is to be permitted to remain in the territory of a Member State other than his own, in search of employment, for not less than three months.[24]

It is to be acknowledged that these statements do not conclude the matter. The European Court's remarks are in the nature of *obiter dicta* since none of the judgments in which they appeared arose from a case involving a person in search of employment: and the minutes of a Council meeting cannot in any case be conclusive. Indeed, there is reason to doubt that they may be taken into account at all, when the Court is interpreting the Treaty.[25] The language of Article 48(3) of the EEC Treaty appears to contain an implication that there is no freedom of movement for those engaged in a speculative search of employment. It states that freedom of movement shall entail the right

(a) to accept offers of employment actually made;
(c) to move freely within the territory of Member States for this purpose.

'This purpose', apparently, is the purpose of accepting offers actually made.

Nevertheless, it is extremely probable that the Court had in mind the language of Article 48(3) when it formulated its *obiter dicta* in the *Levin* and *Royer* cases; and those *dicta* are by no means incompatible with the Treaty. On the contrary, they proceed upon the basis of interpreting Article 48 in the wider context of the Treaty as a whole, which sets out to secure a free labour market, together with specified social objectives. Supply of labour will not match demand, nor will the Community's social objectives be attained, unless those who are actively in search of work are permitted to travel to the parts of the Community where they judge that they are likely to obtain an offer of employment.

THE TERM 'NATIONAL'

Whereas the Treaty confines the right of establishment to nationals of Member States and likewise confines to such nationals the freedom to supply services, it does not expressly provide that only nationals may exercise freedom of movement as workers.[26] It is possible that the omission of the word 'national' from Article 48(1) of the EEC Treaty was deliberate, particularly as that word is used in its progenitor, Article 69(1) of the ECSC Treaty, which speaks of 'workers who are nationals of Member States'.[27] The explanation of the absence of this limitation in Article 48(1) may be that the draftsmen wished to leave open, in 1957, the possibility that the Community might develop a common market in labour corresponding with the common market in goods; accompanied by a common external policy towards labour from third countries and freedom of movement within the Community for established immigrants. In the event, the Community's policy towards nationals of third countries employed on the territory of Member States has not developed in this fashion.[28]

Even in cases involving freedom of establishment, the rights conferred by the Treaty on nationals of third countries seldom match those conferred on nationals of the Member States.[29] In the case of 'workers' Article 1 of Regulation No. 1612/68 provides expressly that freedom of movement is to be enjoyed only by nationals of Member States.

The adoption of nationality as a criterion for identifying the beneficiaries of freedom of movement gives rise, however, to certain difficulties. Not least of these is the fact that in certain Member States the term 'national' has less than a fixed meaning.

In the case of the Federal Republic of Germany, Article 116(1) of the Basic Law reads as follows (in its English translation):

> Unless otherwise provided by law, a German within the meaning of this Basic Law is a person who possesses German citizenship or who has been admitted to the territory of the German Reich as it existed on 31 December 1937 as a refugee or expellee or German stock.

Hence there arises the difficulty of determining whether, in relation to the Federal Republic, the term 'nationals' and its derivatives should be taken to denote those possessing German citizenship or those falling within the enlarged definition given in the Basic Law. The Federal Republic has indicated by means of a Declaration appended to its signature of the Treaty, that the second of those constructions is to be preferred. The consequence of that Declaration is that freedom of movement is extended to the original inhabitants of East Germany and of the parts of Silesia and of Upper Prussia which were annexed by the Soviet Union or transferred to Poland after the Second World War, together with expellees or refugees of German descent.

The United Kingdom appended to its Act of Accession a Declaration to the effect that the term 'nationals' in relation to the United Kingdom means a citizen of the United Kingdom and Colonies or a British subject without citizenship having the right of abode or a citizen of the United Kingdom and Colonies by association with Gibraltar. This definition was unique. It did not correspond to the definition of 'patrials' under the Immigration Act since it included Gibraltarians having no right of abode in the United Kingdom but excluded Commonwealth citizens with patriality. On the entry into force of the British Nationality Act 1981, the United Kingdom made a new Declaration stating that the term 'United Kingdom national' was henceforth to mean a British citizen or a British subject with a right of abode or a British Dependent Territories citizen deriving that status by association with Gibraltar.

While it appears clear that Member States cannot by means of Declarations alter the meaning of expressions in the founding treaties which fall to be determined by Community Law, it is no less clear that 'nationality' is regulated, in principle, in accordance with national law.[30] The Member States' exceptional capacity to regulate by this means the significance attached to a term used in the Treaty owes its origin, therefore, to the rule of public international law that 'it is for the State to determine under its own law who are its nationals'.[31]

The European lawyer cannot, however, remit to the domestic lawyer all questions concerning the nationality of the person asserting the freedoms of movement created by the Treaty. In particular, he must resolve in accordance with Community law the vexed issue of determining whether, or to what extent, an individual may assert his rights under the Treaty against his own State.

Article 1 of Regulation 1612/68 speaks of the right of a national of one Member State to take up an activity as an employed person within the territory of *another* Member State. This language repeats *mutatis mutandis* the words used in Article 52 of the Treaty. These texts might be thought to imply that the Regulation and the Treaty do not confer on nationals the right to enter and take up employment, or to establish themselves, in their own State. If this were so, it would follow that the spouse of a national of a Member State could not assert the right under Community law to remain with him in that State: but could assert the right to remain in another Member State in which he took up employment or in which he was established. It was on this reasoning that the *Oberverwaltungsgericht* of Rheinland-Pfalz reached the paradoxical conclusion in 1974 that the Egyptian husband of a German national in Germany gains under Community law no privileges as the spouse of a worker, whereas the Egyptian husband of an Italian worker in Germany would do so.[32]

In that case, however, the Court proceeded upon the express assumption that Community law does not give rise to any rights as between an individual and the country of which he is a national. That assumption now appears to be very questionable. In Case 115/78, *Knoors* v *Secretary of State*[33] the Court ruled that the reference in Article 52 of the Treaty to 'nationals of a Member State' who wish to establish themselves 'in the territory of another Member State' cannot be taken to exclude from the benefit of Community law a given Member State's own nationals, when the latter have acquired in another Member State a trade qualification. Such persons are, in their State of origin, to be treated no less favourably than nationals of the Member State in which they resided and qualified. It was left to the national court to deduce that a Dutch national who had lived for a long period in Belgium and there qualified as a plumber was entitled to practise as a plumber in the Netherlands, in accordance with Community legislation governing the mutual recognition of qualifications,[34] even though he had no qualification in the Netherlands. Later, in Case 246/80, *Broekmeulen* v *Huisarts Registratie Commissie*[35] the Court was confronted with questions on the interpretation of directives governing the right of establishment of doctors. It indicated that Community law does not permit the competent medical authorities in a Member State to withhold registration from a doctor of medicine who has obtained qualifications in another Member State, which are regarded under the Directive as equivalent to those required in the State in which the doctor proposes to practise, even if he is a national of that State. The Court stated that 'the free movement of persons, the right of establishment and the freedom to provide services ... would not be fully realized if Member States were able to deny the benefit of provisions of Community law to those of their nationals who have availed themselves of the freedom of movement and the right of establishment and who have attained, by those means, the professional qualifications mentioned in the directive in a Member State other than the State whose nationality they hold'.

Those words seem to indicate that the European Court will recognize the right of a worker, no less than the right of a self-employed person, to invoke the Treaty against the authorities in his own State. In Case 175/78, *R* v *Saunders* Mr Advocate General Warner took the view that 'the Treaty, in many ways, confers on the citizens of each Member State rights enforceable against the authorities of that State,' and, the Court as a whole, while not accepting that opinion in its entirety, stated that 'the rights conferred upon workers by Article 48 may lead the Member States to amend their legislation, where necessary, even with respect to their own nationals'.[36] Moreover, in the *Van Duyn* case the Court referred to the general principle of international law whereby States are obliged to admit their own nationals to their territories.[37] We may conclude that an individual's claim to enter and remain in the territory of a Member State of which he is a national may give rise to rights protected by Community law.

This is not to say that the individual's right to enter his own territory or that of his spouse or parent, will be protected *as such* by Community law in all circumstances. As the Court stated in *Knoors* and reiterated subsequently[38] the provisions of the Treaty on freedom of movement cannot be applied to situations which are wholly internal to a Member State, in other words, where there is no factor connecting them to any of the situations envisaged by Community law. Such a connecting factor might exist, for example, in the case of a seasonal worker, who spent part of each year in his or her own country and part in another Member State; for it would scarcely be conducive to the creation of a free labour market if, in such a case, the worker were entitled in the foreign State to privileges created by Community law (such as the right to be accompanied by specified dependants) but were denied those privileges in his own State.[39]

Exceptionally, the Council has declared that refugees of any nationality shall be entitled to particularly favourable consideration when they are established in the territory of one Member State and seek to engage in employment in another such State. The Declaration does not appear to produce direct effects on which an individual may depend but those responsible for the maintenance of immigration control in any State appear to be under an obligation to take it into account in disposing of applications from refugees who fall within its terms.[40]

DEPENDENTS

Article 10 of Regulation 1612/68 sets out comparatively generous rules for the admission of members of the families of migrant workers, irrespective of their nationality. That right is extended to the worker's spouse and their descendants who are under 21 years of age or are dependants; and to dependent relatives in the ascending line of the worker and his spouse. Member States are to 'facilitate the admission' of other members of the worker's family, if they are dependent on him or living under his roof in the country whence he came. For these purposes, the worker must have available for his family housing considered normal for national workers in the region where he is employed.[41]

The European Court has ruled that the companion, in a stable relationship, of a worker who is a national of a Member State cannot qualify as the worker's 'spouse' within the meaning of Article 10.[42] It seems that the term 'spouse' means one who is married to the worker at the time when the spouse is to instal himself or herself; and that the validity of the marriage must be determined in accordance with the private international law of the forum.[43]

It is possible that the distinction between the right conferred on spouses, descendants and dependant relatives on the one hand, and the expectation of facilitated admission, extended to other members of the family on the other, is that the former amounts to a clear and precise entitlement, capable of being enforced by individuals in national courts, whereas the latter is insufficiently clear and precise to produce direct effects.[44] It would be misleading to interpret literally the requirement that the other members of a worker's family, whose admission is to be facilitated, should be 'living under his roof'; that phrase is to be given the more general or colloquial meaning that it bears in the French (*'sous le toît du travailleur'*). What is required is that the worker and other members of his family should in the normal course of events form part of a single establishment, irrespective of the construction or ownership of any building.

The Regulation provides expressly that a worker's spouse is to have the right to move within the territory of the Community to take up any activity as an employed person. The Court has now ruled that this carries with it the right to pursue occupations subject to a system of administrative authorisation, such as the medical profession, if the spouse has the professional qualifications and certificates required by the host state. In this respect, the spouse is entitled to be treated equally with nationals of the host state.[45]

THE RIGHT TO ENTER AND RESIDE IN A MEMBER STATE

The Treaty does not state expressly that a worker, or a person exercising the freedom of establishment or the freedom to supply services, shall be entitled to enter the territory of a Member State. This right is clearly implied, however, in Article 48(3) of the Treaty, which provides that freedom of movement shall entail the right to accept offers of employment actually made, to move freely within the territory of the Member States for this purpose, to stay in a Member State for the purpose of employment and to remain in that State thereafter; and in Article 52 which speaks of the right to take up and pursue activities as self-employed persons. The right to depart, to enter and to reside is conferred expressly in Council Directive 68/360, which provides that Member States shall grant to workers the right to leave their territory in order to take up and pursue activities as employed persons in the territory of other Member States, and shall allow those persons to enter their territory simply on production of a valid identity card or passport. The same Directive provides that Member States shall grant the right of residence in their territory to workers who are able to produce those documents, and that a document entitled a 'Residence Permit for a National of a Member State of the EEC' shall be issued. Those permits are to be valid throughout the territory of the issuing Member State, for a period of at least five years. Council Directive 73/148[46] sets out corresponding rules for nationals of Member States who establish themselves in the territory of other Member States in order to pursue activities as self-employed persons. They, too, are entitled to receive residence permits. The Directive of 1973 provides for the abolition of restrictions on the movement of nationals of Member States wishing to travel to other Member States to provide *or to receive* services and for the dependant relatives of such nationals.

The European Court has stated and reiterated that the residence permit for which these Directives make provision is mere evidence of a right conferred directly by the Treaty. It is in no sense the source of the right. The logical consequence of this reasoning is that a mere failure by a national of a Member State to complete the legal formalities concerning the admission or residence of aliens does not justify a decision ordering his expulsion.[47] The failure of a national of one Member State to report her presence in another would not warrant her deportation.[48] It is open to a Member State to require a national of another such State to obtain a residence permit as proof of his or her right to remain, and even to impose a penalty for failure to obtain such a permit. The host State may impose this obligation, even though no corresponding duty is imposed on its own nationals; but the penalty imposed for a failure to comply with this obligation must never be so great as to amount to a disincentive to the mobility of labour.[49] On the other hand, a Member State may not require a national of another such State to obtain leave to enter its territory nor may it punish him for entering without leave; for his entitlement to enter derives from the Treaty directly. It is not dependent on any form of permission.[50] Indeed, the Court has even stated that freedom to provide services includes the freedom for the recipients of services to go to another Member State in order to receive a service there. The Court added that tourists and students are to be regarded as recipients of services.[51]

DISCRIMINATION

The rights conferred on the worker, or the self-employed person, are not exhausted at the port of entry. On the contrary, once admitted to the territory of another Member State, he is entitled to be treated equally with its nationals. In the case of workers that right, contained in Article 48(2) of the Treaty, is amplified in Article 7 of Regulation No. 1612/68, which proclaims that 'a worker who is a national of a Member State may not, in the territory of another Member State, be treated differently from national workers by reason of his nationality in respect of any conditions of employment and work . . . He shall enjoy the same social and tax advantages as national workers'. The Court's tendency has been to avoid strict or technical constructions of this provision. 'Conditions of work and employment', within the meaning of Article 48(2), are not confined to contractual terms. They embrace statutory protection against disadvantage which would otherwise be occasioned by military service[51] and against dismissal following industrial injury.[52] In Case 65/81, *Reina* v *Landeskreditbank Baden Württemburg*,[53] the Court ruled that 'social advantages' embraced interest-free loans granted to parents by a bank of a German Land, in accordance with a statutory scheme designed to relieve hardship and promote the growth of the population. In a consistent decision on Article 12 of that Regulation[54] the Court ruled that educational grants for school children cannot be reserved for children of nationals of the granting State, but must be extended to the children of nationals of other Member States. More recently, the Court has construed the term 'social advantages' in such a way as to embrace non-pecunary benefits. Where a State permitted the unmarried companions of its nationals, who are not themselves nationals of that Member State, to reside in its territory, it could not lawfully refuse to grant the same advantage to migrant workers who are nationals of other Member States.[55]

The principle of equality of treatment for nationals of the Member States assumes particular importance in cases involving the freedom of establishment; for the exercise of that freedom is apt to be impaired when inadequate provision is made for the recognition in one Member State of qualifications obtained in another. The General Programme for the Abolition of Restrictions on the Freedom of Establishment, drawn up by the Council in 1962, contains an illustrative but inexhaustive list of restrictive provisions and practices to be abolished: and refrains from dealing with the mutual recognition of diplomas, a matter which was left for subsequent directives to be issued by the Council.[56] By the end of the transitional period, less progress had been made in this area than many had desired. Although the Council had adopted a wide range of directives governing freedom of establishment, only a minority of them dealt with the question of qualifications.[57] That question was addressed in a series of measures dealing with the medical, paramedical and veterinary professions; but the degree of consensus reached by the representatives of the professions was not such as to enable the Council to draft the directives with great detail or precision.[58] In the case of other occupations and professions, including the law, there are at present directives on the supply of services only, and none on establishment.[59] The European Court has been left to resolve difficulties arising from the existence of these *lacunae*. In so doing, it has relied on the principle of non-discrimination.

In *Reyners* v *Belgium*[60] a Dutch national who held a legal diploma giving the right to take up the profession of *avocat* in Belgium found himself excluded from that profession by reason of his nationality as a result of a Belgian decree. He challenged that exclusion by an action before the Conseil d'Etat, which asked the European Court to rule on the interpretation of Articles 52, 54 and 57 of the EEC Treaty. That Court began by observing that the rule on equality of treatment with nationals is one of the fundamental legal provisions of the Community. By its essence, that rule was capable of being invoked directly by nationals of the Member States. The fact that the progressive measures to implement the freedom of establishment had not been adopted in accordance with the timetable set out in the Treaty in no way impaired the existence or the direct effectiveness of the rule on equality of treatment. Accordingly, it was not open to one Member State to prohibit nationals of another State from engaging in practice as a lawyer.

The Court took this reasoning one step further in *Thieffry* v *Conseil de l'Ordre des Avocats à la Cour de Paris*[61] where the appellant was denied admission to the Paris Bar, not because he was a Belgian national but because he had a Belgian rather than a French diploma in law. The Court emphasized that freedom of establishment, subject to the observance of professional rules justified by the general good, is one of the objectives of the Treaty. Consequently, if that freedom could be ensured in a Member State under the provisions of the laws in force, or by virtue of the practices of the public service or of professional bodies, a person subject to Community law could not be denied the practical benefit of that freedom solely by virtue of the fact that, for a particular profession, the directives provided for by Article 57 of the Treaty had not yet been adopted. As the appellant's Belgian doctorate was recognized by a French university as equivalent to a French doctorate in law, and as he had obtained a qualifying certificate for the profession of advocate, it was not open to the Ordre des Avocats to demand that he obtain a French national diploma.

The Court's third step was taken in *Patrick v Ministre des Affaires Culturelles*[62] in which the appellant was a British subject and the holder of a certificate issued by the Architectural Association in the United Kingdom. He was denied authorization to practise as an architect in France on the ground that there was no convention between France and the United Kingdom providing for the mutual recognition of qualifications in architecture. The Court ruled that it is not possible to invoke against the direct effect of the rule on equal treatment with nationals, contained in Article 52 of the Treaty, the fact that the Council has failed to issue the directives provided for by Articles 54 and 57 or the fact that certain of the directives actually issued have not fully attained the objectives of non-discrimination required by Article 52. As the appellant's qualification was recognized by the competent French authorities as equivalent to the certificate issued to prospective architects in France, those authorities could not require the appellant to satisfy any other condition. In particular he could not be required to demonstrate that a comparable French qualification would be recognized in the United Kingdom.

It is to be emphasized that in all of these three cases the Court relied upon the direct effectiveness of the Treaty's provisions after the end of the transitional period. They cannot, therefore, be taken as authority for the proposition that individuals may rely on the Treaty's provisions so as to secure the recognition of qualifications in a period prior to the date on which Member States were obliged to act. Indeed, the Court has now decided that Article 52 of the Treaty does not have that form of retrospective effect, even where the Council has, at a later date, adopted measures to regulate the recognition of qualifications in the particular profession.[63]

In the case of the freedom to provide services, a particular difficulty arises. It has been contended that the aim of Articles 59 to 66 of the EEC Treaty is not to remove all restrictions on freedom to supply services, but simply to ensure that foreigners and nationals are treated in the same way. If this were so, national rules which require providers of services to fulfil certain conditions (such as residence in the appropriate State or the acquisition of a licence) would be valid, so long as they were not discriminatory. It is true that the Court has often insisted upon the need to abolish discrimination on grounds of nationality.[64] This does not imply, however, that these Articles are limited to the abolition of discrimination. In Case 279/80, *Alfred Webb*,[65] Mr Advocate General Slynn expressed the view that an element of discrimination is a conclusive but inessential condition of a breach of these Articles. The Court appears to have upheld that view. Where national law subjects the exercise of a particular activity to the holding of a licence (as is the case with employment agencies in most Member States) it may not on that basis restrict the activities of a person established in another Member State who holds a licence issued by the authorities there, if that licence demonstrates that he meets each of the conditions which would otherwise be imposed in the State in which the services are to be supplied, and that those requirements are adequately capable of enforcement.

Nor may a Member State restrict the freedom of establishment of nationals of other Member States by requiring them to sever their professional ties with their countries of origin. Such a policy tends to convert a right of establishment into a mere freedom to supply services. Thus, France acted unlawfully in requiring doctors and dental practitioners established in other Member States to cancel their enrolment in such States, in order to practise in France.[66]

PUBLIC POLICY, PUBLIC SECURITY AND PUBLIC HEALTH

The rights enumerated in Articles 48, 52 and 59 of the EEC Treaty are subject to two principal limitations of which the first, and hitherto the most highly developed, is the exception in the interests of public policy, public security and public health. Article 48(3) states that freedom of movement shall entail specified rights subject to limitations justified on those grounds. By Articles 56 and 66 of the Treaty, limitations may be imposed on the travel of the self-employed, and on recipients of services, in the interests of public policy, security or health.[67] The meaning to be given to this expression is explained in Council Directive 64/221, which states that such limitations must be based on 'the personal conduct of the individual concerned'. The draftsmen of the Directive (which has since been extended to self-employed persons by Directive 75/35) cannot have been unaware of the logical difficulty in distinguishing between individual conduct and general considerations; for it is impossible to justify the exclusion of an individual, by reference to his conduct, without making an assertion, albeit implied, about the categories of persons who should be excluded or expelled. Nor is it possible to apply the elementary principle of treating like cases alike without identifying characteristics of different individuals in general terms. The gist of the Directive nevertheless appears tolerably clear: each case is to be considered upon its merits and general rules for exclusion are to be avoided.

An illustration of the distinction between individual and general considerations is provided in the European Court's ruling in *Carmelo Angelo Bonsignore*.[68] The circumstance giving rise to this case was the conduct of a young Italian man in killing his brother accidentally, while in unlawful possession of a firearm in Germany. Following his conviction, the aliens authority ordered his deportation, a course of action which could be justified under German law only on the basis of its 'general preventive nature' (or its effect as a deterrent upon others). The European Court ruled that such a consideration could not warrant the deportation from one Member State of a worker from another such State. 'As departures from the rules concerning the free movement of persons must be strictly construed, the concept of 'personal conduct' expresses the requirement that a deportation order may only be made for breaches of the peace and public security which might be committed by the individual affected'.

There remain some difficulties in understanding the precise significance in modern law of the Court's words in Case 41/74, *Van Duyn* v *Home Office*,[69] which arose from the ban imposed by the United Kingdom on the admission of persons seeking to work or study at establishments of the Church of Scientology. In that case the European Court refrained from ruling that such a ban was incompatible with Community law, when applied to nationals of other Member States. It reasoned that continuing membership of an organization, which reflects participation in the activities of the body or of the organization as well as identification with its aims and its designs, may be considered a voluntary act of the person concerned and consequently as part of his personal conduct within the meaning of the Directive. It is thought that the Court did not intend to imply by those words that a prohibition upon the admission of all members of a specified organization is permitted, even in the absence of any inquiries into the circumstances of individual members; but rather that in determining whether an individual is to be admitted to the territory of a Member State, its authorities may take into account, along with other conduct, his affiliations including his membership of a prescribed organization.

The next issue to which the Court addressed itself in *Van Duyn* was the fact that the activities of the Church of Scientology, although considered as contrary to the public good, were not prohibited by national law. The Court reasoned that where a Member State considers the activities of a particular organization socially harmful, and has taken administrative measures to counteract those activities, the Member State cannot be required to make such activities unlawful before it can rely on the concept of public policy. That part of the Court's judgment appears no longer to represent the law. In a later case the Court ruled conduct may not be considered as being of a sufficiently serious nature to justify restrictions on the admission or residence of a national of another Member State in a case where the former Member State does not adopt, with respect to the same conduct on the part of its own nationals, repressive measures or other genuine and effective measures intended to combat such conduct. It was left for the national court to infer that the Belgian authorities could not invoke the concept of public policy to justify the removal from Belgium of two French nationals, working as waitresses in conditions which were 'suspect from the point of view of morals'; for no comparable penalty could have been imposed in Belgium against like women having Belgian nationality. Their activities, although considered socially harmful, and discouraged by administrative measures, were not expressly prohibited.[70]

In that judgment the Court emphasized the relevance of the principle of equality of treatment to cases involving restrictions on the freedom of movement. It was by no means the first time that it had applied that principle to that context. In Case 36/75, *Rutili*[71] the European Court ruled that a residence restriction could not be imposed on an Italian trade union activist in France where no such restriction could have been imposed upon a French national. Such a restriction was not to be justified in the case of the Italian by reference to public policy, public security or public health. Likewise in Case 152/73 *Sotgiu v Bundespost*[72] the Court ruled that once a national of one Member State has been admitted to the public service of another such State he is entitled to be treated equally with nationals of that State as regards terms and conditions of employment.

Since the free movement of labour itself constitutes one of the fundamental principles of the European Communities the Court has emphasized that any derogation – including the derogation on grounds of public order or public policy – must be construed restrictively. In Case 30/77 *R. v Bouchereau*[73] it therefore ruled that 'in so far as it may justify certain restrictions on the free movement of persons subject to Community law recourse by a national authority to the concept of public policy presupposes, in any event, the existence, in addition to the perturbation of the social order which any infringement of the law involves, of a genuine and sufficiently serious threat to the requirements of public policy affecting one of the fundamental interests of society'.

Even if a migrant worker has committed in a Member State other than his own an offence of the utmost gravity he will not, necessarily be amenable to deportation. In Case 131/79 *Santilo*,[74] the accused was an Italian national who had been convicted in the United Kingdom of serious sexual offences committed against two prostitutes. He was sentenced to a total of eight years' imprisonment. After serving his sentence, less remission for good behaviour, he was due to be released but was detained under the Immigration Act in order that the Home Secretary might determine whether to follow a recommendation, made by the Court before which he was convicted, that he should be deported to Italy. Santillo contended that he should not be deported until he had been given the opportunity of availing himself of the remedy envisaged by Article 9 of Council Directive No. 64/221. This envisages that in advance of any deportation there shall be obtained an opinion from the competent authority of the host country before which the person concerned shall enjoy rights of defence and legal representation. Santillo's contention was that the administrative remedy must be afforded at the time when the decision to order expulsion is made against him and not at a stage several years earlier when he is first put on trial. The European Court appears to have upheld this argument, in essence, ruling that 'a lapse of time amounting to several years between the recommendation for deportation and the decision by the administration is liable to deprive the recommendation of its function as an opinion within the meaning of Article 9'. Thus, as the offence increases in gravity and the period of imprisonment lengthens, the migrant worker's right to a hearing under Article 9 of the Directive is apt to increase in utility. On the other hand, there may not be inferred from the Directive an obligation for the Member State to permit an alien to remain in its territory for the duration of the proceedings, so long as he is able nevertheless to obtain a fair hearing.[75]

In the case of restrictions based on public health, the Directive provides that refusal of entry may be justified only on the basis of illnesses specified in the Annex. This specifies diseases subject to quarantine listed in the World Health Organization's Regulation No. 2 of 25 May 1951, together with tuberculosis; syphilis and other infectious or parasitic diseases which are the subject of provision for the protection of nationals of the host country.[76]

PUBLIC SERVICE AND OFFICIAL AUTHORITY

The second of the main limitations on freedom of movement is found in the final paragraph of Article 48 of the EEC Treaty, which indicates that this freedom is not to extend to employment in the public service, and in Article 55, which states that freedom of establishment is not to extend to activities connected, even occasionally, with the public service. The limitation contained in Article 55 is applied by analogy to freedom to provide services, by Article 66 of the EEC Treaty.

That Treaty does not define public service or the exercise of official authority. It falls, therefore, upon the Court to provide a definition. This the Court has begun to do, although slowly and cautiously, on the basis of comparative law.

The issue appears to have been raised for the first time in *Sotgiu* v *Bundespost*[77] which concerned an employee of the German post office. The Court found it unnecessary in that case to express an opinion on the concept of 'public service', since it took the view that the limitation contained in the final paragraph of Article 48 applied only in respect of access to employment and not in respect of the treatment of workers once engaged. Mr Advocate General Mayras, however, did not feel free to avoid the issue. He expressed the view that the meaning of the phrase 'public service' cannot vary from State to State and cannot therefore be defined in terms of the legal status under national law of the holder of the office in question. Rather, in his view, it was necessary to have resort to factual criteria based upon the duties which the post entails. In his opinion, the exception for 'public service' will be applicable only if the holder of the office 'possesses a power of discretion with respect to individuals or if his activity involves national interests – in particular those which are concerned with the internal or external security of the State'. His view has the merit of being consistent with the series of judgments of the Court in which it has insisted that any derogation from the freedom of movement must be construed restrictively.

The Court returned to that theme in the *Reyners* case[78] where it concluded that the exception to freedom of establishment created by Article 55 must be restricted to those activities which involve a 'direct and specific connection with the exercise of official authority'. The Court based this conclusion on 'the fundamental character of freedom of establishment', reasoning that the exceptions allowed by Article 55 cannot be given a scope which would exceed their objective. Consequently, the activities of an *avocat* could not be taken to involve the exercise of official authority, even where they involved the compulsory provision of advice or assistance to litigants, or where there is a legal monopoly in respect of those services.

It is not immediately clear what is meant by activities involving a 'direct and specific connexion' with official authority. Possibly the Court meant to qualify the word 'connected', as it appears in the phrase 'activities . . . connected with the exercise of official authority': the *avocat* is not 'connected' with the exercise of official authority by a judge, by reason only of the fact that he assists the judge in the exercise of the latter's function, by presenting the litigant's case in due and proper form. In Case 149/79, *Commission v Belgium*[79] the Court stated that the exception to the freedom of movement for workers, which exists in cases of employment in the public service, applies to 'posts which involve *direct or indirect* participation in the exercise of power conferred by public law and duties designed to safeguard the general interests of the State or of other public authorities'. For the purpose of the free movement of workers, therefore, it seems that the crucial feature is not the directness of any connection between the worker and a person indisputably possessing official functions, but rather the capacity to exercise powers conferred by public law or to discharge responsibility for safeguarding the interests of the State. In its more recent judgment in the same case[80] the Court reiterated that this is the touchstone. The influence of the Opinion of Mr Advocate General Mayras, in the *Sotgiu* case[81] is not difficult to perceive.

Since the principal European systems of social security have a territorial basis, they present two difficulties for migrants. The first is non-recognition by the country of immigration of security rights acquired in the country of emigration. The second is the unavailability of benefits outside the territory of the country in which the title to the benefit is acquired. Hence there arises the necessity of coordinating social security systems within the European Community, so as to remove the barriers that would otherwise restrict the free movement of persons throughout the region. The aspiration of the EEC Treaty[82] is to achieve this objective.

Article 51 of the EEC Treaty was initially implemented by a pair of Regulations made in 1958[83] but these have since been replaced by more modern instruments.[84] These Regulations were made to coordinate social security legislation of Member States in order to remove restrictions to the mobility of labour and abolish inequality of treatment among workers on the basis of their nationality.[85] To achieve these ends, certain rights were placed on a personal rather than a territorial basis. Such rights were originally conferred on 'workers'.[86] In 1983 the Council extended the application of the basic Regulations[87] to include self-employed persons.[88] Further, an unemployed person entitled to benefit in one Member State and seeking work within another Member State may receive unemployment benefits for a maximum of three months in the latter State.[89] It is, however, necessary to quality the beneficiaries with greater precision.

The principal Community legislation on social security schemes applies to employed and self-employed persons who are or have been subject to the legislation of one or more Member States and who are nationals of one of the Member States or who are stateless persons[90] or refugees[91] residing within the territory of one of the Member States. Such persons are by definition insured for one or more of the contingencies covered by the branches of a social security scheme. The legislation also applies to members of the families and survivors of employed and self-employed persons.[92] A member of the family is defined as such by the national legislation which provides the benefit, or by simple dependence upon the employed or self-employed person. A survivor is similarly described by relation to the deceased.[93]

Article 13(1) of Regulation 1408/71 states that:

> Persons to whom this Regulation applies shall be subject to the legislation of a single Member State only.[94]

This rule does not prohibit a Member State, other than that in which the person concerned is employed, from applying its social security legislation to him or her.[95] However, a person who is employed or self-employed in the territory of one Member State is generally subject to the legislation of that State, even if he or she resides in the territory of another State. This rule is modified where the person concerned goes to work in the territory of another State other than that in which he is usually employed;[96] where the person normally works in two or more Member States;[97] and where a person is employed or self-employed in an undertaking which has its registered office or place of business in the territory of another Member State and which straddles common frontiers of those States.[98] A person employed on a ship flying the flag of a Member State is subject to the legislation of that State[99] and civil servants and members of the armed forces are subject to the legislation of the State to which the administration employing them is subject.

Community social security provisions apply to all legislation concerning eight branches of social security laws:[100] sickness and maternity benefits; invalidity benefits, including those intended for the maintenance or improvement of earning capacity; old-age benefits; survivors' benefits; benefits in respect of accidents at work and occupational diseases; death grants; unemployment benefits; and family benefits.[101] An employed or self-employed person residing in the territory of a Member State other than the competent State, who satisfies the conditions of the legislation of that State for entitlement to benefits, is entitled to receive such benefits in the State in which he or she is resident. Benefits in kind are provided on behalf of the competent institution by the institution in the place of residence as though the person concerned were insured with it. Regard must be had to all the legislation which the person has been subject to and to whether the person had completed the requisite periods of insurance[102] before benefit can be awarded. Where the legislation of one Member State makes acquisition of the right to benefits conditional upon completion of periods of insurance or periods of employment, the competent institution of that State must generally take into account, to the extent necessary, periods of insurance, employment or self-employment completed in any other Member State as if they were periods completed under the legislation which it administers.

There are common provisions under the Community social security legislation to determine the State responsible for the provision of benefits. The competent State is the State in which the 'competent institution' is situated. The institution with which the applicant is insured at the time of the application for benefit is normally the competent institution. Alternatively, the competent institution is the one from which the applicant would be entitled to receive benefits on condition of being resident in the territory of the State in which the institution is situated.[103] The distribution of benefits is, however, entrusted to the institution situated at the place at which the applicant resides.

Community regulations contain provisions against the reduction or overlapping of benefits in consequence of migration. Certain specified benefits are preserved against reduction, modification, suspension, withdrawal or confiscation by reason of the fact that the recipient resides in a State other than the one in which the institution responsible for the payment is situated.[104] Moreover, in the case of pensions for invalidity, old age, death or occupational disease, recipients may be in receipt of overlapping benefits in two or more Member States. Normally, Community provisions neither confer nor maintain the right to several benefits of the same kind; indeed, a Member State may reduce or suspend benefit where it is duplicated (except in these cases) even though the right to such benefit was acquired under the legislation of another Member State. Article 15(1) of Regulation 1408/71 lists provisions for the aggregation of insurance contributions in order to satisfy national conditions for entitlement to benefits. The rules prevent the institution of a Member State from applying national rules for the aggregation and apportionment of periods of insurance which might be less favourable to the person concerned.

RECENT PROPOSALS

The present principles of European Community law governing freedom of movement for persons are liable to be altered in pursuance of the Single European Act, which was concluded in February 1986.[105] This Act[106] inserts into the Treaty establishing the European Economic Community a new Article 8A, reading in part as follows:

> The Community shall adopt measures with the aim of progressively establishing the internal market over a period expiring on 31 December 1992 . . .
> The internal market shall comprise an area without internal frontiers in which the free movement of goods, persons, services and capital is ensured.

The language appears to imply that the measures to be adopted in the period expiring at the end of 1992 are to include the reduction or abolition of certain of the frontier controls conducted at the Community's internal borders. This would be consonant with the construction explicitly placed on the same Article by members of the Council, in so far as it refers to the free movement of goods. It is also possible that the measures to be adopted under Article 8A will include those governing freedom of movement for persons other than workers, suppliers and recipients of services and beneficiaries of freedom of establishment.

The Single European Act requires the Commission to report to the Council before the end of 1988 and again before the end of 1990 on progress made towards achieving the internal market.[107] When drawing up its proposals, the Commission is to take into account the 'extent of the effort that certain economies showing differences in development will have to sustain during the period of establishment of the internal market'. The Commission's proposals made in view of these considerations may include derogations in favour of the States concerned but such derogations must be temporary and must cause the least possible disturbance to the functioning of the Common Market.[108] When it acts on the Commission's proposals, in matters falling under the Treaty provisions governing the free movement of workers, the Council is to reach its decisions by qualified majority, in cooperation with the European Parliament and after consulting the Economic and Social Committee.[109]

During the second half of 1986, when the United Kingdom occupied the Presidency of the Council, the British Home Secretary took the initiative of proposing the tightening of the Community's external controls as internal controls are relaxed. The point was first made at a speech to the Anglo-German Association in Bonn on 24 September 1986, but elaborated after a meeting of European Community ministers in London on 20 October 1986. On that date it was announced that a working group had been established to consider urgently:

(i)   stronger checks at external Community frontiers;
(ii)   the contribution which internal checks can make;
(iii)   the role of co-ordination of visa policies of Member States in improving controls;
(iv)   the role and effectiveness of frontier controls at internal frontiers in the fight against terrorism, drugs, crime and illegal immigration;
(v)   exchange of information about the operation of spot check systems;
(vi)   close co-operation to avoid the abuse of passports;
(vii)   measures to achieve a common policy to eliminate the abuse of the right of asylum; and
(viii) examination of ways in which the convenience of Community travellers can be improved without adding to the terrorist threat or the risk of illegal immigration, drug trafficking and other crime.

Further, it was agreed that the Member States would coordinate and (if possible) harmonise their policies on visas.

After a meeting of ministers held on 9 December 1986 it was announced that the working group had made progress, although the extent and nature of the progress was not disclosed.

CONCLUSION

The Community's programme for securing the free movement of labour does not appear to have contributed to an increase in migration for employment across the borders of Member States. On the contrary, it is even possible that it has had some tendency to reduce such migration, by improving the conditions of migrant workers and thereby adding to the costs of their engagement. In 1959, when the programme was in its infancy, some three quarters of the migrant workers within the Community came from the territories of other Member States: but by 1973, when the programme had reached its fruition, the proportions were reversed: three quarters came from countries outside the Community. In the year in which the United Kingdom joined the Community the number of Community nationals taking employment in that country fell, as did the number of United Kingdom nationals taking employment in the other Member States. The nine original Member States may, therefore, have been acting with an excess of caution when they required, in the Greek and in the Spanish and Portuguese Acts of Accession, long transitional periods for the application to Greece, Portugal and Spain of the Community's rules on the subject.[110]

Nevertheless, the Community's provisions governing the free movement of labour remain of rather lively practical interest and of no little symbolic significance. The Court's insistence on the direct effectiveness of these provisions, and upon the narrow construction of any derogating provisions, has had the result of transforming Title III of the EEC Treaty into a charter of widespread practical utility to the employed and the self-employed, both in their own countries and elsewhere in the Community.

NOTES

1. *Infra*, pp. 273–276.
2. Act concerning the Conditions of Accession of the Hellenic Republic, Articles 44–48, annexed to Treaty of Accession, 28 May 1979, O.J. 1969 L291/9 at 26 (transitional periods expiring on 1 January 1986 and 1 January 1988).
3. Act concerning the Conditions of Accession of the Kingdom of Spain and the Portuguese Republic, Articles 55–60, annexed to Treaty of Accession, 12 June 1985, O.J. 1985 L302/9 at 35 (transitional periods expiring on 1 January 1991 and 1 January 1993).
4. *Infra*, note 26. By a Political Declaration annexed to the Single European Act, The Hague, 17 and 28 February 1986, 25 I.L.M. (1986) 506 the Member States agreed that they would cooperate as regards the entry, movement and residence of nationals of third States. *Infra* text at note 12 and Chapter VIII, text at note 3.
5. In the case of the European Coal and Steel Community, Member States undertook to remove any restriction based on nationality upon the employment in the coal and steel sector of workers who are nationals of Member States and who have a recognized qualification, subject to limitations based on public health or public policy: *E.C.S.C. Treaty, 18 April 1951, 261 U.N.T.S. 140, Article 69 (Basic Documents VI.2)*. In the case of the European Atomic Energy Community, Member States made a corresponding undertaking, subject to limitations based on public policy, public security or public health: Euratom Treaty, 25 March 1957, 298 U.N.T.S. 167, Articles 96–97 (*Basic Documents* VI.3). See further E.C.S.C. Decisions of 8 December 1954 and 16 May 1961 E.C. Council Decision 74/494 and Euratom Council Directive of 5 March 1962 (*Basic Documents* VI.4).

216

6. 25 March 1957, 298 U.N.T.S. 11.

7. Under the terms of the Association Agreement of 12 September 1973, O.J. C 113, 24 December 1973 p. 2, the parties agreed to be guided by Articles 48 to 50 of the E.E.C. Treaty for the purpose of progressively securing freedom of movement for workers between them. Acting in pursuance of the Agreement the Council of Association established thereby made Decision 1/80 (Council Doc. 8795/1/80) having among its declared objectives the improvement of the treatment accorded to migrant workers and their families.

8. 24 I.L.M. (1985) 571, Articles 252–254. These establish the principle of non-discrimination on grounds of nationality for individuals, firms and companies establishing themselves or supplying services in the contracting States. For the terms on these matters in the antecedent Treaty of Lomé, 31 October 1979, see O.J. L347 of 22 December 1980, p.2.

9. *Action Programme in Favour of Migrant Workers and their Families.* Com. (74) 2550, p. 1: *Report on the Development of the Social Situation in the Community in 1976,* Commission (1977) para. 55; R. Plender, 'An Incipient Form of European Citizenship', *European Law and the Individual* (ed. Jacobs) 1976 at 40 note 5; A. Durand, 'European Citizenship', 4 E. L. Rev. (1974) 3; W. Boehning, *The Migration of Workers in the United Kingdom and the European Community,* 1972 at p. 81.

10. Case 53/81, *Levin v Staatssecretaris van Justitie,* (1982) ECR 1035 at 1049. See R. Beever, *Trade Unions and Free Labour Movement in the EEC.* 1969.

11. Case 77/82, *Peskeloglou v Bundesanstalt für Arbeit,* (1983) ECR 1085. See L. Berrocal Martin, '*Intégration européenne et libre circulation des travailleurs: quelques éléments d'analyse pour le cas espanol*', 4 Rev. int. eur. (1981) 335. See further R. Plender and J. Perez Santos, *Introduccion al Derecho Comunitario,* 1983 (2nd. reprint), pp. 141–180.

12. Joined Cases 281/85, 283, 284 and 285/85 and 287/85 *Federal Republic of Germany and Others* v. *Commission,* 9 July 1987, not yet reported.

13. *Basic Documents* IV.1. See generally K. Simmonds, 'The EEC Freedoms of Establishment and Supply of Services: A Comparison', *Commercial Operations in Europe* (ed. Goode and Simmonds) 1978, 37; J. Usher, 'Establishment, Services and Lawyers', [1979] S.L.T. 65; D. Bennet, 'EEC Nationals in the United Kingdom: 1. Rights of Entry and Residence', 128 New L.J. (1978) 43; C. Maestripieri, *La libre circulation des personnes et des services dans la CEE,* 1972, 46.

14. Council Regulation 1612/68 of 15 October 1968 on Freedom of Movement for Workers within the Community. O.J. Sp. Ed. 1968, 475 (as amended by Council Regulation 312/76 of 9 February 1976, O.J. 1976 L 39/2) Article 1 and Council Directive 68/360 of 15 October 1968 on the Abolition of Restrictions on Movement and Residence within the Community for Workers and Members of their Families, O.J. 1968, 485, Article 2. See further Council Regulation 1251/70 of 29 June 1970 on the Right of Workers to Remain in the Territories of Member States, O.J.Sp.Ed. 1970, 402.

15. Case 75/63 [1964] ECR 177 at 184. See also Case 17/76, *Brack v Insurance Officer,* [1976] ECR 1429.

16. Case 66/85, *Lawrie-Blum v. Land Baden-Wurttemberg,* 3 July 1986, O.J. 1986 C200/86.

17. The comparative method was employed in Case 149/79, *Commission v. Belgium* [1980] ECR 3881. See further Maestripieri, *supra,* note 13 at 40–42.

18. *Re Expulsion of an Italian National,* [1965] C.M.L.R. 285; *City of Wiesbaden v. Barulli,* [1968] C.M.L.R. 239; Decision of *Verwaltungsgerichtshof Mannheim,* [1965] D.V.BL. 405; Police v. Secchi, [1976] Crim. L. Rev. 392; *Nijssen v. Immigration Officers; London and Sheerness* [1978] Imm. A.R. 2664. In *Giovanni v. Home Secretary.* [1977] Imm. A.R. 85 it was held that a national of another Member State was not a 'worker' when he was relying on public funds and did not intend to take employment.

19. Case 13/76, [1976] ECR 1333 at 1340. See L. Picchio, '*Discriminazioni nel settore sportivo et*

communita europea', 59 Riv. dir. int. (1976) 745; J. Plouvain, *'La libre circulation des sportifs professionels à l'interieur de la Communauté'*, Rev. marché comm. (1978) 516; N. Giltay Veth, *'Uitsluiting van buitenlandse voetballers: mogelijk binnen de EEG?'* 53 Ned. Jur. (1478) 504.

20. EEC Treaty, Article 48(3)(b); Council Directive 64/221 of 15 February 1964, on the Co-ordination of Special Measures concerning the Movement and Residence of Foreign Nationals, O.J. Sp. Ed., 1963–64, 117, Article 1; Regulation 1612/68, *supra*, note 14, Preamble; Directive 68/360, supra, note 14, Article 2.

21. Case 139/85, *Kempf v. Staatssecretaris van Justitie,* 3 June 1986, O.J. 1986 C188/3.

22. *Supra,* note 17 at 512.

23. Case 118/75, [1976] ECR 1185 at 1204.

24. T. Hartley, *EEC Immigration Law,* North Holland (Amsterdam) 1978, 105; 'The Internal Personal Scope of the EEC Immigration Provisions concerning Free Movement of Workers', *European Law and the Individual (ed. Jacobs) 1976, 24; 'The Internal Personal Scope of the EEC Immigration Provisions',* 3 E.L. Rev. (1978) 191 at 193.

25. See the Opinion of Mr Advocate General Slynn in Case 53/81, *Levin, supra,* note *10.* In *R v Secretary of State ex parte Muhammad Avub,* [1983] Imm. A.R. 20 at 27, Forbes, J. concluded that a national of one Member State has the right to enter the territory of another only when he has an offer of employment.

26. See D. Loschak, *'Les ressortissants de la CEE',* 5 Droit soc. (1976) 83; W. Much & J.C. Séché, *'Les droits de l'étranger dans les Communautés européennes',* 2 Cah. dr. eur. (1971) 251; Giuseppe Sperduti, *'La libertà di circolazione e di stabilimento nei paesi della Communità economica europea',* 13 Riv. dir. int. e comp. del lav. (1973) 179.

27. This is the view taken by A. Campbell, *Common Market Law,* Supp. 2, 1971, 226 and by W. Boehning, *supra,* note 9. See further G. Renato *Il processo evolutivo nel diritto communitario per la libera circolazione delle persone,* 1977.

28. D. Duyssens, 'Migrant Workers from Third Countries in the European Community', 14 C.M.L. Rev. (1977) 501; F. Durante & A. Costa, *'La politica sociale e del lavoro delle Communitá europea: riflessi sulla condizione giuridica dei refugiati',* 9 Aff. soc. int. (1981) 193; G. Falchi, *'Le régime définitif de la libre circulation et l'immigration des pays tiers',* 2 Droit Soc (1971) 16; S. Neri, *Le champ d'application du droit communautaire en matière de libre circulation des travailleurs,* 1982.

29. Case 65/77, *Razanatsimba,* [1977] ECR 2229.

30. See *Nationality Decrees in Tunis and Morocco,* P.C.I.J. Ser. B. No. 4 (1923): the *Nottebohm Case,* I.C.J. Rep. (1955) 4. See further K. Simmonds, 'Immigration Control and the Free Movement of Labour: A Problem of Harmonization', 22 I.C.L.Q. (1972) 307 at 319.

31. Hague International Conference for the Codification of International Law, L.O.N. Doc. C. 24. M. 13. 1931, V; Article 1.

32. *Re Residence Permit for an Egyptian National,* [1975] C.M.L.R. 402.

33. [1979] ECR 399.

34. Council Directive No. 64/427 of 7 July 1964, O.J. Sp. Ed. 1963–64, 148.

35. [1981] ECR 2311 at 2329.

36. Case 175/78, *R v Saunders,* [1979] E.C.R. 1129 at 1142 and 1135.

37. Case 41/74, *Van Duyn v Home Office,* [1974] E.C.R. 1337.

38. Case 115/78, *supra* note 33; Case 175/78, R. v. *Saunders,* supra, note 36; Case 298/84, *Lorio* v. *Azienda Autonoma dello Ferrovie dello Stato,* 23 January 1986.

39. Joined Cases 35 and 36/82, *Morson and Jhanjan,* [1982] ECR 2723.

40. Declaration 64/305 of 25 March 1964, J.O. 22 May 1964, No. 78. *Obomalayat* v. *Home Office,* 16 August 1978 (Mars-Jones J., unreported).

41. P. Bianchi, *'Osservazioni sulla libera circolazione dei lavoratori dipendenti all'interno della*

218

Communita europea', 34 Foro Padano (1979) 1; T. Hartley, 'Are British Immigration Rules Contrary to Community Law?' 6 E.L. Rev. (1981) 280; I. Telchini, *'La libertà circolazione nella comunita dei lavoratori dipendenti'*, 8 Ann. Fac. Giur. Genova (1969) 392. Useful guidance of the general principles may be deduced from the decisions of the European Commission and the Court of Human Rights, and decisions of national courts, on the interpretation of Article 8 of the European Convention on Human Rights. See the materials cited in F. Jacobs, *The European Convention on Human Rights,* 1975, 128–135.

42. Case 59/85, *Netherlands v Anna Florence Reed,* 17 April 1986, O.J. 1976, C 122/3.
43. *Grewal v Home Secretary,* [1979–80] Imm. A.R. 119: *R v Home Secretary, ex parte Amarjit Singh Sandhu,* [1983] Imm. A.R. 61.
44. Cf. Case 167/73, *Commission v France,* [1974] E.C.R. at 372 and Case 41/74, *Van Duyn v Home Office, supra,* note 37 at 1348; Case 267/83, *Diatta v Land Berlin,* 13 February 1985, O.J. 1966 C61/3.
45. Case 131/85, *Emir Gül v Regierungspräsident Düsseldorf,* 7 May 1986, O.J. 1986, C 145/7.
46. Council Directive 73/148 of 21 May 1973, on the Abolition of Restrictions on Movement and Residence ... with Regard to Establishment and the Provision of Services, O.J. 1973, L 172/4. For the right to remain in a Member State after employment there, see Council Regulation 1251/70 of 29 June 1970, O.J. Sp. Ed. 1970, 396; and for the right to remain after pursuing self-employed activities see Council Directive 75/34 of 17 December 1974, O.J. 1975 L14/10.
47. Case 48/75, *Jean Noël Royer,* [1976] ECR 497 at 513.
48. Case 118/75, *Watson and Belmann, supra,* note 23 at 1197.
49. Case 8/77, *Sagulo, Brenca and Bakhouche,* [1977] ECR 1495 at 1504.
50. Case 157/79 *R v Pieck* [1979] ECR 2171 at 2184. See further A. Evans, 'Entry Formalities in the European Communities', 6 E.L. Rev. (1981) 3. See further the Commission's Reply to Written Question No 108/85 on the right of abode in the Federal Republic of Germany of Mr Adolfo Ghiani, O.J. 1986 C 78/1.
51. Case 268/82, *Luisi and Carbone v Ministero del Tesoro* [1984] ECR 377 at 403, para. 16.
52. See Case 15/69, *Ugliola,* [1969] ECR 363, and Case 44/72, *Marsman v Rosskamp,* [1972] ECR 1243.
53. [1982] ECR 33.
54. Case 9/74, *Casagrande v. Landeshauptstadt München,* [1974] ECR 773.See also Case 68/74, *Alaimo v. Préfet du Rhône* [1975] ECR 109. The matter is now regulated by Council Directive 77/486 of 25 July 1977, O.J. 1977 L199/32. For the franchise see G. Bertinetto, *'La partecipazione al voto communale dei cittadini dei paesi comunitari e degli altri stranieri in Italia',* 8 Aff. soc. int. (1980) 87.
55. Case 59/85, *Netherlands v. Ann Florence Reed, supra* note 42.
56. J.O. 1962, 36; O.J. Sp. Ed., 2d. Ser. No. 9, p.7. See generally V. Abellan Honrubia, *'Medidas especificas para la libertad de establecimiento en cada sector de actividad',* I Rev. inst. eur. (1974) 1121; G. Biscottini, *'Problemi della circolazione e dello establimento nel Trattato di Roma',* 53 Riv. dir int. (1970) 161; J. Bontemps, *Liberté d'établissement et libre prestation des services dans le marché commun,* 1968; N. Briquet, *'Liberté d'établissement et libre prestation des services',* 13 R.M.C. (1970) 311; F. Capelli, *'La libera professione nella C.E.E. degli anni 80',* 35 Foro Padano (1980) 57; J. Detienne, *'L'Accession aux activités économiques dans la Communauté économique européenne',* 88 Jo. des Trib. (1973) 341, 361, 381; O Lando, 'The Liberal Professions in the European Communities', 8 C.M.L. Rev. (1971) 343; C. Lega, *'Le libere professioni e la liberta di prestazione dei servizi nella C.E.E.',* 24 Riv. dir. del. lav. (1972) 107; P. Leleux & M. Bronkhorst, 'The Impact of European Community Law on the Right of Establishment and the Engagement of Personnel', *Commercial Operations in Europe* (ed. Goode & Simmonds) 1978, 27; C. Maestripieri, 'Freedom

of Establishment and Freedom to Supply Services', 10 C.M.L. Rev. (1973) 150; N. Nagy, '*Le droit de l'établissement et les prestations de services dans la Communauté économique européenne*', 21 Wirt. und Recht (1969) 173; G. Nicolaysen, '*Harmonisierung des Niederlassungsrechts*', 11 Kölner Schriften zum Europarecht (1971) 77; I. Schwartz, '*Le rôle du rapprochement des législations afin de faciliter le droit d'établissement et la libre circulation des services*', 2 Doc. dir. comp. (1980) 5; G. Sperduti, *La libertà di circolazione e di stabilimento nei paesi della Comunità economica europea*', 13 Riv. dir. int. e comp. del. lav. (1973) 179; B. Sundberg-Weitman, *Discrimination on Grounds of Nationality: Free Movement of Workers and Freedom of Establishment under the EEC Treaty*, 1977; V. Tedeschi, '*Le direttive della CEE in terma di stabilimento delle persone e la sede giuridica*', 133 Giur. it. (1981) 256.

57. Council Directive 64/223 of 25 February 1964, Concerning . . . Wholesale Trade, J.O. 1964, 863, O.J. Sp. Ed. 1963–64, 123; Council Directive 64/224 of 25 February 1964 Concerning . . . Activities of Intermediaries in Commerce, Industry and Small Craft Industries, J.O. 1964, 869, O.J. Sp. Ed. 1963–64, 126; Council Directive 68/363 of 15 October 1968, Concerning . . . Self-Employed Persons in Retail Trade, J.O. 1968 L 260/1, O.J. Sp. Ed. 1968, 496; Council Directive 68/365 of 15 October 1968, Concerning . . . Self-Employed Persons in the Food Manufacturing and Beverage Industries, J.O. 1968 L 260/9, O.J. Sp. Ed. 1968, 505; Council Directives 63/261 and 63/262 of 2 April 1963, 67/530, 67/531 and 67/532 of 25 July 1967, 68/415 of 20 December 1968 and 71/18 of 16 December 1970 Concerning Agriculture J.O. 1963, 1323 and 1326, J.O. 1967, 190/1, 190/3 and 190/5, J.O. 1968 L 308/17, J.O. 1971, L8/24, O.J. Sp. Ed. 1963–64, 19 and 22, O.J. Sp. Ed. 1967, 228, 230 and 232, O.J. Sp. Ed. 1968, 589 and O.J. Sp. Ed. 1971, 23; Council Directive 65/264 of 13 May 1965 and 68/369 of 15 October 1968, Concerning the Film Industry, J.O. 1965, 1437, J.O. 1968, L 260/22, O.J. Sp. Ed. 1965–66, 62 and O.J. Sp. Ed. 1968, 520; Council Directive 67/43 of 12 January 1967, Concerning . . . Activities of Self-Employed Persons Concerned with . . . Real Estate, J.O. 1967, 140, O.J. Sp. Ed. 1967, 3; Council Directives 75/368 and 75/369 of 16 June 1975 on Various Activities, O.J. 1975 L 167/22 and L 167/29.

58. Council Directive 75/362 of 16 June 1975, Concerning the Mutual Recognition of Diplomas . . . in Medicine, O.J. 1975, L 167/1; Council Directive 75/363 of 16 June 1975, Concerning the Co-ordination of Provisions . . . in Respect of Activities of Doctors, O.J. 1975, L 169/14; Council Directive 77/452 of 27 June 1977, Concerning the Mutual Recognition of Diplomas . . . of Nurses, O.J. 1977, L 176/1; Council Directive 78/686 of 25 July 1978, Concerning the Mutual Recognition of Diplomas . . . in . . . Dentistry, O.J. 1978, L233/1; Council Directive 78/1026 of 18 December 1978, Concerning the Mutual Recognition of Diplomas . . . in Veterinary Medicine, O.J. 1978, L 362/1; Council Directive 80/154 of 18 December 1979, Concerning the Mutual Recognition of Diplomas . . . in Midwifery, O.J. 1980 L 33/1. See H. Anrys, *Les professions médicales et paramédicales dans le marché commun*, 1971 and '*Les directives médecins: cas test ou acte politique?*' 90 Jo. des Trib. (1975) 453; B. Bonnici, *Les conditions de circulation et d'établissement des médecins dans la Communauté économique européenne*, 1976; J. Guigue, '*La libre circulation de médecins dans les pays du marché commun*', [1978] D. 163; H. Michelmann, 'Credentials, Jurisdiction and Mobility; Physicians in the European Community', 2 Rev. int. eur. (1979) 203; G. Morse, 'Mutual Recognition of Midwifery Qualifications', 5 E.L. Rev. (1980) 222; G. Santoro, *Posizione giuridica del medico nella Comunità economica europea*, 1977; J.C. Séché, '*Les directives du Conseil des Communautés européennes du 16 juin 1975, concernant les activités du médecin*', 12 Cah. dr. eur. (1976) 32; R. Wägenbauer, L*La libre circulation des médecins dan la Communauté européenne: Problèmes actuels*', 12 Cah. dr. eur. (1976) 707, '*La mise en oeuvre de la libre circulation des médecins dans la Communauté européenne*', 208 Rev. marché com. (1977) 311 and '*L'Europe des vétérinaires*', 15 Rev. trim. dr. eur. (1979) 653.

59. Council Directive 77/249 of 22 March 1977 to Facilitate the Effective Exercise by Lawyers of Freedom to Provide Services, O.J. 1977 L 78/17. See M. Bronkhorst, 'Freedom to Provide Services: Lawyers' Freedom under the New Directive', 2 E.L. Rev. (1977) 224; P. De Brauw, 'La libéralisation de profession d'avocat en Europe', 14 Cah. dr. eur. (1978) 33; D. Edward, 'European Community Directive: the Provision of Services by Lawyers', 22 Jo. L. Soc. Scot. (1977) 188; S.P. Laguette, 'L'avocat dans les neuf Etats de la Communauté Européenne', 1978; P. Leach, 'EEC: Moves towards a Directive on Freedom of Establishment for Lawyers in the European Community', 77 Guar. Gaz. (1980) 660; A. O'Caoimh, 'The Implementation of the Directive on Lawyers' Freedom to Provide Services in Ireland', 5 E.L. Rev. (1980) 235; Gil Carlos Rodriguez, 'La libre circulación de los abogados y los médicos en la Communidad Europea', 4 Rev. inst. eur. (1977) 83; P. Wilson 'EEC: Freedom to Provide Services for EEC Lawyers', 19 Harv. Int. L.J. (1978) 379.

60. Case 2/74, [1974] ECR 631 at 649, 652.

61. Case 71/76, [1977] ECR 765 at 777, 778.

62. Case 11/77, [1977] ECR 1199 at 1205.

63. Case 136/78, Ministère Public v Auer, [1979] ECR 437.

64. Case 33/74, Van Binsbergen, [1974] ECR 1299 at 1309; Case 39/75, Coenen v. Sociaal-Economische Raad [1975] ECR 1547; Case 15/78, Société générale Alsacienne de Banque v. Koestler, [1978] ECR 1971 at 1980; Joined Cases 110 and 111/78, Van Wesemael, [1979] ECR 35 at 52; Case 52/79, Debauve, [1980] ECR 833 at 856.

65. [1981] ECR 3305.

66. Case 96/85, Commission v France, 30 April 1986, O.J. 1986 C 136/5.

67. V. Abellan Honrubia, 'Excepciones a la libertad de establecimiento en la C.E.E.', 2 Rev. inst. eur. (1975) 371; W. Bongen, Schranken der Freizügigkeit aus Gründen der offentlichen Ordnung und Sicherheit im Recht der europäischen Wirtschaftsgemeinschaft, 1975; G. Druesne, 'La réserve d'ordre public de l'article 48 du traité de Rome', 12 Rev. trim. dr. eur. (1976) 229; A. Evans, 'Ordre public, public policy and United Kingdom Immigration Law', 3 E.L. Rev. (1978) 370 and 'Ordre public in French Immigration Law', [1980] Pub.L. 132; F. Marx, 'Die Auswanderungsfreiheit des Arbeitnehmers nach europäischem Gemeinschaftsrecht', 8 Europarecht (1973) 133; A. Pauly, 'La libre circulation des personnes dans la Communauté européenne sous le biais des restrictions d'ordre public', 8 Quest. soc. (1977) 19; R. Plender, 'Deportation and EEC Law', [1976] Crim. L. Rev. 676; L. Singer, 'Free Movement of Workers in the European Economic Community: The Public Policy Exception', 29 Stan. L. Rev. (1977) 1283: B. Strachan, 'Deportation and EEC Nationals', 130 New L.J. (1980) 798; J. Verhoeven, 'La police de étrangers: droit du Benelux et de la Communauté économique européenne', 30 Ann. dr. (1970) 427; K. Winkel, 'Das Niederlassungsrecht der freien Berufe im Gemeinsamen Markt', 29 N.J.W. (1976) 446; F. Wooldridge, 'Free Movement of EEC Nationals: the Limitation Based on Public Policy and Public Security', 2 E.L. Rev. (1977) 190.

68. Case 67/74, [1975] ECR 297 at 307.

69. Supra, note 37 at 1349.

70. Joined Cases 115 and 116/81, Adoui and Cornuaille v Belgium, [1982] ECR 1665.

71. [1975] ECR 1219.

72. [1974] ECR 153.

73. [1977] ECR 1999.

74. [1980] ECR 1585. See further Nijssen v Immigration Officers, London and Sheerness, supra note 18; Monteil v Home Secretary, [1983] Imm. A.R. 149.

75. Case 98/79, Pecastaing v Belgium, [1980] ECR 691.

76. Article 4. Diseases or disabilities occurring after the first grant of a residence permit cannot be invoked for the purpose of this derogation.

77. *Supra*, note 72.
78. *Supra*, note 60 at 654.
79. [1980] ECR 3881 at 3900.
80. [1982] ECR 1845, para. 7.
81. *Supra*, note 72.
82. EEC Treaty Article 51.
83. Council Regulations 3/58 and 4/58 of 15 December 1958, OJ. 1958 561, 597. The origins of these Regulations can be traced to Article 69 of the ECSC Treaty which provided for the free movement of workers in the coal and steel industries. Article 69(4) stated that Member States should settle 'among themselves any matter remaining to be dealt with in order to ensure that social security arrangements do not inhibit labour mobility'.
84. Council Regulation 1408/71 of 14 June 1971, O.J. Sp. Ed. 1971, 416, O.J. 1971 L 149/2 and Council Regulation 574/72 of 21 March 1972, O.J. Sp. Ed. 1972, 159. See generally, P. Watson, *Social Security Law of the European Communities*, 1980, p. 30.
85. See Case 20/75 *d'Amico* v *Landesversicherungsanstalt Rheinland-Pfalz*, [1975] ECR 891 at 902; Case 35/73, *Kunz* v *Bundesversicherungsanstalt für Angestellte*, [1973] ECR 1025 at 1037.
86. Originally Regulation 3/58. O.J. Sp. Ed., 1958, 597, covered 'wage earners and other assimilated workers'.
87. Council Regulations 1408/71 of 14 June 1971 and 574/72 of 21 March 1972, *supra*, note 84. 159.
88. Coucil Regulation 2001/83 of 2 June 1983, O.J. 1983 L 72/1.
89. Before departure, the unemployed person must be registered with the employment services of the competent State as a person seeking work and have remained available for work for at least four weeks after becoming unemployed: Regulation 1408/71 Art. 69(1)(a); however, departure may be authorised before expiry of the four weeks: see Case 139/78, *Coccioli* v *Bundesanstalt für Arbeit* [1979] ECR 991. The person must register with the employment services of each of the Member States to which she or he goes: Regulation 1408/71 Article 69(1)(b). If the person does not return within three months of departure to the State which he or she originally left, entitlement to benefit is lost: Regulation 1408/71 Article 69(2). The time limit may be extended: see Joined Cases 41/79, 121/79 and 796/79, *Testa Maggio and Vitale* v *Bundesanstalt für Arbeit*, [1980] ECR 1979.
90. 'Stateless person' has the meaning assigned to it under the Convention of New York, 28 September 1954, 360 U.N.T.S. 117; *Basic Documents* II.4.
91. 'Refugee' has the meaning assigned to it under the Convention of Geneva, 28 July 1951, 189 U.N.T.S. 150; *Basic Documents* III.2.
92. This was not so until 1 July 1982, when Regulation 1390/81 entered into force, broadening the scope of Regulation 1408/71 to include self-employed persons. Although the term 'workers' is no longer used in Community legislation applying in this area, the definitions of 'employed person' and 'self-employed person' are drawn in terms reminiscent of the definition of 'worker' and decisions on the meaning of the term 'worker' will continue to be influential. See Case 19/68, *De Cicco* v *Landesversicherungsanstalt Schwaben*, [1968] ECR 473; Case 23/71 *Janssen* v *Alliance Nationale des Mutualités Chrétiennes*, [1971] ECR 859; Case 63/76, *Vita Inzirillo v. Caisse d'allocations familiales de l'Arondissement de Lyon*, [1976] ECR 2057.
93. Further, the legislation applies to survivors of employed or self-employed persons who have been subject to the legislation of one or more Member States, irrespective of the nationality of these persons, where their survivors are nationals of one of the Member States or stateless persons or refugees residing within the territory of one of the Member States. In Case 40/76, *Kermashcek* v *Bundesanstalt für Arbeit*, [1976] ECR 1669, the Court pointed out that for the

purpose of determining the rights of a member of the family or a survivor, the nationality of the employed or self-employed person from whom those rights derive is irrelevant. The legislation also applies to civil servants and persons who, in accordance with the national legislation applicable, are treated as such, where they are or have been subject to the legislation of a Member State.

94. This rule avoids plurality and overlapping of contributions and liabilities which would result from the simultaneous or alternative application of several legislative systems. The same rule prevents those concerned, in the absence of legislation applying to them, from remaining without protection. See Case 50/75, *Caisse de Pension des employés privés* v *Massonet*, [1975] ECR 1473.

95. The rule applies unless it requires that person to contribute to the financing of an institution which would not accord him or her any supplementary social security protection in respect of the same risk and for the same period. See Case 92/63, *Nonnenmacher* v *Besuur der Sociale Verzekeringsbank*, [1964] ECR 281. If the person is employed simultaneously in the territory of one Member State and self-employed in another, he or she is subject to the legislation of the State in which he or she is engaged: Regulation 1408/71 Article 14c(1)(a). In specified instances Article 14c(1)(b) creates an exception whereby such a person is subject to the legislation of each of the relevant Member States as regards the activity pursued in its territory.

96. Provided that the work does not exceed twelve months and that the person is not replacing another, the person continues to be subject to the legislation of the first Member State. See Case 35/70, *SARL Manpower* v *Caisse primaire d'assurance maladie, Strasbourg*, [1970] ECR 1251, where the Court held that this provision applies to a person who is engaged by an undertaking pursuing its activity in a Member State, is paid by that undertaking, is answerable to it for misconduct, is able to be dismissed by it, and who, on behalf of that undertaking, performs work temporarily in another undertaking in another Member State. If the work exceeds twelve months' duration, the legislation of the first State continues to apply until the completion of the work, subject to the consent if the competent authority of the second State.

97. Persons employed in international transport are subject to the legislation of the State in which the undertaking by which they are employed has its registered office or place of business. Any other person is subject either to the legislation of the State in which he is resident, or, if not residing in the territory of a Member State where he is pursuing the activity, to the legislation of the Member State in which the employer is situated. A person who is permanently resident in one State but who occasionally works in another is subject to the legislation of the first State only insofar as that person is affiliated to the social security schemes of that State; otherwise he is subject to the legislation of the State in which he usually pursues the activity.

98. Such a person is subject to the legislation of the Member State in whose territory the undertaking has its registered office or place of business.

99. Regulation 1408/71 Art. 14(b) establishes special rules applicable to mariners.

100. Regulation 1408/71 Article 4(1)(a) to (h). Complex rules are applicable to particular claimants of these benefits covering the conditions of entitlement. For a general analysis of these rules, see: *Halsbury's Laws of England*, Vol 33 (1982), p. 878, paragraphs 1042 to 1077.

101. The provisions apply to all general and special social security schemes, whether contributory or non-contributory, but do not apply to social or medical assistance, to benefit schemes for victims of war or its consequences, or to special schemes for civil servants and persons treated as such.

102. For example, entitlement to invalidity benefit depends upon whether the person concerned has completed periods of insurance (1) exclusively under legislations according to which the

amount of benefit is determined irrespective of the duration of periods completed, or (2) exclusively under legislations where the duration of periods completed is instrumental to the determination of entitlement or (3) under both types of legislation.

103. Regulation 1408/71, Article 1(o)(i) and (ii).
104. This applies to invalidity, old age or survivors' cash benefits, pensions, death grants, and lump sum payments to remarrying survivors.
105. The Hague, 17 and 28 February 1986; 25 I.L.M. (1986) 206.
106. Article 13.
107. EEC Treaty, Article 8B, inserted by Single European Act, Article 13.
108. EEC Treaty, Article 8C, inserted by Single European Act, Article 13.
109. EEC Treaty, Article 49, inserted by Single European Act, Article 6(3).
110. *Supra*, notes 2 and 3. For the compilation of statistics see Council Regulation 311/76 of 9 February 1976, O.J. 1976 L38/2.

BIBLIOGRAPHY

V. Abellan Honrubia, '*Medidas específicas para la libertad de establecimiento en cada sector de actividad*', 1 Revista de instituciones europeas (1974) 1121.

V. Abellan Honrubia. '*Excepciones a la libertad de establecimiento en la C.E.E.*', 2 Revista de instituciones europeas (1975) 371.

H. Anrys, '*Les directives médecins: cas test ou acte politique?*', 90 Journal des Tribunaux (1975) 453.

A. Barav, and S. Thomson, 'Deportation of EEC Nationals from the United Kingdom in the Light of the Bouchereau Case' [1977–2] LIEI 1.

L. Berrocal Martin, '*Intégration européenne et libre circulation des travailleurs: quelques éléments d'analyse pour le cas espagnol*', 4 Revue de l'intégration européenne (1981) 335;

P. Bianchi, '*Osservazioni sulla libera circolazione dei lavoratori dipendenti all'interno della Comunità europea*', 34 Il foro padano (1979).

G. Biscottini, '*Problemi della circulazione e dello stabilimento nel Trattato di Roma*', 53 Rivista di Diritto Internazionale (1970) 161;

W. Boehning, *The Migration of Workers in the United Kingdom and the European Community*, 1972.

W. Bongen, *Schranken der Freizügigkeit aus Gründen der öffentlichen Ordnung und Sicherheit im Recht der europäischen Wirtschaftsgemeinschaft*, 1975.

J. Bontemps. *Liberté d'établissement et libre prestation des services dans le marché commun*, 1968.

N. Briquet, 'Liberté d'établissement et libre prestation des services', 13 R.M.C. (1970) 311.

M. Bronkhorst, 'Freedom to Provide Services: Lawyers' Freedom under the New Directive', 2 E.L. Rev. (1977) 224.

E. Cerexhe, *Le droit européen: la libre circulation des personnes et des entreprises*, 1982.

P. Daillier, '*Liberté d'accès aux activités professionnelles et droit communautaire: le cas particulier des activités maritimes*', Rev. trim. dr. eur. (1976) 439.

P. De Brauw, '*La libéralisation de profession d'avocat en Europe*', 14 Cah. dr. eur. (1978) 33.

G. Druesne, '*La réserve d'ordre public de l'article 48 du traîté de Rome*', 12 Rev. trim. dr. eur. (1976) 229.

A. Durand, 'European Citizenship', 4 E.L. Rev. (1979) 3.

D. Duyssens, 'Migrant Workers from Third Countries in the European Community', 14 C.M.L. Rev. (1977) 501.

A. Evans, 'Ordre public, public policy and United Kingdom Immigration law', 3 E.L. Rev. (1978) 370.

224

A. Evans, 'Ordre public in French immigration law', (1980) Pub. L. 132.

G. Falchi, '*Le régime définitif de la libre circulation et l'immigration des pays tiers*', II Droit social (1971) 16.

J. Guigue, '*La libre circulation de médecins dans les pays du marché commun*' [1978] Recueil Dalloz Sirey 163.

T. Hartley, 'The Internal Personal Scope of the EEC Immigration Provisions', 3 E.L. Rev. (1978) 191.

T. Hartley, 1978. *EEC Immigration Law*.

T. Hartley, 'Are British Immigration Rules Contrary to Community Law?', 6 E.L. Rev. (1981) 280.

F. Jacobs, 'The Free Movement of Persons within the EEC', 30 C.L.P. (1977) 123.

O. Lando, 'The Liberal Professions in the European Communities', 8 C.M.L. Rev. (1971) 343.

P. Leleux, and M. Bronkhorst, 'The Impact of European Community Law on the Right of Establishment and the Engagement of Personnel', *Commercial Operations in Europe* (ed. Goode and Simmonds) 1978, 27.

C. Lewis, 'Freedom of Movement and Community Law', 75 L. Soc. Gaz. (1978) 818.

D. Loschak, '*Les ressortissants de la C.E.E.*', 5 Dr. Soc. (1976) 83.

C. Maestripieri. '*La libre circulation des personnes et des services dans la C.E.E.*', 1972.

H. Michelmann, 'Credentials, Jurisdiction and Mobility: Physicians in the European Community', 2 Rev. de l'int. eur. (1979) 203.

G. Morse, 'Mutual Recognition of Midwifery Qualifications', 5 E.L. Rev. (1980) 222.

W. Much, and J. Séché, '*Les droits de l'étranger dans les communautés européennes*', II Cah. dr. eur. (1975) 251.

A. O'Caoimh, 'The Implementation of the Directive on Lawyers' Freedom to Provide Services in Ireland', 5 E.L. Rev. (1980) 235.

R. Plender, 'The Right to Free Movement in the European Communities', *Fundamental Rights* (ed. Bridge, Lasok & Perrott) 1973, 306.

R. Plender, 'Deportation and EEC Law', [1976] Crim. L. Rev. 676.

R. Plender, 'An Incipient Form of European Citizenship', *European Law and the Individual* (ed. Jacobs) 1976 at 39;

J.Y. Plouvain, '*La libre circulation des sportifs professionels à l'intérieur de la Communauté*', R.M.C. (1978) 516.

G. Renato, *Il processo evolutivo nel diritto comunitario per la libera circolazione delle persone*, 1977.

F. Rigaux, '*Les migrations des travailleurs dans la C.E.E.*', 2 Rivista de direito e economia (1976) 295.

G. Santoro, *Posizione giuridica del medico nella Comunità economica europea*, 1977.

I. Schwartz, '*Le rôle du rapprochement des législations afin de faciliter le droit d'établissement et la libre circulation des services*', 2 Documentaçao e direito comparado (1980) 5.

J-C. Séché, '*Les directives du Conseil des Communautés européennes du 16 juin 1975 concernant les activités du médecin*', 12 Cah. dr. eur. (1976) 32.

J-C. Séché, 'Free Movement of Workers under Community Law', 14 C.M.L. Rev. (1977) 385.

K. Simmonds, 'Immigration Control and the Free Movement of Labour: A Problem of Harmonisation', 22 I.C.L.Q. (1972) 307.

L. Singer, 'Free Movement of Workers in the European Economic Community: The Public Policy Exception', 29 Stan. L. Rev. (1977) 1283.

B. Strachan, 'Deportation and EEC Nationals', 130 New L.J. (1980) 798.

B. Sundberg-Weitman, *Discrimination on Grounds of Nationality: Free Movement of Workers and Freedom of Establishment under the EEC Treaty*, 1977.

H. Ter Heide, 'The Free Movement of Workers in the Final Phase', 6 C.M.L. Rev. (1969) 466.

J. Usher, 'Establishment, Services and Lawyers', [1979] S.L.T. 65.
C. Vincenzi and T. Connor, *EEC Nationals and Rights to Freedom of Movement in the United Kingdom,* 1986 (Huddersfield Polytechnic).

CHAPTER 7

Council of Europe Conventions

Since its inception in 1949[1] the Council of Europe has devoted no small part of its efforts to the establishment of common standards governing the status and treatment of aliens. The European Convention on Human Rights[2] deals with this question only incidentally, although the Fourth Protocol[3] and the draft Seventh Protocol[4] address it directly. Speaking of the Convention itself, however, the Commission has observed that 'a State which signs and ratifies the European Convention on Human Rights must be understood as agreeing to restrict the free exercise of its rights under general international law, including the right to control the entry and exit of foreigners to the extent and within the limits of the obligations which it has accepted under that Convention'.[5] The restrictions imposed by that Convention are supplemented by further limitations on national powers imposed by five further treaties sponsored by the Council of Europe: the European Convention on Establishment,[6] the European Convention on Extradition,[7] the European Social Charter,[8] the European Convention on Social Security[9] and the European Convention on the Legal Status of Migrant Workers.[10] To these must be added the Agreement[11] and the dozen other instruments governing refugees[12] concluded or adopted under the aegis of the Council of Europe in the period since 1959.

THE EUROPEAN CONVENTION ON HUMAN RIGHTS

In the absence from the European Convention on Human Rights of provisions specifically addressed to the situation of aliens, applicants have tended to base their challenges to national immigration laws or practices on Article 3 (which prohibits inhuman or degrading treatment), Articles 5 and 6 (which protect the liberty of the person and the right to a fair and public hearing), Article 8 (which speaks of respect for private and family life), Article 12 (which deals with the right to marry) and Article 14 (which establishes the principle of non-discrimination).

In its report on the *East African Asians Case* (*Patel and Others* v U.K.)[13] the Commission considered the argument that the United Kingdom's Commonwealth Immigrants Act 1968 entailed a contravention of Article 3. That Act (it will be recalled)[14] was passed at speed in reaction to an influx of citizens of the United Kingdom and Colonies of Asian origin, many of whom were constrained to leave East Africa in consequence of immigration and trades licensing restrictions there. The Commission found that the United Kingdom's enactment discriminated against the applicants on the ground of their colour or race; not, indeed, in form, but in substance and effect. In the Commission's conclusion, discrimination based on race could, in certain circumstances, of itself amount to degrading treatment within the meaning of Article 3. Publicly to single out a group of persons for differential treatment on the basis of race might in certain circumstances, constitute a special form of affront to human dignity. Therefore, differential treatment of a group of persons on the basis of race might amount to degrading treatment when differential treatment on some other ground would raise no such question.

No doubt, this decision turns upon its own particular facts. One of the elements leading the Commission to conclude that the applicants had suffered 'degrading treatment' was the speed with which the Act of 1968 had been passed. Another was the fact that many of those who were excluded from their country of nationality thereby had no other country in which they were entitled to live. Moreover, the Commission's decision was not confirmed by a judgment of the Court, since the Committee of Ministers failed to reach agreement on the disposal of the case, as is required by Article 32 of the Convention. Nevertheless, the decision appears to support the proposition that the maintenance by a Contracting State of immigration legislation will entail a breach of the Convention if in its effect that legislation discriminates on ground of race against a group of persons who are thereby subjected to seriously detrimental treatment. It is not necessary that the group singled out for such treatment must be nationals of the Contracting State. This we may infer since the Commission dismissed the argument advanced by the United Kingdom that the latter had not ratified the fourth Protocol to the Convention, which alone provides for the right to enter one's own country. The Commission's decision in the East African Asians Case stands independently of any proposition contained in the Fourth Protocol.

It is equally firmly established that expulsion, deportation or extradition from a Contracting State may bring about a breach of Article 3. In particular, the repeated expulsion of an alien without identity documents, whose country of origin is unknown, may amount to degrading treatment.[15] Further, the deportation of an alien or the rendition of an offender must be accomplished without ill-treatment, if it is to conform with that Article.[16]

The right under Article 5 to liberty and security of the person is expressly qualified by paragraph (1)(f) thereof. This provides as follows:

> No one shall be deprived of his liberty save in the following cases and in accordance with a procedure prescribed by law:
>
> . . .
>
> (f) the lawful arrest or detention of a person to prevent his effecting an unauthorized entry into the country or of a person against whom action is being taken with a view to deportation or extradition.

In Application 7317/75 *Lynas* v *Switzerland*[17] the Commission placed emphasis upon the word 'justified' and on the opening words of the paragraph, which require observance of a procedure prescribed by law. This language led the Commission to conclude that a detention entails a breach of the Convention if it results from a misuse of power or from a legal process other than one conducted with due diligence.

More recently, the Commission declared admissible an application from a Pakistani national who was deemed to be an 'illegal entrant', liable to be deported from the United Kingdom, although he had been granted leave to enter the country and had not made a positive misrepresentation at the part of entry.[18] In a decision in his case (since overturned) the House of Lords had held that the applicant was under a positive duty of candour on all material facts, including those which denoted a change of circumstances between the issue of the entry certificate and the alien's arrival at the port.[19] The Commission considered it arguable that in these circumstances the applicant's detention and his proposed removal were not 'in accordance with a procedure prescribed by law'.

For present purposes, the principal obstacle to the use of Article 6 of the Convention is that it guarantees a fair hearing in the determination of 'civil rights'. Despite some initial uncertainty, it seems that this expression is to be understood in the sense in which the corresponding expression is used in French ('*droits . . . de caractère civil*'). The claim to enter a State is advanced as a matter of public law and for this reason cannot be characterised as a civil right in the sense of the Convention.

In an early case,[20] an applicant placed reliance on Article 6 in complaining of the absence of an appellate system to challenge a decision whereby a child was refused leave to enter the United Kingdom to join his father. The proceedings were terminated by means of a friendly settlement, in which the Government of the United Kingdom recorded that it had introduced draft legislation to provide for rights of appeal in such cases. This episode appeared to give some force to the suggestion that the claim to enter a State may be characterised as a civil right. More recently, however, in the *Ringeisen Case*[21] the Commission by a majority recorded its view that it would be incompatible with the intentions of the contracting parties to adopt an extensive interpretation of the term 'civil rights and obligations.'

An administrative decision relating to the transfer of ownership or use of land was not a determination of a civil right, even though it had an incidental effect upon proprietary rights.

Building on that decision, the Commission has held that Article 6 does not apply to a decision to deport an alien, since it does not relate to the determination of civil rights and obligations.[22] By parity of reasoning, it has held that Article 6 is not applicable to administrative proceedings on prohibition of entry[23] and that proceedings concerning a request for an entry clearance (or residence permit) do not include the determination of a civil right.[24] Anticipating such decisions, those acting for Mark Hosenball, an American national against whom a deportation order had been made in the United Kingdom, contended that the decision to make the order amounted to a determination of his civil rights: the contested decision effectively terminated private rights that he had enjoyed in the kingdom, including his contractual rights as a journalist. The Commission dismissed the application, taking the view that the rights on which Hosenball relied were affected only incidentally. The contested decision had its primary effect upon rights in public law.[25]

Nevertheless, Article 6 of the Convention applies equally to nationals and to aliens.[26] Indeed, the Contracting Parties undertake to secure to everyone within their jurisdiction the rights and freedoms set out therein.[27] Where those rights and freedoms are qualified in their application to aliens, the Convention says so expressly[28] and there is no express qualification in respect of Article 6.

In European Commission's case-law on Article 8 of the Convention provides a more promising basis for claims by migrants. It has long been established that the refusal to allow a person to take up residence in a particular country might result in the separation of such persons from close members of their family and thereby raise serious problems under Article 8.[29]

In order to identify the obligations which parties to the Convention have accepted in the interests of 'family life', it is necessary to assign a precise meaning to the word 'family'. As Sir James Fawcett observes, it is scarcely possible to define the phrase 'family life', since the content of a family varies from one society to another.[30] Indeed, within any one society different groups of relatives may visualise their families differently. Clearly, the term 'family' normally embraces spouses and their minor unmarried children, but that observation merely postpones the problem of definition.

The Convention is silent on the question of polygamous unions, and on this point Fawcett is non-committal. On principle, it is thought that a polygamous wife and her husband should be regarded as spouses for this purpose if they normally and habitually cohabit and form part of a familial unit. It is also thought that a 'common-law wife' should be treated as a member of the family of any man with whom she habitually lives in a common household. In a number of decisions the Commission has decided that illegitimate children formed part of the 'family' of their mothers and fathers, but in each of these cases the child and the parent had formed part of a single household.[31]

Consistently with these decisions, it seems that a stepchild forms part of the 'family' of the stepmother or stepfather with whom he or she normally lives. In the *Lebeau Case* the German Federal Administrative Tribunal annulled a decree ordering the expulsion of a Belgian national who had resided in Germany together with his German wife, child and two stepchildren. If his expulsion had been put into effect his wife would have been able to follow him to Belgium, but would have been unable to bring with her the two step-children. If the wife had stayed in Germany the legitimate child of the marriage would have been separated either from the father or from the mother. In either case the unity of the family would have been curtailed.[32]

The definition of the word 'family', for the purposes of the European Convention, must be based on fact, rather than on unyielding genealogical rules modified by reservations governing age and status of legitimacy or matrimony. The case-law under Article 8 of the Convention is dominated by the concept of family unity, whereby persons who in fact live together as a family are permitted in law to continue to do so. Thus in 1963 the Commission refused to hold that a man of forty could not be regarded as a member of a single family, along with his parents.[33] Likewise, it may now be taken to be established that the right to respect for family life may be infringed when fiancés are separated.[34] On the other hand, in the case of a homosexual couple the Commission did not find that the relationship fell within the scope of respect for 'family life' within the meaning of the Article.[35]

On more than one occasion, the Commission has stated or implied that the voluntary migration of one of the spouses cannot, in itself, engage any public responsibility under Article 8(1).[36] This rule must be construed restrictively. In *Alam's Case*, an immigrant from Pakistan, resident in Britain, sought to introduce his father to live with him. The British authorities refused to admit the father and Alam claimed that this refusal amounted to a violation of Article 8(1). The Commission found the claim admissible, even though Alam's complaint could not have arisen but for his own voluntary departure from Pakistan.[37] It is thought that the Commission would have reached the same conclusion *a fortiori* if Alam had been seeking to introduce not a father but a wife.

In an early case, a Danish woman, previously resident in Denmark, married a German citizen and went to live with him in Germany. Two years later the couple sought to move to Denmark. Between 1953 and 1956 the Danish authorities repeatedly refused to grant the husband a residence permit. The wife argued that these refusals amounted to violations of respect for her family life. The Commission considered that the couple had maintained their matrimonial home in Germany since 1951, and that it was lawful for them to continue to reside there together. It therefore rejected the application, observing that the applicant seemed to be claiming for her husband the right to live in a country of which he was not a national.[38] The Commission might well have come to a contrary conclusion if the original refusal of the husband's application to enter Denmark had occurred after the date of entry into force of the Convention. It was that refusal which presented the wife with a choice between separation from her husband and departure from her country; but that refusal could not be considered by the Commission because it was made prior to the date on which the Convention began to have effect.

In the *East African Asians Case,* twenty-five applicants who had been denied admission to the United Kingdom alleged that the denials amounted to breaches of Article 8(1).[39] The Commission observed that in only six of the applications could the facts, as they appeared from the submissions of the parties, give rise to any question of a relationship constituting family life within the meaning of Article 8 of the Convention. In three of those six cases members of a family, including husband and wife, were at no time separated but were detained together and released together, and therefore (the Commission concluded) the treatment of those applicants by the immigration authorities could not give rise to any question of interference with family life. In another of those six cases the decision of the authorities requiring the applicant to leave the kingdom was never actually enforced, and was finally reversed, with the result that there was not in fact any violation of family life. In the remaining two cases the Commission found that the applications were admissible, insofar as they raised the question of respect for family life under Article 8.

In those two cases the applicants were denied admission to the United Kingdom although their wives had been admitted to that country and had settled there. On behalf of the United Kingdom it was argued that the place of residence of a family is normally that of the husband, and that Article 8 does not safeguard any right for the husband and wife to live together permanently in any place other than the husband's country of residence or in a country where he is entitled to live. That argument is consistent with the decision of the German Supreme Administrative Court in a case heard in 1955, when the Court expressed the view that the wife had in such circumstances the obligation to follow her husband.[40] The Commission refrained from passing an opinion on that particular question, and the argument may well be inconsistent with Article 14 of the European Convention, which provides expressly that 'the enjoyment of the rights and freedoms set forth in this Convention shall be secured without discrimination on any ground such as sex . . .'.

The guarantees of respect for family life, contained in paragraph 1 of Article 8, are subject to the limitations expressed in paragraph 2, which provides that interference with the right to family unity is permissible if it is

in accordance with the law and is necessary in a democratic society in the interests of national security, public safety or the economic well-being of the country, for the prevention of disorder or crime, for the protection of health or morals, or for the protection of the rights and freedoms of others.

The effect of the second paragraph upon the first has been examined in a number of cases involving the expulsion of one member of a family. In the *Family Unity (Belgium) Case* the Belgian Supreme Court stated:

L'article 8 visé au moyen, permet l'ingérence de l'autorité publique dans l'exercise du droit au respect de la vie familiale d'une personne, lorsque cette ingérence est prévue par la loi et qu'elle constitue, notamment, une mesure nécessaire, dans une société démocratique, à la sûreté publique ou à la défense de l'ordre.[41]

Then the Court concluded that the expulsion in question was justified on the ground of public order. Unfortunately, the Court did not specify the particular threat to public order which justified the expulsion. In *X* v *Belgium*[42] the Commission expressed itself in yet less explicit terms, stating that it had no reason to doubt that the preconditions for the application of paragraph 2 were fulfilled. In a third case involving expulsion from Belgium, a man holding both Belgian and Italian nationality was sentenced to death in Belgium for collaborating with the German army of occupation during the Second World War. His sentence was commuted to penal servitude, and later he was released from detention and expelled. He complained that his expulsion was incompatible with Article 8 of the Convention, since the effect of the expulsion was to separate him from his wife and child who were not in a position to follow him to Italy. The Commission rejected his application, observing that the expulsion was justified in the public interest.[43]

An effort to test the legality of measures allegedly taken in the public interest may thus involve a balancing of the protection of the family against the protection of the public. The same process may be involved when a State seeks to justify its actions by reference to the other grounds, described in Article 8(2), for derogating from the right to respect for family life. Thus a court or the Commission might be justified in assessing the weight to be given to the protection of health or morals or of the rights and freedoms of others. In that context the phrase 'protection of health or morals' relates not only to the protection of requirements of the community as a whole, but also to the protection of requirements of individuals.[44]

Not infrequently the difference between the applicant and the State centres upon the issue of proof. The essential question is whether the applicant is in reality the spouse, child or other relation of a person settled in the territory of the Contracting State. In *Kamal* v *United Kingdom*[45] the applicant was a man who had for many years been settled in the English Midlands. He claimed that his right to respect for family life had been impaired by the refusal of the competent British authorities to issue an entry clearance for the admission to the United Kingdom of a woman from Sylhet, whom he declared to be his wife. The evidence that the couple were married was sufficiently strong to induce an immigration adjudicator to allow the applicant's appeal; but that determination was overturned by the Immigration Appeal Tribunal, which placed reliance upon apparent discrepancies between the accounts given by the applicant and the woman of their family life before the man's emigration. On an application to the Commission, the latter held that a Contracting Party is entitled to establish a domestic verification procedure for the family claims of prospective or settled immigrants. Where there is a complaint that the verification authorities were mistaken in their conclusions, the Commission's rôle is confined to that of determining whether the national authorities acted outside what might reasonably be expected of them. In the instant case, the national authorities had not acted unreasonably.

The European Court of Human Rights has now established that an applicant may rely upon Article 8 of the Convention in conjunction with Article 14. Following a unanimous decision of the Commission, the Court has held that the United Kingdom acted in breach of the Convention in maintaining a system of immigration control whereby the conditions for the admission of husbands to join wives within the jurisdiction were significantly more stringent than the conditions for the admission of wives to join husbands. The element of discrimination in such rules might in certain circumstances have been justified; but it was disproportionate to the aim advanced by the United Kingdom in defence of its legislation.[46] In consequence of that decision, the United Kingdom amended its legislation, essentially so as to impose on wives entering the Kingdom conditions similar to those formerly applied only to husbands.[47]

The right under Article 12 to marry and found a family has been invoked more than once in attempts to resist national deportation proceedings. The Commission has held in such cases that the right under Article 12 is to be read subject to Article 5(1)(f), which preserves the power of the competent national authorities to detain a person against whom proceedings are being taken with a view to deportation.[48] In *R* v *Secretary of State, ex parte Bhajan Singh*,[49] Lord Denning, M.R., adopted and applied the Commission's jurisprudence on the point. It was plain, in his view, that Article 12 does not give people an unlimited right to marry, merely because they are of marriageable age. Article 12 was subject to Article 5(1)(f). A man who is detained as an illegal entrant with a view to his removal has no right to be released in order to marry. In the same case, Lord Denning differed from the view expressed below by Lord Widgery, C.J., who had placed emphasis upon the words 'to found a family' as though a right to marry could not subsist without it. With due respect to Lord Widgery, Lord Denning's view on this point is plainly correct. The phrase 'to marry and found a family' is to be read disjunctively. The right conferred by Article 12 must therefore be protected in the interest of a couple who have no prospect of founding a family (in the sense of bearing or adopting children). Circumstances may arise in which national authorities are bound to admit to their territory for the purposes of marriage and settlement there the fiancé of a resident, particularly if there exist good reasons preventing the couple from cohabiting elsewhere.[50]

The Fourth Protocol to the European Convention has yet to be ratified by eight of the States parties to the Convention. It entered into force for the thirteen parties thereto on 2 May 1968 or on the date of deposit of subsequent instruments of accession. The Protocol requires respect for the right to move freely within the territory of Contracting States and for the right to leave that territory, subject to restrictions such as are necessary in the interests of national security, public safety, public order, the prevention of crime and the protection of the rights of others.[51] The same Protocol prohibits without qualification the collective expulsion of aliens.[52] Equally without qualification it stipulates that no one shall be expelled from the territory of a State of which he is a national nor deprived of the right to enter that territory.[53]

The Commission found no violation of the rule against expulsion of aliens in a case in which the Danish authorities planned to expel 199 Vietnamese children who had been placed temporarily in a Danish hostel. The Commission reasoned that 'collective expulsion of aliens' means any measure of the competent authority compelling aliens as a group to leave the country, except where such a measure is taken on the basis of a reasonable and objective examination of the particular cases of each individual alien.[54] In placing this gloss on the language of the Protocol, the Commission did not import a qualification to the rights set out therein. The Commission's decision took the form of an analysis and interpretation of the words 'collective expulsion'.

By a similar technique, the Commission qualified the protection given by the protocol against expulsion from one's own State. The Commission concluded that extradition to the territory of another Contracting State does not constitute 'expulsion' since it entails no obligation to reside abroad permanently.[55]

Protocol No. 7 (not yet in force) provides in Article 1(1) that

an alien lawfully resident in the territory of a State shall not be expelled therefrom except in pursuance of a decision reached in accordance with law and shall be allowed:
  a) to submit reasons against his expulsion;
  b) to have his case reviewed, and
  c) to be represented for these purposes before the competent authority or a person or persons designated by that authority.

The second paragraph of the same Article qualifies the first. It provides that an alien may be expelled before the exercise of the foregoing rights when such expulsion is necessary in the interests of public order or grounded on reasons of national security. It is to be emphasised that the right protected by this Protocol is that of an alien who is lawfully resident in the territory of the State. In construing that phrase it appears appropriate to have regard to the definitions contained in the European Convention on Social and Medical Assistance[56] and in the Protocol to the European Convention on Establishment.[57] The former provides that residence by an alien is to be considered as lawful so long as there is in force in his case a permit or such other permission as is required by the laws of the country concerned to reside therein.[58] The latter provides that regulations governing the admission, residence and movement of aliens shall be unaffected by the Convention in so far as they are not inconsistent with it. Thus, it is suggested that 'lawful residence' means residence in accordance with rules of national law, in so far as the latter are consistent with those of the terms of the European Convention on Human Rights and its Protocols that are binding on the State concerned.

THE EUROPEAN CONVENTION ON ESTABLISHMENT

Concluded in 1955,[58] the European Convention on Establishment is the world's first multilateral agreement on a subject that is normally regulated by bilateral instruments. It is bold in its coverage of the subject. Indeed, it regulates practically all of the principal legal questions affecting an alien who is permanently resident is a European State: entry, residence, expulsion, the exercise of private rights, judicial and administrative guarantees, individual (political) rights, taxation, compulsory civilian service, expropriation and naturalization. It has, however, attracted many fewer ratifications than the European Convention on Human Rights. Among the States which have yet to ratify it are Austria, France, Spain and Switzerland.[59] Moreover, nothing akin to the right of individual petition exists for those who claim to have suffered in consequence of breaches of the Convention on Establishment. There is a Standing Committee charged with the function of formulating proposals designed to improve the practical implementation of the Convention;[60] and there is a qualified obligation to refer to the International Court of Justice disputes arising between the Contracting Parties.[61]

The Convention begins with a general undertaking on the part of each Contracting State to facilitate the entry of nationals of other Contracting States for temporary visits. It is in the light of this provision that we must read the minutes of the meeting at which the Council of the EEC adopted Directive 68/360 of 15 October 1968. These record that persons looking for work are entitled to remain for a period of three months, the period taken in practice to be the end of a 'temporary' stay within the meaning of the Convention.

Article 3 affords a degree of protection to nationals of one contracting party who are 'lawfully residing' in the territory of another party. A person is considered as lawfully residing if he has conformed with the regulations governing the admission, residence and movement of aliens and also their right to engage in gainful occupations, in so far as those regulations are not inconsistent with the Convention. One who is 'lawfully residing' in this sense may be expelled only if he endangers national security or offends against *ordre public* or morality.[62] Each Contracting State has the right to judge by national criteria the circumstances which constitute a threat to national security or an offence against *ordre public* or morality; but the concept of *ordre public* is to be understood in the wide sense generally accepted in continental countries.[63]

The same Article provides that one who 'has been so lawfully residing' for more than two years shall not be expelled from his State of residence without first being allowed to submit reasons against his expulsion. The alien must be allowed to appeal to some competent authority and to be represented for that purpose before it. The words 'has been so lawfully residing' imply that two years' lawful residence immediately precede the making of the order for expulsion. An exception is made 'where imperative considerations of national security otherwise require'. Plainly, such considerations include not only the nature of the alien's conduct (which is the only issue mentioned in the preceding paragraph) but also issues beyond the control of the alien, such as the protection of the anonymity of informants.[64] The guarantee of a right of appeal, given in this Article of the Convention, is among the most important of its contents. In the case of the United Kingdom, the ratification of the Convention was delayed until the passage of the Immigration Appeals Act 1969.

By Article 3(3), nationals of any Contracting State who have been lawfully residing for more than ten years in the territory of another Contracting State may be expelled only for reasons of national security or for particularly serious offences against *ordre public* or morality. Each Contracting party is to determine whether the reasons for expulsion are of a particularly serious nature, taking account of the behaviour of the individual during his whole period of residence.[65]

The Convention provides for the equal treatment of nationals of Contracting parties in respect of private rights, both personal and proprietary.[66] Further, it provides that nationals of any Contracting party shall enjoy, equally with nationals of Contracting States in which they find themselves, the right of access to courts and the right to obtain legal representation and legal aid.[67] Each party undertakes to authorise nationals of other parties to engage in its territory in any gainful occupation, equally with its own nationals, in the absence of cogent economic or social reasons to the contrary.[68] Again, Contracting parties are free to judge by national criteria the economic and social considerations to be taken into account for this purpose.[69]

It is not difficult to discern in the detailed provisions in this Convention the genesis of some of the modern rules of European Community law governing freedom of movement. It is in the European Convention on Establishment that the draftsmen of the EEC Treaty appear to have found a precedent for the limitation on grounds of public policy, public security and public health.[70] Those who drafted from the Community's Directive of 15 February 1964[71] appear to have derived from the Convention of 1955 the rule that the right of expulsion may be exercised only in individual cases, that is, on the basis of the personal conduct of the individual concerned.[72] Article 48(4) of the EEC Treaty contains more than an echo of Article 13 of the European Convention on Establishment. The former provides for a derogation in the case of 'employment in the public service'. The latter permits Contracting parties to reserve for their own nationals 'the exercise of public functions or of occupations connected with national security or defence'. It is thought that the difficulties presented by Article 48(4) of the EEC Treaty would be reduced if it were read in its historical context, that is, in the light of Article 13 of the Convention of 1955. This should make it clear that 'public service' is defined by reference to the function performed, rather than by reference to the legal characterisation of the office. Moreover, the reference to national security and defence may assist in defining 'public functions' yet more closely, on the principle *cognoscere a sociis*.[73]

As in the case of the EEC Treaty, it remains controversial whether the European Convention on Establishment may be invoked in the interest of nationals of States other than Contracting parties. The only basis on which the Convention could be so invoked is by the medium of a most favoured nation clause in another treaty. There is some support for the view that such a clause may be invoked in conjunction with a multilateral treaty, so as to secure the benefits of that treaty in favour of the nationals of third States which are bound to parties to the multilateral treaty by 'most favoured nation' clauses.[74]

As in the case of the EEC Treaty, there is good reason to believe that the

European Convention on Establishment does not give rise to relevant benefits for nationals of States beyond the organization. The draftsmen of that Convention considered whether to insert in it a provision stating that it could not be invoked in conjunction with a most favoured nation clause in favour of nationals of States outside the Council of Europe. They decided not to insert such a provision but their decision appears to have been made in deference to the principle *pacta tertiis nec nocent nec prosunt*. A third State could not be deprived of a benefit by reason of a provision to which that State is not a party.[75] It is, however, clear from the character of the Convention as a whole that it is designed as a charter specifically for nationals of certain European States. The preamble refers to the special links binding together the States and peoples of the Council of Europe. The Secretary-General of the Council of Europe is entrusted with numerous special functions in relation to the Convention,[76] as is the Committee of Ministers;[77] and of course the Convention is open to accession only by Member States of that organization.[78]

More problematical is the question whether a Member State of the Council of Europe may rely on a most favoured nation clause in a treaty with another such Member, so as to claim for its nationals the benefits of the European Convention on Establishment, when only the latter State is a party to that Convention. Dr Kiss has advanced the argument that it would be incompatible with the express provisions governing ratification of the Convention to permit Member States to invoke it obliquely, by means of most favoured nation clauses.[79] On the other hand, the Convention's provisions governing accession contain nothing unusual other than the restriction of this facility to Members of the Council of Europe. Moreover by invoking the Convention in conjunction with a most favoured nation clause, a State does not assert that it is entitled to be treated as a party to the Convention. It does not in any precise sense evade the mandatory provisions in the Convention relating to accession.

There is a more fundamental objection to the claim that such a State might advance. Authority exists for the proposition that a most favoured nation clause cannot in principle be invoked together with a multilateral treaty.[80] Even if this proposition were accepted as a general rule, it could be applied only with the greatest reservation to the situation here considered. The special links binding Member States of the Council of Europe, to which the parties to the European Convention on Establishment drew attention in the preamble, demand the application of special interpretative techniques in construing instruments governing their mutual relations.[81] The Convention has among its stated objectives the advancement of the process of European unification. It would be consonant with that objective to permit a Member State which has not yet ratified the Convention of 1955 to rely on its terms in conjunction with a most favoured nation clause in a treaty between itself and another Member State. By reciprocity, or by parity of reasoning, a Member State which is a party to the Convention of 1955 should be considered as competent to rely upon it against a Member State which is not a party, in conjunction with a most favoured nation clause binding those two States.[82]

The European Convention on Extradition was concluded in Paris on 13 December 1957.[83] Its principal object is to ensure that Contracting States will surrender to each other, in accordance with the rules set out in the instrument, all persons sought by the requesting State for prosecution, sentence or detention. It has been modified by two subsequent protocols. The first, dated 15 October 1975, excludes war crimes and crimes against humanity from the category of 'political offences' as that expression is used in the Convention of 1957 and defines cases in which extradition can be refused on the ground that the offender has already been brought to trial.[84] The second, dated 17 March 1978, replaces certain of the provisions in the Convention of 1957 in their application to fiscal offences, judgments *in absentia* and amnesties, among other matters.[85] Each of the Protocols has attracted the ratifications of Cyprus, Denmark, the Netherlands and Sweden; in addition the Second Protocol has been ratified by Austria. The Convention of 1957 has, however, been ratified by eighteen States, representing the great majority of the members of the Council of Europe.

While this agreement does not amount to an innovation comparable with the European Convention on Establishment, it signifies a bold initiative on the part of the Council of Europe. Earlier attempts to regulate extradition by multilateral convention had been confined to the American continent and had not been marked by success. Four Latin American treaties on the subject were concluded between 1899 and 1911,[87] followed by a Central American Convention[88] on Extradition and the 'Bustamante Code' on Asylum.[89] In 1933 the second Montevideo Convention was concluded[90] and in the following year a new Convention was concluded between the five Central American republics in order to replace the Central American Convention of 1923.[91] Nevertheless, a League of Nations Committee concluded in 1926 that experience had revealed few aspects of the law of extradition suitable for resolution by multilateral convention.[92] The extradition convention prepared in 1935 by the Harvard Research in International Law was not adopted as a practical model.[93] Not until 1981 did there emerge an Inter-American Convention on Extradition comparable in the breadth of its coverage to the European Convention of 1957.[94] Thus, it is in Latin America that we find the origins of the multilateral regulation of extradition; but in Europe that we find the basis for its present form. Moreover, the influence of the European Convention is not to be detected in multilateral agreements alone. As Professor Bassiouni has observed, its effects have also been felt as a model for bilateral treaties concluded elsewhere.[95]

Article 1 of the European Convention, echoed in Article 1 of the Inter-American Convention, sets out the parties' undertaking to surrender to each other persons who are judicially required for prosecution, or who are being tried or have been sentenced to a penalty involving deprivation of liberty. Both conventions, therefore, are premised upon the 'eliminative method' of defining extraditable offences by reference to the penalties that may be imposed on conviction. They conform in this respect with the prevailing post-war tendency to adopt this device in preference to the 'enumerative method' by which the extraditable offences are defined by reference to categories of crime in municipal domestic law.[96] The principle of double criminality is preserved in the European Convention, in the sense that the offence must be punishable under the laws of the requesting party and the requested party by deprivation of liberty for at least one year.

Article 3 of the European Convention provides that extradition shall not be granted if the offence in respect of which it is requested is regarded by the requested party as a political offence or as one connected to such an offence. The same rule is to apply if the requested party has substantial grounds for believing that a request for extradition for an ordinary criminal offence has been made for the purpose of prosecuting or punishing a person on account of his race, religion, nationality or political opinion. The Convention does not define a political offence, but leaves it to the requested State to do so according to its own criteria. Moreover, the 'political exception' applies not only to political offences as so defined but also to related or connected acts and to ordinary criminal offences prosecuted for political reasons. In all these respects the European Convention is reflected by the Inter-American Convention.[98] The former adds, however, that the killing or attempted killing of a Head of State or of a member of his family shall not be regarded as a political offence. The latter stipulates that the requested State may decide that the fact that the victim performed political functions does not in itself justify the designation of the offence as political

General international law sheds some further light upon the designation of an offence as 'political'. In the *Asylum Case*[99] Judge Alvarez addressed some remarks to the question:

to overthrow the domestic political order of a country must be regarded as a political offence . . . . Since the last two World Wars, two new categories of offences have been established: *international* offences, such as violation of the rights of the individual, genocide, etc. and crimes *against humanity*, the chief one being responsibility for instigating a war.

These two categories of offences cannot be qualified as political.

The punishment of genocide is now regulated by the famous Convention on the subject adopted on the initiative of the United Nations.[100] Article 7 of that Convention states that 'Genocide and the other acts enumerated in Article 3 shall not be considered as political crimes for the purposes of extradition. Originally, the United Kingdom declined to accede to that Convention on the ground that Article 7 would involve a derogation from the right to grant asylum.[101] A later Government of the United Kingdom decided in favour of acceding to the Convention. The necessary amendments to domestic law were made by the Genocide Act 1969. Section 2 of that Act provides that genocide shall be extraditable. Crimes against humanity are generally extraditable because

> the very sanctity of [the principle of non-extradition of political offenders] requires that it should not be abused for sheltering persons who, behind the screen of war, have been responsible for common crimes which have outraged civilized mankind.[102]

As for the express exclusion of killings of Heads of State, this is commonly designated as non-political in domestic law.[103]

The value of international law and of comparative experience in defining the 'political' offence has been reviewed by others.[104] For present purposes it suffices to observe that several rules seem to have emerged. Domestic courts have generally recognized that an offence may be intrinsically political if it is a crime against the State itself or against a political party.[105] Secondly, it is generally recognized that an ordinary crime, such as murder or theft, may be 'political' if it was a means for carrying out a political object.[106] Thirdly, a crime does not normally qualify as 'political' unless it is committed in the furtherance of a struggle for political power.[107] Fourthly, a crime is not political by virtue only of the fact that it was committed by one holding political office, in purported discharge of his duties.[108] Finally, since time brings about changes in the nature of political struggles, many domestic courts adhere to the view that they should adopt a flexible approach towards determining whether a particular crime is 'political'.[109] Not all courts, however, adhere to that view. In Marxist States the courts tend to abide by the theory that the struggle between the proletariat and their oppressors contains changeless characteristics.[110]

Moreover, the dispensation granted in favour of those whose offences have political characteristics is not necessarily confined to the reservation made in the case of 'political' offences. In *Kakis v Republic of Cyprus* the appellant was a political opponent of the then Government of Cyprus. His arrest was sought in connection with the killing of a supporter of the Government. Indeed, that killing was at the heart of the subsequent *coup d'état* and the Turkish intervention on the island. The Divisional Court found that the offence was not 'political', in the absence of evidence sufficiently connecting the killing with the subsequent overthrow of the Government.[111] The House of Lords, however, held that it would be 'unjust and oppressive' to return the appellant for trial in Cyprus, in view of the delay in the commencement of the extradition proceedings. In having regard to that delay, it was appropriate to take into account not only its length but also its character. The character of the delay was affected by the policies towards the accused of successive Cypriot Governments.[112]

The European Convention on Extradition is now supplemented by the European Convention on the Suppression of Terrorism, 1977.[113] The latter has been ratified by fourteen States.[114] Moreover, by a further agreement concluded in Dublin in 1979,[115] nine of the Member States of the European Communities have undertaken to apply the Convention of 1977 in their mutual relations, pending acceptance without reservation of that Convention by all such States. Until 1986 the principal advantage of the Convention of 1979 was that it secured the application of the Convention of 1977 between the United Kingdom and the Republic of Ireland, the second of which had not yet ratified the former of those treaties. In February 1986, however, the Republic signed the Convention of 1977; ratification was to follow completion of domestic legal processes.

The purpose of the Convention of 1977 is to designate certain offences connected with terrorism 'so odious in their methods or results in relation to their motives, that it is no longer justifiable to classify them as 'political offences' for which extradition is not possible'.[116] The offences listed in Article 1 of the Convention as crimes which should not be regarded as political include those within the scope of the Hague Convention on the Unlawful Seizure of Aircraft,[117] the Montreal Convention for the Suppression of Unlawful Acts against the Safety of Civil Aviation,[118] and the New York Convention on Crimes against Internationally Protected Persons.[119] The withdrawal of the exemption for political offences has been justified on the ground of the climate of mutual confidence among like-minded Member States of the Council of Europe. Within the United Kingdom the provisions of the Convention have been applied by the Suppression of Terrorism Act 1978.[120]

THE EUROPEAN SOCIAL CHARTER

The European Social Charter was signed in 1961 and entered into force in 1965.[121] It refers in its preamble to the aim of safeguarding and realising the ideals and principles which are the common heritage of the members of the

244

Council of Europe. It is open to ratification only by Member States of the Council of Europe. It combines a proclamation of general principles, in Part I, with a formulation of relatively precise obligations, in Part II.[122] On ratifying the Charter each Contracting State undertakes to consider Part I as a declaration of the aims it will pursue by all appropriate means.[123] By contrast, parties can within certain limits select the obligations set out in Part II *à la carte*. Each party undertakes to consider itself bound by at least five of seven specified Articles in Part II, together with not less than three of the remaining twelve Articles or twenty-three of the remaining fifty paragraphs.[124] Among the seven specified Articles, five of which must be accepted by all parties, is Article 19. The deals with the right of migrant workers and their families to protection and assistance.

The greater part of the obligations imposed by Article 19 of the European Social Charter are derived from I.L.O. Convention No. 97 concerning Migration for Employment (Revised) 1949.[125] Some, however, reflect the European Convention on Establishment.[126] The Committee of Experts established under Article 25 of the Charter has determined that Article 19 applies only in respect of nationals of Contracting Parties. It does not apply in respect of those from third States.[127] In the case of refugees, however, the Appendix provides that

Each Contracting Party will grant to refugees as defined in the Convention relating to the Status of Refugees, signed at Geneva on 28 July 1951, and lawfully staying in its territory, treatment as favourable as possible, and in any case not less favourable than under the obligations accepted by the Contracting Party under the said Convention and under any other existing international instruments applicable to those refugees.

By the first paragraph of Article 19, Contracting States undertake to secure the maintenance of adequate and free services to assist migrant workers, particularly in obtaining accurate information; and to take appropriate steps against the dissemination of misleading propaganda.[128] The adequacy of the services provided must be assessed in the light of the volume of migration for employment in the State in question. Thus, Ireland was found to have complied with its obligation in view of the enactment of the Employment Agencies Act 1972, which provides for measures against misleading advertising, and in view of the publication of a booklet for foreign migrant workers containing information about such matters as social services and taxation. These modest measures were sufficient to warrant the provisional conclusion that Ireland had met its obligations, given the small number of immigrants to Ireland and the fact that the great majority of emigrants worked in the United Kingdom, for which sufficient information was available.[129]

In the case of the prohibition of misleading propaganda, it is appropriate to take account of both the prevailing social conditions and the law in the State in question. Thus, the Committee of Experts adverted to the lack of evidence of dishonest recruitment practices in Austria and had regard to the maintenance of a pre-entry work permit system, in concluding that Austria had complied with its duty to take 'appropriate' steps against misleading propaganda.[130] In the case of the United Kingdom, the evidence of compliance took the form of material showing that complaints by migrant workers were promptly investigated, together with the language of the Trade Descriptions Act 1968,[131] which prohibits the making of false or misleading statements concerning employment services.[132]

By Article 19(2) Contracting States undertake to adopt appropriate measures to facilitate the departure and reception of migrant workers and to provide appropriate services during the journey.[133] The Committee of Experts has given a broad construction to the word 'reception' as it appears in this context. It relates to the treatment of the alien throughout the weeks after his arrival when he is yet unfamiliar with the country in which he is to work.[134] In determining whether the measures provided in this period are appropriate, the Committee of Experts will take account of the volume and character of migration. Thus, in assessing the measures taken by the Irish and Cypriot Governments with respect to emigration, the Committee had regard to the fact that in each case nearly all the migrant workers tended to travel to one country.[135]

Article 19(3) requires Contracting Parties to promote cooperation, as appropriate, between social services in countries of immigration and emigration. In this context the term 'social services' means all public or private organizations which facilitate the life of emigrants and their families, their adjustment to their new environment and their relations with members of their families who have remained in their country of origin.[136] The Committee of Experts has rejected the argument that it was for each Contracting Party to assess the appropriateness of particular forms of cooperation between social services. The words 'as appropriate' must be understood as applying not to the undertaking itself but to ways of implementing cooperation, depending on the structure of the social services in the countries concerned.[137]

The fourth paragraph of the Article contains its crucial provision. This sets out to guarantee equality of treatment between nationals of Contracting States and migrant workers within their territories, in respect of employment, trades unions and accommodation.[138] The effects of this paragraph, which would otherwise be very extensive indeed, are limited by two qualifications. Firstly, equality is to be guaranteed only in so far as such matters are regulated by law or regulation or are subject to the control of administrative authorities. Thus, discrimination on grounds of nationality, practised by private employers, is unaffected in principle. Secondly, the reference to employment is a reference to conditions of employment once the latter has been obtained. Access to employment is untouched by this Article, but governed instead by Article 18. The latter provides for the liberal application of existing regulations, the simplification of formalities and the reduction of charges payable by foreign workers, the liberalising of regulations governing the employment of foreign workers and the recognition of the right of nationals to leave the territory of their own States in order to accept employment in the territory of other Contracting States. Thus it falls short of imposing any duty to relax conditions governing the engagement of foreign labour.

Despite the two qualifications thus imposed on Article 19(4), its effect has been considerable. The Committee of Experts has interpreted broadly the expression 'employment and working conditions'. This has been taken to include arrangements for training and promotion,[139] grants and allowances paid under schemes for transferring employees to a different place of work within the same Contracting State[140] and arrangements and payments with respect to redundancy.[141] The same Committee has found that France was in breach of Article 19(4) because of restrictions on the exercise by migrant workers of certain functions within French trades unions.[142] The Committee found the United Kingdom to be in breach of its obligation in respect of housing, since migrant workers who were nationals of Contracting States other than European Community States were ineligible to obtain public housing in Northern Ireland, unless employed in key posts.[143] The maintenance of a comparable rule in the Isle of Man entailed no breach of the Article, however, since the ineligibility affected British and other Community nationals along with nationals of other Contracting States. Only native Manxmen and those resident on the island for ten years qualified for the accommodation.[144]

Paragraph (5) provides for the equal treatment of nationals of Contracting States and workers lawfully within their territories with regard to employment taxes, dues or contributions. The language is adopted without alteration from the I.L.O. Convention of 1949.[145] Only taxes on employment are covered, to the exclusion of income and other taxes generally.

By Article 19(6) Contracting States undertake 'to facilitate as far as possible the reunion of the family of a foreign worker permitted to establish himself in the territory'. For the purpose of this provision, the term 'family of a foreign worker' is understood to mean at least his wife and dependent children under the age of 21 years.[146] This provision has few parallels in general multilateral conventions. A comparable stipulation is signally lacking from the I.L.O. Convention of 1949; Article 19(6) is now reflected in Article 12 of the European Convention on the Legal Status of Migrant Workers of 1977.[147]

The obligation imposed by this paragraph is qualified and tentative. The duty is to 'facilitate as far as possible' the objective there described. The use of this expression, which does not appear elsewhere in the Article, indicates that a greater measure of latitude is extended to Contracting Parties in respect of this paragraph than in respect of any other. Thus, a Contracting State is permitted to make the admission of the family contingent on the alien's capacity to maintain them.[148] Equally, it is permitted to exclude from its territory in particularly serious cases those members of the alien's family who are suffering from contagious diseases.[149] Moreover, the admission of the family is to be permitted only when the worker has been 'permitted to establish himself in the territory'. This expression does not appear elsewhere in the Article. It is to be contrasted with the phrase used in the contextual paragraphs, 'workers lawfully within their territories'. The expression used in paragraph (6) seems to imply that the alien is permitted to remain indefinitely, as is generally the case in the United Kingdom only after four years' lawful residence.[150]

Article 19(7) provides that Contracting Parties shall secure for migrant workers 'lawfully within their territories' treatment not less favourable than that of their own nationals in respect of legal proceedings relating to matters referred to in that Article. This language is to be contrasted with that of Article 19(8), which contains protection against the expulsion of such workers 'lawfully residing within their territories'. The insertion of the word 'residing' is to be explained by the fact that the entire paragraph has been adopted from the European Convention on Establishment.[151] The same consideration suggests that the interpretation to be given to Article 19(7) of the European Social Charter should be identical to that of the European Convention on Establishment, save only that the former is limited in its application to migrant workers.[152]

The penultimate paragraph requires Contracting States to permit, within legal limits, the transfer of such parts of the earnings and savings of migrant workers as they may require. The reference to 'legal limits' cannot be taken to mark unqualified acceptance of any exchange or other controls that may be imposed in Contracting States. Such an interpretation would deprive the paragraph of its useful effect. The migrant worker must be permitted to transfer a reasonable amount of earnings and savings, having regard to the situation of the migrant and his family.[153]

Finally, the parties agree to extend the protection and assistance provided for in Article 19 to self-employed migrants 'in so far as such measures apply'. Most of the paragraphs of Article 19 seem capable of being applied equally to the employed and the self-employed. This is not the case with paragraph (4), which provides for equality of treatment in respect of remuneration and trades union rights; nor with paragraph (5), which deals with taxation with regard to employment. It is thought, however, that even those two paragraphs contain provisions applicable to self-employed persons. This is certainly the case with paragraph (4), in so far as it provides for equality of treatment in respect of accommodation. It is possible that the remaining parts of paragraphs (4) and (5) are to be applied to the self-employed by way of analogy. Thus the reference to the benefits of collective bargaining might be taken to extend to the benefits of bargaining conducted by a professional organization, such as are conducted in the United Kingdom between the Lord Chancellor's Department and the Bar Council or the Ministry of Health and the General Medical Council.[154]

THE EUROPEAN CONVENTION ON SOCIAL SECURITY

The European Convention on Social Security[155] is the sequel to the European Code on Social Security, concluded in 1964.[156] The Code has the general object of establishing an improved standard of social security in the European States to which it applies. In Article 73, however, the Code refers to the need for a special instrument governing social security for migrants and aliens. This need is perceived in order to secure the preservation of acquired rights and the establishment of the principle of equality of treatment with nationals of host States. The necessity for such a Convention became apparent particularly in view of the rise in temporary migration for employment in Western Europe, even at a time when permanent migration for employment was beginning to decline.[157]

The Convention terminates as between its parties two interim agreements concluded under the aegis of the Council of Europe in 1953.[158] It also terminates certain bilateral agreements[159] but leaves untouched the social security provisions in the EEC Treaty and those adopted thereunder. It also leaves untouched I.L.O. Conventions on social security ratified by parties to the European Convention on Social Security. That Convention must be read together with the Supplementary Agreement as to its application, which was adopted simultaneously. The purpose of the Supplementary Agreement is to regulate relations between social security institutions and the procedures to be followed for the provision of benefits due in accordance with the Convention. States ratifying the Convention are required to ratify also the Supplementary Agreement. Of the five parties to this pair of instruments, two are exporters of labour (Portugal and Turkey) and the remaining three net importers (Austria, Luxembourg and the Netherlands).

The Convention[160] applies to legislation governing eight categories of social security benefits: sickness and maternity benefits, invalidity benefits, old-age benefits, survivors' benefits, benefits in respect of occupational injuries and diseases, death grants, unemployment benefits and family benefits. In this respect it reflects precisely the principal regulation of the European Community on the subject.[161] The Convention on Social Security[162] applies to three categories of persons. In this respect also it reflects the European Communities' régime, but with the important difference that the Council of Europe Convention applies and has always applied to self-employed persons, in addition to 'workers'.[163] The first category comprises (broadly) all nationals of Contracting Parties and refugees who have been subject to the legislation of one or more such parties. The second comprises survivors of persons who were subject to the legislation of one or more Contracting Parties, irrespective of the nationality of such persons, where the survivors are nationals of a Contracting Party or refugees or stateless persons. The third group consists of civil servants and assimilated persons who are subject to the legislation of a Contracting Party.

The Convention is based upon two fundamental principles, set out respectively in Articles 8 and 14. By Article 8(1)

> Unless otherwise specified in this Convention, persons who are resident in the territory of a Contracting Party and to whom the Convention is applicable shall have the same rights and obligations under the legislation of every Contracting Party as the nationals of such Party.

To this general principle the Convention establishes a number of qualifications. Perhaps the most important is that entitlement to non-contributory benefits, the amount of which does not depend on the length of the period of residence, may within certain limits be made conditional on the beneficiary having resided for a specified period in the territory of the Contracting Party concerned.

Article 14 sets out the general rules for the determination of the legislation applicable. There are four such general rules.

(i) Persons employed in the territory of a Contracting Party are to be subject to the legislation of that Party, even if resident in the territory of another such Party.

(ii) Workers who follow their occupation on board a ship flying the flag of a Contracting Party are to be subject to its legislation.

(iii) Self-employed persons who follow their occupation in the territory of a Contracting Party are to be subject to the legislation of that Party, even if resident in the territory of another such Party.

(iv) Civil servants and assimilated persons are to be subject to the legislation of the Contracting Party in whose administration they are employed.

After establishing these general rules (and itemising many qualifications) the Convention sets out special provisions governing the eight categories of social security benefits in turn.

The Convention has a dual purpose. Firstly, it is a framework convention since it is applicable from its entry into force in respect of only part of its provisions. Implementation of other provisions is dependent on the conclusion of subsequent agreements between Contracting Parties. Secondly, it is a model convention in the sense that the provisions not immediately applicable serve as a model for subsequent bilateral and multilateral agreements.[164] The same is true of the Suppelementary Agreement, although in that case the model administrative agreement is detailed and designed to be adopted without modification. The Convention and Supplementary Agreement aim to make aggregation of benefits possible in respect of both contributory and non-contributory schemes. In the case of contributory schemes, the benefit payable is, in general, proportionate in sum to the number and amount of contributions made. In the case of non-contributory benefits, the general rule is that the beneficiary is to receive, equally with nationals of the Contracting State in question, the benefit payable in the State in which the insured risk occurred.

Periods of insurance completed under the legislation of other Contracting Parties must, under the Convention, be taken into account for the acquisition, maintenance or recovery of the right to benefit. The Convention provides, moreover, that benefits shall be provided in the territory of the other Contracting Party. The right to benefits in kind, and to short-term cash benefits, is generally determined in accordance with the legislation of a single 'competent State'.[165] Benefits in kind are provided by the competent institution of the Contracting State in which the claimant finds himself at the date of the occurrence of the risk. Short-term cash benefits are generally supplied in accordance with the same criterion.

In the case of long-term benefits (in particular, old-age and survivors' pensions) the Convention and Supplementary Agreement provide for the calculation of benefits *pro rata temporis*. Each institution determines the theoretical amount of the pension which would have been due to the claimant under the legislation which it applies if all the periods taken into account for the purposes of aggregation had been completed under that legislation. It then calculates the actual amount due in proportion to the ratio of the periods completed under its legislation to the total of all the periods completed under the various legislations to which the claimant has been subject. The sum total of the benefits due by each of the competent institutions constitutes the pension to which the claimant is entitled. To this rule there is one qualification. Where the amount of the benefit which could be claimed by the person concerned under the legislation of one Contracting Party on the basis of periods completed solely under that legislation is greater than the total amount of the benefits to which he is entitled under the Convention, he is eligible to receive from that Contracting Party a supplement equal to the difference between these two amounts.[166]

The Social Security Convention provides a means of eliminating, as between Contracting States, one of the principal legal obstacles to intra-European migration (other than immigration law itself). Like the European Communities' legislation on which it is based, it contributes to the creation of a single labour market. One author writing recently has claimed that 'the Convention must undoubtedly be the most ambitious exercise in the coordination of social security systems for the protection of migrant workers ever attempted by an international organization'.[167]

THE EUROPEAN CONVENTION ON THE LEGAL STATUS OF MIGRANT WORKERS

Like the European Convention on Social Security, the European Convention on the Legal Status of Migrant Workers[168] has been ratified by five States, three being net exporters of labour (Portugal, Spain and Turkey) and two net importers (the Netherlands and Sweden). It entered into force on 7 May 1983, seventeen years after the making of a decision to include in the Work Programme of the Committee of Ministers a proposal for such a treaty.[169]

The object of the Convention is to regulate the legal situation of migrant workers who are nationals of Member States, so as to ensure as far as possible that they are treated no less favourably than workers who are nationals of the receiving State in all aspects of living and working conditions.[170] In this respect it seeks to apply within the 'Europe of 21' the principle of non-discrimination set out in Article 48(2) of the EEC Treaty, in the case of the 'Europe of 12'.[171] In common with the EEC Treaty, it aspires to have a progressive effect. For this reason it provides for the establishment of a Consultative Committee consisting of representatives of each Contracting Party and with observers from any other Member of the Council of Europe which wishes to send one. The principal functions of the Consultative Committee are to examine proposals for facilitating or improving the application of the Convention, or for amending it; and to draw up periodical reports, for the attention of the Committee of Ministers, containing information about the laws in force in Contracting Parties, in respect of matters governed by the Convention.[172]

By contrast with the European Communities' regime on migrant workers, the European Convention on the Legal Status of Migrant Workers does not aspire to regulate the access of workers of one Contracting State to the labour market of another, nor does it contemplate the establishment of machinery for clearance of vacancies. It is not designed to confer rights on migrant workers (save in very exceptional respects) but to regulate the horizontal relationship between the parties.[173] For this reason, it seems doubtful that individuals can (save in very exceptional cases) rely on its terms as a source of private entitlements, even in Contracting States, like the Netherlands, where the domestic constitution permits individuals to invoke before national courts treaty provisions that are 'binding on anyone'.

Except for the reference to 'acquired rights' in Article 31, the Convention mentions the migrant's rights in only four Articles. Three of these deal only with the principle of equality of treatment: the right of access to the courts and the right to organize are to be respected equally in the cases of migrant workers and nationals, as are rights in respect of accidents and occupational diseases.[174] Only Article 4(1) imposes on Contracting Parties an obligation to guarantee rights to migrant workers, other than on a basis of comparison with local workers.[175] This stipulates that

> Each Contracting Party shall guarantee the following rights to migrant workers:
> - the right to leave the territory of the Contracting Party of which they are nationals;
> - the right to admission to the territory of a Contracting Party in order to take up paid employment after being authorised to do so and obtaining the necessary papers.

The first of these rights exists as a matter of general public international law and is not a matter of controversy in any of the Contracting States. The second is more of a facility than a right since it is contingent on the authorisation of the receiving State.

For these reasons, the title of the European Convention on the Legal Status of Migrant Workers is more ambitious than its content. It is to be characterised as a treaty on establishment rather than as the basis for a system of regulating migrant labour. On the other hand, it must be viewed in the light of a series of resolutions of the Committee of Ministers which have inspired much of the content of the Convention and the policies of the Member States.[176]

In common with the European Conventions on Human Rights,[177] Establishment[178] and the Suppression of Terrorism[179] the European Convention on the Legal Status of Migrant Workers is open to ratification by Members of the Council of Europe only; and any Contracting Party which ceases to be a Member of the Council of Europe ceases six months thereafter to be a party to the Convention.[180] The application of the Convention to the non-metropolitan territories of the parties is subject to express notification by the party concerned, at the point of signature, ratification or accession or at any later date.[181]

For the purposes of the Convention, the term 'migrant worker' is defined to mean a national of a Contracting Party who has been authorised by another Contracting Party to reside in its territory in order to take up paid employment.[182] Thus, the scope of the Convention is restricted in three significant respects. Migrant workers from States outside the Council of Europe are excluded altogether; but these constitute an increasingly important part of the reservoir of labour in Western Europe, and a sector singularly in need of international protection.[183] Secondly, 'undocumented migrants' are excluded, although these, too, are increasingly numerous and vulnerable.[184] Thirdly, the Convention is designed for those in paid employment, to the exclusion of the self-employed and of resident or visitors who are not economically active, including students, tourists and the retired. In the first two of those three respects, the European Convention on the Legal Status of Migrant Workers imposes qualifications on the term 'migrant worker' which are absent in the most closely analogous Convention of the International Labour Organization: Convention No. 143 of 1975.[185]

Further, the application of the European Convention is specifically excluded in the cases of frontier and seasonal workers[186] and in the cases of artists and entertainers,[186] seamen and trainees. The same is true of workers who are nationals of a Contracting Party but are carrying out specific work in the territory of another Contracting Party on behalf of an undertaking having its registered office outside the territory of that party.[188] It is immaterial for these purposes that the registered office is in the territory of the worker's State of nationality, or in that of another Contracting State, or that of a Member State or of a third party.

Certain of the benefits envisaged in the Convention are to be enjoyed by members of the families of migrant workers.[189] The word 'family' and its derivatives are not defined. Article 12(1) provides in part that

> The spouse of a migrant worker ... and the unmarried children thereof, as long as they are considered to be minors by the relevant law of the receiving State, who are dependent on the migrant worker, are authorised ... to join the migrant worker in the territory of a Contracting Party, provided that the latter has available for the family housing considered as normal for national workers in the region where the migrant worker is employed.

It seems clear that in this context the term 'family' is to be understood as embracing only the spouse and unmarried, minor dependent children. From this it probably follows that the term 'family' is to be given the same meaning in every other context in which it appears in the Convention.[190] Thus, the principle of family reunion, and probably the definition to be given to the term 'family', is considerably more narrow in the case of the European Convention on the Legal Status of Migrant Workers than in the case of the corresponding legislation of the European Community. The latter provides for the admission not only of the worker's children but also of his more remote issue and of dependent relatives in the ascending line of the worker and his spouse. Moreover, in the case of children, the Community's regime does not apply a condition against marriage, nor does it authorise the exclusion of a child under 21 who is no longer considered a minor in the law of the State whose territory he seeks to enter.[191] Indeed, the European Convention is even narrower in its use of the term 'family' than I.L.O. Convention No. 143 of 1975.[192]

The principal obligations imposed by the Convention are in Articles 2–7, which deal with the migrant worker's situation before arrival in the host State, and in Articles 8–29,[193] which deal with his situation in that State. Article 2 states that the recruitment of migrant workers may be carried out either by 'named' or by 'unnamed' request. The distinction between named and un-named requests is not that between the recruitment of individuals and that of groups. 'Named' recruitment covers all cases where workers are recruited by name by employers in the Host State or at their request. Unnamed recruitment occurs where labour is recruited on the basis of offers of employment for which anyone with the required qualifications can apply.[194] Although the Contracting State is free to apply either procedure, the recruitment by unnamed request of a migrant worker must be effected via the official authority of the State of origin.

Article 3, which deals with medical examinations, proved during the nego-tiations to be one of the most controversial and bitterly debated of the provisions. Some of the negotiating States insisted that an examination con-ducted in the country of emigration should not be vitiated by a further but inconsistent examination conducted at the point of arrival; whereas others emphasised the primacy of examination conducted in the host country. The result is a compromise which makes no mention of the place of examination. It is, however, implicit in the first paragraph, which speaks of recruitment being preceded by a medical test, that the examination will normally be conducted in the State of origin; for it is there that the recruitment commonly occurs. The second paragraph stipulates, however, that the purpose of the test is to ascertain that the prospective worker is fit for his job and that his state of health will not be such as to endanger public health in the host country. Thus, the principal climatic and sanitary conditions to be borne in mind by the examining physician are those at the destination. Article 3 is to be read in the light of Articles 4(2) and 9(5)(b), which authorise the imposition of restrictions on the worker's admission and the cancellation of his residence permit in the interests of public health.

By Article 5 the Contracting Parties agree that each migrant worker will receive prior to departure a contract of employment or a definite offer of employment. The reference to a definite offer of employment indicates that a written contract is not required. The Article appears to exclude from the Convention those who migrate in the mere hope of obtaining employment at the destination. In this respect it reflects the literal wording of the EEC Treaty, which speaks of the right to accept offers of employment actually made,[195] and is to be contrasted with recent indications from the Court of Justice of the European Communities that there is a right in Community law to travel to other Member States in order to look for employment.[196]

Article 6 creates obligations to provide appropriate information for migrant workers and to seek to prevent misleading propaganda. In these respects it amplifies certain provisions of a Convention promoted by the International Labour Organization in 1949.[197]

The two opening Articles of Chapter III must be read together. They deal with the issuance of work permits and residence permits. The first of them states that each Contracting Party which allows a migrant worker to enter its territory to take up employment shall issue him with a work permit, 'unless he is exempt from this requirement' (as is the case with workers travelling between Member States of the European Communities in accordance with Directive 68/360).[198] The principal obligation imposed thereby is that the work permit may not 'as a rule' bind the worker to the same employer for longer than a year. Since the ensuing Article requires as a general rule that a residence permit shall be issued with a period of validity equal to that of the work permit,[199] it generally follows that a residence permit for a migrant worker will be for a period no longer than one year. There is nothing in the Convention, as there is in Directive 68/360, to prohibit the withdrawal of a residence permit on the ground that the worker is temporarily incapacitated or is involuntarily unemployed.[200] A step in this direction is taken by Article 9(4) of the Convention, however. Quoting from Directive 68/360, this provides that in certain cases of temporary incapacitation or involuntary unemployment, the migrant worker shall be allowed to remain on the territory of the host State for a period which should not be less than five months, for the purposes of Article 25. The latter deals with re-employment.

In view of their importance to the Convention as a whole, the Articles governing work permits and residence permit must be accepted without reservation or not at all. The same is true of Article 12, governing family reunion. This is designed to state the principle that members of the migrant worker's family are authorised to join him at the expiry of a waiting period not exceeding twelve months, if the various conditions provided for in the Convention are met. Since, however, this principle appeared unduly onerous to some of the negotiating States, despite the narrow terms in which the 'family' is defined,[201] Contracting parties are given a facility to declare that family reunion shall be subject to a further condition: that the worker has steady resources, sufficient for their needs. For the same reason, provision is made to enable Contracting parties to derogate from the principle on a temporary basis (but without specific limit of time) in the case of difficulties as to receiving capacity. In the event of such a derogation, any Contracting party may demand a meeting of the Consultative Committee, which is then to be convened by the Secretary General.[202]

With regard to conditions of work, migrant workers are to receive no less favourable treatment than that which applies to national workers by virtue of legislative or administrative provisions, collective labour agreements or custom.[203] It is to be emphasised that the migrant worker's entitlement is to be tested against the national worker's treatment and not merely be reference to the latter's entitlement. This is implied by the words 'treatment . . . which applies to national workers by . . . custom'.

The European Convention requires each Contracting party to permit the transfer of such parts of the migrant worker's earnings or savings as the latter may wish to transfer. The obligation is qualified by the phrase 'according to the arrangements laid down by its legislation'; but this cannot be read so as to embrace arrangements inconsistent with the migrant worker's freedom to choose the proportion of his savings or earnings to be transferred or the place to which they were sent. The arrangements mentioned in the Article must be those designed for the purpose of implementing the principle: for example, regulations governing exchange of currencies and transmission of funds.[204]

By Article 30, every Contracting party is required to assist migrant workers and their families on the occasion of their final return to their State of origin. The Article states expressly that the provision of financial assistance is to be left to the discretion of each Contracting party. States of origin are required to provide host States with certain information to be transmitted to migrant workers, so that the latter will be aware of the conditions on which they will be able to resettle in their States of origin.

The fact that only five States have ratified this Convention, which imposes such modest obligations, illustrates with pellucid clarity the reserve with which most West European States have treated migration for employment since the date when it was opened for signature in November 1977.

EUROPEAN INSTRUMENTS GOVERNING THE STATUS OF REFUGEES

The countries of the Council of Europe lie at the very edge of the world's flood of refugees. Extra-regional arrivals are merely the overflow, the last ripples of refugee waves in far away regions in other continents. Nevertheless, in absolute figures the number of persons seeking asylum in the Member States of the Council of Europe is considerable. The average number over recent years has been estimated at over one hundred thousand per annum.[205]

Faced with a phenomenon of this magnitude, the institutions of the Council of Europe have taken more than one initiative to deal with the situation jointly. The more ambitious of these initiatives have tended to fail for lack of support from the governments of the Member States. By Recommendation 293(1961)[206] the Parliamentary Assembly recommended that an Article on the right of asylum should be included in the Second Protocol to the European Convention on Human Rights. The proposed Article envisaged not merely a right to seek and enjoy asylum but a right to receive it. No such Article was included in the Second Protocol. The Declaration on Territorial Asylum adopted in 1977 reaffirmed only the Member States' right to grant asylum.[207] At about the date of the adoption of that Declaration, there was established within the Council of Europe the Ad Hoc Committee on Stateless Persons and Refugees (known by its French acronym, CAHAR). The latter was entrusted with the drafting of an agreement concerning responsibility for examining asylum requests. Its work did not result in a final draft agreement and CAHAR's efforts were suspended in 1984.

Despite the failure of these major initiatives, the Council of Europe's instruments provide the basis for a regional code on the treatment of refugees. That this is so is the result, in no small measure, of the European Commission and Court of Human Rights, which have applied to the problems of asylum-seekers and refugees several of the key articles of the European Convention of Human Rights.[208]

Although the Parliamentary Assembly has declared that 'the right of asylum is an integral part of the common heritage of European traditions',[209] it has failed to secure governmental agreement on the right to be granted asylum. In the application of the European Convention on Human Rights, circumstances may arise in which a party is obliged to refrain from ignoring an asylum-seeker's plea for assistance, even in advance of his arrival on the soil of that State. Such circumstances may occur when the asylum-seeker presents himself to the commander of a public vessel of a Contracting State, or at its diplomatic premises abroad and claims that he is in distress or in imminent danger of persecution. In such an event two legal questions arise. The first is that of determining whether the fugitive may be said to be 'within the jurisdiction' of the Contracting State and the second is whether the State's inaction in the face of his plea may be said to constitute 'inhuman or degrading treatment' within the meaning of Article 3 of the Convention.

As for the first of those questions, the Commission inclined several years ago to the view that a State may, in certain circumstances, incur liability under the Convention by reason of the acts of its agents abroad.[210] More recently, it has concluded that the authorised agents of a Contracting State, including its diplomatic agents and armed forces, not only remain under its jurisdiction when abroad but bring any other persons within its jurisdiction to the extent that they exercise jurisdiction over such persons.[211] A commander of a public vessel may be said to exercise jurisdiction over an asylum-seeker, found in a small boat on the high seas, when the latter claims to be in distress and asks to be taken aboard the vessel. Likewise, a diplomatic agent exercises jurisdiction in granting or refusing to grant extraterritorial asylum.

As for the second question, it seems clear that the refusal to take an asylum-seeker aboard a public vessel or to admit him to diplomatic premises is capable of amounting to inhuman or degrading treatment. It has been held that a person's expulsion may, in exceptional circumstances, by contrary to Article 3 where there are strong reasons to believe that the person will be subjected to persecution in the country to which he is to be sent.[212] There seems to be no reason why this principle should apply only when the fugitive has reached the territory of the Contracting State. On the contrary, the case for concluding that the Contracting State has subjected an individual to 'inhuman or degrading treatment' is often particularly strong when extraterritorial asylum is denied, either on the high seas or at diplomatic premises; for in these cases the fugitive's suffering may be the imminent or instant consequence of the refusal.[213]

Once the refugee arrives on the soil of a State which is a party to the European Convention on Human Rights, he is protected against *refoulement* to a country where his life or liberty is in serious danger. This is so not only in the application of Article 33 of the Geneva Convention on the Status of Refugees but also in the application of Article 3 of the European Convention on Human Rights. In such cases, the Contracting State returning the refugee is not the agent of 'persecution', within the meaning of the Geneva Convention, but the author of 'inhuman and degrading treatment', within the meaning of Article 3 of the Convention on Human Rights.[214] In assessing whether there is a serious risk of persecution at the fugitive's destination, the European Commission on Human Rights takes account of his conduct in the Contracting State, for the purpose of determining whether it is consistent with that of a genuine refugee.[215] It also takes into account his conduct[216] and treatment[217] in his State of origin, together with the views of the Office of the United Nations High Commissioner for Refugees.[218] In general, a fugitive will not benefit from Article 3 when he is free, on expulsion, to live in another State from which he did not flee and in which he has no reason for fearing persecution.[219] It is only in very exceptional cases that the expulsion of a fugitive to a State party to the European Convention on Human Rights will entail a violation of Article 3; for it is to be presumed that Contracting States will secure to the applicant freedom from inhuman and degrading treatment, which implies *a fortiori* freedom from persecution.[220] As we have seen, however, the repeated expulsion of an alien without identity documents, whose country of origin is unknown, may amount to degrading treatment.[221]

On these points the Parliamentary Assembly and the Committee of Ministers have endorsed the case-law of the European Commission on Human Rights. The nexus between the situation of refugees and the European Convention on Human Rights was established by the Parliamentary Assembly in 1961 in Recommendation 293.[222] In 1965 the Assembly made Recommendation 434. This referred explicitly to the case-law of the European Commission on Human Rights in support of the proposition that the prohibition of in-human treatment embraced a prohibition of *refoulement* of refugees.[223] By Resolution 14(1967) the Committee of Ministers referred to Article 3 of the European Convention on Human Rights and recommended that Member Governments, acting in a particularly liberal and humanitarian spirit, should ensure the application of the principle of *non-refoulement*.[224] In 1977 the Parliamentary Assembly made Recommendation 817, recommending the Committee of Ministers to call on all governments of the Member States to reaffirm their intention of maintaining their liberal attitude towards asylum-seekers. The Recommendation was advanced on the basis of Resolution 14(1967) and having regard to the Geneva Convention and New York Proto-col. [225] In response, the Committee of Ministers adopted the Declaration on Territorial Asylum, 1977.[226] By this Declaration the Member States reaf-firmed, through the Committee, their intention to maintain their liberal atti-tude towards persons seeking asylum on their territory, 'on the basis of the principles set out in Resolution 67(14)'; and reaffirmed their right to grant asylum to those who qualify as refugees within the meaning of the Geneva Convention of 1951 'as well as to any other person they consider worthy of receiving asylum for humanitarian reasons'. It will be noted that the Commit-tee of Ministers carefully avoided any suggestion that there exists a right to receive asylum.

The difference in origins and meaning between 'persecution' in the Geneva Convention and 'inhuman or degrading treatment' in the European Conven-tion on Human Rights is a point of some significance for the asylum-seeker who faces ill-treatment short of persecution. There is no reason in principle why such a person should be unable to rely upon the prohibition of inhuman and degrading treatment in Article 3 of the Convention on Human Rights; nor does the European Commission's case-law on that Article imply that he cannot do so. Moreover, several of the instruments adopted by the Parlia-mentary Assembly and Committee of Ministers address the specific problems of asylum-seekers who may not qualify as refugees in the strict sense of the term. This is the case with those instruments, already mentioned, which call on Member States to apply the principle of *non-refoulement* in a particularly liberal and humanitarian spirit. It is more expecially the case with the As-sembly's Recommendation 773 of 1976 on De Facto Refugees,[227] to which the Committee of Ministers responded in Recommendation R(84)1 on the Protec-tion of Persons not Formally Recognized as Refugees.[228]

The former noted that there are in the Member States of the Council of Europe a considerable number of persons not recognized as refugees, who are unable or unwilling to return to their countries of origin for political, racial, religious or other valid reasons. Thus, it addresses the problem of those who had valid reasons other than reasons of persecution for failing to return to their countries of origin.[229] It recommended the preparation of an appropriate instrument, preferably an agreement, to govern this problem; and invited Member Governments to take several steps in order to relieve the hardship suffered by *de facto* refugees. In particular, it invited them to refrain from denying them admission on the ground that they have found 'protection or asylum elsewhere', save when they will in fact be admitted by another country. The Committee of Ministers' Recommendation, on the other hand, applies only to those who satisfy the criteria for the definition of the term 'refugee', within the meaning of the Geneva Convention, and are not formally recognized as refugees because they have not applied for refugee status or for other reasons. Thus, it leaves unaffected the larger category of '*de facto* refugees' as that term is used in the Parliamentary Assembly's Recommendation. Moreover, even in the case of those who qualify, but have not been formally recognized, as refugees, the Committee of Ministers' Recommendation provides only meagre protection. In essence, it calls on Member States to respect the principle of *non-refoulement* in the case of all refugees within the meaning of the Geneva Convention, whether formally recognized as such or not. Since formal recognition is not a prerequisite of the principle of *non-refoulement* in Article 33 of the Geneva Convention, the Recommendation amounts to a call for observance of existing obligations.[230]

The Committee of Ministers' response to the Parliamentary Assembly's proposal has been more impressive in the case of procedures for the determination of eligibility for asylum. In 1976 the Assembly expressed concern at the widely differing recognition rates in the various States, which resulted, in the view of the Assembly, from the adoption of different criteria and reliance upon inadequate information. It recommended that the Committee of Ministers should consider as one of the Council of Europe's objectives the harmonization of eligibility practice.[231] The Committee responded on 5 November 1981 by adopting its Recommendation on the Harmonisation of National Procedures relating to Asylum.[232] Among the principles contained in that Recommendation, three merit particular attention. Firstly, decisions on requests for asylum should be taken only by central authorities, issued with clear instructions drawing attention especially to the obligation to respect *non-refoulement*. Secondly, pending the decision by the central authority, the applicant should be allowed to stay in the territory of the State, save where the request is manifestly based on grounds having connection with asylum. Thirdly, there should be provision for appeal to a higher administrative authority or to a court of law against the decision on an asylum request, or at least an effective possibility of having the decision reviewed.

The Recommendation thus exceeds the demands made by the Geneva Convention on the Status of Refugees, which is for the most part silent on the question of eligibility procedures. On the other hand, it does not exceed the demands of the European Convention on Human Rights, which may well impose on Member States obligations similar to the principles set out in the Recommendation of 5 November 1981, but enforceable by the Commission and Court. Article 13 of the Convention on Human Rights provides, in effect, that anyone claiming that he has suffered a violation of his rights and freedoms under other Articles of the Convention shall have an effective remedy before a national authority.[233] As we have been, a person who claims that he has been removed to a country of persecution advances, in effect, a claim that he has suffered inhuman or degrading treatment at the hands of the returning State.[234] Such a person is therefore entitled to an effective remedy before a national authority of that State. It seems improbable that the Convention entitles him to a remedy only after his rendition, when it is likely to be comparatively ineffective, and does not also entitle him to a remedy in advance of the rendition, so as to avoid the inhuman or degrading treatment.[235] From this it should follow that he is entitled to an effective remedy against a decision to return him to his country of origin; and that the exercise of that remedy must precede his removal.

The Geneva Convention on the Status of Refugees does not provide that the refugee's immediate family shall be entitled to enter the State of asylum for the purpose of living with him nor that they shall enjoy the same status as the refugee. Family reunification is by no means unconditional in the case of refugees admitted to Council of Europe States. In certain of the German *Länder*, for example, such reunification is contingent on the refugee's ability to provide accommodation considered as normal by local standards.[236] The European Commission on Human Rights has held that the exclusion of a person from a country in which his close relations live may raise a question under Article 8 of the Convention on Human Rights, which protects the rights to family life.[237] This is particularly the case where it is impossible for the family to be reunited in the country of origin,[238] as is generally the case with refugees. Indeed, it is possible to imagine circumstances in which a member of the family of a refugee might under the Convention gain a certain status of irremovability in the territory in which he has been granted asylum. The Commission has acknowledged the possibility that the Convention might forbid the deportation of parents of small children who cannot themselves be removed from the territory of a Contracting State in which they were born.[239] By parity of reasoning, it appears that the close relation of a refugee may not be amenable to deportation when the refugee cannot be removed from the State of asylum. Indeed, as regards refugees there may be a particularly strong case for the application of this reasoning. The objection to the removal of a small child from the State in which he or she was born is, very commonly, that the child has acquired the nationality of his birthplace: it is wrong in principle to confront a child with a choice between exile and separation from his parents. In the case of refugees, however, the objection to their removal is the serious risk of persecution. If a member of the immediate family of a refugee were deported to the country of origin of the refugee, the latter would be presented with a choice between exposure to a serious risk of persecution and separation from his immediate family.

One of the problems presented by the reunification of refugees' families is addressed in Article 6 of the European Agreement on Transfer of Responsibility for Refugees, 1980.[240] This provides that in the event of the transfer of responsibility for a refugee, the State accepting the responsibility shall facilitate the admission to its territory of the refugee's spouse and minor or dependent children. Since that Agreement as a whole is concerned with transfers of responsibility from one Contracting State to another, it might be contended that Article 6 imposes a duty to facilitate the admission of members of a refugee's family only when the latter are present in the territory of another Contracting State. The Article cannot bear that construction. It is made clear both in the context and in the Explanatory Report published by the Council of Europe that the object of Article 6 is not to relieve Contracting States of responsibility for members of the family of refugees but to promote 'the interest of family reunification and for humanitarian reasons'.

The principal rule established by that Agreement is set out in Article 2. Where a refugee has been issued by one Contracting State with a Convention Travel Document, in accordance with the Geneva Convention of 1951, and settles thereafter in another Contracting State, the second assumes responsibility for him on permitting him to remain in its territory permanently, or for a period exceeding the validity of his document, or on the expiry of two years of actual and continuous stay in the second State with the agreement of its authorities. From the date of transfer of responsbility, the first State ceases to be under a duty to extend or renew the Travel Document and the second State assumes the duty to issue a new Travel Document to the refugee.

The European Agreement of 1980 is one of only two treaties concluded under the aegis of the Council of Europe for the purpose of ameliorating the condition of refugees. The other is the European Agreement on the Abolition of Visas for Refugees, 1959.[241] In essence, this follows the pattern of traditional visa abolition agreements, save that the beneficiaries are not nationals of the Contracting States but refugees lawfully resident in the territory of a Contracting Party and holding a valid Convention Travel Document.

The ultimate legal step in the assimilation of refugees in their country of asylum is the grant of local nationality. With a view to facilitating the naturalization of refugees the Parliamentary Assembly made Recommendation 564 (1969).[242] This invites member governments to facilitate the naturalization of refugees *inter alia* by a liberal interpretation of the legal requirements in respect of naturalization and by making every effort to remove or at least reduce legal obstacles to naturalization, such as the minimum period of residence when it exceeds five years. In 1970 the Committee of Ministers resolved to transmit the Assembly's Recommendation to governments, inviting them to take such action as is possible for them.[243]

NOTES

1. Statute of the Council of Europe, London, 5 May 1949, 87 U.N.T.S. 103; parties (21) include Austria, Belgium, Cyprus, Denmark, France, Federal Republic of Germany, Greece, Iceland, Ireland, Italy, Liechtenstein, Luxembourg, Malta, Netherlands, Norway, Portugal, Spain, Sweden, Switzerland, Turkey, United Kingdom.
2. Rome, 4 November 1950; 213 U.N.T.S. 221; *Basic Documents* V.1.
3. 16 September 1963; 58 A.J.I.L. 334; *Basic Documents* V.2.
4. 27 November 1984; Council of Europe No. 117 (ratified by France and Sweden and requiring seven ratifications in all in order to enter into force).
5. Application No. 434/58, II Ybk. (1958–59) 354, 372.
6. Paris, 13 December 1955, 529 U.N.T.S. 141; *Basic Documents* V.3.
7. Paris, 13 December 1957, 359 U.N.T.S. 276; *Basic Documents* V.4.
8. Turin, 18 October 1961, 529 U.N.T.S. 89; *Basic Documents* V.5.
9. Paris, 14 December 1972, E.T.S. 78; *Basic Documents* V.6.
10. Strasbourg, 24 November 1977, E.T.S. 93; *Basic Documents* V.7.
11. Strasbourg, 20 April 1959, 376 U.N.T.S. 85; *Basic Documents* IV.1.
12. See *Basic Documents* IV.2 to IV.13.
13. Applications Nos 4403/70–4419–70, 4422/70, 4423/70, 4434/70, 4443/70 and 4446/70–4486/70, 10 I.L.M. (1971) 6.
14. *Supra*, Chapter IV, text at note 78.
15. Application No. 7612/76, *Giama v Belgium*, XXIII Ybk. (1980) 428.
16. Application No. 6242/73, *Brückmann v Federal Republic of Germany*, 6 D.R. (1977) 57.
17. XX Ybk. (1976) 413.
18. Application No. 9174/80, *X v United Kingdom*, 5 E.H.R.R. (1983) 242.
19. *Zamir v Secretary of State*, [1980] 2 All E.R. 768; see now *Khawaja v Secretary of State*, [1983] 1 All E.R. 765.
20. Application No. 2991/66, *Alam v United Kingdom*, X Ybk. (1976) 478. See further Z. Nedjati, *Human Rights under the European Convention*, 1978, 108–112.
21. Application No. 2614/65, *Ringeisen v Austria*, XI Ybk. (1968) 268 (decision on admissibility). F. Jacobs, *The European Convention on Human Rights*, 1974, p. 79 at 80 (extract from report).
22. Application No. 7729/76, *Agee v United Kingdom*, 7 D.R. (1977) 164.
23. Application Nos. 7289/75 and 7349/75, *X and Y v Switzerland*, 9 D.R. (1978) 57.
24. Application No. 8244/79, *Uppal v United Kingdom*, 17 D.R. (1980) 149.
25. Application No. 7902/77, *X v United Kingdom*, 9 D.R. (1978) 224.
26. J. Fawcett, *The Application of the European Convention on Human Rights*, 1969, p. 18.
27. Article 1.
28. See Article 16.
29. Application No. 1855/63, *X v Denmark*, VIII Ybk (1965) 200.
30. *Supra*, note 26, p. 188.

31. Application Nos. 514/59, *X* v *Austria* III Ybk. (1960) 197; 1855/63, *X* v *Denmark, supra,* note 29; Applications Nos. 7289/75 and 7349/76, *X* v *Switzerland,* 9 D.R. (1978) 57; Application No. 6833/74, *Marckx* v *Belgium,* 3 D.R. (1975) 112; Application No 7626/76, *X* v *United Kingdom,* 11 D.R. (1978) 160.

32. *Deutsches Verwaltungsblatt,* 1957, p. 57.

33. Application No. 1855/63, *X* v *Denmark, supra,* note 29; Fawcett, *supra,* note 26 p. 188.

34. Applications Nos. 9214/80, 9473/81 and 9474/81, *Abdulaziz, Cabales and Balkandali,* 7 E.H.R.R. (1985) 471.

35. Application No. 9369/81, *X and Y* v *United Kingdom,* 3 May 1983 (not reported); see A Drzemczewski, *The Position of Aliens in relation to the European Convention on Human Rights,* 1985, p. 23.

36. Application No. 1477/62, *X* v *Belgium,* VI Ybk. (1963) 620, 628; Application No 858/60, *X* v *Belgium,* IV Ybk. (1961) 224; Application No. 2535/65, *X* v *Germany,* 16 July 1965, not reported.

37. *Supra,* note 20.

38. Application No. 238/56, *X* v *Denmark,* I Ybk. (1955–1957) 205.

39. *Patel et al.* v *United Kingdom, supra,* note 13.

40. *Matrimonial Home (Germany) Case,* [1953] E.B. 58; Fawcett, *supra,* note 26, p. 193.

41. [1960] J.T. 573; III Ybk. (1960) 624.

42. Application No. 858/60, *X* v *Belgium* IV Ybk. (1961) 224.

43. Application No. 312/57, *X* v *Belgium,* II Ybk. (1958–1959) 352, 353.

44. Application No. 911/60, *X* v *Sweden* IV Ybk. (1961) 198, 216; see Fawcett, *supra,* note 26, p. 191; A. Macheret, *L'immigration étrangère en Suisse a l'heure de l'integration européenne,* 1969, p. 193.

45. Application No. 8378/78, 20 D.R. (1983) 168.

46. Applications Nos. 9214/80, 9473/81 and 9474/81, *Abdulaziz, Cabales and Balkandali* v *United Kingdom, supra,* note 34.

47. H.C. 503, 15 July 1985, paras 41–47.

48. Application No. 7175/75, *X* v *Germany,* 6 D.R. (1977) 138; Application No. 7031/75, *X* v *Switzerland,* 6 D.R. (1977) 124; Application No. 5269/71, *X and Y* v *United Kingdom,* XV Ybk. (1972) 564.

49. [1975] 2 All E.R. 1981.

50. In *Bhajan Singh, supra,* note 49 at 1083, Lord Denning expressed the view that 'when anyone is considering a problem concerning human rights, we should seek to solve it in the light of the Convention'. He subsequently qualified that statement. See *R* v *Home Secretary ex parte Phansopkar,* [1975] 3 All E.R. 497; *R* v *Chief Immigration Officer, ex parte Salamat Bibi,* [1976] 3 All E.R. 843.

51. Article 2.

52. Article 4.

53. Article 3.

54. Application No. 7011/75, *Becker* v *Denmark,* XIX Ybk. (1976) 416; *infra,* Chapter XIII at note 183.

55. Application No. 6189/73, *X* v *Austria,* C.D. 214.

56. Paris, 11 December 1953, 218 U.N.T.S. 255.

57. Paris, 13 December 1955, 529 U.N.T.S. 141, *Basic Documents* V.3.

58. *Supra,* note 6; *Basic Documents* V.3. See Council of Europe, *Commentary on the European Convention on Establishment adopted by the Standing Committee,* 1980.

59. Austria, France, Iceland and Turkey have signed the Convention without yet ratifying it. Cf. European Convention on Establishment of Companies, Strasbourg, 20 January 1966, E.T.S. No. 57.

60. See the periodical reports of the Standing Committee, in particular the first such report, 1971, the second, 1974, and the third, 1977.
61. Articles 24 and 31 and Protocol, section IX.
62. Article 3(1).
63. Protocol, sections I and III.
64. Article 4. See *R* v *Home Secretary ex parte Hosenball*, [1977] 3 All E.R. 452; cf. note 25, *supra*.
65. Protocol, section I(b).
66. Article 4.
67. Articles 7 and 8.
68. Article 10.
69. Protocol, section I(a)(2).
70. EEC Treaty, Rome, 25 March 1957, 298 U.N.T.S. 11, Article 48(3); *Basic Documents* VI.1.
71. Directive 64/221 of 15 February 1964, O.J. Sp. Ed. 1963–4,117 Article 3; *Basic Documents* VI.5.
72. Protocol, section III(c).
73. See Case 149/79, *Commission* v *Belgium*, [1980] E.C.R. 3881.
74. See A. Kiss, 'La convention européenne d'établissement et la clause de la nation plus favorisée', [1957] A.F.D.I. 478 at 482, note 8.
75. See A. Piot, 'La clause de la nation plus favorisée', Rev. crit. dr. int. (1956) 14; P. Mamopoulos, 'La Convention européenne d'établissement', 7 Rev. hell. dr. int. (1955) 32 at 183.
76. See Articles 6(1)(a) and (b), 14, 26(3), 28(2), 29, 31(3), 33(1) and 34.
77. See Article 24(5), (6).
78. Article 34(1).
79. *Supra,* note 74 at p. 482.
80. See J. Ebner, *La clause de la nation plus favorisée*, 1931; G. Schwarzenberger, 'The Most Favoured Nation Standard in British State Practice', 22 B.Y.I.L. (1945) 109.
81. Cf. R. Plender, 'The Interpretation of Community Acts by Reference to the Intentions of the Authors', 2 Ybk. E.L. (1982) 57.
82. On the European Convention on Establishment generally, see F. Rigaux, *'La convention européenne d'établissement: origine, analyse et commentaire'*, 60 R.G.D.I.P. (1957) 5; P. Maitland, *Task for Giants*, 1957.
83. *Supra*, note 7.
84. Strasbourg, 15 October 1975, E.T.S. No. 86.
85. Strasbourg, 17 March 1978, E.T.S. No. 98.
86. Belgium, Malta, Portugal and the United Kingdom have yet to ratify it.
87. Montevideo, 23 January 1899 (Argentina, Bolivia, Paraguay, Peru, Uruguay) 18 Martens 432; Mexico, 28 January 1902 (*idem*) 6 Martens 185; 20 December 1907 (Costa Rica, Guatemala, Honduras, Nicaragua, San Salvador) 3 Martens 117; Caracas, 18 July 1911 (Bolivia, Colombia, Ecuador, Peru, Venezuela) 2 *Tratados y acuerdos de Venezuela* 435.
88. Washington, 7 February 1923 (Nicaragua, El Salvador, Costa Rica, Honduras, Guatemala), 2 Hudson 954.
89. Havana, 20 February 1928, 4 Hudson 2412.
90. Montevideo, 26 December 1933, 6 Hudson 597.
91. Guatemala, 12 April 1934, 6 Hudson 833 (parties as in note 88, *supra*).
92. L.O.N. Doc. C51 M.28 1926 V.
93. 29 A.J.I.L. (1935) Supp. 21.
94. Caracas, 25 February 1981, 20 I.L.M. (1981) 723.
95. M. Cherif Bassiouni, *International Extradition and World Public Order*, 1974, p. 22.

96. The eliminative method was used, however, in the Convention of 7 February 1923, *supra*, note 88. See also extradition treaty of 12 June 1942 between Germany and Italy, 149 B.F.S.P. 686 and Treaty of Ankara, 29 March 1946 between Iraq and Turkey, Article 2, 37 U.N.T.S. 389.
97. Article 2. The same principle is applied to the Inter-American Convention, *supra*, note 94, Article 3.
98. *Supra*, note 94, Article 4(4).
99. I.C.J. Rep. (1950) 266, 298.
100. Convention on the Prevention and Punishment of Genocide, New york, 9 December 1948, 78 U.N.T.S. 278. For the character of this Convention generally see the Advisory Opinion on *Reservations to the Genocide Convention*, I.C.J. Rep. (1951) 15.
101. 663 H.C. Deb. col. 422 (Rt. Hon. Edward Heath, Lord Privy Seal, 18 July 1962).
102. Sir Hersch Lauterpacht, 'The Law of Nations and the Punishment of War Crimes', 21 B.Y.I.L. (1944) 58, 90.
103. See the United Kingdom's Fugitive Offenders Act 1967, section 4(5); Belgium's Extradition Laws of 22 March 1856, Art. 1 and 1 October 1963, Art. 6. See further the United States-Venezuela Extradition Treaty of 21 January 1922, 49 L.N.T.S. 435, Article 3.
104. D. O'Connell, *International Law*, 1970, Vol. II, pp. 726–29; D. Greig, *International Law*, 1976 pp. 410, 411, 412–19, 428, 429; Bassiouni, *supra*, note 95, pp. 370–428; J. Gutteridge, 'The Notion of Political Offences in the Law of Extradition', 31 B.Y.I.L. (1954) 430; M. Garcia-Mora, 'Present Status of Political Offences in the Law of Extradition and Asylum', 14 U. Pitts. L.R. (1952–3) 371; L. Deere, 'Political Offences in the Law and Practice of Extradition', 27 A.J.I.L. (1933) 247; A. Evans, 'Reflections upon the Political Offence in International Practice', 57 A.J.I.L. (1963) 1; L. Green, 'Political Offences, War Crimes and Extradition', 11 I.C.L.Q. (1962) 329; S. Sinha, *Asylum in International Law*, 1971; C. van den Wijngaert, *The Political Offence Exception to Extradition*, 1980.
105. See the judgment of the Chilean Supreme Court in *Matter of the Extradition of Hector José Campora and Others*, VI Rev. D.I.C.D. (1957) No. 12, 143, 53 A.J.I.L. (1959) 693); see also correspondence on extradition of Horacio Julio Coiscon, a revolutionary, VI Whitman 804–6; Denmark, *Collaboration with the Enemy Case*, 4 B.S.B.D.I. (1948) 128, 14 A.D. (1947) 146 (No. 71); *Re de Serclaes* (1952–II) F.I. 129, 19 I.L.R. (1952) 366 (No. 78).
106. *In Re Fabijan*, A.G. St. Vol. 67 (1933), 7 A.D. (1933–4) 360 (No. 156); *In Re Giovanni Gatti*, (1947–II) Sirey, 48 14 A.D. (1947) 145 (No. 70); *In Re Ficorilli*, 77 A.T.F.S. (1951–I) 18 I.L.R. (1951) 345 (No. 110).
107. *Re Castioni*, [1891] 1 Q.B. 149; *Re Meunier* [1894] 2 Q.B. 415; *U.S. v Artukovic,* 170 F. Supp. 383 (1959); *In Re Richard Eckermann*, 26 G. de los T. (No. 35) (1929) 5 A.D. (1929–30) 293 (No. 189); *Ramos v Diaz*, 179 F. Supp. 459 (1959).
108. *In Re Ezeta*, 62 F. 972 (1894); *In Re González*, 217 F. Supp. 717 (1963); *In Re Ockert*, 59 E.S.B. (1933–I) 136, 7 A.D. (1933–4) 369 (No. 157); *In Re Camporini*, 50 E.S.B. (1924–I) 299, 2 A.D. (1923–4) 283 (No. 164).
109. *R v Governor, Brixton Prison, ex parte Kolczynski*, [1955] 1 Q.B. 540.
110. For the Soviet concept of political offences, see T. Taracouzio, *The Soviet Union and International Law*, 1935, p. 146–7.
111. That Court and the House of Lords had no cause to apply the European Convention on Extradition, since it had not been ratified by the United Kingdom.
112. [1978] 2 All E.R. 634.
113. Strasbourg, 27 January 1977, E.T.S. No. 90.
114. Austria, Cyprus, Denmark, Federal Republic of Germany, Iceland, Liechtenstein, Luxembourg, Norway, Portugal, Spain, Sweden, Switzerland, Turkey, United Kingdom.
115. 4 December 1979, Cmnd. 7823 (Agreement concerning the Application of the 1977 Europe-

an Convention on the Suppression of Terrorism among the Member States of the European Communities).

116. Cmnd. 7031, *Explanatory Report*, para. 2.
117. 16 December 1970, 860 U.N.T.S. 105.
118. 23 September 1971, 10 I.l.M. (1971) 1151.
119. 14 December 1973, 13 I.l.M. (1974) 41.
120. I. Stanbrook. *The Law and Practice of Extradition*, 1980, p. 94.
121. *Supra*, note 8.
122. Sir O. Kahn-Freund, 'The European Social Charter' in F. Jacobs, ed., *European Law and the Individual*, 1976, 181 at 182.
123. Article 20(1)(a).
124. Article 20(1)(b), (c).
125. Geneva, 1 July 1949, 120 U.N.T.S. 71; *Basic Documents* VII.2.
126. *Supra*, note 58.
127. I C.E. 81, cited by D. Harris, *The European Social Charter*, 1984, 158.
128. Cf. I.L.O. Convention No. 97, Articles 2 and 3; *supra*, note 125.
129. III C.E. 89; VI C.E. 117.
130. IV C.E. 113.
131. Section 14.
132. III C.E. 87; IV C.E. 114.
133. Cf. I.L.O. Convention No. 97, Article 4; *supra*, note 125.
134. Harris, *supra*, note 127 at 164.
135. III C.E. 89; IV C.E. 116.
136. III C.E. 91; cited by Harris, *supra*, note 127 at 167.
137. II C.E. 90.
138. Cf. I.L.O. Convention No. 97, Article 6(1)(a); *supra*, note 125.
139. III C.E. 92.
140. III C.E. 94.
141. IV C.E. 119.
142. VI C.E. 121.
143. VI C.E. 122.
144. VII C.E. 103.
145. Cf. I.L.O. Convention No. 97, Article 6(1)(c); *supra*, note 125.
146. Appendix to the Social Charter.
147. Strasbourg, 24 November 1977; E.T.S. No. 93; *Basic Documents* V.7.
148. III C.E. 96.
149. III C.E. 95.
150. Harris, *supra*, note 127 at 175–76.
151. Article 3(1). *Supra,* text at note 61.
152. See, however, the materials assembled by Harris, *supra*, note 127 at 180–86.
153. I C.E. 86.
154. See further D. Pugsley, 'The European Social Charter', [1969] Ann. A.A.A. 39; W. Wiese, '*Europäische Sozialcharta*', 16 Jahrbuch für internationales Recht (1973) 328; G. Tessari, '*Considerazioni sulla carta sociale europea, l'integrazione sociale europea e il Consiglio d'Europa*', 14 Riv. dir. eur. (1974) 235; W. Wiebringhaus, '*Convention européenne des droits de l'homme et la Charte sociale européenne*', 8 Rev. dr. de l'homme (1975) 527.
155. *Supra*, note 9.
156. Strasbourg, 16 April 1964; 648 U.N.T.S. 235; see M. Taquet, '*Code européen de sécurité sociale*', 30 Rev. trim. dr. belge (1970) 45.
157. G. Veldkamp and M. Raetsen, 'Temporary Work Agencies and Western European Social Legislation', 107 Int. Lab. Rev. (1973) 117.

158. European Interim Agreement on Social Security Schemes Relating to Old Age, Invalidity and Survivors and Protocol, Paris, 11 December 1953, 218 U.N.T.S. 211; European Interim Agreement on Social Security other than Schemes for Old Age, Invalidity and Survivors and Protocol, Paris, 11 December 1953, 218 U.N.T.S. 153.
159. Article 5.
160. Article 2.
161. Council Regulation 1408/71 of 14 June 1971 on the Application of Social Security Schemes, O.J. Sp. Ed. 1971, 416, Article 4, as replaced by Council Regulation 2001/83 of 2 June 1983, amending and updating Regulation 1408/71, O.J. 1983 L230/6.
162. Article 4.
163. Council Regulation 1408/71, *supra,* note 161, Article 2.
164. Council of Europe, *Guide to the Application of the European Convention on Social Security and Supplementary Agreement thereto* and Forms CE1 to CE29, 1976, p. 19.
165. In relation to a social insurance scheme, this means, broadly, the State where there is situated the institution with which the claimant is insured when he claims benefit, or the institution from which is is entitled to receive benefit or would be entitled to receive benefit if he were resident in the territory of that State, or in which is situated the institution designated by the competent authority of the Contracting Party concerned. In relation to schemes other than social insurance schemes, this means, broadly, the State in which is situated the institution designated by the competent authority of the Contracting State concerned.
166. Article 34. See Council of Europe, *Explanatory Reports on the European Convention on Social Security and on the Supplementary Agreement for the Application of the European Convention on Social Security,* 1973, p. 65.
167. P. Watson, *Social Security in the Law of the European Communities, 1980, 28. See further I. Vimars, 'Social Security for Migrant Workers in the Framework of the Council of Europe', 120 Int. Lab. Rev. (1981) 291.*
168. *Supra,* note 10.
169. For the drafting history of the Convention, see H. Golsong, '*La convention européenne relative au statut juridique du travailleur migrant*', in Société française pour le droit international, *Les travailleurs étrangers et le droit international,* 1978 at 226–231.
170. Preamble, paragraph 2.
171. Treaty establishing the European Economic Community, Rome, 25 March 1957, 298 U.N.T.S. 11; *Basic Documents* VI; *supra* Chapter VI at note 51.
172. Article 33.
173. Golsong, *supra,* note 169 at 249.
174. Articles 26, 28 and 20 respectively.
175. The point is remarkable since the preamble refers to the aim of the Council of Europe in 'respecting human rights and fundamental freedoms'. No reservations to Article 4 are permitted.
176. Resolution (76)11 on equality of treatment of national workers and migrant workers in respect of training, vocational training and retraining, Assembly Doc. 4063, Annex I (cf. Article 14); Resolution (76)12 on the educational and health entitlements of children educated in foreign countries, Assembly Doc. 4063, Annex II (cf. Article 12) Resolution (76)25 on the model contract of employment or engagement of a migrant worker, Assembly Doc. 4063 Annex III (cf. Article 5); Resolution (78)4 governing the social and economic repercussions for migrant workers of recessions and economic crises, Assembly Doc. 4156, (cf. Article 24).
177. *Supra,* note 2, Article 65(3).
178. *Supra,* note 6, Article 33(3).

179. *Supra,* note 113, Article 15.
180. Articles 34(1), 37(3).
181. Article 35.
182. Article 1(1).
183. See the comments at the Council of Europe's Colloquy in Funchal, *Human Rights of Aliens in Europe,* 1985 at 34 and 273.
184. General Assembly Res. 3449(XXX) of 9 December 1975, United Nations G.A. Res. (1975) p. 90.
185. Geneva, 24 June 1975, Cmnd. 6674, *Basic Documents* VII.5.
186. According to the definition applied by the Joint Committee, which was entrusted with the drafting, frontier workers are nationals of one Member State who, while retaining their residence in the frontier area of their home country, to which they normally return every day, go to work in the frontier area of a neighbouring Member State: *Explanatory Report on the European Convention on the Legal Status of Migrant Workers,* Council of Europe, 1978, p. 8. The definition is adopted from EEC Council Regulation 1408/71 of 14 June 1971, O.J. Sp. Ed. 1971, 416, Article 1(f). For a definition of a 'seasonal worker', see *ibid.,* Article 1(g).
187. The expression is not defined but see *Home Secretary* v *Stillwaggon,* [1975] Imm, A.R. 132.
188. Article 1(2). The exclusion reflects Article 11(2) of I.L.O. Convention No. 143, *supra,* note 185.
189. See Articles 7 (travel), 9(3) (residence permits), 10 (information on reception), 12 (family reunion), 15 (teaching in mother tongue), 18 (social security) and 19 (social and medical assistance).
190. Golsong, *supra,* note 169 at 235. The converse cannot be excluded: it would be possible to read the term 'family' in Article 18, which deals social security benefits, as meaning those who are defined as families by the law of the State whose social security system is in issue. Such a construction would be compatible with the European Convention on Social Security, *supra,* note 9.
191. Council Regulation 1612/68 of 15 October 1968, O.J. Sp. Ed. 1968, 475, *Basic Documents* VI.6, Article 10.
192. *Supra,* note 185, Article 13(2) (which includes parents).
193. Chapters II and III respectively.
194. *Explanatory Report, supra,* note 186, p. 9.
195. Article 48(3)(a).
196. *Supra,* Chapter VI, text at note 22.
197. Convention No 97 concerning Migration for Employment (Revised), Geneva, 1 July 1949, 120 U.N.T.S. 72, *Basic Documents* VII.2, Articles 2 and 3.
198. Council Directive 68/360 of 15 October 1968, O.J. Sp. Ed. 1968, 41, *Basic Documents* VI.7.
199. Article 9(2); cf. Article 8(2).
200. *Surpa,* note 198, Article 7.
201. *Surpa,* text at note 198.
202. Article 33(3).
203. Article 16.
204. *Explanatory Report, supra,* note 186, p. 22; cf. I.L.O. Convention No. 82 Concerning Social Policy (Non-Metropolitan Territories) 1947, Geneva, 11 July 1947, 218 U.N.T.S. 345, *Basic Documents* VII.1, Article 11.
205. A.H.J. Swart, 'Problems Connected with the Admission of Asylum-Seekers to the Territory of Member States', paper delivered at the Lund Colloquium, Council of Europe and Raoul Wallenberg Institute, September 1986, p. 5.
206. *Basic Documents* IV.2.
207. *Basic Documents* IV.10.

208. *Basic Documents* V.1. See R. Plender, *Problems Raised by Certain Aspects of the Present Situation of Refugees from the Standpoint of the European Convention of Human Rights*, Council of Europe, Human Rights Files No. 9, 1984.
209. Recommendation 434 (1965) on the Right of Asylum.
210. Applications Nos. 6780/74 and 6950/74, *Cyprus v Turkey*, 2 D.R. (1975) 125 at 136–137.
211. Application No. 8007/77, *Cyprus v Turkey*, 13 D.R. (1979) 85.
212. Application No. 2134/64, *X v Austria and Yugoslavia*, VI Ybk. (1964) 314; Application No. 6315/73, *X v Germany*, 1 D.R. (1973) 73; Application No. 7011/75, *Becker v Denmark*, 4 D.R. (1976) 205.
213. See Application No. 1611/62, *X v Austria*, VIII Ybk. (1965) 158 at 168.
214. Applications Nos, 4162/69, 32 C.D. (1970) 87 at 95; 9012/80, *X v Switzerland, 24 D.R. (1981) 201 at 219. See also Amerkrane v United Kingdom*, 44 C.D. (1973) 101.
215. Application No. 7216/75, *X v Germany*, 4 D.R. (1976) 101.
216. Application No. 10032/82, *X v Sweden*, 5 October 1983, not reported.
217. Application No. 74165.76, *X v Denmark*, 7 D.R. (1977) 153.
218. Application No. 8581/79, *X v United Kingdom*, 6 March 1980, not reported.
219. Application No. 7237/75, *X v Denmark*, 5 D.R. (1976) 144.
220. Application No. 8088/77, *X v Netherlands*, 15 December 1977, not reported. Where, however, the Contracting State did not accept the right of individual petition, different considerations applied: Application No. 9822/82, *X v Spain*, not reported.
221. Application No. 76112/76, *Giama v Belgium*, XXIII Ybk. (1980) 428, *supra*, note 15.
222. *Basic Documents* IV.2.
223. *Basic Documents* IV.3.
224. *Basic Documents* IV.4.
225. *Basic Documents* IV.9.
226. *Basic Documents* IV.10.
227. *Basic Documents* IV.7.
228. *Basic Documents* IV.13.
229. See, however, Article 5(II)(ii)(a).
230. There is, perhaps, some encouragement to be derived from the Recommendation since it asserts in the preamble that 'the principle of *non-refoulement* has been recognized as a general principle applicable to all persons'.
231. Recommendation 787(1976) on Harmonisation of Eligibility Practice, *Basic Documents*, IV.8.
232. Recommendation R(81)16, *Basic Documents*, IV.12.
233. *Vagrancy Cases*, European Court of Human Rights, Series A, No. 12 (1971), paragraph 95; *Swedish Engine Drivers Case*, European Court of Human Rights, Series A, No. 20 (1976) paragraph 50; *Klass and Others*, European Court of Human Rights, Series A, No. 28 (1978).
234. *Supra*, text at note 214.
235. The European Commission on Human Rights appears to have accepted that an asylum-seeker is entitled to such a remedy: Application No. 9856/82, *X v United Kingdom*, not yet reported. In that case the application was based on Article 13 of the Convention. It was dismissed on the 'wholly exceptional' ground that the respondent State had admitted the Applicant and altered its procedures.
236. Baden-Württemberg: *Auslanderordnung* (Aliens Decree) of 15 December 1981, Article 38(4)(5); Berlin: *Auslanderordnung* (Aliens Decree) of 22 September 1980, as amended on 21 July 1982, Articles 2(3)(1)(1)(b) and 2(3)(1)(2); Bremen: *Auslandergesetz* (Aliens Law) of 21 october 1982, Articles 2(3)(1)(3) and 2(3)(1)(4); Niedersachsen: *Auslandergesetz* (Aliens Law) of 30 July 1982, Article 4.
237. Application No. 6357/73, *X v Germany*, 1 D.R. (1975) 77.

271

238. Application No. 8245/78, *X v United Kingdom*, 23 D.R. (1981) 98; Application No. 9478/81, *X v Germany*, 27 D.R. (1982) 243.
239. Application No. 8244/78, *Uppal and Singh v United Kingdom*, 17 D.R. (1980) 149 and 20 D.R. (1980) 29; Application No 8245/78, *X v United Kingdom*, 24 D.R. (1981) 98.
240. Strasbourg, 6 October 1980; Cmnd. 8127; *Basic Documents* IV.11.
241. Strasbourg, 20 April 1959; 376 U.N.T.S. 85; *Basic Documents* IV.1.
242. *Basic Documents* IV.5.
243. Resolution 70(2) on the Acquisition by Refugees of Nationality; *Basic Documents* IV.6.

BIBLIOGRAPHY

Council of Europe, *Guide to the Application of the European Convention on Social Security and Supplementary Agreement Thereto and Forms CE1 to CE29*, 1976.
Council of Europe, *Commentary on the European Convention on Establishment adopted by the Standing Committee*, 1980.
Council of Europe, *Human Rights of Aliens in Europe*, 1985.
A. Drzemczewski, *The Position of Aliens in relation to the European Convention on Human Rights*, 1985.
H. Golsong, '*La convention européenne relative au statut juridique du travailleur migrant*' in Sociéte française pour le droit international, *Les travailleurs étrangers et le droit international*, 1978, 226.
D. Harris, *The European Social Charter*, 1984.
O. Kahn-Freund, 'The European Social Charter' in F. Jacobs, ed., *European Law and the Individual*, 1976, 181.
A. Kiss, '*La convention européenne d'établissement et la clause de la nation plus favorisée*', [1957] A.F.D.I. 478.
P. Mamopoulos, '*La convention européenne d'établissement*', 7 Rev. hell. dr. int. (1955) 32.
C. Palmer, *The European Convention on Human Rights and United Kingdom Immigration Law*, 1981.
R. Plender, *Problems Raised by Certain Aspects of the Present Situation of Refugees from the Standpoint of the European Convention on Human Rights*, 1984.
D. Pugsley, 'The European Social Charter', [1969] Ann. A.A.A. 39.
F. Rigaux, '*La convention européenne d'établissement: origine, analyse et commentaire*', 60 R.G.D.I.P. (1957) 5.
A. Swart, 'The Legal Status of Aliens: Clauses in Council of Europe Instruments Relating to the Rights of Aliens', 11 Neths. Ybk. Int. L. (1980) 3.
M. Taquet, '*Code européenne de sécurité sociale*', 30 Rev. trim. dr. belge (1970) 45.

CHAPTER 8

Other Regional Arrangements

The European arrangements for freedom of movement, concluded under the aegis of the European Communities, the Council of Europe and (to a lesser extent) the European Free Trade Area have had an influence beyond the confines of the subcontinent in which they are applied. In particular, they are reflected in the *Communauté économique de l'Afrique de l'Ouest* (C.E.A.O.), the Economic Community of West African States (ECOWAS), the Central African Community and the Caribbean Community. The distinct system of freedom of movement applied in the case of the Andean Pact owes its origins more to the work of the I.L.O. than to that of the European institutions. Those arrangements and kindred organizations will be considered later in this Chapter. It is, however, to another European system that we must first devote our attention.

THE BENELUX SYSTEM

The system established under the Treaty establishing the Benelux Economic Union[1] merits special consideration since it is not only the precursor of the arrangements made within the European Communities but also an indication of the form that may be assumed by the Communities' régime of the future. By a treaty dated 14 June 1985, France, the Federal Republic of Germany and the Benelux States agreed to seek means of abolishing controls on the movement of persons between their territories and of harmonizing their controls on immigration from third countries, including their policies on the issuance of visas. Pending the achievement of that objective, the same five States agreed to pursue a policy of cooperating in the reduction of delays for travellers between their territories. From 15 June 1985, vehicular traffic would generally be permitted to cross the parties' common frontiers without stopping, where only tourist passengers were carried and a green disc was displayed on the windscreen. From 1 January 1986 administrative measures would be adopted for the purpose of reducing delays at the common borders of the five States for other traffic.[2] By a Political Declaration annexed to the Single European Act[3] the twelve Member States of the European Community undertook to 'cooperate . . . in particular as regards the entry, movement and residence of nationals of third countries'.

The system established under the Benelux treaty is itself the culmination of a dozen agreements concluded between 1945 and 1958 by the three Benelux States together, or by two of the three in variously-constituted pairs. The post-war process began even before the armistice with an exchange of notes between Belgium and Luxembourg on the re-establishment of freedom of movement for persons: a freedom abrogated by conditions of warfare.[4] When this had been amplified by a supplementary agreement of 1949,[5] it established an arrangement whereby nationals of those two States could travel to one another's territory without the necessity of a passport, but with national identity cards or aliens' cards issued by contracting States of residence. In 1950 Belgium and the Netherlands reached an agreement on travel without passports: certificates of nationality or national identity cards were to be accepted by each contracting State in respect of nationals of the other such State.[6] A few days later, Belgium and Luxembourg replaced their agreements of 1945 and 1949 with a new arrangement whereby nationals of those two States were admissible to the territory of the other State bearing any of five documents.[7] The new Belgo-Luxembourg arrangement was then extended to embrace nationals of those States bearing aliens' identity cards issued by the Swiss authorities.[8]

In March 1953, Belgium and the Netherlands reached an Agreement for the Liberalization of Minor Frontier Traffic[9] which made provision for nationals of either State to cross their common border at any time between sunrise and sunset. This was amended two years later so as to permit crossings of the border at any time.[10] There followed a succession of treaties governing seamen and refugees[11] and an agreement on the removal of undesirable persons.[12] On 7 June 1956 the three Benelux States concluded at The Hague a Labour Treaty[13] providing for the free movement of nationals of contracting States, in the event of their employment by private employers in other such States. The object of the Treaty was to establish a common labour market. Pending its entry into force, the same three States concluded a Provisional Labour Agreement[14] whereby salaried workers who were nationals of any one of the contracting States were entitled to accept offers of employment from a private employer in another such State on equal terms with nationals of that State.[15]

The Treaty establishing the Benelux Economic Union was concluded at The Hague on 3 February 1958 and entered into force on 1 November 1960.[16] That Treaty places the free movement of persons at the forefront of its objectives. By Article 1(1) an Economic Union is established between the Kingdom of

Belgium, the Grand Duchy of Luxembourg and the Kingdom of the Netherlands, entailing the free movement of persons, goods, capital and services. Article 2 provides that the nationals of each High Contracting Party may freely enter and leave the territory of any other Contracting Party; and that they shall enjoy the same treatment as nationals of that State as regards freedom of movement, sojourn and settlement; and freedom to carry on a trade or occupation, including the rendering of services.[17] Article 55 stipulates that a further Convention shall be concluded for the purpose of determining the provisions which may be applied by one Contracting State to nationals of another such State, in the interests of public order, public security, public health or morality, with regard to their entering or leaving its territory, to their freedom of movement, of sojourn and of establishment therein, and to their expulsion.

In accordance with that Article, two new Conventions were concluded between the Benelux States on 11 April 1960.[18] One of these is essentially a Convention on Establishment, although it begins with the broad statement that nationals of each of the Contracting Parties may enter the territory of the other Contracting Party on the sole condition of being in possession of a valid identity document.[19] It replaces the bilateral treaties on establishment labour formerly in force between the Netherlands and her two partners in Benelux.[20] The Convention provides that nationals of each of the Contracting Parties shall have the right to establish themselves in the territory of the other Contracting Parties, provided they have adequate means of subsistence and are of good character. Once established, such nationals may be expelled only if they endanger public order or national security. A Committee on Freedom of Movement and Establishment is set up to supervise the application of the Convention.[21]

The second of the Conventions concluded on 11 April 1960 is entitled the 'Convention concerning the Transfer of Entry and Exit Controls to the External Frontiers of the Benelux Territory'.[22] It provided expressly that from the moment of its entry into force each of the parties should abolish entry and exit controls at the internal frontiers and effect at the external frontier a control valid for the whole of the Benelux territory.[23] From this it followed that there must be a common policy both on the internal plane and *vis-à-vis* third States. A common visa was established for the Benelux territory. Persons who are not nationals of any of the Benelux States were to be admitted to Benelux territory, provided that they had adequate means of subsistence or were in a position to support themselves by legally authorised work.[24] Such a person was to be free, after entering Benelux territory lawfully, to travel in each of the Benelux countries during a period to be fixed by the Ministerial Working Party established in accordance with the Benelux Treaty. Moreover, such a person, if he had a residence permit issued in one Benelux country, could travel in the other two Benelux countries on the strength of that permit alone.[25] The parties undertook to harmonize their laws relating to the punishment of infringements of the provisions concerning the entry and movement of foreigners: but they reserved the right temporarily to re-establish entry and exit controls at the internal frontiers for reasons of public order or national security.[26]

The Ministerial Working Party has amplified the Convention concerning the Transfer of Entry and Exit Controls twice: first for the purpose of elaborating on the provisions governing the admission of aliens to Benelux territory and later for the purpose of elaborating on the system of reporting of aliens' whereabouts, the right of refugees to take employment, the deportation of aliens, the definition of undesirable aliens and the possibility of maintaining controls on aliens within Benelux territory and on their admission to that territory. Further, a series of agreements has been concluded between the Benelux Community and third States not only for securing the abolition of visas on a reciprocal basis, but also to simplify transit more generally.[27]

THE WEST AFRICAN COMMUNITIES

In the space of some seven months, beginning in October 1978, the two economic communities of West Africa concluded separate agreements on the free movement of persons. Both of the agreements have their inspiration in European instruments.[28]

Article 39 of the Treaty establishing the *Communauté économique de l'Afrique de l'Ouest*[29] (C.E.A.O.) states that the objectives of the Community shall include the realization of a homogeneous and integrated economic area within which persons, services, goods and capital may move freely. With the purpose of achieving that objective, the Member States of the C.E.A.O. concluded an agreement dated 27 October 1978,[30] which begins with the following Article:

> *Sous réserve des dispositions de lois de police et de sûreté publique, ainsi que des prescriptions de la réglementation sanitaire, les ressortissants des Etats Membres pourront librement entrer sur le territoire de l'un quelconque des Etats Membres, y voyager, y séjourner et en sortir sur simple présentation du passeport national en cours de validité sans qu'il soit exigé l'accomplissement d'aucune formalité préalable telle que visa d'entrée ou de sortie.*

Article 2 provides that freedom of movement will extend to establishment. By Article 3, nationals of Member States are to enjoy the same rights as nationals of the States in which they find themselves, with the exception of political rights.

The agreement of 27 October 1978 has been compared with the European Convention on Establishment[31] with which it has indeed some similarities, notably in its terms governing the equal treatment of nationals. No less obvious are its points of similarity with the European Communities' system, most particularly in the pattern of linking freedom of movement for persons, services, goods and capital. Indeed, the economic climate in which the C.E.A.O. originated was tempered by the enlargement of the European Communities no less than by the dissolution of the *Union douanière des Etats de l'Afrique de l'Ouest*.[32] Both of these events gave the French-speaking States of West Africa reason to conclude an agreement which would enable them to withstand jointly the combined economic strength of their principal trading partners.[33] For this reason, and because an unusual degree of mobility of labour was achieved under the preceding regional arrangements between the same States,[34] the agreement of 27 October 1978 sets out in remarkably broad terms the principle of equality of treatment and the right to enter and settle in neighbouring States.

That agreement enunciates in Article 1 two countervailing principles: derogations are permitted in the interests of public health and in those of public order. The latter is not defined in the agreement; but it clearly embraces restrictions imposed in the interests of internal and external security. Of this, one African author has remarked:

> *Dans une Afrique qui est souvent en proie à des soubresauts politiques, il y a cependant lieu de craindre qu'elles soient appliquées de manière à entraver la circulation des opposants politiques des gouvernements en place.*[35]

A more fundamental restriction is imposed by the C.E.A.O. Treaty on the exercise of freedom of establishment. Article 39(2) of that Treaty stipulates that the freedom shall be subject to national provisions governing the public service and related occupations and governing professions regulated by law. The reference to public service in that Article echoes Article 48(4) of the E.E.C. Treaty,[36] although an attempt has been made in the C.E.A.O. Treaty to enlarge the compass of the expression by mentioning related occupations. Particular problems are created, however, by professions regulated by law (*professions réglementées*), which can comprise not only the liberal professions but (in the countries concerned) may extend even to such activities as those of transporters and drivers.[37] Such occupations may in principle be reserved for local nationals; but each Member State is required, in effect, to submit to the Council of Ministers a list of the occupations that it proposes to reserve for its own nationals. It is for the Council to take a decision; and in the event of disagreement the matter may be resolved by inter-State proceedings before the Community's Court of Arbitration.[38]

The Economic Community of West African States (ECOWAS) was established in 1975 to promote cooperation and development in economic, social and cultural affairs between West African States.[39] There are sixteen parties, including the parties to the C.E.A.O. Treaty.[40] The founding Treaty of E.C.O.W.A.S., like that of the European Economic Community, contains an elaborate preamble referring to the objective of removing obstacles to the free movement of goods, capital and persons. There follows a list of the activities in which the Community is to engage. These include 'the abolition as between Member States of the obstacles to the free movement of persons . . .'. Article 27 of the Treaty declares the intention of creating a Community citizenship to be acquired automatically by citizens of the Member States. It provides for the taking of measures to exempt Community citizens from the necessity of holding visas and residence permits in the event of their travel within the territory of the Community. It also envisages the progressive establishment of the right of each Community citizen to obtain employment and engage in commercial and industrial activities anywhere in the Community, on equal terms with other Community nationals.[41] Individuals have, however, no *locus standi* before the Tribunal established by the Treaty to settle differences between Member States.

The objectives foreseen by the founding Treaty of E.C.O.W.A.S. were fulfilled in part by a Protocol concluded in Dakar on 29 May 1979.[42] The Protocol sets out a programme designed to be achieved in a period of fifteen years, in three phases of five years measured from June 1980. During the first phase, the right of entry was to be secured together with the abolition of visas. The second phase was to be devoted to achievement of the right of residence and the third to the right of 'establishment' (meaning the right to take up employment as well as the right to set up in business).

In pursuance of the first phase, any citizen of the Community who wishes to enter the territory of another Member State may do so on production of a valid travel document and international health certificate. A citizen of the Community may visit any Member State for a period not exceeding ninety days, without the necessity of presenting or possessing a visa, provided that he enters the territory of the State at an official entry point. Such a citizen is, however, required to obtain permission from the appropriate authorities if he wishes to extend his stay beyond ninety days.[43] Special counters are established at entry points of Member States for the purpose of dealing jointly with the entry formalities of their own nationals and other Community citizens. There is, however, an important safeguard clause: each Member State reserves the right to refuse admission to 'any citizen who comes within the category of inadmissible immigrants' according to local law.

It will be noted that during the first phase E.C.O.W.A.S. citizens were not granted the right to take up employment without permit; but many such citizens did so, as did citizens of Chad, a State not belonging to the Community. It is for this reason that citizens of E.C.O.W.A.S. States were captured, together with Chadian nationals, by the Nigerian announcements dated 17 January 1983 and 28 February 1983 that foreign nationals who were illegally employed on federal territory should depart within fourteen days (if unskilled) or should either regularize their stay or depart (if skilled).[44]

The second phase of the Protocol on freedom of movement was due to begin on 4 June 1985. In April of that year, however, the Nigerian Government demanded the departure by 10 May 1985 of aliens unlawfully present on federal territory. The enforced departure of some two million persons created an atmosphere unsuited to the implementation of the second phase, which was therefore not initiated until 18 June 1986 (in time for the meeting of the Heads of State of E.C.O.W.A.S. at Abidjan, Nigeria on 30 June). As it entered into force, the Nigerian Minister for Internal Affairs announced that Nigeria would impose unilaterally conditions on its implementation. Only migrants of six professions would be allowed unrestricted admission: doctors (of medicine), engineers, surveyors, teachers and bilingual secretaries; and these would be permitted to stay only if they found employment within six months of their arrival.

Thus, the provisions relating to the free movement of persons under the E.C.O.W.A.S. Treaty have proved more troublesome in their implementation than those of the C.E.A.O., although more modest in conception. They have been among the casualties of the fall in oil prices which has struck so severely the economy of Nigeria, the principal power in the E.C.O.W.A.S. It is possible, however, particularly in the event of a rise in oil revenues, that the arrangements within the C.E.A.O. may have an influence upon the E.C.O.W.A.S. comparable with the influence that the Benelux system aspires to produce on the European Community.[45] Even if this should not transpire, the provisions concluded under the aegis of the E.C.O.W.A.S. appear ambitious and imaginative when compared to those in comparable African organizations.

An embryonic system for freedom of movement was created by the French-speaking States of West Africa by means of the Treaty of Tananarive, which constituted the Union of African and Malagasy States (U.A.M.C.E.).[44] The system was extended to the Central African Economic and Customs Union (U.D.E.A.C.) in 1964.[47] It survived the transformation of the first of those unions into the African and Malagasy Common Organization[48] which was dissolved following a decision taken in March 1985 that it had fulfilled its objectives. The system so created has matured into the arrangements now applied within the *Communauté économique de l'Afrique de l'Ouest* (C.E.A.O.). It was never applied other than in the French-speaking States.

Provisions on freedom of movement for persons were conspicuous in their

absence from the Treaty for East African Cooperation[49] as they are in the
Treaty for the Establishment of a Preferential Trade Area for Eastern and
Southern African States.[50]

The Economic Community of Central African States was established by
Treaty at Libreville on 19 October 1983.[51] It was set up under the aegis of the
United Nations Economic Commission for Africa and was intended to provide
a Central African Community parallel to the E.C.O.W.A.S. Community.
Initially, ten States signed the Treaty. Although attending the Conference,
Angola did not sign the Treaty until later, owing to its economic and political
situation at the time.[52] Four of the signatory States, the Cameroons, the
Central African Republic, Congo and Gabon, were members of the *Union
douanière et économique de l'Afrique centrale*.[53] These States, it has been
suggested,[54] inherited a planned economic development from France, which
was essentially integrative.

It is Article 4 of the Treaty which sets out the main aims of the Community:
to promote and enhance a harmonious cooperation and a balanced and self-
maintaining development in all fields of economic and social activity. Article 3
requires observation of principles of sovereignty and independence, but Article 4(2)(e) states as a main aim of the Community the gradual abolition
between Member States of obstacles to the free movement of people, goods,
services and capital, and to the rights of establishment. Citizens of Member
States are deemed to be citizens of the Community.[55] A Protocol on Freedom
of Movement and Right to Establishment lays down procedures to achieve
these ends.[56]

The Protocol applies to the nationals of a Member State travelling to
another Member State as tourists or for personal reasons; as businessmen; in
order to exercise remunerated activities – as workers; or to carry on an
unsalaried liberal or craft professions – as freelance professionals.[57] Nationals
of a Member State of the Community who travel, stay or become established in
the territory of another Member State are to enjoy the same rights and
freedoms as the nationals of the host State except for political rights. The
Protocol requires the abolition of obstacles to free movement, the coordination of national laws and increased accessibility to non-salaried work
during the transitional period[58] (Article 6 of the Treaty provides for such a
period of twelve years). The Protocol requires freedom of movement to
become effective within four years and the right of establishment within twelve
years of the entry into force of the Treaty.[59]

Article 3 of the Protocol sets out to facilitate freedom of movement of nationals of Member States, provided they hold a national identity card, a valid passport or a *laissez-passer,* together with an international health *carnet.* Tourists must prove that they can support themselves and will not take up employment during their stay. They are generally allowed entry for a period not exceeding three months. Business travellers must hold a special certificate issued by the National Chamber of Commerce of each Member State before they are allowed entry. Freedom of movement for workers is to be established, subject to limitations on the grounds of public order, public safety and public health. The freedom is to entail the right to move within the territories of Member States to accept employment; to stay in the territory of a Member State for the purpose of employment, in accordance with national laws; and to remain within a State after the termination of employment '. . . with a view to finding further work or becoming established in such a State'.[60]

Article 4 deals with the right of establishment. This includes the right of access to unsalaried occupations, both in the liberal professions and in the crafts, together with the right to set up and manage enterprises under conditions defined by national legislation. The Secretary-General is required to study activities for which freedom of establishment makes a particularly useful contribution to the expansion of production and trade. Governments of Member States retain, however, the sovereign right to expel nationals to other Member States. The State of nationality of the expellee is to be informed immediately of any action taken in this regard and appropriate steps should be taken to safeguard the property and interests of the expelled person.

THE CARIBBEAN COMMUNITY

The Treaty establishing the Caribbean Free Trade Association[61] provided in Article 20 for a limited freedom of establishment. Member Territories agreed that restrictions in the establishment and operation of Member Territories should not be applied in such a way as to frustrate the benefits that would otherwise accrue by reason of the removal of customs duties and quantitative restrictions under that agreement. This principle was qualified by the following reservation: Member Territories were to remain free to impose measures for the control of entry, residence, activity and departure of persons where such measures are justified by reasons of public order, public health or morality or national security.[62] In the wording of this Article, as in that of many others, the CARIFTA Treaty followed the Treaty establishing the European Free Trade Area.[63]

The Treaty establishing the Caribbean Community was concluded in 1973, when CARIFTA was dissolved.[64] Article 4 of that Treaty states that the Community shall have among its objectives 'activities in the fields specified in the Schedule and referred to in Article 18 . . .'. The Schedule lists sixteen areas of functional cooperation, the twelfth of them being 'travel within the region'. Article 18 provides in part that in furtherance of the objectives set out in Article 4 of the Treaty, Member States will make every effort to cooperate in the areas set out in the Schedule.

This commitment, although expressed in guarded terms, is made by the CARICOM States in addition to an undertaking comparable with that made in the former CARIFTA Treaty. Article 35(1) of the Annex to the CARICOM Treaty reads as follows:

> Each Member State recognizes that restrictions on the establishment and operation of economic enterprises therein by nationals of other Member States should not be applied, through accord to such persons of treatment which is less favourable than accorded in such matters to nationals of that Member State, in such a way as to frustrate the benefits expected from such removal or absence of duties as is required by this Annex.

There follows, as in the case of the CARIFTA Treaty, an explicit reservation to preserve Member States' freedom to impose controls justified by reasons of public order, public health or morality, or national security. Thus, the tradition established by the E.F.T.A. Treaty is preserved; although in the case of CARICOM a further reservation has been added:

> Nothing in this Treaty shall be construed as requiring, or imposing any obligation on, a Member State to grant freedom of movement to persons into its territory whether or not such persons are nationals of other Member States of the Common Market.[65]

Since the conclusion of the CARICOM Treaty, the Member States (collectively or in part) have taken three steps to advance the cause of promoting 'travel within the region'. The first was an oral agreement between the Premiers of Grenada, Saint Lucia and Saint Vincent containing the following points:

> (1) In order to eliminate barriers to better communication and association among the States; and without prejudice to, or frustration of the constitutional aspiration(s) of any such State, there shall be effective August 1, 1972, complete freedom of movement among the States of persons belonging to; or being permanent residents of; or accepted visitors of any of these States.
> (2) Persons belonging to any of these States shall not be subject to any restrictions on their right to work in any of these States.
> (3) Persons belonging to any of these States shall not be subject to any restrictions on their right to hold land in any of these States.[66]

The second step was taken during the inaugural meeting of the Conference of Heads of Government of CARICOM at Castries in Saint Lucia on 15 July 1974, when the concept of a common travel document was approved and it was agreed that a common immigration card would be used for CARICOM nationals travelling in the region. The third was an agreement between the Members of the Organization of Eastern Caribbean States (which are also members of CARICOM) reached in Sam Lord's Castle in St Philip, Barbados between 1 and 4 July 1986. This provides that Member States will facilitate the movement of in transit passengers through international airports on arrival from or departure to countries without international airports.[67]

THE ANDEAN PACT

In May 1969, Bolivia, Chile, Colombia, Ecuador and Peru concluded the agreement on Andean Subregional Integration known as the Pact of Cartagena.[68] Venezuela joined the Andean Group on 13 February 1973.[69] On 24 November 1969 the Pact came into force. The Pact of Cartagena has aims allied to those of the Montevideo Treaty which established the Latin American Association of Free Trade in 1969.[70] For the purpose of applying the Pact of Cartagena the Member States undertook to fulfil conditions stipulated by the corresponding institutions established for the purposes of the Free Trade Association.[71]

The supreme authority of the Organization is the Andean Group Commission consisting of one representative from each Member State. The Commission's policies are formulated, and their implementation supervised, by a three member Board or Junta. The institutional structure of the group comprises a consultative committee responsible for liaison between the Junta and the Member States; an Economic and Social Committee; the Andean Development Corporation; the Andean Reserve Fund; a Court of Justice; the Andean Parliament; and the Andean Council of Foreign Ministers.

The objectives of the Agreement are set out in Chapter One. Article 1 aims to promote a balanced and harmonious development of Member States' economies, by means of economic integration as envisaged in the Montevideo Treaty, and to create a climate favourable to the conversion of the Latin American Free Trade Association into a common market. Such a development is aimed at bringing about a more equal distribution of benefits gained by Member States and so reducing the existing differences between them. Article 3 lists means of achieving these goals, including 'coordination of . . . social policies'.

Following a meeting of Employment Ministers in Quito in March 1973,[72] a declaration was made stressing that to carry out the objectives of the Pact of

Cartagena the main aspects requiring attention were the socio-labour problems of integration. This was to be achieved through the intervention of the Employment Ministers and the effective and permanent participation of the workers and employers. Further, it has stated that in order to permit all workers to exercise their rights it was essential to include the law of social security among the subjects of integration. The main lines of action to be taken were seen as:

(a) the harmonization of labour law and social security which would guarantee equal social protection and structuring of the economy, thus reflecting the governments' will to place full emphasis on workers' benefits in the integration process;

(b) the coordination, expansion and improvement of professional training schemes to enable workers to acquire higher levels of cultural and technical knowledge;

(c) the establishment of a subregional system of migration, easing the problems of workforce mobility;

(d) the creation of structures to enable workers and employers to participate in the development programme;

(e) the search for solutions to problems of unemployment and under-employment to make better use of human resources; and

(f) the creation of a system of financial support for the encouragement of the foregoing priorities and for social welfare programmes.

These obligations formed the basis for the Simon Rodriguez Agreement on Socio-Labour Integration which was signed after a second meeting of Employment Ministers of the Andean Group which took place in Caracas in October 1973.[73] The Ministers approved a document called the Andean Common Policy on Social Security and passed a resolution which embraces the situations of the skilled migrant worker, the frontier worker and the temporary worker. In addition, the meeting considered the situation of workers in an irregular situation and the harmonization of labour legislation of the different States in the region.

In particular, the Ministers agreed to encourage their governments to ratify various agreements adopted by the International Labour Organization designed specifically to improve the rights of migrant workers in respect of welfare, trade union membership, protection from discrimination on grounds of race and sex and in respect of social policies.[74] It was agreed to apply the principles of free association for workers, to encourage workers' organizations and collective bargaining aimed at improving working and living conditions in Member States. The Ministers emphasized the importance of the working relationship between the Simon Rodriguez Agreement and the Andean Pact.[75] (Article 26 of the Pact of Cartagena requires Member States to initiate a coordinated procedure in their development planning and in the harmonization of their economic and social policies).

Five Councils have been established by the Commission of Delegates of the Employment Ministers.[76] The purpose of these bodies is to make policy recommendations in their respective areas of responsibility. They are to collaborate with the Board, or Junta, in the implementation of policies and they are to disseminate information on the progress of integration in the region.

The Employment Ministers of the Member States of the Andean Pact have developed a Common Policy on National Legislation on Migrant Labour.[77] A Code of Practice establishes definitions and general principles and makes provisions for the setting up of administrative processes for the contracting of migrant workers.[78] The main objective of the Common Policy is to harmonize the legislation of the Member States.

Chapter One of the Code of Practice deals with uniform definitions. The migrant worker, as defined in clause e), Part I of the Ministers' Resolution, falls into three categories: the qualified or skilled worker, the frontier worker and the temporary worker. The Council, in describing a frontier worker, has emphasized two points. Firstly, the worker must live 'near' to the border (the degree of proximity is not defined). As there is no common criterion amongst the countries of the area, a worker's claim to qualify as a frontier worker is apt to depend upon national laws of the country of emigration, which may differ from the laws of the country of immigration. The resultant problems may be resolved by bilateral arrangements. Secondly, the Council requires that a worker can be considered as a migrant only if he crosses the border to offer his services in return for payment. The only entitlement to seek and accept offers of employment abroad arises when uses is made of Migration Employment Agencies.

As regards temporary workers, the Ministers' definition requires that the worker should go to another Member State to offer his labour for a short time only. The Council for Social Affairs has explained that this means that the worker must carry out seasonal work or other short term work.

Chapter Two of the Code of Practice requires Member States, in fulfilling their own demands for migrant labour, to first look to the employment centres of the Andean area. Both the Junta and Council allow more leeway in that they only require States 'preferably' to find their labour within the region. The Council allows States to 'appeal to other areas if their respective plans for economic and social development call for it'. The movement of labour is promoted by means of cooperation between Labour Migration Offices, through the exchange of national reports. These offices may make regulations as to their national labour requirements, although the Council has advocated a restriction of this power. The Code of Practice demands that national authorities should not impede the entry and departure of migrant workers under contract.[79] From this it appears that national authorities should refrain from exercising their powers to make administrative rulings in such a way as to hinder movement between Member States.

It is clear[80] that Member States may conclude bilateral agreements for the purpose of solving special problems. They cannot, however, establish subordinate regulations under such agreements. The Junta's Report suggested that States, in making these agreements, ought to be obliged to inform the Conference of Employment Ministers of the Simon Rodriguez Agreement and the Commission of the Pact of Cartagena.

Point seven in Chapter Three of the Code of Practice establishes the duties of the Labour Migration Offices. They are as follows:
1) the execution of the Labour Migration Policy of each country;
2) the control of migrant workers' movements;
3) the determination of needs of migrant workers and their rights under national law; and
4) participation in negotiations for the employment of temporary workers and frontier workers.

The procedure for recruitment depends upon the level of demand in the country of immigration and on the practice of the relevant Labour Migration Office.[81] Demand is assessed by reference to the kind of work involved, the type of contract and the duration of employment. The Junta suggested that special visas be issued to migrants and sought to define the 'family' of the migrant worker and to define demand more precisely. The Council for Social Affairs took up that suggestion. It proposed a Code of Practice to determine such matters. The Labour Office of the country of emigration will inform the migrant within thirty days if employment is available in the country of immigration. Documents are provided for visa applications. The workers' qualifications, experience, aptitude and state of health are verified. Requests from applicants with criminal records are not processed. If the worker is accepted, he is provided with a contract signed by the employers. The Labour Office ensures that the contract complies with conditions made in the offer of employment and with conditions agreed by both parties, and with the national labour legislation of the country of employment.[82]

Upon arrival, workers must go to the Labour Office of the host country. Travel facilities are provided for the migrant and his family on the journey to and from the country of immigration.[83] Points 25 and 26 of the Code of Practice cover principles of non-discrimination, whether based on sex, race, religion or nationality. Equal treatment of migrants with national workers is ensured in accordance with the legislation of the country of immigration. Point 28 allows for all migrants to remit savings to their country of origin and to export with them all personal effects acquired with their wages.

Temporary migrant workers are required to carry a work contract which gives details of the holder's employment. The migrant is guaranteed the right to enter at the beginning and to depart at the end of his contract and is assured that his income will be taxed only in the country in which he is working. The employer is to provide transport for temporary and frontier workers as well as occasional board and lodging, in accordance with the standards established for local workers under the national law of the host State.[84]

Chapter Nine of the Code of Practice as signed by the Employment Ministers deals with the question of undocumented migrant workers.[85] The Code aims to regularize the position of undocumented migrants who entered countries before the Code entered into operation. It proposes the creation of information and documentation centres coupled with an information campaign aimed at areas with a high proportion of irregular workers.[86] To avoid deportation and obtain the relevant documents, a migrant must produce national identification papers and prove that he has been engaged in employment which is lawful in all respects other than immigration law. For reasons of State sovereignty the country of immigration retains the right to deny a worker permission to stay in the country. His removal is to comply with all principles of human rights.[87]

Quite separate arrangements have been made within the Andean Pact to ensure the transferability of social security entitlements. The Employment Ministers of the Andean Region established the Andean Charter for Social Security[88] to guarantee the equality of treatment and the conservation of the rights of migrant workers covered by respective national legislation of the Member States. As with the Labour Migration Charter, this agreement was passed on to the Commission of the Pact of Cartagena. Both the Junta of the Pact and Council for Social Affairs have issued reports on social security code of practice.

The Charter applies to three main branches of social security: illness and maternity; invalidity, old age and death; and industrial accidents and illnesses. It is applicable to specialized and general social security systems, including the obligations of the employer. The benefits of the Charter extend to members of the family of migrant workers; and the benefits may be claimed by any such persons without discrimination on grounds of nationality.[89] The object of the instrument is to secure aggregation of periods of insurance and to avoid duplication of contributions. To these ends, it creates an administrative commission.

The Andean Pact and the instruments adopted thereunder do not aspire to produce the transnational qualities seen in European Community law. It is the duty of contracting States to secure the observation of the Pact and its subordinate instruments in the domestic legal system. Recent Colombian[90] legislation is designed to fulfil this obligation, as is some older legislation adopted in Peru[91] and Ecuador.[92]

It is within the Nordic Community that the relaxation of national controls on migration by means of international agreement has reached its most advanced stage of development. The Nordic Community's instruments on the matter may be classed within three groups, dealing respectively with the passport union, the common labour market and the recognition of social security entitlements.[93]

By a Protocol dated 22 May 1954 the Danish, Finnish, Norwegian and Swedish Governments decided that as from 1 July that year nationals of those four countries should no longer be required to have a passport or other travel document when travelling between those countries, nor to be in possession of a residence permit when residing in a Scandinavian country other than their own.[94] By a subsequent exchange of notes, Iceland participated in the agreement.[95] The arrangements so made were extended by a Convention concluded in 1957 which made provision for the waiver of passport control at the intra-Nordic frontiers.[96] Since the practical benefits of that Convention are enjoyed by nationals of States other than Nordic States, the Convention establishes common standards for the maintenance of passport control on the part of all parties.

The essential features of the Nordic labour market were set by an agreement concluded on 22 May 1954, simultaneously with the Protocol on the passport union.[97] This abolished work permits for Nordic nationals employed in Nordic States and provided for administrative cooperation to match the supply of labour with demand. A series of subsequent agreements amplifies the principles established in 1954, notably by making provision for mutual recognition of qualifications.[98]

The Nordic Social Security Convention of 5 March 1981 has as its object the establishment of a system in which nationals of Denmark, Finland, Iceland, Norway and Sweden, while working in any of those countries, shall enjoy the same social security benefits as nationals of the State of employment, irrespective of the nationality of the worker.[99] The benefits of the Convention are extended to refugees established within any of those States and to nationals of those States who are resident in Nordic countries other than their own but not employed.

NOTES

1. The Hague, 3 February 1959, 5 Ybk. (1959) 167. See generally, J.W. Schneider, 'The Benelux Court', 4 Neths. Ybk. Int. L. (1973) 193.
2. Treaty of Schengen, 14 June 1985, J.O.R.F. 5 August 1986, Articles 1, 2, 3, 4, 5, 17, 18, 20.
3. Luxembourg, 17 February 1986 and The Hague, 28 February 1986, Bull. Supp. 2/86, p. 25.

4. 17 and 28 April 1945, 41 U.N.T.S. 265.
5. 2 and 15 July 1949, 41 U.N.T.S. 13.
6. 22 and 29 March 1950, 68 U.N.T.S. 45.
7. 6 April 1950, 65 U.N.T.S. 147.
8. 13 and 19 September 1950, 79 U.N.T.S. 328.
9. 26 March 1953, 165 U.N.T.S. 297.
10. 24 February and 5 March 1955, 213 U.N.T.S. 387.
11. Belgo-Luxembourg Agreement of 4 April 1955, 211 U.N.T.S. 571; Netherlands-Luxembourg Agreement of 4 May 1955, 292 U.N.T.S. 17; Belgo-Netherlands Agreement of 29 July 1954 and 13 January 1955, 210 U.N.T.S. 63 and 16 February 1955, 211 U.N.T.S. 49.
12. Belgo-Netherlands Agreement of 14 January – 4 February 1958, 330 U.N.T.S. 83.
13. 381 U.N.T.S. 158.
14. Brussels, 20 March 1957, *Bulletin trimestriel Benelux* No. 1 June 1957, p. 31.
15. See D. Turack, *The Passport in International Law*, 1971, at 89–93.
16. 381 U.N.T.S. 165; Annex IX.6.
17. By Article 6, 'Without prejudice to the provisions of Articles 2 to 5 above, the High Contracting Parties shall jointly ensure that no law or regulation, in particular public health regulations, should unduly hinder freedom of movement'.
18. Brussels, 11 April 1960. Benelux Convention Establishment, VIII *Ann. Eur.* (1960) 169; Convention concerning the Transfer of Entry and Exit Controls to the External Frontiers of Benelux Territory, 374 U.N.T.S. 3; *Basic Documents* IX.7.
19. On the entry into force of the Convention the Benelux Committee of Ministers made a Decision specifying the kinds of identity documents that would be accepted for such purposes: 1 October 1963, *Bulletin Benelux*, 1963–5, p. 41.
20. Agreement with Belgium, Geneva, 20 February 1933 and Protocol and Exchange of Notes, Brussels, 7 January 1936, 165, L.N.T.S. 383; Agreement with Luxembourg, The Hague, 1 April 1933, 179 L.N.T.S. 11. See J. Schneider, 'The Netherlands and Benelux' in T.M.C. Asser Institute, *International Law in the Netherlands*, 1979, Vol. II, p. 99.
21. Articles 2, 4 and 8.
22. Brussels, 11 April 1960; VII *Ann. Eur.* (1960) 175; 374 U.N.T.S. 3.
23. Article 2.
24. Article 4.
25. Articles 5 and 8.
26. Articles 11 and 12.
27. J. van Winkel, 'Het Personenverkeer in de Benelux', 30 *Sociaal-Economische Wetgeving; Tijdschrift voor Europees, Nederlands en Belgisch Sociaal Recht* (1982) 552. The arrangements made by the ministerial Working Party are published in *Nederlands Tractatenblad* 1971 No. 107 and *Nederlands Tractatenblad* 1978 No. 171. The Interparliamentary Benelux Council presented to the Governments a review of achievements in the first twenty-five years with proposals for future action. For the text, see *Nederlandse Staatscourant* 10 May 1982.
28. See I. Fall, '*De la liberté de circulation et d'établissement dans les communautés de l'Afrique de l'ouest*', 34 Rev. jur. et pol., indep. et coop. (1980) 92; O. Goundian, '*Liberté de circulation en Afrique francophone*', 34 Rev. jur. et pol., indep. et coop. (1980) 45 at 62–63.
29. Abidjan, 17 April 1973; parties: Burkina Faso, Ivory Coast, Mali, Mauritania, Niger, Senegal. The agreement was foreshadowed by the brief *Protocole d'Accord* of Bamako, 21 May 1970: A. Peaslee, *International Governmental Organizations*, 3rd. ed., 1974, Part I, p. 1365.
30. Dakar, 27 October 1978; parties as in Treaty of Abidjan, *supra*, note 29. 'Subject to the provisions of laws governing police and public security, as well as the requirements of public health, nationals of Member States may enter the territory of any other Member State without restriction and may travel and remain there and leave such territory simply on production of a

290

valid national passport, without being required to comply with any antecedent formality, such as the obtention of a visa for entry or departure'.

31. Goundian, *supra,* note 28, at 62.
32. Abidjan, 3 June 1966; Peaslee, *supra,* note 29, p. 1361.
33. Fall, *supra,* note 28, at 95.
34. See M. Crowder, *West Africa under Colonial Rule,* 1968; and see *infra,* text at notes 46–48.
35. Fall, *supra,* note 28 at 98: 'In an Africa which is often a prey to political somersaults, there is, however, reason to fear that they will be applied in such a manner as to curtail the free movement of political opponents of the government of the time'.
36. *Supra,* Chapter VI, text at note 76.
37. Fall, *supra,* note 28 at 99.
38. C.E.A.O. Treaty, *supra,* note 29, Article 15.
39. Lagos, 28 May 1975, 14 I.L.M. (1975) 1200.
40. Benin, Burkina Faso, Cape Verde, Gambia, Ghana, Guinea, Guinea-Bissau, Ivory Coast, Liberia, Mali, Mauritania, Niger, Nigeria, Senegal, Sierra Leone, Togo. For antecedents see Articles of Association for the Establishment of an Economic Community of West Africa, Accra, 4 May 1967, 595 U.N.T.S. 287.
41. O. Yerokun, 'The Economic Community of West Africa; Its Evolution and Scope', 20 Ind. J.I.L. (1980) 284 at 298–299 and 304–305; R. Onwuka, 'The ECOWAS Protocol on Freedom of Movement of Persons: A Threat to Nigerian Security?' 81 *African Affairs* (1982) No. 323, p. 199.
42. *West Africa,* 25 May 1981, p. 1153.
43. Article 3(2).
44. *Infra,* Chapter 12, text at note 8.
45. See J. Gautron, '*La Communauté économique de l'Afrique de l'ouest: antécédents et perspectives*', A.F.D.I. (1975) 197.
46. 8 September 1961; parties as in Treaty of Tananarive, *infra,* note 48.
47. Brazzaville, 8 December 1964, 4 I.L.M. (1964) 699; parties: Cameroon, Central African Republic, Congo-Brazzaville, Gabon, Chad.
48. Tananarive, 27 June 1966, 637 U.N.T.S. 247; parties: Central African Republic, Upper Volta, Gabon, Niger, Dahomey, Madagascar, Ivory Coast, Senegal, Chad, Cameroon, Congo-Brazzaville, Togo.
49. Nairobi, 6 June 1967; Peaslee, *supra,* note 29, p. 382; parties: Kenya, Tanzania, Uganda.
50. Lusaka, 21 December 1981, 21 I.L.M. (1982) 479; signed by Comoros, Djibouti, Ethiopia, Kenya, Malawi, Mauritius, Somalia, Uganda, Zambia. For African organizations generally, see M. Ajomo, 'Regional Economic Organizations: The African Experience', 25 I.C.L.Q. (1976) 93.
51. 23. I.L.M. (1984), 945.
52. *West Africa,* 31 October 1983, at 2540.
53. Treaty establishing a Central African Economic and Customs Union, *supra,* note 47.
54. M. Marasinghe, 'Review of Regional Economic Integration in Africa with Particular Reference to Equatorial Africa', 33 I.C.L.Q. (1984) 39 at 55.
55. Article 40.
56. Annex VII to the Treaty, *supra,* note 50, at 987.
57. Article 2(2).
58. Article 2(4).
59. Article 5(1).
60. Article 3(4).
61. Antigua, 30 April 1968, 7 I.L.M. (1968) 935; parties: Antigua, Barbados, Dominica, Grenada, Guyana, Jamaica, Montserrat, St. Kitts-Nevis-Anguilla, Trinidad and Tobago.

62. Article 20(5).
63. Stockholm, 4 January 1960, 370 U.N.T.S. 3, Article 16; parties (at that time): Austria, Denmark, Norway, Portugal, Sweden, Switzerland, United Kingdom. See K. Simmonds, 'International Economic Organizations in Central and Latin America and the Caribbean: Regionalism and Subregionalism in the Integration Process', 19 I.C.L.Q. (1970) 376 at 390.
64. Chaguaranas, 4 July 1973, 947 U.N.T.S. 17. See C. Dundas, 'The Law and Practice of the Caribbean Community', (1979) West Indian L.J. 19 and *ibid.*, 'The Law of the Caribbean Community: A Statement', (1980) West Indian L.J. 13.
65. Annex, Article 38.
66. Letter dated 8 June 1973 from Ms Monica Joseph, Attorney General of St Vincent to D. Turack, as quoted in his article 'Freedom of Movement in the Caribbean Community', 11 Denver Jo. Int. L. and Pol. (1981) 37 at 45.
67. Turack, *supra,* note 66 at 46, and letter from B. Pollard, Legal Consultant, Caribbean Community Secretariat, 14 November 1986.
68. Bogotá, 26 May 1969, 8 I.L.M. (1969) 910. Venezuela took part in the negotiations but did not sign the agreement. For the Protocol on Special Treatment of Adherence by Venezuela, see 8 I.L.M. (1969) 939. Panama is an Associate Member, and Chile withdrew in October 1976. See further M. Casanova, '*La aproximación de las legislaciones relativas a la migración laboral y seguridad social en el Acuerdo de Cartagena*', 8 *Derecho de la Integración* (1975) 11.
69. *Decisión 70 de la Comisión del Acuerdo de Cartagena conteniendo las condiciones para la adhesión de Venezuela al Acuerdo y Acta final de las negociaciones entre la Comisión del Acuerdo de Cartagena y el Gobierno de Venezuela para la adhesión de dicho pais al Acuerdo,* Lima, 13 February 1973, effective at 1 January 1974. In October 1972 Mexico became a working partner cooperating in financial and industrial development.
70. Montevideo, 19 July 1969; superseded by Treaty establishing the Latin American Integration Association, Montevideo, 12 August 1980, 20 I.L.M. (1981) 672.
71. Resolution 201 (CM-II VI-E); 203 (CM-II VI-E); 222 (VII). Resolution 179 (CEP), 9 July 1979, declares the compatibility of the Cartagena Pact with the Montevideo Treaty.
72. Participating States were Bolivia, Colombia, Chile, Ecuador, Peru and Venezuela. 20 March to 2 April 1973.
73. Those participating were the Employment Ministers of Colombia, Chile, Ecuador, Peru and Venezuela, the Bolivian Ambassador to Venezuela, government advisors and representatives of employers' and workers' organizations and representatives of international organizations. Caracas 22–27 October 1973. The meeting guidelines were formulated in the agenda and documents of the Commission of Delegates of Ministers held in Bogotá in August and September 1973.
74. I.L.O. Conventions: No. 48, Geneva, 22 July 1935, 8 Hudson 144; No. 87, Geneva, 9 July 1948, 68 U.N.T.S. 17; No. 88, Geneva, 9 July 1948, 70 U.N.T.S. 85; No. 97, Geneva, 1 July 1949, 120 U.N.T.S. 131; No. 98, Geneva, 1 July 1949, 96 U.N.T.S. 257; No. 102, Geneva, 28 June 1952, 210 U.N.T.S. 131; No. 111, Geneva, 25 June 1958, 362 U.N.T.S. 31; No. 114, Geneva, 19 June 1959, 413 U.N.T.S. 59; No. 117, Geneva, 22 June 1962, 494 U.N.T.S. 249; No. 118, Geneva, 28 June 1962, 494 U.N.T.S. 271; No. 121, Geneva, 8 July 1964, 602 U.N.T.S. 259; No. 122, Geneva, 9 July 1964, 569 U.N.T.S. 65; No. 128, Geneva, 29 June 1967, 699 U.N.T.S. 185; No. 130, Geneva, 25 June 1969, 826 U.N.T.S. 3; and No. 131, Geneva, 22 June 1970, 825 U.N.T.S. 77.
75. The Conference of Employment Ministers held Ordinary Meetings once a year, the venue rotating amongst the Member States. At the request of at least three members an Extraordinary Meeting can be held (Article 8). The Secretary for Coordination is the permanent body of the Agreement and is based in the Ecuador Ministry of Employment in Quito (Article 11).
76. Councils for: Planning; Exchange and Monetary Affairs; Finance; Fiscal Policies; and International Trade.

292

77. The Second Conference of Employment Ministers of the Pact of Cartagena held in Caracas 22–26 October 1973 gave full support to a research programme on labour migration. The Organization of American States produced such a report: *Andean Labour Migration,* 5 G Ser II V, MLA I L, as submitted to the Technical Meeting on Andean Labour Migration, Lima, 17–21 June 1974.
78. The Junta and the Council for Social Affairs have also made studies and recommendations on this policy and their views have brought new elements into consideration, changing the emphasis of some of the Ministers' proposals.
79. Point 4.
80. Point 6.
81. Point 8.
82. Point 6 (c) and (d).
83. Points 22, 23 and 24.
84. Chapter VII, points 20 and 21.
85. Chapter 9 of the Junta's Report and Chapter 8 of the report issued by the Council for Social Affairs.
86. Points 30, 31 and 32.
87. Points 33 and 34. In addition, point 36 proposes that the fact that a worker does not possess papers or that he is to be repatriated should in no way diminish his labour rights which protect him from his employer.
88. Second Conference of Employment Ministers, *supra,* note 77. *Derecho de la Integración* No. 17, p. 108 *et seq.*
89. Points 3, 4 and 5.
90. Decreto No. 1000 of 26 March 1986.
91. Circular of 21 October 1983.
92. Decreto No. 1899 (Ley de Migracion) and Decreto No. 1900 (Reglamento para Ley de Migracion), 30 December 1971.
93. See generally W. von Eyber, 'Inter-Nordic Legislative Cooperation', 6 *Scandinavian Studies in Law* (1962) 63; H. Kling, *La Cooperation Internordique,* 1965 at 99; G. Petrer, 'Scandinavian Cooperation', 2 Ann. Eur. (1956) 60.
94. Copenhagen, 22 May 1954, 198 U.N.T.S. 47.
95. Stockholm, 3 November 1955, 199 U.N.T.S. 29.
96. Copenhagen, 12 July 1957, 322 U.N.T.S. 245.
97. *Supra,* note 94.
98. Oslo, 28 June 1976, Swedish Treaty Series No. 118 (1976); Sverdborg, 25 August 1981, Swedish Treaty Series No. 103 (1983); Copenhagen, 6 March 1982, Swedish Treaty Series No. 92 (1983).
99. Copenhagen, 5 March 1981, Swedish Treaty Series No. 50 (1982).

BIBLIOGRAPHY

M. Casanova, 'La aproximación de las legislaciones relativas a la migración laborial y seguridad social en el Acuerdo de Cartagena', 8 *Derecho de la integración* (1975) 11.

I. Fall, *'De la liberté de circulation et d'établissement dans les communautés de l'Afrique de l'Ouest'*, 34 Rev. jur. et pol., indep. et coop. (1980) 92.

O. Goundian, *'Liberté de circulation en Afrique francophone'*, 34 Rev. jur. et pol., indep. et coop. (1980) 45.

R. Onwuka, 'The ECOWAS Protocol on Freedom of Movement of Persons: A Threat to Nigerian Security', 81 *African Affairs* (1982) 199.

293

G. Petren, 'Scandinavian cooperation', 2 Ann. Eur. (1956) 60.

J. Schneider, 'The Benelux Court', 4 Neths. Ybk. Int. L. (1973) 193.

E. Theuser, *Fri Bevaelighed for Arbejdskraft, Etablering og Tjenesteydelser i Ef og Norden*, 1984.

D. Turack, *The Passport in International Law,* 1971.

J. van Winkel, '*Het Personenverkeer in de Benelux*', 30 *Sociaal-Economische Wetgeving* (1982) 552.

CHAPTER 9

Migration for Employment

There is a basis for maintaining that migration for employment was the first type of migration to be subjected to systematic international regulation. In recent years, and for more than half a century, the principal agent in the establishment of the regulatory system has been the International Labour Organization. So great has been the influence of that institution in this sphere, and so unusual are the arrangements made for the enforcement of conventions and the implementation of recommendations adopted under the aegis of that body, that we must begin with an account of its origins and constitution.

THE INTERNATIONAL LABOUR ORGANIZATION

The history of the International Labour Organization can be traced to 1897, when the International Association for Labour Organizations was established by private parties. Its permanent office was located in Basle in 1901 and given the name 'The International Labour Office'. This institution stimulated the first official conference of governmental representatives concerned with labour in Berne, four years later. In the period before the First World War the International Labour Office established itself as a forum for the conclusion of multilateral conventions dealing with questions of employment. Perhaps the best known of its products was the International Convention respecting the Prohibition of Night Work for Women in Industrial Employment.[1] During the course of the Great War a campaign was waged by labour organizations within the allied and neutral States to place the International Labour Office on a more durable and official basis. Resolutions adopted by the General Federation of Trades Unions of Great Britain (in 1916) and by workers' congresses in allied and neutral States (in 1917) called for the insertion of provisions to this effect in the peace treaty.

Accordingly, Part XIII of the Treaty of Versailles[2] established the constitution of the I.L.O. as a public international institution. The preamble to that part of the Treaty recorded that 'conditions of labour exist involving such injustice, hardship and privation to large numbers of persons as to produce unrest so great that the peace and harmony of the world are imperilled; and an improvement in these conditions is urgently required; as for example . . . the . . . protection of the interests of workers when employed in countries other than their own'. During the inter-war period, the organization promoted several conventions designed wholly or in part to protect migrants for employment.

Among them was the Convention concerning the Simplification of the Inspection of Emigrants on board Ship[3] which established two principles in particular. The first was the principle that the official inspection carried out on board an emigrant vessel for the protection of emigrants should be undertaken by not more than one government; the second was that the inspector should ensure the observance of the rights which emigrants possess under the laws of the country whose flag the vessel flies, or such other law as is applicable, or under international agreements, or the terms of their contracts of transportation.[4] That Convention remains in force, but the I.L.O. ceased in April 1986 to promote its ratification, reasoning that migration by ship had practically ceased to exist. Two further agreements concluded in 1926 aspired to improve the legal position of seamen, by regulating their articles of agreement[5] and the conditions of their repatriation.[6]

A Convention concerning Forced or Compulsory Labour,[7] concluded under the aegis of the organization, imposed restrictions on the use of forced or compulsory labour, meaning any work or service exacted from a person under the menace of any penalty and for which the worker has not offered himself voluntarily. That convention contained two elements of special relevance to migrants for employment: in general, forced or compulsory labour was to be remunerated at rates not less than those prevailing in the district in which the labour is employed or in the district from which the labour was recruited, which ever may be the higher; and except in case of special necessity, persons from whom forced or compulsory labour might be exacted should not be transferred to districts where the food and climate differ so considerably from those to which they have been accustomed as to endanger their health.[8]

By a pair of conventions, one concluded in 1936[9] and the other in 1939,[10] members of the organization regulated the recruitment and employment of 'indigenous workers', meaning those belonging or assimilated to the indigenous populations of their dependent territories or to dependent indigenous populations of their home territories. In particular, the Contracting States agreed to take such measures as might be necessary to avoid the risk of pressure being brought to bear on the populations concerned by or on behalf of employers to obtain the labour required; and to take into account, before granting permission to recruit in any area, the possible effects of the withdrawal of adult males on the social life of the population concerned.[11] Workers who were brought to the place of employment by the employer or a person acting on the employer's behalf were to be entitled to be repatriated at the employer's expense, not only at the expiration of the period of employment but also in other instances, including the worker's inability to fulfil the contract owing to illness or accident. Where a contract made in one territory related to employment in another, the worker's rights were to be enlarged and his enjoyment of those rights supervised in accordance with the treaty.[12]

In 1939 the International Labour Conference approved a Migration for Employment Convention and made the first Migration for Employment Recommendation and a related measure, the Migration for Employment (Cooperation between States) Recommendation.[13] The Convention never gained sufficient ratifications to enter into force; but it was a forerunner for the Convention of the same title adopted in 1949.

At the conclusion of the Second World War, the constitution of the International Labour Organization was revised, notably in the light of a Declaration made in Philadelphia on 10 May 1944. The latter, which is now annexed to the Constitution, sets out the organization's fundamental principles, among which is the principle that labour is not a commodity and that all human beings have the right to pursue their material well-being and spiritual development in conditions of dignity.[14]

In its present form, the I.L.O. is unique among international organizations in that it has as its principal organs tripartite regulatory bodies on which representatives of employers and employees are given a status equal to that of governments. The plenary or parliamentary organ of the organization is the International Labour Conference. This is composed of two delegates representing governments, and one each representing workers and employers. All are nominated by the Governments of Member States; but those delegates representing workers' organizations or employers' organizations must be chosen by agreement with the organizations concerned. The administrative or secretarial body is the International Labour Office, situated in Geneva and staffed by an international secretariat. Between the two organs there exists a governing body, composed of two groups in equal numbers: the one representing Governments of Member States and the other representing their employers' and employees' organizations. The governing body supervises the International Labour Office and arranges for the conduct of preliminary studies into matters to be raised before the International Labour Conference.[15]

The latter is competent to adopt Conventions or Recommendations. In either event, two thirds of the votes cast on a final vote are required for the adoption of the measure. In the case of Conventions, each Member State undertakes to bring the instrument before the authorities within whose competence it lies to enact the legislation made necessary thereby. If the competent

298

authorities consent to the adoption of the legislation, the Member State will communicate its formal ratification; if not, its obligations in respect of that Convention are extinguished. In the case of Recommendations, each Member State undertakes to bring the instrument before the authority within whose competence the matter lies for enactment of legislation. There is a further obligation: to report at appropriate intervals at the request of the governing body on the Member State's law and practice with respect to the Recommendation.[16]

Each Member State undertakes to report to the International Labour Office every second year (on the more important conventions) or every four years (in other cases) on the measures it has taken to give effect to the provisions of Conventions to which it is a party.[17] Representations may be made to the International Labour Office by any independent association of employers or employees that a Member State has failed to secure in any respect the effective observance of any Convention to which it is a party.[18] Any Member may file a complaint with the I.L.O. if not satisfied that any other Member is securing the effective observance of a Convention to which it is a party.[19] On the receipt of such a complaint, the governing body may appoint a commission of enquiry and make recommendations to the Government of the Member State concerned. Each of the Governments concerned, if it does not accept the recommendations of the governing body, may refer the complaint to the International Court of Justice, which may appoint assessors and must receive any information communicated by the International Labour Office. That information may include representations made by employers, employees or their respective associations.[20]

THE MIGRATION FOR EMPLOYMENT CONVENTION (REVISED) 1949

By the summer of 1948 international migration for employment had become an issue of major international concern and a source of friction between the principal powers. The United Nations Organization had a permanent interest in the subject by reason of Article I(ii) and (iii) of the Charter.[21] The World Bank[22] and the International Refugee Organization[23] concerned themselves with the subject, as objects of economic and humanitarian concern. An incidental interest was expressed by U.N.E.S.C.O. and F.A.O. Above all, the International Labour Organization maintained an interest by reason of the Declaration of Philadelphia and the moribund but influential Convention of 1939.[24] The American Federation of Labour had called upon the Economic and Social Committee to promote the adoption in Europe of the I.L.O.'s Convention and Recommendations of 1939, so as to reduce the difficulties which might otherwise arise from the absorbing of millions of refugees. The

Soviet Union, on the other hand, argued that countries should create high standards of living at home by promoting progressive social policies, rather than exploit migrant workers and the countries from which they came. At the same time it demanded the repatriation of 'quislings, traitors and war criminals'.[25]

Such were the circumstances in which the governing body of the I.L.O. convened a meeting of its Permanent Migration Committee in January 1949. The Committee endorsed a decision taken by the governing body in the preceding March to revise the Migration for Employment Convention and Recommendations. The product of the Conference was the Convention concerning Migration for Employment (Revised) 1949: [26] a Treaty now ratified by 38 States. Based on a model proposed by the United States, it consists of a relatively general treaty together with three specific annexes. The first deals with recruitment and conditions of work for those recruited other than under government-sponsored arrangements; the second deals with recruitment and conditions of work for those recruited under government-sponsored arrangements; and the third deals with the importation of personal effects and tools.

Whereas the Convention of 1939 had provided in rather general terms for equality of treatment between migrants and nationals[27] the new Convention stipulates that immigrants will enjoy treatment no less favourable than that accorded to nationals in respect of remuneration, membership of trades unions and accommodation,[28] 'in so far as such matters are regulated by law or regulations, or are subject to the control of the administrative authorities'. The addition of accommodation to the areas in which immigrants and nationals were to be treated equally proved both controversial (at the time) and influential (later). Moreover, the Convention of 1949 specified that equality in respect of trade union rights was to entail 'enjoyment of the benefits of collective bargaining': the phrase was absent from the Convention of 1939 and its insertion in that of 1949 has proved to be an additional obstacle to the ratification of the instrument by the States of Eastern Europe.

In some respects, however, the Convention of 1949 proved more modest than its sponsors had desired. Thus, Article 4 provides that 'measures shall be taken as appropriate by each Member, within its jurisdiction, to facilitate the departure, journey and reception of migrants for employment'. The measures to be taken in accordance with that Article are spelled out in the first two Annexes: they include the simplification of administrative formalities, the provision of interpretative services, 'any necessary assistance during an initial period in the settlement of the migrants' and the safeguarding of their welfare.[29] Contrary to the wishes of the workers' group, the Convention fails to state that the measures to be taken shall include the provision of financial assistance; and those measures are not included in the text but in the Annex (so that they can be excluded by Contracting States[30]). Only in the Annex relating to government-sponsored migration is it stated that the competent authorities are bound to take appropriate measures to assist those migrants for employment who are considered unsuitable for the employment for which they were recruited.[31] The Convention provides (subject to qualifications) that a migrant for employment admitted on a permanent basis, and any member of his family admitted to accompany or join him, shall not be returned to his country of origin if he becomes unable to pursue his occupation by reason of an illness or injury arising after his admission.[32] This provision, although expressed subject to qualifications, met with opposition from an important country of immigration, Canada.[33] Representatives of that State argued that it would impose an intolerable burden on countries which admitted migrants for employment on a permanent basis without a probationary period. Accordingly, the provision was qualified further. Where migrants for employment are admitted on a permanent basis on arrival, the competent authority of the State of employment may reserve the power to deport them and their dependants, in the event of incapacity to work, if such incapacity arises within a reasonable period, which may not exceed five years measured from the date of arrival.[34]

Like the Convention of 1939, that of 1949 requires the parties to take steps against misleading propaganda relating to immigration and emigration,[35] and to secure the maintenance of an adequate service designed to supply information to migrants.[36] Like the Convention of 1939, that of 1949 is inapplicable to frontier workers and seamen. Also excluded from the Convention of 1949 is the 'short-term entry of members of the liberal professions and artistes'. Migration for employment is defined as meaning the migration of a person from one country to another with a view to being employed otherwise than on his own account.[37] The definition excludes many of those who were eligible for protection under the Convention on indigenous workers: those who migrated within the borders of a State, including those travelling from colonial to metropolitan territories.

Nevertheless, the Convention of 1949 remains to be ratified by a significant proportion of the world's States of immigration, including Argentina, Australia, Canada, South Africa and the United States. Certain of the West European countries of immigration have ratified the Convention itself while excluding the Annexes: France excluded Annex II and the United Kingdom excluded both Annexes I and II.

THE MIGRATION FOR EMPLOYMENT RECOMMENDATION (REVISED) 1949

In place of the two Recommendations adopted in 1939 – one dealing with the direct recruitment of migrants and the other with cooperation between States relating to that issue – the International Labour Conference of 1949 adopted a single Recommendation concerning Migration for Employment. To this was annexed a Model Agreement on Temporary and Permanent Migration for Employment, which was to be used by Members of the Organization as inspiration for bilateral agreements, to be concluded in accordance with paragraph 21 of the Recommendation.

The first section of the Recommendation, covering paragraphs 1–3, deals with points of definition. Migration for employment is given the same signification in the Recommendation as in the Convention.[38] The Recommendation is, however, so framed as to embrace refugees and displaced persons. Accordingly, and at the request of the Preparatory Commission for the International Refugee Organization, the Recommendation contains a statement to the effect that wherever reference is made to the competent authority of a State of emigration, a body established in accordance with an international instrument should take the place of that body, in the case of refugees and displaced persons.[39]

Paragraph 4 of the Recommendation, which constitutes a section by itself, creates a general duty to facilitate the movement of manpower from areas of labour surplus to those of labour deficiency. The next section, comprising paragraphs 5–12, deals with the provision of information and measures for facilitating migration generally. Paragraphs 6 and 7, which were inserted on the initiative of the Swiss Government, are designed to provide for the exchange of information between Member States via the International Labour Office in conformity with Article 1 of the Convention. These paragraphs require States to supply information about their emigration and immigration laws respectively.

The key paragraph in this part of the Recommendation is paragraph 10 (numbered 9 in the proposed text). This was also the product of a Swiss proposal. It sets out five means by which States are to facilitate migration. By contrast, the original version of paragraph 9 listed seven means: the parties have excluded from the list obligations in respect of insurance and naturalization. Moreover, in the version approved by the Conference, the five remaining means of assisting migration are expressed in more guarded terms than in the original.[40] Migration should be facilitated 'by such measures as may be appropriate' to ensure that migrants for employment are provided in case of necessity with accommodation, food and clothing; and to ensure vocational training and access to schools. States are to take appropriate measures to permit the transfer of migrant workers' earnings 'taking into account the limits allowed by national laws'. They are also to take appropriate measures to arrange for the transfer of migrants' capital to the country of employment 'within the limits allowed by national laws'.

Paragraphs 13–15 are carried over from the Recommendation of 1939 dealing with the recruitment of migrants. In the main, they deal with the regulation of persons or bodies undertaking the operations of recruitment, introduction and placing of migrants.

The following section comprises provisions concerning equality of treatment generally. It was taken over from the 1939 Recommendation (paragraph 12). The Swiss Government, in the course of the discussion of this provision, proposed its deletion. The United States, on the other hand, asked that it should be included in the Convention. In the event, it was decided to retain it in the Recommendation in its original form.[41]

In present economic circumstances it is, perhaps, in paragraphs 18–20 that the greatest significance lies. These deal with the removal of migrants to their countries of origin on account of indigence or unemployment and with the availability of social assistance at the destination. Paragraph 18 is expressed in guarded terms. It applies only to migrants for employment regularly admitted to the territory of a Member. Members are asked to refrain 'as far as possible' from removing such persons. The recommendation to refrain from such action applies only in the absence of an agreement to this effect between the countries of immigration and emigration concerned. Such agreements, however, must conform with paragraph 18(2), which excludes 'in principle' the possibility of removing on these grounds a migrant who has been in the country of immigration for five years; and the principle inspiring this paragraph has been elaborated in the Recommendation of 1975.

Paragraph 20 recommends that a State's provisions governing poor relief, unemployment relief and the promotion of re-employment should extend to nationals of that State on their return from another State in which they or the head of their family have been employed.

THE MIGRANT WORKERS (SUPPLEMENTARY PROVISIONS) CONVENTION 1975

For twenty years following the adoption of the Migration for Employment Recommendation (Revised) 1949 demand for labour in the industrialized States remained at a high level. In such circumstances, few voices were raised to challenge the proposition that States should pursue a policy of facilitating the international distribution of manpower from areas of labour surplus to areas of deficiency. That proposition was reiterated in Recommendation No. 122 concerning Employment Policy, although there was a suggestion that migration for employment can be damaging to developing countries.[42] Paragraph 33 of that Recommendation read as follows:

International migration of workers for employment which is consistent with the economic needs of the countries of emigration and immigration, including migration from developing countries to industrialized countries, should be facilitated, taking into account the provisions of the Migration for Employment Convention and Recommendation (Revised) 1949, and the Equality of Treatment (Social Security) Convention 1962.[43]

By 1975, however, the effects of the recession had become perceptible in the deliberations of the International Labour Conference. The new mood affected both the preamble and the contents of the Convention concerning Migrations in Abusive Conditions and the Promotion of Equality of Opportunity and Treatment of Migrant Workers (in short, the Migrant Workers (Supplementary Provisions) Convention 1975).[44] The preamble refers to the 'need to avoid the excessive and uncontrolled or unassisted increase of migratory movements', 'the desirability of encouraging the transfer of capital and technology rather than the transfer of workers', and 'the existence of illicit and clandestine trafficking in labour'. In this context, the reference to the 'right of everyone to leave any country, including his own' is merely adjectival. It is designed to ensure that the international approval of new standards applicable to clandestine immigration cannot be construed as a sanctioning of controls on emigration contrary to the International Covenant on Civil and Political Rights.

During the course of the deliberations on the text of the Convention, several Members desired to have the expression 'migrant workers' defined so as to include for some and exclude for others various categories of migrant workers, such as short-term seasonal workers, short-term workers and frontier workers.[45] No definition appears in Part I of the Convention of 1975, which deals with migrations in abusive conditions, and the expression must therefore be construed in a broad sense to include temporary as well as permanent migration. For the purposes of Part II, which deals with equality of opportunity, a definition is given on the basis of the definition of 'migration for employment' in the Convention of 1949.[46] The groups excluded from Part II of the Convention of 1975 include not only the three categories excluded from the Convention of 1949,[47] but also persons coming specifically for the purposes of education or training and employees of organizations or undertakings who have been admitted temporarily to that country at the request of their employer to undertake specific duties or assignments for a limited and defined period of time, and who are required to leave that country on the completion of their duties or assignments.

The greater part of the provisions of Part I of the Convention of 1975 are devoted to the suppression of clandestine migration. The tone is set by Article 2 (originally Article 1 of the Office's draft) which requires States Parties to seek to detect any movements of migrants for employment contravening relevant international instruments or national laws. This Article must be read in the most general sense. Its purpose is to ascertain whether such movements are taking place and not to require States to investigate penal offences. It was on the basis of such a construction of its own draft that the Office decided to make no change, in response to the United Kingdom's objection that it appeared to set different standards for different States, according to their participation in international agreements or the form of their national laws.[48] By Article 3, Contracting States agree to take all necessary and appropriate measures to suppress migration in abusive conditions, including measures against organizers of clandestine migration. To this end, they are to exchange information[49] and generally to collaborate for the purpose of ensuring 'that the authors of manpower trafficking can be prosecuted whatever the country from which they exercise their activities'.[50] That language is not to be read as imposing a duty to ensure that there is jurisdiction in a Contracting State to try an individual for a relevant offence committed abroad. The Article merely describes and defines the purpose of the forms of international collaboration set out in the antecedent provisions.[51]

Article 6 reads in part as follows: 'Provision shall be made under national laws . . . for the definition and the application of administrative, civil and penal sanctions, which include imprisonment in their range, in respect of the illegal employment of migrant workers'. The Article falls short of requiring the Parties to make provision for the imposition of penal sanctions on the employers of migrant workers 'in an irregular situation'.[52] It presupposes that national law renders unlawful the employer's act, not the alien's presence. Moreover, since national law is to define the sanctions, that law may determine whether they shall be administrative, civil or penal.

Part II of the Convention aspires to establish the principle of equality of opportunity and treatment. By Article 10, each party undertakes to pursue a national policy designed to guarantee equality of opportunity and treatment 'for persons who as migrant workers or as members of their families are lawfully within its territory'. The Article fails to specify that it is concerned with equality as between migrants on the one hand and nationals on the other, rather than equality as between migrants of diverse nationalities. That the former construction is intended appears with sufficient clarity from the accompanying Recommendation[53] which states in Article 2 that migrant workers and members of their families lawfully within the territory of a Member should enjoy effective equality of opportunity and treatment with nationals of the Member concerned. Such equality is to be promoted, in the case of Parties to the Convention, in respect of employment and occupation, social security, trade union and cultural rights and individual and collective freedoms.

On ratifying the Convention, Member States are free to exclude either Part I or Part II. Despite this fact, the Convention has hitherto attracted only fifteen ratifications; and of the Parties to that instrument only one (Venezuela) is a major country of immigration.

Whereas the first Part of the Convention of 1975 is entitled 'Migrations in abusive conditions' and is largely devoted to the suppression of clandestine migration, the accompanying Recommendation is practically silent on these issues. It begins with a section on equality of opportunity and treatment, which amplifies Part II of the Convention.[54] Such equality is to be assured in nine respects, listed in Article 2. These include housing and the benefits of social services and remuneration for work of equal value. In the last of these respects the Recommendation is expressed in particularly broad terms, exceeding by a perceptible margin equal remuneration for equal work. It seems that Member States are called upon to make an assessment of the respective values of work performed by migrants and work performed by nationals, and to take steps to secure the equal rating of these types of employment.[55] By paragraph 6, however, a Member may make the free choice of employment subject to conditions that the migrant worker has resided lawfully in its territory for the purposes of employment for a period not exceeding two years.

Section II of the Recommendation, which accounts for 21 of the 34 paragraphs, deals with social policy, particularly in respect of family reunification, the protection of migrant workers' health and social services. The general principle to be applied in these three areas is that migrant workers and their families should be able to share in the advantages enjoyed by nationals of the host State, while taking into account such special needs as they may have pending their adaptation to society there.[56]

One of the advantages enjoyed by nationals of the host State is the freedom to live together. Accordingly, the Recommendation states that all possible measures should be taken to facilitate the reunification of families of migrant workers as rapidly as possible. That proposition is made subject to an important qualification. A prerequisite for reunification should be that the worker has, for his family, appropriate accommodation which meets the standards normally applicable to the nationals of the country of employment.[57]

The principle that migrant workers and their families should be able to share in advantages enjoyed by nationals of the host State also permeates the paragraphs of the Recommendation devoted to social services. Migrant workers and their families should benefit from the activities of social services under the same conditions as nationals of the country of employment. Furthermore, social services should be entrusted with certain functions related to the special needs of migrant workers and their families, particularly in assisting them to adapt to the conditions in the host country.[58]

The subsection concerned with the protection of the health of migrant workers contains no rule dealing with equality of treatment; but the omission is probably without significance, since the Recommendation provides elsewhere[59] that migrant workers and members of their families should enjoy effective equality with nationals of the host State in respect of health facilities. Rather, the subsection describes measures to be taken to prevent any special health risks to which migrant workers may be exposed.

Paragraph 18 of the Migration for Employment Recommendation (Revised) 1949 provides that Members should, as far as possible, refrain from removing from their territory, on account of lack of means or the state of the employment market, a migrant worker regularly admitted thereto.[60] Paragraph 30 of the Recommendation of 1975 adds that the loss by such a migrant worker of his employment should not in itself imply the withdrawal of his authorisation of residence. Furthermore, a migrant worker who is the object of an expulsion order should have a right of appeal before an administrative or judicial instance 'according to conditions laid down in national laws or regulations'.[61] Those ten words must be taken to mean that national law will determine such matters as the form and procedure of any appeal rather than its availability. The opposite construction would rob the antecedent words of their useful effect.

OTHER I.L.O. INSTRUMENTS

The Conventions of 1936 and 1939 on indigenous workers[62] were followed in 1947 by a new Convention concerning Social Policy in non-Metropolitan Territories.[63] Like the earlier Conventions, this dealt with social and labour policy in general but devoted one Part to migrant workers. The Articles in this Part of the Convention do not presuppose that the worker has migrated across an international border: they are equally applicable to migration within the borders of a dependent territory. The terms and conditions of the employment of migrant workers are to take account of normal family needs; and when workers move from low-cost areas to those of higher cost, account is to be taken of the increased cost of living resulting from the change.[64] Where, however, the labour resources of an area are used in an area under different administration (whether subject to the same sovereign or not) the competent authorities of the two areas are to enter into agreements, whenever necessary or desirable, for the purpose of regulating matters of common concern.[65]

Convention No. 117 concerning Basic Aims and Standards of Social Policy[66] is also devoted to issues broader in compass than the situation of migrant workers. It contains statements of social objectives in terms sufficiently broad to exact the support of States as diverse as Syria and Israel, Kuwait and Vietnam. The Part dealing with migrant workers is, however, based on the corresponding Part of the Convention of 1947 on Social Policy in non-Metropolitan Territories. Indeed, the latter Convention follows the wording of the earlier one *verbatim,* in these respects, save for the amendments made necessary by the application of the Convention of 1962 to the metropolitan territories of the States concerned.

The International Labour Organization has promoted two major Conventions dealing with social security entitlements, one in 1962[67] and one in 1982.[68] The guiding principle of the earlier Convention is as follows: each Contracting State will grant within its territory to nationals of any other for which the Convention is in force equality of treatment with its own nationals, both as regards coverage and as regards the right to benefits, in respect of every branch of social security for which it has accepted the obligations of the Convention.[69] Article 1 lists nine branches of social security, from medical care to family benefit. It stipulates that each Member may accept the obligations of the Convention in respect of any one or more of them. Thus, Contracting States may qualify any obligations they may assume under the Convention by selecting branches of social security *à la carte.* Moreover, by way of departure from the normal practice of the International Labour Organization, the Convention of 1962 is to be applied strictly on a basis of reciprocity.[70]

The Convention of 1982, on the other hand, applies to all nine of the branches of social security listed in Article 1, subject to any qualifications made by bilateral agreement between the Parties.[71] Moreover, the Convention of 1982 aspires to achieve ambitions exceeding formal equality of treatment: its objectives include the maintenance of rights in the course of acquisition, the maintenance of acquired rights and the provision of benefits abroad, together with the provision of administrative assistance. Hitherto it has attracted only two ratifications.

The International Labour Office (rather than the Council of Europe) was sponsor of a European agreement concluded in 1980 to regulate the provision of medical care to persons during temporary residence.[72] This aims to avoid conflicts of law and their consequences of lack of protection for workers. It also aspires to avoid undue plurality of contributions, or plurality of other liabilities.

The Recommendation on Employment Policy of 1964[73] at paragraph 33 encouraged States to recognize the interests of developing countries. In 1955 Recommendation No. 100 Concerning Protection of Migrant Workers in Underdeveloped Countries[74] touched upon these issues. The emphasis was on improving conditions under which free movement of such migrants may be encouraged. Part III of the Recommendation considered circumstances where the migration of workers from developing countries was to be discouraged in the interests of the workers or their country and community of origin. Measures were to be taken to improve conditions of life and to raise standards of living in the areas from which the migrations usually began. In addition, however, paragraph 17(b) urged a more rational use of manpower and increased productivity in the areas of immigration to remove the need for migrant workers from developing countries. The Recommendation went on to list at length rights and benefits, on the basis of parity with nationals, that were to be afforded to migrant workers.

In June 1983 the International Labour Conference examined proposals for a new Recommendation on Employment Policy to supplement that of 1974. The Employment Policy (Supplementary Provisions) Recommendation No. 169 of 1984 placed emphasis on the promotion of employment in the home countries of potential migrants.[75] Given high levels of unemployment in the countries of traditional immigration, the International Labour Conference initiated a policy of attempting to persuade industrialized States to invest in developing States, to transfer technical knowledge and increase trade as a way of reducing the outflow. In addition, the countries of emigration were urged to cooperate in this effort to re-attract their nationals from abroad. Further measures were suggested to find alternatives to migration (paragraph 40); to prevent abuses in employment and recruitment (paragraphs 41 and 43) and to encourage the voluntary return of nationals with scarce skills to their countries of origin (paragraph 42).

For some years now the International Labour Organization has been encouraging States bordering South Africa to reduce their dependence on that country and to curtail their supply of migrant workers there. The Conference on Migratory Labour in Southern Africa, held in Lusaka in 1978, under the auspices of the United Nations Economic Commission for Africa, adopted a Charter of Rights for Workers in South Africa. The International Labour Conference in 1981 adopted a Declaration on the Policy of Apartheid in South Africa, the sequel to a similar Declaration made in 1964. The permanent Committee on Apartheid of the International Labour Conference has also urged trade unions to organize campaigns to ensure that their members do not emigrate to South Africa and to exert pressure for the closure of South African recruitment offices.[76]

OTHER INTERNATIONAL INSTRUMENTS

Bilateral treaties have been employed to effect or facilitate the transfer of labour on a regular basis since the middle of the last century. In general, the provisions governing this matter in earlier treaties tended to be brief: the beneficiaries of assisted-passage migration were commonly imported as a solution to specific and temporary problems of manpower shortage or to aid the economic development of the receiving State. More recent treaties have tended to contain more detailed administrative regulations for the creation of links between the States of emigration and immigration and to facilitate the passage of migrant workers. Moreover, modern bilateral arrangements commonly contain provisions designed for the protection of workers abroad. Indeed, it has been argued that such treaties now constitute a major source of international legal norms in the protection of the human rights of aliens.[77]

Early post-war agreements between Australia and the United Kingdom made no mention of the rights of such migrants and there was no fear of discrimination on racial or ethnic grounds.[78] Australia later negotiated assisted passages and settlement for over 200,000 refugees with the International Refugee Organization. Australia's right of selection was subject to the requirement that it was not to be carried out with any discrimination on racial or religious grounds. Language and social instruction were also provided. There was not at this stage any guarantee of equal treatment with Australian nationals. In the 1950's Australia concluded bilateral treaties with the Netherlands, Italy and West Germany.[79] Article 6 of the Dutch agreement of 1951 related to family reunion and provided for a 'reasonable ratio' of family units to the number of migrants. Paragraph 13 of the schedule to the agreement guaranteed 'normal' social service benefits, implying equality of treatment in this area. Although the Italian agreement applied only to Italians of European descent, Article 7 entitled the migrant, during the two year period or work under government supervision, to wages, accommodation and general conditions of employment equal to those of Australian nationals. Article 17 allowed repatriation of funds to Italy for the support of dependant relatives or for any other justified reason.

European agreements of the period governing the transfer of labour tended to contain more explicit provisions governing human rights. An agreement between Belgium and Spain in 1956[80] allowed members of the immediate family of the migrant worker to join him once he had completed three months' government-supervised work. Their admission was subject, however, to the availability of accommodation. Almost all of the bilateral European agreements contained guarantees of equal pay, equal conditions of work and equal benefits in respect of social policy, health and safety; equality in this context denoted equality with national workers.

From the mid-1950's Western European industrialized States concluded similar agreements with governments of developing countries (as well as poorer European States).[81] Provisions were commonly contained within these treaties for the right of migrants to remain in Western Europe after the expiration of their contracts of employment. Often the migrant was required to take up a new contract and he continued to be supervised by the government. Nevertheless, there was a restriction of a host State's ability to expel aliens from its territory at will.

In Australia in 1956 a second Dutch agreement[82] provided for equality of treatment for Dutch migrants in the areas of wages and conditions of employment generally – beyond the initial three-year period. Whereas the first agreement with the Netherlands[83] expressly stated the purpose of the agreement to be 'the necessity of fostering the development of certain branches of both primary and secondary industries which are of vital importance to the Australian economy . . .', the second agreement was directed more specifically at the protection of the workers. Subsequent Australian treaties placed increasing emphasis on workers' rights. Article 24 of a treaty with Italy dated 1967[84] created a Charter of Rights exceeding any comparable provisions in such a bilateral agreement. Among the rights protected are rights of entry and sojourn (subject to national laws); equality with nationals before the law; freedom of religion and of association; the right not to be expelled from the host State except in accordance with the laws; equality of educational opportunity and social security benefits and ownership of property; and equality of treatment with respect to the right to establish business enterprises. Charters of rights are also to be found in agreements concluded by Australia subsequently.[85]

In the United States, national policies on migrant workers have been dominated in recent years by the problem of illegal or clandestine migration.[86] The absence of bilateral treaty arrangements to deal with this issues has proved an aggravating or complicating factor. Indeed, it has proved impossible to attain sufficient consensus to achieve even domestic legislation. The U.S. Bracero agreement with Mexico was discontinued in 1984. Since then the inflow of migrants has been largely unregulated.[87] In 1981 the Administration introduced the Temporary Mexican Workers Act under Title VI of the Omnibus Immigration Control Act.[88] This would have authorised the admission of 50,000 Mexican migrant workers to take employment lasting between nine and twelve months in states and in occupations where there was a shortage of local workers. The migrants would have been entitled to normal working conditions and wages but would not have been entitled to bring families with them nor to receive full welfare benefits. Neither this proposed legislation nor its successor was adopted by Congress.

Accordingly, it remained necessary to apply in the United States section 212(a)(14) of the Immigration and Nationality Act. This required that there must be insufficient able, willing and qualified available workers in the United States before a migrant would be admitted. Moreover, the employment of such aliens must not have been such as to affect adversely the wages and working conditions of the workers in the United States similarly employed.

On 17 October 1986, however, Congress finally passed the Immigration Reform and Control Bill. The Bill received Presidential assent and entered into force on 1 January 1987. It provided for an amnesty to be extended to those aliens in an irregular situation who had been resident in the United States continuously since a date not later than 1 January 1982. It also provided for the imposition of fines of not less than US $250 nor more than US $10,000 on employers of aliens in an irregular situation unless such employers could show that they had taken reasonable steps to satisfy themselves that the aliens were present lawfully.[89]

Since the start of the present world recession, the current trend has been to encourage the return of migrant workers or at least to discourage their movement to industrialized States. In 1980 France and Algeria concluded an agreement for the orderly return of migrant workers whom France was no longer able to employ.[90] The agreement provided for professional training; aid to finance businesses of returning migrants in Algeria; and a cash grant to those who did not benefit from either of the first two categories. It remains to be seen whether other States will follow this example. For the present, the instrument which commands the greatest attention for draftsmen of new bilateral agreements is not the Franco-Algerian treaty but a Convention in the making.

The Draft United Nations Migrant Workers Convention is the product of the United Nations' investigation of illicit and clandestine labour trafficking and of the migration of skilled workers from developing countries.[91] By the late 1970s the United Nations was becoming interested in the broader aspects of migration for employment and in general in the human rights of aliens. In 1974 Baroness Elles produced for the Sub-Commission on Prevention of Discrimination and Protection of Minorities a draft Declaration on the Human Rights of Individuals who are not Citizens of the Country in which they live.[92] After several revisions, a draft declaration on International Provisions Protecting the Human Rights of Non-Citizens was finally adopted by the Sub-Commission.[93] In 1979 the General Assembly decided to draft a general Convention on the human rights of migrant workers and their families. The Assembly established a Working Group to elaborate this Convention.[94] A comprehensive Convention is envisaged, covering all of the principal human rights to which legal and illegal migrant workers are entitled. Thus, its scope is intended to exceed that of the instruments of the International Labour Organization and the European Convention on the Legal Status of Migrant Workers.[95] In short, the draft Convention places the emphasis on the status of aliens as members of the population of the countries in which they live, even in the event of their illegal presence,[96] rather than as elements in economic policy related primarily to the labour market. It aspires to ameliorate the conditions of such aliens, particularly by securing an improvement in their conditions of employment.

The draft Convention has been prepared at a time of increasingly restrictive national provisions governing the admission of migrants for employment. In the following pages an account is given of the domestic laws and practices on migration for employment in States in all five continents.

In order to enter or remain in the United Kingdom for the purposes of employment (save for temporary employment of an exceptional nature) a non-citizen requires a work permit.[97] These are issued by the Department of Employment[98] and the number awarded each year depends upon the Department's assessment of the market's needs. Ordinarily, a work permit will not be issued if alternative labour is available locally. Several categories of employment are considered to be 'permit free'.[99] These are:

(a) ministers of religion;
(b) representatives of overseas companies which have no office or subsidiary in the United Kingdom;
(c) representatives of overseas newspapers and broadcasting agencies;
(d) doctors and dentists coming to take up professional appointments;
(e) private servants of diplomats;
(f) employees of international organizations of which the United Kingdom is a member;
(g) teachers coming under approved exchange schemes;
(h) seamen under contract to join ships in British waters;
(i) operational staff of overseas airlines; and
(j) seasonal workers at agricultural camps.

An entry clearance certificate is needed by any non-citizen, other than a national of a European Community State, seeking admission for the purposes of establishing himself in the United Kingdom in business or in self-employment[100] or as a writer, artist[101] or person of independent means.[102] However, those who have been legally admitted for these employment purposes are eligible to have the limit on their stay removed after they have been in the United Kingdom for four years.[103]

Migrant workers are able to enter the United Kingdom accompanied by a spouse and children under eighteen for the period of authorised stay, provided certain conditions are met.[104] In particular, the husband or father must be able and willing to maintain and accommodate his dependants without recourse to public funds, in accommodation of his own which he occupies himself.

Only workers between 23 and 53 years of age are eligible to obtain permits. A genuine vacancy must exist as permits are only issued for named overseas workers coming to fill a specified post. Generally, the vacancy must be in an occupation serviced by the Professional and Executive Recruitment which includes employment in professional, managerial, administrative, executive technical and scientific occupations. The worker must have an adequate command of the English language. There are eight categories of posts which will qualify for the issue of a permit and a permit will only be issued for jobs requiring workers in these categories. The eight categories are:

(1) those holding recognized professional qualifications;
(2) administrative and executive staff;
(3) highly qualified technicians having specialised experience;
(4) key workers with a high or scarce qualification in an industry requiring specific expert knowledge or skills;
(5) highly skilled and experienced workers for senior posts in hotel and catering establishments with the requisite qualifications;
(6) entertainers and sportsmen/women who meet the appropriate skills criteria;
(7) people coming for a limited period of training on the job or work experience approved by the Department of Employment;
(8) other persons only if, in the opinion of the Secretary of State for Employment, their employment is in the national interest.

The Department of Employment enjoys a wide discretion in determining whether to grant or withhold a permit to an applicant. Against its decision there is no right of statutory appeal.[105] Moreover, a non-citizen who has been granted leave to enter for temporary purposes (other than those of employment) has no claim to remain for any other purpose. In general, applications to remain for employment from persons admitted as visitors or students or from persons admitted for other temporary purposes should be refused without reference to the Department of Employment, unless the conditions subject to which the applicant was admitted left him free to take employment without the consent of the Secretary of State for Employment.[106] The Court of Appeal has suggested, however, that the Home Secretary cannot refuse unconsidered every application to vary limited leave by a person who has been refused a work permit by the Department of Employment.[107] Circumstances might arise in which such a refusal could be corrected by way of judicial review.

In 1984, 5,040 permits were awarded for admission to perform work for twelve months and 8,060 for less than twelve months.[108]

The United Kingdom maintains no system of imposing sanctions on employers of migrants in an irregular situation. An employer is in the same position as any other person, in that he commits an offence if he knowingly harbours an illegal entrant or assists in the commission of an offence against the Immigration Act.[109] The Commission of the European Communities has urged the United Kingdom to adopt a system of employer sanctions; its demand met with some resistance in the national and European Parliaments.[110]

Amnesties for illegal entrants have not been part of the United Kingdom's system of immigration regulation as they have been in certain other European countries, including France. In April 1974 the Home Secretary announced a limited amnesty for a specific purpose: to relieve of summary removal those who were exposed to that sanction following the decision of the House of Lords in *Azam and Others* v *Home Secretary*.[111] In the subsequent five years, some 2,430 applications were made to benefit from this amnesty; 621 (or 26%) of the applicants were found to be ineligible. In 1977 the amnesty was extended to cover those who had entered by deception between 1968 and 1973. 641 persons applied to benefit from the amnesty and 178 (or 28%) were found ineligible.[112]

WEST GERMAN PRACTICE

The Federal Republic of Germany began importing foreign workers or *gast-arbeiter* in 1955 and by 1973 it had a population of 2.6 million such workers. Although the active recruitment of foreign workers was halted in 1973, the number of foreigners living in the country continued to grow as dependants arrived from home countries and births of alien residents outpaced those of returning foreigners. By 1984 there were 4.4 million foreigners residing legally within the Federal Republic, 57% of whom had been there for more than ten years and 73% for more than six years.[113]

The legal instruments controlling the admission of migrant workers into the Federal Republic can be divided into two groups: general regulations applicable to all aliens (including migrant workers) and specific measures governing the admission of aliens who were specially recruited, together with members of their families. The basis of the general regulations continues to be the Aliens Act or *Auslandergesetz* of 1965,[114] which imposes the requirement to hold a residence permit, and the Work Promotion Law or *Arbeitsforderungsgesetz* of 1969, which imposes the requirement to hold a work permit.[115] The latter is amplified by the Work Permit Decree or *Arbeitserlaubnisverordnung* of 1971.[116]

Aliens, other than nationals of Member States of the European Communities, may not enter the Federal Republic with a view to remaining for more than three months, unless they are in possession of a residence permit, which is issued at the discretion of the authorities. The authorities' decision on the issuance of a residence permit is based on the 'interests' of the Federal Republic. The official policy is that the Federal Republic is not an immigration country.[117] Federal administrative guidelines provide that initial residence permits will be issued only for a one-year period, after which an extension for a two-year period may be granted. After five years of uninterrupted lawful residence, an alien may obtain a residence permit of indefinite duration, and after eight years lawful residence he may obtain a permanent residence permit, provided that he possess a special work permit and has adequate housing and a sufficient knowledge of the German language.[118] The Federal Administrative Court has held, however, that the longer an alien resides in West Germany, the stronger is his claim to remain. It follows that an alien's length of residence is to be taken into account in the event of a proposal to deport him; and in some cases a duty to approve a further stay arises.[119]

Work permits may be specific or non-specific. A specific work permit is issued for a particular job at a designated place of employment. Its issuance is conditioned by the state of the labour market. A non-specific permit is not restricted in location or duration and is granted only to those who have been employed in the Federal Republic for five years without interruption. A permanent work permit is granted to an alien only after ten years' residence.[120] Nationals of Member States of the European Communities are, of course, exonerated of the obligation to hold a work permit.[121] In 1976 the regulations were tightened to restrict immigration for employment: spouses who entered after November 1974 and children who entered after 1976 were no longer allowed to take employment.[122] In 1981 the *Arbeitsforderungsgesetz* (Law on Promotion of Employment) was strengthened by two measures. Firstly, it was provided that the issuance of a work permit for first employment was to be subject to a prior period of residence. Secondly, a sixth order dated 24 September 1981 stated that in order to qualify for a work permit as the spouse of an alien employee, an applicant should have lived in Germany for four years, or for three years if there is a serious shortage of labour in the sector concerned.[123]

Non-specific work permits are available to aliens married to German citizens, to political refugees and the spouses of Turkish workers who have resided in the territory of the Federal Republic for at least five years.[124]

The majority of migrant workers in the Federal Republic did not arrive in consequence of individual initiatives but in pursuance of programmes of recruitment.[125] Recruitment agreements were concluded between the Federal Republic of Germany and Italy,[126] Spain,[127] Greece,[128] Turkey,[129] Morocco,[130] Tunisia,[131] and finally Yugoslavia.[132] Such agreements provided for systems of 'State recruitment', whereby the labour authorities collected applications from German companies wishing to employ foreign labour and transmitted details of available labour to recruitment offices in the countries of emigration, after checking that the priority of the German domestic labour reservoir had been respected and that the contracts of employment conformed with a statutory model. The agreements with countries of emigration also made provision for 'visa recruitment', whereby the prospective employer nominated an aspiring immigrant and requested the issuance of a visa by the German mission in the country of emigration.From November 1973, however, the programmes of recruitment have been suspended: indeed, the system has been put into reverse.

In 1981 civil penalties of up to 50,000DM were provided for the employment of a foreign national (other than a European Community national) without a work permit.[133] In June 1985 this law was strengthened: the employment of more than five migrant workers without permits, contrary to the *Arbeits-forderungsgesetz*, became an offence punishable with imprisonment for up to one year and, in the event of a particularly serious infringement, imprisonment for a period not exceeding three years.[134]

In the past, the Federal Republic offered assistance to create employment in the countries of origin of migrant workers, together with legal and technical assistance and aid in planning, for the purpose of encouraging migrant workers to return home.[135] By a measure adopted in 1983, cash incentives were paid[136] to induce *gastarbeiter* to return home when they had no employment in Germany. To receive the inducement the worker had to leave with his whole family. In addition, returning workers were free to withdraw funds from savings accounts and pension funds without tax deductions.[137] The measure was applied for a temporary period only, ending in June 1984. It appears unlikely to be reintroduced.

FRENCH PRACTICE

Prior to the Second World War, immigration into France was organized by an association of the employers most affected by immigration, the *Société Générale d'Immigration*. From 1945, however, private recruitment was replaced by a public monopoly, the *Office Nationale de l'Immigration,* created as an intermediary between migrant and employer. It was envisaged that an alien wishing to migrate to France for the purposes of employment would apply in his country of origin to the O.N.I. which would organise the journey and secure respect for correct legal procedures, in the event of an offer of employment to the applicant. Employers would make their demands for labour known to the O.N.I. and satisfy that body that they were in a position to provide suitable housing and conditions of employment.[138]

Prior to its most recent reforms French law provided for a system of controlling migration for employment by work permits and residence permits. Work permits were available in three categories, denominated 'A', 'B' and 'C', valid for one year, three years and ten years respectively. Permits in the first two categories authorised the alien to take designated employment in a specified place, whereas 'C' permits bore no restrictions on the employment that might be taken. Residence permits were also available in three categories, valid for one year, three years or ten years. They were described as *cartes de séjour 'temporaires', 'ordinaires'* or *'priviligiées',*[139] The period of validity of a residence permit did not necessarily coincide with that of a work permit issued to the same migrant workers: for the former was controlled by the Department of Employment and the latter by the Department of the Interior. Since the adoption of the Law of 29 October 1981, the residence permit and work permit have been merged into a single document which may be issued for a period not exceeding three years.

As in the case of the Federal Republic of Germany, immigration into France for employment has been regulated not only by the general law but also by a series of bilateral treaty arrangements designed to facilitate the admission of workers from the contracting States. During the period between 1950 and 1963, the principal suppliers of labour under these treaty arrangements were the countries of Southern Europe.[140] Thereafter, until 1973, France's European partners in this exercise were replaced by certain of the States of North Africa.[141] The pattern is complicated, however, by the position of Algeria. Prior to the independence of that country in 1962, and for the first six years thereafter, migration for employment from Algeria to France was uncontrolled. In pursuance of a bilateral treaty concluded in 1968 a quota was established, initially at the rate of 35,000 migrants *per annum*,[142] but in 1973 the quota was abolished.[143] Indeed, in 1964 France concluded an exchange of notes with Canada to regulate the migration to that country of French settlers from North Africa, mainly from Algeria.[144]

The ambitions of draftsmen of the statutes and treaties have, however, often been frustrated in practice. Regular immigration in accordance with the statutory plan has been replaced in many instances by irregular migration for employment. The role of the *Office Nationale de l'Immigration* has in recent years been confined to the admission of the families of migrant workers. In the face of this trend, several French governments have pursued a policy of regularising the status of workers in an irregular situation. Between 1948 and 1981 more than 1,400,000 aliens benefited from regularisation of status, after remaining beyond the period of temporary employment arranged via the O.N.I. or taking employment although admitted for the purposes of visits.[145] In the first few years of the post-war period, 'regularisation' was taken up by about one migrant worker in ten but by 1968 it was estimated that 82% of the migrant workers in France were beneficiaries of regularisation.[146] Two administrative circulars issued in summer 1981 made provision for the regularisation of the status of alien workers who had entered France prior to January 1981 and had 'stable employment'.[147] At the same time, judicial and administrative sanctions were imposed on the employers of aliens in an irregular situation.[148] These sanctions included imprisonment for three months to a year and a fine of not less than 2,000 francs and not more than 20,000 francs for a first offence. A second offence within three years of the first attracted a maximum penalty of three years' imprisonment; and a fine not exceeding 40,000 francs for every alien illegally employed. In addition, as an administrative sanction, the employer could be required to pay to the O.N.I. a contribution of up to 2,000 times the minimum guaranteed wage for each worker employed in an irregular situation.

The *Loi Bonnet* of 10 January 1980 became the principal legal means of resisting clandestine immigration for employment. This added five grounds for expulsion[149] to that already existing under Article 23 of the *Ordonnance* of 1945, which provided for removal of an alien whose presence constituted a threat to public order. The *Loi Bonnet* was amended by Article 5 of the law of 29 October 1981, which reduced the powers of the administration and augmented the powers of the judges.[150] Expulsion of a foreigner can only be carried out if his presence constitutes a 'grave' menace to the public order; and the expulsion of seven categories of foreigner was prohibited. The *Loi Bonnet* was later repealed save in so far as it applies to French Overseas Departments, where it will cease to have effect in November 1986.[151]

From September 1977 the government offered cash incentives (of 10,000 French francs, plus an air fare) to alien workers who wished to be repatriated. In order to qualify the applicant had to hold a valid residence permit and work permit and who that he had been gainfully employed in France for five years.

THE NETHERLANDS

In the Netherlands, the Foreign Employees Labour Act 1978[152] regulates the employment of migrant workers, requiring an employer to procure for an alien an employment permit before any contract of employment can be made. Section 7 of the Act provides for the refusal of a permit on certain grounds. Primarily, the company concerned may not exceed a limited number of aliens' work permits allotted to it.[153] An alien without a residence permit will not be granted a work permit. Where a sufficient supply of labour in the relevant labour market exists or is expected to exist at the time in respect of which the application is made, the permit will be refused. Section 8(2) sets out four further grounds for the non-admittance of migrants for employment. Firstly, an alien is to be denied a permit if he originates from a country with which the Netherlands have not concluded an agreement on recruitment, and a sufficient supply of labour is available from the countries with which such agreements have been concluded. Secondly, a permit will be refused if the alien originates from a country with which the Netherlands have concluded an agreement on recruitment, but was not recruited through this agreement. Thirdly, it will be refused if the worker is under 18 or over 35 years of age.[154] Lastly, it will be refused where there is no suitable housing available. Very few aliens are now recruited by the Dutch government. After working for three years in the Netherlands, an alien worker is no longer subject to permit requirements.

The 1965 Aliens Act regulates self-employed aliens by means of conditional residence permits. Such a worker must show that his proposed activities serve Dutch interests.

The Canadian system of assessment of those eligible for admission for employment differs significantly from those of the principal industrialized States. Instead of maintaining immigration quotas,[155] the Canadian scheme is based on a points system, whereby any prospective immigrants who score a requisite number of points are normally allowed to enter for settlement. The system applies only to independent immigrants under Section 115 of the 1976–77 Immigration Act and Schedule 1[156] of the accompanying Regulations. These aliens are known as 'unsponsored' immigrants, as opposed to 'sponsored' immigrants in family class, to whom different criteria are applied under Regulations 4 to 6.

The points systems is designed to bring immigration into line with Canada's labour market needs. Emphasis is placed on practical training, experience and capability of the applicant. Employment-related factors account for almost half of the total possible rating points that can be awarded. Other criteria include the presence of friends or relatives to aid settlement in Canada, linguistic ability and personal and financial suitability for integration. All immigrants must meet the minimum number of required assessment points in order to receive immigration visas. Entrepreneurs must earn at least 25 points; assisted relatives 20 to 35 points; and those with arranged employment or a designated occupation 50 points out of 100. In addition, applicants must meet requirements of job experience or necessary skills and training. For example, any migrant worker who does not receive at least one point for the job experience factor must either have a pre-arranged job in Canada, and a signed statement of the prospective employer's willingness to engage an inexperienced applicant, or be qualified and prepared to work in a designated occupation in an area Canada identifies as having a shortage of workers in that occupation. Section 11(3) of the Act allows an Immigration Officer discretion in the grant or refusal of a visa irrespective of these criteria. In addition, migrants for employment are required to possess employment visas.[157] Regulation 26(1) (3) and (4) set up a system whereby a work permit can be issued only if there is no qualified Canadian citizen available for the work.[158] In 1973 Canada instituted a large scale regularisation or amnesty programme, repeated ten years later in 1983. In 1976, employer sanctions were established as part of a campaign to reduce clandestine immigration.[159]

AUSTRALIAN PRACTICE

In the Commonwealth of Australia it is a fundamental provision of the Migration Act[160] that a non-citizen may not enter the territory of the Commonwealth without an entry permit. This may be granted subject to a condition imposing restrictions with respect to the work that may be performed by the holder in Australia. Such restrictions may include a prohibition on performing any work, or work other than specified work, without the written permission of an immigration officer.[161] Thus, while work permits as such are neither required nor issued, the entry permit has become a vehicle for controlling the employment of migrants.

While the Migration Act[162] does not make express provision for the establishment of quotas, it has been the recent practice of Australian governments to announce maximum numbers of entry permits to be issued each year for migrants for settlement; and to endeavour not to exceed the numbers so announced. Currently the target is set at between 80,000 and 90,000 permits per year: the figure has remained unchanged since 1983–84. Moreover, the Australian Government considers that the admission of refugees and family reunion should account for the majority of permits issued.[163]

The allocation of entry permits between applicants has been regulated since 1978 by a system not dissimilar to that employed in Canada. All applicants are assessed in accordance with the Numerical Multifactor Assessment System (NUMAS), so as to give weight to such factors as family ties in Australia, occupational skills in demand in Australia, the applicant's literacy in his mother tongue, his knowledge of English and his prospects of successful settlement and integration.

Australia has not found itself called upon to embark on a programme of amnesties of the scale seen in France; but in 1973, 1976 and 1980 short programmes were announced by ministerial statement to regularize the condition of migrants in an irregular situation. Employer sanctions are not applied in Australia; but in common with any other person an employer commits an offence, punishable with imprisonment for a period not exceeding six months or a fine of $1,000, if he aids or incites a non-citizen to remain in Australia in circumstances in which he would become a prohibited non-citizen.[164]

UNITED STATES PRACTICE

The administration of primary immigration control in the United States continues to be based upon the allocation of visas according to 'preference classes' within a global annual quota, currently maintained at the level of 270,000 visas annually.[165] There are six preference classes, of which four are based on close family relationships to United States citizens or aliens permanently living in the country. The remaining two categories provide for the allocation of visas to aliens entering for the purpose of employment. The first such category is reserved for members of the professions and for aliens who demonstrate exceptional ability in the sciences or arts, such as will substantially benefit the welfare of the United States. The second is reserved for qualified immigrants performing labour for which a shortage of employable and willing persons exists in the United States.[166] An alien who qualifies for a preference visa is entitled to bring his children and spouse. These family members are accorded the same status as the alien and their admission reduces the number of visas available for other aliens seeking admission.[167]

Aliens wishing to enter for work under the third or sixth preferences must receive 'labor certifications' indicating that their employment in the United States will not adversely affect the wages and working conditions of American workers and that nationals are not able to fill the jobs such migrants seek.[168] The worker must obtain an offer of employment from a United States business that will sponsor the applicant. The employer must first make a *bona fide* effort to find qualified local labour, and must report on the response to these efforts to the Department of Labor.

In the case of three groups of occupations, the Department of Labor has determined that there are insufficient qualified workers in the domestic labour reservoir. Applications from migrant workers whose occupations fall within this designated list will receive a 'blanket labor certification'.[169] The first group includes physical therapists, physicians, surgeons and qualified nurses. In each of these cases professional qualifications are strictly required and physicians and surgeons must take a Visa Qualifying Examination to indicate professional competence comparable with that required by United States Medical Schools.[170] The second blanket grouping covers aliens of exceptional ability and international recognition in the fields of the arts or sciences. Applicants must give evidence of their skills, experience, ability and expertise, supported with documentary evidence of published work, awards, prizes and international recognition.[171] The third grouping covers admission to pursue a religious vocation. The applicant must show that at least half of his or her time in the United States will be devoted to this work.[172]

Separate provision is made for the admission to the United States of intra-company transferees. This includes not only those admitted for settlement in the first instance but also those permitted to remain in the United States after admission on a temporary visa in management or executive capacities.[173] Special visas are issued to those who enter the United States for a temporary period to conduct business, make investments or to work. In the case of those entering for skilled or unskilled work, there applies the requirement that there should be no available alternative employee in the domestic labour reservoir. The number of aliens entering as temporary workers – between 20,000 and 35,000 each year – is dwarfed by the number of aliens in an irregular situation.[174]

In most of the developing States of Africa, as in North America and Western Europe, the current recession has been accompanied by a strengthening of the controls in the admission of aliens for employment. In several of those States, the pattern is complicated by two elements: firstly, a tendency to require the employment of local citizens, particularly in economically important industries, in order to increase national control of the national economy; and secondly, respect for the relevant provisions of the treaties and instruments of the newly-established African economic communities.

In Nigeria, the basic rule is that no person other than a citizen is permitted to take employment without the written consent of the Chief Federal Immigration Officer. Non-citizens entering Nigeria for the purpose of employment may be divided into three categories. The first consists of those entering in order to take up employment in Federal or Regional government departments, including public corporations and institutes of higher education. These are not subject to any quota restrictions. The second group consists of employees of governmental organizations and private companies and organizations. These are subject to 'expatriate quota restriction', the annual quota being established periodically by the federal government. The third group consists of expatriates making short visits to Nigeria in order to perform specialized work.

Visas issued for the admission of aliens falling into the first two of these three groups are normally issued on a temporary basis initially, for three months, and are extended on the employer's application. Applications for the admission of workers falling into the third group must be made by the prospective employer; and when issued, visas for entrants within this group normally have a maximum period of validity of six months.[175]

Certain areas of employment are reserved for Nigerian nationals, notably finance, the administration, marketing and technical posts. Accordingly, visas will not normally be issued for aliens seeking to occupy positions in these areas. In principle, an employment visa for an expatriate will not be renewed more than five times nor extended so that the period of validity exceeds ten years in all. Where the visa is renewed more than once, a Nigerian citizen should be employed as an understudy, to take over the employment in due course. As a rule, no person other than a citizen of Nigeria may establish or take over any trade or business or register or take over any company without the written consent of the Minister of Internal Affairs. Certain enterprises are exclusively reserved for Nigerian citizens or associations, whereas others may be the subject of foreign investment undertaking in partnership with Nigerian citizens or associations, provided that the Nigerian participation in the equity amounts to not less than 40 or 60 per cent according to the nature of the enterprise and the size of the total investment.[176] In this context, 'Nigerian citizen or association' embraces 'any person of African descent, not being a citizen of Nigeria, who is a national of any country in Africa which is a member country of the Organization of African Unity, and who continues to reside and carry on business in Nigeria', if the country of which he is a national extends a similar facility to Nigerians.[177]

In Ghana, residence permits are issued for aliens desiring to take up paid employment or to engage in any trade, business or profession, subject to the condition that the migrant worker shall not work in any occupation except as specified in the permit.[178] Permits are issued for two years at a time, subject to ministerial discretion. Where application is made for a residence permit authorising the holder to take paid employment, the prospective employer must make out a case for the grant of the permit from the immigrant quota.[179] The employer must give details of the prospective employee's qualifications, skills and suitability. The principal consideration made by the inter-departmental committee, which advises the immigration authorities on the grant of permits, is the availability of Ghanaians with comparable qualifications and skills.

Since 1973 Ghana has applied a selective alien employment tax to discourage the employment of aliens and since 1985 an immigrant quota has been established for expatriates in designated enterprises.[180] The admission to Ghana of aliens seeking to establish businesses in importing and exporting is specifically forbidden, save in the case of those who propose to bring specified amounts of foreign capital into the country. The same rule applies in the case of aliens who propose to establish themselves in industrial occupations in Ghana on their own account.[181]

In Tanzania, two categories of residence permits are available for those seeking to engage in employment. Class A permits are issued to those wishing to engage in any trade, business or profession or in agriculture, animal husbandry or prospecting for minerals, on deposit of a sum to cover the cost of repatriating the applicant and his dependants together with an additional 25% of that sum. Class A permits contain limitations on the place where the holder may live, his occupation and the duration of his employment. Class B permits are issued to those who have been offered specific employment in Tanzania and have the requisite skills and qualifications. In such cases, the employer acts as guarantor of any costs incurred in repatriation.[182] The immigration legislation has been applied for some twenty years for the purpose or reducing the number of positions in employment and trade that may be undertaken by non-citizens.[183] Uganda,[184] Kenya[185] and Zambia[186] have followed the same pattern, while making use in addition of trades licensing law.

The countries of East and Central Africa appear to have been less concerned by clandestine African migration than their neighbours to the south, where systems of sanctions have been applied to employers of migrants in an irregular situation. In Zimbabwe, a system of sanctions was imposed in 1976[187] and in Botswana this was done in 1981.[188]

CONCLUSION

During the present recession, as during the last, the most pervasive and visible trend in comparative migration law has been the imposition of new restrictions on migration for employment.[189] The phenomenon is observed particularly, but by no means exclusively, in the States of Western Europe, North America and Australasia, which had been the principal importers of labour in the decade ending in 1973. Moreover, the trend is perceptible even in laws other than immigration laws. Thus, in the case of India the restrictions imposed under the Foreigners Act 1948 on the admission of aliens for employment are relatively meagre. Under the exchange control laws, however, an alien is required to obtain the permission of the Reserve Bank of India before accepting employment as agent of any person or company in a trading or commercial transaction.[190]

In such circumstances, many of the bilateral arrangements governing migration for employment which were concluded in the quarter century after the war have been abrogated or permitted to lapse. The existing multilateral treaties governing the treatment of migrant workers have tended to assume greater significance as a source of protection for migrants exposed to new restrictions upon their presence abroad. Progress in concluding new multilateral agreements, however, has been slow and the response to the more technical of the new Conventions has been disappointing.[191]

It is possible to discern a tendency, both at the international and at the domestic level to secure equality of treatment between migrant and domestic workers in respect of certain conditions of employment, including remuneration. This tendency is by no means universal; but it has probably gained some impetus from the recession: for it is to the advantage of the domestic labour force to ensure that it is not in competition with migrant workers remunerated at a lower rate. The prohibition of racial discrimination in the selection and treatment of migrants for employment has found very general acceptance and might even have matured into a legal principle. (The Nigerian Decree of 1977 restricts to Nigerians and others of 'African descent' the opportunity to engage in certain enterprises as investors: but leaves intact the principal of non-discrimination in employment). It must be emphasized, however, that the rule whereby migrant workers are entitled to equality of treatment with nationals of the State of employment is accepted only in a few defined respects. In certain European countries, the migrant worker is commonly denied the opportunity to have his family living with him; and in certain of the developing countries of Africa, the skilled foreign worker is admitted on a temporary basis only, pending his replacement by local labour.

For the present, the principal concern of the main multinational agencies is to secure by international action a reduction in the volume of clandestine or abusive migration. To this end, a majority of States appear to have expressed their support for the introduction and maintenance of systems for the imposition of sanctions on employers of aliens in an irregular situation; and a framework has been established for technical cooperation, including systematic contact and exchange of information between States, in consultation with representative organizations of employers and workers.

NOTES

1. Berne, 26 September 1906, U.K.T.S. 21 (1910). See also Convention on the Prohibition of Use of White (Yellow) Phosphorus in the Manufacture of Matches, Berne, 26 September 1906, U.K.T.S. 4 (1909).
2. Versailles, 28 June 1919; 13 A.J.I.L. Supp. (1919) 151 at 361.
3. Geneva, 5 June 1926; I.L.O. No. 21; 38 U.N.T.S. 281.
4. Articles 2(1) and 5(1).
5. Convention concerning Seamen's Articles of Agreement, Geneva, 24 June 1926; I.L.O. No. 22; 38 U.N.T.S. 295.
6. Convention concerning the Repatriation of Seamen, Geneva, 23 June 1926; I.L.O. No. 23; 38 U.N.T.S. 315.
7. Geneva, 28 June 1930; I.L.O. No. 29; 39 U.N.T.S. 55.
8. Articles 14 and 16.
9. Convention concerning the Regulation of Certain Special Systems of Recruiting Workers, Geneva, 20 June 1936; I.L.O. No. 50; 40 U.N.T.S. 110.
10. Convention concerning the Regulation of Written Contracts of Employment of Indigenous Workers, Geneva, 27 June 1939; I.L.O. No. 64; 40 U.N.T.S. 282.
11. Convention No. 50, *supra*, note 9, Articles 4 and 5.
12. Convention No. 64, *supra*, note 10, especially Article 19.
13. Convention No. 66: Recommendations Nos 61 and 62. See *I.L.O. Conventions and Recommendations, 1919–1966*, pp. 438, 443 and 447.
14. For amendments of the Constitution of the I.L.O. to the present date, see Instrument of Amendment, Montreal, 9 October 1946, 15 U.N.T.S. 35; Instrument of Amendment, Geneva, 25 June 1953, 191 U.N.T.S. 143; Instrument of Amendment, Geneva, 22 June 1962, 466 U.N.T.S. 323; Instrument of Amendment, Geneva, 22 June 1972, U.K.T.S. 110 (1975).
15. D. O'Connell, *International Law*, 1970, Vol. II, p. 756.
16. Article 19(5).
17. Article 22.
18. Article 24.
19. Article 26.
20. See generally, A. Alcock, *History of the International Labour Organization*, 1971; C. Jenks, *The International Protection of Trade Union Freedom*, 1957; G. Johnson, *The International Labour Organization*, 1970; P. Périgord, *The International Labor Organization*, 1926; A. Thomas, *The International Labour Organization*, 1931.

21. U.N. Charter, San Francisco, 26 June 1945; 1 U.N.T.S. xvi. Purposes include 'respect for the principle of equal rights' and 'international cooperation in solving international problems of a . . . social . . . character'.
22. Articles of Association, Washington, 27 December 1945; 2 U.N.T.S. 134.
23. Constitution, New York, 15 December 1946; 18 U.N.T.S. 53.
24. *Supra,* note 13.
25. H. Jacobson, *The Soviet Union and the Economic and Social Activities of the United Nations,* 1955, p. 61.
26. Geneva, 1 July 1949; I.L.O. No. 97, 120 U.N.T.S. 71; *Basic Documents* VII.2.
27. Article 6 (mention was made of remuneration and trade union rights).
28. Article 6(1)(a).
29. Annex I, Article 6; Annex II, Article 7.
30. Article 14.
31. Annex II, Article 10.
32. Article 8(1).
33. Alcock, *supra,* note 20 at 25.
34. Article 8(2).
35. 1939 Convention, Article 1; 1949 Convention, Article 3.
36. 1939 Convention, Article 2; 1949 Convention, Article 2.
37. 1939 Convention, Article 8; 1949 Convention, Article 11.
38. Convention, Article 11; Recommendation, Article 1(a). For the text of the Recommendation (No. 86) see *Basic Documents* VIII.1.
39. International Labour Conference, *Migration for Employment.* Report XI (1) 32nd Sess. 1948, p. 36.
40. *Ibid.,* p. 109.
41. *Ibid.,* p. 48.
42. 17 June 1964.
43. Geneva, 6 June 1942; I.L.O. No. 118; 494 U.N.T.S. 271; *Basic Documents* VII.4.
44. Geneva, 24 June 1975; I.L.O. No. 143; Cmnd. 6674; *Basic Documents* VII.4.
45. International Labour Conference, *Migrant Workers,* Report V (1), 60th Sess. 1975, p. 4.
46. Article 11 of the Convention of 1975; c.f. Article 11 of the Convention of 1949; *supra,* note 37.
47. Viz: frontier workers, artistes and members of the liberal professions who have entered on a short-term basis and seamen.
48. International Labour Conference, *Migrant Workers,* Report V (2), 60th Sess. 1975, p. 11.
49. Article 4.
50. Article 5.
51. International Labour Conference, *supra,* note 48, p. 13.
52. The expression is preferred by the General Assembly of the United Nations. See G.A. Res 3449 (XXX) of 9 December 1975, 29 U.N. Ybk. (1975) 641.
53. Recommendation No. 151 concerning Migrant Workers, 1975, *Basic Documents* VIII.3.
54. Recommendation No. 151; *Basic Documents VIII.3.*
55. Analogy may be made with Council Directive 75/117 of 10 February 1975 on the Principle of Equal Pay for Men and Women, O.J. 1975 L 45/19, Article 1, as interpreted in Case 61/81 *Commission* v *United Kingdom,* [1982] E.C.R. 2601.
56. Paragraph 9.
57. Paragraph 13.
58. Paragraphs 23 and 24.
59. Paragraph 2(i).
60. *Supra,* text at note 41.

61. Paragraph 33.
62. *Supra,* notes 11 and 12.
63. Geneva, 11 July 1947; No. 82; 214 U.N.T.S. 33; *Basic Documents* VII.1.
64. Articles 10 and 13.
65. Article 12.
66. Geneva, 22 June 1962; No. 117; 494 U.N.T.S. 249; *Basic Documents* VII.3.
67. Geneva, 28 June 1962; No. 118; 494 U.N.T.S. 271; *Basic Documents* VII.4.
68. Geneva, 21 June 1982; No. 157; *Basic Documents* VII.7.
69. Article 3(1).
70. Article 3(3).
71. Article 4(1), (3)(a).
72. Geneva, 17 October 1980; 22 I.L.M. (1983) 553; *Basic Documents* VII.6.
73. *Supra,* note 42. Paragraph 33 states: 'International migration of workers for employment which is consistent with the economic needs of the countries of emigration and immigration, including migration from developing countries to industrialized countries, should be facilitated . . .'. See H. Kellerson, 'International Labour Conventions and Recommendations on Migrant Workers' in A. Dummett, ed., *Towards a Just Immigration Policy,* 1986, at 41.
74. *Basic Documents* VIII.2. See further I.L.O. Recommendation No. 166 concerning Termination of Employment.
75. Convention No. 122 of 1964 provides that '. . . with a view to stimulating economic growth and development, raising levels of living, meeting manpower requirements and overcoming unemployment, each Member shall declare and pursue, as a major goal, an active policy designed to promote full productivity and freely chosen employment' (Article 1(1)). Recommendation No. 169 of 1984 urged Members to adopt policies to '. . . create more employment opportunities and better conditions of work in countries of emigration so as to reduce the need to migrate to find employment' and '. . . to ensure that international migration takes place under conditions designed to promote full, productive and freely chosen employment' (paragraph 39).
76. International Labour Conference, 66th Session, 1980, Record of Proceedings, pp. 25/8–25/10, Point IV(5). See A. Trebilcock, 'Migrant Workers: An Overview of International Labour Standards', in Max Planck Institute for Comparative Public Law and International Law, *The Legal Position of Aliens in National and International Law,* 1985, p. 10.
77. See R. Lillich, *The Human Rights of Aliens in Contemporary International Law,* 1984 at p. 108; and see generally R. Lillich and S. Neff, 'The Promotion of Human Rights through Bilateral Treaties: The Australian Experience with Migration and Settlement Agreements', 8 Aust. Ybk. I.L. (1978–1980), 142 at 160.
78. U.K. Free Passage Migration Agreement (1946) and U.K. Assisted Passage Migration Agreement (1946). The texts of these agreements do not appear in any official treaty series. For a description of their content see Parker (Under-Secretary of State for Dominion Affairs) 5 March 1946, 420 H.C. Deb. (5th Ser.), cols. 186–8.
79. Netherlands: Agreement for Assisted Migration, Canberra, 22 February 1951, 128 U.N.T.S. 115; Italy, Agreement on Assisted Migration, Melbourne, 29 March 1951, 131 U.N.T.S. 187; Federal Republic of Germany: Agreement on Assisted Migration, Bonn, 29 August 1952, 184 U.N.T.S. 147.
80. Convention respecting Emigration, Brussels, 28 November 1956, 308 U.N.T.S. 285. For similar provisions, see Convention concerning the Employment and Residence in Belgium of Tunisian Workers, Tunis, 7 August 1969, 696 U.N.T.S. 73; Convention concerning the Employment and Residence in Belgium of Algerian Workers and their Families, Algiers, 8 January 1970, 717 U.N.T.S. 321; and for Yugoslav Workers, Belgrade, 23 July 1970; 784 U.N.T.S. 223.

81. Agreement between France and Greece concerning Emigration, Paris, 13 May 1954, 222 U.N.T.S. 299; Agreement between Netherlands and Portugal concerning Migration, Recruitment and Employment of Portuguese Workers, Lisbon, 22 November 1963, 492 U.N.T.S. 31; Agreement between Austria and Turkey concerning the Recruitment and Employment of Turkish Workers, Vienna, 15 May 1964, 515 U.N.T.S. 108; Convention between Morocco and the Netherlands concerning the Recruitment and Placement of Moroccan Workers, The Hague, 14 May 1969, 686 U.N.T.S. 139.

82. Netherlands Assisted Migration Agreement, The Hague, 1 August 1956, 280 U.N.T.S. 3.

83. *Supra,* note 79.

84. Migration and Settlement Agreement (1967), Aust.T.S. 1971 No. 13, cited by Lillich and Neff, *supra,* note 77 at p. 156.

85. Turkey: Agreement concerning the Residence and Employment of Turkish Citizens in Australia, Canberra, 5 October 1967, 660 U.N.T.S. 55; Yugoslavia: Agreement on the Residence and Employment of Yugoslav Citizens in Australia, Canberra, 12 February 1970, 742 U.N.T.S. 299.

86. Argentina and Venezuela, like the United States, have large numbers of illegal entrants owing to the difficulties of controlling border crossing. Imported labour comes chiefly from neighbouring States – from Bolivia, Chile and Paraguay, into Argentina, from Colombia into Venezuela, and from Mexico into the United States. It is estimated that there are over 10 million illegal aliens in the United States. See Lillich, *supra,* note 77 at 111; and R. Silva, 'The International Protection of Migrant Workers', 12 Israel Ybk. H.R.

87. G. Kiser and M. Kiser, *Mexican Workers in the United States: Historical and Political Perspectives,* 1979; P. Ehrlich, L. Bilderback and A. Ehrlich, *The Golden Door: International Migration, Mexico and the United States,* 1979.

88. Section 1765, 97th Cong., 1st Sess. S 601 (1981). This was replaced by Section 529, 98th Cong., 1st Sess. (1983). The Simpson-Mazzoli Bill which also foundered when the U.S. House of Representatives and Senate failed to reach agreement in 1984.

89. See 99 Cong. 2d. Sess. Report 99–1000. The Act amends the Immigration and Nationality Act 1952 by adding after section 274 a new section 274A (unlawful employment of aliens) and amends the Migrant and Seasonal Agricultural Worker Protection Act 1983 accordingly. It also prohibits discrimination based on national origin or citizenship status as an unfair employment practice and provides for the legalization of the status of aliens who demonstrate, on application made within twelve months, that they entered the United States before 1 January 1982 and resided there continuously thereafter in an unlawful status: section 201, inserting section 245A into Immigration and Nationality Act 1952. In the case of non-immigrants who entered before 1 January 1982, they must show that their period of authorised stay expired before that date or that their unlawful status was known to the Government before that date: ibid.

90. For text see *Décret No. 80–1150 du 30 décembre 1980 portant publication de l'échange de lettres franco-algérien du 18 septembre 1980 relatif au retour en Algérie de travailleurs algériens et de leurs familles',* J.O.R.F. 4 January 1981 at 162. See Lillich, *supra,* note 77 at 110.

91. The U.N. Institute for Training and Research has been the principal agent in the study of the economic and social effects of skilled migration. See W. Glaser and G. Habers, *Brain Drain, Emigration and Return. Findings of UNITAR Multinational Comparative Survey of Professional Personnel of Developing Countries who Study Abroad,* 1978. See also UNCTAD report, 'The Reverse Transfer of Technology', Doc. TD/B/C/6/47 (1979).

92. D. Elles: U.N. Doc. E/CN.4/Sub.2/L/598 (1974) and U.N. Doc. E/CN.4/Sub.2/392/Rev 1 (1980.

93. U.N. Doc. E/CN.4/1336 (1978).

94. G.A. Res. 34/172, 34 U.N.G.A.O.R. Supp. (No. 46) 188–9, U.N. Doc. A/34/46 (1979) and see also Report of the Secretary General: 'Measures to Improve the Situation and Ensure the Human Rights and Dignity of all Migrant Workers', Addendum, U.N. Doc. A/34/535/Add. 1 (1979).

95. For a collation of the articles contained in the text of 'Draft International Convention on the Protection of the Rights of all Migrant Workers and their Families', see Lillich, *supra*, note 77, Appendix C, p. 135.

96. It has been estimated that between 14 and 20 million people are living and working in countries in which they are not citizens and do not have an immigrant status: P. Martin and F. Houston, 'The Future of International Labour Migration', 33 Jo. Int. Aff. (1979) 311.

97. Statement of Changes in Immigration Rules, H.C. 169, paragraph 27. Exceptions are made in the cases of Commonwealth citizens with a grandparent born in the United Kingdom, those entering for 'working holidays' under reciprocal arrangements with Commonwealth countries and those entering as *au pairs*. See paragraphs 26, 29 and 30.

98. Department of Manpower Services. The current regulations were introduced to come into effect from 1 January 1980. See Leaflet 'OW 5' issued by the Department of Employment.

99. H.C. 119, paragraphs 31–34, amended by H.C. 293. The earlier Immigration Rules for Control on Entry, H.C. 79, paragraph 26, provided for the entry of nine groups of migrants for employment without first obtaining work permits. Prior to these Rules, control was administered under the Aliens Order 1953, S.I. 1671, Article 4(1); Instructions to Immigration Officers, Cmnd. 3064, paragraph 21, Cmnd. 4398 paragraph 29 and Cmnd. 4296, paragraph 25.

100. H.C. 169, paragraph 35. See *Haji and Others* v *Home Secretary*, [1978] Imm. A.R. 26.

101. H.C. 169, paragraph 37. See *Home Secretary* v *Stillwaggon*, [1975] Imm. A.R. 132.

102. H.C. 169, paragraph 36. See *Home Secretary* v *Evgeniou*, [1978] Imm. A.R. 89.

103. H.C. 169, paragraph 133.

104. H.C. 169, paragraph 40.

105. Immigration Act 1971, section 14.

106. H.C. 169, paragraph 100. In the antecedent rule (H.C. 80 and H.C. 82, paragraph 5) it was stated that such applications were 'normally' to be refused. In interpreting the word 'normally', the Tribunal held that departures from the normal rule were to be permitted in the case of exceptional circumstances, such as strong personal and compassionate reasons, or reasons involving an aspect of vital public interest. See *Home Secretary* v *Stillwaggon, supra,* note 101; *Home Secretary* v *Sarwar,* [1978] Imm. A.R. 190; *Home Secretary* v *Moussa*, (1976) Imm. A.R. 78. On the other hand, the Immigration Rules were not intended to deal with industrial matters and accordingly it was not open to an applicant to rely upon the abnormal nature of the work, as requiring a person with overseas experience, such as a baker of Greek pitta bread: *Nicolaides* v *Home Secretary,* [1978] Imm. A.R. 67. The word 'normally' has been eliminated from the current rules, but it is possible that the former case-law is to be applied in the context of the opening words of paragraph 100 of H.C. 169, which states that 'in regard to variation of leave to enter with a view to employment, the general position is' as described in the text above.

107. *Pearson* v *Immigration Appeal Tribunal,* [1978] Imm. A.R. 212 at 225. See further *Lim Chow Tom* v *Home Secretary,* [1975] Imm. A.R. 137; *Chulvi* v *Home Secretary,* [1976] Imm. A.R. 133; *Latiff* v *Home Secretary,* [1972] Imm. A.R. 76.

108. Cmnd. 9544, Table 12. See generally V. Bevan, *The Development of British Immigration Law,* 1986 at 276–285.

109. Immigration Act 1971, section 25, as amended by British Nationality Act 1981, section 39(6) and schedule 4 paragraph 6.

110. 933 H.C. Deb., col. 1995, 24 June 1977 (Dr Shirley Summerskill) and O.J. 1978 D. 234/37, 10 October 1978.

330

111. (1973) 2 All E.R. 765. For the terms of the amnesty, see the statement of the Rt. Hon. Roy Jenkins, Home Secretary, dated 11 April 1974, 637 H.C. Deb., col 637.
112. I. Macdonald, *Immigration Law and Practice in the United Kingdom*, 1983, 398–399.
113. H. Schild, '*Kommunalwahlrecht für Ausländer?*' (1985), *Die Offentliche Verwaltung* 664 at 665, citing *Statistiches Jahrbuch der Bundesrepublik Deutschland* (1985) 19. For general accounts, see P. Martin and M. Miller, 'Guestworkers: Lessons from Western Europe', 33 Ind. Lab. Rel. Rev. (1980) 315 and 'The Legal Rights of Guestworkers', 24 Colum. J. Tran. L. (1986) 311. See further M. Zuleeg, *Einwanderungsland Bundesrepublik Deutschland Juristenzeitung,* (1983) 425.
114. *Auslandergesetz* (Aliens Law) of 28 April 1965, B G Bl 1965 I, 353.
115. *Arbeitsforderungsgesetz* (Work Promotion Law) of 25 June 1969, B G Bl. 1969 I, 582, as amended by *Gesetz zur Anderung des Arbeitsforderungsgesetz* (Law on Amendment of Work Promotion Law) of 3 August 1981, B G Bl 1981 I, 802.
116. *Arbeitserlaubnisverordnung* (Work Permit Decree) of 2 March 1971, B G Bl. 1971 I, 152, as amended by *Verordnung zur Anderung* (Amendment Decree) of 8 January 1973, B G Bl 1973 I, 18 and by *Verordnungen zur Anderung* (Amendment Decrees) of 22 February 1974, B G Bl 1974 I, 365, 7 July 1976, B G Bl 1976 I, 1782, 29 August 1978 B G Bl I, 1531 and 30 May 1980, B G Bl I, 638.
117. *Indian National,* Judgement of Bavarian *Volksgerichtshof* (BayVGH) 4 June 1969, 22 N.J.W. (1970) 1012.
118. *Allgemeine Verwalterungsvorschrift zum Auslandergesetz mit Wirking,* 1 October 1978.
119. *In the Matter of G,* Judgment of the Bundesverfassungsgericht, 26 September 1978, 49 BVerfG.E. (1978) 168, 185.
120. H. Esser and H. Korte, 'Federal Republic of Germany' in T. Hanmer (ed.) *European Immigration Policy: A Comparative Study,* 1985, 165 at 185.
121. A. Evans, 'Entry Formalities in the European Communities', 6 E.L. Rev. (1981) 3; *supra,* Chapter 6, note 50.
122. '*Stichtagsregelung*' or *Verordnung zur Durchführung des Auslandergesetzs* (Order based on Date of Arrival) of 29 June 1976, B G Bl 1976 I, 1717.
123. *Gesetz zur Anderung des Arbeitsforderungsgesetz* (Work Promotion Amendment Law) of 3 August 1981, B G Bl 1981 I, 802: *Arbeitserlaubnisverordnung* of (Sixth Order) 24 September 1981, B G Bl 1981 I, 1042. See Case 77/82, *Peskeloglou* v *Bundesanstalt für Arbeit,* [1983] E.C.R. 1085 at 1088.
124. M. Quaas, 'The Legal Status of Foreign Workers: The Federal Republic of Germany', 6 Comp. L.Y. (1982) 33.
125. Esser and Korte, *supra,* note 120 at 186.
126. Bonn, 5 May 1953, 1969 II, 134.
127. Bonn, 25 January 1952, *Bolétin Oficial,* 1953, 1616; Bonn, 29 March 1960, *Bolétin Oficial,* 1960, 505.
128. Bonn, 18 February 1960, BAnz 1960, 173; Bonn, 30 March 1961, BAnz 1961, 25.
129. Bonn, 30 September 1964, BAnz 1968, 22; Bonn, 15 June 1971, *Resmî Gazete* 1971, 2409; Bonn, 7 December 1972, B G Bl 1973 II, 747, 755.
130. Bonn, 21 May 1963, B G Bl 1971 II, 1365.
131. Bonn, 18 October 1965, B G Bl 1966 II, 57.
132. Bonn, 12 October 1968, B G Bl 1969 II, 1107.
133. *Gesetz zur Bekämpfung des illegalen Beschäftigung* (Law on the Suppression of Illegal Employment) of 15 December 1981, B G Bl 1981 I, 1390.
134. *Gesetz zur Regulung der gewerbsmässiger Arbeitnehmerüberlassung* (Law on the Protection of Subcontracted Labour) of 25 June 1985, B G Bl 1985 I, 1069, section 15(a)(2).
135. A credit programme to assist with the creation of new businesses in the home country led to

38,000 jobs and 200,000 shareholders but the rate of return was too slow.

136. *Gesetz zur Förderung der Ruckkehrbereitschaft von Ausländer* (Act to Promote the Preparation of Foreign Workers to Return) of 28 November 1983, B G Bl 1983 I, 1377.

137. Applications for reimbursement of contributions to the pension fund totalled 140,000, whilst applications for repatriation assistance totalled 16,870. Approximately 5% and 16% of these applications respectively were denied.

138. G. Verbunt, 'France' in T. Hammer (ed.) *European Immigration Law: A Comparative Study,* 1985, 127 at 138.

139. *Ordonnance* No. 45–2658 of 2 November 1945, J.O.R.F. 11 January 1945, p. 71, D. 1946 (L) 24; B.L.D. 1945, 474; amended, Law No. 84–622 of 17 July 1984, J.O.R.F. 19 July 1984, p. 2324, D. 1984 (L) 458.

140. Italy: Rome, 21 March 1951, G.U. 1953, No. 22, and exchange of notes, 2 August 1963, 18 *Diritto Internazionale* (1964) 254; Spain: 17 March 1956, 1 *Censo de Tratados Internacionales* 228, 27 June 1957, *Bolétin Oficial* 1957, 1409, San Sebastian, 29 August 1964, J.O.R.F. 7 January 1965, 171; exchange of letters 2 August 1968, J.O.R.F. 18 September 1969, 9323; Portugal: 30 October 1958, *Recueil des traités et accords de la France* 1956, 16.

141. Morocco: Paris, 1 June 1963, J.O.R.F. 2 August 1963, p. 7161, *Recueil des traités et accords de la France* 1963, No. 52; Tunisia, Paris, 9 August 1963, *Recueil des traités et accords de la France,* 1963, No. 70.

142. Algiers, 27 December, 677 U.N.T.S. 339.

143. In place there was a new agreement on social security,Paris, 23 January 1973, 964 U.N.T.S. 248.

144. 22 July 1964, 1 *Recueil général des traités de la France,* Ser. II, *Accords bilatéraux non-publiés,* ed., R. Pinto and H. Rollet, 1976, 430. See generally R. Lanpue, *'Conventions d'établissement entre la France et les Etats Africains',* 34 Rev. Jur. and Pol. (1980) 456.

145. *Service des Etudes et de la Statistique, Ministre des Affaires Sociales et de la Solidarité Nationale: Immigration Clandestine, La Régularisation des travailleurs 'Sans Papiers',* Supp. No. 106 (1983) p. 9.

146. *Ibid.* at p. 10.

147. 11 and 27 August 1981, D. 1981 (L), 340, J.O.R.F. 25 September 1981, p. 8681; and 22 October 1981, D. 1981 (L) 384, J.O.R.F. 28 November 1981, p. 10396. See R. Aymard, *'Politique française d'immigration',* 34 Rev. Jur. et Pol. (1980) 444.

148. Decree No. 81–891 of 1 October 1981, J.O.R.F. 2 October 1981, p. 2687, D. (L) 1981, 345.

149. Law No. 80-9 of 10 January 1980; J.O.R.F. 11 January 1980, p. 71; D. 1980 (L) 79. See D. Turpin, *'Réforme de l'ordonnance du 2 novembre 1945 sur la condition des étrangers par la loi du 10 janvier 1980',* 69 Rev. crit. dr. int. priv. (1980) 41.

150. Law No. 81-973 of 29 October 1981; J.O.R.F. 30 October 1981, p. 2970, D. 1980 (L) 361.

151. Law No. 84-622 of 17 July 1984; J.O.R.F. 19 July 1984, p. 2324; D. 1984 (L) 458. See J. Vincent, *'Nouveau régime de l'entrée et du séjour des étrangers en France',* 33 Rev. admin. (1980) 363.

152. Act of 9 November 1978 (Stb. 1978 No. 737), replacing Act on Aliens' Work Permits of 20 February 1964 (Stb. 1984 No. 72) entered into force 1 November 1979 by Royal Decree 26 October 1979 (Stb. 1979 No. 567).

153. Sections 12–16. The Minister for Social Affairs may fix the maximum number of permits allocated to each company. The maximum may not be less than 20 aliens per company.

154. 45 years if a skilled worker.

155. In the past, Canada employed quota systems, notably to reduce immigration from Japan, India, Pakistan and Ceylon (Sri Lanka). Nowadays, however, immigration levels are set for the year and the priorities of processing immigrant applications are occasionally adjusted. See J. Grey *Immigration Law in Canada,* 1984, at 19.

332

156. Regulations 8 to 11.
157. Immigration Act 1976–77, section 10 and 16(2), Regulations 18–20.
158. This 'Canadians First' policy is reflected in other sections in the Immigration Act itself, notably sections 3(a)(b)(h), 10 and 26(1)(b) (relating to the employment of aliens in Canada).
159. The sanctions against employers remain largely unenforced owing to difficulties in proving violations. The estimated number of illegal immigrants has been considerably revised; most are overstayers entering through airports. Total immigration to Canada fell from 143,000 in 1980 to 88,000 in 1984. Parliamentary Reports indicate that up to 175,000 immigrants a year are needed to sustain population growth: *Employment and Immigration Canada, Report to Parliament on the Review of Future Directions for Immigration* Levels (June 1985), p. 5.
160. Migration Act 1958 (No. 62) section 6(1) as amended by Migration Amendment Act 1979 (No. 117), Migration Amendment (No. 2) Act (1980) (No. 175) and Migration Amendment Act 1983 (No. 112).
161. Migration Act 1958 (No. 62) section 6(6A).
162. Nor is such provision made by the Migration Regulations 1959 (No. 35) as amended by those of 1959 (No.89), 1964 (No. 158), 1966 (No. 86), 1970 (No. 41), 1976 (No. 225) and 1979 (No. 234). The Regulations govern *inter alia* the documents to be presented by passengers arriving on overseas vessels, the procedures to be followed by commissioners and prescribed authorities, the provision of maintenance guarantees and the running of immigrant centres.
163. *Migrant Entry Handbook,* Australian Government Publication Service, 1983.
164. Migration Act 1958 (No. 62) section 30(2) as amended by Migration Act 1966 (No. 10), Migration Amendment Act 1979 (no. 117), Migration Amendment Act 1983 (No. 112) and Taxation Laws Amendment Act 1984 (No. 123).
165. Immigration and Nationality Act 1952, section 201, as amended by Act of 11 September 1957, P.L. 85–816, section 10 and Act of 3 October 1965, P.L. 89–236, sections 1 and 22(b), 8 U.S.C.A. para. 1151. This figure does not include resident aliens who seek to re-enter the United States after a temporary visit abroad. Nor does it include other special and numerically insignificant groups defined in section 101(1)(27) of the Act of 1952.
166. Immigration and Nationality Act 1952, section 203(a)(3)(6), amended by Act of 11 September 1957, P.L. 85–316, section 3, Act of 22 September 1959, P.L. 86–363, sections 1–3 and Act of 3 October 1965, P.L. 89–236, sections 3, 22(d); 8 U.S.C.A. para. 1153.
167. Immigration and Nationality Act 1952, section 203(a)(9).
168. Immigration and Nationality Act 1952, section 201(9) as amended (*supra,* note 166). The scope of judicial review in cases of denial of preference classification is limited to a determination of whether the Attorney General has abused his discretion in denying the classification required: *Asuncion* v *District Director of U.S. Immigration and Naturalisation Service,* 427 F. 2d. 523 (1970).
169. Immigration and Nationality Act 1952, section 101(a)(15)(H)(i), (iii); 8 C.F.R. para. 214.2 (2)(iv) and 214.2(4)(iv).
170. Immigration and Nationality Act 1952, section 101(a)(15)(H)(i);8 C.F.R. para. 214.2(2)(i).
171. Immigration and Nationality Act 1952, section 101(a)(27)(C); 22 C.F.R. para. 42.25.
172. Immigration and Nationality Act 1952, section 101(a)(15)(L); 8 C.F.R. para. 214.2 (1)(l) (iii).
173. Immigration and Nationality Act 1952, section 101(a)(15)(H)(ii); 8 C.F.R. para. 214.2(3).
174. A. Aleinikoff, 'U.S. Immigration, Nationality and Refugee Law', in Max Planck Institute, *The Legal Position of Aliens in National and International Law,* 1985, Vol. 4, p. 46.
175. Immigration Act 1963, No. 6, section 8(1), amended by Immigration Amendment Decree, No. 8, of 1972.
176. Nigerian Enterprises Promotion Decree 1977, No. 3, sections 4–6 and Schedules 1–3.

177. *Ibid.* section 23(1)(b).
178. Aliens Act 1963, No. 160, section 10 as amended by Aliens (Amendment) Act 1965, No. 265.
179. Aliens Regulations 1963, L.I. 265, Reg. 7.
180. Selective Alien Employment Tax Decree 1973, N.R.C.D. No. 201; Investment Code 1985, P.N.D.C.L. 116, section 15(b).
181. Import and Export Trade and Industry (Specification of Minimum Foreign Capital Investment by Non-Ghanaian Citizens) Act 1980, Act 402, section 6.
182. Immigration Act 1972 (No. 8), Part III, sections 11–13.
183. R. Plender, 'The Exodus of Asians from East and Central Africa: Some Comparative and International Law Aspects', 19 A.J. Comp. L. (1971) 287.
184. Immigration Act 1969, No. 19, and Trade (Licensing) Act 1969, No. 14.
185. Immigration Act 1967, No. 25; Trade Licensing Act 1967, No. 33.
186. Immigration and Deportation Act 1965, No. 29; Trade Licensing Act 1968, No. 41.
187. Foreign Migratory Labour (Amendment) Act No. 7 of 1976, section 3, amending Foreign Migratory Labour Act 1958, Statute Law of Rhodesia, consolidated 1974. By the Employment Act No. 13 of 1980, section 17(1), no person may carry on the business of recruiting labourers for employment in Zimbabwe except in terms of a recruiting permit.
188. Employment of Non-Citizens Act 1981 (No. 11), section 4.
189. Cf. H. Fields, 'Closing Immigration throughout the World', 26 A.J.I.L. (1982) 671 and R. Plender, 'Recent Trends in National Immigration Control', 35 I.C.L.Q. (1986), 531.
190. Foreign Exchange Regulation Act 1973, No. 46.
191. See, for example, Convention No. 157 concerning Rights in Social Security, Geneva, 21 June 1982, I.L.O. Official Bulletin (1982) Series A No. 2, p. 61; *Basic Documents* VII.7.

BIBLIOGRAPHY

T. Ansay, 'Legal Problems of Migrant Workers', 156 *Hague Recueil* (1977) 7.

J. Birks and C. Sinclair, *Arab Manpower: The Crisis of Development*, I.L.O. 1980.

C. Sinclair, *International Migration and Development in the Arab Region*, I.L.O. 1980.

W. Böhning, *Studies in International Labour Migration*, 1984.

J. Claydon, 'International Protection of the Welfare of Migrant Workers' in *The International Law and Policy of Human Welfare,* ed: R. St John Macdonald, D. Johnston and G. Morris, 1978 at 347.

K. Doehring, 'Non-discrimination and Equal Treatment under the European Human Rights Convention and West German Constitution', 18 A.J. Comp. L. (1970) 30.

W. Gormley, 'The Growing Protection of Human Rights and Labour Standards by the I.L.O.', 9 Banaras L.J. (1973) 1.

W. Gould, 'The Rights of Wage-Earners, of Human Rights and International Labour Standards', 3 Ind. Rel. Law. J. (Berkeley Cal.) (1979) 489.

C. Jenks, *Human Rights and International Labour Standards,* 1960.

H. Kellerson, 'International Labour Conventions and Recommendations on Migrant Workers' in *Towards a Just Immigration Policy,* ed. A. Dummett, 1986 at 33.

V. Leary, *International Labour Conventions and National Law: The Effectiveness of the Automatic Incorporation of Treaties in National Legal Systems,* 1982.

R. Lillich, *The Human Rights of Aliens in Contemporary International Law,* 1984.

R. Lillich and S. Neff, 'The Promotion of Human Rights through Bilateral Treaties', 8 Aust. Y.I.L. (1978Â80) 142.

A. Lopez Valdez, 'Labour Mobility: The Global Bracero Problem', Proc. A.S.I.L. (1979) 119.

334

P. Maggs and L. Lee, 'North African Migrants under West European Law', 11 Texas Int. L.J. (1976) 225.

W. Paati Ofusu-Amaah, 'Restrictions of Aliens in Business in Ghana and Kenya', 8 Int. Law. (1974) 452.

A. Panley and R. Diedrich, 'Migrant Workers and Civil Liberties', European University Institute Working Paper No. 45, Florence 1983.

S. Rugege, *Legal Aspects of Labour Migration from Lesotho to the Southern African Mines*, I.L.O. 1979.

R. Silva, 'The International Protection of Migrant Workers', 12 Israel Ybk. H.R. (1982) 62.

S. Strichter, *Migrant Labourers: African Society Today*, 1985.

E. Thomas, *Immigrant Workers in Europe: Their Legal Status, A Comparative Study*, UNESCO 1982.

U.N. Department of Social Affairs, *Protection of Migrants*, U.N. New York (1952), U.N. Doc. ST/SOA/IS.

J. Van der Ven, 'The Right to Work as a Human Right', 11 Howard L.J. (1965) 397.

N. Valticos, 'The Role of the ILO: Future Perspectives', in *Human Rights: 30 Years after the Universal Declaration*, ed. B. Ramcharan, 1979.

M. Warzazi, *Exploitation of Labour through Illicit and Clandestine Trafficking*, U.N. New York, 1974, U.N. Doc. E/CN.4/Sub/2/352.

CHAPTER 10

Temporary Migration

At its session in Geneva held in 1892 the Institute of International Law distinguished between permanent and temporary migration. It suggested that the power to deny admittance to aliens seeking to enter for temporary purposes should be exercised with particular circumspection:

> *Un état peut, à titre exceptionnel, d'admettre des étrangers que temporaire-*
> *ment et sous défense pour eux de se domicilier dans le territoire, pourvu que,*
> *autant que faire se pourra, la défense soit notifiée individuellement et par écrit.*
> *L'interdiction cesse d'avoir effet si elle n'est pas répétée periodiquement dans*
> *des delais n'excedant pas deux ans.*[1]

An aspiration cognate with that expressed by the Institute inspired two more modern instruments, to which States have subscribed. In the Declaration on Principles of International Law concerning Friendly Relations and Cooperation between States, the General Assembly of the United Nations reaffirmed and amplified the duty of States to cooperate in the economic, social and cultural fields.[2] On the basis of this Declaration, at least one author has been led to conclude that a State cannot in conformity with international law close its borders to all foreigners, including mere visitors.[3] Secondly, in the Final Act of the Helsinki Conference on Security and Cooperation in Europe, the participating States declared themselves to be 'aware of the contribution made by international tourism to the development of mutual understanding among peoples, to increased knowledge of other countries' achievements in various fields [and] to economic, social and cultural progress'. They expressed their intention to encourage an increase in tourism and to collaborate in efforts to resolve the problems arising from the temporary employment of foreign labour.[4]

At the regional level, the intention to treat temporary migration with particular liberality tends to be expressed in more precise terms. Thus, Article 1 of the European Convention on Establishment provides that Contracting

States will facilitate the entry of nationals of other parties for temporary visits, except when this would be contrary to *ordre public,* national security, public health or morality.[5]

With the possible exception of the European Convention on Establishment, these instruments are not sources of formal legal obligations.[6] Nevertheless, they appear to embody one of those 'norms of various degrees of cogency, persuasiveness and consensus' which play a part in modifying the conduct of States.[7] The same is true of certain of the declarations appearing in the constitutions of international organizations. As Judge Dillard observed in his Separate Opinion in the *I.C.A.O. Council* case, multilateral treaties establishing functioning institutions frequently contain articles that represent ideals and aspirations which, being hortatory, are not considered to be legally binding.[8] Into this category falls the preamble in the Constitution of U.N.E.S.C.O., which affirms that the parties will develop and increase the means of communication between their peoples.[9] Into the same category falls Article 3 of the Statutes of the World Tourism Organization, to which 110 States have subscribed. This records that the fundamental aim is to be the development of tourism with a view to contributing to economic development, international understanding, peace, prosperity and respect for human rights.[10]

No doubt, self-interest plays a greater part than legal norms in influencing States to extend greater liberality to temporary migrants than to prospective settlers. Nevertheless, the multilateral and regional instruments which call on States to facilitate the admission of aliens for temporary visits are not to be ignored. At least, they may be relevant factors to be taken into account in construing the multilateral, regional and bilateral arrangements which now regulate temporary migration.

TEMPORARY MIGRATION FOR LUCRATIVE PURPOSES

The Model Agreement on Temporary and Permanent Migration for Employment, drafted by the International Labour Organization, aspires to establish a standard to be observed by members of that Organization in the event of the migration for employment of any person other than a frontier worker, seaman, artiste or member of a liberal profession admitted for a short term.[11] Since the passages in the Model Agreement which are printed in italics are stated to refer primarily to permanent migration, we are enabled to draw from the typography some deductions about the distinctions that may properly be drawn between permanent and temporary migrants for employment.

The Organization has consistently printed in italics the provisions in the Agreement governing the admission of members of the families of migrant workers. This suggests that a receiving State is in general under no duty to permit the residence within its territory of the families of temporary migrants for employment; and if such an inference can properly be drawn from the Model Agreement, it is consonant with State practice.

Also printed in italics are the provisions governing the action to be taken by the competent authorities of the host State to facilitate migrants' adaptation to the climatic, economic and social conditions in the host State and to facilitate naturalization. The Organization has concluded that it is inappropriate to call on States to take such measures in the interests of temporary migrants for employment. The same is true of Article 18, which deals with access to trades and occupations and the right to acquire property; and Article 21, which deals with the maintenance of social security entitlements.

Article 1(3)(f) of the Model Agreement requires the competent authority of the territory of emigration periodically to furnish information to the competent authority of the territory of immigration concerning *the provisions in force regarding the export of capital*. The typography suggests that the supply of this information is generally inappropriate in the event of temporary migration for employment, presumably because controls on the export of capital are seldom an impediment to short-term migration. The fact remains that such controls are susceptible to impede the movement of persons between States, when applied in a sufficiently rigorous or indiscriminate manner. The Court of Justice of the European Communities has ruled that there is an obligation under Article 67 of the EEC Treaty to liberalize capital requirements 'to the extent necessary to ensure the proper functioning of the common market'.[12] That expression must be taken to embrace the liberalizing of capital movements to the extent necessary to secure the free supply of services in accordance with the Treaty.[13]

Part II of I.L.O. Convention No. 143 of 1975 deals with equality of opportunity and treatment. It does not apply to frontier workers, artistes and members of the liberal professions who have entered the country on a short-term basis; nor does it apply to seamen or to persons coming specifically for the purposes of training or education.[14] The exclusion of short-term entrants of these kinds is not an unusual feature of multilateral conventions regulating the status of migrant workers, even at a regional level.[15] In the case of the European Communities, however, limits are imposed on the power of Member States to regulate the admission to their territories of nationals of other such States, even in the case of frontier workers, seamen and members of the liberal professions.

A frontier worker is defined for these purposes as a worker who, while having his residence in the territory of a Member State to which he returns as a rule, each day or at least once a week, is employed in the territory of another Member State.[16] Thus the expression is sufficiently broad to embrace such cases as that of the businessman or official who works in one Member State and habitually returns by aeroplane each weekend to his country of origin in another Member State, remote from the one in which he is employed. Frontier workers, thus defined, are assured a right of residence in their countries of employment without the necessity of receiving a residence permit. A similar facility is extended to seasonal workers and to workers pursuing activities as employed persons, where the activities are not expected to last for more than three months.[17]

In the case of seamen we have the authority of the Court of Justice of the European Communities for the proposition that sea transport remains at present subject to the general rules of the Treaty, including the rules relating to the free movement of workers.[18] The same is true of air transport.[19] There is therefore no basis for regarding the temporary admission of seamen or aircrew as a matter falling outside Title III, Chapter 1 of the EEC Treaty. This is so even though Article 84(2) authorizes the Council to decide whether appropriate provisions may be laid down for sea and air transport. Far from excluding the application of Title III, Chapter 1 to sea and air transport, that Article provides only that the special provisions found elsewhere in the Treaty, relating to transport, shall not automatically apply to these matters.

In the case of the liberal professions the European Court has explicitly rejected the argument whereby the freedom to supply services, under Article 59 of the EEC Treaty, was alleged to mean no more than the right of a national of one Member State to be treated no less favourably than a national of the State in which the services are supplied. Such an interpretation would have entailed undesirable results. Where a State licensed the practice of a particular profession or occupation on the condition that the individual concerned should maintain an office within that State's jurisdiction, with books and records available for inspection by the competent regulatory authority, nationals of other Member States would be inhibited from supplying services there on a short-term basis. By this means, the freedom to supply services would be equated with the freedom of establishment. The Court therefore began by stating that the freedom to supply services may be restricted only by provisions which are imposed on all persons operating in the Member State in which the service is to be provided. The Court then added that such restrictions are permissible only in so far as the public interest is not safeguarded by the provisions to which the provider of the service is subject in the Member State of his establishment.[20] It follows that where the individual concerned has been licensed in his country of origin to exercise his professional activity, and wishes to supply services in another Member State, the authorities of the latter must take into account the licence already issued in his State of origin. The second State may not require a duplication of guarantees already provided.

It is, however, by means of bilateral agreements that temporary migration for employment is most commonly regulated. In Southern Africa contract labour agreements assume a special significance, both for economic and for political reasons. The treaty relations between Mozambique and South Africa on this matter are old-established; and have been the subject of recent differences between those States.

In 1875 an agreement was concluded between the Portuguese authorities in Mozambique and the British authorities in South Africa sanctioning the voluntary emigration of African labourers from Lourenço Marques to Natal.[21] A similar agreement reached in the following year provided for the emigration of African labourers from the same point of origin to the Cape of Good Hope.[22] The agreements achieved their objectives amply. By 1889, 58% of the mine workers in 44 South African mines originated in Mozambique. The relationship between the two dependencies was sealed by a *Modus Vivendi* concluded on 18 December 1901 by the High Commissioner for South Africa and the Mozambican Governor-General.[23] By this arrangement the Portuguese authorities received thirteen shillings for each worker plus sixpence more for each month's service beyond the initial contract period of one year. Furthermore, half of each worker's salary was paid directly to the Portuguese authorities in gold at a favourable rate of exchange; and a specified percentage of imports to Transvaal and exports from the same source were diverted through the port of Lourenço Marques. The treaty of 1901 was replaced in 1909 by new arrangement designed to afford a degree of protection to the migrant worker, notably by prohibiting the forced renewal of the contract of employment.[24]

On 11 September 1928 the Union of South Africa and the Government of the Portuguese Republic concluded the agreement 'regulating the introduction of native labour from Mozambique into the province of the Transvaal' and other matters.[25] This agreement is still in force, although amended from time to time. It provides for the regulation of medical inspection and of workers' rights, in case of industrial injuries or occupational diseases. It limits the period of contract to one year, subject to an extensions of six months. Thereafter, re-employment is prohibited until the worker has resided for six months in Mozambique. Since 1964, it has been provided that a Portuguese (or Mozambican) worker shall not be treated less favourably than a South African worker employed on work of the same kind.[26] The agreement regulates the number of workers to be recruited and the method of payment.

Mozambican mine workers may be recruited only by one organization which represents all the mines, while agricultural workers must be recruited through one labour office and on condition that the prospective employer has a 'no objection certificate'. Both categories of employees are restricted to lengths of contracts not exceeding eighteen months. Thereafter they may not be recruited again until they have spent at least six months in Mozambique. Those employed in mines are housed in special compounds for males only, provided by proprietors of the mines.

From the earliest dates the agreements with Mozambique have made provision for a system of deferred payment. The present agreement provides that after the first six months of employment, 60% of the employee's net pay is to be deferred and transferred through the Institute of Labour. Migrant workers are not subject to South African taxes, under the agreement, but it appears that there is no objection to the levying of Mozambican tax. It is reported that an unpublished agreement was concluded between the South African and Portuguese authorities whereby deferred payments would be made by the former to the latter in gold at a price expressed in Rands and at a rate favourable to the Portuguese. The gold was to be sold by the South African authorities on the world market and the profit yielded to the Portuguese authorities.[27] It is further reported that in 1975 the profit resulting from this arrangement (and yielded to the Mozambican authorities) amounted to R.150 million.[28] In that year South Africa ceased to apply this arrangement in Mozambique's favour in view of the strained relations between the two States. Between 1975 and 1978 the number of Mozambicans employed in South Africa fell from over 150,000 to under 50,000. In the same period migration from Lesotho was relatively stable, as was migration from Botswana, Malawi, Swaziland and Zambia, and migration from Angola and Zimbabwe increased.[29]

In 1984 the South African and Mozambican governments concluded the Nkomati Accord, by which each State undertook to respect the other's sovereignty and independence and to take steps to prevent the illegal crossing of their common border, in particular by terrorists.[30] On 5 October 1986, however, a South African military vehicle struck a land mine in the vicinity of that border and six South African soldiers lost their lives. The South African authorities immediately announced a decision to return to Mozambique some 13,000 Mozambican workers and to return to other countries in the region a further 9,000 persons, declared (in each case) to be illegally present. The South African President announced that on the expiry of their contracts other Mozambicans would be returned.

South Africa has concluded with others of its neighbours treaties governing the use of migrant labour. Malawi signed an agreement in 1965 with the recruiting agency of the Chamber of Mines. In 1967 the Governments of the two States ratified a formal agreement or treaty.[31] This envisages contracts of one year's, eighteen months' or two years' duration. Unlike the Mozambican agreement, it does not regulate contractual terms governing minimum wages, food, clothing and general conditions of employment; but in common with the

Mozambican agreement it provides for deferred pay and remittances. It states expressly that all Malawians employed on external contracts are required to pay taxes.

The labour agreements with Botswana,[32] Lesotho[33] and Swaziland[34] are in similar form (apart from minor differences, mostly relating to methods of recruitment). The maximum period of contract is fixed at two years; but in other respects the conditions of employment are not prescribed. All three agreements state that deductions will be made from the worker's wages where the contracts so specify and that the sums deducted will be sent to the relevant authorities. In 1974, the Government of Lesotho required a minimum of 60% deduction for deferred pay for all Basotho mine workers. This money was to be paid to the Lesotho Bank.[35]

The position in South Africa of migrant workers from Zimbabwe remains unsettled. At the time of the Federation of Rhodesia and Nyasaland, migrant labourers from the federation were subjected in South Africa to the Workmen's Compensation Agreement of 11 October 1958. By a formal agreement concluded in 1964 between the Government of Southern Rhodesia and the Government of South Africa the application of the Workmen's Compensation Agreement to Rhodesian workers was confirmed.[36] In February 1981 the Zimbabwean Government refused to allow the representatives of the South African Chamber of Mines to maintain an office in Zimbabwe for the purpose of recruiting migrant workers. At the same time the Zimbabwean authorities stated that the migration of Zimbabweans to South Africa for the purposes of temporary employment was to be discouraged, although not forbidden. The South African authorities responded by failing to renew the contracts of Zimbabwean employees, other than long-term employees in the mines. The number of Zimbabweans in South Africa has now fallen very considerably; but it appears that those who remain are still subjected to the Workmen's Compensation Agreement of 1958.

Indeed, the number of registered foreign black workers in South Africa generally has fallen by some 40% since 1983 (Namibian workers being included as foreign). The fall is explained in part by the imposition of South African restrictions on the recruitment of women or families from Botswana, Lesotho and Swaziland; in part by the effects of the recession; and in part by the policy adopted by the front-line States.

The labour agreements between South Africa and the front-line States have been accommodated by straightforward means in the former's immigration legislation. This provides that no person shall enter the territory of the Republic other than at a port of entry where he must satisfy an immigration officer that he is not a prohibited person. A person is not a prohibited person if he enters the Republic for the purpose of employment under such conditions as may be prescribed from time to time or in pursuance of a convention with the government of a neighbouring territory or in accordance with an approved scheme of recruitment and repatriation.[37]

At a conference on Migratory Labour in Southern Africa held in Lusaka in 1978 under the auspices of the United Nations Economic Commission for Africa, delegates expressed objections to the system of migratory labour, as an element in the policy of *apartheid*. They adopted a charter of rights for migrant workers in the region.[38] In 1981 the International Labour Organization adopted a Declaration on the Policy of Apartheid in South Africa which referred to the need of the front-line States to reduce their dependence on South Africa in general and on migratory labour in particular. The same Declaration called for the provision of long-term solutions to the regional difficulties which give rise to the phenomenon. Among the solutions proposed was the promotion of public works programmes in the front-line States.[39]

In 1979 the authors of a working paper commissioned by the International Labour Office published a plan for the progressive elimination of the front-line States' dependence on remittances from migrant labourers. Their proposal was that the States concerned should form an Association of Home Countries of Migrants (A.H.C.M.) and should provide the 367,000 migrant workers from their territories with decent alternative opportunities for employment. To this end they contended that the A.H.C.M. should bring pressure to bear on South Africa to pay for the creation of alternative employment opportunities within the A.H.C.M. economies; to counter possible South African retrenchment, they argued that a fund should be established by voluntary contributions from Member States of the United Nations.[40] Neither of these proposals has been adopted, nor does there appear to be any immediate prospect of their adoption. Indeed, certain of the front-line States depend heavily upon the remittances of migrant labourers working in South Africa. This is particularly the case with Lesotho, which supplies 40% of South Africa's migrant labour.

TONGAN CONTRACT LABOUR IN NEW ZEALAND

While the South African system of temporary labour migration operates on a particularly large scale, and has attracted special international attention by reason of the policy of *apartheid,* it is by no means the only internationally-regulated system of temporary labour migration between developed and developing States.[41] The temporary migration of Tongans to New Zealand, a relatively modern phenomenon, is governed by a Memorandum of Understanding concluded in October 1974.[42] It entered into force on 1 January 1975, making formal the arrangements previously applied *ad hoc.*

The central feature of the Memorandum is the introduction of a four-month work permit scheme. Employers are required to arrange accommodation for the Tongan workers, of a standard approved by the Department of Labour. They are required to advance air fares, to pay insurance premiums covering accidents and sickness and to guarantee continuous employment throughout the contractual period. The Tongan workers are responsible for signing and abiding by the terms of their contracts of employment, including any term providing for the deduction form their wages of a sum to cover air fares; to remain in the employment of the nominated employer; and to leave New Zealand at the expiry of the contract.

It is envisaged that the scheme will be extended to allow a longer stay in New Zealand, normally of six months but with the possibility of an extension for up to one year. The phased provision of hostel accommodation to introduce newcomers to life in New Zealand is planned; and it is proposed to introduce agreed arrangements for the employment of Island workers which would ensure that they receive training of a character such as to assist and sustain the development of Tonga.

Temporary migration for employment between Indian States is, of course, regulated by the Act rather than by treaty.[43] In common with certain of the treaties examined above, however, the Indian enactment provides for the licensing of employers who are to engage contract labourers and defines both their duties and the conditions of service of the migrant workers.

STUDENTS AND STUDENT EMPLOYEES

The network of cultural agreements and of similar agreements regulating the admission of foreign students is very extensive; but it is predominantly composed of bilateral arrangements. The German Democratic Republic has been particularly energetic in concluding treaties to regulate the admission of students from States with which it maintains friendly relations. The treaties show sufficient similarity with one another to have matured into a standard form.[44]

Within Western Europe a distinct species of bilateral arrangement has emerged. By a long series of treaties concluded since 1948, West European States have made provision for the admission[45] or exchange[46] of 'student employees'. Such agreements typically contain mutual undertakings by the contracting States to admit each other's nationals who are under the age of thirty and desire to enter the territory of a contracting State other than their own and to remain there for a limited period in order to improve their occupational and linguistic knowledge by taking employment in that State. Commonly, the agreements provide that the period of student employment shall be limited to one year and that they shall enjoy the same conditions of work and remuneration as nationals of the State in which they are engaged.

A regional arrangement concluded under the auspices of the Brussels Treaty Organization[47] provides for the admission of student employees within Belgium, France, Luxembourg, the Netherlands and the United Kingdom. For the purposes of that Convention a student employee is defined as a national of one of the contracting parties going to the territory of another contracting party in order to improve his or her linguistic and occupational knowledge by taking employment with an employer. It is stated that 'in general they shall not be more than 30 years of age'. Subject to the provisions of the Convention, each party undertakes to grant in respect of student employees any necessary authorisation to work and remain in its territory. Employment is limited to one year, although in exceptional circumstances the work visa may be extended for an additional six months.

TOURISM

The principal universal agreements governing the promotion of tourism fall short of imposing on contracting States a legal duty to admit each other's nationals, even for visits;[48] and the same appears true of the Final Act of the Helsinki Conference.[49] At the regional level, however, such an obligation has been imposed: it is to be found in the European Agreement on Regulations governing the Movement of Persons between Member States of the Council of Europe.[50]

This provides in Article 1 that nationals of the contracting parties may enter or leave the territory of another party on presentation of one of the documents listed in the Appendix. The documents so listed include passports, identity cards and other certificates (including birth certificates) as is appropriate in the case of each contracting State. The same Article provides in a subsequent paragraph that the facility of entering or leaving the contracting State's territory shall be available for only three months. Hence there arises by necessary implication a right to enter the territory of a contracting State other than one's own for such a period.[51] Each party reserves the right to forbid nationals of another party whom it considers undesirable to enter or stay in its territory.[52] Provision is also made for delaying the entry into force of the Convention, or suspending its operation temporarily, on grounds relating to *ordre public*, security or health, in respect of all or some of the other parties.[53] In 1980, this power was invoked by several States for the purpose of suspending the operation of the Convention in favour of Turkey. Switzerland invoked that power in relation to Turkey in July 1982.

A separate agreement sponsored by the Council of Europe is designed to facilitate the travel of young persons who are nationals of contracting States on collective passports.[54] It is limited in operation to travel for non-lucrative purposes. The collective passport is valid for groups of five to fifty young persons, under the age of 21, on visits to contracting States for periods not exceeding three months. The European Agreement on the Abolition of Visas for Refugees likewise provides for the admission for three months of a person holding the documents specified therein.[55]

The European Agreement on Au Pair Placement[56] describes an *au pair* as neither a worker nor a student, but as someone temporarily received by a family. In exchange for certain services, the young foreigner protected by the Convention works abroad in order to improve his or her linguistic and occupation knowledge. Article 3 envisages placement for an initial period of one year, renewable for a maximum of two further years.

PASSENGERS IN TRANSIT

A qualified obligation to permit foreign nationals to pass through national territory in transit appears to arise from two multilateral conventions. The first of these cases is relatively clear. The Agreement concerning the Preparation of a Transit Card for Emigrants[57] provides in Article 11 that contracting States shall allow emigrants holding valid national passports and transit cards to pass through their territories without visas.

The second case is that of the Statute on the International Regime of Maritime Ports.[58] This does not impose expressly a duty to permit the transit of foreign nationals; but such a duty appears to be implied. In particular, Article 17 provides that no contracting State is bound thereby to permit the transit of passengers whose admission to its territories is forbidden on grounds of public health or security. As regards traffic other than transit traffic, it is provided that no contracting State is bound by the Statute to permit the transportation of passengers whose admission is prohibited by national laws. This seems to imply that the contracting parties are bound to admit to their territories transit passengers whose admission, even if previously prohibited by national laws, is not forbidden on the grounds of public health or security.

Although the regulation of temporary migration by multilateral and bilateral treaty is exceptional, in the sense that most States enjoy a very wide margin of discretion in this area, the domestic immigration laws of most States are affected by constraints imposed by international law or assumed by international engagements.

DOMESTIC LAW IN THE UNITED STATES

Aliens seeking admission to the United States for temporary purposes are designated 'non-immigrants'. They are neither required to obtain labour certifications nor is their admission subject to numerical restrictions. On the other hand, they are subject to limitation on the period for which they remain and are generally prohibited from taking employment.

The Immigration and Nationality Act establishes thirteen major non-immigrant classifications, as follows:

(1) Foreign government officials and representatives, assigned visa symbols A-1 to A-3.
(2) Temporary visitors for business or pleasure, respectively assigned visa symbols B-1 or B-2.
(3) Aliens in transit through the United States, assigned visa symbols C-1 to C-3.
(4) Alien seamen or airmen, assigned visa symbol D.
(5) Treaty traders and treaty investors, respectively assigned visa symbols E-1 and E-2.
(6) Students, assigned visa symbols F-1 and F-2.
(7) Representatives of international organizations, assigned visa symbols G-1 and G-5.
(8) Temporary workers, assigned visa symbols H-1 to H-4.
(9) Representatives of non-U.S. press, radio, film or other information media, assigned visa symbol I.
(10) Exchange visitors, assigned visa symbols J-1 or J-2.
(11) Fiancé(e)s of U.S. citizens, assigned visa symbols K-1 and K-2.
(12) Intra-company transferees, assigned visa symbols L-1 or L-2.
(13) Students attending vocational programmes, assigned visa symbols M-1 and M-2.[59]

It will be noted that six of these categories are designed for those entering temporarily for lucrative purposes. Of these six, the most numerous category is for those entering temporarily on business (holders of B-1 visas). To qualify for admission on this basis, the applicant must demonstrate that he seeks to enter the United States temporarily for the purpose of conducting a lawful professional or commercial activity in that country while retaining his principal place of business elsewhere. Further, he must demonstrate that adequate financial arrangements have been made for his stay in the United States and that it is open to him to return to the country in which he maintains his principal place of business on the termination of his work in the United States.

The United States maintains treaties of trade with thirty-nine States[60] and treaties of investment with twenty-nine States[61] and provides accordingly for the admission of nationals of such States as treaty traders or treaty investors. Aliens entering in either of these categories are non-immigrants but the visas providing for their admission will be renewed indefinitely, so long as the business activity for which they were issued continues to exist. A national of a State bound to the United States by a treaty of trade is eligible to receive a treaty trader visa if he seeks to carry on substantial trade between the United States and the State of which he is a national. The trader's spouse and unmarried children under twenty-one years of age are eligible to receive the same status as is conferred on him.

A national of a State bound to the United States by a treaty of investment is eligible to receive a treaty investor visa if he seeks admission solely to develop and direct the operations of an enterprise in which he has invested a substantial amount of capital, or in which he is in the process of investing such capital. Neither the Act nor the Foreign Affairs Manual specifies in dollars the amount of capital considered to be 'substantial'. It is understood that in practice the investment of $100,000 will commonly be regarded as substantial if it is sufficient for the launching of the type of business proposed or if it amounts to a significant proportion of the total sum invested. Like the treaty trader, the treaty investor is assured that his spouse and unmarried children under twenty-one years of age are eligible to receive the status conferred on him.

The condition of temporary workers admitted as intra-company transferees has been considered in the preceding chapter; as has the condition of workers bearing 'H' visas; but it may be added that special protection has been afforded to migrant and seasonal agricultural workers since 1983. By an Act passed on 14 January of that year, it is an offence for a person other than the holder of a certificate of registration to engage in farm labour contracting activities. Migrant and seasonal workers have been given statutory rights to receive certain information and their employers are in principle responsible for ensuring that they have adequate health and housing.[62] By section 211(a)(20) of the Immigration and Nationality Act, applications to enter the United States for temporary purposes must first be made at United States consulates abroad. Issuance of a visa is no guarantee of admission: a second check takes place at the port of entry. Visas are commonly granted with periods of validity of six months; however, the issuance of visas of indefinite duration, valid for multiple entries, is increasingly frequent, particularly in the case of B-1–B-2 visas and E-1–E-2 visas issued to nationals of States other than those from which there appears to be the greatest demand for settlement in the United States.

Canadian and Mexican nationals may apply for border crossing cards that authorize temporary visits to the United States. Aliens in transit may enter the United States without a visa; but this facility is not extended to nationals of Afghanistan, Cuba, Iran or Iraq.[63]

Non-immigrants other than transit passengers, crewmen and fiancé(e)s may apply for extension of their visas not less than fifteen or more than sixty days before the date of scheduled expiry.

Where grounds exist for doubting that the alien will leave the United States at the expiry of his visa, he may be admitted on condition that he provides a bond, returnable on departure.

DOMESTIC LAW IN THE SOVIET UNION

The basic legal provisions applicable to aliens in the Soviet Union are now to be found in a Law of 24 June 1981[64] together with three sets of Regulations. The first set of Regulations, together with Articles 24–27 of the Law, deal with the admission of aliens.[65] The remaining two sets of Regulations entered into force simultaneously on 1 July 1984: they deal with the transit and residence of aliens respectively.[66]

Admission to Soviet territory is contingent on the presentation of a visa issued to aliens by Soviet missions abroad or, exceptionally, Soviet representatives duly authorised to issue such documents. In appropriate cases, which are not defined, visas may be issued at the port of entry. Following the conclusion of the Final Act of the Helsinki Conference on Security and Cooperation in Europe, the Soviet Union announced that it had taken two administrative measures to simplify the issuance of entry visas. First, visas for temporary residence were to be issued within ten days of the submission of the necessary documents to the appropriate Soviet consulate. Second, visas would no longer be required for travellers arriving on Soviet or foreign vessels in Soviet ports for the purposes of transit only, or for transit passengers on foreign aircraft passing through the Soviet Union. Furthermore, duly accredited foreign correspondents in Moscow and their families would be eligible to receive visas for multiple entries and exits.[67]

Visas for admission to the Soviet Union for temporary purposes may be issued for the purposes of business, tourism, participation in conferences, visits to exhibitions or fairs, study, professional training or education, charitable purposes, work in accordance with intergovernmental agreements or private purposes. Applicants for visas other than tourist visas must support their applications by written invitations from the appropriate Soviet organizations or letters of invitation from Soviet relatives or friends.[68] Those entering for the purposes of tourism must obtain in advance travellers' cheques denominated in hard currencies (such as U.S. dollars) in amounts sufficient to meet the costs of their stay.[69]

The new Regulations governing the transit of foreign citizens through Soviet territory provide[70] that the transit of foreign citizens by air, rail and sea is permitted on presentation of documents valid for the alien's admission to a country contiguous with the Soviet Union, together with appropriate travel documents and confirmation of the date and place of exit from the Soviet Union. Transit by road is permitted only pursuant to inter-State agreements, on presentation of documents valid for admission to the contiguous country.[71] In principle, transit visas are issued with no right to stop in the territory of the Soviet Union but exceptionally they may be issued with the right to stop in one or several points, even for foreign nationals travelling by private car, provided that the latter employ Intourist autotours. In the latter case, however, the alien must obtain an appropriate tourist visa with an indication of stopping points before arrival in the Soviet Union.[72] Entry to Soviet territory without Intourist autotours, for private travel by motor vehicle, is permitted only for citizens of countries with which the Soviet Union has entered into agreements concerning the mutual abolition of visas, and even then on condition that the journey in the Soviet Union occupies no more than twenty-four hours.[73] By Regulation 11:

> Foreign citizens in transit across territory of the USSR by road, including those engaged in international automobile transportation, may use only those roads which are open for international automobile communication. Stops for meals, rest or overnight accommodation may be taken only at approved motels or camp-sites.[74]

Foreign citizens travelling by train are expressly authorized to alight from their train at railway stations for the period of the train's stop as indicated in the timetable.[75] The Regulations make special provision for forced stops, including those occasioned by calamities.[76] Residents of the Soviet Union who provide foreign nationals with accommodation or transport must report the fact to the authorities responsible for internal affairs within twenty-four hours.[77]

The Regulations governing the residence of foreign citizens in the Soviet Union contain provisions to regulate the processing of documents of aliens present for temporary purposes,[78] the movement of aliens in the Soviet Union[79] and the grant of leave to remain permanently in the Soviet Union.[80]

With two groups of exceptions, all aliens residing temporarily in the Soviet Union are obliged to register with the authorities responsible for internal affairs. Registration takes the form of the submission of the alien's passport and accompanying correspondence to the appropriate authorities within forty-eight hours of arrival.[81] Registration can be effected by the hotel in which the alien is residing. The first group of persons exempted from this obligation includes secretaries, members and candidates for office in the Communist Party of the Soviet Union or the Communist or Labour Parties of foreign countries, together with heads of States and governments, members of parliamentary delegations, holders of United Nations passports and crew members of foreign warships duly admitted by the chief of the Soviet garrison at the port of arrival. This exemption is unconditional. The second exempted group consists of persons exempted on a basis of reciprocity. The group includes members of diplomatic missions, their families and staff, employees of departments of foreign countries and senior representatives of forces belonging to the Warsaw Pact.[82]

Foreign nationals residing temporarily or permanently in the Soviet Union require permission in order to change their place of residence or to travel to points not indicated in the residence permit.[83] By Article 29 of the new Regulations:

> Visits to places other than those specified in the alien's reception plan or in his entry document may be authorized by the authorities responsible for internal affairs on the basis of written applications made by the ministries, departments and organizations receiving such persons in the Soviet Union.

The entry, temporary stay and residence of aliens in Soviet border zones, in the border land and in places closed for foreigners are forbidden, save when special permission is granted by the authorities responsible for internal affairs or by the armed forces, or when the alien's entry visa or invitational telegram makes provision for an appropriate dispensation.[84]

DOMESTIC LAW IN THE UNITED KINGDOM

A person who is subject to immigration control will be admitted to the United Kingdom if he can show that he is genuinely seeking entry for the period of the visit and can demonstrate that he has sufficient means to support himself and accompanying dependants for the duration of his intended stay, and can meet the cost of his accommodation and return travel.[85] If the immigration officer is not satisfied on any of these points, he should refuse the application. In particular, leave should be refused 'where there is reason to believe that the passenger's real purpose is to take employment or that he may become a charge on public funds'.[86]

Visitors need not apply for entry clearances but may do so in order to ascertain in advance that they are eligible for entry into the United Kingdom. Entry clearance, however, is no guarantee of admission as an immigration officer is authorized to refuse to admit a bearer of such a certificate who appears to him to be ineligible.[87] Countries whose citizens require visas for entry into the United Kingdom are listed in the Appendix to the Statement of Changes in the Immigration Rules H.C. 169 (as amended). Originally, all such countries were foreign States, but in June 1985 Sri Lanka was included and in November 1986 citizens of India, Pakistan, Bangladesh, Nigeria and Ghana were required to hold valid visas prior to entry. A visit must be of ascertainable duration[88] and since 1980 the Immigration Rules have provided for admission for a period of six months, which may be extended up to one year.[89]

In most cases the principal obstacle to admission as a visitor consists in the assessment made by the immigration officer as to the intentions of the applicant. The officer will examine the applicant's personal circumstances to decide whether there is a sufficient incentive to return home. It has been determined that doubts about a person's intentions must be based on evidence rather than on mere suspicion.[90]

To gain entry clearance for admission as a student, the applicant must establish that it is genuinely his intention to follow a full-time course of study,[91] and to leave the country on completion of his studies.[92] In *Patel*[93] Dillon, L.J. observed that a person who intends to leave only if he cannot by lawful means avoid doing so fails to discharge the burden of proving that he intends to depart on completion of his education.

In assessing an applicant's intentions, immigration officers will consider his background, any relatives he has in the United Kingdom, his academic ability and record, his employment prospects at home and whether he sought to gain entrance to a similar course at home.[94] The course must be at 'a university, a polytechnic or further educational establishment, an independent school or any *bona fide* private education institution'.[95] The course of study should occupy the whole or a substantial part of the applicant's time. Correspondence or training courses will not suffice.[96]

THE COMMONWEALTH

The idea that any British subject – or at least any European British subject – should be entitled to free entry to any part of the Dominions was surrendered by 1901. By 1933 'the Dominions definitely [had] closed their doors to the migration of Indians'.[97] After the introduction of the system of tiered citizenships, in the period from 1946–1950, a Commonwealth citizen had in each Commonwealth country only such rights of entry as local law might allow.[98] A certain tradition of liberality in matters of immigration control persisted between Commonwealth countries even after 1962; in particular, there was a tendency to exonerate Commonwealth citizens of the requirement to bear visas for temporary admission; but nowadays the tradition has ceased to apply.[99]

In Barbados all persons other than citizens of Barbados are subject to control under the Immigration Act (although residents of Barbados enjoy a qualified right of entry). The Act provides for the admission of two classes of 'permitted entrants'. The first consists of diplomats, students and those entering for employment or other lucrative purposes or for purposes approved by the Minister. Entrants in this first category may be admitted for periods of any length, save that students and persons entering for 'other purposes approved by the Minister' may not be allowed to remain for more than three years in the first instance. The second category consists of passengers in transit, visitors, members of the crew of ships or aircraft; sportsmen and sportswomen; artists; and those entering in pursuance of cultural exchanges or visiting for medical treatment. Such persons may be admitted for periods not exceeding six months. No distinction is to be drawn for these purposes between Commonwealth citizens and others.[100]

In Antigua and Barbuda, special treatment of the kind formerly extended to Commonwealth citizens is now reserved for British and United States citizens. In outline, the scheme is similar to that of Barbados: temporary migrants, divided into categories after the Barbadian pattern, are admissible to the islands for statutory periods, but with a possibility of remaining for up to twelve months as visitors or passengers in transit. The Passport and Visa (Exemption) Order of 1985 sets out categories of persons exempted from visa requirements. These are: British citizens and citizens of the United States and Canada visiting for no more than six months, provided that they are in possession of return tickets; transit passengers staying no more than fourteen days with tickets to onward destinations; and officials of the Caribbean Community, the Organization of American States and the United Nations with official travel documents.[101]

The Zimbabwe Immigration Act[102] makes provision for the admission without visas of visitors who are beneficiaries of international arrangements to which Zimbabwe is a party. A similar exoneration is extended to persons domiciled in Zimbabwe, together with aircrew, students, diplomats and overseas workers entering under approved schemes of recruitment. The Immigration Regulations[103] provide that no visitor may remain in Zimbabwe longer than six months, unless he has obtained the permission of the Chief Immigration Officer; nor longer than twelve months, unless he is in possession of a permit of the kind required for intending immigrants.

Mauritian immigration law continues to distinguish between Commonwealth citizens and aliens, to the extent of conferring on the former the status of 'resident' if they were ordinarily resident in Mauritius for seven years preceding 14 December 1968. No such distinction is drawn, however, for the purposes of the rules governing the admission to Mauritius of temporary migrants. For this group, Mauritian law creates generous exemptions, as befits a country largely dependent on tourism; but among the twelve classes of temporary migrants exempted from the principal controls are persons who come to Mauritius under the provisions of any treaty or agreement between Mauritius and another country and whose admission to Mauritius is approved by the Minister.[104]

In the Seychelles, visitors' permits are valid for three months, though they may be extended up to a maximum of twelve months. No distinction is drawn between Commonwealth citizens and others; and although exonerations are created for crew members, diplomats and passengers in transit, no special facility is established for beneficiaries of international arrangements. The point is probably without significance, however, since the discretionary power conferred on the Minister is sufficient to enable him to ensure that beneficiaries of those engagements receive visitors' permits (or, in the case of temporary migrants for lucrative purposes, 'gainful occupation permits').[105]

In India the former Passport (Entry into India) Rules 1950[106] required any prospective visitor to obtain permission to enter from a diplomatic mission or consul abroad. This rule was repealed in March 1981; and arrangements made for the issuance of a temporary landing permit on arrival in India. Since the outbreak of communal violence in the Punjab in June 1984 a visa system has been re-introduced even for Commonwealth citizens.[107] A transit visa is issued for fifteen days and a stay for business purposes is allowed for ninety days or as required. Students are admitted for up to one year in the first instance depending upon the overall duration of the course of study; and for employment, workers' visas are extended from year to year. Extension of a visa is at the discretion of the immigration authorities.[108]

In Canada the Immigration Act 1976 describes a visitor as a person lawfully in Canada or seeking to come into Canada for a temporary purpose.[109] The visitor's leave to enter is always granted for a limited period[110] unless the entrant is a citizen of the United States, or is a native of St Pierre or Miquelon or is otherwise exempted from the obligation to carry a passport.[111] In general, admission is authorized through the issuance of a visa and the examination at the port of entry. Unless otherwise specified, a visitor is not allowed to remain in Canada for longer than three months.[112]

In Australia, no 'immigrant' may enter the territory of the Commonwealth without an entry permit; but the term 'immigrant' is defined to include a person intending to enter for a temporary stay only, where he would be an immigrant if he intended to stay permanently. No distinction is drawn in this respect between British subjects, Irish citizens and British protected persons on the one hand and aliens on the other. Only aliens, however, are amenable to deportation under section 12 of the Migration Act, so that in this respect the former privileges of Commonwealth citizens persists. For temporary visitors, admission is normally made conditional on the prohibition of paid employment and a stay of not more than six months. Students are admitted to Australia if accepted at an educational institution and on payment of a visa fee intended to offset to some extent the cost of educational facilities provided. Certain young persons aged 18 to 25 may be admitted to work for a maximum of three months in any one job: this scheme is established only for citizens of the United Kingdom and Japan, which provide reciprocal arrangements for young Australians. The maximum length of the working holiday is one year. Special temporary permits are also granted to experts, consultants, performing artists, sports competitors and those who come for medical treatment.[114]

A temporary residence permit may be extended at any time but subject to the condition that the holder remain in Australia no longer than the specified period.[115]

THE PRACTICE OF JAPAN

It is the Immigration Control and Refugee Recognition Act of 1951 (as amended) which controls temporary migration into Japan. Article 4(4) of that Act provides for the admission of aliens who seek to stay in Japan for short periods with the following purposes: sightseeing, rest and recuperation, to engage in sporting activities, to visit relatives, tours of inspection, attendance at short courses, participation in meetings or other similar purposes. A valid passport is required for all passengers entering Japan, as is a visa issued by a consular officer abroad; but visas are not required in the cases of nationals of States which exonerate Japanese nationals of the requirement of a visa.[116] The period of stay is prescribed by the Ministry of Justice Ordinance: it is not to exceed three years. Also permitted to enter the country are aliens seeking to pursue a specific branch of study or to receive education at an academic or educational institution and those who are accepted by a public or private organization in Japan to acquire industrial techniques or skills. Aliens in these latter categories must apply prior to landing for a certificate of eligibility for the pertinent status of residence, to the Minister of Justice.[117]

Article 14 and 15 of the Act deal with transit through Japan. Not more than three days is allowed for this purpose. A variation of status after arrival in Japan is permitted by the Minister of Justice only if there are reasonable grounds for the change and if the application for variation is supported by documentary or other evidence indicating that the applicant has the requisite qualifications to assume the new status. Variation of status from that of temporary visitor will not be granted unless there arise special unavoidable circumstances.[118] An extension of permission to stay is granted if the alien can demonstrate reasonable grounds for this facility.[119]

The Japanese Immigration Control Act provides for the deposit of a bail bond, not exceeding two million yen, which may be demanded as a condition of admission of an alien. In such an event the bond is returned to the alien on the grant of leave to remain in Japan or on the making of an order to leave Japan. The bond is forfeited if the alien absconds or fails to appear at a hearing of his claim to remain in Japan.[120]

CONCLUSION

International law imposes relatively few constraints upon the power of the State to control at its will the admission and stay of foreign visitors. The customary rules applying in this area remain rudimentary, (save in special cases, such as those of diplomatic envoys and military personnel); although they do provide a basis for maintaining that a State cannot close its borders to all aliens. The rules of law established by treaties open to universal participation are also meagre; although the International Labour Office has had some success in establishing minimum standards for the treatment of temporary migrants for employment. Nevertheless, by means of regional arrangements and by a wide network of bilateral treaties, most States have submitted to a degree of international regulation in respect of the national control of visitors. By reciprocal arrangements and courses of action based more upon a cordial understanding between the participants than upon a sense of obligation, other States have from time to time extended privileges to visitors possessing each other's nationalities.

Thus, in the United States, the categories of 'treaty trader' and 'treaty investor' depend upon almost exclusively international engagements. In the Soviet Union, the effects of the Final Act of the Helsinki Conference are perceptible in the rules governing the issuance of visas; and bilateral arrangements are reflected in the rules governing transport by road and exoneration from registration. Of the informal arrangements applicable in this area, the most noteworthy has long been the facility in the Commonwealth, whereby at one time British subjects were exonerated from immigration control and more recently were relieved of the requirement to hold visas. That arrangement, informal as it was, has now broken down; and although the remains of the arrangement are still perceptible in the laws of Commonwealth countries as diverse as Mauritius and Australia, the remnants may be considered purely vestigial.

Bilateral and regional arrangements continue to play a part in fashioning the immigration laws of many Commonwealth countries, however: from the United Kingdom's provisions relating to nationals of European Community States to Zimbabwe's generalized exoneration from visa requirements for nationals of States bound to Zimbabwe by international agreements. Even in the case of Japan, the influence of bilateral arrangements may be discerned. A temporary migrant to Japan benefits from special facilities when seeking to have his status changed to that of a permanent resident, if he is the spouse or child of a Korean national and is the beneficiary of the agreement between Korea and Japan governing the treatment of such persons.[121]

356

1. 12 Ann. I.D.I. (1892–4) at 221, Article 13. For the distinction between temporary and permanent migration, see A. Roth, *The Minimum Standard of International Law applied to Aliens,* 1949, p. 46 and P. Fauchille, *Traité de droit international public,* 1921, Vol. I, p. 891.
2. G.A. Res. 2625 (XXV) of 24 October 1970, 9 I.L.M. (1970) 1292 at 1296.
3. M. Bogdan, 'Admission of Tourists and the Law of Nations', 37 Z.a.öR.V. (1977) 87 at 88.
4. Helsinki, 1 August 1975, 14 I.L.M. (1975) 1292 at 1310; *Basic Documents* I.4.
5. Paris, 13 December 1955, 529 U.N.T.S. 141; *Basic Documents* V.3.
6. In the case of the Final Act of the Conference on Security and Cooperation in Europe, paragraph 4 of the final section records that the Act 'is not eligible for registration under Article 102 of the Charter of the United Nations'.
7. R. Baxter, 'International Law in "Her Infinite Variety" ', 19 I.C.L.Q. (1980) 549.
8. *India* v. *Pakistan,* I.C.J. Rep. (1972) 46 at 107 n. 1.
9. London, 16 November 1948, 4 U.N.T.S. 276.
10. Mexico City, 27 September 1970, 27 U.S.T. 2213.
11. Annexed to Recommendation No. 86 concerning Migration for Employment (Revised) 1949, *Basic Documents* VIII.1.
12. Case 203/80, *Casati,* [1981] E.C.R. 2595 at 2614.
13. M. Petersen, 'Capital Movements and Payments under the EEC Treaty after Casati', 7 E.L. Rev. (1982) 167.
14. Convention No. 143 concerning Migrant Workers (Suplementary Provisions) 1975, *Basic Documents* VII.5, Article 11(2), *supra,* Chapter IX, text at note 47.
15. Cf. European Convention on the Legal Status of Migrant Workers, Strasbourg, 24 November 1977, E.T.S. 93; *Basic Documents* V.7, Article 1(2).
16. Council Directive 68/360 of 15 October 1968, O.J. Sp. Ed. 1968, 485, *Basic Documents* VI.7, Article 8(1)(b). Cf. Convention on Frontier Workers, Brussels, 17 April 1950, 131 U.N.T.S. 99.
17. *Ibid.,* Article 8(1)(a), (c).
18. Case 167/73, *Commission* v *French Republic,* [1974] E.C.R. 359 at 371.
19. *Ibid.* See also Case 43/75, *Defrenne* v *Sabena, S.A.,* [1976] E.C.R. 455.
20. Joined Cases 110 and 111/78, *Van Wesemeel,* [1979] E.C.R. 35; Case 279/80, *Webb,* [1981] E.C.R. 3305.
21. Lourenço Marques, 2 August 1875, 67 B.F.S.P. 1291.
22. Lisbon, 18 July 1876, 72 B.F.S.P. 1143.
23. Lourenço Marques, 18 December 1901, 95 B.F.S.P. 931.
24. Pretoria, 1 April 1909, 102 B.F.S.P. 110. Revised by Treaty of Lisbon, 31 March 1923, 18 L.N.T.S. 30.
25. Pretoria, 11 September 1928, 98 L.N.T.S. 9. Revised by Agreement of Lourenço Marques, 12 July 1934, 197 L.N.T.S. 306; Exchange of Notes, Lisbon, 8 June 1936, S.A.T.S. 1936 No. 5; Exchange of Notes, Lisbon, 2 May 1940, 144 B.F.S.P. 201; Agreement of Lisbon, 13 October 1964 and 1 January 1965, S.A.T.S. 1964 No. 11; Exchange of Notes, Pretoria, 1 January and 26 March 1970, S.A.T.S. 1970 No. 3.
26. Article 18.
27. R. First, *Black Gold: The Mozambican Miner, Proletarian and Peasant,* 1983, 221–222. See also J. Harlon, *Beggar Your Neighbour,* Chapter 12.
28. J. Kalley, *A Chronological and Subject Analysis of South Africa's Multilateral and Bilateral Treaties, 1806–1979,* 1985, 152.
29. F. De Vletter, *Recent Trends and Prospects of Black Migration to South Africa,* 1985, Table 1.

30. 16 March 1984, published by the two Governments.
31. Blantyre, 1 August 1967, S.A.T.S. 1967, No. 10.
32. Pretoria and Gabarone, 24 December 1973, S.A.T.S. 1973, No. 3.
33. Pretoria and Maseru, 24 August 1973, S.A.T.S. 1973, No. 1.
34. Pretoria, 22 August 1986, S.A.T.S. 1986, No. 3.
35. De Vletter, *supra*, note 29, at p. 23.
36. Salisbury, 3 June 1964, S.A.T.S. 1964, No. 3.
37. Admission of Persons to the Republic Regulation Act, No 59 of 1972 (as amended by Admission of Persons to the Republic Regulation Act, No 42 of 1978, Admission of Persons to the Republic Regulation Act, No 6 of 1979, Admission of Persons to the Republic Regulation Act, No 29 of 1980, Republic of South Africa Constitution Second Amendment Act, No 101 of 1981, Heraldry Amendment Act, No 22 of 1982 and Aliens and Immigration Laws Amendment Act, No 49 of 1984). See in particular sections 14(1), 32 and 33 of the Act of 1972. The term 'prohibited person' is broadly defined under section 13(1). In particular, it embraces 'any person or category of persons deemed by the Minister on economic grounds or on account of standards or habits of life to be unsuited to the requirements of the Republic or any particular province thereof'. For the meaning of the prohibition of entry other than at approved ports of entry, see *S* v. *Natali,* [1973] 2 S.A. 490.
38. W. Böhning, ed., *Black Migration to South Africa: A Selection of Policy-Oriented Research,* 1981.
39. Point 6(a).
40. C. Stahl and W. Böhning, *Reducing Migration Dependence in Southern Africa,* 1979.
41. See also M. Miller and D. Yeres, *A Massive Temporary Worker Programme for the United States: Solution or Mirage?* I.L.O., 1979; C. Luroga, *Season Labour Migration in Tanzania: the Case of Ludewa District,* 1982; J. Gaude. *The Temporary Migration Phenomenon in the Sierra of Ecuador,* 1981.
42. J. de Bres and R. Campbell, 'Temporary Labour Migration between Tonga and New Zealand', 112 Int. Lab. Rev. (1975) 445.
43. Inter-State Migrant Workmen (Regulation of Employment and Conditions of Service) Act, No. 30 of 1979.
44. Treaties with: Bulgaria, Berlin, 10 October 1961, 9 D.A.R.D.D.R. 319; Ghana, Berlin, 14 May 1964, 12 D.A.R.D.D.R. 746; Guinea, Conakry, 29 May 1964, 12 D.A.R.D.D.R. 759; China, Beijing, 27 December 1954, 2 D.A.R.D.D.R. 407; U.S.S.R., Berlin, 21 February 1958, 6 D.A.R.D.D.R. 425; Korea (North), Pyonyang, 7 December 1959, 7 D.A.R.D.D.R. 384; Hungary, Budapest, 11 May 1962, 10 D.A.R.D.D.R. 497; Mali, Bamako, 3 June 1964, 12 D.A.R.D.D.R. 849; Mongolia, Berlin, 28 May 1965, 336 D.Z. 51; China, Beijing, 15 July 1965, 1965 Agreements of the People's Republic of China 94.
45. United Kingdom-France, Arrangement, Paris 16 May 1928, 80 L.N.T.S. 257; Netherlands-France, Exchange of Notes, Paris, 16 and 29 October 1930, 125 L.N.T.S. 29; United Kingdom-Netherlands Exchange of Notes, London, 12 January, 23 March and 9 April 1931, 125 L.N.T.S. 41; France-Sweden Exchange of Notes, Paris, 9 June 1934, 154 L.N.T.S. 101; Denmark-France Arrangement, Paris, 28 January 1935, 158 L.N.T.S. 11; France-Netherlands Agreement, Paris, 2 June 1948, 70 U.N.T.S. 105; Belgium-Finland Arrangement, Brussels, 20 March 1951, 110 U.N.T.S. 27; Belgium-Tunisia Agreement, Tunis, 7 August 1969, 696 U.N.T.S. 99.
46. Denmark-Switzerland Exchange of Notes, Copenhagen, 21 February 1948, 14 U.N.T.S. 321; Sweden-Switzerland Exchange of Notes, Berne, 16 March 1948, 197 U.N.T.S. 39; Netherlands-Sweden Exchange of Notes, The Hague, 6 July 1949, 197 U.N.T.S. 189; France-Turkey Agreement, Paris, 22 December 1950, 98 U.N.T.S. 11; Netherlands-Switzerland Exchange of Notes, Berne, 20 November 1952, 163 U.N.T.S. 121; Sweden-Germany Agree-

ment, Bonn, 15 May 1953, 227 U.N.T.S. 195; Netherlands-Italy Agreement, Rome, 4 June 1954, 289 U.N.T.S. 261; Denmark-Austria Exchange of Notes, Copenhagen, 7 September 1954, 292 U.N.T.S. 45; Sweden-Austria Exchange of Notes, Vienna, 3 November 1955, 262 U.N.T.S. 289; Belgium-Austria Exchange of Letters, Brussels, 20 January 1956, 248 U.N.T.S. 3; Netherlands-Ireland Agreement, Dublin, 28 May 1959, 344 U.N.T.S. 95; United States-Spain Exchange of Notes, Madrid, 13 and 21 July 1960, 393 U.N.T.S. 289; Finland-Italy Agreement, Helsinki, 18 February 1961, 434 U.N.T.S. 199; Finland-Austria Exchange of Notes, Helsinki, 1 February 1962, 425 U.N.T.S. 33; Netherlands-Denmark Agreement, Copenhagen, 20 June 1967, 619 U.N.T.S. 67.

47. Convention concerning Student Employees, Brussels, 17 April 1950, U.K.T.S. 1951 No. 8. For the Brussels Treaty, 17 March 1948, see U.K.T.S. 1949, No. 1.

48. Constitution of U.N.E.S.C.O., *supra,* note 9; Statutes of the World Tourism Organization, *supra,* note 10.

49. *Supra,* note 4.

50. Paris, 13 December 1957, 315 U.N.T.S. 139. Parties (13) include: Austria, Belgium, France, Federal Republic of Germany, Greece, Italy, Luxembourg, Malta, Netherlands, Portugal, Spain, Switzerland, Turkey.

51. The right is acknowledged in the minutes of the meeting of the Council of the European Communities at which Directive 68/360 of 15 October 1968 was adopted: O.J. Sp. Ed. 1968, 485. Article 3 of the Convention provides that 'the foregoing provisions shall in no way prejudice the laws and regulations governing visits by aliens in the territory of any Contracting Party'. The word 'visits' must, however, be understood in the light of the French *'sejour',* meaning conditions of stay rather than admission.

52. Article 6.

53. Article 7.

54. European Agreement on Travel by Young Persons on Collective Passports, Paris, 16 December 1961, E.T.S. No. 37, 544 U.N.T.S. 19.

55. Strasbourg, 4 December 1963, E.T.S. No. 31.

56. Strasbourg, 24 November 1969, E.T.S. No. 68.

57. L.N. Off. Jo. Special Supplement No. 193.

58. Geneva, 9 December 1923, 58 L.N.T.S. 285; 119 B.F.S.P. 568. See also Convention and Statute on Freedom of Transit, Barcelona, 20 April 1921, 7 L.N.T.S. 11.

59. Immigration and Nationality Act 1952, section 214(b); 22 C.F.R. 41.10. See generally, *Karnruth* v *U.S., ex parte Albro,* 279 U.S. 231 (1929).

60. Argentina: Treaty of Friendship, Commerce and Navigation, (Article II), San José, 27 July 1853; 5 Bevans 61. Austria: Treaty of Friendship, Commerce and Consular Rights, (Article I), Vienna, 19 June 1928; 5 Bevans 341; Belgium: Treaty of Friendship, Establishment and Navigation, (Article II), Brussels, 21 February 1961; 480 U.N.T.S. 149. Bolivia: Treaty of Peace, Friendship, Commerce and Navigation, (Article III), La Paz, 13 May 1858; 5 Bevans 721. Brunei: Treaty of Peace, Friendship, Commerce and Navigation, (Article II), Brunei, 23 June 1850, 5 Bevans 1080. China (Taiwan): Treaty of Friendship, Commerce and Navigation, (Article II), Nanking, 4 November 1946; 6 Bevans 761; (Pursuant to Section 6 of the Taiwan Relations Act, P.L. 96–8, 93 Stat. 14, and Executive Order 12143, 44 F.R. 37191, this agreement, which was concluded with the Taiwan authorities prior to 1 January 1979, is administered on a non-governmental basis by the American Institute in Taiwan, a non-profit District of Columbia corporation, and constitutes neither recognition of the Taiwan authorities nor the continuation of any official relationship with Taiwan.) Colombia: Treaty of Peace, Amity, Navigation and Commerce, (Article III), Bogota, 12 December 1846; 6 Bevans 868. Costa Rica: Treaty of Friendship, Commerce and Navigation, (Article II), Washington, 10 July 1851; 6 Bevans 1013. Denmark: Treaty of Friendship, Commerce and

Navigation, (Article II), Copenhagen, 1 October 1951; 421 U.N.T.S. 105. Estonia: Treaty of Friendship, Commerce and Consular Rights, (Article I), Washington, 23 December 1925; 7 Bevans 620. Ethiopia: Treaty of Amity and Economic Relations, (Article VI), Addis Ababa, 7 September 1951; 206 U.N.T.S. 41. Finland: Treaty of Friendship, Commerce and Consular Rights, (Article I), Washington, 13 February 1934; 7 Bevans 718. France: Convention of Establishment, (Article II), Paris, 25 November 1959; 401 U.N.T.S. 75. Federal Republic of Germany: Treaty of Friendship, Commerce and Navigation, Washington, 29 October 1954; 273 U.N.T.S. 3. Greece: Treaty of Friendship, Commerce and Navigation, (Article II), Athens, 3 August 1951; 224 U.N.T.S. 279. Honduras: Treaty of Friendship, Commerce and Consular Rights, (Article I), Tegucigalpa, 7 December 1927; 8 Bevans 905. Iran: Treaty of Amity, Economic Relations and Consular Rights, Tehran, 15 August 1955; 284 U.N.T.S. 93 (still in force: see *United States Diplomatic and Consular Staff in Iran*, I.C.J. Rep. (1980) 3, 28 and *Schering Corp.* v *Iran*, 5 Iran-U.S. C.T.R. (1984-I) 361, 381). Ireland: Treaty of Friendship, Commerce and Navigation, (Article I), Dublin, 21 January 1950; 206 U.N.T.S. 269. Israel: Treaty of Friendship, Commerce and Navigation, (Article II), Washington, 23 August 1951; 219 U.N.T.S. 237. Italy: Treaty of Friendship, Commerce and Navigation, (Article I and Article XXIV, paragraph 7), Rome, 2 February 1948; 9 Bevans 261. Japan: Treaty of Friendship, Commerce and Navigation, (Article I), Tokyo, 2 April 1953; 206 U.N.T.S. 143. Republic of Korea: Treaty of Friendship, Commerce and Navigation, (Article II), Seoul, 28 November 1956; 302 U.N.T.S. 281. Latvia: Treaty of Friendship, Commerce and Consular Rights, (Article I), Riga, 20 April 1928, 80 L.N.T.S. 35. Liberia: Treaty of Friendship, Commerce and Navigation, (Article I), Monrovia, 8 August 1938; 201 L.N.T.S. 163. Luxembourg: Treaty of Friendship, Establishment and Navigation, (Article II), Luxembourg, 23 February 1952; 474 U.N.T.S. 3. Netherlands: Treaty of Friendship, Commerce and Navigation, (Article II), The Hague, 27 March 1956; 285 U.N.T.S. 231. Norway: Treaty of Commerce and Navigation, (Article I), Stockholm, 4 July 1827; 11 Bevans 876; and Treaty of Friendship, Commerce and Consular Rights, Washington, 5 June 1928; 134 L.N.T.S. 81. Oman: Treaty of Amity, Economic Relations and Consular Rights, (Article II), Salalah, 20 December 1958; 380 U.N.T.S. 181. Pakistan: Treaty of Friendship and Commerce, Washington, 12 November 1959; 404 U.N.T.S. 259. Paraguay: Treaty of Friendship, Commerce and Navigation, (Article II), Asunción, 4 February 1859; 10 Bevans 888. Philippines: On 6 September 1955, pursuant to Article V of the revised Trade Agreement between the United States and the Republic of the Philippines, notes were exchanged between the two Governments implementing the provisions of the Act of 18 June 1954, which renders Philippine nationals eligible for non-immigrant classification as treaty investors under the provisions of section 101(a)(15)(E)(ii) of the Act, although there is no commercial treaty in force between the two countries; 238 U.N.T.S. 109. Spain: Treaty of Friendship and General Relations, (Article II), Madrid, 3 July 1902; 11 Bevans 628. Surinam: Treaty of Friendship, Commerce and Navigation, (Article II), The Hague, 27 March 1956; 285 U.N.T.S. 231. Switzerland: Convention of Friendship, Commerce and Extradition, (Article I), Bern, 25 November 1850; 11 Bevans 894. Thailand: Treaty of Amity and Economic Relations, Bangkok, 29 May 1966; 652 U.N.T.S. 253. Togo: Treaty of Amity and Economic Relations, (Article I), Lomé, 8 February 1966; 680 U.N.T.S. 159. Turkey: Treaty of Establishment and Sojourn, (Article I), Ankara, 28 October 1931; 11 Bevans 1127; 138 L.N.T.S. 345. United Kingdom: Convention to Regulate Commerce, (Article I), London, 3 July 1815, 12 Bevans 49. (The Convention which entered into force in 1815 applies only to British territory in Europe and to 'inhabitants' of such territory. This term, as used in the Convention, means 'one who resides actually and permanently in a given place, and has his domicile there'. Also, in order to qualify for treaty investor status under this treaty, the alien must be a national of the United Kingdom.) Yugoslavia: Treaty of Commerce, (Article I), Belgrade, 14 October 1881, 12 Bevans 1227.

61. Argentina: Treaty of Friendship, Commerce and Navigation, (Article II), San José, 27 July 1853; 5 Bevans 61. Austria: Treaty of Friendship, Commerce and Consular Rights, (Article I), Vienna, 19 June 1928; 5 Bevans 341; Belgium: Treaty of Friendship, Establishment and Navigation, (Article II), Brussels, 21 February 1961; 480 U.N.T.S. 149. China (Taiwan): Treaty of Friendship, Commerce and Navigation, (Article II), Nanking, 4 November 1946; 6 Bevans 761; (*supra,* note 60). Colombia: Treaty of Peace, Amity, Navigation and Commerce, (Article III), Bogotà, 12 December 1846; 6 Bevans 868. Costa Rica: Treaty of Friendship, Commerce and Navigation, (Article II), Washington, 10 July 1851; 6 Bevans 1013. Ethiopia: Treaty of Amity and Economic Relations, (Article VI), Addis Ababa, 7 September 1951; 206 U.N.T.S. 41. France: Convention of Establishment, (Article II), Paris, 25 November 1959; 401 U.N.T.S. 75. Federal Republic of Germany: Treaty of Friendship, Commerce and Navigation, Washington, 29 October 1954; 273 U.N.T.S. 3. Honduras: Treaty of Friendship, Commerce and Consular Rights, (Article I), Tegucigalpa, 7 December 1927; 8 Bevans 905; Iran: Treaty of Amity, Economic Relations and Consular Rights, Tehran, 15 August 1955; 284 U.N.T.S. 93 (*supra,* note 60). Italy: Treaty of Friendship, Commerce and Navigation, (Article I and Article XXIV, paragraph 7), Rome, 2 February 1948; 9 Bevans 261. Japan: Treaty of Friendship, Commerce and Navigation, (Article I), Tokyo, 2 April 1953; 206 U.N.T.S. 143. Republic of Korea: Treaty of Friendship, Commerce and Navigation, (Article II), Seoul, 28 November 1956; 302 U.N.T.S. 281. Liberia: Treaty of Friendship, Commerce and Navigation, (Article I), Monrovia, 8 August 1938; 201 L.N.T.S. 163. Luxembourg: Treaty of Friendship, Establishment and Navigation, (Article II), Luxembourg, 23 February 1952; 474 U.N.T.S. 3. Netherlands: Treaty of Friendship, Commerce and Navigation, (Article II), The Hague, 27 March 1956; 285 U.N.T.S. 231. Norway: Treaty of Commerce and Navigation, (Article I), Stockholm, 4 July 1827; 11 Bevans 876; and Treaty of Friendship, Commerce and Consular Rights, Washington, 5 June 1928; 134 L.N.T.S. 81. Oman: Treaty of Amity, Economic Relations and Consular Rights, (Article II), Salalah, 20 December 1958; 380 U.N.T.S. 181. Pakistan: Treaty of Friendship and Commerce, Washington, 12 November 1959; 404 U.N.T.S. 259. Paraguay: Treaty of Friendship, Commerce and Navigation, (Article II), Asunciòn, 4 February 1859; 10 Bevans 888. Philippines: On 6 September 1955, pursuant to Article V of the revised Trade Agreement between the United States and the Republic of the Philippines, notes were exchanged between the two Governments implementing the provisions of the Act of 18 June 1954, which renders Philippine nationals eligible for non-immigrant classification as treaty investors under the provisions of section 101(a)(15)(E)(ii) of the Act, although there is no commercial treaty in force between the two countries; 238 U.N.T.S. 109. Spain: Treaty of Friendship and General Relations, (Article II), Madrid, 3 July 1902; 11 Bevans 628. Surinam: Treaty of Friendship, Commerce and Navigation, (Article II), The Hague, 27 March 1956; 285 U.N.T.S. 231. Switzerland: Convention of Friendship, Commerce and Extradition, (Article I), Bern, 25 November 1850; 11 Bevans 894. Thailand: Treaty of Amity and Economic Relations, Bangkok, 29 May 1966; 652 U.N.T.S. 253. Togo: Treaty of Amity and Economic Relations, (Article I), Lomé, 8 February 1966; 680 U.N.T.S. 159. United Kingdom: Convention to Regulate Commerce, (Article I), London, 3 July 1815, 12 Bevans 49 (*supra,* note 60). Yugoslavia: Treaty of Commerce, (Article I), Belgrade, 14 October 1881, 12 Bevans 1227.
62. Migrant and Seasonal Agricultural Worker Protection Act 1983, 96 Stat. 2583, sections 101, 201, 202, 203, 403.
63. 8 C.F.R. para. 212.1. The Immigration and Nationality Service has proposed that a similar restriction be imposed on nationals of Bangladesh, India, Pakistan and Sri Lanka.
64. Law of 24 June 1981 on the Legal Status of Foreign Citizens in the USSR; Constitution of the USSR, 1977, Article 37.
65. Regulations of 22 September 1970, *Vedomosti S.S.S.R.,* 1970, No. 18, Article 139.

66. *Vedomosti S.S.S.R.*, 1984, No. 21, Article 113; ratified by Decision of the Council of Ministers of the USSR on 10 May 1984, No. 433.
67. *On the Way which was Opened in the Helsinki Documents and Materials,* Moscow, 1980, pp. 365 ff.
68. *Encyclopaedia of the Economic and Foreign Relations of the Soviet Union,* 1983, p. 452.
69. M. Boguslavski, '*Uber die Rechtsstellung der Ausländer in der USSR*', in *Die Rechtsstellung von Ausländern nach Staatlichen Recht und Volkerrecht,* Max-Planck Institute, 1985, Vol. 4 at p. 7.
70. Reg. 3.
71. Reg. 4.
72. Regs. 6, 9(1).
73. Reg. 9(2).
74. By Reg. 34 of the Regulations governing the residence of foreign citizens in the Soviet Union: 'Foreign citizens including those engaged in international automobile transportation may use only those roads which are open for international automobile transportation'.
75. Reg. 12.
76. Reg. 14.
77. Reg. 19.
78. Regs. 12–27.
79. Regs. 28–36.
80. Regs. 6–11.
81. Reg. 15.
82. Regs. 19 and 21.
83. Reg. 28.
84. Reg. 32.
85. Statement of Changes in the Immigration Rules, 1983, H.C. 169, paras. 17 and 20; formerly Immigration Rules, Control on Entry, para. 15, Instructions to Immigration Officers, Cmnd. 4296 and 4298 para. 12.
86. H.C. 169 para. 17. See S. Grant, 'Immigration Laws and Visitors', 129 Sol. Jo. (1985) at 387. If the Immigration Officer is not satisfied that the entrant will leave at the end of the period in respect of which the application was made, he has no discretion to grant leave to enter: *Visa Officer Cairo* v *Malek,* [1979–80] Imm. A.R. 111.
87. *Mustun* v *Home Secretary,* [1972] Imm. A.R. 97, now incorporated in H.C. 169 rule 17. An entry clearance can only be used once: *Andronicou* v *Chief Immigration Officer London (Heathrow) Airport,* [1974] Imm. A.R. 87. There is no restriction on the number of visits a person may make and no specific time period need have elapsed between visits.
88. *Hashim* v *Home Secretary,* [1982] Imm. A.R. 113.
89. H.C. 169 rules 20 and 103. In 1984 17,335 entrants (excluding EEC nationals) were refused admission. Others were admitted for less than the period requested. Nationals of the new Commonwealth countries accounted for a disproportionately large number of those refused admission: Commission for Radical Equality Report 1984, paras. 6. 9. 2–6.
90. *Entry Certificate Officer, New Delhi* v *Bhambra,* [1973] Imm. A.R. 14.
91. Government White Paper 1965, para. 22, Cmnd 2739. See generally, V. Bevan, *The Development of British Immigration Law,* 1986, at 276 *et seq. C.* v *Entry Clearance Officer, Hong Kong,* [1976] Imm. A.R. 165; *R* v *Chief Immigration Officer, Gatwick, ex parte Kharrazi,* [1980] 3 All E.R. 373. Reasonable suspicion by the entry clearance officer that the entrant has ulterior motives is sufficient to warrant refusal of entry: *Goffar* v *Entry Clearance Officer, Dacca,* [1975] Imm. A.R. 142.
92. *Islam* v *Entry Clearance Officer, Dacca,* [1974] Imm. A.R. 83.
93. *Patel* v *Immigration Appeal Tribunal,* [1983] Imm. A.R. 76.

94. On these issues, see generally: *R* v *Immigration Appeal Tribunal, ex parte Khan*, [1975] Imm. A.R. 26; *Islam* v *Entry Clearance Officer, Dacca, supra*, note 92; *Ghosh* v *Entry Clearance Officer, Calcutta*, [1976] Imm. A.R. 60; and *Sae-Heng* v *Visa Officer, Bangkok*, [1978–80] Imm. A.R. 69.

95. *Wedad* v *Home Secretary*, [1979–80] Imm. A.R. 27, where it was decided that full-time study with a firm of solicitors, by means of articles of training, did not amount to study in an 'educational institution'. See also *Entry Certificate Officer, Lagos* v *Amusu, [1974] Imm. A.R. 16*.

96. As a rule, not less than fifteen hours' study each week amounts to study for a substantial part of the applicant's time. See further, *Kpoma* v *Home Secretary*, [1973] Imm. A.R. 25.

97. A. Berriedale-Keith, *The Constitutional Law of the British Dominions*, 1933, pp. 6, 485.

98. Sir I. Jennings, *Constitutional Laws of the Commonwealth*, 1957, p. 20. See also S. de Smith, *The New Commonwealth and its Constitutions*, 1964, p. 37.

99. See now Sir K. Roberts-Wray, *Commonwealth and Colonial Law*, 1966, p. 96; Sir W. Dale, *The Modern Commonwealth*, 1983, p. 303.

100. Immigration Act 1976, Cap. 190, section 13 and second schedule.

101. Immigration and Passport Act 1946, Cap. 150, sections 13(1)(a) (former privileges of British subjects) and 33 (power to make regulations); Immigration and Passport (Amendment) Regulations 1981, S.I. 22/81; Passport and Visa (Exemption) Order 1985, S.I. 42/85.

102. No. 18 of 1979, Section 29(2) as amended by High Court of Zimbabwe Act, No. 29 of 1981, Part LXXIX; Refugee Act No. 13 of 1983, section 21(e); Citizenship of Zimbabwe Act No. 23 of 1984, section 24.

103. R.G.N. No. 273 of 1979, Reg. 10.

104. Immigration Act 1973. Revised Laws of Mauritius 1981 No. 83, sections 5 and 7.

105. Seychelles Immigration Decree 1979, No. 18, sections 13 and 14(2) as amended by the Immigration (Amendment) Act 1982, No. 17, which provides for a dependants' permit and Immigration (Amendment) Act 1985, No. 6, which at section 12(2) substitutes the word 'spouse' for 'wife' in the old Act.

106. Rule 5 (iv); also rule 34; and also for exemption for Nepalese and Bhutanese see rule 4.

107. This facility was suspended with effect from 24 June 1984. *Gazette of India, Extraordinary*, 16 June 1984. For other visitors this facility was suspended on 5 November 1982 for one month in view of the threat of extremist activities during Asiad IX, held at that time in New Delhi – *Gazette of India, Extraordinary*, Pt. 11, 5 3(ii). It was again suspended on 9 December 1982 until 31 March 1983 because of the ensuing non-aligned meeting and on 30 March of that year the suspension was extended indefinitely.

108. Foreigners Order 1948, Article 7.

109. R.S.C. 1952, C 325 section 2(f). The end of the period of admittance signifies automatic lapse of immigration status: *Re Morrison*, (1974) 47 D.L.R. (3d) 255 (Fed. C.A.).

110. Section 26(1) 1976 Act. See generally, J. Grey, *Immigration Law in Canada*, 1984, pp. 17 *et seq*.

111. 'Every immigrant and visitor must have a visa before appearing at a port of entry (except in prescribed cases)': Immigration Act 1976, section 9(1). 'A visa may only be issued if the visa officer is satisfied that the immigrant or visitor meets the requirements of the Act': *ibid.*, section 9(4). The 'requirement that any person seeking to enter Canada present himself for examination at a port of entry' is imposed by section 12(1). The cases of *Ainsooni* v *M.E.I.*, 78–1103, unreported judgement of Immigration Appeals Board 1 December 1979, and *M.E.I.* v *Gudino*, (1982) 2 F.C. 40, 124, D.L.R. (3d) 748, 38, N.R., 361 (C.A.) establish that a person not in possession of a visa may be turned back at the border. In *De Luca* v *M.M.I.*, (1976), 1 F.C. 226 (F.C.A.) it was held that to be allowed into Canada as a tourist the stay must be for a specified length of time as well as a limited one. The desire to remain for as long

as possible is inconsistent with being a genuine visitor: *Gill* v *M.E.I.,* (1981), 1 F.C. 615 (F.C.A.). In *Piangos* v *M.M.I.,* (1977) 14 N.R. 440 (F.C.A.) it was held that *having* the intention of staying as long as possible, and, if possible, permanently, upon coming to Canada, negates visitor status. It is the temporary nature of the stay, not the person's reasons for going to Canada that are decisive: *Shafi-Javid* v *M.M.I.,* (1977) 1 F.C. 509 (F.C.A.).

112. Immigration Act 1976, section 26(2), sections 16(1)(b) and 17(2)(c) allow for visa extension at the discretion of the immigration officer.

113. Migration Act 1958–73, sections 5, 6.

114. Migration Regulations 1959 No. 35 amended by 1964 No. 158, 1966, No. 86, 1970, No. 41, 1976. No. 225, 1979, No. 234.

115. In *Haj-Ismail* v *Minister for Immigration and Ethnic Affairs,* (1981), 36 ALR 516, it was stated *obiter* that in a case where an extension of a temporary permit was necessary to complete studies and the entrant had a 'legitimate expectation' that he would be permitted to complete his studies, natural justice required that the applicant be heard before a deportation order was issued.

116. Article 6. Nor is a visa required if the alien's passport already contains a re-entry visa issued under Article 26, or if the entrant has a Refugee Travel Document as defined under Article 61-2-6.

117. Article 4(6).

118. Articles 21 and 22.

119. Article 70 provides for punishment by penal servitude or imprisonment not exceeding three years or a fine not exceeding 300,000 yen for any person contravening these rules.

120. Article 13(3), (4), (5).

121. Special Immigration Law for Enforcement of the Agreement on the Legal Status and Treatment of the Nationals of the Republic of Korea residing in Japan, Law No. 146 of 1965. See also Imperial Ordinance concerning the Orders to be Issued in Consequence of the Acceptance of the Potsdam Declaration, Law No. 126 of 1952.

BIBLIOGRAPHY

J. Birks and C. Sinclair, *International Migration and Development in the Arab Region,* 1980.

M. Bogdan, 'Admission of Tourists and the Law of Nations', 37 ZaöRV (1977) 87.

W. Böhning (ed), *Black Migration to South Africa: A Selection of Policy-Oriented Research,* 1981.

J. de Bres and R. Campbell, 'Temporary Labour Migration between Tonga and New Zealand', 112 Int. Lab. Rev. (1975) 445.

F. de Vletter, *Recent Trends and Prospects of Black Migration to South Africa,* 1985.

R. First, *Black Gold: The Mozambican Miner, Proletarian and Peasant,* 1983.

R.D. Fraado and M. Artan, 'Temporary Employment of Foreign Nationals: The "M" Visa', 14 Int. Lawyer (1980) 235.

J. Grande, *The Temporary Migration Phenomenon in the Sierra of Ecuador,* 1981.

J. Harlon, *Beggar Your Neighbour,* 1986.

A. Hicks, 'Admission of Foreign Domestic Helpers: Some Legal Issues', 13 Hong Kong L.J. (1983) 194.

C. Luroga, *Season Labour Migration in Tanzania: The Case of Ludewa District,* 1982.

C. Manuelli, '*La Protection internationale de voyageur non-privilegié*' in R. St J. Macdonald, D.M. Douglas and G.L. Morris (eds) *The International Law and Policy of Human Rights,* 1978.

M. Miller and D. Yeres, *A Massive Temporary Worker Programme for the United States: Solution or Mirage?* 1979.

C. Stahl and W. Böhning, *Reducing Migration Dependence in Southern Africa,* 1979.

A. Tizzano, '*Circulazione dei Servizi nella Communità Economica Europea*', 19 Diritto Comunitario e degli Scambi internazionale (1980) 125.

CHAPTER 11

Family Reunification

Several of the multilateral legal instruments governing the protection of human rights place emphasis on the sanctity and unity of the family. Article 12 of the Universal Declaration of Human Rights proclaims that 'no-one shall be subjected to arbitrary interference with his ... family'. Article 16(3) asserts that 'the family is the natural and fundamental group unit of society and is entitled to protection by society and the State'.[1] That assertion is echoed in the International Covenant on Economic, Social and Cultural Rights, while the International Covenant on Civil and Political Rights states that no-one shall be subjected to arbitrary or unlawful interference with his family. Later, that instrument emphasizes the primacy of the family and adds that 'the right of men and women of marriageable age to marry and to found a family shall be recognized'.[2] The International Convention on the Elimination of All Forms of Racial Discrimination guarantees the right to marry and to choose a spouse without distinction as to race, colour or national or ethnic origin.[3]

At the regional level, the Final Act of the Helsinki Conference on Security and Cooperation in Europe sets standards in respect of contacts and regular meetings on the basis of family ties; the reunification of families; and marriages between citizens of different States.[4] The European Convention on Human Rights proclaims the right to respect for family life.[5] The American Convention on Human Rights reiterates the principles governing family rights promulgated in the International Covenant on Civil and Political Rights of 1966.[6] The African Charter on Human Rights declares that 'the State shall have the duty to assist the family which is the custodian of morals and traditional values recognized by the community'.[7]

Among all these proclamations, only one addresses specifically the problems arising in the event of the residence of members of a family in two States. The exception is the Final Act of the Helsinki Conference, but that document considers the issue principally in the context of emigration rather than immigration. Moreover, its force lies more in the political than in the legal sphere.[8] The Universal Declaration of Human Rights, which also exists in the hinterland between politics and law,[9] contains no suggestion that the protection of the family, envisaged in Article 16(3), encompasses the right of members of the family to enter a State's territory in order to live there with close relatives. On the contrary, by proscribing interference with the right to family life only when it is arbitrary, the framers of the Declaration signified that certain restrictions upon admission for the purposes of family reunion may indeed be imposed. On the other hand, the use of the term 'arbitrary' in place of the words 'illegal' or 'illegitimate' indicates that States are not free to impose any restrictions whatever.[10] The term 'arbitrary' was intended to have a meaning closer to 'unjust' than to 'illegal'.[11]

The point is made yet more clearly in the International Covenant on Civil and Political Rights, which prohibits 'arbitrary or unlawful' interference with the family. The implication is that interference which is lawful may nevertheless be arbitrary; and obstacles to family reunion arising from the operation of immigration laws may or may not be 'arbitrary'. The framers of the Covenant were not oblivious of the difficulties presented by immigration control in this context. Indeed, during the course of the negotiations a suggestion was made that programmes should be initiated to facilitate the reunion of families split after the Second World War.[12] They chose to avoid any specific mention of the subject in the text, in the interests of consensus.[13] In the case of the International Convention on the Elimination of All Forms of Racial Discrimination, the principal concern of the draftsmen of Article 5(d)(iv) was to establish a basis for resisting the maintenance of laws against miscegenation.[14]

Of the three regional conventions governing human rights, the African Charter goes furthest in advocating active assistance for the family. The assertion is made, however, without mention of migration. The European Convention is silent on that topic also; but as we have seen, the Commission has observed in this context that a State ratifying the Convention must be understood as agreeing to restrict the free exercise of its right to control the entry and exit of foreigners.[15] Indeed, the Commission appears to have adopted the language employed by the draftsmen of the Universal Declaration, in upholding the view that the expulsion of an individual or a decision refusing to admit that individual to a State's territory offends against Article 8 of the Convention if it results in the 'arbitrary' separation of members of a family.[16]

Even if they are taken together, these international and regional provisions do not amount to evidence of a right to family reunification in general international law. They do, however, establish the widespread acceptance of the moral or political proposition that States should facilitate the admission to their territories of members of the families of their own citizens or residents, at least when it would be unreasonable to expect the family to be reunited elsewhere. Thereby, they influence the content of bilateral agreements and domestic law.[17] Indeed, the special position of the family, as a fundamental unit of society entitled to the protection of the State, is the subject of explicit constitutional provisions in at least fifty countries.[18]

THE FAMILIES OF NATIONALS

The strongest claim to enter a State's territory can often be advanced by members of the immediate family of a national of that State; for if they are denied admission, the national is confronted with a choice between expatriation and disruption of the unity of the family.

The law of the United States, therefore, provides that the 'immediate relatives' of United States citizens shall be admissible to the territory of the United States subject only to qualitative and documentary restrictions. They are exempted from numerical restrictions. 'Immediate relatives' are defined to mean the spouses, children and parents of U.S. citizens.[19] Adult children do not qualify for this exemption but benefit from the availability of immigrant visas in the first preference category.[20] Twenty per cent, a total of 54,000 visas annually, are made available to qualified immigrants who are the unmarried sons and daughters of U.S. citizens. The fourth preference is reserved for married sons and daughters of U.S. citizens. Ten per cent of the visas available annually, plus any visas not used by the first three preference groups, are made available for those falling into this category.[21]

In the United Kingdom the right of abode is conferred upon Commonwealth citizens who enjoyed that right on the eve of the entry into force of the British Nationality Act 1981[22] as the children or wives of citizens of the United Kingdom and Colonies.[23] Furthermore, section 1(5) of the Immigration Act 1971 requires that the immigration rules shall be so framed that Commonwealth citizens settled[24] in the United Kingdom at the coming into force of that Act and their wives and children shall be no less free to come and go than if the Act had not been passed. In order to benefit from this provision, the wife or child must have been ordinarily resident in the kingdom on 1 January 1973; but it seems that she or he need not have been physically present at that date.[25] The wives and children who are protected by section 1(5) of the Act of 1971 do not enjoy a right of abode, but only the assurance that they will be treated no less favourably than they were to have been treated in accordance with the Instructions to Immigration Officers[26] in force at the end of 1972.[27]

In the Federal Republic of Germany, the legal rules and administrative regulations governing family reunification must conform with Article 6 of the Basic Law. The first three paragraphs of that Article provide as follows:

(1) Marriage and family shall enjoy the special protection of the State;
(2) The care and upbringing or children are a natural right of, and a duty

primarily incumbent on, the parents. The national community shall watch over their endeavours in this respect;

(3) Children may not be separated from their families against the will of the persons entitled to bring them up, except pursuant to a law, if those so entitled fail or the children are otherwise threatened with neglect.

The Federal Administrative Court has held that Article 6 prohibits the enactment of a law which imposes excessive restrictions on the admission to Germany of the spouse of a national, thereby confronting the German with a choice between expatriation and effective dissolution of the bond between man and wife.[28] Thus, the deportation of the alien spouse of a German national is impermissible, at least where it is a penalty for minor criminal offences.[29] It may be justified, however, in the event of the commission of a major offence by the alien, for in the application of Article 6, the principle of proportionality is to govern the exercise of administrative power.[30] The principles developed for the foreign spouses of German nationals apply equally to the foreign parents of minor German children.[31] The same is not the case, however, for the adult children of a German parent. There is not normally the kind of *Lebensgemeinschaft* (life community) between adult children and their parents that is required to maintain the family ties protected by Article 6 of the Basic Law. The admission to Germany of the children of German nationals is less frequently problematical than the admission to the United States or the United Kingdom of children of nationals of those countries, since in the Federal Republic of Germany nationality is generally transmitted to the children in accordance with the principle of *jus sanguinis*.

In France, Law No. 84–622 of 17 June 1984 provides that a residence permit shall be issued as a matter of right to certain aliens who benefit from the principle of family reunification. Among those aliens are the spouse of a French national and the child under twenty of such a national, if dependent on that national, and the parents or grandparents of the national, subject to a similar qualification. Alien parents of French children residing in France are also entitled to a residence permit to authorise their stay in France until the children attain the age of majority.

It seems that European Community law protects in certain circumstances the right of a person's spouse, children and other dependent relatives to live with that person in his or her own country; but this right is protected obliquely. Article 10(1) of Council Regulation 1612/68 provides that

The following shall, irrespective of their nationality, have the right to install themselves with a worker who is a national of one Member State and is employed on the territory of another Member State:

(a) his spouse and their descendants who are under the age of 21 years or are dependants;

(b) dependent relatives in the ascending line of the worker and his spouse.[32]

The Article envisages rights of entry only for dependants of nationals of one Member State employed in another. Thus the *Oberverwaltungsgericht* of Rheinland-Pfalz reached the conclusion in 1975 that the Egyptian husband of a German national in Germany gained no privileges under Community law as the spouse of a worker, whereas the Egyptian husband of an Italian woman employed in Germany would gain such privileges.[33] The judgment now appears to be superseded by a series of rulings of the European Court which establish a principle of 'reverse discrimination'. Within the sphere of application of the Treaty, a national is entitled to invoke against his own State those rights that can be invoked against the same State in like circumstances by nationals of another Member State. Among those rights is the entitlement to be accompanied by specified dependants when entering the State as a worker.

With this exception, international arrangements tend to leave untouched the admission to a State's territory of the foreign dependants of that State's nationals. The unification of a family within the territory of a State in which the head of the family lives and in which he is a national is not in general an issue impinging upon the interests of foreign States. Even in the case of the European Convention on Human Rights, the Fourth Protocol protects the right of entry of a national, to the exclusion of his dependants; and in the interpretation of Article 8 of the Convention the Commission has adopted the German concept of *Lebensgemeinschaft:* it seems that that Article is not infringed if the family can reside together elsewhere.[34]

For two categories of migrants, however, there exist networks of treaties and other arrangements designed to ensure reunification of the family. Those categories are migrant workers and refugees.

THE FAMILIES OF MIGRANT WORKERS

At a series of conferences of the I.L.O., members of that organization have made recommendations relating to dependants of migrant workers. The Migration for Employment Recommendation 1939 (No. 61)[35] advised that the members of the family of a migrant for employment, who desire to accompany or to join him, should receive special facilities for that purpose, including priority over other applicants for admission, a simplification of the administrative formalities and a reduction of the payments required. In that context the members of the family of a migrant for employment were deemed to consist of his wife and minor children 'and other members of his family dependent on him'. Most I.L.O. Conventions deal with family reunification only obliquely by reference to members of workers' families 'authorised to accompany or join them'[36] or by requirements to take account of workers' 'normal family needs'.[37] However, Article 13 of Convention No. 143 of 1975 concerning Migrant Workers (Supplementary Provisions) calls on Member States to take all necessary measures which fall within their competence and to collaborate with other Members to facilitate the reunification of the families of all migrant workers legally residing in their territory.[38]

The Migration for Employment Recommendation (Revised) (No. 86) adopted by the International Labour Conference in 1949 contained more explicit provisions to the same effect. For the purposes of the later Recommendation, the members of a family of a migrant for employment were defined as including his wife and minor children. The paragraph continued: 'favourable consideration should be given to requests for the inclusion of other members of the family dependent upon the migrant'. Moreover, the movement of the members of the family of a migrant for employment was to be 'specially facilitated' both by the country of emigration and by the country of immigration.[39] Paragraph 16(1) went on to advise that migrants for employment authorised to reside in a territory, and members of their family authorised to accompany or join them, should, as far as possible, be admitted to employment in the same conditions as nationals. According to paragraph 16(2) of this Recommendation: 'In countries in which the employment of migrants is subject to restrictions, these restrictions should as far as possible ... (b) cease to apply to the wife and children of an age to work who have been authorised to accompany or join the migrant, at the same time as they cease to apply to the migrant'. Annexed to Recommendation No. 86 is the Model Agreement on Temporary and Permanent Migration which envisaged that countries of emigration and immigration would conclude bilateral agreements to govern the categories of members of migrants' families authorised to accompany or join them.[40]

Repeating many of the provisions of this Recommendation and Model Agreement is Recommendation No. 151 concerning Migrant Workers, adopted in 1975. Part II, section A deals specifically with the Reunification of Families; and paragraph 13(1) states that 'All possible measures should be taken both by countries of employment and by countries of origin to facilitate the reunification of families of migrant workers as rapidly as possible. These measures should include, as necessary, national laws or regulations and bilateral and multilateral arrangements'. The family is to include the spouse, dependent children, father and mother.[41] The worker is required to have appropriate accommodation for his family; however, States are required to assist migrants in obtaining housing, to encourage the construction of housing for families and to provide services for the reception of the families of migrant workers. Paragraph 17 provides that where a migrant worker who has been employed for at least a year, cannot be joined by his family he should be entitled either to visit his country of origin without losing any rights to which he is entitled or to be visited by his family during his annual paid holiday. Member States are urged to consider giving financial assistance to the migrant worker towards the cost of this travel.

In bilateral agreements more specific provisions are commonly to be found. Such agreements often regulate the permanent settlement of members of the family of a migrant worker.[42] An agreement between France and Portugal[43] made in 1977 provides at Article 6(1):

Les autorités françaises favorisent le regroupement familial des travailleurs portugais employés en France. A ce titre, le conjoint et les enfant mineurs (fils de moins de 18 et filles de moins de 21 ans) du travailleurs sont admis dans les conditions de la législation française et conformément aux dispositions prévues à l'annexe II du présent Accord.

Articles 6(2) and (3) continue:

Les autorités compétentes françaises accorderont une attention particulière à la situation des ascendants du travailleur ou de son conjoint qui désireraient bénéficier du regroupement familial et ... recommenderont aux organismes gestionnaires des logements sociaux d'admettre les inscriptions des travailleurs portugais désireux de se faire rejoindre par leurs familles demeurées au Portugal.

By reason of Articles 1 and 13 of this treaty these provisions are applicable to both permanent and seasonal workers. A similar agreement between Belgium and Algeria[44] provides for Algerian workers who are 'employed and settled' in Belgium to be joined by their families on completion of three months' work, provided that they have suitable living accommodation available. An agreement between Italy and Switzerland required that a worker's employment and position in the country be sufficiently 'stable and durable' before family reunification could be considered.[45] Tunisian workers admitted to Belgium pursuant to a Convention of 1969[46] had to complete three months' work and find suitable accommodation before being reunited with a wife and dependent minor children. Both this treaty and another between Morocco and the Netherlands, under which employees had to have worked for two years before being joined by a family,[47] provide for employers and government agencies to assist the employee in finding accommodation for the family. Under Article 11 of an Agreement on Manpower between the Gabonese Republic and Cameroon[48] the accommodation is to be provided by employers so as to enable families to be reunited with workers. Article 6 of a similar agreement between Belgium and Italy of 11 July 1966 states that the government of the country of immigration will reimburse the travel costs of family members, including at least three dependent children, so as to enable them to be reunited with workers.[49]

Other bilateral instruments govern the treatment of families after their arrival. For example, an Exchange of Notes between France and San Marino is designed to enable workers of the latter State to benefit in France from the advantages enjoyed there by Italian nationals, particularly in respect of family allowances.[50] An agreement between Belgium and Tunisia[51] states that the wife and children of a Tunisian worker may take up employment 'if the situation of the labour market so permits'. The matter is governed more comprehensively in two Conventions concluded by France, with the Cameroon[52] and Portugal.[53] These require extensive documentation from families intending to be reunited with migrant workers employed in France. The first Convention provides that Cameroonian citizens travelling to France must hold a valid passport and visa, an international certificate of vaccination and a medical certificate. They must also guarantee their repatriation by holding a return ticket, by deposit of money or by bankers' warranty. The second Convention provides that an office for family migration in France and a corresponding mission in Portugal will deal with all questions relating to family reunification. In particular, the bureaux will coordinate their requirements for medical examination and travel documents for families intending to travel. The Director General responsible for emigration undertakes to inform families of living conditions in France, to take appropriate measures to ensure the best material and moral conditions and to take such measures as may be appropriate to assist families and to facilitate their emigration with the minimum delay.

The European Convention on the Legal Status of Migrant Workers[54] in Article 12 envisages that the spouse and unmarried minor dependants of a migrant worker will be permitted to join him in the territory of a contracting party. States are free to make this right conditional upon the worker having steady resources sufficient to meet the needs of his family and they may impose a waiting period not exceeding twelve months before a family may be reunited.

THE FAMILIES OF REFUGEES

In none of the main instruments concluded for the protection of refugees is the principle of family reunification guaranteed. This is so despite the fact that those fleeing persecution are often forced to leave behind family members who in turn may face disadvantage. Only in the Final Act of the United Nations Conference of Plenipotentiaries on the Status of Refugees and Stateless Persons[55] were recommendations made on the subject. The Conference considered that the family is the fundamental group unit of society, that family unity is an essential right of the refugee and that such unity is constantly threatened. Delegates recommended governments to take the necessary measures for the protection of the refugee's family, especially with a view to:

'(1) ensuring that the unity of the refugee's family is maintained, particularly in cases where the head of the family has fulfilled the necessary conditions for admission to a particular country; (2) the protection of refugees who are minors, in particular unaccompanied children and girls with special reference to guardianship and adoption'.

The desideratum expressed in the Final Act of the Conference of Plenipotentiaries has now been amplified by the Executive Committee of the Programme of the United Nations High Commissioner for Refugees. In Conclusion No. 9 (XXVIII) on Family Reunion, the Executive Committee affirmed that the UNHCR performed a coordinating role with a view to promoting the reunion of separated refugee families through appropriate interventions with governments and with intergovernmental and non-governmental organizations. In a later Conclusion[56] the Committee encouraged countries of asylum and countries of origin to facilitate family reunification with the least possible delay, for humanitarian reasons. Given the recognized right of everyone to leave any country including his own, countries of origin should grant exit permission to family members of refugees to enable them to join the refugee abroad. Countries of asylum were requested to apply liberal criteria in identifying those family members who can be admitted with a view to promoting a comprehensive reunification of the family. The absence of documentary proof of the formal validity of a marriage or of the filiation of children should not *per se* be considered as an impediment to reunification. The Executive Committee called upon governments to assist the refugees who are heads of families by providing economic aid and housing facilities for their dependants and by granting to those dependants the same legal immigration status as the head of the family. As regards unaccompanied minor refugee children, the Office of the UNHCR called upon States to endeavour to trace their relatives and to clarify their family situation before their resettlement.

Perhaps the main multilateral effort to achieve family reunification, coordinated by UNHCR, was the programme for 'orderly departure from Vietnam'.[57] In January 1979, Vietnam announced that it would permit the emigration of those who wished to leave, subject to certain exceptions. The Office of the United Nations High Commissioner despatched missions to Vietnam in March and May of that year, and the initiative resulted in a Memorandum of Understanding designed to facilitate the legal emigration of family members and 'other humanitarian cases'. The resettlement of Vietnamese nationals emigrating in accordance with the Memorandum of Understanding was then achieved both by the unilateral action of receiving States and by informal bilateral arrangements between those States and the UNHCR or Vietnam or both. One of the difficulties encountered in framing such arrangements was the necessity of taking account of the extended family known in Indo-China, by contrast with the nuclear family known in the principal receiving States.[58]

Both Japan[59] and Australia[60] had concluded bilateral agreements with the Government of South Vietnam concerning the orderly departure programme. On 22 April 1975, faced with a large-scale influx of Vietnamese 'boat people', the Australian Government announced that those eligible for temporary entry and family reunification would include: the spouse and children under 21 of Vietnamese students and Australian citizens of Vietnamese origin and those Vietnamese with a long and close association with the Australian presence in Vietnam whose life was considered to be in danger (on a case by case basis). Today in Australia family reunification is still given a high priority in the policies governing the immigration programme.

In the United States the spouse and unmarried children under 21 may accompany or join a refugee resident in America and may assume the same immigration status as that person.[61] An asylee may include his family in the application and all are eligible for permanent resident status one year after attaining refugee or asylee status.[62] In the law of the United Kingdom, a recognized refugee is seen as a person liable to remain and who therefore is allowed family reunification on the same basis as persons settled in the country. In Canada, the dependants of a Convention refugee seeking resettlement are considered with him when he applies for an entry visa. If the person makes a claim for refugee status from within Canada and his family is with him, then any dependants are liable to be included on a deportation order. Accordingly they may participate in an inquiry and the result of the inquiry will affect the family members in the same way as it does the principal applicant.

In the Netherlands, the dependants of a recognized refugee are admitted by reason of the family tie and are not usually subject to an independent procedure of recognition. Article 6 of the Law 38/80 of Portugal states: 'the grant of asylum shall apply to the spouse and minor children of the applicant and may apply also to other members of his extended family'.

THE DEFINITION OF THE FAMILY

Save in so far as States have accepted specific obligations to extend privileges to defined members of the families of their own nationals, or migrant worker or refugees, they remain free to admit or exclude the foreign dependants of their residents. At the same time, they are subject to a certain political or moral predisposition so to conduct their immigration policies as to avoid unnecessary disruption to family life. In these circumstances, national rules respecting family reunification present the greatest divergencies. In the principal States of immigration in the industrialised Western world, the basic provisions governing the definition of the family are sufficiently proximate to bear comparison; but even among States in this group the disparities are often striking.

In the United Kingdom, the following may be admitted as members of the family of a person settled in the country: the spouse, children and (under more rigorous conditions) the fiancé or fiancée, parents, grandparents, siblings and aunts and uncles. In all cases entry clearances are required, except where the entrant is admissible as a member of a worker's family in accordance with European Community law; or where the applicant for admission or residence is a wife who acquired the right of abode upon marriage; or where the applicant has already entered under another category and seeks variation of leave on the basis of a family relationship.[63] The entry clearance will be refused unless the immigration officer is satisfied that there will be adequate resources and accommodation for the parties without recourse to public funds.[64]

Those entering as spouses may be given leave to do so for up to twelve months, but this is extended indefinitely if the Home Secretary is satisfied at the end of that period that the marriage has not terminated and the couple intend to continue living together as spouses.[65] Where a person is admitted as a fiancé or fiancée, leave will normally be given for three months and a prohibition on employment imposed; but the entrant is advised to apply for the variation of the conditions of admission once the marriage has taken place.[66] In the event of an application for variation being made after the marriage, leave to remain for a further twelve months will normally be granted, provided that the marriage subsists and did not take place after the making of a deportation order or a recommendation to deport.[67] At the end of those twelve months, indefinite leave will normally be given if the marriage has not been terminated and the parties intend to live together permanently as man and wife.[68] A person admitted in any capacity other than that of spouse, fiancé or fiancée may apply for the relaxation of his or her conditions of admission following marriage to a person settled in the United Kingdom. Where conditions are relaxed in response to such an application, there will be imposed on the applicant the same conditions as are imposed on a person admitted as fiancé or fiancée.[69]

The immigration rules provide for the admission of a child together with a parent or to join a parent settled in the United Kingdom. The word 'parent' is defined so as to include both parents of an illegitimate child; step-parents, provided that the corresponding natural parent has died; and adoptive parents, provided that there has been a genuine transfer of responsibility which was not arranged so as to facilitate admission.[70] If both parents are living (whatever their matrimonial status), a child will be admitted to accompany or join one parent only if that parent has sole responsibility for the child's upbringing, or if there are serious or compelling family or other considerations making the child's exclusion undesirable; and if suitable arrangements for the child's care have been made.[71] 'Sole responsibility' is not to be construed literally but is a question of fact, to be determined according to the degree of parental support, genuine interest and affection.[72] On the other hand, a strict construction is applied to the phrase 'serious and compelling family or other ... considerations'.[73]

To qualify as a child the applicant must normally be under eighteen years of age. Those over eighteen may be admitted as dependants only in the most exceptional compassionate circumstances, in the same fashion as remoter relations. This rule is relaxed, however, in the case of fully dependant unmarried daughters under 21 years of age, who formed part of the family unit overseas and have no other close relations to whom they can turn.[74]

In order to qualify for admission as a parent or grandparent, an applicant must be a widowed mother or a widowed father over sixty-five years of age. The parent or grandparent must be wholly or mainly dependent upon sons or daughters settled in the United Kingdom who have the means to maintain the parent or grandparent and any other relations admitted with them.[75] Parents or grandparents who do not fulfil the normal age requirements may be admitted in the most exceptional compassionate circumstances, if they are living alone and have a standard of living substantially below that of their own country.[76] In the same exceptional compassionate circumstances, sons and daughters who do not otherwise qualify for admission may be given leave to enter, as may sisters, brothers, uncles and aunts.[77]

In Canada the Immigration Act makes explicit the aim of achieving family reunification[78] but the provision to that effect is construed as a statement of policy only. It does not override the other provisions of the Act, including the requirement that the wife of a Canadian citizen should obtain a visa before arriving at a port of entry.[79] Nevertheless, the Act provides for the admission, subject to documentary requirement, for members of a 'family', meaning the father, mother and any dependent children.[80] The Immigration Regulations define the 'family class' whose members are eligible for admission as sponsored immigrants.[81] That class includes fiancés or fiancées, parents or grandparents over sixty years of age who are widowed or incapable of working, unmarried children under 21 years of age and unmarried orphaned brothers, sisters, nephews, nieces and grandchildren under 21 years of age. The same Regulations permit a resident of Canada who has no other members of his family living with him to sponsor as a member of the family class any relative regardless of age or relationship.[82]

In general, the admission of dependants is discretionary: the sponsor must undertake to provide for the dependant and the immigration officer must be satisfied that the undertaking is likely to be honoured. In making his assessment, the officer must consider whether the sponsor's means are so reduced that he is living below the official poverty line.[83] This discretion is absent, however, in the case of members of the 'family', that is, the sponsor's spouse and unmarried children under 21 years of age.[84] Indeed, in the case of spouses (and presumably in the case of dependent minor children) the visa officer is under a duty to issue the visa, when the statutory conditions are fulfilled.[85]

In the case of fiancés or fiancées, sponsorship is permitted only when there is no impediment to the marriage and the parties intend that the ceremony of marriage will be celebrated within ninety days of entry to Canada.[86] The rule has been subjected to criticism on the ground that the difficulties entailed in securing divorces in certain of the Canadian provinces are formidable; and couples who have lived together for considerable periods or have children may not qualify as fiancés.

To be eligible for admission as the child of a Canadian sponsor, the applicant may be the legitimate or illegitimate child of a female sponsor but only the legitimate child of a male sponsor.[87] A challenge to this was launched in *René Germain* v *Malouin*, on the ground that the rule violated the principle of sexual equality.[88] The challenge failed although it was later established that an illegitimate child in Canada may sponsor the admission of both his father and his mother.[89] Unlike the word 'child', the words 'father' and 'mother' are not given a statutory definition.

More remote relations falling within the 'family class' are assessed on a points system. Thereby they receive priority over other applicants for admission, but no form of right of entry.[90]

In France the spouse and children under the age of eighteen of an alien bearing a residence permit are authorised to reside with that alien. A similar right is extended to spouses and children of refugees enjoying asylum in France, stateless persons who have been resident in France for three years and aliens who have lived in France for fifteen years or at all times since reaching the age of ten.[91] More distant relations, including the parents and grandparents of an alien resident, may be granted residence permits authorising them to live in France when they formed part of the family unit in the country of origin together with an alien bearing a French residence permit, and where the reunification of the family is warranted for humanitarian reasons.[92] The *Conseil d'Etat* has ruled that the powers of the administration must be exercised in conformity with a general rule of law which guarantees the alien's right to live a normal family life.[93]

Children under 18 years of age are immune from deportation from France, as are aliens who are married to French nationals and have been so married for

378

at least six months. A similar immunity is extended to the father or mother of a
French national resident in France.[94]

In each of these cases, as in the United States, the law establishes a policy of
admitting the nuclear family of a settled immigrant and permitting the admission in certain circumstances of remoter relations. This policy is not universally
observed, even among Western States. In the Netherlands, the Aliens' Circular[95] provides for the admission of spouses and minor children (including minor
children of one of the spouses not born of the marriage, if they belonged to the
family abroad). It also envisages the admission of other family members, if
they belonged to the family abroad or were entirely dependent on the family
member resident in the Netherlands. The Circular adds, however, that unmarried partners of Dutch nationals or of aliens who have been granted asylum
or who hold establishment permits in the Netherlands are eligible for admission. This is so in the case of homosexual as well as heterosexual part-
nerships.[96] Moreover, the admission to the Netherlands of nationals of Surinam and members of their families was regulated in accordance with a bilateral
treaty which gave an extended definition to the 'family'.[97] Article 5(2) identified the members of the family as the spouse, those with whom the national
had a lasting and exclusive personal relationship, minor children who actually
belonged to the family of the persons concerned and over whom one of those
persons exercised authority and other family members who actually belonged
to the family and were dependent on the person concerned.

Moreover, the Dutch Aliens Decree[98] contains a radical provision designed
to protect the unity of the family of Dutch nationals and holders of establishment permits, together with aliens admitted as refugees. The spouse and
children under 21 years of age of these persons obtain a special title of
residence as members of the family, which may be held in conjunction with
another immigration permit or status. Those benefitting from this title are
protected from expulsion from the Netherlands, without qualification, so long
as the family tie subsists and the family lives together.[98]

The extended definition of 'family' found in the treaty between the Netherlands and Surinam is by no means unique. The Danish Aliens Act permits
family reunification in the case of those 'closely connected through relatives or
in a similar manner with a person permanently resident in Denmark'.[99] Swedish law contemplates the admission as dependant of a person in a 'serious
relationship' with a Swedish national or resident.[100] In Ghana, the former
immigration regulations defined a family as including the wife, husband,
mother, father, step-father, step-mother, son, daughter, step-son and step-
daughter.[101] In 1975, however, the definition was deleted.[102] A residence
permit will now be issued to anyone who establishes to the satisfaction of the
immigration officer that he is in fact dependant upon a Ghanaian national or
resident. In this context, relationships of consanguinity are material but inconclusive.

The Constitution of Kenya does not specifically guarantee the right to family unity, nor does the Immigration Act of 1967 specifically provide that the dependants of Kenyan nationals or residents shall enjoy the right to enter that country. Nevertheless, a person who holds Kenyan citizenship or a Kenyan entry permit, and is thereby entitled to reside in Kenya, may apply for a pass to authorize any of his dependants to reside there with him. The Immigration Regulations do not prescribe any degree of relationship to determine who may, and who may not, be treated as a 'dependant'. Instead, the immigration officer has the power to issue a dependant's pass if he is satisfied that the person on whose behalf the application was made is in fact dependent for his maintenance on the applicant, and if the applicant is financially capable of caring for the putative dependant.[103]

Similarly, under Barbadian law, the element of dependence is emphasized, and the element of consanguinity is correspondingly eclipsed. Thus, a person who is genealogically a remote relative of a Barbadian resident may nevertheless qualify as his 'dependant'. Such dependants enjoy, in effect, the right to enter Barbados.[104]

Jamaican law also confers statutory rights of entry on the dependants of certain residents, but this right is only conferred on persons seeking to enter the island under the Immigration Restriction (Commonwealth Citizens) Law, 1945. For the purposes of that Law, a person qualifies as a 'dependant' if he or she is the wife, or is the child or step-child or adopted child under sixteen of a person who 'belongs' to Jamaica, or is in civil, military or diplomatic service there. Furthermore, a Commonwealth citizen has a right of entry in Jamaica if he 'belongs' to the island, and a citizen 'belongs' to the island if he is the dependant of a person domiciled there.[105] A Jamaican domicile cannot normally be acquired for this purpose until the *de cujus* has been resident in the island for two years,[106] but on satisfying the requirements for the acquisition of a Jamaican domicile, an immigrant to that island may introduce his dependants to live with him – for they will then 'belong' to Jamaica. Once admitted, they will not necessarily have the right to take employment in Jamaica. Nevertheless, if the head of the household takes Jamaican citizenship, other members of the family become free to take paid work in the island: wives and certain widows of Jamaican citizens have been exempted from the Foreign Nationals and Commonwealth Citizens (Employment) Act.[107]

Alien dependants do not enjoy any right of entry under Jamaican law. However, in practice the alien spouse and minor children of a Jamaican resident are normally admitted to the island if the resident is able to maintain them.[108] More remote alien relatives of Jamaican residents are permitted to enter the island if commercial or humanitarian considerations demonstrate the wisdom of admitting them.

If the national rules governing the definition of the family present more divergencies than points of similarity, the collective experience of the principal States of immigration has nevertheless presented some common problems. One of these is the 'marriage of convenience', meaning a ceremony of marriage undergone with the object of gaining admission to a State and with the intention that the marriage will be dissolved when that object is accomplished. During the last twenty years or so there has emerged a widespread tendency to disregard such marriages for the purposes of identifying spouses who are qualified to be admitted as such.

Indeed, the origins of the trend can be traced to an earlier date. In a case decided in 1930, *Nachimson* v *Nachimson,* the purported marriage had been solemnized in Moscow at a time when Russian law provided for automatic divorce, on the application of either party. The court rejected the argument that the ease with which the marriage might be dissolved made the marriage void; but in rejecting the argument, Lawrence, L.J., stated that

> the present case might possibly have assumed a different complexion if it had been proved ... that the marriage in question had been a complete sham.[109]

The judge's suggestion failed to receive the endorsement of the English and South African courts a generation later, when they were confronted with applications for decrees of nullity, presented by parties who had undergone ceremonies of marriage for immigration purposes.[110] In the light of this case-law, it appears that an immigration officer was not entitled at common law to treat such a marriage as void for the purpose of applying the immigration rules.

The United Kingdom's present immigration rules therefore address the issue; but since those rules were altered in 1985, without retrospective effect, it is necessary to consider separately those cases in which applications for entry clearances are made after 15 July 1985 and those cases in which applications were made before that date. Where the application is made after 15 July 1985, the entry clearance officer will authorize the admission of a spouse, irrespective of sex, only if three conditions are satisfied. Firstly, the parties must have met. Secondly, they must intend to live together as spouses. Thirdly, the marriage must not have been entered into primarily to obtain admission into the United Kingdom.[111] From this it appears sufficiently clearly that the new rules strikes at marriages which are in no sense mere shams. A marriage entered into primarily for the purpose of immigration is captured by the rule, even when the couple genuinely intend to live together indefinitely.[112]

Spouses who applied for entry clearances before 15 July 1985 are treated differently, according to the sex of the applicant.[113] In the case of a wife, she need not fulfil the requirements as to primary purpose. The husband must fulfil that requirement, although he is not entirely subject to the regime which operated prior to the new rules, since he is not obliged to meet the accommodation and maintenance requirements nor can he be refused leave to enter on grounds of restricted returnability or on medical grounds. Furthermore, the requirement that the wife be a British citizen, which applied prior to 1985, has been abolished even for transitional cases.[114]

In the United States, the federal courts have established that parties to a 'sham' marriage are not to be regarded as spouses within the meaning of the Immigration Act.[115] A marriage is a 'sham' if it was entered into for the sole purpose of securing admission to the United States, without the intention of establishing a *bona fide* marital relationship;[116] or if the parties 'did not intend to establish a life together at the time they were married'.[117] Parties to a sham marriage, if alien, are liable to deportation.[118] If a marriage between a resident and an alien breaks down within two years of the alien's admission to the United States, the inference may be drawn that the marriage was arranged so as to gain admission of the alien.[119]

In the Federal Republic of Germany, a marriage contracted exclusively for the purpose of gaining an entitlement to reside on federal territory, between a couple who do not live together, is not invalid. Such a marriage is, however, unprotected by Article 6 of the Basic Law.[120] The public interest in preventing such marriages (designated '*Scheinehe*') is a priority of the Republic.[121] Therefore, in the exercise of its discretion, the aliens authority may refuse to permit the alien party to the marriage to remain on federal territory. Moreover, if the purpose of the marriage is discovered after the grant of permission to reside, that permission may be withdrawn.[122]

Recent Belgian legislation is designed to discourage the practice of celebrating marriages of convenience (or '*marriages bidons*') for the purpose of overcoming immigration controls. The *Procureur du Roi* may apply for the annulment of a marriage on the ground that the parties entered into it exclusively for the purpose of acquiring or preserving right of residence. Furthermore, an alien admitted to Belgium as a dependant may not in turn bring a spouse to the kingdom other than with the authorization of the Minister of Justice.[123]

Although the position in Canada is less certain, it appears that a party to a marriage of convenience is inadmissible as a spouse.[124] In *M.E.I. v Robbins*, the court held that a visa officer is precluded from inquiring into the purposes for which parties to a valid marriage contracted it.[125] The decision suggests that a marriage which is intended by the parties to be a genuine union of indefinite duration is not to be treated as a sham by reason of motives of one or other partner. Different considerations arise when the parties do not intend to cohabit, but to dissolve the marriage once the immigration formalities have been fulfilled. Where this intention is demonstrated, there is no need to inquire into the parties' motives.[126] The English and South African authorities which suggest that such a marriage is not voidable[127] are easily distinguishable, in view of the express language of the Canadian immigration regulations.

It can scarcely be maintained that a party to the European Convention on Human Rights infringes Article 12 of that Treaty if it expels or declines to admit to its territory a person who has undergone a marriage of convenience with one of its nationals or residents. The right to marry and found a family, under Article 12 of the Convention, is subject to the qualifications expressed in that Article and also to others that must be inferred from contextual provisions. For this reason the Court of Appeal held in *R* v *Home Secretary, ex parte Bhajan Singh*[128] that a person who was lawfully detained with a view to deportation was not entitled to rely upon Article 12 for the purpose of securing his release to marry a girl of sixteen resident in England. In that case the Lord Chief Justice had taken the view, at first instance, that the marriage was a 'sham'. Indeed, it was conceded that neither party had contemplated marriage until after the applicant's arrest, and that the prospective bride had not thought of it until the day before the initiation of the legal proceedings. The Court of Appeal, however, took the view that the marriage was intended to be genuine; and that Court's conclusions as to Article 12 of the Convention must apply to marriages of convenience *a fortiori*.

THE POLYGAMOUS WIFE

The basis for the assessment of the validity of a marriage for the purposes of immigration is commonly to be found in the familiar rules of private international law of the forum. Thus, questions of essential validity may be referred to the law of the place of celebration and questions of capacity to the laws of the parties' domiciles or nationalities or to that of the intended matrimonial domicile. The rules of private international law are, however, apt to be qualified by special rules of policy in the context of immigration, particularly in cases involving the recognition of the validity of marriages.

In the United States, the tribunals charged with the determination of immigration appeals have been required to apply the rule which subjects questions of formal validity to the *lex loci contractus*.[129] Thus, a marriage registered in accordance with Article 739 of the Japanese Civil Code at a time when the male party to the ceremony was in the United States was recognized as valid.[130] In *Won Man Gin* v *Dulles*, Justice Sweeney upheld the validity of a marriage celebrated in China by 'one of the usual ceremonies, such as the exchanging of red cards, with the bride riding to the house of the groom in a red sedan chair'.[131] There is something of a presumption in favour of the formal validity of a marriage celebrated abroad.[132] The same is true in the event of a dispute as to the essential validity of the marriage: it appears that a voidable marriage will be recognized until annulled, even though the effect of the annulment may be to render the union void *ab initio*.[133]

In the case of polygamous marriages, the prevailing American view[134] is that such marriages will not be recognized for the purpose of giving rise to the relationship of 'spouses' or 'children' as defined in the Immigration and Nationality Act. This is so even though the marriage may be valid according to the law of the place in which it was contracted. Moreover, the invalidity of the polygamous marriage is not removed by the subsequent divorce of the first wife. This view is based upon venerable but relatively ancient judicial authority.[135] The harshness of the rule is mitigated in the case of children of such marriages, since they may be admitted under the fifth preference category as legal half-brothers or half-sisters, in common with illegitimate children.[136] In the case of spouses, however, there is no scope for such mitigation, even where the first marriage has been dissolved at the date of the application for an immigrant visa.

In the United Kingdom, the polygamous wife is at present eligible for admission, in principle. Where the second or subsequent marriage was contracted during the subsistence of the first marriage, and at a time when the parties were domiciled in a jurisdiction in which polygamous marriages are recognized, the second wife qualifies for admission as a 'spouse' within the meaning of the Immigration Rules.[137] Indeed, the Immigration Act declares specifically that the word 'wife' includes each of two or more wives for the purposes of deportation.[138] Where, on the other hand, either party is domiciled in England and Wales at the time of celebration of the polygamous marriage abroad, the marriage will be void. For this purpose a marriage may be polygamous although at its inception neither party had any spouse additional to the other.[139] Thus, where a man domiciled in England undergoes a ceremony of marriage in Muslim form in Pakistan with a woman domiciled there, the woman is ineligible for admission as his wife, unless he was unmarried at the time of the celebration of the marriage and the marriage is incapable of becoming polygamous in fact.[140] The last condition will normally be fulfilled if the wife establishes a domicile in England with her husband.

Formerly, the immigration rules provided that a woman who has been living in permanent association with a man might be admitted 'as if she were his wife', due account being taken of any local custom or tradition tending to establish the permanence of the association.[141] The Immigration Appeal Tribunal held that this rule was not sufficiently broad to permit the admission of a woman who was a party to a polygamous marriage contracted with a man then domiciled in England, during the lifetime of the first wife.[142] That decision was subject to telling criticism[143] and was distinguished by the same Tribunal in a later case, in which the husband believed that he had divorced the first wife and taken the second wife to the exclusion of all others.[144] Since August 1985, the rule permitting the admission of unmarried cohabiting partners has been abolished, save for transitional cases (principally cases in which an application for entry clearance was made before 15 July 1985).[145] It follows that the contentious decision of the Tribunal has been deprived of much of its significance.

According to a leading Canadian authority, polygamous marriages will not be recognized for the purposes of sponsorship in Canada. This rule is said to be based on a rule grounded in public policy, since 'no provincial marriage law recognizes the legal validity of common law or polygamous marriages'.[146] It is, of course, appreciated that no such law recognizes the validity of such a marriage when it depends for its validity upon the law of a Canadian province; but different considerations arise in the case of a marriage contracted in a foreign jurisdiction, in which the parties are domiciled.[147] If the parties to such a marriage are not to be treated as spouses for the purposes of immigration, notwithstanding the validity of both marriages in accordance with the *lex loci contractus,* the rule requiring the courts to disregard the marriage must be made on a principal or public policy applying specifically in the context of immigration, rather than in the conflict of laws.[148]

Moreover, it is not obvious that a monogamous State experiencing immigration from polygamous States must as a matter of public policy always decline to treat a polygamous wife as a spouse for the purposes of immigration. In France, the *Conseil d'Etat* has held that the Minister of the Interior was not entitled to make a deportation order against a polygamous wife, on the ground of *ordre public,* even though her husband was living in France with the other of his two wives and her children.[149] That decision was followed by the German *Bundesverwaltungsgericht* in 1985. It held that the grant of a residence permit to the second (polygamous) wife of a Jordanian national was not to be excluded. The protection of the family envisaged by Article 6 of the Basic Law extended to polygamous marriages where there were children of the union. In such cases, polygamous marriages were not to be treated as identical with monogamous marriages, but they gave rise to relationships which had to be weighed against the State's interest in maintaining immigration control.[150]

THE SEVERANCE OF FAMILY TIES

The severance of family ties, particularly in the event of divorce of a couple, or the attainment of majority or independence by their children, generally leaves unaffected the position in immigration law of those who have already established their status as permanent residents. The coincidence of State practice on the point is remarkable and is consonant with the phenomenon which we have observed elsewhere: that aliens who have satisfied a residential qualification commonly receive an indefinite right of residence or relief from liability to deportation.[151]

Thus, in Argentina, an alien who loses his status as permanent resident by reason of a change in his family situation, may apply for restoration of that status on the basis of his own connections with that country.[152] A similar rule applies in Chile.[153] In France, a member of the family within the statutory limits of consanguinity is eligible to receive a residence permit and no provision is made for the withdrawal of the permit in the event of severance of family connections.[154] The silence of the governing legal provisions produces a similar effect in Canada,[155] Yugoslavia,[156] and the United Kingdom.[157] It is also true of the United States, save that the dissolution of a marriage occurring within two years of the admission of one of the spouses to the United States, as spouse, will give rise to the rebuttable presumption that the marriage was one of convenience.[158] In some States, a statutory period of residence must be completed in order that the alien may gain a right of residence,[159] and in others the family ties must exist for a statutory period.[160]

Where, however, the dependant has not yet established the status of a permanent resident, the dissolution of the family bond is apt to bring about the severance of his claim to remain; although the nature of his connections with the country of immigration, as well as the length of his period of residence, is likely to be taken into account by the administrative authorities in determining whether to require the alien to depart.[161]

NOTES

1. New York, 10 December 1948, 43 A.J.I.L. (1949) Supp. 127 (*Basic Documents* I.1). See N. Robinson, *The Universal Declaration of Human Rights: Its Origin, Significance, Application and Interpretation*, 1958, pp. 117–118; R. Verdoot, *Naissance et Signification de la Déclaration universelle des droits de l'homme*, 1964, pp. 138–143.
2. International Covenant on Economic, Social and Cultural Rights, New York, 16 December 1966, 6 I.L.M. (1967) 360, Article 10; International Covenant on Civil and Political Rights, New York, 16 December 1966, 6 I.L.M. (1967) 368 (*Basic Documents* I.2), Articles 17 and 23.
3. New York, 7 March 1966, 60 U.N.T.S. 195 (*Basic Documents* I.3), Article 5(d)(iv).
4. Final Act of the Conference on Security and Cooperation in Europe, Helsinki, 1 August 1975, 14 I.L.M. (1975) 1293; Cooperation in Humanitarian and Other Fields, 1; Human Contacts (a), (b) and (c); (*Basic Documents* I.4), elaborated in the Concluding Document of the Madrid Session of the Conference, 9 September 1983, 22 I.L.M. (1983) 1395.
5. Rome, 4 November 1950, 213 U.N.T.S. 223 (*Basic Documents* V.1), Article 8.
6. San José, 22 November 1969, 9 I.L.M. 99 (*Basic Documents* IX.4), Article 17.

7. Banjul, 26 June 1981, 21 I.L.M. (1982) 58 (*Basic Documents* IX.5), Article 18(2).

8. See generally A. Bloed and P. van Dijk, *Essays in Human Rights and the Helsinki Process*, 1985, 1–8.

9. For the rejection of the Universal Declaration as a legal instrument, see H. Lauterpacht, 'The Universal Declaration of Human Rights', 25 B.Y.I.L. (1948) 354 at 356–365 and R. Cassin, '*La déclaration universelle et la mise en oeuvre des droits de l'homme*', 79 Hague *Recueil* (1951–II) 237 at 290–296.

10. The Saudi Arabian delegate considered the word 'illegal' and proposed the word 'illegitimate'; but his proposal was rejected; American and British delegates expressed the view that the word 'arbitrary' was broader in meaning: UNGAOR Vol. 3, Part I, Third Committee (1948) at 276, 310, 352, 354.

11. P. Hassan, 'The Word 'Arbitrary' as used in the Universal Declaration of Human Rights: 'Illegal' or 'Unjust'?' 10 Harv. Int. L.J. (1969) 225.

12. U.N. Doc. A/33/40 paras. 165, 181 (1978); L. Henkin (ed.), *The International Bill of Rights: The Covenant on Civil and Political Rights,* 1981, 205.

13. The principal instruments adopted by the United Nations or under its auspices for the purpose of implementing the right to family unity are not concerned with the issue of migration at all. See the Convention on Consent to Marriage, Minimum Age for Marriage and Registration of Marriages, U.N.G.A. Res. 1763 (XVII), New York, 10 December 1962, 521 U.N.T.S. 231; the Declaration of the Rights of the Child, U.N.G.A. Res. 1386 (XIV) of 20 November 1959; and the Declaration on the Promotion among Youth of the Ideals of Peace, U.N.G.A. Res. 2037 (XX) of 7 December 1965.

14. New York, 7 March 1966, 60 U.N.T.S. 195; N. Lerner, *The U.N. Convention on the Elimination of All Forms of Racial Discrimination,* 1980, p. 58.

15. Application No. 434/50, *X* v *Sweden,* II Ybk. (1959) 354; Application No. 2142/64, *X* v Austria and Yugoslavia, VII Ybk. (1964) 314; Application No. 6315/73, *X* v *Germany,* XVII Ybk. (1974) 480.

16. Application No. 434/50, *supra* note 15.

17. Thus, during a Parliamentary debate in the United Kingdom, one Member referred to 'the inherent right of a man to have his wife and children with him': 717 H.C. Deb., Cols. 1062–1063, 1066–1067 (2 August 1965).

18. Albania: Constitution of 28 December 1976, Articles 17 and 19; Algeria: Constitution of 9 November 1976, Article 17; Argentina: Constitution of 1853, Article 14; Bolivia: Constitution 2 February 1967, Article 193; Brazil: Constitution of 17 October 1969, Article 167; Bulgaria: Constitution of 18 May 1971, Article 72; Burma: Constitution of 3 January 1974, Article 37; Byelorussian S.S.R.: Constitution of 19 February 1937, Article 97; Cameroon: Constitution of 20 May 1972, Preamble; Central African Republic: Constitution of 1 February 1981, Preamble; The Congo: Constitution of 9 July 1979, Article 51; Costa Rica: Constitution of November 1949, Article 43; Cuba: Constitution of 24 February 1976, Article 26; Czechoslovakia: Constitution of 11 July 1960, Article 15; Dominican Republic: Constitution of 25 July 1978, Articles 29 and 30; Ecuador: Constitution of 25 May 1967, Article 19; Egypt: Constitution of 22 May 1980, Article 19; El Salvador: Constitution of 15 December 1983, Article 179, and Labour Code, Article 182; Gabon: Constitution of May 1975, Article 1; German Democratic Republic: Constitution of 7 October 1979, Articles 18 and 30; Federal Republic of Germany: Constitution of 1949, Article 6; Guatemala: Constitution of 31 May 1985, Article 85; Honduras: Constitution of 11 January 1982, Articles 109, 118, 124; Hungary: Constitution of 20 August 1949, Articles 50 and 51; India: Constitution of 26 November 1949, Article 38; Iraq: Interim Constitution of 16 July 1970, Articles 5 and 15; Ireland: Constitution of 6 December 1922, Article 41; Italy: Constitution of 22 December 1947, Article 29; Democratic Republic of Korea: Constitution of 27 December 1972, Article

23; Kuwait: Constitution of 11 November 1969, Article 9; Libyan Arab Republic: Constitution of 18 January 1974, Article 33; Madagascar: Constitution of 29 April 1959, Preamble; Panama: Constitution of 1 March 1946, Article 54; Paraguay: Constitution of 25 August 1967, Article 85; Poland: Constitution of 22 July 1952, Article 67; Portugal: Constitution of 2 April 1976, Article 12; Romania: Constitution of 21 August 1965, Article 23; Rwanda: Constitution of 20 December 1978, Article 26; Senegal: Constitution of 8 March 1963, Article 14; Somalia: Constitution of August 1979, Article 31; Spain: Constitution of 29 December 1978, Article 22; Switzerland: Constitution of 31 January 1874, Article 34D; Syrian Arab Republic: Constitution of 13 March 1975, Article 20; Turkey: Constitution of 9 November 1982, Article 35; Ukrainian S.S.R.: Constitution of 30 January 1937, Article 102; Uruguay: Constitution of 27 June 1976, Article 40; Venezuela: Constitution of 23 January 1961, Article 73; Democratic Republic of Vietnam: Constitution of 18 December 1980, Article 24; Democratic Republic of Yemen: Constitution of 31 October 1978, Article 6.

19. Immigration and Nationality Act 1952, section 201(a)(b).
20. Section 203 (a)(1). See C. Gordon and H. Rosenfield, *Immigration Law and Procedure 1959–1986,* Vol. I, para 2–27(b); T. Aleinikoff and D. Martin, *Immigration: Process and Policy,* 1985, p. 101.
21. Section 203 (a)(4).
22. I.e. 31 December 1982: section 53(2).
23. British Nationality Act 1981, section 39(2), amending Immigration Act 1971, section 2 (paraphrased).
24. A person is settled in the United Kingdom if he is ordinarily resident there without being subject under the immigration laws to any restrictions on the period for which he may remain: Immigration Act 1971, section 2(3)(d).
25. *R v Home Secretary, ex parte Mughal,* [1973] 3 All E.R. 796.
26. Cmnd. 4298 (admission); Cmnd. 4295 (after entry).
27. *Afuah Foriwaa Poku v Home Secretary,* [1986] Imm. A.R. 119; *R v Immigration Appeal Tribunal, ex parte L. Ruhul,* [1986] Imm. A.R. 27; D. Marrington, 'Commitment and Contradiction in Immigration Law', 6 *Legal Studies* (1986) 272.
28. See, among other decisions, *Turkish National,* decision of Senate dated 18 September 1984, 70 B.Verw.G. 127 (No. 21).
29. *Jordanian National,* decision of Senate dated 20 May 1980, 60 B.Verw.G. 126 (No. 18).
30. *Greek National,* B.VerW.G. 4 August 1983, Inf. Ausl.R. 1983, 308; *Turkish National,* B.VerW.G. 19 August 1983, NVwZ 1983, 667.
31. *Michael Peter T.,* decision of Senate date 18 January 1979, 57 B.Verw.G. 229 (No. 31).
32. Council Regulation 1612/68 of 15 October 1968 on Freedom of Movement for Workers within the Community, O.J. Sp. Ed. 1968, 475 (*Basic Documents* VI.6).
33. *Re Residence Permit for an Egyptian National,* [1975] C.M.L.R. 402.
34. *Supra,* Chapter VII, text at note 38.
35. Paragraph 10(1)(2). For earlier instruments and a comparative study, see I.L.O. Migration Laws and Treaties, Vols I, II and III, Geneva, 1928–1929 and UNIDROIT International Institute for the Unification of Private Law, Compilation of Laws on the Legal Status of Aliens, Rome, 1953.
36. Convention No. 97 concerning Migration for Employment (Revised) 1949, Article 5(a); see *Basic Documents* VII.2.
37. Convention No. 82 concerning Social Policy (Non-Metropolitan Territories) 1947, Article 10: see *Basic Documents* VII.1; and also Convention No. 117 concerning Basic Aims and Standards of Social Policy 1962, Article 6: see *Basic Documents* VII.3.
38. Geneva, 24 June 1975, Cmnd. 6674; *Basic Documents* VII.5.
39. Paragraph 15(2), (3); see *Basic Documents* VIII.1.

388

40. Article 5(1)(b).
41. Paragraph 15; see *Basic Documents* VIII.3.
42. See generally: *Migrant Workers: General Survey by the Committee of Experts on the Application of Conventions and Recommendations,* International Labour Conference, 66th session 1980, Report III, Part 4.B. at p. 120, 'Reunification of Families'.
43. *Accord relatif à l'immigration, à la situation et à la promotion sociale des travailleurs portugais et de leur famille en France (ensemble quatre annexes),* Lisbon, 11 January 1977, J.O.R.F. 17 May 1977 p. 2787.
44. Convention concerning the Employment and Residence in Belgium of Algerian workers and their families, Algiers, 8 January 1970, 717 U.N.T.S. 321.
45. Rome, 10 August 1964, *Legge 16 febbraio 1965 n. 61. Ratifica e esecuzione dell'Accordo tra l'Italia e la Svizzera relativo all'emigrazione dei lavoratori italiani in Svizzera con Protocollo finale e Dichiarazione Comuni,* Article 13, G.U. No. 54 2 March 1965, p. 988.
46. Convention concerning the Employment and Residence in Belgium of Tunisian Workers (with annexes), Tunis, 7 August 1969, 695 U.N.T.S. 73, Article XIII.
47. Convention concerning the Recruitment and Placement of Moroccan Workers in the Netherlands, The Hague, 14 May 1969, 686 U.N.T.S. 139, Article 17. A Convention respecting Emigration between Belgium and Spain (Brussels 28 November 1956, 308 U.N.T.S. 285) contains no such limitations but provides for the straightforward issue of visas to dependants of those settled in the territory of the contracting parties.
48. Cooperation Agreement on Manpower between the Gabonese Republic and the United Republic of Cameroon. Ratified by Decree No. 77–125 of 6 May 1977, Yaoundé, 9 August 1974 (Official Gazette of the United Republic of Cameroon, 15 May 1977, No. 10, p. 999.
49. See also: Convention concerning Emigration of Portuguese Workers and their Families, 15 April 1976, 1976 *Diario do Goberno* p. 117; *Protocole relatif à la formation professionelle des adultes, Décret no. 63–779 du 27 juillet 1963 portant publication de la Convention de main d'oeuvre entre la France et le Maroc du 1 juin 1963, fait à Rabat,* Article 11, J.O.R.F. 2 August 1963, p. 7161.
50. Paris, 21 May 1965. *Décret no. 65–461 du 15 juin 1965 portant publication.* J.O.R.R. 21 and 22 June 1965, p. 5155.
51. *Supra,* note 46, Article XIV.
52. *Convention rélative à la circulation des personnes, signée à Yaoundé le 26 juin 1976,* Article 9. *Décret no. 77–1215 du 25 octobre 1977 portant publication,* J.O.R.F. 7 and 8 November 1977, p. 5351.
53. *Supra,* note 43, Annexe II, *Regroupement Familiale.*
54. Strasbourg, 24 November 1977, E.T.S. No. 93; *Basic Documents* V.7.
55. Pursuant to U.N.G.A. Res. 429(V) of 14 December 1950. The Conference met at Geneva from 2 to 25 July 1951. The Final Act was signed on 28 July 1951. The Conference noted with satisfaction that according to the official commentary of the Ad Hoc Committee on Statelessness and Related Problems (E/1618, p. 40), the rights granted to a refugee are extended to members of his family: Recommendation IV.B.
56. No. 24 (XXXII), Family Reunification. Conclusion endorsed by the Executive Committee of the High Commissioner's Programme upon the recommendation of the sub-committee of the whole on International Protection of Refugees.
57. Report of the Secretary-General on the Meeting on Refugees and Displaced Persons in South East Asia, Geneva, 20–21 July 1979, and subsequent developments. U.N. Doc. A/34/627. On UNHCR's activities in promoting family reunion, see Note on International Protection, U.N. Doc. A/AC.96/538, annexe, 5–9 (28th session of the Executive Committee, 1977).
58. Incorporating recognition of such relationships in resettlement programmes can in turn

cause problems, as where other migrant groups perceive themselves disadvantaged by comparison. See U.N. Docs. A/AC.96/599, paras 26–36; A/AC.96/601, paras. 54, 57(4).

59. Agreement on Resettlement of Vietnamese Refugees, 20 May 1970, *O Van Kien Ngoai-Giao* 326; 3 October 1973, *Joyakushu* 759 and 30 March 1974, *Joyakushu* 1055.
60. See Australian Population and Immigration Council, *Immigration Rules and Australia's Population, A Green Paper,* Canberra, 1977, AGPS, and also L. Benyei, 'Refugee Problems of the Third World – From an Australian Perspective', 24 AWR Bulletin 1986, p. 47.
61. Immigration and Nationality Act 1952, section 207(c)(2).
62. Immigration and Nationality Act 1952, section 208(c) and 209. From 1968 to 1976, the number of visas available for immigration from the Western Hemisphere was reduced each year to take account of the number of Cuban refugees granted permanent resident status in that year under the Cuban Adjustment Act 1966. In *Silva v Bell,* 605 F.2d. 978, the Circuit Court ruled that this practice was unlawful and had to be corrected retrospectively.
63. H.C. 169, paras. 41–44, 46–48, 50–63, 66 and 133, as substituted by H.C. 503, paras. 10–14. R. White (contributor), *Stair Memorial Encyclopaedia of the Law of Scotland,* Immigration, para. 159. The sponsor must show that he is present in the kingdom and settled there or is being admitted on the same occasion for settlement. See *Arshad v Immigration Officer, London (Heathrow) Airport,* [1977] Imm. A.R. 19; *Immigration Appeal Tribunal v Manek,* [1978] Imm. A.R. 131 (C.A.).
64. H.C. 169, para. 46, as substituted by H.C. 503, para 10.
65. H.C. 169, paras 77 and 125, as substituted by H.C. 503, paras. 10 and 22.
66. H.C. 169, para 42, as substituted by H.C. 503, para. 8.
67. H.C. 169, para. 123, as substituted by H.C. 503, para. 22.
68. H.C. 169, para. 125, as substituted by H.C. 503, para. 22.
69. H.C. 169, para. 124, as substituted by H.C. 503, para. 22.
70. H.C. 169, para. 50, as amended by H.C. 503, para. 11. *J. Pereira and Another v Entry Clearance Officer, Bridgetown,* [1979–80] Imm. A.R. 79. The adoption need not be one recognized under ordinary rules of English or Scots private international law but must be valid where it occurred: *Malik v Home Secretary,* [1972] Imm. A.R. 37.
71. H.C. 169, para. 50(e), (f), as amended by H.C. 503, para. 11.
72. White, *supra* note 63 at para. 174. See also, *McGillivray v Home Secretary,* [1972] Imm. A.R. 63; *Emanuel v Home Secretary,* [1972] Imm. A.R. 69; *Martin v Home Secretary,* [1972] Imm. A.R. 71; *Home Secretary v Pusey,* [1972] Imm. A.R. 240; *Bovell and Others v Entry Clearance Officer, Georgetown, Guyana,* [1973] Imm. A.R. 37; *Sloley v Entry Clearance Officer, Kingston, Jamaica,* [1973] Imm. A.R. 54; *Eugene v Entry Clearance Officer, Bridgetown,* [1975] Imm. A.R. 111; *Entry Clearance Officer, Kingston, Jamaica v Martin (S.S.),* [1978] Imm. A.R. 100.
73. *Howard v Home Secretary,* [1972] Imm. A.R. 93; *Rennie v Entry Clearance Officer, Kingston, Jamaica,* [1979] Imm. A.R. 117; *Entry Clearance Officer, Kingston, Jamaica v Thompson,* [1981] Imm. A.R. 148; *R v Immigration Appeal Tribunal, ex parte Fojor Uddin and Nur Uddin,* [1986] Imm. A.R. 203.
74. H.C. 169, para. 51, as amended by H.C. 503, para. 13; *Bernard v Entry Clearance Officer, Kingston, Jamaica,* [1976] Imm. A.R. 7; *Harmail Singh v Immigration Appeal Tribunal,* [1978] Imm. A.R. 1401.
75. H.C. 169, para. 52, as amended by H.C. 503, para. 14. *Phillips v Entry Clearance Officer, Kingston, Jamaica,* [1973] Imm. A.R. 47.
76. *Mukhopadyay v Entry Clearance Officer, Calcutta,* [1975] Imm. A.R. 42.
77. *Harder Kaur and Others v Entry Clearance Officer, New Delhi,* [1979–80] Imm. A.R. 76.
78. Immigration Act 1976, S.C. 1976–77, cap. 52, section 3(c).
79. *Boudjaklian v M.E.I.,* [1979] N.R. 3.17.

80. Section 2(1).
81. Immigration Regulations 1978, S.O.R. 78–172 [1978] 112, Canada Gazette, Part II, 757, 24 February 1978, made pursuant to section 115(i)(b) and (c) of the Act.
82. Regulations 4 and 5.
83. Regulation 6(2).
84. Regulation 6(1)(d).
85. *M.E.I.* v *Robbins,* (1983) N.R. 195. See F. Ringham, Case Comments, 19 U.B.C.L. Rev. (1985) 97.
86. J. Grey, *Immigration Law in Canada,* 1984, p. 140.
87. Regulation 2.
88. (1978) 2 F.C. 14, 80 D.L.R. (3d) 659, affirmed, *sub. nom. Germain* v *M.E.I.,* (1979) 2 F.C. 784, 101 D.L.R. (3d) 384.
89. *Gill* v *M.E.I.,* (1979) 2 F.C. 782, 102 D.L.R. (3d) 341; see generally, J. Grey, *supra,* note 86 at p. 137.
90. See generally F. Hawkins, 'Immigration and Citizenship Laws in the United States, Canada and Australia', paper for Conference on International Migration in the Arab World, U.N.E.C.E., Nicosia, 11–16 May 1981, pp. 14–24.
91. Law No. 84–622 of 17 July 1984, D (L) 1984, 458, amending Ordonnance 45–2658 of 2 November 1945, Article 15. The family is defined more broadly in the case of nationals of Member States of the European Communities and members of consular or diplomatic missions in France.
92. In such an event, the permit is not issued as a matter of right but may be refused where the head of the family does not possess sufficient means to provide for the family or where his presence or that of members of the family would constitute a threat to *ordre public.*
93. *El Kaamouchi,* decision of 8 December 1978, *Rec. Cons. d'Et* 1978, p. 501 (note).
94. Law No. 81–973 of 29 October 1981 D (L) 1981, 361, Article 5, amending Ordonnance 45–2658 of 2 November 1945, Article 23.
95. Aliens Circular (loose leaf) 1982, published pursuant to Aliens Regulations 1966.
96. In Case 59/85, *Netherlands* v *Anna Florence Reed,* 17 April 1986, O.J. 1976 C122/3, the Court of Justice of the European Communities ruled that such a partner is not a 'spouse' for the purposes of Article 10 of Council Regulation 1612/68, O.J. Sp. Ed. 1968, 475. Where, however, a State admits the partners of its own nationals it must extend a similar facility to the partners of nationals of other European Community States.
97. Agreement between the Kingdom of the Netherlands and the Republic of Surinam concerning the Temporary and Permanent Residence of their Respective Nationals, Paramaribo, 25 November 1975, 1041 U.N.T.S. 316 (expired after five years' operation).
98. Aliens Decree 1966, section 47, made in implementation of the Aliens Act 1965, section 10.
99. Aliens Act, No. 226, 8 June 1983, section 9(2)(i).
100. Aliens Regulations, 25 January 1957, *Forskrifter om Lutendingers adgang til riket;* G. Melander, in *Legal Position of Aliens in National and International Law,* Max Planck Institute, Swedish Abstract, p. 27.
101. Aliens (Registration) Amendment Regulations 1974, L.I. 883.
102. Aliens Registration (Amendment No. 2) Regulations 1975, L.I. 1052.
103. Immigration Regulations 1967, Legal Notice No. 235, paragraph 15.
104. Immigration Act 1952, section 2(1)(d).
105. Section 2(3)(b)(d).
106. Section 2(1).
107. Foreign Nationals and Commonwealth Citizens (Employment) Exemptions Regulations, 1964, *Jamaica Gazette Supplement,* Vol. LXXXVIII, No. 149, 26 November 1964, No. 369.
108. The principal alien is ineligible for admission unless he is in a position to support himself and

his dependants (if any) in Jamaica: Aliens Law, 1945–48, section 6(a).

109. [1930] P. 217, 233.
110. *Silver* v *Silver*, [1955] 2 All E.R. 614; *Martens* v *Martens*, [1952] 3 S.A. 771, 776; approved by Karminski, J. in *H.* v *H.*, [1953] 2 All E.R. 1232.
111. H.C. 169, para. 46, as substituted by H.C. 503, para. 10. The rule that the parties must 'have met' requires that they should be acquainted with one another. A brief meeting when the couple were infants does not suffice: *Reural Raj* v *Entry Clearance Officer, New Delhi*, [1985] Imm. A.R. 151.
112. *R* v *Immigration Appeal Tribunal, ex parte Bhatia, The Times* L.R., 12 April 1985 (Divisional Court).
113. The change in 1985 was brought about in consequence of the decision of the European Court of Human Rights in Applications Nos. 9214/80, 9473/81 and 9474/81, *Abdulaziz, Cabales and Balkandali* v *United Kingdom*, 28 May 1985, 7 EHRR (1985) 471.
114. H.C. 503, para. 30.
115. *Scott* v *Immigration and Naturalisation Service*, 350 F. 2d. 279 (1965); *U.S.* v *Rubenstein*, 151 F. 2d. 915 (1945). See also *Ex parte Lee Yum Bo, Re Morony*, (1964) 6 F.L.R. 235.
116. *Lutwak* v *U.S.*, 344 U.S. 604 (1954); *In the Matter of M.*, I.D. 968 (1958).
117. *Bark* v *Immigration and Naturalisation Service*, 511 F. 2d. 1200 (1975).
118. Immigration and Nationality Act 1952, section 241(c). See T. Roberts, 'Marital Status and the Alien', 62 *Interpreter Releases* (1985) 64 at 76.
119. Immigration and Nationality Act 1952, section 212(a)(19).
120. *Supra,* text at note 28.
121. Max Planck Institut für Ausländisches, Offentliches Recht und Völkerrecht, *The Legal Protection of Aliens in National and International Law,* 1985, German National Report by K. Hailbronner at p. 37.
122. *Yugoslav National,* BVerwG. 23 March 1982, NJW 1982, 1956.
123. Law of 15 December 1980, Article 10(3) (in force 16 August 1984).
124. Immigration Regulations, Reg. 4(3).
125. (1984) 1 D.L.R. (4th) 380.
126. *Re Jiminez-Perez* v *M.E.I.,* 15 A.C.W.S. (2d) 310 (Fed. C.A.); cited by C. Wydrzynski, *Canadian Immigration Law and Procedure,* 1983, at p. 133.
127. *Supra,* note 110.
128. [1975] 2 All E.R. 1081.
129. J. Beale, *A Treatise on the Conflict of Laws,* 1935, Vol. II, 669.
130. *In the Matter of H.H.,* 6 I.N. 278 (1954).
131. 131 F. Supp. 549 (1955).
132. *In the Matter of M.D.,* 3 I.N. 485 (1949); *Karanos* v *Murff,* 170 F. Supp. 182 (1959).
133. *In the Matter of S.,* 7 I.N. 247 (1956). However, in *In the Matter of F.,* 9 I.N. 275 (1961), the Board of Immigration Appeals regarded as valid a marriage celebrated three years before one of the parties secured the annulment of a previous marriage.
134. Gordon and Rosenfield, *supra,* note 20, Vol. I. para. 2–18a(4).
135. *Hi* v *Weedin,* 21 F. 2d. 801 (1927); *In the Matter of C.,* 4 I.N. 632 (1952); *In the Matter of H.,* 9 I.N. 640 (1962).
136. *In the Matter of Mahal,* 12 I.N. 409 (1967).
137. H.C. 503, paragraph 10. The principle is enunciated in *Dicey on the Conflict of Laws,* ed. J. Morris and Others, 1980, Vol. I, p. 320, Rule 38: 'A marriage which is polygamous under Rule 35 and not invalid under Rule 36 or 37 will be recognized in England as a valid marriage unless there is some strong reason to the contrary'.
138. Immigration Act 1971, section 5(4).
139. Matrimonial Causes Act 1973, section 11(d).

140. *Husain* v *Husain,* [1983] 4 Fam. 339 (C.A.).
141. H.C. 169, para. 49.
142. *Zahra* v *Visa Officer, Islamabad,* (1979–80) Imm. A.R. 48.
143. I. Macdonald, *Immigration Law and Practice,* 1983, p. 214 (note).
144. *Khoja,* TH/77412/81 (2343).
145. H.C. 503, para. 29.
146. *Supra,* note 126, p. 103.
147. So in *Lee Sheck Yew* v *Attorney General for British Columbia,* [1924] 1 D.L.R. 1166, the two (polygamous) wives of a man domiciled in China were entitled to be treated as his 'wife' for the purposes of fixing the rate of succession duty payable on the administration of his Canadian estate.
148. Cf. *Sidhu* v *M.E.I.,* 14 June 1978, C.L.I.C. No. 1.31.
149. *Minister of the Interior* v *Montcho,* 11 July 1980, *Rec. Cons. d'Et.,* 1980, p. 315.
150. *Jordanian National (No. 2),* decision of 30 April 1985, 40 J.Z. (1985) 740.
151. *Supra,* Chapter V, text at notes 1–17.
152. Decree No. 4418 of 1965, Article 17.
153. Supreme Decree No. 597 of 1984, Article 141.
154. *Supra,* text at notes 91–94.
155. See Immigration Regulations 1978, Reg. 6(1) (obligations of sponsorship).
156. See Aliens Act 1974.
157. The onus is on the secretary of state: *Home Secretary* v. *Anseereegaroo,* [1981] Imm. A.R. 30.
158. *Supra,* note 119.
159. Aliens Act 1983, section 19(2).
160. See Ass. S. Thomson, 'The Legal Position of the Spouse and Family Members' in Max Planck Institute, *The Legal Position of Aliens in National and International Law,* at p. 19.
161. E.g. Spain: Aliens Law, 1 June 1985, Article 13.

BIBLIOGRAPHY

D. Danilov and M. Nerheim, 'Marriage, Divorce, the Alien and Washington Law', 19 Gonzaga L. Rev. (1983–4) 308.

A. Harakas, 'Canadian Immigration Law and the Canadian Charter of Rights and Freedoms', Detroit Coll. of L. Rev. (1985) 1089.

C. Hyde, 'Aspects of Marriage between Persons of Differing Nationality', 24 A.J.I.L. (1930) 742.

A. Khan, 'Adoption and Immigration', 130 Sol. Jo. (1985), 213.

R. Lillich (ed) C. Newdick, *The Family in International Law,* 1980; 'Immigration, Marriage and the Primary Purposes Rule', 135 New L.J. (1985), 816.

R. Plender, 'Relatives' Rights and Absolute Discretion', 2 New Community (1972–73), 177.

F. Ringham, Case Comments, 19 UBCL Rev. (1985), 97.

A. Robertson (ed.), *Privacy and Human Rights,* 1973.

CHAPTER 12

Refugees

Since the establishment of the Office of the United Nations High Commissioner for Refugees in 1950, the world's population of asylum-seekers has altered significantly. Approximately 98% now originate in developing countries rather than in Eastern Europe; two-thirds are from Africa and Asia. Their numbers have grown at a disturbing rate and currently approach twelve million.[1]

There is as yet no consensus on the definition of 'refugee'[2], although treaties and State practice contribute to an understanding of the term. For present purposes we may define a refugee as a person outside his country of nationality who is seeking or has received asylum in a foreign country as a means of protection against persecution in his own. The word 'asylum' will be used to connote 'the protection which a State grants *on its territory* to a person who comes to seek it.[3]

A refugee so defined is an alien of a special kind, since he or she is unwilling or unable to return to his or her country of nationality. It is primarily (though not exclusively) in this respect that the treatment of refugees becomes a matter for international concern. The refugee is estranged from his State of nationality, but as a general rule his State of nationality is the only entity capable of defending his interests on the international plane. That State is in normal circumstances the only one which is obliged by international law to admit him to its territory. Furthermore, there is a close relationship between the problems of refugees and the maintenance of international peace and security. The allegation that proper treatment has not been accorded to refugees may become the catalyst in an international conflagration, as the United Nations has recognized with respect to the situation in the Middle East.[4] For this reason, political considerations are apt to play an important rôle in decisions on the grant of asylum.[5] It is in part to reduce the influence of such considerations that there arises the necessity of resolving such matters in accordance with legal criteria. In fact the status and treatment of refugees have been matters of concern for the international community and for international lawyers in particular since a relatively early date.[6]

This chapter is concerned exclusively with territorial asylum, in contradistinction to extraterritorial asylum (that is, asylum granted not within the jurisdiction of a State, but within the territory of another country, normally in the legations or ships of the State of refuge). Extraterritorial asylum has been the subject of much informative writing, but there is no adquate measure of agreement as to its basis in general international law,[7] and it appears to be at best local usage.[8]

The present chapter will be addressed firstly to the existence and content of the so-called 'right of asylum'.[9] Next, we will examine the definition of a 'refugee' contained in the Geneva Convention and New York Protocol relating to the Status of Refugees in the light of the existing case-law.[10] Some attention will be given to the identification of countries of first asylum. We will then consider the principle of *non-refoulement,* in order to see whether it embodies a rule of customary international law. Finally, we will deal with the meaning and loss of refugee status.

CHANGING ATTITUDES AMONG THE WRITERS

The traditional view is that the right of asylum is no more than the right of each State to grant asylum to a fugitive alien. In part, this view is based on the premise that international law gives rise to rights and duties only between States;[11] and in part on the premise that States are free to exclude aliens from their territories. In accordance with the traditional thesis, Professor de Visscher wrote:

> Ce que l'on appelle le droit d'asile n'est autre chose que la facilité pour tout Etat d'offrir asile à qui le demande.[12]

Dr Weis, in similar vein, observed in 1953 that:

> According to general international law as at present constituted, the so-called right of asylum is a right of States, not the individual.[13]

Professor O'Connell also argued that a State is not obliged to admit aliens to its territory[14] and Miss Morgenstern concluded:

> There can be no doubt that the individual has no general right of asylum.[15]

Remarks to a similar effect can be found in the works of Oppenheim,[16] Barcía-Mora,[17] Krenz,[18] Nanda,[19] Bevan[20] and Jankovic,[21] among others.

Some writers express the view that a State may have an obligation *vis-à-vis* the international community or *vis-à-vis* the individual to admit to its territories a person fleeing from political, religious or racial persecution. Scelle is among the more emphatic of them:

> Les formes compliquées de l'institution ont pour raison d'être l'effort fait pour tourner le dogme de la souveraineté. Aujourd'hui cet effort est inutile: les gouvernements ont non seulement le droit, mais le devoir de pratiquer l'asile.[22]

Although few concur with Scelle's judgement as a statement of *lex lata,* there has been a trend towards accepting it *de lege ferenda.* That trend has been influenced by García-Mora's monograph. The eighth edition of Oppenheim contains a passage reading as follows:

> At present it is probable that the so-called right of asylum is nothing but the competence of every State to allow a prosecuted alien to enter and remain on its territory under its protection.[23]

The first six words of that passage did not appear in earlier editions, and their insertion in the edition of 1952 is a testament not only to Sir Hersch Lauterpacht's thinking but also to more recent developments of international law on the subject. Dr Weis has observed that it would not nowadays be easy to find a State which would go to the length of claiming that it is entitled to return a refugee to a country of persecution.[24] Professor Grahl-Madsen has said:

> Our generation has witnessed an impressive development towards an internationally-guaranteed right for the individual to be granted asylum ... the right to gain admission to a country of refuge still belongs to the moral sphere but it has been strengthened by the adoption of the Declaration on Territorial Asylum and Resolution (67) 14 by the General Assembly of the United Nations and the Committee of Ministers of the Council of Europe respectively.

He adds that the adoption of these instruments goes 'beyond the principle of *non-refoulement* to include non-rejection at the frontier and this gives refugees a moral choice to be given asylum if they are in need of it'.[25]

Article 14(1) of the Universal Declaration of Human Rights establishes the standard that everyone has 'the right to seek and to enjoy asylum'. Commenting on that Article, Professor Greig has pointed out that a case can be made for the proposition that a right of asylum has been established by the practice of States as part of customary international law. It could be argued, for example, that one can hardly 'enjoy' asylum without it being granted; that the moral force of the declaration has in time brought about legal consequences; and that a variety of other instruments, such as the O.A.U. Convention governing the Specific Aspects of Refugee Problems in Africa and the American Convention of Human Rights and the U.N. and European Declarations on Territorial Asylum, have reinforced the sense of legal obligation (the *opinio juris* required in the formation of customary rules). Professor Greig concludes, however, that such a case is not convincing. The language employed is for the most part qualified, emphasising the right of the State to decide, rather than of the individual alien to claim to be entitled to admission.[26]

The OAU Convention of 1969 goes some way further than the Universal Declaration: it provides that Member States shall use their best endeavours consistent with their respective legislations to receive refugees. Of this Dr Goodwin-Gill has stated:

> Despite the encouraging tone of the O.A.U. Convention, neither this instrument nor any other permits the conclusion that States have accepted an international obligation to grant asylum to refugees, in the sense of lasting protection against persecution and/or the exercise of jurisdiction by another State.[27]

In order to measure the extent to which the traditional view has been displaced, reference may be made to international conventions, the practice of international organizations, diplomatic intercourse, the determinations of international judicial tribunals and the practice of States, including domestic constitutions, judicial decisions, and the contents of immigration laws.

INTERNATIONAL CONVENTIONS AND SIMILAR INSTRUMENTS

The Convention Relating to the International Status of Refugees, 1933, provided in Article 3(2) that contracting States should not refuse entry to refugees at the borders of their countries of origin.[28] It was ratified by few States and was concerned with *refoulement* rather than with the refugee's more general right to be granted asylum.[29] The Constitution of the International Refugee Organization of 1946[30] urged States to cooperate in its main function of resettling refugees, but it stopped short of imposing a duty to grant asylum.

Article 14(1) of the Universal Declaration of Human Rights[31] proclaims that:

> Everyone has the right to seek and to enjoy in other countries asylum from persecution.

The original draft of that article (then Article 12) contained significantly different wording:

> Everyone has the right to seek *and be granted* in other countries asylum from persecution.[32]

That draft was opposed by the United Kingdom, the Commonwealth of Australia and the Kingdom of Saudi Arabia, delegates from those States arguing that refugees are not admitted under any obligation, and that the recognition of a right to be granted asylum would violate State sovereignty.[33] The wording was amended accordingly. In a comment on that change, Miss Morgenstern wrote:

> the amendment ... from the point of view of the individual – for whose protection the whole Declaration is intended – makes the right of asylum meaningless.[34]

Dr Weis quotes the late Sir Hersch Lauterpacht as describing the article as adopted as: '... artificial to the point of flippancy.'[35]

Nevertheless, the value of Article 14(1) of the Universal Declaration must not be underestimated. It does imply that, although an asylum-seeker has no right to be granted admission in a foreign State, equally a State which has granted asylum to a refugee must not remove him to the country whence he came.[36] That Article not only carries moral authority, but embodies the logical prerequisite of any rule of international law governing the individual's right to asylum.[37] Moreover, Article 14(1) of the Universal Declaration provided the inspiration for regional instruments which impose more positive obligations. Article 27 of the American Declaration of the Rights and Duties of Man states that:

> Every person has the right, in cases of pursuit not resulting from ordinary crimes, to seek *and receive* asylum in foreign territory, in accordance with the laws of each country and with international agreements.[38]

In establishing the Office of the United Nations High Commissioner for Refugees, the General Assembly of the United Nations urged States to cooperate with the High Commissioner, *inter alia,* by admitting refugees.[39] The Conference of Plenipotentiaries on the Status of Refugees and Stateless Persons, in drafting the 1951 Convention relating to the Status of Refugees, recommended: 'that governments continue to receive refugees in their territories and that they act in concert in a true spirit of international cooperation in order that these refugees may find asylum and the possibility of resettlement.[40]

As many as 100[41] States have ratified or acceded to the 1951 Convention as amended by the 1967 Protocol,[42] but, as we shall see, the Convention is silent on the so-called right of asylum. The Declaration on Territorial Asylum made by the General Assembly in 1967[43] has gone some way to extending to the universal plane the most basic principle of the 1951 Convention: the rule against *refoulement*. By that Declaration, adopted unanimously, the General Assembly proclaimed that no-one entitled to invoke Article 14 of the Universal Declaration should be subjected to measures such as rejection at the frontier or, if he has already entered the territory in which he seeks asylum, expulsion or compulsory return to any State where he may be subjected to persecution. It is to be emphasized that the Declaration speakes of persons entitled to invoke Article 14 of the Universal Declaration. It seems clear, therefore, that the right of asylum mentioned in that Article is the right of the individual. The editor of *Oppenheim* and Dr Weis appear to be too pessimistic in characterising the right of asylum as that of the State alone.

In 1977 a Draft Convention on Territorial Asylum was abandoned after representatives failed to reach agreement on the text. The Draft had envisaged that States would be under an obligation to use their best endeavours to ensure non-rejection of asylum-seekers at the frontier. Even that proposal proved controversial some States favouring the substitution of the word 'endeavour' for 'use best endeavours' and others calling for the deletion of the Article altogether. In the event, much of the discussion was devoted to the definition of the word 'refugee' and the reiteration or enlargement of national discretion in the grant of asylum.[44] Dr Weis wrote this epitaph to the Draft Convention and to the so-called right to be granted asylum:

> In this situation it seems unlikely that a Convention on Territorial Asylum which constituted progress from the legal and humanitarian angles could be concluded in the near future on a universal level within the framework of the United Nations and still less likely that it would be widely ratified.[45]

On this point, his assessment is plainly correct.

More definite obligations are imposed by certain of the specialized conventions on the law of refugees, including the Agreement Relating to Refugee Seamen of 1957 and its amending Protocol of 1973.[46] Article 1 defines a 'refugee seaman' as a refugee within the meaning of the 1951 Convention and Protocol, who is 'serving as a seafarer in any capacity on a mercantile ship, or habitually earns his living as a seafarer on such ship'. The objective of the agreement is to determine the links which a refugee seaman may have with contracting States, with a view to establishing entitlement to residence and/or the issue of travel documents.[47] Refugees also benefit from provisions in a wide variety of international instruments dealing with such matters as safety at sea, social security, migration for employment and even the protection of copy-right.[48] Moreover, refugees and aslyum-seekers may gain from legal machinery established on a regional basis. Indeed, if the right to be granted asylum is not established at the universal level, it exists at least in inchoate form in African and American regional instruments.

The Convention of 1954 on Territorial Asylum in America declared that the territorial State has the right to grant asylum; that other States have the duty to respect asylum so granted; and that States are exempted from any obligation to surrender or expel persons 'sought for political offences' or 'persecuted for political reasons or offences'.[49] Article 22(7) of the American Convention on Human Rights adopted in 1969 established a right of asylum, although in qualified terms:

> Every person has the right to seek and be granted asylum in a foreign territory in accordance with the legislation of the State and international conventions in the event he is being pursued for political offences or related common crimes.[50]

At the meeting of the General Assembly of the Organization of American States held on 2 December 1985 an effort was made to respond to the problems of refugees in Central America.[51] By a Resolution adopted on that date, the Assembly placed emphasis on the necessity for finding durable solutions; and made extensive reference to the Cartagena Declaration on Refugees of November 1984. This Declaration enlarges the definition of refugee from the wording of the 1951 Convention by including victims of 'violence', 'conflicts' and 'mass human rights violations'.

As we have seen, the Organization of African Unity's Convention of 1969[52] also establishes a qualified expectation to granted asylum. Using the same language as the original Draft Convention on Territorial Asylum, prepared for the United Nations, Article II proclaims that Member States 'shall use their best endeavours consistent with their respective legislations to receive refugees and to secure the settlement' of those unable or unwilling to be repatriated. It provides further that asylum is to be seen as a peaceful and friendly act and a refugee 'may' be granted temporary residence pending resettlement.

THE PRACTICE OF INTERNATIONAL ORGANIZATIONS

The first international organization established for the systematic assistance of refugees was the League of Nations High Commissariat for Russian Refugees, with Dr Frijthof Nansen as its head. By Arrangements dated 1922 and 1926 provision was made for the issuance of identity certificates or 'Nansen passports' to Russian and Armenian refugees. By a further Arrangement dated 1928 the Commissariat's functions were expanded to deal with some non-Russian refugees.[53] Between 1924 and 1929 the International Labour Organization was responsible for the provision of material assistance to refugees and from 1930 onwards a series of agencies succeeded one another in taking similar responsibilities. In the period preceding the war, three international agreements were concluded to regulate the reception of refugees from German (apart from the Geneva Convention of 1933 and the Montevideo Convention of 1928).[54] None envisaged a right of asylum.

The massive post-war migratory movements, and the consequential demand for an international agency to deal with the problems of refugees, led to the creation of the United Nations Relief and Rehabilitation Agency and the Intergovernmental Committee for Refugees. When those two bodies ceased to operate in 1947 they had attended to the movement of some seven million persons in Europe, but there were still some 1.6 million persons in refugee camps in that continent.[55] By Resolution 302(IV) of 8 December 1948 the General Assembly established the United Nations Relief and Works Agency to care for Palestinian refugees. In the same period, the United Nations established the International Refugee Organization (I.R.O.) to succeed U.N.R.R.A. and I.C.R. The preamble to the Constitution of the I.R.O. referred to repatriation as 'the principal task of the Organization'. Yet, during the existence of the I.R.O. (1947 to February 1952), less than six per cent of the refugees under its mandate chose to be repatriated. The United States, which had been committed to taking up to forty per cent of the persons under the I.R.O.'s mandate, and to furnishing up to sixty per cent of the Organization's budget, was extremely sensitive towards the insistence of the Communist States on forcible repatriation. The Foreign Affairs Committee of the U.S. House of Representatives, in its preliminary report of April 1951 on the Mutual Security Act, therefore imposed the following condition for further U.S. financial contributions:

> No sum shall be spent . . . or put at the disposal of an international bureau, institution or organization which includes in its membership States which do not take part in the free movement of international emigrants or immigrants.

This much criticized move heralded the demise of the I.R.O.[56]

Shortly before the I.R.O.'s demise, however, the General Assembly of the United Nations passed a resolution appointing a United Nations High Commissioner for Refugees.[57] The latter was charged with the task of protecting the legal rights of refugees and displaced persons formerly under the mandate of the I.R.O.[58] The High Commissioner is to promote the conclusion of international conventions providing for the legal protection of refugees, to supervise the application of those conventions, and, if necessary, to promote their amendment. In the exercise of its functions of 'protection' the High Commission seeks to persuade Governments to accept refugees and in the exercise of its functions of 'assistance' provides assistance and emergency relief to refugees in need.[59]

The small budget[60] of the Office tends to confine its activities to administering relief and legal aid to refugees and appealing to parties to the Convention and other members of the United Nations to admit refugees individually or collectively and to effect adjustments in their immigration laws.[61] By way of exception, the High Commissioner's Office has been called upon to undertake specific and more extensive tasks on an *ad hoc* basis. In May 1979 the UNHCR concluded with the Government of Vietnam a Memorandum of Understanding on the Orderly Departure of Persons from Vietnam.[62] A Conference in Geneva of representatives of concerned governments followed and bilateral diplomatic exchanges, initiated by UNHCR, were placed on a formal basis with the object of resolving the crisis brought about by the efflux of Indo-Chinese refugees.

The UNHCR has been obliged to adapt so as to meet the changing demands of international refugee assistance and to the reluctance of its principal contributor States to accept large numbers of refugees in their territories. In January 1985 the new High Commissioner said

> ... the principal concern is no longer emergency relief, but the organization of the daily lives of the populations concerned once these have become sedentary or semi-sedentary.[63]

The formal division of the Office into two sections, one devoted to 'protection' and other to 'assistance' was abandoned in 1986. The Office is now organized principally on a geographical basis. The five regional bureaux deal independently with these twin issues. Protection, in particular, is likely to be organized on a regional basis. The Executive Committee meets yearly to determine the broad policy but the emphasis has now moved away from Headquarters and into the field. In addition a new legal division has been established. This is the 'Refugee Law and Doctrine' division dealing with the development of refugee law on a global basis.

When the International Refugee Organization ended its operations, Belgium and the United States sponsored the Brussels Resolution, whereby those two nations, together with several of their allies, established a Provisional Committee ón Refugees. In October of 1952 that Provisional Committee was formalized into the Intergovernmental Committee for European Migration (I.C.E.M.). The Constitution of I.C.E.M. provided[64] that the basic objective of the Organization should be the transport of migrants for whom existing facilities are inadequate, and who could not otherwise be moved, from European countries having surplus population to countries overseas which offer opportunities for orderly immigration. Essentially, the Organization was concerned in its early years with migration between Europe and the Americas, Southern Africa and Israel. More recently, it has devoted its attention to migration from non-European points of departure and has abandoned the word 'European' in its title.

Every movement sponsored by the I.C.M. involves an agreement between that Committee, the migrant and the country of immigration. In appropriate cases, the movement will also involve the agreement of the country of emigration and any voluntary agency or individual sponsor interested in the migration of the refugee concerned. The I.C.M. normally employs ordinary commercial transport facilities and companies, but not infrequently it charters ships or aircraft. It also assists member Governments in the development of their migration programmes.[65]

The foregoing summary of the main functions of two major international organizations involved in the resettlement of refugees – admittedly brief and incomplete[66] – demonstrates, at least, that these organiations are principally concerned with the administration of relief and the coordination of national migration policies. While the efforts of such international organizations may be directed towards the reduction of the financial, administrative and legal restrictions on the movement of refugees, the existence and constitutions of those organizations in no way assure the individual refugee of a right of asylum, either under the domestic law of contracting States, or under general international law.

DIPLOMATIC PRACTICE AND COMMENTS

There is no shortage of diplomatic comments on the alleged existence of an individual's right to be granted asylum under customary international law. Candour demands that it be recognized that these diplomatic comments have frequently been influenced by the national interests and foreign policies of the States concerned.

In 1957 the Government of France submitted to the Human Rights Committee of the United Nations a Draft Declaration on the Right of Asylum. Article 2 of that Draft envisaged that

> Every person whose life, physical integrity or liberty is threatened, in violation of the principles of the Universal Declaration of Human Rights, shall be regarded as entitled to seek asylum.

In their comments on the Draft, several Governments expressed the view that the decision to grant or withhold asylum falls within the exclusive competence of the State in which refuge is sought. Peru, therefore, stressed that the grant of asylum must be voluntary, and a similar view was espoused by the representative of the United Kingdom. The Indian representative stated that in the understanding of his Government, an individual has no right of asylum, and a State has no duty to grant asylum, but a State is competent to grant territorial asylum if it chooses to do so.[67]

Several States, however, support the view that asylum may be a right enjoyed by an individual by virtue of international law. At the Eighth Session of the Human Rights Commission (1952) Uruguay, Chile and Yugoslavia jointly presented for inclusion in the Draft International Covenant on Human Rights a plan whereby asylum would be granted to all persons charged with political offences

> ... and, in particular, to all persons accused or persecuted because of their participation in the struggle for national independence or political freedom or because of their activities for the achievement of the purpose and principles set forth in the Charter of the United Nations and the Universal Declaration of Human Rights.

The Union of Soviet Socialist Republics proposed that the right of asylum should be guaranteed to

> ... all persons persecuted for their activities in defence of democratic interests, for their scientific work, or for their participation in the struggle for national liberation.[68]

Among the members of the Asian-African Legal Consultative Committee, Iraq and the United Arab Republic maintained that

> ... asylum to political refugees is a well-established institution under customary international law.

That statement is, of course, ambiguous: it is not clear whether the statement refers to the individual's right to enjoy asylum or to the State's right to confer it.[69]

During a parliamentary debate on the denial of asylum to Leon Trotsky, the Home Secretary of the United Kingdom reported that no alien has the right to be given asylum in Britain, at least if it would be contrary to the interests of the country to admit him.[70] In 1983 France declared that

> The right of asylum is secure. France has taken pride in it for centuries. It will be strictly respected. Candidates for refugee status can feel assured of guaranteed impartiality, understanding and assistance.[71]

On the other hand, in the same year a representative of the U.S. Coordinator for Refugee Affairs described the moral determinants underlying U.S. refugee law. The perspective of 'shared humanity' would oblige the United States to assist all casualties of political and religious persecution and would thus impose an enormous burden upon that country. 'Ally responsiveness', on the other hand, obliges the United States to grant asylum only to

> ... people who come from fallen allied democratic regimes or who served as support troops in conflicts to preserve Western values.[72]

At the Conference convened by the United Nations in 1977 to create a Convention on Territorial Asylum, the representative of the Federal Republic of Germany suggested a provision whereby individuals faced with persecution for political reasons would be given a right to be granted asylum. This proposal received little support, even from the Western European States which traditionally grant asylum for humanitarian reasons.[73]

DOMESTIC CONSTITUTIONS

Constitutional guarantees of a right to be granted asylum are common, and this fact may contribute towards the formation of an international legal assurance of such a right. This is so not only because such provisions may, in appropriate circumstances, constitute evidence of general principles of law, but also because they may demonstrate that States regard themselves as being under a moral duty to extend their protection to those suffering from persecution. As García-Mora observes, the recognition of that moral duty is a *sine qua non* for the realization of a right under international law to be granted asylum.[74] Furthermore, domestic constitutional provisions may be expressed in such a manner as to constitute evidence of a rule of international law. Article 10 of the Italian Constitution of 1947 begins by stating that the Italian juridical order conforms with generally recognized norms of international law, and that the juridical condition of foreigners in Italy is regulated in conformity with international norms and standards. The Article then proceeds to declare that any alien who is prevented in his own country from exercising the democratic liberties guaranteed in the Italian Constitution shall have the right to asylum in the Republic, on conditions laid down by law.[75] That Article does not define the right of asylum, but it is thought that in Italian law the right of asylum consists in freedom from *refoulement,* rather than in assurance of admission to Italy, as a State of refuge.[76]

In other Western European constitutions written shortly after the conclusion of the Second World War there are provisions comparable with those contained in Article 10 of the Italian Constitution. The preamble to the French Constitution of 1946 provided that any person persecuted on account of his activities in the cause of liberty had the right of asylum within the territories of the Republic. That provision is confirmed in the French Constitution of 1958. Article 16(2) of the Federal German Constitution of 1949 provides that persons persecuted for political reasons enjoy the right of asylum. The context suggests, however, that the word '*asylrecht*' in Article 16(2) connotes no more than *non-refoulement.* The constitutions of the United Kingdom and of Switzerland contain no guarantee of any right of asylum. A resolution of the Swiss Federal Council of 1921 declared that

> L'étranger n'a pas droit d'asile. L'Etat a simplement la faculté, en vertu de sa souveraineté, d'admettre sur son territoire un étranger.[77]

The constitutions of numerous Eastern European States also contain provisions to guarantee a right of asylum, and these provisions show marked similarities with one another, and common marked differences to the guarantees of asylum contained in the Constitutions of France, Italy and the Federal Republic of Germany. The paradigm is Article 38 of the Constitution of the USSR, which provides:

> The USSR grants the right of asylum to foreigners, persecuted for defending the interests of the working people and the cause of peace, for participating in revolutionary or national liberation movements, or for progressive socio-political, scientific or other creative activities.[78]

Very similar wording is to be found in the constitutions of Albania,[79] Poland,[80] Roumania,[81] the Mongolian People's Republic,[82] Bulgaria,[83] the Democratic People's Republic of Korea,[84] Czechoslovakia[85] and Hungary.[86]

The Constitution of the German Democratic Republic provides that:

> The G.D.R. can grant asylum to citizens of other States or stateless persons if they are being persecuted for political, scientific or cultural activity in the defence of peace, democracy, the interests of the working people, or because of their participation in a social or national struggle for liberation.[87]

It is thought that this German provision, Article 38 of the Constitution of the USSR and other provisions fashioned after the Soviet model refer to the removal of refugees rather than to their admission in the first instance. There is some authority to the contrary, but of this ideological grouping (if indeed it belongs to the group at all) only the Constitution of Yugoslavia 'guarantees' a right of asylum.[88] These constitutional provisions refer to Socialist principles, with the result that only a person who is considered to have been 'persecuted for defending the interests of the working people' benefits from the right of asylum. According to García-Mora:

> ... it can readily be seen [from the Constitutional provisions of the Iron Curtain countries] that asylum is guaranteed only to those who are persecuted for the particular interests and policies of the State of refuge. Consequently, a person fleeing from the persecution of a Communist State will not obtain refuge in another ... Thus, there can be little doubt that under the Constitutional provisions of the countries behind the Iron Curtain, the right of asylum is considerably restricted ...[89]

Within the group of countries influenced by Chinese practice there is another series of constitutional safeguards of the right of asylum. Under the Constitution of the People's Republic of China there is a

> ... grant of the right of residence to any foreign national persecuted for supporting a just cause, for taking part in revolutionary movements, or for engaging in scientific work.[90]

The Constitution of the Democratic Republic of Vietnam contains a provision similar to the Chinese one and in addition guarantees asylum to any foreign national persecuted for 'demanding freedom'.[91] Again, the Popular Revolutionary Republic of Guinea accords rights of asylum for similar reasons in Article 14 of its 1982 Constitution.[92]

Latin American constitutions have a greater tendency to confer on refugees of all political complexions the right to be granted territorial asylum. Under the Constitution of El Salvador, that State grants asylum to any foreigner who desires to reside in its territory except in those cases provided for by domestic or international law. These exceptions may not include anyone who is being prosecuted solely for political reasons.[93] The Costa Rican Constitution is scarcely less explicit. It provides that Costa Rican territory shall be a refuge for any person persecuted for political reasons.[94]

Article 116 of the Venezuelan Constitution states that the Republic recognizes asylum on behalf of any person subject to persecution or who is in danger for political reason under the conditions and requirements established by law and rules of international law.[95] In similar vein, the Guatemalan Constitution provides that Guatemala recognizes the right of asylum and extends it to political refugees who seek protection under its flag, provided that they respect the sovereignty and the laws of the nation.[96] Thereafter, the Guatemalan Constitution forbids the *refoulement* of political refugees. At some length, the Nicaraguan Constitution provides that

> The Right of Asylum ... is guaranteed to any person being persecuted for fighting for the cause of peace and justice, or for the recognition of the extension of the human, civil, political, social and economic and cultural rights of individuals or groups. If for any reason it is deemed necessary to expel an exile, he may never be sent to a country where he might be persecuted.[97]

A right to be granted asylum is not, however, recognized throughout Latin America. Under the Constitution of Haiti, it is provided that the right of asylum is extended to political refugees subject to the condition that they shall abide by local law.[98] The condition by which that right is qualified indicates that the Haitian concept of asylum is rather less demanding than the Salvadorean concept; it consists primarily in freedom from extradition rather than in the right to enter the country as a political refugee.

The determinant elements in the Cuban constitutional development are the revolutionary laws which regulate Cuban Socialist creation.[99] Article 13 of the 1979 Constitution proclaims:

> The Republic of Cuba grants asylum to those who are persecuted because of the struggle for the democratic rights of the majorities; for national liberation; against imperialism, fascism, colonialism and neo-colonialism; for the abolition of racial discrimination; for the rights of workers, peasants and students and the redress of their grievances; for their political, scientific, artistic and literary activities; for socialism and peace.[100]

The right to be granted asylum is not commonly guaranteed in the constitutions of Arab States. Nevertheless, Islamic constitutions very frequently forbid the extradition of political offenders.[101]

The constitutions of several African territories formerly under French rule provide for the adoption of principles laid down by the Universal Declaration of Human Rights.[102] Since that Declaration does not proclaim a right to be granted asylum, it cannot properly be maintained that the appropiate constitutions of francophone territories in Africa confer any such right in domestic law.[103]

408

Under Section 1(3) of the United Kingdom's Aliens Act of 1905 political and religious refugees were exempted from the substantive requirements of immigration control. The Aliens Restriction Act of 1914 and 1919 contained no similar exempting clauses, but that omission is scarcely surprising in view of the origins of the enactments. No such exempting provision was inserted into the Immigration Act of 1971. That omission is mitigated by a provision in the Immigration Rules,[104] whereby a person is not to be turned away if the only country to which he could be removed is one to which he is unwilling to go owing to well-founded fear of persecution for reasons of race religion, nationality, membership of a particular social group or political opinion. Leave to enter the United Kingdom will not be refused if removal would be contrary to the provisions of the Convention and Protocol relating to the Status of Refugees.[105] Immigration officers are instructed to report the case of an asylum-seeker to the Home Office and to admit or refuse to admit the alien in accordance with the instructions given to him by the Home Office.[106] An immigration officer is under a duty to follow the immigration rules; but the existing precedents suggest that he is not under a duty to abide by the international conventions governing refugees.[107]

French law has given greater definition to the expression 'refugee'. In 1832, when the French National Assembly debated the Law Relative to Alien Refugees who will Reside in France, the *Garde-des-Sceaux* explained that the essential element in refugee status is the absence of diplomatic or consular protection. The term *étrangers réfugiés* connoted

> ... ceux qui, sans passeport, sans relations avec aucune espèce d'ambassadeur, se trouvent évidemment dans l'Etat.[108]

Under the law providing for the creation of a French Office for the Protection of Refugees and Stateless Persons it is stated that the Office (OFPRA) recognizes as a refugee any person who falls within the mandate of the UNHCR, or within the definition contained in Article 1 of the Geneva Convention.[109] (As we shall see, the mandate of the UNHCR embraces numerous persons who do not fall within the definition contained in Article 1 of the Geneva Convention since the High Commissioner's competence has been extended from time to time by General Assembly resolutions.[110])

In the Netherlands the Aliens Act of 1965 and a subsequent Royal Decree continues to constitute the essential national source of the law on asylum and refugees. Section 15 of the Act concerns the admission of refugees, while sections 6 and 22 contain special regulations with regard to them. The Royal Decree on Aliens of 1966, Sections 104 to 106, implement Section 32 of the

1951 Convention. The revised Constitution of 1983 at Article 93 ensures that provisions of Conventions and decisions by international organizations which by their content are binding on everyone, shall have this binding effect from the date of publication. In other words, the Netherlands' international treaty commitments have direct effect and may be invoked in court by any party.[111] The Administrative Law Review Act 1978, and a circular letter from the Ministry of Justice dated 21 February 1974 (revised with effect from 1 February 1983) set out in greater detail the criteria for the grant of refugee status in the Netherlands.

The laws of some Scandinavian countries contain some of the more explicit statutory guarantees of the right to be granted asylum, in that the definition of a 'refugee' is broader than in the 1951 Convention. In Norway Section 2(2) of the Aliens Act 1956 contains a definition of a 'refugee' corresponding with Article 1A(2) of the Convention. The definition also inlcudes those fleeing their countries of origin for 'other political reasons' and 'persons who, having committed a political offence, may be subjected to severe punishment'. In Sweden, the Aliens Act 1975 affords protection to the so-called *de facto* refugees, a category considerably broader than normally defined in municipal legislation.[112]

The Norwegian Aliens Act, Section 2(1) provides that political refugees shall be given asylum if there are no special reasons to the contrary and Section 17(3) prohibits forcible return.[113] In Sweden, provision is made for the grant of asylum to those who qualify as refugees within the meaning of the Geneva Convention and come directly from a country of persecution.[114] By a *refoulement* agreement between Sweden and the Federal Republic of Germany, an asylum-seeker may be returned from one of these States to the other if he was present for not less than two weeks in that other State before claiming asylum in the State from which he is returned.[115] In the Danish Consolidated Act on the Entry of Aliens into Denmark 1973 provision is made for the purpose of ensuring the *non-refoulement* of refugees as defined in the Geneva Convention.[116]

In the Federal Republic of Germany the Aliens Law[117] extends the right of asylum (an expression used in the Basic Law[118]) to refugees within the meaning of Article 1 of the 1951 Convention and to other aliens who are persecuted on political grounds. The Federal Constitutional Court has interpreted this right as one directly enforceable against the legislative, executive and judicial branches.[119] The Asylum Procedure Law 1982[120] has been introduced, however, with the object of increasing the speed of processing refugee claims.

Just as the constitutions of some Latin American countries provide that political refugees shall have the right to be granted asylum, so the immigration laws of those countries frequently implement the political refugee's right. A law of Ecuador, for example, specifically provided that persons persecuted for political reasons should be admitted.[121] In Argentina treaty law is incorporated into national law after approval by congress and ratification by the executive.[122] At the Sixth Congress of the Ibero-American Union of Lawyers[123] it was declared that the granting of asylum and assistance to refugees amounts to an international custom in the area of Ibero-America. It has been reported that the principle of *non-refoulement* has always been respected in Argentina and no precedents exist to the contrary.[124]

In Africa, States have been encouraged to grant asylum by the 1969 O.A.U. Convention. Few countries incorporate this instrument into national practice or have their own municipal legislation. Nevertheless, there is a tradition of refugee assistance in Africa. Sudan, in its passage of the 1974 Regulation of Asylum Act,[125] has set an example in the provision of legal protection for refugees.

In the United States the essential domestic source of law on refugees and asylees is the Refugee Act 1980,[126] initiated to bring United States law into conformity with the Geneva Convention following ratification of the 1967 Protocol in 1968. The Refugee Act added a definition of refugee;[127] established a process for deciding how many refugees to admit from overseas each year:[128] authorised the Attorney General to grant asylum to aliens who apply for such status at the border;[129] and made provision for benefits to be supplied to refugees admitted to the United States.[130] Administrative regulations govern the procedures by which aliens may enter as refugees, together with family reunification.[131] United States legislation also makes provision for annual intakes of refugees from among groups of specific humanitarian interest to the United States.[132]

By means of 'parole power'[133] (now substantially restricted to the provisions on refugees) and 'extended voluntary departure'[134] the United States authorities may permit the entry or continued residence of aliens who do not meet the definition of a refugee. By these means the normal Immigration and Naturalization Service procedures regarding aliens may be extended; and once conditions have become stable in the alien's State of origin, the authorities are able to re-evaluate such aliens' status. (Often, however, it is considered unconscionable to deport these people if they have established links with the United States over time.)

The Refugee Act requires a Presidential determination, following extensive consultation with Congress, of the number of refugees of 'special humanitarian concern' who are to be admitted to the United States from abroad. (Such refugees are those who fail to qualify for admission by meeting the statutory definition). The Presidential determination allocates the maximum number (or 'ceiling') among various refugee groups.[135] In addition, the Refugee Act makes provision for 'unforeseen emergency refugee situations' by authorising a new round of consultations followed by a second Presidential determination in such circumstances. Waiting lists are maintained for each refugee group designed by the Presidential determination. By regulation,[136]

> ... refugees or groups of refugees may be selected from these lists in a manner that will best support the policies and interests of the United States.

DOMESTIC JUDICIAL PROCEEDINGS

Although numerous States make specific provision, in their constitutions and immigration laws, for the admission of refugees, domestic courts in those countries have often had cause to reject the argument that under international law the individual is entitled to enter a country if he seeks to do so as a refugee. In *U.S.* v *Insull*[137] an Illinois District Court (Sullivan, J.) argued as follows:

> It is contended by the defendant that, being in British Columbia, a British province, he could not be removed without the permission of the British Columbia authorities ... No asylum is guaranteed to defendant in Canada, and if a treaty did cover the offence charged it would be political, and not judicial ...

The Court then cited the statement of Marshall, C.J. in *Foster* v *Neilson*,[138] to the effect that treaties do not generally effect, of themselves, the object to be accomplished, but merely are executed by the parties. The Court continued:

> The right of the Hellenic Republic or Turkey to give asylum to the defendant is different from the right of the defendant to demand security in such asylum. The Hellenic Republic or Turkey, through their sovereignties, if, unlawfully invaded, may demand reparation and a surrender of the abducted party ... [but] the defendant cannot before this court invoke the right of asylum either in the Hellenic Republic or Turkey ...

In other cases domestic courts have dealt with the issue not on a procedural, but on a substantive basis, and have flatly denied the existence of any right of asylum owed to the individual. In *Ker* v *Illinois* the appellant had been kidnapped in Peru and brought from that country to the United States. The Supreme Court of the United States observed that the extradition treaty between the U.S. and Peru did not provide that a party fleeing from the United States to escape punishment for a crime becomes thereby entitled to an asylum in the country to which he has fled. The Court added that the Government of Peru undoubtedly retained the right to order Ker of the country on his arrival. From these findings the Court deduced that Ker had no right of asylum.[139] In

412

Chandler v *U.S.* it was held expressly that the right of asylum is that of the State, not that of the fugitive.[140]

The practice of the United States suggests strongly that a distinction is to be drawn between the principle whereby a refugee may not be returned to a country of persecution and the claimed or postulated principle that an individual may have a right to be granted asylum. Where an objection is made during the course of an exclusion or deportation hearing to the return of a fugitive to a country of persecution, the immigration judge must adjourn the hearing in order to obtain an advisory opinion from the State Department's Bureau of Human Rights and Humanitarian Affairs.[141] The asylum-seeker may appeal against any adverse decision reached by the immigration judge.[142] In the determination of his claim, the asylum-seeker enjoys certain procedural and constitutional rights including a guarantee of due process[143] and a right to be informed of his entitlement.[144] Conversely, in the case of an application for asylum made at a port of entry or to a district office of the Immigration and Naturalization Service there is no right of appeal against denial (although the claim to asylum can be advanced in subsequent deportation proceedings) and it seems that an alien seeking asylum at the border is not entitled to invoke constitutional protection.[145] There is even a basis for believing that a different standard of proof applies in the case of applications for asylum under section 208 of the Immigration and Nationality Act and objections to *refoulement* under section 243(h).[146]

The question whether there is a right to be granted asylum does not seem to have been considered directly by the courts of the United Kingdom, although in the *Soblen* case there was an oblique reference to the point.[147] Stevenson, J. observed that it is clear

> ... that the question of an alien being a political refugee or a fugitive offender, convicted of, or wanted for, an offence of a political character appears to be one which is for the Home Secretary, a matter to be taken into consideration by him ... [T]he court is prevented from getting to the point of considering whether the applicant has a claim to be treated as a political refugee [and] any suggestion by Low, J. in *Sarno's* Case[148] that that was a matter for the courts is wrong ... 'By international law, every state has the power to prevent aliens, whether friendly or enemy, from entering its territory ...

In *Two Citizens of Chile*,[149] the Tribunal held that the immigration authority must determine appeals in accordance with the Immigration Act and rules: the Geneva Convention and the Universal Declaration of Human Rights might be of value only in interpreting that Act and those rules. That decision is based on the established and unassailable principle of English law that a domestic court is bound to apply an Act of Parliament in preference to a treaty. The point was not argued that where the Act and rule confer a discretion, that discretion should be exercised in conformity with the treaty.[150] A series of decisions dealing with the rights of asylum-seekers to appeal against decisions entailing their removal from the United Kingdom presuppose that the asylum-seeker's presence is unlawful at the material time. The presupposition suggests that there is no right to be granted asylum in domestic law.[151]

In two German cases early in the present century, the courts explicitly stated that the grant or refusal of asylum falls within the discretion of the State to which the refugee has fled, and that the refugee has no claim or right to be granted asylum. In the first of those cases the court expressed itself as follows:

Asyl zu gewähren oder zu versagen, ist ein Recht das Zuflucthsstaates; der Flüchtling hat darauf keinen Anspruch.[152]

In the second case, the German court merely observed that

Dadurch allein, dass es dem Täter gelungen ist, die Grenze dieses Staates zu überschreiten erwirbt er keinen Anspruch auf Straflosigkeit und auf Schutz gegen strafrechtliche Verfolgung.[153]

In *Re de Saint-Antoine de Fleury* the Belgian *Cour de Cassation* quashed the appellant's claim to be a political refugee;[154] and in in *Re Ouakli, Abdi and Zouche,* the same court dismissed an appeal brought by aliens who had entered Belgian territory without proper papers and, three days later, had submitted a formal request to be regarded as refugees.[155] In reaching these conclusions the Court relied on the Royal Order of 3 December 1953, which provided that penalties for unlawful entry might be imposed unless the refugees presented themselves without delay to the appropriate authorities, and showed good cause for their illegal entry. The *Cour de Cassation* interpreted that item in the light of the similar provision contained in Article 31 of the Geneva Convention.

The situation may be different in a State which has not only incorporated the Convention of 1951 into domestic law but also created a right of asylum domestically. In the Netherlands the *Raad van Staat* has accepted the direct effect of the 1951 Convention. The definition of a refugee in Article 1A(2) of the Convention is identical with a corresponding provision in Dutch legislation.[156] The Royal Decree of 10 January 1974 has created a category of 'persons entitled to asylum'. They are persons who for humanitarian reasons cannot reasonably be required to return to their country of origin, considering the political situation there.[157]

One judicial decision in particular has established the existence of limitations on the Government's discretion in the grant of asylum.[158] It was decided that Eritreans from Ethiopia seeking asylum in the Netherlands are to be considered *prima facie* as entitled to refugee status. Although other groups have been refused this facility,[159] the acknowledgement that all Eritreans are so entitled implies that it is not open to the Government to contend that each application must be established individually, without reference to the treatment of the group as a whole.

In the Federal Republic of Germany, Article 16(2) of the Basic Law states '*Politisch Verfolge geniessen Asylrecht*': those persecuted for political reasons have the right to be granted asylum. Article 3 of the Asylum Procedure Law *Asylverfahrensgesetz* provides that those granted asylum shall enjoy as a minimum the standard of protection required by the Geneva Convention of 1951.

Not even the Geneva Convention, however, confers on every refugee the right to enter and settle down in the State of his choice. In *Bermudez de Madriaga* v *Ministro Interno* the Italian *Consiglio di Stato* dismissed the appellant's argument that Article 10 of the Italian Constitution was violated by the attachment of conditions to a residence permit.[160] The Court then referred to the Geneva Convention of 1951. It held that although the appellant was a 'refugee' within the meaning of the Convention, and although that Convention had been adopted into Italian law by the Act of July 24th, 1954, there was no violation of the Convention or the Act by the administrative decision to limit the period of validity of the appellant's residence permit. On an interpretation of the Convention and of the Act, the Court concluded that the admission of refugees to the territories of Contracting Parties is within the discretionary power of the latters' administrative authorities.

The alleged existence of an individual's right to be granted asylum seems not to have been the subject of a definitive ruling by an international tribunal. In the *Asylum Case*[161] the International Court was, of course, concerned with specialised aspects of the law on extraterritorial asylum. Nonetheless, some of the Court's remarks in that case may shed light on the current state of general international law on territorial asylum. The Court implied that the receiving State did have the right to grant diplomatic asylum if it chose to do so, and that implication leads to the conclusion that (at least among Latin American States in 1950) a State might equally grant territorial asylum. Later the Court concluded that it was impossible to infer from the Havana Convention that a person accused of political crimes was thereby entitled to asylum. In his dissenting judgement, Judge Alvarez made a remark to a similar effect, although the latter did not restrict his comment to the Convention alone:

> . . . it is the State from which asylum is requested that must decide whether it wishes to grant it or not.

Taken as a whole, the soruces examined in the foregoing pages suggest that no State is obliged by current international law to admit to its territory a person who establishes that he is a refugee. Indeed, it is significant in this context that the Geneva Convention of 1951 is silent on the question of the State's alleged duty to grant asylum.

THE DEFINITION OF REFUGEE

The principal basis for the international legal protection of refugees continues to be found in the definition contained in Article 1A(2) of the Geneva Convention of 1951 as extended by the New York Protocol. The refugee is (primarily) a person who is outside his country of nationality and unable or unwilling to return to it owing to well-founded fear of being persecuted for reasons of race, religion, nationality, membership of a particular social group or political opinion. Contracting States may treat as a refugee one who meets the primary definition 'as a result of events occurring in Europe' provided that they make a declaration to this effect on signing, ratifying or acceding to the Convention.[162] By a subsidiary provision, designed to preserve the status of the dwindling number of beneficiaries of antecedent arrangments, the Geneva Convention also provides that a person is to be a refugee if he was considered as such under the Arrangements of 12 May 1926 and 30 June 1928 or under the Conventions of 28 October 1933 and 10 February 1938, the Protocol of 14 September 1939 or the Constitution of the International Refugee Organization.[163] The provisions of the Convention do not apply to those who are receiving protection from other United Nations agencies. Further, those provisions do not apply to any person with respect to whom there are serious reasons for considering that he has committed a crime against peace, a war crime or a crime against humanity, or a serious non-political crime outside his country of refuge, prior to his admission to that country as a refugee. Nor does the Convention apply to a person who is guilty of acts contrary to the purposes and principles of the United Nations.[164]

The use of the definition contained in the Geneva Convention persists even though the world's population of displaced persons has grown in size and altered in character so greatly that the Convention of 1951 now embraces only one half of the world's displaced persons. The OAU Convention first defines a refugee in the language used in the Geneva Convention, and then adds that the term shall also apply to every person who, owing to external aggression, occupation, foreign domination or events seriously disturbing public order in part or the whole of his country of origin is compelled to seek refuge else-where.[165] For the same reason, the mandate of the United Nations High Commissioner has on many occasions been extended by the General Assembly or the Economic and Social Council to cover refugees who would otherwise have fallen outside his competence.[166] The functions of the High Commissioner in the exercise of 'good offices' beyond the terms of the Convention continue to grow in significance and number. In January 1985 the High Commissioner authorised the grant of assistance to displaced persons in the Sudan who had been uprooted as a combination of natural and man-made disasters, stating that 'it would be pointless to engage in a debate over the status of the persons concerned'.

Nevertheless, it is by reference to the terms of the Geneva Convention, adapted to the conditions of the laws of the Contracting States in which it is applied, that individuals' claims for asylum are most commonly tested. It is to those terms that we must now turn our attention.

(a) Well-founded fear

The Ad Hoc Committee on Statelessness and Related Problems commented twice on the meaning of the phrase 'well-founded fear'. In a Draft Report of 15 February 1950 the Committee stated that the words require an applicant to give a 'plausible account' of why he fears persecution.[167] In the Final Report, it was said that the applicant must show 'good reason' to fear persecution,[168] which required the adduction of evidence of an objective risk. The applicant was not, however, required to prove the existence of those conditions objectively, nor that he would be singled out for persecution.[169] In the interests of equity, any State which required adduction of objective evidence should share with the applicant the information it has in support of the applicant's claim.[170] If such support is unavailable, the State should afford the applicant the benefit of the doubt.

Thus, the appraisal requires an enquiry into both the subjective and the objective element in the fear. According to the UNHCR Handbook on Procedures and Criteria for Determining Refugee Status,[171] the determination of refugee status will

... primarily require an evaluation of the applicant's statements rather than a judgement of the situation prevailing in his country of origin.[172]

At a recent Seminar of the European Consultation on Refugees and Exiles, it was found that jurisprudence in the six participating States had tended to place emphasis on the objective element. Moreover, many States required evidence of actual past persecution. The participants at the Seminar concluded, however, that such a requirement was not to be found in the definition.[173]

In practice, it is seldom the existence of the fear but its foundation that provokes difficulty. The United Kingdom's case-law suggests that the applicant need not show that it is more probable than not that he will be persecuted in his country of origin. Initially, this was indeed required[174] but recent jurisprudence illustrates a departure from that test.[175] In the case of *Kazie*[176] the applicant was merely required to establish 'a serious possibility' or 'substantial grounds for thinking' or 'a reasonable chance' of persecution. In *Enninful* v *Home Secretary*,[177] the Tribunal ruled that a person facing a less than even chance of persecution could properly be found to have a well-founded fear. In applying these tests, the Tribunal will of course take account of objective evidence of conditions in the country of origin.[178]

In the United States the appellate authorities have required a 'realistic likelihood' of persecution. While authorities can examine background information on political and social conditions, it is agreed that:

> ... persecution cannot be proven by the introduction of documentary evidence, not pertaining to the applicant individually, that depicts a general lack of freedom or the probability of human rights abuses in the alien's native land ... instead, the alien must introduce sufficient credible evidence that supports his individual claim of persecution.[179]

It has been suggested that an applicant for asylum must show that he will be 'singled out'[180] for persecution. It is thought, however, that the suggestion cannot be taken literally; what is meant is that the applicant does not discharge his burden of proof merely be showing that he originates in a State experiencing wide-scale breakdowns in civil order or a State that is generally repressive.[181]

In Canada, Wilson, J. stated in the case of *Kwiatkowsky* v *M.E.I.*:

> He may, as a subjective matter, fear persecution if he is returned to his homeland, but his fear must be assessed objectively in order to determine if there is a foundation for it.[182]

The statement sheds light on the burden of proof: the applicant need not show that his fears will be fulfilled but that they have a foundation.

(b) Persecution

The persecution that the refugee fears consists primarily in a serious disadvantage, including jeopardy to life, physical integrity or liberty. This is suggested by Article 31–33 of the Convention, which speak of threats to life or freedom. It seems, however, that any other serious disadvantage will constitute persecution when it gives rise to intolerable psychological pressure. This is suggested by Swiss law, which speaks in this context of threats to life, limb or liberty and *'les mesures qui entrainent une pression psychique insupportable.*[183] Admittedly, the Swiss law adopts the definition in the Geneva Convention subject to an important amendment: the words 'serious disadvantage' (*sérieux préjudices*) are applied in place of 'persecution'; but the standard suggested by Swiss law is also applied in the United States[184] and is apparently applied in the Netherlands, where the law provides that persecution entails a contravention of basic rights and refers in this context to the European Convention on Human Rights.[185] Conversely, discrimination on racial or social grounds does not itself amount to persecution, even when it entails a loss of livelihood or denial of university education.[186] Economic disadvantage will amount to persecution only when it is so grave as to produce intolerable consequences.[187]

Punishment may amount to persecution if its severity is grossly disproportionate to the offence.[188] Even in such cases, however, it is necessary to establish a nexus between the persecution and the reasons identified in the Convention. If, therefore, a law which is neutral upon its face can be said to have been drafted with the object of penalising members of one of the groups identified in Article 1 of the Geneva Convention, or if it is designed for netural purposes but is applied with particular rigour to members of such a group, it can be said to constitute persecution for the reasons set out in the Convention. A national law which imposes serious penalties for unlawful departure *Republikflucht*) is apt to give rise to persecution in this sense, in as much as it is designed to deal with the political disenchanted. It has been held, therefore, that severe punishment for *'Republikflucht'* (or unauthorized stay abroad) amounts to a justified fear of persecution within the meaning of the Convention when the offence was inspired by reasons set out in Article 1(A)(2) or the punishment inflicted for those reasons.[189] A similar problem arises in the case of disproportionate penalties for failure to engage in military service. In *Doonetas,* the United Kingdom's Immigration Appeal Tribunal has held that a Jehovah's Witness who faced several long successive periods of imprisonment for conscientious refusal to engage in military service had no claim for asylum. The Tribunal considered that 'the sort of sentences being imposed in Greece for refusal of military service amount to persecution' but that the persecution was not 'for reasons of religion or political opinion'.[190] The decision appears correct, for the sentence imposed on Jehovah's Witnesses were no different form those imposed on others refusing to engage in military service, whether on conscientious grounds or otherwise. Serious difficulties arise from such decisions; but they may be resolved by the practice of granting the protection of the Convention to persons who are not covered by it, in accordance with the hope expressed by the Conference of Plenipotentiaries in paragraph E of the preamble. Indeed, that was the solution adopted in the case of the Greek conscientious objector, who was permitted to remain in the United Kingdom 'outside the rules'.

In general, the persecution feared must be committed by the State rather than by fellow citizens but there is persecution within the meaning of the Convention when the State condones the acts committed by a sector of the population against another.[191] It seems unnecessary for the applicant to prove that he will be singled out for the treatment constituting persecution. In a recent English case, Taylor, J. observed that it would be of little comfort to a Tamil family to know they were being persecuted as Tamils rather than as individuals.[192] The correctness of his conclusion is confirmed by the very wording of the Convention, in so far as it speaks of persecution for reasons of membership of specified groups.

(c) 'Race'

The criteria for persecution will frequently overlap and often there will be more than one element combined in one person. On race, the UNHCR Handbook states that:

Race ... has to be understood in its widest sense to include all kinds of ethnic groups that are referred to as 'races' in common usage. Frequently it will also entail membership of a specific social group of common descent from-ing a minority within a larger population. Discrimination for reasons of race has found world-wide condemnation as one of the most striking violations of human rights. Racial discrimination, therefore, represents an important element in determining the existence of persecution.

Racial discrimination has received particularly detailed attention from the international community during the last quarter century; and it seems likely that the language used in other multilateral instruments on the question will shed light on the use of the word 'race' in the Geneva Convention. This is the case, in particular, with Article 1 of the International Convention on the Elimination of All Forms of Racial Discrimination, which defines 'racial discrimination' as discrimination based on race, colour, descent or national or ethnic origin.[193]

Two elements must be distinguished: the identification of 'persecution' in the context of racial intolerance; and the meaning of the expression 'for reasons of race'. In the United Kingdom case of *Ali (MMH)*[194] Kenyan citizens of Asian origin who feared discrimination under Kenya's policy of African-ization were 'far from showing that they had a well-founded fear of persecu-tion'. From this we may deduce that discrimination based on race is not 'persecution' in the sense in which that word is used in the Convention, even if accompanied by some governmental acts. Canadian case-law is consistent with this view.[195] The Immigration Appeal Board noted in the case of *Iyar*[196] that where racial persecution is in issue, a mere feeling of unease, without any evidence of actual harrassment or maltreatment by reason of race, is not evidence of persecution.[197] In the case of the South African apartheid laws, the Dutch authorities have held that discriminatory measures applied by the authorities do not *in themselves* amount to 'persecution'.[198]

National attempts to define 'race' in this context have seldom proved enlightening. The Canadian Immigration Manual says that the term 'race'

> denotes not only major ethnic groups such as black, white, European, African, etc., but also embraces the social concept, e.g. Jews, Gypsies, a particular tribe or minority, racial or ethnic.[199]

It is thought, however, that the crucial determinant is seldom, if ever, the definition of 'race'. The question is whether the persecution is for reason of race. It is therefore for the national authority of the receiving country to determine whether the persecutor is actuated by considerations which appear to him to be racial.[200]

(d) Religion

Although freedom of thought, conscience and religion is proclaimed in several modern international conventions[201] and religious intolerance was described in the Genocide Study as 'one of the decisive causes of genocide',[202] progress on the drafting of an international declaration on religious freedom has been extremely slow. Where, therefore, religious persecution is in issue, national authorities cannot derive as much guidance from international conventions as in cases involving racial discrimination. Indeed, official discouragement of religious practice is common, and some States, such as Iran, maintain constitutional provisions explicitly limiting religious freedom. Such case-law as is available suggests that it is insufficient to be a fugitive from such a country and desirous of manifesting one's faith. Nor is it sufficient that the fugitive objects to the secular propaganda issued in his country of origin.

In several Canadian cases individuals who were unable to practise their religious beliefs freely for fear of reprisals failed to secure recognition of their status as refugees: but the decisions are best explained on the ground that the hardship of which the individuals complained did not emanate from governmental policies.[203] In *Billas* v *M.E.I.* a Jehovah's Witness failed to establish that punishment for proselytizing amounted to persecution, where the prohibition applied indiscriminately to all faiths.[204] A similar decision was reached in the United Kingdom in *Atibo* v *Immigration Officer,* where the applicant was a member of an evangelical church from Mozambique, where proselytizing was prohibited.[205]

These cases shed more light on the meaning of the word 'persecution' than on the word 'religion'. Indeed, it was common ground that the appellants were motivated by religious concerns. Different issues would arise in the event of the persecution of a sect identified by their ethical or atheistic views. The word 'religion' in its natural and accustomed sense is concerned with man's relations with God rather than with the moral order.[206] An atheistic or ethical sect may be better regarded as a 'social group' than as a religious group, for the purposes of the Convention. It is thought, however, that the distinction is of little practical significance for the persecutor's perception is of greater relevance than the theologian's or the etymologist's definition. The persecution of a group on the ground that they amount to a religious group (in an atheistic society) or to a group of infidels (in an intolerant theistic State) amounts to persecution for reasons of religion within the meaning of the Convention.

Furthermore, the existing authorities are consonant with the view that severe punishment for engaging in observances common to religions in general amounts to persecution for reasons of religion. It seems, therefore, that those who are prohibited from engaging in ordinary religious rites or ceremonies, in private or in premises dedicated to that purpose, together with other adherents to the same faith, are persecuted for reasons of religion.

(e) Nationality

The term 'nationality' as it appears in Article 1 of the Geneva Convention is to be understood in a broad sense, to embrace not only citizenship but also membership of an ethnic or linguistic group.[207] A Dutch court has held that the treatment experienced by Eritreans in Ethiopia amounted to persecution for reason of nationality.[208] Later, another court added that the claim would fail only if persecution by the Ethiopian authorities could be shown to be absent in the case of any particular Eritrean asylum-seeker.[209]

(f) Social groups

The criterion of membership of a particular social group is of particularly uncertain limits. Introduced by the Swedish representative of the Ad Hoc Committee,[210] it was intended to ensure that the Convention would embrace those, particularly in Eastern Europe during the Cold War, who were persecuted because of their membership of a social class.

Professor Grahl-Madsen[211] lists many examples of social groups which have suffered persecution because of a common denominator in their background. Dr Goodwin-Gill[212] states the essential element in any description to be the factor of shared interests, values or background – a combination of matters of choice with other matters over which members of the group have no control.

The UNHCR *Handbook* mentions people of a similar background, habits or social status: the identifying feature is that the persecuting government is averse to the common element of social attachment shared by members of the group, whose political outlook, antecedents or economic activities may be an obstacle to the government's policies.[213]

The place given to the protection of 'social groups' in the Geneva Convention is unusual but by no means unique. Article 2 of the 1948 Universal Declaration of Human Rights prohibits distinctions on grounds of 'national and social origin, property, birth or other status'. This form of words is repeated in Article 2 of the 1966 Convenants on Economic, Social and Cultural Rights and on Civil and Political Rights.[214]

Among the more troublesome issues currently arising in this context is the question whether sex or sexual conduct is an identifying characteristic of a social group. In their report 'Sexual Violence Against Women Refugees' de Neef and de Reuter argue that women are sufficiently homogeneous to qualify as a social group.[215] Others have equated the fact of being a woman with low social and economic status so as to contend that they qualify for inclusion in the Convention.[216] While it seems unlikely that even the term 'social group' is sufficiently elastic to embrace one half of mankind, it is strongly arguable that sex may be an element in the identification of such a group. This may be the case, for example, when conduct tolerated in members of one sex is not tolerated in members of the other sex.

Case-law is sparse and inconsistent and deals mostly with homosexuals who fear persecution for transgressing the social and sexual mores.[217] In the Dutch case of *W.R.* v *Secretary of State for Justice,* the Court held that persecution on account of membership of a particular social group, reasonably interpreted, could include persecution on account of sexual disposition.[218] A United States court in *Matter of Acosta* listed sex, along with colour and kinship as characteristics which may identify members of a social group. The court added, however, that the characteristic must be beyond the power of the individual to change, or it must be so fundamental to the identity or conscience of the person that it ought not to be required to be changed.[219] Conversely, there is Canadian authority suggesting that neither sex nor sexual disposition amounts to an identifying characteristic of a social group.[220]

The Office of the UNHCR has endorsed the view that those who are singled out for persecution by reason of any characteristic shared with others form a 'social group' together with those others. In October 1985 the Executive Committee

> recognized that States, in the exercise of their sovereignty, are free to adopt the interpretation that women asylum-seekers who face harsh or inhuman treatment due their having transgressed the social mores of the society in

which they live may be considered as a 'particular social group' within the meaning of Article 1A(2) of the 1951 U.N. Refugee Convention.[221]

This principle has also been endorsed by resolution of the European Parliament.[222] While it falls short of requiring States to apply the principle therein, the Executive Committee's resolution offers a workable solution to claims based on sex or on sexual disposition. It suggests that women who face persecution for engaging in acts that would be tolerated in the case of men form a social group within the meaning of the Convention.

(g) Political opinion

The term 'political opinion' must be understood in the context of the network of international conventions and declarations governing freedom of opinion and expression.[223] So interpreted, the expression referes to any opinion on a matter on which the machinery of the State may be engaged.[224] In the case of political opinion, as in the case of religion, there arises with some frequency the problem of determining whether persecution is practised 'for reason of' the victim's persuasion, when it takes the form of punishment for activities in which he engaged in consequence of that persuasion. In the Canadian case of *Musial* v *M.E.I.*[225] Pratte, J. stated:

A person who is punished for having violated an ordinary law of general application is punished for the offence he has committed, not for the political opinions that may have induced him to commit it.

This statement is equally capable of being applied in the context of draft evasion and *Republikflucht*. Several cases arising in the United Kingdom illustrate the difficulty of the issue.

In *Church* the applicant had fled South Africa to avoid conscription in the armed forces. The adjudicator distinguished the case of *Doonetas* on the ground that the Greek army had been active only in defense of the country, whereas the South African army was instrumental in 'repression' contrary to U.N. General Assembly Resolution 33/165.[226] The proper distinction may be, however, that in *Church,* unlike *Doonetas,* the applicant had conscientious objections to the particular policies pursued by the armed forces. The nature of the objection identified the applicant as a member of a political group, together with like-minded persons. In later cases the appellants were required to show that they would suffer discrimination in comparison with other draft evaders. In order to establish that they would suffer persecution for reason of political opinion it was necessary to identify a nexus between the political opinion and the nature of the punishment.[227] It is arguable, therefore, that such

424

a nexus is established where the conscript refuses to serve in armed forces on the ground that the objects in good faith to the policies being implemented by them.[228]

This view gains some support from judicial decisions in other jurisdictions (although it must be admitted that there is some equivocal Dutch authority to the contrary[229]). In France it has been determined that an applicant qualifies if he has expressed an opinion in public, directly or indirectly.[230] A refusal to engage in military service, expressed on grounds of opposition to a particular policy, may well amount to a public expression of opinion 'direct or indirect'. A similar issue has recently arisen in the United States against the background of large-scale influxes from El Salvador and Haiti. The Court of Appeals has said

> when a person is aware of contending political forces and affirmatively chooses not to join any faction, that choice is a political one.[231]

THE COUNTRY OF FIRST ASYLUM

In the absence of a widely accepted system for distributing refugees between States able and willing to grant asylum to them,[232] there has developed an informal practice of returning refugees from countries of second or subsequent arrival to countries of 'first asylum'. A country of first asylum is to be described only in broad terms, since consensus on its definition is absent. Such a country may be taken to mean any State in which the asylum-seeker remained for a significant period in the interval between his departure from his country of origin and his arrival in a State which is unwilling or unable to permit him to reside on its soil. In the absence of universal agreement upon the principle and on the definition of a country of first asylum, the State which returns an asylum-seeker from its territory to a State other than that of his nationality cannot in general insist that he be admitted to the State to which he is sent. The authorities of that State may return him whence he came or remit him to another State. The human victims of this procedure have become known as 'refugees in orbit'.

The practice of returning asylum-seekers to countries of first asylum finds a basis (of sorts) in the Geneva Convention itself. By Article 31(1), Contracting States undertake not to impose penalties, on account of their illegal entry or presence, on refugees 'coming directly from a territory where their life or freedom was threatened'. While that provision refers to penalties only, it implies that a distinction may properly be drawn between those arriving directly and those doing so indirectly.

The domestic laws of certain of the Contracting States contain more or less explicit references to the practice of identifying countries of first asylum. In the Federal Republic of Germany, Article 2 of the *Asylverfahrensgesetz*[234] provides expressly that a person shall not be entitled to asylum if he has already been recognized as a refugee in another State or found protection there. In the United Kingdom the Immigration Rules require that it be shown that 'the only country to which a person can be removed is one to which he is unwilling to go owing to well-founded fear of being persecuted'.[235] In *Two Citizens of Chile*[236] the Immigration Appeal Tribunal held that the rule was not fulfilled where appellants showed that they had no legal right to return to a country in which they spent a year after leaving Chile but before arriving in the United Kingdom. In the United States the Supreme Court held in 1971 that the concept of 'resettlement', although not mentioned in the Immigration and Nationality Act, was not irrelevant to claims for conditional entry. It was one of the factors which the Immigration and Naturalization Service must take into account to determine whether a refugee seeks asylum in the United States as a consequence of his flight in search of a refuge.[237] In 1980, the Refugee Act made that limitation explicit.

The draft Convention on Territorial Asylum considered at the Conference held in Geneva in 1977 proposed to set a seal of approval on the practice of identifying countries of first asylum by adding the following additional paragraph to Article 1:

> Asylum should not be refused by a Contracting State solely on the ground that it could be sought from another State. However, where it appears that a person requesting asylum from a Contracting State already has a connexion or close links with another State, the Contracting State may, if it appears fair and reasonable, require him first to request asylum from that State.

The language of that draft Article indicates, however, that participating States were then far from reaching agreement upon the connections or close links which were to be taken into account for this purpose. Although Professor Melander has drafted a Convention designed to serve that purpose,[238] agreement on the terms of a multilateral instrument is still lacking: and in so far as the matter is settled by treaty, this is done on a bilateral basis.

NON-REFOULEMENT IN THEORY

Refoulement may be defined as an administrative act, regulated as to its exercise by rules of international law, whereby the authorities appointed by a State refuse to admit a particular person to the State's territory, and thereupon return him to the country whence he came.[239] The term is to be distinguished from the various forms of expulsion (including extradition). According to Lapradelle and Niboyet:

> *L'expulsion se distingue du refoulement en ce que l'expulsion s'applique à l'étranger qui a été admis à pénétrer dans un pays et qui y a été effectivement séjourné un temps plus ou moins long, tandis que le refoulement atteint l'étranger non admis et classé comme indésirable, au moment où il tente de franchir la frontière.*[240]

Indeed, in the Geneva Convention, Article 32 protects from expulsion those refugees who are lawfully present in territories of Contracting States, whereas Article 33 prohibits their *refoulement*.

The distinction must not be drawn, however, in an excessively literal manner. *Refoulement* is apt to describe the return of a person seeking admission, or admitted temporarily or conditionally. Indeed, anyone presenting himself at a frontier will normally be within the State's jurisdiction. It is for this reason, and the better to maintain control, that national law may deem an alien unadmitted, even when he is physically present at the port, and provide for a power to refuse admission, which may amount to *refoulement*. Similarly, national law may authorise the deportation of an alien, notwithstanding any presumption that he is unadmitted.[241] In the *Soblen Case*[242] the United Kingdom authorities first attempted to secure the appellant's removal to the United States under Article 1(1) of the Aliens Order of 1953 (which dealt with refusal of leave to land in the United Kingdom). Later, the Home Secretary sought to ensure Dr Soblen's return to the United States under Article 20(2)(b) of the 1953 Order (which dealt with deportation of aliens in the public interest). The Vacation Court[243] and the Court of Appeal[244] held that it was open to the Home Secretary to initiate proceedings under Article 20(2)(b) in respect of a person who had been denied leave to land in the kingdom although by statute that person was deemed not to have landed. Article 33(1) of the Geneva Convention suggests further more that a distinction is not to be drawn in literal terms between expulsion and *refoulement*.

That Article requires Contracting States to refrain from the expulsion or return (*refoulement*) of refugees to the frontiers of territories where their lives or freedoms would be threatened for any of the reasons set out in Article 1. In this context the term '*refoulement*' appears to bear a broad meaning, as is emphasised by the phrase in which it is qualified: 'in any manner'. The aim of the prohibition is to ensure that the refugee will not be returned to any State including that from which he fled, whether by '*refoulement*' in the traditional sense of the term or by expulsion. Moreover, in Article 33(1) there is no limitation (as there is in Article 32) to persons 'lawfully' in the territory of the State of refuge. The prohibition on *refoulement* appears to apply to all those at the frontier, whether or not they have been '*admis à pénétrer*'. This conclusion is confirmed in authoritative national decisions.[245] In the application of that rule, certain of the States of Africa and Asia and a few developed States have allowed large numbers of asylum-seekers to cross borders and remain pending a solution.[246]

Article 33(2) provides that the benefit of the antecedent paragraph may not be claimed by a refugee when there are reasonable grounds for regarding him as a danger to the security of the country where he is; nor by a refugee who has been convicted by a final judgment of a particularly serious crime and constitutes a danger to the community. Since this paragraph constitutes an exception to a fundamental general principle, it must be interpreted restrictively, in common with all such paragraphs. Moreover, in applying this paragraph, the principle of proportionality operates. In the words of the United Kingdom's representative at the Conference, the question is whether the danger faced by the refugee outweighs the danger to public security or to the community if he were permitted to stay.[247] In some States, including the Federal Republic of Germany, refugees sentenced to long periods of imprisonment may be put to the choice of serving their term in prison or returning home. Paragraph (2) applies primarily but not exclusively to the case in which a refugee engages in acts prejudicial to security or is convicted in the State of asylum. Circumstances may be imagined, however, in which activities in some other country make the refugee's presence inimical to the interests of the State or community in which he has asylum; and in such cases paragraph (2) may be invoked.

Few issues in this area are more controversial or important than the question whether *non-refoulement* amounts to a rule of customary law, binding on all States irrespective of the Geneva Convention. Dr Goodwin-Gill has argued that the evidence relating to the meaning and scope of *non-refoulement* in its conventional sense also amply supports the conclusion that today the principle forms part of general international law.[248] The widespread acceptance of the Geneva Convention, coupled with the express prohibition of reservations to Article 33, tends to support his conclusion,[249] as does the trend in authoritative modern writing. Indeed, as early as 1953 Dr Weis suggested that Article 33 simply codifies the practice of civilized States.[250] He stopped short of asserting that this practice had matured into positive law. The principle of *non-refoulement* was a usage which led to the adoption of the proposition that a State should not refuse admission to a refugee. In other words, it should grant him at least temporary asylum if non-admission was tantamount to surrender to the country of persecution.[251]

In 1965 Dr Schnyder, the then High Commissioner for Refugees, wrote that the principles of non-rejection and temporary asylum were becoming more and more recognized.[252] Eleven years later, however, his successor concluded that not all States accepted a rule of non-rejection.[253] Professor Grahl-Madsen wrote that the principle of *non-refoulement* was more important as a moral means of convincing a government that as a basis for legal argument.[254] It is thought, however, that modern developments afford a basis for reaching a more positive development.[255]

NON-REFOULEMENT: CONVENTIONS AND DECLARATIONS

The practice of withholding the extradition of political offenders may have originated in Europe[256] but it was in Latin America that asylum appears to have gained an institutional status in a multilateral agreement concerned with penal law.[257] Several such agreements embodied a rule against *refoulement*; and such a rule is also to be found in the Convention relating to the International Status of Refugees, 1933[258] and the Constitution of the International Refugee Organization, precursors of the Geneva Convention of 1951.

The principle now finds expression in Article 33 of the Geneva Convention. The fundamental character of that Article is emphasized by the prohibition of reservations to it. In this respect Article 33 is to be contrasted with Articles 31 and 32 (dealing with the punishment of those present unlawfully and the expulsion of refugees other than to countries of persecution).

Had the Geneva Convention and the antecedent treaties not been followed by other and more specific engagements, the rule against *refoulement* might have remained particular rather than general, conventional rather than customary. The rule contained in Article 33 is, however, supplemented by more specialized and regional instruments[259] and in particular the subject was reviewed at the Conference in Arusha of the Organization of African Unity. The Conference there recommended that the protection of individuals by the principle of *non-refoulement* be observed.[260] The O.A.U.'s Convention elaborates the principle of *non-refoulement* in Article 11. Paragraph (3) includes among the proscribed measures 'rejection at the frontier', thereby making it clear that an asylum-seeker's admission to the territory of a State is not a precondition for benefit from the principle. Paragraph (4) is designed to ensure the practice of burden-sharing 'in the spirit of African solidarity and international cooperation'. This paragraph acknowledges and addresses the practical difficulties created by application of the principle of *non-refoulement* in cases of the arrival of asylum-seekers *en masse*. Paragraph (5) makes explicit the duty to grant temporary refuge pending resettlement.[261]

The terms of international declarations formally made often have a greater value than those of treaties in establishing rules of general international law. Although commonly lacking a treaty's obligatory force, a declaration may well be phrased as an expression of a principle recognized as binding on all. This is the case with the General Assembly's Declaration on Territorial Asylum of 1977, which provides that no one entitled to seek asylum shall be subjected to measures such as rejection at the frontier or, if he has already entered the territory in which he seeks asylum, expulsion or compulsory return to any State where he may be subjected to persecution.[262]

A resolution adopted by the Committee of Ministers of the Council of Europe in the same year expresses the same principle in even more explicit language: no one shall be subjected to refusal of admission at the frontier or any other measure which would have the result of compelling him to return to a country of persecution.[263]

The force of the principle contained in such declarations or treaties is emphasized by the restrictive terms in which the scope of any permissible derogations is expressed. The General Assembly's Declaration permits derogation only 'in order to safeguard the population, as in cases of a mass influx of persons' and that of the Council of Europe envisages derogations in order to safeguard national security or to protect the community from serious danger. The O.A.U. Convention declares the principle without exception: no right of derogation for reasons of national security is permitted, although in cases of difficulty 'in continuing to grant asylum' appeal may be made directly to other Member States and through the Organization.

NON-REFOULEMENT: DIPLOMATIC PRACTICE AND COMMENT

Even examination of early diplomatic practice yields some support for the view that the principle of *non-refoulement* was recognized internationally.[264] The Convention on Territorial Asylum adopted at the Tenth Inter-American Conference at Caracas in 1954 provides in Article IV that the 'right of extradition' is not applicable in connection with persons who are sought for political offences or for common offences committed for political ends, or when extradition is sought for political motives. If, as the context seems to imply, the 'right of extradition' covered by those articles is the right of the pursuing State to seek the extradition of the offender, the Convention implies that the pursuing State may not effectively demand the return of a political refugee to its territory, by way of extradition. In its report to the Conference, the United States delegation observed that its Government's position on the Convention on Territorial Asylum was predicated on the conclusion that there was no need for a treaty on this subject because those articles which, in general, restate existing international law do not need to be incorporated in a conventional agreement in order to be binding.[265]

Since the relevant articles of the Convention, and consequently the statement of the U.S. delegation, refer only to the expulsion of political refugees and not to *refoulement* generally, we cannot necessarily infer that, in the opinion of the U.S. Government, existing international law required a State to refrain from any form of *refoulement* of such refugees. Nevertheless, on 11 December 1952, Mrs Franklin D. Roosevelt, United States delegate to the Seventh Regular Session of the General Assembly, stated that the United States 'would never force a refugee to return to his country against his will'.[266] A statement to much the same effect was made in the U.K. Parliament by the Home Secretary in 1954.[267]

As has been observed, the practice of granting temporary asylum tends to be applied by States which are unwilling to grant permanent asylum but feel constrained to refrain from *refoulement*.[268] In response to a request for an assurance that temporary asylum would be extended to persons claiming and appearing to be political refugees, the United Kingdom's Home Secretary confirmed that his Government had no intention of surrendering its right to grant asylum.[269]

In recent years the principle of *non-refoulement* has been placed under some strain and efforts have been made on the part of several States to diminish its effect. The latter serve, however, to underscore the growing, if reluctant practice of acknowledging the existence of the principle as a binding obligation. In 1976 the UNHCR Director of Protection referred to recurring violations of the basic rights of refugees, in particular that of *non-refoulement*'.[270] The following year the Executive Committee of the High Commissioner's programme produced recommendations to resist this trend.[271]

Again, in 1977, the Conference on Territorial Asylum produced evidence of a desire for a restricted interpretation of *non-refoulement*. The Turkish delegate observed that in exceptional cases *non-refoulement* might be claimed by a great number of persons whose massive influx may constitute a serious problem to the security of a Contracting State. In such an event, the receiving State should be free to return the refugees whence they came. His observation accounts for the qualification inserted into the ensuing Declaration; but the reluctance with which that qualification was made, the guarded terms in which it is expressed and the explicit comments of other delegates on the point serve to reinforce the fundamental nature of the rule against *refoulement*.[272] A similar inference may be drawn from the proceedings of the Conference held at Arusha on the Situation of Refugees in Africa.[273] The Conference expressly re-affirmed the principle of *non-refoulement* and supported the practice of granting of temporary asylum.[274]

At the meeting in 1981 of the Executive Committee of the UNHCR measures were adopted for the protection of asylum-seekers in situations of large-scale influx.[275] The first requirement was that they 'should be admitted to the State in which they first seek refuge ... the fundamental principle of *non-refoulement* – including non-rejection at the frontier – must be scrupulously observed'.[276] The General Assembly of the United Nations has supported the principle by calling on States in which refugees are found to avoid 'any action that may cause human suffering' and to observe scrupulously the principle of *non-refoulement*.[277] Indeed, the report of the Thirty-Third Session of the UNHCR Executive Committee in October 1982 went so far as to refer to the principle of *non-refoulement* as a 'peremptory rule of international law'.[278] While the latter assertion appears somewhat audacious, it is significant that the Executive Committee felt able to make it. Their assertion lends credence and weight to the argument that the principle of *non-refoulement* has matured into a rule of customary law, at least.[279]

NON-REFOULEMENT: DOMESTIC LAW

During the early years of the present century, it would have been remarkable to discover, at least in the case-law of the common law courts, judicial acknowledgment of the principle of *non-refoulement* as a rule of customary law. Indeed, in *The State (Duggan)* v *Tapley,* the Irish Supreme Court expressly rejected the claim that there is a recognized principle of international law preventing the extradition of refugees.[280]

Judicial recognition of that principle appears to have become more widespread as a result of developments in treaty law rather than customary law. Moreover, the continental courts were the *fora* in which the recognition first occurred. In *Keledjian Garabad* v *Public Prosecutor,* an Armenian refugee, apparently protected by the 1933 Convention on the International Status of Refugees, was made the subject of an expulsion order in France.[281] He appealed against the decision to make the order, alleging that under the Convention he could not be expelled other than on the grounds of national security or public order. On this point the Court sought the guidance of the delegate in France of the League of Nations for the Nansen Office. The latter certified that under the Convention the contracting parties were obliged to refrain from sending refugees back to the frontiers of their countries of origin, but to undertake to obtain for them, through the appointed channels, the necessary visas to secure their admission to another country, and that these provisions were applicable even to refugees expelled for reasons of public order. In following this advice the Court implied that under the 1933 Convention, the expulsion of a refugee could take place only if another country were willing to admit him. Similarly, in *Brozoza's Case* the Court of Appeals of Toulouse reversed an order made by the *Tribunal Correctionel* for the imprisonment of a stateless person who had failed to comply with an order to leave the country. The Court of Appeals took the view that the Convention of 1933 excluded punishment in such cases.[282]

Today, few of the refugee-receiving States have failed to ratify the Geneva

Convention of 1951, and the effects of widespread accession to the Geneva Convention are discernible in State practice. Writing for the Max Planck Institute, Dr Rainer Hofmann has commented as follows:

> In all countries even persons still being at the frontier seem to be protected against *refoulement* to a country where their lives or freedom would be threatened on account of their race, religion, nationality, membership of a particular social group or political opinion. This result confirms the widely shared view that the fundamental principle of *non-refoulement* in its wide sense nowadays forms part of international customary law.[283]

Almost without exception, modern domestic legislatures insert into their immigration laws provisions which actively forbid the return of political or other refugees to countries from which they have fled. Examples of this approach are numerous. Section 17(3) of the Norwegian Aliens Act of 1956 forbids the return of refugees in this manner. Moreover, its application is not dependent upon a determination of refugee status and so it may be invoked by anybody fearing persecution upon his deportation.

Under Dutch law the principle of *non-refoulement* is applied if the alien claims to be a refugee. An asylum-seeker will only be removed in exceptional cases, before he has requested admission as a refugee, with permission of the Minister of Justice under Sections 6 and 22 of the 1965 Aliens Act.[284] In Belgium Article 72 of the Royal Decree of 8th October 1981 requires that any alien at the frontier without the requisite documents and claiming asylum will be admitted to the kingdom. The asylum-seeker is given a document declaring his protected status under Article 25[285] and he is then free from *refoulement*. In Australia the principle of *non-refoulement* is not explicitly recognized in law. It is well-understood, however, in executive practice.[286]

In some jurisdictions a person who has been denied admission to the State's territory, or is about to be deported from it, may appeal on the question of the country to which he is expected to be sent. Where appeals on this question are readily available and the appellate tribunal is instructed to allow appeals on the ground that the appellant's return would expose him to persecution, the result may be similar to that achieved by the statutory proscription of the return of refugees.

In the United Kingdom appeals on this question may be brought under Section 17(1) of the Immigration Act 1971 (provided that the case is one in respect of which a right of appeal lies). The adjudicator (or the Immigration Appeal Tribunal) will allow the appeal if he or it considers that the authorities 'should have . . . exercised differently' their discretionary power to select the appellant's destination.[287] A deportation order is not to be made against a person if the only country to which he can go is one to which he is unwilling to go owing to a well-founded fear of being persecuted.[288]

In the United States it is argued that by incorporating the principle of *non-refoulement* into Section 243(h) of the 1980 Refugee Act, Congress has given aliens a right not to be returned; and aliens enjoy a status accordingly. An alien must, however, affirmatively request the relief before the Government has any obligation to consider whether or not return would lead to persecution.[289] The Immigration and Naturalization Service will not deport an alien who has requested asylum (under Section 208 of the Walter-McCarren Act), nor will they deport one who has requested withholding of deportation (under Section 243(h)) until any appeals have been heard. If the alien succeeds in his appeal, this gives him no formal status but simply applies the principle of *non-refoulement.* The Government is then free to seek the alien's deportation to another country[290] in which his life or freedom would not be threatened.

Naturally, there remain among the parties to the Geneva Convention several States, dualist in their tradition, which hold that it is not open to a litigant in domestic courts to rely upon the principle of *non-refoulement* in the face of inconsistent domestic legislation. Such is the law in the United Kingdom[291] and in Australia,[292] Canada [293] and Lesotho.[294] The case-law in these jurisdictions is, of course, perfectly consistent with the proposition that the principle of *non-refoulement* is acceptable and established as a general principle of international law.

Indeed, that case-law is for the most part consistent with the view that an official exercising a discretionary power should take that principle into account in determining how to exercise his discretion.[295] The congruence of national law on the principle of *non-refoulement,* even in the case of States not parties to the 1951 Convention and 1967 Protocol, is so striking that it appears to constitute a basis for recognizing that principle as one of general application.

REFUGEE STATUS

Once admitted to the territory of a State party to the Geneva Convention of 1951, a refugee may expect to benefit from the provisions of the Convention governing equality of treatment, juridical status, gainful employment, welfare and administrative measures.

The principle of equality of treatment is expressed in two main provisions. By Article 3 Contracting States agree to apply the provisions of the Convention to refugees without discrimination as to race, religion or country of origin. By Article 7 those States undertake to accord to refugees the same treatment as is accorded to aliens generally, save where the Convention contains more favourable stipulations. Indeed, it might be thought that Article 3 prohibits discrimination in respect of the admission of refugees with a view to the grant of asylum, while Article 7 protects refugees from discrimination after their

434

admission. Such a construction would be incorrect. The principle of non-discrimination is to be applied, in accordance with Article 3, in the implementation of 'the provisions of this Convention'. While the provisions of the Convention regulate the return or *refoulement* of refugees, they do not govern the selection of those who are to be granted asylum. Moreover, an examination of the *travaux préparatoires* makes it clear that the Article is inapplicable to the grant of asylum. The *Ad Hoc* Committee recorded the following statement:

> In Article 3 the Committee decided to clarify the meaning of the Article . . . to make it clear that it was not intended to apply to special conditions of immigration imposed on aliens but only to the treatment of aliens within the territory of a Contracting State.[296]

Thus, Article (7)1 sets out the minimum standard of treatment that a refugee may expect: he is to be treated no less favourably than aliens generally. The prohibition of discrimination on grounds of race, religion or country of origin is a special instance of the minimum standard enjoyed by other aliens. In so far as the Convention confers on refugees privileges exceeding those conferred on aliens generally, the rule in Article 3 assumes its full significance: the benefits so conferred are to be enjoyed without discrimination.

Conversely, the guarantee of equality of treatment with aliens generally is not qualified by any reference to the provisions of the Convention. A refugee may claim equality of treatment with aliens generally even in respect of matters falling outside that instrument. Moreover, by Article 7(2), refugees are to enjoy exemption from legislative reciprocity in the territory of Contracting States after three years' residence there. Thus, a French court held that a Spanish refugee was entitled to the renewal of an agricultural lease, even though a French law of 28 May 1943 reserved to aliens the right to equality of treatment with French nationals in respect of agricultural tenancies, on condition that the alien's law of nationality conferred analogous privileges on French nationals.[297]

Indeed, in two respect the refugee is entitled to be treated more favourable than other aliens, even in the absence of subsequent specific provisions in the Convention. Article 4 requires Contracting States to accord to refugees treatment at least as favourable as that accorded to their nationals with respect to freedom to practise their religion.[298] Article 8 establishes the general principle that exceptional measures taken against the person, property or interests of a foreign State shall not be applied to refugees who are nationals of that State, solely on account of their nationality. The sentence embodying that general principle is taken directly from Article 44 of the Geneva Convention on the Protection of Civilian Persons in Time of War.[299] Nevertheless, the wording was opposed by the United Kingdom on the ground that she wished to reserve the right to intern enemy aliens in time of war and otherwise protect herself against 'fifth columnists'.[300] Accordingly, the principle is qualified; and Contracting States which are unable to apply the general principle are to grant exemptions 'in appropriate cases'.

Articles 12 to 16 of the Geneva Convention form Chapter II of that instrument and govern juridical status. The principal provision is Article 12(1), which establishes the rule that a refugee's personal status shall be governed by the law of his domicile or, if he has no domicile, by the law of his country of residence. The term 'personal status' is not defined; but it must be taken to embrace legal capacity (including capacity to contract, to marry and to inherit) together with family rights (including legitimacy and efficacy of marriage). The rule set out in Article 12 conforms with the rule applied in the Geneva Convention of 1933[301] whereas the agreements of 1936 and 1938 dealing with refugees coming from Germany provided that where the refugee retained a nationality, his personal status should be governed by the law of the State of nationality; and the law of the domicile or residence should be applied only to those who had lost their nationality.[302]

The principle set out in Article 12 has been applied very widely before and after the conclusion of the Convention. In *May* v *May and Lehmann*[303] the Petitioner was a German Jewish refugee admitted temporarily to the United Kingdom in 1939 with a view to settlement in the United States. Some few months later, following the outbreak of war, he was interned as an enemy alien, to be released in 1941. A year later, he petitioned in an English court for divorce. Pilcher, J. found that he had established a domicile in England, even though he was an alien and liable to be deported at any time; and accordingly the court had jurisdiction.

In application of the principle contained in Article 12 of the Geneva Convention, a French court has held that the matrimonial régime of a couple of Roumanian refugees was unaffected by a Roumanian law dated 25 January 1953 governing the 'community of goods'. The couple had acquired a French domicile in advance of that date and at the time of their marriage the principle of separation of goods had been applied in Roumania.[304] Similarly, the Swiss Federal Tribunal declined to recognize a decree of divorce pronounced in Budapest in relation to a couple of Hungarian refugees. At the time of the pronouncement of that decree, both were domiciled in Switzerland.[305]

Contracting States undertake to accord to refugees the most favourable treatment possible in respect of movable and immovable property, and in any event not less favourable treatment than is accorded to aliens generally in similar circumstances.[306] In respect of artistic rights and industrial property, the refugee is to be accorded the same protection as is given to nationals of the State of habitual residence.[307] The refugee's rights of association under the

Convention are confined to non-political and non-profit making associations and trades unions. In such cases, a refugee lawfully staying in the territory of a Contracting State is to be given the most favourable treatment accorded to nationals of a foreign country, in the same circumstances.[308]

By Article 16 a refugee is to have free access to the courts of law of all Contracting States and is to enjoy in the Contracting State in which he has his habitual residence equality of treatment with nationals of that State as regards legal assistance and exemption from *cautio judicatum soli*. These provisions reproduce corresponding provisions in the Convention of 1933.[309] To this is added a new requirement: as regards legal assistance, exemption from *cautio judicatum soli* and access to the courts, a refugee is to be accorded in any Contracting State the treatment granted to a national of his country of habitual residence.[310]

Among the most important of the provisions in the Geneva Convention of 1951 is Article 17. This provides that each Contracting State shall grant to refugees lawfully staying in their territory the most favourable treatment accorded to nationals of a foreign country in the same circumstances, as regards the right to engage in wage-earning employment. Articles 18 and 19 provide that Contracting States shall accord to such refugees treatment 'not less favourable than that accorded to aliens generally in the same circumstances' as regards self-employment and the liberal professions respectively. Article 17, which deals with employment, reflects a provision in the Arrangement concerning the Legal Status of Russian and Armenian Refugees of 30 June 1928,[311] but there is no precedent for Articles 18 and 19. Moreover, a distinction is drawn between equality of treatment with 'foreign nationals' in Article 17 and equality of treatment with 'aliens generally' in Articles 18 and 19. The former is intended to establish in favour of refugees a most favoured nation clause. The latter is designed to ensure merely that refugees are treated no less favourably than aliens generally, in other words, that they are not penalized on account of their status as refugees. Beyond this, Articles 18 and 19 exhort Contracting States to ensure in favour of refugees 'treatment as favourable as possible'.

The standard of protection granted to refugees in the event of their engagement in self-employment or their entry into the liberal professions is extended to them also in respect of housing and public education other than elementary education. In so far as such matters are subject to the control of public authorities, refugees are to receive treatment as favourable as possible and, in any event, no less favourable treatment than is accorded to aliens generally in the same circumstances.[312] Thus, in so far as a Contracting State remits the fees of aliens generally for secondary or further education, it is obliged to remit those fees for refugees, and in so far as it recognizes foreign school certificates or diplomas generally, it is obliged to recognized them when they are issued to refugees.

In all other respects, the chapter of the Convention dealing with welfare assures for the refugee equality of treatment with nationals of the State in question. Thus, national treatment is to be assured in respect of elementary education and (on condition that the alien is lawfully staying in the State in question) the national standard is applied in respect of public relief, labour legislation and social security.[313]

The principal administrative measure adopted for the benefit of refugees is the grant of the Convention Travel Document. Save where compelling reasons of national security or public order otherwise require, Contracting States undertake to issue Convention Travel Documents to refugees lawfully staying in their territory for the purpose of travel outside that territory. By paragraph 13(1) of the Schedule, each Contracting State undertakes that the holder of a travel document issued by it will be readmitted to its territory at any time during the period of its validity; and by paragraph 5 the document shall be valid for one or two years. Thus, the Convention Travel Document is the visible emblem of the refugee's status, the ostensible guarantee of his readmission to the country of asylum.

The Convention does not state that travel documents are to be issued 'on request', for in some States, such as the Federal Republic of Germany, they are issued automatically as a form of alien's identity card. Elsewhere, they are issued on the refugee's application. Moreover, provision is made in Article 28 for the issuance of Convention Travel Documents to refugees who are not 'lawfully staying' in the issuing State. The grant of such a document to such a refugee will be appropriate when he is resident in a State which is not a party to the Convention, or is a refugee as a result of events occurring beyond Europe, whereas his State of residence has exercised its right under Article 1B(1)(a) of the Convention to treat as refugees only those who fear persecution as a result of events occurring in Europe.[314] Moreover, by Article 27, Contracting States undertake to issue identity papers to any refugee in their territory who does not possess a valid travel document. No condition as to lawful residence is imposed.

The refugee's freedom of movement within the borders of Contracting States is protected by Article 26 of the Convention. This provides that each Contracting State shall accord to refugees lawfully in its territory the right to move freely within it, subject to any regulations applicable to aliens generally in similar circumstances. The proviso permitting restrictions of the kind applied to aliens generally appears apt to embrace only those restrictions on travel or residence which are in fact of general application. Thus, they do not (apparently) permit the imposition of restrictions on an individual refugee, even in the exercise of a general power.[315]

438

Refugee status may be lost by the voluntary act of the refugee or by a change of circumstances in his country of origin. Further, the Convention does not apply to those who receive protection or assistance from organs or agencies of the United Nations other than the Office of the United Nations High Commissioner for Refugees; nor to those who are treated as nationals of the country in which they have taken residence.[316]

Foremost among the voluntary acts which result in loss of refugee status are those which amount to re-availment of the protection of the country of nationality. According to the UNHCR *Handbook,*[317] this provision implies three requirements. First, the refugee must act voluntarily, and this condition is not met when he is obliged by circumstances beyond his control to have recourse to a measure of protection from his own country. Second, he must have the requisite intention, a condition which is not met when the refugee merely obtains documents from national authorities for which foreigners would likewise have to apply. Third, he must actually obtain the protection: thus status is not lost by a refugee who applies unsuccessfully to be resettled in his country of origin.

In general, a refugee forfeits his status if he renews the passport issued by his country of nationality, for by so doing he avails himself of its protection. On the other hand, it seems clear that the status is not lost by a refugee who returns for a short visit to the country which he left owing to fear of persecution. This is implied by Article 1C(4), which envisages the loss of refugee status in the event of a refugee's voluntary re-establishment in his country of origin. The voluntary re-acquisition of the nationality of the refugee's country of origin is also a basis for the loss of refugee status. According to the *Handbook,* the granting of nationality by operation of law does not imply voluntary re-acquisition unless the nationality has been expressly or impliedly accepted. Thus, it appears that the re-acquisition of a nationality of origin by sympathetic naturalization (as in the case of marriage) is not to be considered as an acquisition by voluntary act, unless it is contingent upon an option expressly exercised the refugee.

A refugee loses that status on the acquisition of a new nationality if he enjoys the protection of the country of nationality. This is so whether the new nationality is that of his country of asylum or of any other State. The acquisition by Jewish refugees of Israeli nationality under the Law of the Return[318] will therefore have the effect of depriving them of their status as refugees in a country other than Israel which is a party to the Convention. A change of circumstances in the refugee's country of nationality or former residence will result in a loss of refugee status if it is of such a nature that he is able to return there or can no longer continue to refuse to avail himself of that country's protection. By way of exception, a refugee who was considered as such under the Arrangements of 1926 or 1928 or under the Conventions of 1933 and 1938 or under the Protocol of 1939 or the Constitution of the International Refugee Organization will not lose that status in consequence of a change of circumstances which enables him to return to his country of former habitual residence, if he is able to invoke compelling reasons arising out of previous persecution for refusing to return there.[319] The exception appears to have been created specifically in order to preserve the status as refugees of Russian, Armenian and Jewish victims of persecution in the Soviet Union and in Germany.

Since Palestinian refugees are eligible to receive the protection or assistance of the United Nations Relief and Works Agency, they are ineligible for protection in accordance with the Geneva Convention of 1951 when 'at present receiving' that protection or assistance. It follows that the Office of the United Nations High Commissioner has no significant functions to perform in relation to the majority of the Palestinian refugees in those Middle Eastern countries in which the U.N.R.W.A. is active, and particularly in relation to refugees in camps administered by that agency. A Palestinian refugee outside the area of operation of the U.N.R.W.A. is, however, ineligible to receive the protection or assistance of that agency. Accordingly, he falls within the competence of the United Nations High Commissioner, until his return to the area in which protection or assistance is extended by the U.N.R.W.A.[320] Indeed, it seems that a Palestinian refugee within the U.N.R.W.A.'s area of operation falls within the competence of the United Nations High Commissioner only if he is unable to obtain the protection or assistance of the U.N.R.W.A., as is the case, for example, with Palestinians who failed to register for the protection of that agency in 1949 and find themselves in the Lebanon, where the government will not at present accept late registration.

By Article 1 E, the Convention is not to apply to a person who is recognized by the competent authorities of the country in which he has taken residence as having the rights and obligations which are attached to the possession of the nationality of that country. This provision has been inserted specifically to deal with such cases as those of the *Volkdeutsche:* persons of German ethnic origin who are regarded by the authorities of the Federal Republic of Germany as possessing German nationality in conformity with Article 116 of the Basic Law. A refugee does not lose his status as such by reason only of the fact that the State in which he finds himself draws no material distinction on grounds of nationality between him and its own nationals.

440

NOTES

1. Since 1970, 800,000 Haitians have left Haiti. Since 1979 over 500,000 Salvadoreans have left El Salvador. Over 40,000 Sudanese fled to Ethiopia in 1984 to escape civil war. In 1985 there were over one million Eritreans and Tigreans in Sudan. In 1978 the invasion of Cambodia by Vietnam forced several hundred thousand Cambodians to flee into Thailand. See: U.S. Committee for Refugees, American Council for Nationalities Service, *World Refugee Survey*, 1983, 69; UNHCR *Refugees Magazine* No. 24 December 1985; E. Lentini, 'The Definition of Refugee in International Law: Proposals for the Future', 5 B.C. Third World L.J. (1985) 183.; R. Chamberlain, 'The Mass Migration of Refugees and International Law', 7 Fletcher Forum (1983) 93 at 103–41; A. Fragoman, 'The Refugee: A Problem of Definition', 3 Case W. Res. J.I.L. (1970) 45 at 58.

2. For a catalogue of definitions of the term 'refugee' in international legal instruments, see Asian-African Legal Consultative Committee, *The Rights of Refugees: Report of the Committee and Background Materials*, 1986, pp. 23–27. See also F. Schnyder '*Les aspects juridiques actuels du problème des réfugiés*', 114 Hague *Recueil* (1965-II) 339, 362–363; O. Kimminich, *Der Internationale Rechtsstatus des Fluchtlings*, 1962, p. 15. Writing in 1963 A. Bouscaren estimated that the military and political shocks since 1945 had displaced forty million refugees: *International Migration since 1945*, 1969, p. 21. See further, A. Fragoman, *supra*, note 1.

3. This definition is taken from Article 1 of the Resolution on Asylum, adopted by the Institute of International Law at its Bath Session 1950: 43(1) Ann. I.D.I. (1950) 157; 45 A.J.I.L. (1951) Supp. p. 15.

4. D. Peretz, 'The Arab Refugees – A Changing Problem', 41 For. Aff. (1962–3) 558. See also S. Spitzer, 'World Tensions and International Law', 3 S.L.J. (1961) 175; J. Stebbing, 'UNRWA: An Instrument of Peace in the Middle East', 8 Int. Rel. May 1985; G. Tomeh, 'Legal Status of Arab Refugees', 33 L. and Contemp. Prob. (1968) 110.

5. Note, 'Political Legitimacy in the Law of Political Asylum', 99 Harv. L. Rev. (1985) 450.

6. For the history and development of the international law on refugees, see M. García-Mora, *International Law and Asylum as a Human Right*, 1956, pp. 23–41; A. Grahl-Madsen, *The Status of Refugees in International Law*, 1966, Vol. I pp. 9–25; E. Reale, '*Le droit d'asile*', 63 Hague *Recueil* (1938-I) 469; Shih Shun Liu, *Extraterritoriality: its Rise and its Decline*, 1925; E. Nys, *Les origines du droit international*, 1894, p. 274.

7. F. Morgenstern argues that in regard to extraterritorial asylum the crucial problem is that of reconciling the conflicting claims of State sovereignty and humanitarianism: 'Extraterritorial Asylum', 25 B.Y.I.L. (1948) 236, 261. See also H. Helfant, *The Trujillo Doctrine of Humanitarian Diplomatic Asylum*, 1947. Some writers conclude that diplomatic asylum owes more to considerations decency than to principles of law: C. De Visscher, '*Théories et Réalités en Droit International Public*', 1970, p. 225; F. Krenz, 'The Refugee as a Subject of International Law', 15 I.C.L.Q. (1966) 90, 91. See also A. Bahramy, *Le droit d'asile*, 1938; B. Ulloa, '*El Asilo Diplomatico*' [1950] I.A.J.Y. 40; R. Deustua, '*Derecho de Asilo*', 7 R.D.I. (1947) 23; P. Guggenheim, '*Traité de Droit International Public*', 1967, Vol. I. pp. 505–506; A. McNair, 'Extradition and Extraterritorial Asylum', 27 B.Y.I.L. (1951) 172.

8. García-Mora, *supra*, note 6. The argument that a right of diplomatic asylum does exist among a number of Latin American States has been propounded and substantiated by numerous authors. See the Convention on Diplomatic Asylum, Caracas, 28 March 1954, 161 BFSP 510 (*Basic Documents* IX.3) and C. Ronning, *Diplomatic Asylum: Legal Norms and Political Reality in Latin American Relations*, 1965, and *The Legal Status of the Institution of Diplomatic Asylum in Latin America as Determined by Practice and Conventions*, 1958; L. Zarate, *El. Asilo en el Derecho Internacional Americano*, 1957. When Article 14 of the

Universal Declaration of Human Rights was under discussion, the French delegate opposed the attempts by delegates of Uruguay and Bolivia to include a provision dealing with extraterritorial asylum, arguing that extraterritorial asylum was 'a specifically Latin American tradition': U.N.G.A.O.R. 3d Sess. Pt. I, 3d c'tee, p. 342: (1948). E. Denza, *Diplomatic Law*, 1976, pp. 72, 79, 99. See also *Tekle* v *Visa Officer, Prague* [1986] Imm. A.R. 71, where it was held that despite the Vienna Convention on Diplomatic Relations 1961 which established that foreign missions are *ipso facto* part of the territory of the nation they represent, an application for political asylum made at a British Embassy abroad will fail under paragraph 73 of the Immigration Rules H.C. 169.

9. This issue has attracted a great deal of writing in recent years. See H. Wierer, '*Asylrecht*' in *Handbuch des Internationalen Fluchtungsrechts*, ed. W. Schnatzel and T. Veiter, 1960; A. Frantz, *Das Asylrecht der politisch Verfolgten Fremden nach Internationalem und Deutschen Recht*, 1963, Vol. III, p. 81. See also A. Raestad, '*Le droit d'asile*' 19 R.D.I.L.C. (1938) 115; L. Koziebrodski, *Le droit d'asile*, 1962, p. 336; J. Simpson, *The Refugee Problem: Report of a Survey*, 1939; J. Stoessinger, *The Refugee and the World Community*, 1956; J. Vernant, *The Refugee in the Post-War World*, 1953; J. Stone, *Legal Controls of International Conflicts*, 1954, p. xxxiv; P. Guggenheim, *supra*, note 7, p. 367; M. Sibert, '*Traite de droit international public*', 1951, Vol. I, p. 573; G. Scelle, *Précis de droit des gens*, 1932, Vol. II, pp. 48–50. There is, however, no doubt that States enjoy, *vis-à-vis* one another, the right to extend territorial asylum to aliens, other than in those cases in which that right may be limited by treaties such as treaties of extradition. During the discussions on the constitution of the International Refugee Organization, several Eastern European States expressly admitted the existence of a right of asylum in this sense, though they sought to limit the right by the Convention: U.N. Economic and Social Council, Off. Rec. First Year, 2d sess., p. 543; Journal of the General Assembly, 2d Part of First sess., p. 794. See also R. Lillich, *The Human Rights of Aliens in Contemporary International Law*, 1984, pp. 34–35, 62–69.

10. Convention relating to the Status of Refugees, Geneva 28 July 1951, 189 U.N.T.S. 150; *Basic Documents* III.2; Protocol relating to the Status of Refugees, New York, 31 January 1967, 606 U.N.T.S. 267, *Basic Documents* III.3.

11. On the procedural capacity of individuals in international law in general, see H. Lauterpacht, 'The Subjects of the Law of Nations', 63 L.Q.R. (1947) 438, cont'd 64 L.Q.R. (1948) 97. See also I. Brownlie, *Principles of Public International Law*, 1979, pp. 314 and 558; G. Goodwin-Gill, *The Refugee in International Law*, 1983, 101 *et seq*.

12. *Supra*, note 7, p. 223.

13. 'Legal Aspects of the Convention of 25 July 1951 Relating to the Status of Refugees', 30 B.Y.I.L. (1953), 478, 481.

14. D. O'Connell, *International Law* 1970, Vol. II, p. 740.

15. 'The Right of Asylum', 26 B.Y.I.L. (1949) 327, 335 and see also M. Sibert, *supra* note 9, p. 574: '*Quels que soient le nombre et la qualité de ceux auxquelles il s'applique, l'asile n'est jamais pour eux un droit*' and A. Raestad, *supra* note 9, p. 115: '*Le droit d'asile signifie . . . au point de vue de droit international, un droit exercé par un Etat à l'égard d'un autre Etat*'.

16. L. Oppenheim, *International Law*, 1955, Vol. I, p. 671.

17. *Supra* note 6 p.v.

18. *Supra* note 7 p. 115.

19. V. Nanda, 'World Refugee Assistance: The Role of International Law and Institutions', 9 Hofstra L. Rev. (1981) 449.

20. V. Bevan, *The Development of British Immigration Law*, 1986, 214: 'the so-called Right of Asylum is certainly not a right possessed by the alien to demand that the State into whose territory he has entered with the intention of escaping persecution in some other State should grant protection and asylum. For such State need not grant these things'.

442

21. B. Jankovic, *Public International Law,* 1984, 235.
22. *Supra,* note 9, p. 49.
23. *Supra,* note 16, Vol. I, p. 678.
24. *Legal Aspects of the Problem of Asylum.* Appendix I to Committee Report, International Law Association, Conference at Tokyo, 1964, p. 49.
25. A. Grahl-Madsen *Territorial Asylum,* 1980, p. 43. See also S. Sinha, 'An Anthropocentric View of Asylum in International Law', 10 Colum. J. Trans. L. (1971) 78, 101–102.
26. D. Greig, 'The Protection of Refugees and Customary International Law', 8 Aust. Y.I.L. (1983) 130. See also D. Greig, *International Law,* 1976, at 443: 'it has proved as difficult as ever to obtain agreement on a substantial modification of the principle of State sovereignty in favour of the position of the refugee', and J. Starke, *Introduction to International Law,* 1977, p. 227: 'Nevertheless, it would be unwise to carry too far the idea that the obligations accepted by States under the Convention and Protocol are exclusively obligations *inter se.* The view which one takes on this question is inevitably coloured by one's view on the whole nature of international law – whether, that is, it is a system confined to regulating relations between States or whether it has wider import'.
27. *Supra* note 11, p. 107 (looking at the period 1945–1970); he continues at p. 109: 'The 1970s were characterized by wide ranging activity. Some progress could be noted on the level of individual protection and certain major refugee problems were resolved through repatriation and resettlement, but hopes and expectations centring on asylum were dashed by the failure of the 1977 United Nations Conference'. See also P. Hyndman, 'Asylum and *Non-Refoulement* – are these Obligations owed to Refugees under International Law?', 57 Phillipines L.J. (1982) 43, 55: 'Although States are still resisting binding obligations to grant asylum in the sense of granting a right of permanent settlement, State practice ... does indicate an acceptance of humanitarian obligations – an acceptance that refugees who arrive at foreign borders seeking admission should not be rejected, whether such rejection would mean a return across the border to the country fled, or the sending of the refugee upon a further dangerous journey to seek admission at another frontier, and that they should be given temporary refuge at least, provided that it is placed within a wider context of international cooperation. As well, the necessity for this assumption of responsibility at the international level seems to be gaining increasing acceptance'.
28. Geneva, 28 October 1933, 159 L.N.T.S. 199; emphasis added. U.N. Dept of Social Affairs, *A Study of Statelessness,* 1949, U.N. Doc. E/1112/add 1, p. 75.
29. See K. Mettenberg *Freis Geleit und Exterritorialitat,* 1929, *passim,* L.N. Off. Jo. (1934) 373.
30. New York, 15 December 1946, 18 U.N.T.S. 3.
31. Universal Declaration of Human Rights, U.N.G.A. Res. 217 A III of 10 December 1948, U.N. Doc. A/811, *Basic Documents* I.1; J. Joyce, *Human Rights: International Documents,* 1978, Vol. I, p. 10; K. Vasak, ed., *The International Dimensions of Human Rights,* 1982, at pp. 24–28.
32. U.N. Doc A/C 3/285 Rev. 1 (1948), emphasis added.
33. U.N. Doc A/C 3/SR 121, pp. 4, 6.
34. F. Morgenstern, 'The Right of Asylum', 26 B.Y.I.L. (1949) 327, 337.
35. P. Weis, 'Draft United Nations Convention on Territorial Asylum', 50 B.Y.I.L. (1979) at 151; and see also P. Weis, 'The United Nations Declaration on Territorial Asylum', 7 Can. Y.B.I.L. (1969) 92; and R. Plender, 'Admission of Refugees Draft Convention on Territorial Asylum', 15 San Diego L. Rev. (1979) 45.
36. U.N. Doc A/C 3/SR 121 p. 5; and F. Krenz, *supra* note 7, p. 107. However, U.N.G.A. Res. 2312 (xxii) refers to persons 'entitled' to invoke Article 14. O'Connell describes this resolution as 'vague and ambitious' and he claims that the provisions of the Universal Declaration are (in this respect at least) merely exhortatory. *Supra,* note 14, Vol. II, p. 740/41. Sir Hersch

Lauterpacht, in a famous article on the subject, wrote that: '[n]ot being a legal instrument, the Declaration would appear to be outside international law' – 'The Universal Declaration of Human Rights', 25 B.Y.I.L. (1948) 354, 369.

37. F. Krenz, *supra* note 7, p. 103. See E. Kunz, 'The United Nations Declaration on Human Rights' 43 A.J.I.L. (1949) 316; and M. Garcia-Mora, *supra* note 6, pp. 145–151.

38. Bogotá, 30 March-2 May 1948, 43 A.J.I.L. (1949) Supp 133; emphasis added. Article 3 of the Convention on Political Asylum adopted at the Pan-American Conference of 1933 stated that asylum is an institution of humanitarian character and is therefore not subject to reciprocity: Montevideo, 3–26 December 1933, 28 A.J.I.L. (1934) Supp. 70.

39. U.N.G.A. Res 428 (v) of 14 December 1950.

40. Recommendation IV D.

41. States parties to 1967 Protocol only: 3.
States parties to Convention only or Convention and Protocol: 100
States parties to either one or both: 103

42. *Supra,* note 10.

43. Adopted by the General Assembly on 14 December 1967 by U.N.G.A. Res. 2312 (xxii).

44. Article 1 of the draft text prepared by a group of experts under the auspices of the Carnegie Endowment for International Peace in consultation with UNHCR proposed that contracting States 'acting in an international and humanitarian spirit, shall use [their] best endeavours to grant asylum in [their] territory, which . . . includes permission to remain in that territory'. U.N. Doc. A. 8712.

45. P. Weis, 'Draft Convention on Territorial Asylum', *supra* note 35 at 169.

46. The Hague, 23 November 1957, 506 U.N.T.S. 125; *Basic Documents* III.4; The Hague, 12 June 1973, 965 U.N.T.S. 445; *Basic Documents* III.5.

47. See B. Grant, *The Boat People* 1980, 68–72; J. Pugash, 'The Dilemma of the Sea Refugee: Rescue without Refuge', 18 Harv. I.L.J. (1977) 577. Article 11 of the 1951 Convention requires contracting States to give 'sympathetic consideration' to the establishment within their territory of 'refugees regularly serving as crew members' on ships flying their flag.

48. Note in particular the Convention on the International Tracing Service, Bonn, 16 June 1955, 219 U.N.T.S. 379 and see further G. Goodwin-Gill, *supra* note 11, at 163 n. 64.

49. Caracas, 28 March 1984, 10th Inter-American Conference, text: O.A.S. Official Records OEA/Ser X/1 Treaty Series 34, Articles 1–4.

50. San José, 22 November 1969, 9 I.L.M. (1970) 673, 682; *Basic Documents* IX.4.

51. UNHCR *Refugees Magazine,* No. 27 March 1986.

52. Addis Ababa, 10 September 1969, 1001 U.N.T.S. 46; *Basic Documents* III.7.

53. Arrangement with regard to the Issue of Identity Certificates to Russian Refugees, Geneva, 5 July 1922, 13 L.N.T.S. 237; Arrangement relating to the Issue of Identity Certificates to Russian and Armenian Refugees, Geneva, 12 May 1926, 89 L.N.T.S. 47; Arrangment concerning the Extension to Other Categories of Refugees of Certain Measures in Favour of Russian and Armenian Refugees, Geneva, 30 June 1928, 93 L.N.T.S. 377.

54. Provisional Arrangement concerning the Status of Refugees coming from Germany, Geneva, 4 July 1936, 171 L.N.T.S. 75; Convention concerning the Status of Refugees coming from Germany, Geneva, 10 February 1938, 192 L.N.T.S. 59; Additional Protocol to the Provisional Arrangement of 1936 and Convention of 1938, Geneva, 14 September 1939, 198 L.N.T.S. 141.

55. See R. Ristalhuber, 'The International Refugee Organization', *International Conciliation,* 1951; D. Taft and R. Robbins, *International Migrations,* 1955, p. 240; P. Ladame, *Le Rôle des Migrations dans le monde libre,* 1958, p. 254.

56. G. Scelle in '*Le Problème de l'apatride devant la Commission du droit International de l'O.N.U.*', 52 *Friedenswarte* (1953–4) 142, 152, referred to '*considerations sordides dont*

certaines ont contribue à la suppression de l'O.I.R.' At the time of the creation of the I.R.O. by U.N.G.A. Res. 62, U.N. Doc. A/64/Add.1, it was thought that it could complete its work by 1950: L. Holborn, *The I.R.O.: Its History and Work, 1946–1952.* The I.R.O. assisted about 1,620,000 refugees: G. Goodwin-Gill, 'Entry and Exclusion of Refugees', [1982] Mich. Y.B. Int. L.S. 291. The *Ad Hoc* Committee on Statelessness and Related Problems set up to form the 1951 Convention said: 'The definition of the term 'refugee' given in the Constitution of the I.R.O. was invaluable as a guide'; U.N. Doc. E/AC 32.SR2. 8. The criterion of 'persecution or well-founded fear of persecution – for good and sufficient reasons' was first stated as a ground for refugee status in the revised draft of the refugee definition proposed by the United Kingdom. U.N. Doc. E/AC 32/L2/Rev. 1 at 1 (1950).

57. Res. 428 (V), (1950).

58. Res. 319 (IV) (1950). See H. Trémaud, *'Réfugiés sous mandat du Haut Commissaire des Nations Unies'*, 63 R.G.D.I.P. (1959) 478.

59. See D. Taft and R. Robbins, *supra* note 55, p. 245. See also Chapter I of the Statute of the UNHCR and U.N.G.A. Executive Committee of the High Commissioner's programme 'Financing of Transport of Refugees', U.N. Doc. A/AC 96/126, 20 March 1950, p. 4. See generally L. Holborn, *Refugees: A Problem of Our Time: The Work of the UNHCR 1951–1972,* 1975, Vol 1 at 72–73, 170–171, 327–328 and 401–403.

60. US $ 328 million in 1984. In January 1986 UNHCR was suffering a financial shortfall of some US $ 40 million for its planned 1985 operational budget.

61. A. Bouscaren, *supra* note 2, p. 17; see F. Kirgis, in *International Organizations in their Legal Settings,* 1977, 443–61, argues that a 'mobilization of shame' can change State actions.

62. U.N. Doc. A/C 3/34/7 1979. See generally J. Kumin, 'Orderly Departure from Vietnam', UNHCR *Refugees Magazine* No. 6 June 1982.

63. Jean-Pierre Hocké, Press Conference, Geneva, 17 January 1986; and see also interview with Kazuo Chiba, Chairman, 36th Session of UNHCR's Executive Committee, Ambassador, Permanent Representative of Japan to the U.N. Office, Geneva, UNHCR *Refugees Magazine,* No. 26 February 1986 p. 42.

64. Chapter 1, Article 1, paragraph (a).

65. A. Bouscaren, *supra* note 2, p. 35; I.C.E.M. *Handbook* 1960, p. 12.

66. For more detailed treatment of the subject see M. Proudfoot, *European Refugees 1939–1952,* 1956; A. Grahl-Madsen, *supra* note 6, Vol. I, pp. 18, 55, 171, 305–332; G. Goodwin-Gill, *supra* note 11, p. 127; and generally, L. Holborn, *supra* note 59, esp. at pp. 55–150.

67. U.N. Doc E/CN 4/781 pp. 5–6, 10 and Add. 1, p. 2.

68. U.N. Doc. E/CN 4/L 184 and E/CN 4/L 191.

69. Asian African Legal Consultative Committee, *op. cit.* p. 57.

70. 230 H.C. Deb. Col. 603, 18 July 1929.

71. M. Claude Cheysson – Minister for External Relations – in reply to a Parliamentary question to the National Assembly, December 7th 1983: *Bulletin d'Information en langue anglaise du 20 décembre 1983.* See generally, T. Cox, 'Well-founded fear of being persecuted': The Sources and Application of a Criterion of Refugee Status', 10(2) Brooklyn J.I.L. (1984) at 358.

72. *World Refugee Survey, supra* note 1 at 47: statement of Richard Feen, Special Consultant to the Office of the U.S. Coordinator for Refugee Affairs.

73. K. Hailbronner, 'Refugees and Asylum: The West German case', *The Washington Quarterly,* Fall 1985, 183.

74. *Supra,* note 6, p. 156.

75. G.U. 298 27 December 1947.

76. III E.D., pp. 222, 225. See *Bermudez de Madariaga* v *Ministro Interno,* 42 R.D.I. (1959) 652.

77. 23 February 1921. Cited by F. Morgenstern, 'The Right of Asylum', 26 B.Y.I.L. (1949) 327 at 335.

78. W. Simmons, *The Constitutions of the Communist World,* 1980, p. 351. Constitution of 7 October 1977.
79. Art. 65; W. Simmons, *ibid.,* p. 7; Constitution of 28 December 1976.
80. Art. 88; *ibid.* p. 287; Constitution of 22 July 1952 (as amended to 1976).
81. Art. 38; *ibid.* p. 317; Constitution of 21 August 1965 (as amended to 1975).
82. Art. 83; *ibid.* p. 261; Constitution of 6 July 1960.
83. Art. 65; *ibid.* p. 37; Constitution of 18 May 1971 (includes the grant of asylum from persecution for fighting racial discrimination).
84. Art. 66; *ibid.* p. 231; Constitution of 27 December 1972.
85. Art. 33; *ibid.* p. 139; Constitution of 11 July 1960 (as amended to 1978).
86. Art. 67; *ibid.* p. 175; Constitution of 20 August 1949 (as amended).
87. Art. 23 (2); *ibid.* p. 163; Constitution of 7 October 1974.
88. Art. 202; *ibid.* p. 427; Constitution of 21 February 1974.
89. *Supra,* note 6, pp. 155–6, 160.
90. Art. 59; *ibid.* p. 75; Constitution of 5 March 1978.
91. Art. 37; *ibid.* p. 399; Constitution of 1 January 1960.
92. A. Blaustein and G. Flanz, *Constitutions of the Countries of the World,* Vol. VI, issued February 1985. Art 14, Constitution of 14 May 1982.
93. Art. 28. New Constitution approved on 15 December 1983. The formula is identical with that employed in Article 153 of the former 1962 Constitution.
94. Art. 31. Constitution of November 1949, as amended 15 June 1977.
95. Art. 116. Constitution of May 1973.
96. Art. 17. Fundamental Statute of Government. Decree Law 24-82 as amended by Decree Law 36-82.
97. Art. 16. Statute on the Rights and Guarantees of the Nicaraguan People. Decree No. 52 of September 1979.
98. Art. 47. Constitution of 31 August 1983.
99. *Hoy* (newspaper) April 24th 1964, p. 2. See generally T. Draper, 'On the Cuban Constitutional Problem' in J. Triska (ed.) *Constitutions of the Communist Party States,* 1968, p. 256.
100. Art. 13. Constitution of 24 February 1976.
101. Syrian Arab Republic: Art. 34, Constitution of 13 March 1975; Islamic Republic of Iran: Art. 155, Constitution of 1358 of the Solar Year, Blaustein and Flanz, *supra.,* note 92 Vol. VII, issued April 1980; Jordan: Art 21(1), Constitution as amended, 1 August 1984; Kuwait: Art. 46, Constitution of 1962; Democratic Republic of Yemen: Art. 55, Constitution as amended 31 October 1978; Egypt: Art. 53, Constitution of 22 May 1980.
102. Togo: Art. 27, Constitution of 30 December 1979; Gabon: Preamble, Constitution of May 1975; Mali: Preamble, Constitution of 2 June 1974; Central African Republic: Preamble, Constitution of 1 February 1981; Senegal: Preamble, Constitution of 8 March 1963 (as amended); Ivory Coast: Preamble, Constitution of 1960; Zaire: Preamble, Constitution of 24 June 1967 (as amended to 15 February 1978).
103. The Constitution of Chad makes no reference to asylum. The Constitution of Tunisia – Art. 17, 1 June 1959 (as amended) states that political refugees shall not be extradited.
104. For the interpretation of immigration rules in the light of international conventions, see *Birdi* v *Home Secretary, The Times* L.R. 12 February 1975; *R* v *Home Secretary, ex parte Phansopkar,* [1975] 3 All ER 497, (C.A.); *R* v *Home Secretary, ex parte Akhtar,* [1975] 1 W.L.R. 1717 (CA). See, however, text at note 295.
105. Statement of Changes in Immigration Rules, H.C. 169 Part VII: Asylum, para 73.
106. The Immigration Rules deal with refugees and asylum at five points: twice in the section dealing with control on entry (at paragraphs 16 and 73), and three times in the section dealing with control after entry (at paragraphs 134, 153 and 165).

446

107. *R* v *Chief Immigration Officer, Heathrow, ex parte Salamat Bibi*, [1976] 3 All ER 843 at 847; *R* v *Immigration Appeal Tribunal, ex parte Murugandarajah*, 16 July 1984 (C.A.) (unreported); for judgment of High Court, see [1983] Imm. A.R. 141.
108. 1832 Duvergier Rep. 210, cited by A. Grahl-Madsen, *supra*, note 6, p. 95 Vol. I.
109. Law No. 52-893 of 25 July 1952; *Encyclopédie*, 11, 52, S 164. The Geneva Convention is applicable in France by virtue of the Presidential Decree No. 54-1055 of 14 October 1954, D. 1954, 432.
110. *Infra*, note 166.
111. In *K* v *S, Raad van Staat*, 20 December 1977, RV (1977) 97 the Council of State accepted the direct effect of Article 16 of the 1951 Convention, and interpreted the provision as meaning that persons claiming to be refugees may appeal to the Dutch Administrative Court against decisions denying recognition as such, notwithstanding limitations on appeals imposed by section 34 of the Aliens Act 1965.
112. For definitions of the term '*de facto* refugee', see: P. Weis, 'Convention Refugees and De Facto Refugees', 4 A.W.R. Bull. (1974), 181; G. Goodwin-Gill, *supra* note 11, p. 18; G. Jaeger, *Study of Irregular Movements*, 1985 (UNHCR Restricted Access).
113. This is not dependent upon recognition of refugee status and may be invoked by anyone fearing persecution upon deportation. Norwegian treaty commitments have direct effect in so far as they do not infringe on private acquired rights: *A.* v *The State, Norsk Retstidende* (1984) p. 1175. The definition of 'political refugee' corresponds with Article 1(A)(2) of the 1951 Convention, with the addition of 'other political reasons', and 'persons who, having committed a political offence, may be subjected to severe punishment'. If refugee status is denied, an applicant may be granted the right of residence on humanitarian grounds, and this will usually be the case where *non-refoulement* provisions prevent deportation. There is no procedure for withdrawal of refugee status.
114. *Utlanningslagen: Svensk Författnignssamling*, 1980, No. 376.
115. Exchange of Notes constituting an Agreement concerning the reciprocal obligations to accept certain persons deported from the other country, Bonn, 31 May 1954, BAnz 1954 No. 120. Similar provisions can be found, *inter alia*, in the Inter-Nordic Convention on the Waiver of Passport Control, Copenhagen, 12 July 1957, 322 U.N.T.S. 245 (S.O. 1958 24, amended, S.O. 1963 20 and S.O. 1973 43). If it is ascertained that an asylum-seeker has entered Sweden irregularly, having arrived via another Nordic country party to this Convention, he will normally be returned to the country in which he first entered the passport area: *Rikspolisstyrelsens Cirkular*, C.M. 1/85, page 3.
116. See generally H. Gammeltoft-Hansen, '*The Status of Refugees in Denmark*', International Institute of Humanitarian Law, 1985.
117. *Ausländergesetz* (Aliens Law) of 28 April 1965, BGBl 1965 I, 353; *Verordnung zür Durchführung Ausländergesetz* (Supplementary Decree on Aliens Law) of 10 September 1965, BGBl 1965 I, 1341; and *Asylumverordnung* (Asylum Decree) of 6 January 1953, BGBl 1953 I, 3.
118. *Supra*, text at note 76.
119. The right of asylum may be forfeited if used for subversion of the free and democratic order; Hailbronner, *supra* note 73, p. 183 *et seq.*; A. Randelshofer, Commentary on Art. 16(2) of the Basic Law, Maunz-Dürig-Herzog, *Grundgesetz* Supplement May 1985.
120. *Asylverfahrensgesetz* (Asylum Procedure Law) of 16 July 1982: 1982 BGBl 1, 94. Opportunities for appeal and review originally built into the asylum process led to large-scale abuse by those seeking to remain in the Federal Republic for economic reasons, and amendments to combat this were introduced progressively from 1977 onwards, culminating in a thorough revision in 1982.
121. Aliens Law of February 1938, Article 3.

122. The Constitution of 1853 (as amended) entrusts the Congress with legislative power in the matter, by Article 67(ii). Law No. 22439 of 1981, repealing Law No. 817 of 1876, regulates immigration generally. Decree No. 4418 of 1965 refers to refugees and asylees.

123. Ambassador Cocca (Argentina, November 1984) observed that the granting of refugee status by a State ought not to be seen as an unfriendly act but rather as a pacific humanitarian action.

124. Max Planck Institute for Comparative Public Law and International Law, *Heidelberg Colloquium* 11–14 September 1985, *The Legal Position of Aliens in National and International Law*, Section E, 'The Law of Asylum and Refugees', Argentina abstract, p. 41 *et seq.*

125. 1974 Act No. 45. Sudan Gazette No. 1162 Legis. Supp. (1974) 183. See generally, P. Nobel, 'Refugee Law in the Sudan', Scandinavian Institute of African Studies, Report No. 64.

126. P. L. No. 96-212, 94 Stat. 102. U.S. legislation now expressly incorporates the definition of 'refugee' found in the Convention and Protocol. The Refugee Act 1980 added Sections 207 and 208 to the Immigration and Nationality Act 1952, relating to the admission of refugees and asylees respectively. Since the Act of 1980 came into effect, over 400,000 aliens have entered the U.S. under these provisions (the vast majority as refugees under Section 207.

127. Immigration and Nationality Act, 1952, section 101(a)(42).

128. Immigration and Nationality Act, 1952, section 207 subsection(b) authorises the President to make emergency refugee admissions to respond to unanticipated humanitarian crises.

129. Immigration and Nationality Act, 1952, section 208 subsection(a)(4) specifically excludes from asylum those who have 'ordered, incited, assisted or otherwise participated' in the persecution of others. Excluded from adjustment of status to permanent resident are those asylees who are security risks, Nazi collaborators or those convicted of trafficking in narcotics.

130. Immigration and Nationality Act, 1952, sections 411–414.

131. 8. C.F.R. sections 207, 208.

132. See generally P. Woods, 'The Term "Refugee" in International and Municipal Law: An Inadequate Definition in the Light of the Cuban Boatlift', 5 A.S.I.L.S. Int. L.J. (1981) p. 52 *et seq.* Over two thirds of all admissions in this category from October 1980 to September 1984 came from South East Asia.

133. Immigration and Nationality Act, 1952, section 212(d)(5). 400,000 Indo-Chinese entered the United States under Parole Power following the fall of Saigon (1975–80), and 125,000 Cubans entered in the Mariel Boatlift (1980). The Act of 28 October 1977, 91 Stat. 1223, provided for the conferment of permanent resident status on the Indo-Chinese.

134. Max Planck Institute, *supra* note 124. U.S.A. abstract by A. Aleinikoff, section C. 111.4.

135. See also the Simpson-Mazzoli Bill or 'Immigration Reform and Control Act' 1983 (S. 529, 98th Cong., 1st Sess; 129 Cong. Rec., S. 6969-70, 18 May 1983) for a proposed legislative response. The Bill aspired to set a limit of 425,000 new immigrants per year excluding refugees.

136. 8 C.F.R. S 207 5.

137. 8 F. Supp. 310 (1934); 7 A.D. (1933–4) 188 (No. 75).

138. 27 U.S. (2 Pet.) 253, 314 (1829).

139. 119 U.S., 436, 442, (1886).

140. 171 F. 2d. 921, 935 (1948).

141. 8 C.F.R. para 208.10.

142. Appeal lies to the Board of Immigration Appeals and thence to a Federal District Court in the case of an exclusion order or to the Federal Court of Appeals in the case of a deportation order.

143. *Haitian Refugee Center* v *Smith*, 676 F. 2d. 1023 (1982).

144. *Nunez* v *Boldin,* 537 F. Supp. 578 (1982). See 'Political Legitimacy in the Law of Political Asylum', Harv. L. Rev. *supra* note 5, p. 461.

145. 727 F. 2d. 957 (1984).

146. *Immigration and Naturalization Service* v *Stevic,* 104 S. Ct. 2489, 2501 (1984). See also *Bolanos-Hernandes* v *Immigration and Naturalization Service,* 749 F. 2d. 1316, 1321 (1984), which affords authority for the view that the 'well-founded fear' standard is 'more generous' than the 'clear probability' test. The decision in *Carvajal-Munos* v *Immigration and Natural-ization Service,* 743 F. 2d. 562 (1984) suggested that immigration judges should establish separate procedures for determining asylum claims and claims under Section 243(h). See generally: C. Edwards, 'Political Asylum and With-holding of Deportation: Defining the Appropriate Standard of Proof under the Refugee Act of 1980', 21 San Diego L. Rev. (1983–84) 171; A. Helton, '*I.N.S.* v *Stevic:* Standards of Proof in Refugee Cases involving Political Asylum and Withholding of Deportation', 87 W. Va. L.R. (1985) 787.

147. *R* v *Brixton Prison (Governor), ex parte Soblen* [1962] 3 All ER 641, 656.

148. *R* v *Brixton Prison (Governor), ex parte Sarno,* [1916] 2 K.B. 742.

149. *Home Secretary* v *Two Citizens of Chile (cross appeals)* [1977] Imm. A.R. 36. See also *Home Secretary* v *X,* [1978] Imm. A.R. 13 at 17.

150. The decision was, however, followed in *Dartash* v *Home Secretary,* 16 May 1983, TH/94291/82 (2713).

151. *R* v *Immigration Appeal Tribunal, ex parte Kandia Nandakumara Sri Murugandarajah, supra* note 107; *R* v *Immigration Appeal Tribunal, ex parte Musisi,* [1984] Imm A.R. 175; *R* v *Immigration Appeal Tribunal, ex parte Enwia, ex parte A.S.,* [1983] 2 All ER 1045; see also *Molefi* v *Legal Adviser* [1970] 3 All ER 724.

152. *Asylum (Germany) Case,* 30 R.G. St. Vol. 30 (1900) 99, 101.

153. *Asylum (Germany) (No. 2) Case,* 51 J.W. (1922-II) 1588, 1589.

154. [1953-1] P.b. 724; 20 I.L.R. (1953) 286.

155. [1961-1] P.b. 271; 31 I.L.R. (1960), 327.,

156. Supra, note 111 and see also *S.K.* v *The State Secretary for Justice, Raad van Staat,* 16 October 1980, R.V. (1981) 1.

157. Members of this group are referred to as 'persons entitled to asylum' under Royal Decree 1 October 1974, R.V. (1974) 1. Alternatively, they are known as persons with 'B' status, as opposed to persons admitted as refugees who have 'A' status.

158. *K.T.* v *State Secretary for Justice, Raad van Staat,* 10 April 1979, R.V. (1979) 3, G.V. No. D. 12–18; and see also *N.N.* v *State Secretary for Justice, Raad van Staat,* 14 January 1982, G.V. No. D. 12–57, R.V. (1982) 5.

159. *Iraqi Kurds: Raad van Staat* 27 March 1980, G.V. No. D. 12–38, and *Black South Africans, N.N.H.* v *State Secretary for Justice, Raad van Staat,* 16 May 1979, R.V. (1979) 6.

160. 42 R.D.I. (1959) 652; 26 I.L.R. (1958-11) 500. A. Cassesse, '*Sul soggiorno del rifugiato politico in Italia*', 42 R.D.I. (1959) 653–661.

161. (1950) I.C.J. Rep. 266, 282, 284, 297. For a clarification of this case, see the *Haya de la Torre Case* (1951) I.C.J. Rep. 71. For discussion of the cases see De Visscher, *supra* note 7, pp. 225–6; O'Connell, *supra,* note 14, pp. 734–6; A. Evans, 'The Colombian-Peruvian Asylum Case: Termination of the Judicial Phase', 45 A.J.I.L. (1951) 755; Goodwin-Gill, *supra* note 11, pp. 102–3.

162. *Supra,* note 42 and *Basic Documents* III.2 and III.3. The Convention of 1951 applied only to refugees who acquired such status 'as a result of events occurring before 1 January 1951'. By Article (B)(1), States may, on signature, ratification or accession, limit their obligations to refugees resulting from 'events occurring in Europe'. Brazil, Italy, Madagascar, Malta, Monaco, Paraguay and Turkey, in accordance with Article 1(B)(1) of the Convention, limit their responsibilities to 'events occuring in Europe before 1 January 1950'. The temporal limitation is in effect removed by the Protocol of 1967.

449

163. Arrangement relating to the Issue of Identity Certificates to Russian and Armenian Refugees, *supra,* note 53; Arrangement concerning the Extension to Other Categories of Refugees of Certain Measures taken in Favour of Russian and Armenian Refugees, *supra,* note 53; Convention relating to the International Status of Refugees, *supra,* note 28; Convention concerning the Status of Refugees coming from Germany, supra, note 54.

164. Article 1 F. For the meaning of 'crimes against peace', see Charter of the International Military Tribunal, London, 8 August 1945, 82 U.N.T.S. 279, Article 6(a). For 'war crimes', see *ibid.,* Article 6(b). For 'crimes against humanity' see *ibid.,* Article 6(c) and U.N.G.A. Res. 3068 (xxviii) of 30 November 1973, characterizing *apartheid* as a crime against humanity; and see generally Lord Wright, 'War Crimes under International Law', 62 L.Q.R. (1946) 51. Serious non-political crimes are not defined; by contrast, the Constitution of the I.R.O. referred to extradition crimes. Acts contrary to the purposes and principles of the United Nations are also undefined and uncertainty is compounded by the absence of any requirement that the offender by 'convicted' of such acts. All that is required is that he be 'guilty'. The purposes of the United Nations are defined in Article 1 of the Charter, San Francisco, 26 June 1945, 1 U.N.T.S. xvi. They include the maintenance of international peace and security, the development of friendly relations between nations, the achievement of international cooperation and the harmonizing of actions of nations. The principles of the United Nations are set out in Article 2. They include the sovereign equality of members the pacific settlement of disputes and abstention from the threat or use of force. It is thought that engaging in military activities of a State other than one's own for mercenary gain amounts to an activity contrary to the purposes and principles of the United Nations, at least when it entails the unlawful use of force by that State: see Convention on the Elimination of Mercenarism in Africa, Benin, 3 May 1982 (not in force).

165. *Supra,* note 52.

166. U.N.G.A. Res. 1129 (xi) of 21 November 1956 on Hungarian refugees; 1389 (XIV) of 20 November 1959 on refugees from Algeria and Morocco; 1500 (xv) of 5 December 1960 on refugee from Algeria, Morocco and Tunisia; 1671 (XVI) of 18 December 1961 on Angolan refugees in the Congo; 1672 (XVI) of 18 December 1961 on refugees from Algeria in Morocco and Tunisia; 1784 (XVII) of 7 December 1962 on Chinese refugees in Hong Kong; 2040 (XX) of 7 December 1965 on refugees in Africa; 2958 (XXVII) of 12 December 1972 on Sudanese refugees returning from abroad; 3143 (XXVIII) of 14 December 1973 on the report of the U.N. High Commissioner for Refugees; 3454 (XXX) of 9 December 1975 on humanitarian assistance to Indo-Chinese displaced persons. See also ECOSOC Res. 1655 (LII), 1705 (LIII), 1741 (LV), 1799 (LV), 1877 (LVII) and 2011 (LXI).

167. U.N. Doc. E/AC 32/L 38 (1950) E/1618, reprinted in U.N. Ybk. (1950) 569.

168. E/1618 – E/AC 32/5: 'The expression well-founded fear of being the victim of persecution means that a person has been actually a victim of persecution or he can show good reason why he fears persecution'. Cf. T. Cox, *supra,* note 71 at 342.

169. See Grahl-Madsen, *supra* note 6, at 180.

170. The majority of European States maintain government-sponsored agencies responsible for assisting refugees with the presentation of their cases: C. Avery, 'Refugee Status Decision-Making: The Systems of Ten Countries', 19 Stan. J.I.L. (1984) 235.

171. *Handbook on Procedures and Criteria for Determining Refugee Status,* Geneva, September 1979. In the United Kingdom there can be no judicially enforceable obligation to follow the UNHCR *Handbook: R v Home Secretary, ex parte Huseyin Budgaycay and Michael Nedilow Santis,* [1986] Imm. A.R. 8.

172. *Ibid* at Chap. II B(2), paragraph 37 p. 11.

173. European Lawyers Workshop on the Implementation of Article 1A of the Geneva Convention, Paris, 4–5 May 1985, under aegis of European Consultation on Refugees and Exiles and

France Terre d'Asile, report at p. 3. Participating States: France, Federal Republic of Germany, Netherlands, Sweden, Switzerland, United States.

174. *Habtu Kahsai Haitu* v *Home Secretary,* 1 December 1977, TH/3926/76.

175. In 1983, *Genet Woldu* v *Home Secretary,* 8 June 1983, TH/93591/82 (2705), it was held that there had to be a 'reasonably grounded expectation of persecution and that the expectation must be higher than a mere remote possibility but need not be higher than a probability of persecution'. In *Khera and Khanaja,* [1983] 2 W.L.R. 321 a 'serious possibility' of such treatment was required.

176. *Kazie* v *Home Secretary,* [1984] Imm. A.R. 10. Reference was made to *Fernadez* v *Government of Singapore,* [1971] 2 All ER 691 at 696, where Lord Diplock observed that 'there is no general rule of English law that when a court is required . . . to take account of what may happen in the future and to base legal consequences on the likelihood of its happening, it must ignore any possibility of something happening merely because the odds on its happening are fractionally less than evens'.

177. *Enninful* v *Home Secretary,* 30 August 1984, TH/119683/84 (3423).

178. But see *Atibo* v *Immigration Officer, London (Heathrow) Airport,* [1978] Imm. A.R. 93 and *Doonetas* v *Home Secretary,* 14 October 1976, TH/12339/75 (820), (Individual not persecuted for reasons set out in Convention when punished for breach of law of general application regarding public meetings and national service respectively).

179. *Dally* v *Immigration and Naturalization Service,* 744 F. 2d. 1191 (1984).

180. *Carvajal-Munos* v *Immigration and Naturalization Service, supra* note 146.

181. However, see *Bolanos-Hernandez, supra,* note 146, where it was said, 'the significance of a specific threat to an individual's life or freedom is not lessened by the fact that the individual resides in a country where the lives and freedom of a large number of people are threatened'. See also *Matter of Acosta,* Interim Decision (B.I.A. March 1 1985); *In Re Acosta Solozano,* Interim Decision No. 2986 (B.I.A. 1985) and *Martinez-Romero* v *Immigration and Naturalization Service,* 692 F. 2d. 595 (9th Cir. 1982). In its *amicus* brief, in *Immigration and Naturalization Service* v *Luz Marina Cardoza-Fonseca,* (U.S. Supreme Court, No. 85-72, 9 March 1987, 55 L.W. 4313), the UNHCR submitted that there is 'good reason' to fear persecution where subjective fear is based on an objective situation which makes that fear plausible. The Supreme Court ruled that in order to satisfy section 243(h) it is not necessary to show that it is more likely than not that the alien will face persecution.

182. *Kwiatowsky* v *M.E.I.* [1982] 2 S.C.R. 856. See also *Nunez Veloso et al.* v *M.E.I.* (I.A.B. 79-1017, 79-1017A) and *Rajudeen* v *M.E.I.,* (1984) 55 N.R. 129 (F.C.A.). The House of Lords was invited to follow the dictum in the *Kwiatowsky* case in *R* v *Home Secretary ex parte Sivakumarar and others* (pending).

183. Loi sur l'asile, 5 October 1979, F.F. 1979 II 977.

184. Formerly, the law of the United States required 'physical persecution' as a basis for withholding deportation. In 1965 there was substituted the test of 'persecution'. In *Kovac* v *I.N.S.,* 407 F 2d. 102, 106 (1969), this was described as a 'significant, broadening change'.

185. Netherlands Royal Decree 9 August 1972 A.B. (1973) 19 G.V. D. 12-2.

186. *Ali (MMH)* v *Home Secretary,* [1978] Imm. A.R. 126 (policy of Africanization in Kenya); *Kurlapski* v *Home Secretary,* TH/5911.75, 17 December 1975 (unreported), ('social engineering' in Poland).

187. *S. C.* v *State Secretary for Justice, Raad van Staat,* 21 February 1983, G.V. No. D. 12-79, A.B. (1983) No. 583, R.V. (1983) 2. In this case the *Raad* accepted a well-founded fear of discriminatory treatment on the sole ground that the asylum-seeker had contravened section 217 of the Hungarian Penal Code. For Canadian cases, see *Jankowski* v *M.E.I.,* [1982] 1 F.C. 290 (C.A.). In the latter, Pratte, J. stated: 'a person who is punished for having violated an ordinary law of general application is punished for the offence he has committed, not for the

political opinions that may have induced him to commit it. In my opinion, therefore, the board was right in assuming that a person who has violated the laws of his country of origin by evading ordinary military service and who merely fears persecution and punishment for that offence in accordance with those laws cannot be said to fear persecution of his political opinions even, if he was prompted to commit that offence by his political beliefs.'

188. *Berdo* v *Immigration and Naturalization Service*, 432 F. 2d. 645, 650 (1970); see also *Kovac* v *Immigration and Naturalization Service*, 407 F. 2d. 102, 107 (1969); *Sagermark* v *Immigration and Naturalization Service*, 767 F. 2d. 645, 650 (1980); *Minnulla* v *Immigration and Naturalization Service*, 706 F. 2d. 831 (1983); *Haitian Refugee Center* v *Civiletti*, 503 F. Supp. 442 (S.D. Fla 1980) aff'd as modified 676 F. 2d. 1023 (1982) at 509; *Raass* v *Immigration and Naturalization Service*, 692 F. 2d. 596 (1982).

189. *A.Z.* v *State Secretary for Justice, Raad van Staat*, 30 September 1982, G.V. No. D. 12-72, R.V. (1982) 8; *Klager, Bundesverwaltungsgericht*, 26 October 1971, B. Verw. G.E. Bd. 39, No. 6 at p. 27. In Austria a ministerial directive provides expressly for the grant of asylum in such instances: Directive of the Minister of the Interior, 22, 501/4–II/0/75, part ii.

190. *Doonetas* v *Home Secretary*, approved and applied in *Atibo* v *Immigration Officer, supra,* note 178. See also *Sovich* v *Esperdy, 206 F. Supp. 558 (1963); Glavic* v *Beachie,* 225 F. Supp. 24 (1963). Council of Europe Resolution 337 (1967) calls for recognition of a right of conscientious objection.

191. In *Rajudeen* v *M.E.I., supra* note 182 at 135, Stone, J. said: 'obviously, an individual cannot be considered as a 'Convention refugee' only because he has suffered in his homeland from the outrageous behaviour of his fellow citizens. To my mind, in order to satisfy the definition, the persecution complained of must have been committed or condoned by the State itself and consist either of conduct directed by the State towards the individual or in it knowingly tolerating the behaviour of private citizens, or refusing or being unable to protect the individual from such behaviour.' Conversely, Goodwin-Gill argues that where the protection of the Government is in fact unavailable, persecution may result, for the concept is not limited to actions of governments: *supra,* note 11 at 43.

192. *R* v *Home Secretary, ex parte Selladurai Jeyakumaran,* CO/290/84, 28 June 1985, Queen's Bench.

193. *Supra,* note 10.

194. *Supra,* note 186.

195. See C. Wydrzynski, *Canadian Immigration Law: Special Classes 2. Definition of Convention Refugee,* 1983 at p. 319. Systematic denial of employment because of race or political opinion can amount to persecution within the Convention: *Tounkara* v *M.E.I.,* I.A.B. 80-1044, 8 September 1981, C.L.I.C. No. 38.11; *Alarcon,* I.A.B. 81-9200, 23 May 1981, C.L.I.C. No. 33.11; *Gajardo* v *M.E.I.,* I.A.B. 80-6284, 11 December 1981, C.L.I.C. No. 41.9.

196. *Iyar,* I.A.B. 79-1237, 15 January 1980, C.L.I.C. No. 29.9 at p. 7 of unreported judgment of Chairman Scott.

197. The only instances where the Board has deviated from these basic principles has been to recognize claims arising out of civil wars which were directed against specific racial minorities and cound be justifiably described as genocide: *Abubakar* v *M.E.I.,* I.A.B. 76-6125, 26 August 1977; *Kifletsion et al.* v *M.E.I.,* I.A.B. 79-1136, 29 February 1980.

198. Generally South African conscientious objectors are given *de facto* refugee status, See *N.B.* v *State Secretary for Justice, Raad van Staat,* Afdeling Rechtspraak, 4 June 1981, G.V. No. D. 12-46, R.V. (1981) 3, A.R.O.B. TB/S Jur. III No. 264.

199. Immigration Manual I.S. 13.07(1)(a)(i), entitled 'refugee definition'.

200. Analogy may be drawn with the similar problem arising in the case of the Race Relations Act 1976 in the United Kingdom. See *Showboat Entertainment Centre* v *Owen,* [1984] 1 All E.R. 836; *Mandla* v *Lee,* [1983] 1 All E.R. 1062.

201. Universal Declaration of Human Rights, U.N.G.A. Res. 217 A (III) 10 December 1948, Article 18 *Basic Documents* I.1); International Covenant on Civil and Political Rights, 16 December 1966, U.K.T.S. 6 (1977), Article 18 (*Basic Documents* I.2); European Convention on Human Rights 4 November 1950, 213 U.N.T.S. 221. Article 9 (*Basic Documents* V.1).

202. U.N. Doc. E/CN 4/Sub. 2/416, cited by W. McKean, *Equality and Discrimination under International Law,* 1983, at 121.

203. The cases are reviewed by Wydrzynski, *supra* note 195, at pp. 327 and 201.

204. *Billas* v *M.E.I.* I.A.B. 79-1166, 7 July 1980, C.L.I.C. No. 27.10. See also *Kwiatowsky* v *M.E.I.* (1983) *supra* note 182.

205. *Atibo* v *Immigration Officer, supra,* note 178.

206. *R* v *Registrar General, ex parte Segerdal,* [1970] 3 All E.R. 886; *Bowman* v *Secular Society,* [1916-17] All E.R. at 19–20; *Barrelat and Others* v *Attorney-General,* [1980] 3 All E.R. 918; *Re Thackrah,* [1939] 2 All E.R. 4; *Re Nesbitt's Will Trusts,* [1953] 1 All E.R. 936. It is of course acknowledged that care must be exercised in applying in one context interpretations of a word used in another.

207. This must be so, for otherwise the Convention would protect those persecuted by a State for belonging to it: a state of affairs too extraordinary to be within the contemplation of the draftsmen. Foreign minorities are eligible to be protected by the States of which they are nationals and for this reason excluded from the Convention.

208. *K.T.* v *Secretary of State of Justice, Raad van Staat,* Judicial Division, 10.4.79, R.V. [1979] No. 3, G.V. No. D. 12-18.

209. *N.N.* v *State Secretary, supra,* note 158; *S.K.* v *State Secretary,* 16 October 1980, G.V. No. D. 12-44, R.V. (1981) 1; *F.D.* v *State Secretary,* 17 September 1981, T.M.C. Asser Institute's Collection No. 1736.

210. Mr Petrén. U.N. Doc. A/CONF 2/SR 3 at 14 (19.11.51) and see generally A. Helton, *Persecution on Account of Membership of a Social Group as a Basis for Refugee Status,* p. 41 note 16.

211. *Supra,* note 6 at 219.

212. *Supra,* note 11 at 30.

213. *Supra,* note 171, page 19, paragraphs 77 and 78.

214. New York, 16 December 1966, Annex to U.N.G.A. Res. 2200 (XXX), U.K.T.S. 6 (1977); *Basic Documents* I.2 and I.3.

215. C. de Neef and S. de Ruiter, *Sexual Violence against Women Refugees. A Report on the Nature and Consequences of Sexual Violence These Women have Suffered Elsewhere,* 1985.

216. M. Meijer, *Oppression of Women and Refugee Status,* 1985. See also: World Conference on the U.N. Decade for Women (1980), U.N. Doc. A/CONF 94/24 14–30 July 1980, Copenhagen. 'Refugee Women', UNHCR Roundtable, Geneva, 25 April 1985.

217. See, however, the Tribunal's decision in *Mahshid Mahmoudi Gilani* TH 9515/85, 25 February 1987. The applicant claimed asylum on the ground of persecution in Iran based on the fact of being a woman.

218. *Raad van Staat,* Judicial Division, 13.8.81, G.V. No. D. 12-51, R.V. (1981) No. 5, A.R.O.B. TB/S Jur. III No. 283. See Netherlands Records of the Second Chamber of Parliament 15 649, nr. 16.

219. *Matter of Acosta, supra* note 182.

220. *Astudillo* v *M.E.I.* (1979), 31 NR 121 (Fed. C.A.). See generally J. Grey, *Immigration Law in Canada,* 1984, at 125.

221. 1984 UNHCR Report: *The Situation of Refugee Women the World Over,* adopted by U.N.G.A. Res. 35/135; 1985 UNHCR Report: *Note on Refugee Women and International Protection* EC/SCP/39, 8.7.85 and U.N. Doc. A/AC 96/671 (9.10.85).

453

222. O.J. C 127/137 (13 April 1984).
223. Universal Declaration of Human Rights, *supra*, note 31, Article 19; International Covenant on Civil and political Rights, New York, 16 December 1966, *supra*, note 214, Article 19; European Convention on Human Rights, Rome, 4 November 1950, 213 U.N.T.S. 221, Article 9.
224. Goodwin-Gill, *supra*, note 11 at 31.
225. [1982] 1 F.C. 290 (C.A.).
226. *Church v Home Secretary,* 16 March 1982, TH/69153/80 (2288).
227. *Goldman and Van Zyl,* Appeals heard jointly, TH/97569/82 (2616) and TH/97524/80, 18 February 1983.
228. See also *Swick* v *Home Secretary,* 2 September 1983, TH/98626/82 (2892), *Alexander* v *Home Secretary,* 12 January 1984, TH/115481/83, *Matkov* v *Home Secretary,* 24 May 1984, TH/106300/83 (3331), *Mazel* v *Home Secretary,* 7 January 1985, TH/120591/84, *Miller* v *Home Secretary,* 4 November 1985, TH/120585/84, *Khorshidian* v *Home Secretary,* 20 May 1985, TH/1105/85 (4402) and *Salamat* v *Home Secretary,* 22 March 1985, TH/704/85.
229. *A.D.A.* v *Secretary of State,* [1978] 4 April 1978, G.V. No. D. 12-13, R.V. (1978) No. 13, A.B. (1979) No. 77.
230. *MacNair* Case, *Conseil d'Etat,* 18 April 1980, *Recueil des decisions du Conseil d'Etat,* 1980, p. 189; A.J.D.A. 1980, No. 11, p. 609.
231. *Bolanos-Hernandes, supra,* note 146. See also *Re McMullen* v *Immigration and Naturalization Service,* 658 F. 2d. 1312 (1981).
232. The regrettable expression 'burden-sharing' has now become the established usage to describe such a system. It exists in inchoate form, notably in the case of refugees rescued at sea, for whom maritime and coastal States appear to have achieved some degree of consensus. See U.N. Docs. A/AC.96/549, para. 53.3 and A/AC.96/601, para. 62.
233. G. Melander, *Refugees in Orbit,* 1978.
234. *Supra,* note 120.
235. H.C. 169, paragraph 236.
236. *Supra,* note 149.
237. *Rosenberg* v *Yee Chien Woo,* 402 U.S. 49 (1971).
238. *Supra,* note 233 at 113–115. For bilateral conventions, see note 115, *supra,* and H. Battifol and P. Lagarde, *Droit international privé,* 1970, 198.
239. The definition employed in the Sirey *Dictionnare de la terminologie du droit international* is as follows: '*Acte par lequel les autorités établies à la frontiere s'opposent à l'entrée sur le territoire d'un Etat d'étrangers qui cherchent à y pénétrer'.* The expression may also be taken to apply in those very exceptional cases when States seek to secure the removal and return of persons who do not seek to enter their territories: *Re Lannoy,* [1942] 2 K.B. 281.
240. A. Lapradelle and J. Niboyet: *Repertoire de droit international,* 1929-31, p. 109.
241. *A Study on Statelessness* (U.N. Doc. E. 1112 and Add 1 1949 at 60) defines 'reconduction' as 'the mere physical act of ejecting from the national territory a person who has gained entry or is residing therein irregularly' and 'expulsion' as 'the juridical decision taken by the judicial and administrative authorities whereby an individual is ordered to leave the territory of the country'. The study observes that the terminology varies, but for its purposes the term *refoulement* (reconduction) was not used to signify the act of preventing a foreigner present at the frontier from entering the national territory.
242. *Supra,* note 147.
243. Stephenson, J., [1962] 3 All ER 641, 651.
244. Lord Denning, M.R., [1962] 3 All ER 641, 658; Donovan, L.J., *ibid.* at 663; Pearson, L.J., *ibid.* at 669.
245. *Refugee (Germany) Case,* 28 I.L.R. (1959) 297; *Expulsion of Alien (Austria) Case,* 28 I.L.R.

(1963) 310; *Homeless Alien (Germany) Case,* 28 I.L.R. (1958) 503; *Chim Ming* v *Marks,* 505 F. 2d. 1170 (1974).

246. See generally D. Martin, 'New Developments in Refugee Law and Current Problems: Asylum Concept; Solidarity and the Concept of Burden Sharing': *Symposium on the Promotion, Dissemination and Teaching of Fundamental Human Rights of Refugees, Tokyo, 7–11 December 1981,* at p. 61. 'Australia has taken the lead in pressing the 'temporary refuge' proposal, notably in the 1979 and 1980 meetings of the Executive Committee of the High Commissioner's Programme.' See also F. Feliciano, *'Non-refoulement*: Some Reflections on the Content, Function and Status of the Principle and Rule', *ibid.* at 20.

247. A/Conf. 2/SR. 16.

248. G. Goodwin-Gill, *supra* note 11, pp. 142–143, 218–219.

249. See Greig, *supra,* note 26, p. 132, on 'law making' powers of international refugee instruments.

250. Weis, *supra,* note 13, at 482–3.

251. In an article published in 1966, Dr Weis argued in favour of extending the principle of *non-refoulement* to non-rejection at the frontier, for otherwise the grant of asylum would depend on 'fortuitous circumstance': 'Territorial Asylum', 6 Ind. J.I.L. (1966) 173 at 183. It seems strongly arguable, however, that *non-refoulement* already extends to non-rejection at the frontier (of the State of persecution). The language of Article 33 of the 1951 Convention is to be contrasted with that of Articles 31 and 32 which speak of aliens being 'present' or 'in the territory' of the State of refuge.

252. F. Schnyder, *supra,* note 2.

253. H.H. Prince Sadruddin Aga Khan, 'Legal Problems Relating to Refugees and Displaced Persons', 149 Hague *Recueil* (1976-1) 287 at p. 318.

254. A. Grahl-Madsen. *Territorial Asylum,* 1980, at p. 42.

255. The view here advanced is shared by Dr Goodwin-Gill, *supra,* note 11, p. 97. Moreover, Professor Grahl-Madsen appears to have resiled from the view taken in 1980: 'International Refugee Law Today and Tomorrow', 20 Ar. V. (1982) 411.

256. *'C'était surtout l'Angleterre qui, au siecle dernier, avait favorisée la doctrine de la non-extradition pour faits politiques. Elle était devenue depuis 1848 une sorte de lieu d'asile pour les réfugiés politiques de tout le continent'*: A. Merighnac, *Droit international,* 1907, p. 735.

257. Treaty on International Penal Law, Montevideo, 23 January 1889, 18 M.N.R.G. (2nd Ser) 432, Article 20; cf. Convention on Political Asylum, Montevideo, 3–26 December 1933, *supra,* note 38; Convention on Asylum, Havana, 20 February 1928, 132 L.N.T.S. 323 and Treaty on Asylum and Refuge, Montevideo, 4 August 1939, VIII *Hudson* 404 (which contained no comparable provisions).

258. *Supra,* note 28.

259. *Supra,* text at notes 46–54.

260. U.N. Doc. A/AC 96/INF 158 p. 9. See also G. Melander, L. Eriksson, P. Nobel (S.I.A.S.) *An Analysing Account of the Conference on the African Refugee Problem,* Arusha, May 1979.

261. J.I. Garvey, 'Towards a Reformulation of International Refugee Law', 26 Harv. I.L.J. (1985) 483 at 494. See Article 2(2), U.N. Declaration on Territorial Asylum: 'burden sharing' is the principle that 'where a State finds difficulty in granting or continuing to grant asylum, States individually or jointly through the U.N. shall consider in a spirit of international solidarity appropriate measures to lighten the burden on that State' by offers of resettlement or by financial or other material assistance.

262. Art. 3 (1) U.N.G.A. Res. 2312 (XXII) of 14 December 1967; *Basic Documents* III.6.

263. Res. 14 (1967) on Asylum to Persons in Danger of Persecution, adopted 29 June 1967 (*Basic Documents* IV.4) Article 2.

264. The recommendation of the Intergovernmental Advisory Commission for Refugees, to the effect that Governments should not expel or refuse entry to refugees unable lawfully to enter other countries, would have imposed on States the burden of admitting extra categories of persons to their territories. Such a burden was not easily undertaken. Indeed, the Commission considered itself forced to observe that 'in spite of its repeated recommendations . . . in practice the procedure concerning the expulsion of refugees has not altered'. Still less had there been an alteration in the procedure concerning the *refoulement* of refugees. The Government of the United States observed that it was 'not in a position, under existing laws, to give effect to the recommendation' and the reply of the Swiss Government was equally negative.

265. M. Whiteman, *Digest of International Law*, Vol. VIII, p. 662.

266. U.N.G.A.O.R. 7th Sess. 3d. C'tee, p. 331; A/C 3/SR. 472 (1952).

267. 529 H.C. Deb. Col. 4 (Written Answers, 21 June 1954).

268. Whiteman, *supra* note 265, Vol. VIII, p. 676.

269. 472 H.C. Deb. Col. 443 (9 March 1950).

270. Report of the Executive Committee of the High Commissioner's Programme. 27th Session (A/AC 96/534) 11.

271. Report, 28th Session (A/AC 96/549) 13. See also EC/SCP/2 'Note on *Non-refoulement*'.

272. U.N. Doc. A/CONF 78/C 1/L 28/Rev. 1 adopted in the Committee of the Whole by 24 votes to 20, with 40 abstentions.

273. May 1979, Tanzania. See Melander, Eriksson and Nobel, *supra,* note 260.

274. 'Note on International Protection' (A/AC 96/567) 3. See also A/AC 96/527 11, 13, 15 for views of the Executive Committee.

275. Report of the 32nd Session (A/AC 96/601) 15. 22 October 1981.

276. *Ibid.* at 16.

277. U.N.G.A. Res. 34/60 and 34/61 of 29 November 1979; 36/125 of 14 December 1981.

278. A/AC 96/614 of 21 October 1982 at 13. But see Report of 35th Session U.N.G.A. Doc. 12A (A/39/12/Add 1) Conclusion No. 33 General (c) where the Executive Committee 'noted with concern that in different parts of the world the fundamental principle of *non-refoulement* had been violated'.

279. It follows that the person protected by this rule of customary law is entitled to certain minimal procedural guarantees: for these are to be understood in light of 'the paramount duty of States to abide by the principle of *non-refoulement*': G. Goodwin-Gill, 'The Determination of Refugee Status: Problems of Access to Procedures and the Standard of Proof', *International Institute of Humanitarian Law Yearbook* (1985) 56 at 59. See further Goodwin-Gill, 'International Law and the Detention of Refugees and Asylum-Seekers', 20 International Migration Review (1986) 193.

280. [1952] I.R. 62; 18 I.L.R. (1951) 336.

281. 8 A.D. (1935–1937) 305, 306 (No. 137).

282. 8 A.D. (1935–1937) 308 (No. 139). However, a contrary conclusion was reached by the Esthonian Council of State in *George Talma et al.* v *Minister of the Interior,* 8 A.D. (1935–1937) 313 (No. 142). Moreover, there was no general rule in French law to the effect that a Stateless person may not be expelled: *Krichel,* 52 J.D.I. (1925), 709.

283. Max Planck Institute, *supra* note 124, p. 13.

284. 16 Neths. Ybk. Int. L. (1985) 376 referring to Convention on the Prevention and Punishment of Crimes Against Internationally Protected Persons, including Diplomatic Agents, New York, 14 December 1973, 28 U.S.T. 1975.

285. *Section 2 Chapitre III du titre II de l'Arreté Royal concernant L'entrée et le séjour réguliers des candidats réfugiés.*

286. *Max Planck Institute, supra note 124, Australia abstract by I. Shearer, p. 41.*

287. Section 19(1)(ii). Formerly Aliens (Appeals) Order, 1970, Article 7(1)(a)(ii); Immigration Appeals Act 1969 Section 8(1)(a)(ii).
288. H.C. 169 para 165.
289. See, however, *Nunez* v *Boldin, supra,* note 144, *Orantes-Hernandes* v *Smith,* 541 F. Supp. 351 (C.D. Cal. 1982). See generally: Note: 'Protecting Aliens from Persecution Without Overloading the INS: Should Illegal Aliens Receive Notice of the Right to Apply for Asylum?' 69 Va. L. Rev. (1983) 901.
290. I.e. the country from which the alien last entered the U.S. or from which he embarked, or in which he was born, or in which the place of his birth is situated when his deportation is ordered, or which has sovereignty over his birthplace at the time of his birth, or in which he resided prior to entering the country from which he entered the United States, or (if deportation to any of the foregoing countries is impracticable) any country which is willing to accept him. For rights of appeal see notes 141–146, *supra.*
291. *R* v *Chief Immigration Officer, ex parte Salamat Bibi,* [1976] 3 All ER 843 and [1976] 1 WLR 979. See also *R* v *Immigration Appeal Tribunal, ex parte Murugandarajah, supra,* note 107, in which Woolf, J. reaffirmed that the Geneva Convention and New York Protocol do not form part of United Kingdom law nor are they sources of rights or obligations on which individuals in the United Kingdom may rely; but in a situation of doubt or ambiguity regard may be had to their terms for the purpose of interpreting domestic provisions.
292. *Simsek* v *Minister for Immigration,* [1982] 40 ALR 61.
293. *M.E.I.* v *Hudnik,* [1980] 1 F.C. 180 (F.C.A.) and *Re Vincent* v *M.E.I.,* [1983] 148 DLR (3d) 385 (F.C.A.).
294. *Molefi* v *Legal Adviser, supra* note 151.
295. See *R* v *Secretary of State, ex parte Phansopkar,* [1975] 3 All ER 497; Cf. *R.* v *Chief Immigration Officer, ex parte Salamat Bibi, supra,* note 291. See above, text at note 104.
296. E/1850 p. 11.
297. *Waquet* v *Agut,* Cour d'Appel, Orleans, 27 April 1927, 56 Rev. crit. dr. int. priv. (1976) 702. See also *Guerre* v *Gutersohn,* 1954, D. 539 (1933 Convention).
298. The original draft, proposed by the Holy See, would have gone further. It read as follows: 'The Contracting Parties shall grant refugees within their territories complete freedom to practise their religions, both in public and in private ...'. A/Conf. 2/Sr. 30, p. 10.
299. 12 August 1949, 75 U.N.T.S. 31.
300. E/AC 32/L. 40. p. 36.
301. *Supra,* note 28, Article 4.
302. *Supra,* note 54, Article 6.
303. [1946] 2 All E.R. 146.
304. *Cismiuglu* v *Dane Seicaru,* Tribunal de grande instance de la Seine, 18 April 1966, 56 Rev. crit. dr. int. priv. (1967) 324.
305. *Dax* v *Dax,* 20 October 1975, 105 A.T.F.S. (1975-II) 1.
306. Articles 13 and 6.
307. Article 14.
308. Article 15.
309. *Supra,* note 28, Article 6.
310. Article 16(3). For 'habitual residence' in this context, see *Ilitsch* v *Banque Franco-Serbe,* 1954 D. Somm. 71 (Tribunal de la Seine, 14 May 1954) and *Grundul* v *Bryner,* 83 A.T.F.S. (1951-I) 16 (Tribunal fédéeral).
311. *Supra,* note 53, Recommendation No. 6.
312. Articles 21 and 22.
313. Articles 22(12), 23, 24.
314. *Supra,* note 162.

315. French Commission de Recours, No. 7,313 of 8 February 1973.
316. Article 1C, D and E.
317. *Supra,* note 171, paragraph 119.
318. 5710-1950; see materials cited at Introduction, note 40, *supra.*
319. Article 1 C(5)(6).
320. The suggestion to the contrary in the Home Office's affidavit in *Alsamrat Mustafa,* TH/104224 (84), 14 December 1984, appears plainly mistaken. Indeed, that affidavit is in error in stating that the area of operation of the U.N.R.W.A. applies to Egypt! The operations of the U.N.R.W.A. are confined to Jordan, Syria, the Lebanon and the Gaza Strip.

BIBLIOGRAPHY

H.H. Prince S. Aga Khan, 'Legal Problems Relating to Refugees and Displaced Persons', 149 Hague *Recueil* (1976-I), 287.
S. Aiboni, *Protection of Refugees in Africa,* 1978.
Y. Altamini, *Die Palastina Fluchtlinge und die Vereinten Nationen,* 1970.
L. Bolestra-Koziebrodski, *Le droit d'asile,* 1962.
T. Cox, 'Well-Founded Fear of Being Persecuted: The Sources and Application of a Criterion of Refugee Status', 10 Brooklyn J.I.L. (1984).
J. Dascal, *Derecho de asilo en la 55 Conferencia de la International Law Association,* 4458 *Jurisprudencia Argentina* (1974) 2.
A. Evans, 'Political Refugees and the United States Immigration Laws', 66 A.J.I.L. (1972) 571.
I. Foighel. 'Legal Status of the Boat People', 48 *Acta Scandinavia* (1979) 21.
D. Fowler, 'The Developing Jurisdiction of the United Nations High Commissioner for Refugees', 7 Rev. dr. de l'homme (1974) 119;
A. Fragomen: 'The Refugee: A Problem of Definition', 3–4 Case W. Reserve J.I.L. (1970–72) 45.
G. Goodwin-Gill, *The Refugee in International Law,* 1983.
G. Goodwin-Gill, 'The Determination of Refugee Status: Problems of Access to Procedures and the Standard of Proof', *International Institute of Humanitarian Law Yearbook* (1985) 56.
G. Goodwin-Gill, 'Entry and Exclusion of Refugees: The Obligations of States and the Protection Function of the Office of the UNHCR', [1982] Ybk. I.L.S. 291.
G. Goodwin-Gill, 'International Law and the Detention of Refugees and Asylum Seekers', 20 International Migration Review (1986) 193.
G. Goodwin-Gill, 'Non-Refoulment and the New Asylum-Seekers'. 26 Va. J.I.L. (1986) 897.
A. Grahl-Madsen, *The Status of Refugees in International Law, 1966.*
A. Grahl-Madsen: *'Expulsion of Refugees', 33 Acta Scandinavia* (1963) 4.
D. Greig, 'The Protection of Refugees and Customary International Law', 8 Aust. Y. I.L. (1983) 108.
K. Hailbronner. 'Non-Refoulement and 'Humanitarian' Refugees', 26 Va. J.I.L. (1986) 857.
L. Holborn, *Refugees: A Problem of Our Time. The Work of UNHCR 1951–1972,* 1975.
E. Jahn, 'The Work of the African-Asian Legal Consultative Committee on the Legal Status of Refugees', 27 ZaoRV (1967) 122.
E. Johnson, 'Refugees, Deportees and Illegal Immigrants', 9 Syd. L.R. (1980) 11.
W. Kalin, *Das Prinzip der Non-Refoulement,* 1982.
F. Kellogg, 'Refugees and Human Rights: The Path Ahead', 19 Dept. of State Bull. (1973) 375.
F. Krenz, 'The Refugee as a Subject of International Law', 15 I.C.L.Q. (1966) 90.
E. Lentini, 'The Definition of Refugee in International Law: Proposals for the Future', 5 B.C. Third World L.J. (1985) 183.

458

D. Levy, *Transnational Legal Problems of Refugees*, 1982.

D. Martin, 'Large Scale Migrations of Asylum Seekers', 156 Hague *Recueil* (1982) 598.

G. Melander, 'Refugees in Orbit', 16. A.W.R. Bull. (1978) 59–75.

V. Nanda, World Refugee Assistance: The Role of International law and Institutions', 9 Hofstra L. Rev. (1980–81) 449.

J. Patronogic, 'Interrelationship between General Principles of Law and Fundamental Humanitarian Principles Applicable to the Protection of Refugees', 27 Annales du droit Int. Med. (1977) 50.

R. Plender, 'Admission of Refugees: Draft Convention on Territorial Asylum', 15 San Diego L. Rev. (1977) 45–62.

R. Plender, 'Comments on the Draft Convention on Territorial Asylum', [1976] Proc. A.S.I.L. 75.

J. Schechtman, *The Refugee in the World: Displacement and Integration*, 1963.

W. Schnatzel and T. Veiter (eds), *Handbüch des Internationalen Fluchtlingsrecht*, 1960.

F. Schnyder, '*Les aspects juridiques actuels du problème des réfugiés*', 114 (1965-I) Hague Recueil 341.

Y. Shinada, 'The Concept of Political Refugee in International Law', 19 Jap. Ann. Int. L. (1975) 24.

S. Sinha, 'An Anthropocentric View of Asylum in International Law', 10 Colum. J. Trans. L. (1971) 78–110.

S. Sinha, *Asylum and International Law*, 1971.

M. Udina, '*La Protezione Internazionale dei refugiati e degli apolidi*', 25 Comunita Internazionale (1970) 524.

M. Uibopuu, 'In Search of a Most Favourable Status for Refugees', 14 A.W.R. Bull. (1976) 149.

M. Uibopuu, '*Der Schutz der Fluchtlings in Rahmen des Europartes*', 21 Archiv des Völkerrechts (1983) 60.

E. Vierdag, ' "Asylum" and "Refugee" in International Law', 24 Neths. I.L.R. (1977) 287.

P. Weis, 'Human Rights and Refugees', 10 International Migration (1972) 20.

P. Weis, 'The Development of Refugee Law: Transnational Legal Problems of Refugees', [1982] Mich. Ybk. I.L.S. 27.

P. Weis, 'The Convention of the O.A.U. Governing the Specific Aspects of Refugee Problems in Africa', 3 Human Rights J. (1970) 449.

P. Woods, 'The Term "Refugee" in International and Municipal Law: An Inadequate Definition in the Light of the Cuban Boatlift', 5 A.S.I.L.S. Int. L.J. (1981) 39.

M. Zuleeg. *Arbeitseinsatz von Asylbewerben*, 1982.

CHAPTER 13

The Expulsion of Aliens

That a State has in general the right to expel aliens from its territory is not in doubt. The right has long been acknowledged;[1] and has its corollary (if not its precise counterpart) in the duty of each State to readmit to its territory those of its nationals who have been lawfully expelled from other States.[2] In recent years it has become increasingly apparent, however, that the right of expulsion is subject to significant restrictions imposed by public international law.[3] Such restrictions apply both in the case of collective expulsion and in the case of the expulsion of individuals.

Of the limits imposed by international law on the State's right to expel aliens individually, those which are most frequently encountered have been examined elsewhere in this book.[4] They derive from treaty engagements and from the rules governing exceptional duties to admit aliens, notably in cases of acquired rights. Besides these cases, a State engages international responsibility if it expels an alien without cause or in an unnecessarily injurious manner. Three generations ago, Borchard concluded that

> Arbitrary expulsions, either without any or on insufficient cause, either in the provisions of municipal law or of a treaty, or under harsh or violent circumstances unnecessarily injurious to the person affected have given rise to diplomatic claims and to awards by arbitral commissions.[5]

As we shall see, recent claims and awards confirm the existence of limitations of both substance and form on the State's power of expulsion.

Collective expulsion is explicitly prohibited in several of the modern conventions dealing with the protection of fundamental rights and freedoms.[6] Thus the question arises whether those conventions embody in this respect a rule of customary international law. In order to address that question, we must define our terms. For present purposes, we shall not use the expression so broadly as to encompass the deportation of a plurality of aliens whose common factor is an element which would warrant their deportation individually.[7] The

460

expression 'mass expulsion' (or 'collective expulsion') will be used, as in the Banjul Charter, to denote the deportation of a group of aliens defined by reference to their common nationality, race or religious affiliation. It will, however, embrace expulsions effected by means of governmental coercion of any kind, whether or not designated as a formal act of deportation or expulsion[8] in the law of the expelling State. Collective or mass expulsion, thus defined, has occurred with disturbing frequency in recent years. Among the events falling into this category are the expulsion of British and French nationals from Egypt in 1956; the expulsion of Iranians from Iraq in 1969; the enforced exodus of Asians from Uganda in 1972; the deportation of Gabonese nationals from Benin in 1978; the departure under coercion of ethnic Chinese residents of Vietnam in 1979; the 'chasing of the Banyarwanda' in 1982, when 75,000 persons from three ethnic groups were driven from Uganda into refugee camps in Rwanda, Burundi and the Sudan; and the expulsion from Nigeria in 1983 of nationals of other E.C.O.W.A.S. States, principally Ghanaians.

THE JUSTIFICATION FOR EXPULSION OF INDIVIDUALS

While it is uncontroversial that it is for the expelling State to determine whether there is sufficient cause to remove from its territory any individual alien who is lawfully present there,[9] it may now be taken to be established that the State's discretion in this respect is not unqualified. In principle, the alien is entitled to treatment no less favourable than the 'minimum standard' required by international law.[10] His expulsion arbitrarily or without good cause may well amount to treatment below that of the minimum standard. It is on this basis that we must understand Judge Read's observation in the *Nottebohm Case* that a State which decides to admit an alien thereby assumes an obligation towards his State of nationality to afford him reasonable and fair treatment.[11]

Thus, in so far as a State has a right arbitrarily to exclude an alien, that right is not matched by a corresponding discretionary competence to expel him arbitrarily. In 1907 the United States Secretary of State declared that

The Government of the United States neither questions nor denies the existence of the sovereign right to expel an undesirable resident. It cannot be overlooked, however, that such a right is of a very high nature and that *justification must be great and convincing.*[12]

In one of the Mexican Claims cases, the Umpire required the expelling State to show that it had good reason from the expulsion of a United States consul.[13] That decision appears to go further than is warranted by precedent, at least if we leave aside the consul's status as such, since the Umpire seems to suggest that there must be an objective justification tested by standards set by international law, whereas precedent establishes that it is in principle for the expelling State to decide whether expulsion is warranted.[14] The rule appears to be that the expelling State must, if required to do so by the State of nationality, advance a reason for the expulsion, which could reasonably and properly lead it to the conclusion that such an action is warranted in the public interest.[15]

The classical writers acknowledged a power to expel aliens but often asserted that the power may be exercised only for cause. Grotius wrote of the sovereign right to expel aliens who challenge the established political order of the expelling State and indulge in seditious activities there.[16] Pufedorff[17] echoed this sentiment. In early diplomatic correspondence the same principle is expressed with the same qualification.

The American Secretary of State Fish stated in 1869 that 'the power to expel from its territory *persons who are dangerous to the internal or external security of the State* is an essential attribute of sovereignty'.[18] Ten years later another Secretary of State advised his ambassador in Mexico that he would be fully justified in protesting vigorously in the event of the expulsion of a United States citizen 'without just steps to assure the grounds of such expulsion, and in bringing the facts to the immediate knowledge of the Department'.[19] In the case of the expulsion from Haiti of an American citizen named *Eugene Wiener*, the State Department 'held that Haiti, having assumed the responsibility of expelling a citizen of a friendly power, without giving him any hearing, producing evidence against him or allowing him an opportunity for defence, was thereupon bound either to establish by proofs that there was good ground for the expulsion, or else to indemnify the expelled person for the damage he has sustained'.[20] In 1966, the British Government announced that it reserved the right to make representations to any foreign or Commonwealth government which exercised its power of expulsion in an arbitrary or unjusted manner.[21]

The evidence furnished by the classical writers and by State practice is reinforced by decisions of arbitral tribunals. It must be acknowledged that the latter have been concerned with the expelling State's duty to advance reasons for the expulsion before an international tribunal rather than with a duty to state reasons to the authorities of the State of nationality.[22] The arbitral decisions are, at least, consistent with the view that the expelling State is under a duty to advance reasons.

The *locus classicus* is the *Boffolo Case*[23] in which Umpire Ralson found that expulsion should be resorted to only in extreme instances and must be accomplished in the manner least injurious to the alien. He added that 'the country exercising the power must, when occasion demands, state reasons of such expulsion before an international tribunal, and an insufficient reason or none being advanced, accept the consequences'. It was even suggested in the

Paquet Case[24] that a refusal to state reasons for expulsion would warrant the inference that the expelling State had exercised its power arbitrarily. Moreover, in two early decisions[25] the arbitrators held that an expelling State could not, in time of peace, advance a mere suspicion as a ground for expelling an alien.

In the event of the expulsions from South Africa in 1900, the Commission established by the British Government stated that mere assertions that a certain person was undesirable or was concerned in a plot are 'useless, without authenticated reasons and proofs'.[26] In *Loubriel's Case*,[27] 'motives of internal order', 'reasons of gravity' and 'facts well known to the Government of Venezuela' were deemed to be too vague.

An expelling State does not discharge its liability by advancing its reasons accurately and with sufficient particularity, unless the reasons so advanced could properly lead it to the conclusion that the expulsion was justified. Diplomatic practice of the latter part of the last century appears to establish that at that date a State was not entitled to complain of the expulsion of one of its nationals for ethnic or racial reasons, even though it might deplore the ignorance of true principles of government which lead to the adoption of a discriminatory policy of expulsion.[28] Modern practice, on the other hand, establishes the impermissibility of racial discrimination in this respect.[29] A State which is actuated by racial considerations in determining to expel an alien nowadays will seldom acknowledge the fact.

NATIONAL LEGISLATION

The French Ordinance of 1945 made provision in apparently broad terms for the expulsion of aliens.[30] Indeed, the breadth of discretion conferred thereby on the Minister of the Interior is apt to be taken as evidence of the paucity of the controls imposed by international law in this regard.[31] The Ordinance authorised the Minister of the Interior (or the Prefect in frontier *Départements*) to expel aliens whose presence constitutes a threat to *l'ordre public*.[32] No doubt, that expression is susceptible of an extensive interpretation in cases involving the political activities of aliens hostile to the government.[33]

It must be emphasised, however, that even before the reform of 29 October 1981,[34] the power of expulsion was limited in several important respects. The act of expulsion had to be based on the personal conduct of the individual concerned and not on a policy designed to apply to a class of aliens generally or even to serve as a deterrent.[35] Following the reform, expulsion may be ordered only in the event of a serious threat to public order; and several categories of aliens are immune from the procedure.[36] The alien is entitled to appear before a tribunal of three persons, convened for the purpose of affording protection against the arbitrary exercise of the statutory power. He is entitled to the assistance of counsel and of an interpreter. The tribunal's intervention is obligatory, save in cases of great urgency, when expulsion is ordered in the interests of national security.[37]

Apart from expulsion (or deportation), French law knows a procedure for summary removal (*'reconduction à la frontiére'*). This procedure may be employed only in the case of aliens who are present unlawfully; but even in such cases the intervention of a *tribunal correctionel* is required.

In the Soviet Union, the ground for expulsion is expressed broadly: this course of action may be taken in the interests of the public good.[38] The power is to be exercised on the basis of the individual's conduct exclusively.[39]

In the United Kingdom, also, there is power to make a deportation order against an alien when the Secretary of State deems this action conductive to the public good.[40] The Immigration Rules indicate that general rules about the circumstances in which deportation is justified cannot be laid down and each case will be considered carefully in the light of the circumstances known to the Secretary of State.[41] Although the breadth of this provision has been criticised,[42] its most frequent use has been to deport those convicted of criminal offences.[43] The remaining cases in which the power has been invoked appear to fall into two categories: cases in which the subject of the deportation order entered into a marriage of convenience for the purpose of remaining in the kingdom[44] and cases in which the decision was made on ground of national security.[45] Moreover, there has been a judicial suggestion that the power is not as broad as the language might at first suggest.[46] There is a right to appeal to the Immigration Appeal Tribunal against any decision to make a deportation order on this ground, save in cases in which the decision was made 'in the interests of national security or of the relations between the United Kingdom and any other country or for other reasons of a political nature.'[47] Even in the latter case, there is a non-statutory advisory procedure and the person whose deportation is proposed will be informed, as far as possible, of the nature of the allegations against him and will be given the opportunity to appear before the advisers and to make representations to them.[48] On the very rare occasions on which this procedure has been used, legal representation has invariably been permitted.[49]

The remaining grounds on which a person may be deported from the United Kingdom are articulated with greater precision in the Immigration Act and Rules. A non-citizen who has only limited leave to remain in the kingdom may be deported if he fails to observe a condition of his leave or remains beyond the time allotted to him.[50] In such cases, deportation will normally be the proper course, but account is to be taken of all the circumstances, including the individual's age, length of residence in the United Kingdom and strength of connections with that country, his personal history, domestic circumstances, compassionate circumstances and any representations received on his behalf.[51] A non-citizen may also be deported if, having reached the age of 17, he is convicted of an offence punishable with imprisonment and is thereupon recommended for deportation by a court empowered to do so.[52] In deciding whether to make the recommendation the Court will consider whether the person's continued presence is detrimental because of the seriousness of the crime or length of criminal record.[53] It seems that the Court will ignore considerations of general deterrence[54] but will take into account the effect of deportation on the family and other innocent persons.[55] In considering whether to act on the recommendation, the Home Secretary will take into account all the circumstances, including those that are taken into account in the case of overstayers,[56] together with the nature of the offence and the criminal record of the person in respect of whom the recommendation was made.[57]

A non-citizen may be deported if another person to whose family he belongs is or has been ordered to be deported.[58] For these purposes, a man's wife and his or her children under eighteen are regarded as belonging to his family, and a woman's children under eighteen are regarded as being members of her family.[59] The power to deport members of the family lapses eight weeks after the departure of the principal deportee.[60] In considering whether to require a wife and children to leave with the head of the family, the Home Secretary must take into account all relevant factors known to him, including the length of residence in the country, their ties with the country other than as dependants of the principal deportee, the wife's ability to maintain herself and her children in the United Kingdom for the foreseeable future, any compassionate circumstances and any representations received.[61]

Where a recommendation for deportation is made following conviction of an offence, the offender may appeal against the making of the recommendation as though it were part of the sentence.[62] There is a right to appeal to an adjudicator (with an opportunity of further appeal to the Immigration Appeal Tribunal) against any decision to make a deportation order on the ground that the person concerned failed to observe a condition of leave or remained beyond the time allotted by leave to remain in the country.[63] Where a decision is made to deport a person on the ground that he or she belongs to the family of another person who has been ordered to be deported, there is a right of appeal directly to the Immigration Appeal Tribunal.[64] In each of these cases (as in cases in which the decision was based on 'conduciveness to the public good') the appellate authority is to allow the appeal if it considers that the decision was not in accordance with the law or with any immigration rules applicable to the case; or the decision involved the exercise of discretion which should have been exercised differently.[65]

Where a person arriving in the United Kingdom is refused leave to enter, the immigration officer may give directions for his removal from the country.[66]

There is also a power to give directions for the removal of illegal entrants who have not been given leave to enter.[67] In such cases the normal provisions as to appeals are inapplicable. For this reason the definition of an 'illegal entrant' assumes particular significance.[68] In at least one case heard in 1976 it appears to have been assumed without argument that a person is an illegal entrant where he gains admission by the practice of deception.[69] In 1978 the Court of Appeal held that where, on the evidence taken as a whole, the officer had reasonable grounds for concluding that an entrant was in the country illegally, the Court would not interfere with his detention as an illegal entrant.[70] Later, in *Zamir*, the House of Lords went further: the officer's decision on the issue could be called in question in the courts only if there were no grounds on which he could have acted or if no reasonable person could have decided as the officer did. Their Lordships added that an alien seeking leave to enter was under a positive duty of candour on all material facts.[71] That decision proved controversial since it appeared to expose to removal, without the appellate rights attendant upon deportation, an alien whose only vice was a failure to advance information which was not asked of him. The decision has now been reviewed by the House of Lords in *Khawaja* v *Home Secretary*. In that case their Lordships reaffirmed that the term 'illegal entrant' embraces one who gains admission by deception; but added that non-disclosure of a material fact does not by itself constitute deception. There must be a positive misrepresentation, although exceptionally this could take the form of silence coupled with conduct.[72] The decision has been followed in *Ali*[73] and *Lapnid*[74] and appears to represent settled law.

In the United States the Immigration and Nationality Act spells out in detail the grounds on which an alien 'shall' be deported, but sets out thereafter in equal detail the grounds on which relief from deportation may be obtained.[75] An alien, including an alien crewman,[76] is to be deported if at the time of entry he was within any of the classes of alien then excludable by law[77] or if at the time of the making or the order he is in the United States in violation of the immigration law.[78] Such an alien is to be deported if, within five years of entry, he becomes institutionalized at public expense because of mental disease, defect or deficiency, unless he can show that the disorder did not arise prior to his admission to the United States.[79]

An alien in the United States is to be deported if he is convicted of a crime involving moral turpitude[80] committed within five years after entry and is sentenced to imprisonment for a year or more. Likewise, he is to be deported if he is convicted at any time after entry of two crimes involving moral turpitude, not arising out of a single scheme of criminal misconduct, irrespective of any sentence of imprisonment.[81] The phrase 'moral turpitude' has been criticised as vague'[82] but it is sufficiently precise to constitute a standard for deportation.[83] The guiding principle seems to be the intent with which the offence was committed.[84] An offence involving fraud or dishonesty therefore is an offence of moral turpitude.[85] In determining whether the element of dishonest intent is present, the court sitting in review will not go beyond the record of conviction.[86] United States courts have held that the following offences involved moral turpitude: perjury,[87] burglary,[88] conspiracy to defraud,[89] soliciting men for immoral purposes,[90] forgery[91] and embezzlement.[92] It has been decided that 'as a general proposition' the intentional taking of human life, without justification, if criminal, involves moral turpitude.[93] One authoritative, if elderly, commentary indicates that moral turpitude is involved in 'serious sexual offences, such as common law or statutory rape . . . being a lewd person in speech and behaviour, frequenting houses of ill-fame and evil repute, and conducting oneself in a lewd, wanton and lascivious manner'.[94] On the other hand, it is established that adultery, when criminal by the law of the place where it took place, is not morally turpitudinous.[95] An alien did not commit an offence involving moral turpitude when he re-entered the United States following his deportation.[96] Not did he commit such an offence when his negligent driving resulted in the death of another.[97] It has even been held that moral turpitude is not entailed when an alien is convicted of possessing a jimmy or crow-bar with the intention of using it for an unknown crime.[98] An attempt to avoid the payment of tax does not involve moral turpitude even if it amounts to a felony.[99]

An alien is to be deported if he fails to comply with the statutory requirement[100] to register his change of address, unless he satisfies the Attorney-General that the failure was reasonably excusable or not willful.[101] Likewise, he is to be deported if convicted of failing to apply for registration and fingerprinting.[102] Under section 241(a)(b) of the Act of 1952, aliens falling into any of eight categories are subject to deportation. All eight comprise aliens engaging in activities or organizations or advocating tenets subversive of the Government of the United States. Following subsections provide for the deportation of aliens engaged in other activities prejudicial to the United States and for those convicted of any violation of the Alien Registration Act 1940 within five years of entry, or of two such violations at any time.[103] An alien is to be deported if he commits certain breaches of immigration law: by failing to maintain his non-immigrant status, or entering the United States unlawfully from Canada or Mexico or by aiding another person's illegal entry.[104] He is also deportable if convicted of any of a number of specified offences, irrespective of moral turpitude. The offences include importation of persons of immoral purposes, and possession of particular firearms together with a series of crimes connected with the security, armed forces or foreign relations of the United States.[105] In the last of these categories, mere commission of the offence does not render the alien deportable; it is required additionally that the Attorney-General finds him to be an undesirable resident. Drug addicts and those convicted of dealing in drugs are to be deported, as are those engaged in prostitution, whether convicted or not.[106] The Act further provides that a person shall be deported if he has within five years of entry become a public charge from causes not affirmatively shown to have arisen after entry or if, during the period beginning on 23 March 1933 and ending on 9 Mary 1945 he participated in the persecution of any person in association with the Nazi Government of Germany or the governments of its occupied territories or allies.[107]

Relief from deportation may be obtained temporarily or permanently. Temporary deferral of deportation may be granted at the discretion of the Immigration and Naturalization Service when there are compelling humanitarian factors.[108] The Attorney-General on advice from the Secretary of State may grant temporary relief to aliens individually or in groups who originate in countries to which it would be dangerous or otherwise inadvisable to return.[109] Permanent deferral of deportation may be ordered by a deportation judge in favour of aliens who have lived in the United States and have been of good moral character for not less than seven years, provided that such aliens can show that their deportation would result in extreme hardship to them or to members of their family who are U.S. citizens or are lawful permanent residents.[110] The Attorney-General may suspend an alien's deportation and adjust his status to that of an alien lawfully admitted for permanent residence if he has been inspected and admitted on parole to the United States, did not enter illegally and is not excludable, provided that an immigrant visa is available at the time of application.[111] The Attorney-General may, furthermore, waive the deportation of an alien who is deportable because of fraudulent entry, if the alien is the spouse, parent or child of a U.S. citizen or of a lawful permanent resident alien, possessed an immigrant visa at the port of entry and was otherwise admissible.[112] There is power in the Attorney-General to grant a permanent dispensation in the case of long-term residents;[113] and the alien may seek relief from deportation by applying for asylum.[114]

A deportable alien may be permitted to leave the country voluntarily so as to avoid being deported,[115] one of the consequences of deportation being the obligation to obtain special permission to enter the United States for a period of five years thereafter.

Although the United States is unusual in the precision with which it identifies the grounds for an alien's expulsion and for relief from that process, few States assert in their domestic laws a power to deport aliens without cause. Generally, the power of expulsion is maintained on the ground of the individual's conduct, including his voluntary membership of a group.[116] The interests of national security are almost invariably a ground for expulsion of an alien.[117] The appraisal of those interests is more often than not made by the administrative authorities in the first instance. Very commonly, an alien's deportation may be ordered in the interests of public health,[118] or on account of the alien's criminal behaviour[119] or immoral conduct (including prostitution and use of narcotics)[120] and of course for breach of immigration law.[121]

While this survey tends to confirm the impossibility of devising an exclusive list of the grounds on which States may expel aliens,[122] it reveals sufficient congruence of State practice to support the view that the expulsion of an alien without cause amounts to a breach of international practice such as to warrant a remonstrance from the State of nationality. Indeed, it seems that a claim for reparation may be due where loss is suffered by the alien.[123]

THE FRONTIER OF EXPULSION

From the proposition that a State is in general under no obligation to admit aliens to its territory, it follows that a State may not in principle expel him other than to his country of nationality, unless the State of destination agrees to accept him.[124] National law commonly makes provision for the deportation or expulsion of aliens to a wide variety of jurisdictions. Thus, in the United Kingdom there is power to order the removal of a non-citizen to a country of which he is a national or citizen; or a country or territory in which he obtained a passport or other document of identity; or a country or territory in which he embarked or in which he was engaged as a member of the crew of the ship or aircraft in which he arrived in the United Kingdom to join; or any country or territory to which there is reason to believe that he will be admitted.[125] In the United States the alien may be deported to any country designated by him, if that country is willing to admit him; and in the absence of that country's confirmation that it is willing to do so, he may be deported to any country of which he is a subject, national or citizen; or to the country from which he last entered the United States; or to the country in which he was born or in which his place of birth is situated at the time of deportation; or to any country in which he resided prior to entering the country from which he entered the United States; or to any country which is willing to accept him.[126]

The breadth of discretion conferred upon the national authorities is in no way inconsistent with the general principle that an alien cannot be deported to a State other than that of his nationality against the will of such State. Indeed, it happens not infrequently that national authorities, acting in accordance with a power undoubtedly expressed in national law, expel an alien to a third State where the national authorities exercise a power, equally undoubted under domestic law, to remit him whence he came.

The act of sending an alien to a country which is unwilling and under no obligation to admit him does not in normal circumstances engage international responsibility, either towards the State to which he is conducted or towards any State having an interest (by treaty or otherwise) in the maintenance of the alien's fundamental rights. Circumstances may arise, however, in which the repeated expulsion of an alien to States unwilling to accept him may entail a breach of the specific obligations undertaken by the expelling State in a Convention designed to protect human rights.[127] Moreover, the expulsion of an alien will entail a breach of the Geneva Convention on the Legal Status of Refugees if he is a refugee and is returned in any manner whatsoever to the frontiers of territories where his life or freedom would be threatened on account of his race, nationality, membership of a particular social group or political opinion.[128]

In 1892 the Institute of International Law resolved that expulsion may not degenerate into a disguised extradition, when extradition would not be available.[129] Modern State practice shows that that resolution is not an expression of *lex lata*. In *R v Brixton Prison, ex parte Soblen*[130] it was alleged that the Home Secretary had authorised the alien's deportation in order to secure his rendition to the United States as a fugitive, who was not amenable to extradition by reason of the political nature of his offence. The Court found no objection to the deportation but stated that it was not satisfied that the United States authorities had sought Dr Soblen's return. From this we may infer that the Court would have quashed the deportation order if (but only if) satisfied that it was made *mala fide*, and not for the reasons stated in the Aliens Order.[131] The *Soblen* case does not stand alone. The Israeli Supreme Court has upheld as valid the deportation of an alien to a country in which he was liable to arrest even though he could not have been extradited for the offence.[132] It seems from the legislative provisions in force in Canada,[133] India,[134] and Nigeria[135] that no objection may be raised to the making of directions for an alien's deportation from those countries on the ground that his arrest is sought in the jurisdiction to which he is to be removed. While the opposite rule applies in some other countries, perhaps constituting the majority,[136] there is no consensus on the point, and the most that can be said is that an exercise in comparative law yields support for the proposition that States may not select arbitrarily the destination to which an alien is to be sent. In Dr Goodwin-Gill's words, 'Due process excludes arbitrariness and the requirement flows from international law itself'.[137]

HARSH TREATMENT

In his report to the Institute of International Law in 1888 Mr Rolin-Jacquemyns formulated the following rule:

'The individual expelled has the double quality of being a man and a citizen of another State. As a human being he has the right to be exempt from needless harsh treatment and from unjust detriment to his interests; in his capacity of citizen of another State has a right to invoke the protection of his country against unduly rigorous treatment and against spoliation of his property. The act of expulsion ought to conform to its direct, essential object, which is to relieve the soil of an obnoxious guest. The right of national sovereignty does not require to permit more.[138]

In similar vein, Calvo maintained that when a government expels a foreigner in a harsh, inconsiderate manner (*'avec des formes blessantes'*) the latter's State of nationality has a right to base a claim on the expulsion as a violation of international law.[139]

The views so expressed may be supported by reference to State practice of the period. Thus, in the *Scandella* case[140] of 1898, the United States protested to Venezuela at the manner in which the authorities in the latter country expelled a United States citizen. He was suddenly arrested, thrown into prison and denied communication with his family and friends. He was then taken under guard to a steamer and deported to Trinidad. His wife and children were left without funds and his property stolen or sacked. The Venezuelan authorities agreed to pay compensation amounting to $1600 in American gold, in addition to reimbursement for the property taken or destroyed.

The principle enunciated by Rolin-Jacquemyns and by Calvo has survived with remarkably few modifications the turbulent century that followed them. In the *Maal* case (which was decided on a basis of equity), Venezuela again agreed to pay compensation for the indignities practised on an alien expellee, including his stripping in public.[141] In the *Jaurett* case, Secretary of State Root advised his minister in Caracas to advance a claim on behalf of a citizen of the United States who had been expelled at twenty-four hours notice. He advised that 'the manner and method of expulsion should not be humiliating, for it is not the purpose to humiliate and inconvenience the resident expelled but to save the State from dangers . . .'. The Venezuelan Government agreed to pay $3000 by way of 'indemnity on account of the injury caused him by virtue of his forcible expulsion'.[142] Although the precedent so established is diplomatic rather than judicial, it assumes particular importance since the element of harshness consisted in the peremptoriness of the decision and the shortness of notice, together with its timing (after closing hours on a Saturday). No physical ill-treatment was alleged.

In *Dillon's* case[143] the Mexican-U.S. Claims Commission reaffirmed that there is a basis for a claim when unnecessary force is employed or improper treatment inflicted on the alien. The matter was ventilated again in the *Chevereau* case between Great Britain and France in 1931.[144] The arbitrator there held that Britain was liable to pay damages to France for the arrest of a

French citizen on suspicion of spying in the British zone of influence in Persia. The arbitrator proclaimed that

> The detained person must be treated in a manner fitting his station, and which conforms to the standard habitually practised among civilised nations.

On the evidence before him he found that there was a *prima facie* reason for the arrest of Chevereau and he acquitted the British of his maltreatment during detention; but found that it was the duty of the British authorities to initiate without delay an enquiry into the charges made against him and to permit the alien to defend himself against them.[145]

More recently, American[146] and British practice has yielded further support for the proposition that a State acts in breach of international law if it expels an alien by unnecessarily harsh means. In 1967 the British Government made 'strong representations' to the Kenya Government which had decided to expel at twenty-four hours notice twelve United Kingdom citizens. Objection was taken to the peremptoriness of the expulsion and to the Kenyan conduct in arresting the twelve at night and keeping them under armed guard until their departure.[147]

It may be added that a failure on the part of an expelling State promptly to notify the consulate of an alien's State of nationality of his detention which a view to deportation will entail a breach of the Vienna Convention on Consular Relations, if both are parties to that treaty.[148] That Convention also requires that aliens should be free to communicate with the consular officers of their State, and *vice versa*, and that consular officials shall have the right to visit nationals of their State and to arrange for their legal representation.[149] In the latter respects the Convention appears to represent established international usage which has matured into a rule of customary law.[150]

PROCEDURAL GUARANTEES

It will be recalled that the principal vice imputed to Great Britain in the *Chevereau* case[151] was its failure to initiate an enquiry into the allegations against the alien, and to afford the latter an opportunity of presenting his case. The arbitrator's conclusion raises the question whether an alien is entitled as a matter of customary law to any form of hearing. Dr Goodwin-Gill goes so far as to assert 'that there can be no doubt . . . that international law requires that there be available some procedure whereby the underlying legality of executive action can be questioned, such as the writ of *habeas corpus* in common law jurisdictions'.[152]

It is plain that there is no general obligation in international law to afford a judicial review of the merits of a decision to expel an alien.[153] Indeed, relatively few systems of law can be found in which every decision to deport an alien attracts a right of appeal; and in some the courts have expressly refrained from inferring the existence of such a right.[154] Moreover, the distinction between review of merits and review of underlying legality appears insufficiently established in State practice, particularly in civilian jurisdictions, to constitute the basis of a rule of customary law universal in application.[155]

There is, however, some support for the proposition that a decision to deport an alien from a territory in which he is lawfully present is arbitrary, save where there are overwhelming considerations of national security to the contrary, unless he is informed of the allegations against him and is afforded an opportunity to advance reasons against his deportation, before some competent authority independent of those proposing to deport him. Such a proposition is a reflection of the general rule of law known in England as *audi alteram partem*[156] and in France as part of the *droits de la défense*.[157] The principle has been expressed by the Court of Justice of the European Communities on the basis of comparative law, as follows: 'a person whose interests are perceptibly affected by a decision taken by a public authority must be given the opportunity to make his point of view known'.[158] The same principle finds expression in Article 23 of the Constitution of the U.S.S.R.[159] and may properly claim to be a general principle of law, within the meaning of Article 38(1)(c) of the Statute of the International Court of Justice.

The principle appears to be reflected in Article 13(2) of the International Covenant on Civil and Political Rights.[160] This provides in part that an alien lawfully in the territory of a State party to that Covenant shall, except where compelling reasons of national security otherwise require, be allowed to have his case reviewed by a competent authority.[161] The Article as a whole appears to go further than customary law requires.[162] In particular, there is insufficient basis in State practice to maintain that States which are not bound by that Article are obliged to allow aliens to be represented; and the language of the Article implies a greater degree of formality in the review than is required by application of customary law or general principles of law.[163] For this reason the Article represents an important addition to the alien's procedural guarantees, in States that have agreed to be bound by it. Nevertheless, the *travaux préparatoires* of the Article reveal no evidence for the proposition that the principle applied in the *Chevereau case*[164] no longer represents good law. On the contrary, they appear to reveal a silent acceptance of the proposition that the alien must be given an opportunity to refute the allegation made against him, save in case of grave necessity.[165]

The expulsion of aliens *en masse* will entail, more frequently than their expulsion individually, breaches of the principles described in the foregoing pages. In particular, the obligation to advance a reason which could justify the expulsion must apply with particular force where numerous aliens are deported, most especially where all are of one nationality; and modern experience has shown that expulsion *en masse* is liable to be accompanied by harsh treatment and unaccompanied by respect for the principle *audi alteram partem*. Nevertheless, it seems that an expulsion does not contravene international law by reason only of the fact that it entails the removal of numerous aliens.

The Institute of International law, in its progressive report of 1892, contemplated that[166]

L'expulsion extraordinaire (ou en masse) définitive s'applique à des catégories d'individus; quand elle a été prononcée, les expulsés ne sont pas libres de revenir dans le pays . . .

In 1984 Dr Luke Lee of the United States Department of State presented to the American Society of International Law a Draft Declaration of Principles of International Law on Mass Expulsion.[167] This purported to 'declare' certain principles of international law on the matter. The Draft Declaration did not indicate that expulsion *en masse* is always illegal. Rather, it stated that:

Mass expulsion of aliens, whether long-term residents, migrant workers, refugees or stateless persons, must not be arbitrary or discriminatory in its application, or serve as a pretext for genocide, confiscation of property or reprisal. The power of expulsion must be exercised in conformity with the principles of good faith, proportionality and justifiability, with due regard to the basic human rights of the individual concerned.

Indeed, while it is easy to appreciate that the expulsion of aliens *en masse* is apt to entail breaches of principles by which States are bound even when expelling aliens individually, it is not easy to discover a reason why a massive expulsion should be unlawful *per se*. Nor is there support in State practice for such a proposition. On the contrary, circumstances may arise in which the size of the alien community, relative to the resources of the host State, is a factor to be taken into account in determining whether the expulsion is arbitrary.[168]

If the expulsion of aliens *en masse* does not necessarily entail a breach of international law, it must follow *a fortiori* that an agreement governing the exchange of populations is not inherently unlawful. The contrary is suggested in Principle 6 of Dr Lee's Draft Declaration, which reads as follows:

Compulsory transfers or exchanges of population by treaties are as inherently objectionable as unilateral expulsions, and any such treaties today are to be considered null and void as inconsistent with those peremptory norms of expulsion law from which no derogation can be permitted (*jus cogens*).[169]

The first proposition contained in the Principle is, however, an overstatement, for in the event of an agreement the State of destination generally waives, by necessary implication, any objection that it might otherwise advance on the basis of duties owed by the expelling State to the State of destination as such. The second proposition is advanced without authority and, it is submitted, in the face of precedent to the contrary. By the Treaty of Lausanne and a subsequent Agreement on its implementation,[170] Greece and Turkey made provision for the exchange of their populations. The circumstances surrounding those agreements were justly criticised by Séfériades, principally on the ground that their terms were not observed in fact, and the failure to apply those terms enured to the detriment of the populations concerned;[171] but in its Advisory Opinion on the *Interpretation of the Greco-Turkish Agreement of 1 December 1926*[172] the Permanent Court said not a word to suggest that the treaty entailed a breach of any rule of international law. Nor does it appear that any such suggestion was made in connection with the euphemistically entitled 'emigration agreement' between Turkey and Roumania of 4 September 1936.[173] Several modern, if informal agreements governing exchanges of populations have been implemented without protest on the ground suggested by Dr Lee. Among them are those governing exchanges between India and Pakistan, Pakistan and Bangladesh and Sri Lanka and India.[174] Although none of these transfers of population was 'compulsory' in the most formal and technical sense of the word, none was accomplished without governmental encouragement and in the first two instances, at least, the migration took place in conditions of severe dislocation. The evidence suggests that the agreements are not invalid. This is not to deny the necessity of scrutinising with care both the terms and the manner of implementing such agreements, for they are apt to disturb acquired rights and to entail arbitrariness and undue harshness in their execution.

Special problems are presented in the event of the expulsion *en masse* of aliens who are illegally present in the State taking that action. Such aliens cannot in principle claim to have acquired or vested rights to remain on foreign soil, nor is it possible to rely in their cases on Article 13(2) of the Covenant on Civil and Political Rights.[175] Moreover, the numbers of undocumented migrants present in a wide variety of States, as diverse as Colombia, France, Kenya, Kuwait, the United States and Venezuela, are such as to arouse widespread domestic and international concern.[176] As in the case of other categories of aliens, the expulsion *en masse* of undocumented workers is not inherently unlawful; but it may be carried out only in conformity with obligations imposed both by customary international law and by specific treaty obligations. Of the principles of customary international law governing such cases, the prohibition of arbitrary conduct and the rule of proportionality are likely to prove particularly apt; reasons must be advanced which could reasonably and properly lead the expelling State to the conclusion that its action is necessary in the public interest. The Migrant Workers (Supplementary Benefits) Convention[177] requires Contracting States to adopt 'all appropriate measures' to suppress illegal immigration, including measures against their employers. The Draft Convention on the Rights of All Migrant Workers and their Families[178] proposes that migrants should be eligible for special protection of their basic human rights when present in the territory of a Contracting State 'in an irregular situation'. In this respect it echoes the General Assembly's Resolution of 9 December 1975,[179] adopted by 130 votes to none, which calls on Member States to remind their competent administrative agencies of their obligation to respect the human rights of all migrants, including those that are non-documented or irregular.

Explicit prohibitions of collective expulsion are to be found in several regional instruments governing human rights. In particular, the Fourth Protocol to the European Convention on Human Rights[180] and the American Convention on Human Rights[181] prohibit the practice, but without defining it. In the former case, it appears from the *travaux préparatoires* that the Committee of Experts regarded the prohibition of collective expulsion as a specific manifestation of the rule against arbitrary expulsion of aliens, which finds expression also in Article 3 of the European Convention on Establishment.[182] In an application arising from the proposed repatriation by Denmark of 199 Vietnamese children, the Commission ruled that 'collective expulsion of aliens' means 'any measure of the competent authority compelling aliens as a group to leave the country, except where such a measure is taken after and on the basis of a reasonable and objective examination of the particular cases of each individual alien of the group'.[183] There is reason to believe that the prohibition of collective expulsion in the American Convention on Human Rights is to be understood in a similar spirit, not least because it must be read in the context of Article 22(6) of that Convention, which provides that an alien lawfully in the territory of a State party may be expelled from it only pursuant to a decision reached in accordance with the law.

The African Charter on Human and People's Rights (the 'Banjul Charter') prohibits mass expulsion in a more limited sense:[184]

The mass expulsion of non-nationals shall be prohibited. Mass expulsion shall be that which is aimed at national, racial, ethnic or religious groups.

There is good reason to believe that in this respect the Banjul Charter reflects a rule of modern customary law. As the European Commission on Human Rights has observed, it is generally recognized that a special importance should be attached nowadays to discrimination based on race and that publicly to single out a group of persons for differential treatment on the basis of race might, in certain circumstances, constitute a special form of affront to human dignity.[185] Discrimination based on nationality constitutes, in this context, a special form of affront to the State whose nationals are expelled and warrants remonstrance according to traditional rules of international law, at least in the absence of special circumstances such as the outbreak of hostilities.[186] Although the prohibition of religious discrimination is less well established in international law than the prohibition of discrimination on racial or national grounds, a strong case can be made for the proposition that the expulsion of a religious group, without a reasonable and objective examination of the case of each member, is inherently arbitrary.[187]

It is true that the International Convention on the Elimination of All Forms of Racial Discrimination,[188] so far as it is material, prohibits racial discrimination only in respect of limitations on freedom of movement and residence within the borders of the State and in respect of limitations on the right to leave any country including one's own and to return to it. Thus it is silent on the question of discrimination in respect of expulsion. No significance is to be attached to this circumstance, however, since the civil rights listed in that Convention are taken from the Universal Declaration of Human Rights[189] which was silent on expulsion generally; and this was so less for reason of principle than because of European preoccupations in 1948. It is also true that the United Nations failed to respond to the Ugandan expulsion of Asians in 1972 by condemning its discriminatory nature. A proposal before the Sub-Committee on Human Rights to express concern at the Ugandan action was defeated by fourteen votes to one, with six members abstaining. A proposal to add the words 'an expulsion' to a motion condemning racial discrimination in immigration policies was defeated with only three votes in its favour. The Sub-Committee's inactivity is regrettable, but it cannot be construed as an endorsement of the legality of the expulsion. Members of the Sub-Committee were unwilling to support an initiative originating in an ex-colonial power and criticising a former dependency on racial grounds. Moreover, the illegality of the Ugandan action was the subject of protest in other *fora*, including the Commonwealth;[190] and the Ugandan action would have been the subject of a General Assembly debate had not several African States agreed to intervene with President Amin for the purpose of inducing him to moderate his threats.[191]

The racially discriminatory nature of the Ugandan expulsion appears with sufficient clarity from the principal legislative provisions adopted for the purpose: the Immigration (Cancellation of Entry Permits and Certificates of Residence) Decree, 1972 (No. 17) and the Declaration of Assets (non-Citizen Asians) Decree 1972 (No. 27).[192] Moreover, there is no doubt that some units of the Ugandan armed forces failed to distinguish between Asian residents of Ugandan nationality and those with British nationality in implementing the legislation; nor can it be disputed that the implementation was accompanied by harassment of Asians and looting of their properties. In 1975 the Ugandan Government agreed to pay compensation to the Government of Asians concerned.[193] In January 1976 the Ugandan Government paid compensation to India for the losses sustained by its nationals. In 1977 it paid compensation to the Office of the United Nations High Commissioner for Refugees for losses sustained by Asians of undetermined nationality. The United Kingdom advanced in 1976 a claim for compensation in respect of losses suffered by Asians of British nationality. Despite repeated protestations on the part of the Foreign Office that it attached importance to the issue, the claim was still outstanding in 1986, by which date the United Kingdom had limited its claim to the value of the expropriated property.[194]

On principles similar to those applying in the case of Uganda it has been argued that the expulsion of Benin nationals from Gabon[195] and of Ghanaian nationals from Nigeria[196] entailed breaches of international law. The argument carries conviction.[197]

These considerations support the conclusion that, while the expulsion of aliens *en masse* is not prohibited as such, by customary international law, the right to effect such an expulsion is very closely circumscribed.[198] Firstly, in the case of mass expulsion as in the case of any other, the expelling State must advance a cogent justification in the national interest. The expelling State may not claim the exclusive right to determine whether justification exists,[199] although a margin of appreciation is apparently permitted. Secondly, the collective expulsion of nationals of one or more specified States violates the principles of good neighbourliness enshrined in the Charter of the United Nations and is an unfriendly act, warranting, in the absence of very special circumstances, a protest from the State or States whose nationals are affected and a demand for compensation for any losses incurred by them. Thirdly, the expulsion of a group designated by race is both morally and legally offensive. It excites not only public distaste but a positive obligation to rectify the wrong.[200] To this it must be added that important limitations have been imposed by international conventions governing respect for human rights and freedoms.

In all of these respects the power of expulsion is typical of the competences possessed by States with respect to the entry and residence of aliens. Formerly characterised as aspects of the State's absolute discretion, these powers are regulated and controlled, both as to their substance and as to their form, by a system of rules now sufficiently advanced and cohesive to be described as the international law of migration.

NOTES

1. Sir A. Cockburn, *Nationality*, 1869, 138; N. Mackenzie, *The Legal Status of Aliens in Pacific Countries*, 1937, 286; W. Friedman, O. Lissitsyn and R. Pugh, *International Law*, 1969, 553; S. Oda, 'The Individual in International Law' in M. Sørensen, ed., *Manual of Public International Law*, 1968, p. 482; G. Schwarzenberger, *International Law*, 1957, Vol. I, pp. 360–361; L. Oppenheim, *International Law*, 1955, Vol. I, p. 646; *Musgrove* v *Chun Teeong Toy*, [1891] A.C. 272; *Nishimura Ekiu* v *United States*, 142 U.S. 651 (1892).

2. *Supra*, Chapter IV, text at note 1. The duty and its corollary are not coextensive. See *infra*, text at notes 10–11.

3. G. Goodwin-Gill, *International Law and the Movement of Persons between States*, 1978, pp. 201–310, and 'The Limits of the Power of Expulsion in Public International Law', 47 B.Y.I.L. (1974–5) 55; see further the debate of the Institute of International Law, '*Règles internationales sur l'admission et l'expulsion des étrangers*', 12 Ann.I.D.I. (1892–4) 218 at 223 (*supra*, Chapter II at note 91).

4. *Supra*, Chapters V–VIII.

5. E. Borchard, *The Diplomatic Protection of Citizens Abroad*, 1915, p. 57.

6. *Infra*, text at notes 180, 181, 184.

7. Analogy may be drawn with the judgment of the European Court in Case 41/74, *Van Duyn* v *Home Office*, [1974] E.C.R. 1337 at 1349, paragraph 17, where it was held that present association, reflecting participation in the activities of a group, may be considered as 'personal conduct' within the meaning of a provision requiring any act of deportation to be based on the personal conduct of the individual concerned.

8. For the purpose of describing the deportation of aliens in groups of any kind, irrespective of any national, racial or religious criterion, we shall use the expression 'expulsion *en masse*'.

9. In *Ben Tillett's* case in 6 B.D.I.L. (1898) 124 at 147, the arbitrator observed that the State 'in the plenitude of its sovereignty' judges the scope of the acts leading to the alien's exclusion from its territory.

10. *Administrative Decision No. 5, U.S. v Germany, VII U.N.R.I.A.A. (1924) 119; Neer Claim, U.S. v Mexico*, IV U.N.R.I.A.A. (1926) 60; *Hines* v *Davidowitz et al.*, 312 U.S. 52 (1941); see generally, R. Lillich, *International Claims; their Adjudication by National Commissions*, 1962.

11. I.C.J. Rep. (1955) at p. 47.

12. III Hackworth's *Digest* 690 (emphasis added).

13. The *Chase Case, U.S. v Mexico*, IV Moore I.A. 3336.

14. An equally extreme statement, in the opposite sense, was made by Mr Cledwyn Hughes as Minister of State at the Commonwealth Office on 8 March 1966, when asked whether he proposed to protest at the expulsion of a British journalist from Zambia: 'The expulsion of journalists from Zambia is a matter for the Zambian Government to decide': 725 H.C. Deb., col. 1880.

15. 'Some writers have essayed to enumerate the legitimate causes of expulsion. The effort is useless. The reasons may be summed up and condensed in a single word: the public interest of the State': IV Moore *Digest* 68.

16. H. Grotius, *De Jure ac Pacis, Libri Tres*, 1651, Book II, Chap. II, p. xvi.

17. S. Pufendorf, *De Jure Naturae et Gentium, Libri Octo*, 1866, Book III, Chap. III, para. 10.

18. IV Moore *Digest* 74.

19. *Ibid.*, p. 76. In 1939 Secretary of State Hull instructed Ambassador Bullitt in Paris that 'the French authorities would recognize our right to be informed of the grounds and evidence on which expulsion was based': *Bitzer* case, 8 *Whiteman's Digest* 851 (1939).

20. *Ibid.*, p. 87. D. O'Connell in *International Law*, 1970, Vol. II, p. 707, states that the

requirement that the expelling State prove its legitimate grounds for deportation has not been persisted in, and the tendency has been to allow States a general competence to allow aliens to leave, but to engage them in international responsibility with respect to the manner of expulsion. It is thought, however, that the paucity of convincing modern evidence on this issue reflects only the fact that States seldom expel aliens without advancing some cause.

21. 733 H.C. Deb., col. 1223.
22. Hence Goodwin-Gill states that 'it is doubtful to what extent the requirement of explicit reasons applies in cases other than those submitted to arbitration': *supra* note 3 at p. 232. Apart from specific obligations imposed by reason of the *compromis*, the submission of a dispute to arbitration does not in principle alter the obligations of the States in respect of the question posed. Accordingly, an obligation to advance reasons to the arbitrator ought in principle to be matched by a corresponding obligation owed to the State of nationality when the latter seeks to resolve the difference by diplomatic means.
23. X U.N.R.I.A.A. (1903) 528 at 531. See also *Orazio de Attellis* case, IV Moore I.A. p. 3333.
24. IX U.N.R.I.A.A. (1903) 323.
25. *Zerman's* case, IV Moore I.A. (1903) 3348 *Lorenzo Oliva* (1903), M. Whiteman, *Damages in International Law,* 1937, Vol. I, p. 507, cited by Goodwin-Gill, *supra* note 3 at p. 231.
26. 6 B.D.I.L. at 218.
27. III Hackworth 699. See also *Davidson's Case*, 6 B.D.I.L. (1855) 114; *Furst's Case*, (1860) *ibid.*, p. 119; and *Gallenga's Case* (ibid.) where it was observed that the revocation of the residence permit was for 'political reasons' and no complaint was therefore made. See also debate on expulsions from Austria, 683 H.C. Deb., col. 164 (Written Answers) 1964 and A. Evans, 'The Political Status of Aliens in International Law, Municipal Law and European Community Law', 30 I.C.L.Q. (1981) 20.
28. See the views of Secretary of State Fish on the expulsion of Jewish Americans from Russia, 9 June 1874, 51 Cong. I Sess. 24, 25, cited in IV Moore *Digest* at 112; also cases of *Rosenstrauss*, 1873, *ibid.* at 112; *Pinkos and Wilczynski*, 1888, *ibid.* at 114 and *Lewisohn*, a British national, 1881, *ibid.* at 122. In March 1882 the United States declined to join with Liberia in protesting at a Spanish law prohibiting the landing of foreign negroes in Cuba save on payment of a deposit of $ 1000; *ibid* at 109.
29. W. McKean, *Equality and Discrimination under International Law,* 1983, at 152–166 and 193; Goodwin-Gill, *supra* note 3 at 275.
30. Ordonnance 45–2658 of 2 November 1945, J.O.R.F. 4 nov. p. 7225, Article 23.
31. A. Kiss, *Répertoire de la pratique française en matière de droit international public,* 1962–72, Vol. 4, p. 403; D. O'Connell, *supra* note 20, at 709 note 9.
32. A. Evans, 'Ordre Public, Public Policy and U.K. Immigration Law', 3 E.L. Rev. (1978) 372.
33. C. Rousseau, '*Chronique des faits internationaux,* 78 R.G.D.I.P. (1974) 1139 at 1143: '*Plusieurs incidents survenus depuis l'été 1973 ont toutefois montré que la départ est parfois délicat à opérer dans ce domaine entre l'atteinte authentique à l'ordre public et le seul fait par l'étranger en cause de déployer une activité contraire aux vues professées par le gouvernement du moment.*'
34. Loi No. 81–973 of 29 October 1981, D. 1981(L)361.
35. *Dridi, Conseil d'Etat,* 21 January 1977, D. 1977, 527. Cf. Case 67/74, *Bonsignore* v *Oberstadtdirektor der Stadt Köln,* [1975] E.C.R. 279; and Case 48/75, *Royer,* [1976] E.C.R. 497.
36. Victims of industrial accidents rendering them at least 20% incapacitated and aliens who have not been convicted of offences punishable with at least one month's imprisonment, save where there is an 'overwhelming necessity' for expulsion.
37. Loi No. 81–973, *supra* note 34, Article 5; Cf. *Cohn-Bendit, Conseil d'Etat,* 22 December 1978, D. 1979, 155.
38. Law of 24 June 1981 on the Status of Aliens in the Soviet Union, *Vedomosti S.S.S.R.* (1981) No. 26, Article 30.

39. M. Boguslawski, 'Uber die Rechtstellung von Ausländern nach Staatlichen Recht und Volkerrecht', Max Planck Colloquium, 1985, Vol. 4, p. 20.
40. Immigration Act 1971, section 3(5)(b).
41. H.C. 169, para. 159. Cf. H.C. 80, para. 43 and H.C. 52, para. 50, which began 'the cases in which deportation is justified on the ground that it will be conducive to the public good are likely to continue to be few in number. Judging from past experience, most of the cases in this category will be cases in which a court has convicted the person but has decided to leave the question of deportation to the Appeal Tribunal and the Secretary of State.'
42. L. Grant and I. Martin, *Immigration Law and Practice*, 1982, 232–233.
43. A. Evans, *Immigration Law*, 1983, 271. See 12 H.C. Deb. (N.S.) col. 87, 11 November 1981.
44. *R v Immigration Appeal Tribunal, ex parte Cheema and Others*, [1982] Imm. A.R. 124 (C.A.); *R v Immigration Appeal Tribunal, ex parte Khan*, [1983] 2 All E.R. 420 (C.A.).
45. *R v Home Secretary, ex parte Hosenball*, [1977] 3 All E.R. 452 (C.A.); *Agee v Rt. Hon. R.K. Murray*, 1977, S.L.T. (Notes) 54; B. Hepple, 'Aliens and Administrative Justice: the Deutschke Case', 34 M.L.R. (1971) 501.
46. Lord Bridge in *Khawaja v Secretary of State*, [1983] 1 All E.R. 765 at 787: 'I cannot suppose that this power was ever intended to be invoked as a means of deporting a perfectly respectable established resident on the grounds arising from the circumstances of his original entry'.
47. Immigration Act 1971, section 15(1)(a), (3), (7).
48. H.C. 169, para 150.
49. See, however, *Caprino v United Kingdom*, [1982] 4 E.C.H.R. 97.
50. Immigration Act 1971, section 3(5)(a).
51. H.C. 169, paras. 156 and 158. Acquittal of an offence of overstaying does not preclude deportation on this ground but is a material circumstance to be taken into account: *R v Immigration Appeal Tribunal, ex parte Vashist, The Times*, L.R., 18 January 1983 (C.A.).
52. Immigration Act 1971, section 3(6). H.C. 169, para. 156.
53. *R v Nazari*, [1980] 3 All E.R. 880.
54. *R v Caird*, (1970) 54 Cr. App. Rep. 499 at 510.
55. *R v Nazari, supra* note 53 at 885.
56. *Supra*, text at note 51.
57. H.C. 169, para. 156. See further *R v Serry, The Times* L.R., 31 October 1980 (receipt of supplementary benefit immaterial in case of minor offence).
58. Immigration Act 1971, section 3(5)(c). See *R v Immigration Appeal Tribunal, ex parte Mehmet*, [1978] Imm. A.R. 46.
59. Immigration Act 1971, section 5(4).
60. Immigration Act 1971, section 15(2).
61. H.C. 169, para. 161.
62. It seems from *R v Nazari, supra* note 53 at 885, that the appellant may not raise in the course of such an appeal an argument based on circumstances in the country to which it is proposed to return him. Such circumstances are to be taken into account by the Home Secretary, presumably as 'relevant factors' or 'compassionate circumstances' within the meaning of H.C. 169, para. 156.
63. Immigration Act 1971, section 15(1).
64. Immigration Act 1971, section 15(7)(b).
65. Immigration Act 1971, section 19(1).
66. Immigration Act 1971, schedule 2, para. 8(1).
67. Immigration Act 1971, schedule 2, para. 9.
68. By section 32 of the Immigration Act 1971, 'illegal entrant' means a person unlawfully entering or seeking to enter in breach of a deportation order or of the immigration laws.

This, however, merely postpones the definitional problem. See A. Nicol, *Illegal Entrants*, 1969, esp. at pp. 28–31.

69. *R* v *Bangoo and Others*, [1976] Crim. L.R. 746.
70. *R* v *Home Secretary, ex parte Hussain*, [1978] 2 All E.R. 423.
71. *Zamir* v *Home Secretary*, [1980] 2 All E.R. 768.
72. [1983] 1 All E.R. 765.
73. *Ali* v *Home Secretary*, [1984] 1 All E.R. 1009.
74. *R* v *Home Secretary, ex parte Lapnid*, [1984] 3 All E.R. 257.
75. Immigration and Nationality Act 1952, as amended, section 241(a), 8 U.S.C.S. para. 1251.
76. *In re Dubbiosi*, 191 F. Supp. 65 (1961) (alien crewman did not 'enter' the United States so as to be subject to deportation when arrested and imprisoned for assisting stowaways).
77. The grounds of exclusion are set out in corresponding detail in section 212(a) of the Immigration and Nationality Act 1952. The principal excludable classes are aliens who are insane, mentally retarded, narcotic drug addicts, afflicted with any contagious disease, paupers, vagrants, persons convicted of offences of moral turpitude or for two or more offences for which the aggregate sentences imposed was of five years or more, polygamists, prostitutes, stowaways, drug traffickers, revolutionaries,participants in Mazi persecution and aliens seeking to engage in employment without permits.
78. *Savoretti* v *U.S., ex parte Pincus*, 214 F. 2d. 314 (1954); *Landon* v *Clarke*, 239 F. 2d. 631 (1956); *U.S.* v *Lehmann*, 264 F. 2d. 237 (1959); *Mesina* v *Rosenberg*, 278 F. 2d. 291 (1960); *U.S.* v *Esperdy*, 315 F. 2d. 673 (1963); *Marantan* v *I.N.S.*, 425 F. 2d. 693 (1970).
79. *Foley, ex rel. Schenck* v *Ward*, 13 F. Supp. 915 (1936), where it was held that examination more than five years after entry showing the appellant to be mentally defective did not render her deportable in the absence of evidence of deficiency at the time of admission.
80. Cf. 'good moral character' for the purposes of naturalization: *supra*, Chapter I, note 178. The Act of 1952 provides that such aliens 'shall' be deported, on order of the Attorney-General.
81. Immigration and Nationality Act 1952, as amended, section 241(a)(4).
82. See the remarks of Maris, J. in *U.S. ex rel. Manzella* v *Zimmermann*, 71 F. Supp. 534 at 537 (1947).
83. *Jordan* v *De George*, 341 U.S. 223 (1951). The same applies *a fortiori* in the case of exclusion: *Ex parte Isojoki*, 22 F. 151 (1915).
84. *U.S. ex rel. Schladzien* v *Warden of Eastern State Penitentiary*, 45 F. 2d. 204 (1930).
85. *Guarneri* v *Kessler*, 98 F. 2d. 580 (1938).
86. *The Washington*, 19 F. Supp. 719 (1937).
87. *U.S. ex rel. Karpay* v *Uhl*, 70 F. 2d. 792 (1934).
88. *Baer* v *Norene*, 79 F. 2d. 340 (1935).
89. *U.S. ex rel. Carrolo* v *Bode*, 204 F. 2d. 220 (1953); *Jordan* v *De George*, 341 U.S. 223 (1951).
90. *Barbouris* v *Esperdy*, 269 F. 2d. 621 (1959).
91. *U.S. ex rel. Robinson* v *Day*, 51 F. 2d. 1022 (1931).
92. *The Washington, supra* note 86.
93. *Pillisz* v *Smith*, 46 F. 2d. 769 (1931).
94. U.S. Supreme Court Reports Annotated (Commentary), 95 L. Ed. October 1950, Term 340–341.
95. *U.S. ex rel. Huber* v *Sibray*, 178 F. 144 (1910).
96. *Rodriguez* v *Campbell*, 8 F. 2d. 983 (1925).
97. *In re Schiaro Di Cola*, 7 F. Supp. 194 (1934).
98. *U.S. ex rel. Guarino* v *Uhl*, 107 F. 2d. 399 (1939).
99. *U.S.* v *Carrollo*, 30 F. Supp. 3 (1939).
100. Immigration and Nationality Act 1952, as amended, section 265, 8 U.S.C.S. para 1305.

482

101. Immigration and Nationality Act 1952, as amended, section 241(a)(5).
102. Immigration and Nationality Act 1952, as amended, section 266(c); Alien Registration Act 1940, section 36(c); Alien Registration Act 1938.
103. Immigration and Nationality Act 1952, as amended, section 241(a)(7), (15), (16).
104. *Ibid.*, paras. (9), (10), (13).
105. *Ibid.*, paras. (18), (14) and (17) in that order.
106. *Ibid.*, paras. (11), (12).
107. *Ibid.*, paras. (8), (18). See *U.S.* v *Walus*, 453 F. Supp. 699 (1978), *Digest of United States Practice in International Law*, 1978, 331.
108. 8 C.F.R. 243.4.
109. *Hotel and Restaurant Employees Union, Local 25* v *Smith*, 594 F. Supp. 502 (1984).
110. 8 C.F.R. 242 17(a); Immigration and Nationality Act 1952, section 244; *I.N.S.* v *Jong Ha Wang*, 450 U.S. 139 (1981).
111. Immigration and Nationality Act 1952, section 245(a).
112. *Ibid.*, sections 212(c) and 249, 8 C.F.R. 212.3 and 8 C.F.R. 249.2.
113. Immigration and Nationality Act 1952, section 243(h).
114. *Ibid.*, section 242(b).
115. Immigration and Nationality Act 1952, section 244, U.S.C.S. para. 1254.
116. In Turkey there is, however, a power to expel foreign gypsies, wandering nomads and stateless persons: Act on Residence and Travel of Aliens, No. 5683 of 15 July 1980, Article 26.
117. E.g. Australia: Migration Act, 1958, sections 12, 14; Belgium: Law of 15 December 1980, Article 20(1); Chile: Law No. 12, 927 of 6 August 1956, Article 3; Denmark: Aliens Act No. 226 of 8 June 1983, Section 12; Federal Republic of Germany: *Ausländergesetz* (Aliens Law) of 28 April 1965, BGBl. 1965 I, 353, Art. 10; Ghana: Aliens Act 1933, Section 12; India: Foreigners Act 1946, section 2(c), as interpreted in *Hans Muller* v *Superintendent, Presidency Gaol*, [1955] A.I.R. 367 (S.C.); Ireland: Aliens Order 1946, section 13; Netherlands: Aliens Act 1965, section 12; Nigeria: Immigration Act, No. 6 of 1963, as amended by Decree No. 8 of 1972; Norway: Aliens Act 1956, section 15; Poland: Aliens Law of 29 March 1963, Dz. U. 1963 No. 15, Article 9; Portugal: Decree Law 264–B181, Article 42; Turkey: *supra* note 116, Article 19.
118. E.g. Belgium: Law of 15 December 1980, Article 7(6); Canada: Immigration Act, S.C. 1976–77, cap. 52, as amended, section 32; Federal Republic of Germany: *supra* note 117, *loc. cit.*; Luxembourg: Law of 28 March 1972, Article 9; Nigeria: Immigration Act 1963, section 17; Portugal: Law of 28 March 1972, Article 9; Nigeria: Immigration Act 1963, section 17; Portugal: *supra* note 117, *loc. cit.*
119. E.g. Denmark: Aliens Act No. 226 of 8 June 1983, Article 25(1); Norway: Aliens Act 1956, sector 13(1)(d); Portugal: *supra* note 117, *loc. cit.*; Sweden: Aliens Act (*Utlanningslag*) No. 376 of 1980, Prop. 1979/80:96, section 40; Turkey: *supra* note 115, Article 22.
120. E.g. Denmark: Aliens Act No. 226 of 8 June 1983, Article 25(2); Nigeria: Immigration Act No. 6 of 1963, section 17(1)(g)–(h); Portugal: *supra* note 117, *loc. cit.*; Sweden: Aliens Act, *supra* note 118, section 43.
121. E.g. Belgium: Law of 15 December 1980, Article 7(1); Norway: Aliens Act 1956, section 13(1)(a); Portugal: *supra* note 117, *loc. cit.*; Soviet Union: Law of 24 June 1981, *supra* note 38, Article 30.
122. Attempts of devise such tests have been made, but often with more zeal than conviction. See D. O'Connell, *supra* note 20 at 709–710. See further the Resolution of the Institute of International Law, Article 28, 12 Ann.I.D.I. (1892) at 223.
123. For analyses of the law governing State responsibility in this area, see Professor Riphagen's report to the International Law Commission, I.L.C. Ybk. (1984–II) 99.

483

124. D. O'Connell, *supra* note 20 at 710.
125. Immigration Act 1971, schedule 2 paras. 8(1)(c), 12(2)(c).
126. Immigration and Nationality Act 1952, section 243; 8 U.S.C.S. para. 1253.
127. European Convention on Human Rights, Rome, 4 November 1950, 213 U.N.T.S. 221, Article 3: *Basic Documents* V.1; Application No. 8100/77, *X* v *Germany,* not reported; Application No. 7612/76, *Manitu Giama* v *Belgium,* XXIII Ybk. (1980) 428.
128. 28 July 1951, 189 U.N.T.S. 150: *Basic Documents* III.2; Article 33, read with Article 1.
129. 12 Ann.I.D.I. (1892) at 223.
130. [1963] 2 Q.B. 243.
131. Aliens Order 1953, S.I. No. 1671.
132. *Joanovici,* (1958) 12 Sup. Ct. 646.
133. Immigration Act, S.C. 1976–77, cap. 52, section 54(2).
134. A. Sinha, *Law of Citizens and Aliens in India,* 1962 at 22.
135. Immigration Act No. 6 of 1963, as amended, section 17.
136. For Australia, see *Znaty* v *Minister for Immigration,* 126 C.L.R. (1976) 1; *Barton* v *Commonwealth,* 131 C.L.R. (1974) 477. For Japan, see Law No. 68 of 21 July 1953, Article 2(1). In France the trial of *Klaus Barbie* came about in consequence of his deportation, rather than extradition, which constituted no jurisdictional impediment in the French courts: 6 October 1983, 1984 D. 113.
137. *Supra,* note 3 at 227, See further F. Hassan, 'The Word "Arbitrary" in the Universal Declaration of Human Rights: "Illegal" or "Unjust"?', 10 Harv. Int. L.J. (1969) 228.
138. 'Right of Expulsion of Foreigners', 20 R.D.I. 498.
139. *Dictionnaire de droit international,* title 'Expulsion'.
140. IV Moore *Digest* 108.
141. X U.N.R.I.A.A. (1903) 730.
142. III Hackworth's *Digest* 690 (1907).
143. IV U.N.R.I.A.A. (1928) 368.
144. 6 A.D. (1931), 205.
145. A similar complaint was advanced by Secretary of State Root in the *Jaurett* case, *supra* note 142.
146. In a letter dated 15 December 1961 from Secretary of State Dutton to Congressman Udall, the former expressed on behalf of the Administration the conclusion that 'under generally accepted principles of international law a State may expel an alien whenever it wishes, provided it does not carry out the expulsion in an arbitrary manner, such as by using unnecessary force to effect the expulsion or otherwise mistreating the alien': 8 Whitman's *Digest* 861. See also *Yugoslavia Claim No. 44, ibid.* at p. 860 and R. Lillich, ed., *International Law of State Responsibility for Injuries to Aliens,* 1983, 236.
147. 750 H.C. Deb., col. 98 (10 July 1967).
148. Vienna, 24 April 1963, 596 U.N.T.S. 261, Article 36(1)(b).
149. *Ibid.,* Article 36(1)(a), 36(1)(c).
150. See *Bigelow* v *Princess Zizianoff, Gazette du Palais,* 4 March 1928; P. Cahier and L. Lee, *International Conciliation,* 1969, 63.
151. *Supra,* note 144.
152. *Supra,* note 3 at 275.
153. Dr Goodwin-Gill concedes the point but contends that the contrary may be advanced *de lege ferenda.*
154. See the decision of the Ghanaian Supreme Court in *Captan* v *Minister of the Interior,* [1970] 2 G. and G. 457. Even in the case of Canada, where appellate procedures are very well developed, section 72(1) of the Immigration Act, S.C. 1976–77, C. 52 makes provision for appeals in the case of permanent residents only.

155. See for example Netherlands Aliens Act 1965, section 29; Norwegian Administrative Procedures Act 1968, section 28(1) and *State* v *Czardas*, Norsk Retstidende (1955) 953. For France, see text at note 37, *supra*. Cf. Australian Administrative Decisions (Judicial Review) Act 1977, section 3(4) and in India: *Union of India* v *H. Mohmed*, [1954] A.I.R. 505 (Bom.).

156. Alternatively, *audiatur et altera pars: Ridge* v *Baldwin*, [1964] A.C. 40. The principle applies also in Scotland; *Melloch* v *Aberdeen Corporation*, [1971] 1 W.L.R. 1578; in Denmark: P. Andersen, *Dansk Forvaltningsret*, 1965, 337; in the Federal Republic of Germany: E. Forsthoff, *Lehrbuch der Verwaltungsrechts*, 1973, Vol. I, 235; and in Ireland: J. Kelly, *Fundamental Rights in the Irish Law and Constitutions*, 1967, 313–314.

157. G. Vedel, *Cours de droit administratif*, 1961, 536.

158. Case 17/74, *Transocean Marine Paint* v *Commission*, [1974] E.C.R. 1063 at 1080.

159. *Supra*, Chapter III, text at note 152.

160. New York, 16 December 1966; 6 I.L.M. (1967) 368: *Basic Documents* I.2.

161. The wording is derived from that of Article 3(2) of the European Convention on Establishment, Paris, 13 December 1955; 529 U.N.T.S. 141: *Basic Documents* V.3. Several European States failed to ratify that Convention until the late 1960's, by which time they had established appellate procedures in order to meet the requirements of Article 3(2).

162. France, Iceland, Mexico and the United Kingdom have made reservations in respect of that Article, in the latter case the reservation relating exclusively to Hong Kong. See *United Nations Multilateral Treaties Deposited with the Secretary-General*, 1982 at 123, 124, 125, 128. Cf. Goodwin-Gill's comments on Articles 14, 16 and 26 of the Covenant as embodiments of customary law: *supra note 3 at 275, note 3*.

163. The International Covenant speaks of the alien's right to have his case reviewed, whereas the European Convention speaks of a right of appeal; moreover, the Covenant speaks of review by a competent authority 'or persons especially designated by a competent authority', thereby making plain that judicial review is not the only form of review contemplated.

164. *Supra*, note 144.

165. See Report of the Third Committee, U.N. Doc. A/6546, 13 December 1966 and U.N. Doc. A/P.V. 1496.

166. 12 Ann.I.D.I. (1892) 223 (Article 23).

167. 78 Proc. A.S.I.L. (1984) 342 at 345.

168. Comparison may be made with Lord Denning's comments on the duty of admission of nationals in *Thakrar* v *Home Secretary*, [1974] 2 All E.R. 261 at 266: 'Is it to be said that by international law every one of them has a right if expelled to come into these small islands? Surely not. This country would not have room for them. It is not as if it was only one or two coming. They come not as single files but in batallions. Mass expulsions on this scale have never hitherto come within the cognizance of international law'.

169. *Sed quaere. Supra* note 167, *loc. cit.*

170. 30 January 1923, 32 L.N.T.S. 75; 1 December 1926, 68 L.N.T.S. 11.

171. S. Séfériades, *'L'échange des populations'*, 28 Hague *Recueil* (1928) 311.

172. P.C.I.J. Ser. B., No. 16 (1926).

173. 195 L.N.T.S. 429.

174. The agreement between India and Sri Lanka was concluded by Exchange of Notes dated 30 October 1964 ('the Shastri-Banderanayake pact'). This provided that of an estimated population of 975,000 stateless Tamils in Sri Lanka, 525,000 would be granted Indian citizenship and would be 'repatriated' to India; 300,000 would be granted Sri Lankan citizenship, the transfer being achieved by stages, not more than 35,000 to receive citizenship in any year, on application. By a further agreement concluded between Mrs Bandaranayake and Mrs Gandhi by notes dated 27 November and 4 December 1968, it was agreed that the number

being 'repatriated' would be increased by 10%. By a further agreement dated 27 January 1974, each State agreed to confer its citizenship and right of residence on 75,000 Tamils. The agreements were implemented in Sri Lanka by the Indo-Ceylon Agreement Implementation Act 1967 (No. 14) and the Indo-Ceylon Agreement Implementation (Amendment) Act 1971 (No. 43).

175. *Supra*, note 160.
176. R. Plender, 'Recent Trends in National Immigration Control', 35 I.C.L.Q. (1986) 531.
177. I.L.O. Convention No. 143, Geneva, 24 June 1975, Cmnd. 6624; *Basic Documents* VII.5.
178. U.N. Doc. A/C.3.39/4(xxxix).
179. U.N.G.A. Res. 3449(XXX); 29 U.N. Ybk. (1975) 641–642.
180. Strasbourg, 16 September 1963; E.T.S. No. 46; *Basic Documents* V.2; Article 4.
181. San José, 22 November 1969; 9 I.L.M. (1970) 673; *Basic Documents* IX.4; Article 22(9).
182. Paris, 13 December 1955; 529 U.N.T.S. 141; *Basic Documents* V.3. See W. Pahr, '*Das 4 Zusatsprotokoll zur Europäischen Menschenrechtskonvention*' [1964] Juristische Blätte 187; M. Sand, '*Le quatrième Protocole additionel à la Convention européenne des Droits de l'Homme*', [1964] A.F.D.I. 569.
183. Application 7011/75, *Becker* v *Denmark*, XIX Ybk. (1976) 416, 1454; 4 D.R. (1976) 215 at 235, *supra*, Chapter VII at note 54.
184. Banjul, 26 June 1981; 21 I.L.M. (1982) 58; *Basic Documents* IX.5; Article 12(5).
185. Applications Nos. 4403/70–4419/70, 4422/70, 4423/70, 4434/70, 4443/70 and 4476/70–4486/70 *Patel et al.* v *United Kingdom* (*East African Asians Cases*), 10 I.L.M. (1971) 6.
186. In the case of the proposed expulsion from Egypt of British and French nationals in 1956, the British Foreign Secretary reported that the Swiss Minister in Cairo had protested on behalf of the United Kingdom, describing the action as 'barbarous': 8 Whitman's *Digest* at 858.
187. See F. Capotorti, Special Rapporteur of the United Nations Sub-Commission on Prevention of Discrimination, *Study on the Rights of Persons Belonging to Ethnic, Religious and Linguistic Minorities*, E/CN.4/Sub.2/384/Rev.1 (1969); McKean, *supra*, note 29, at 62.
188. New York, 7 March 1966; 60 U.N.T.S. 195; *Basic Documents* I.3; Article 5(d)(i) and (ii).
189. U.N.G.A. Res. 217 A(iii); 43 A.J.I.L. (1949) Supp. p. 127; *Basic Documents* I.1.
190. Academic literature also supports the view that the expulsion was unlawful. See R. Chhangani, 'Expulsion of Asians and International Law', 12 Ind. J.I.L. (1972) 400; R. Plender, 'Expulsion of Aliens', 9 Rev. Int. Comm. Jur. (1972) 19; G. Goodwin-Gill, *supra*, note 3 at 215; R. Nogel, 'Human Rights and Uganda's Expulsion of its Alien Minority', 3 Denver Jo. Int. L. and Pol. (1973) 107.
191. *New York Times*, 30 September 1972, p. 3, col. 4, cited in R. Lillich, ed., *supra* note 146 at 236.
192. Made under the Immigration Act 1969 (No. 19) section 9(1); Immigration Regulations 1969 (No. 165). The latter Decree was signed on 4 or 5 October 1972 but made retrospective to 9 August. See Plender, *supra* note 190.
193. The Properties and Business (Acquisition) Decree 1975 (No. 11) and Assets of Departed Asians (Amendment) Decree 1975 (No. 12).
194. The claim was based on internal Ugandan law, the Expropriated Properties Act 1982, apparently to the exclusion of international law. See 46 H.C. Deb. (6th Ser.) 174–5 (20 July 1983; 50 H.C. Deb. (6th Ser.) 308 (7 December 1983) and 86 H.C. Deb. (6th Ser.) 195–6, 13 November 1983.
195. R. Chhangani, 'Expulsion of Benin Nationals and International Law', 21 Ind. J.I.L. (1981) 147.
196. T. Austin, 'The Nigerian Expulsion Order', 21 Colum. J. Trans. L. (1983) 641.
197. For the Iraqi expulsion of Iranians, the exodus of aliens from Ghana, the closing of the borders of Togo, the expulsion of Kurds from Iraq, reciprocal expulsions between Kenya

and Tanzania and expulsions from Zanzibar, see the materials cited by Goodwin-Gill, *supra* note 3 at 217–218.

198. Professor Agrawalla maintains that mass expulsion is diminishing along with gradual disappearance of totalitarian ideologies and the advent of true constitutionalism. His comments seem excessively optimistic: *International Law: Indian Courts and Legislature*, 1965, 186.

199. In 1934 Yugoslavia expelled a great number of Hungarian subjects; the latter State contended that the action was not justified by reference to unemployment, the cause cited by Yugoslavia. See A. Toynbee, *Survey of International Affairs, 1934.*

200. For the purpose of determining whether a policy is racially discriminatory, it appears appropriate to have regard to its 'pith and substance' rather than its mere form: *Pillai* v *Mudanayake*, [1953] A.C. 514; *Guinn* v *Beal*, 238 U.S. 1 (1915).

BIBLIOGRAPHY

R. Chhangani, 'Expulsion of Uganda Asians and International Law', 12 Ind. J.I.L. (1972) 400.

R. Chhangani, 'Legal Status of Aliens in Nigeria', 23 J. Ind. L. Inst. (1981) 269.

V. Krishna Iyer, 'Mass Expulsion as a Violation of Human Rights', 13 Ind. J.I.L. (1973) 169.

R. Nogel, 'Human Rights and Uganda's Expulsion of its Asian Minority', 3 Denver J. Int. L. and Pol (1973) 107.

K. Kotecha, 'Shortchanged: Uganda Citizenship Laws and how they were applied to the Asian Minority', 9 Int. Law. (1975).

R. Plender, 'Expulsion of Aliens', 9 Rev. Int. Comm. Jur. (1972) 19.

S. Séfériades, *'L'échange des populations'*, 28 Hague *Recueil* (1928) 311.

A. de Zayas, 'International Law and Mass Population Transfers', 16 Harv. Int. L.J. (1975) 207.

Table of Cases

492

Case 118/75, Watson and Belmann
  [1976] ECR 1185   Ch: 3 N: 129
                                                     Ch: 6 N: 23
                                                     Ch: 6 N: 48

Case 13/76, Dona v Montero
  [1976] ECR 1333   Ch: 6 N: 20
Case 17/76, Brack v Insurance Officer
  [1976] ECR 1429   Ch: 6 N: 15
Case 40/76, Kermashcek v Bundesanstalt fur Arbeit
  [1976] ECR 1669   Ch: 6 N: 93
Case 63/76, Vita Inzirillo v Caisse d'allocations familiales de
l'Arrodnissment de Lyon
  [1976] ECR 2057   Ch: 6 N: 92
Case 71/76, Thieffry v Conseil de l'Ordre des Avocats a la cour de Paris
  [1977] ECR 765   Ch: 6 N: 61
Case 8/77, Brenca and Bakhouche
  [1977] ECR 1495   Ch: 6 N: 49
Case 11/77, Patrick v Ministre des Affaires Culturelles
  [1977] ECR 1199   Ch: 6 N: 62
Case 30/77, R v Bouchereau
  [1977] ECR 1999   Ch: 3 N: 127
                                                     Ch: 6 N: 73

Case 65/77, Razanatsimba
  [1977] ECR 2229   Ch: 6 N: 29
Case 15/78, Society generale Alsacienne de Banque v Koestler
  [1978] ECR 1971   Ch: 6 N: 64
Cases 110/78 and 111/78 (joined), Van Wesemeel
  [1979] ECR 35   Ch: 6 N: 64
                                                     Ch: 10 N: 20

Case 115/78, Knoors v Secretary of State
  [1979] ECR 389   Ch: 6 N: 33, 38
Case 136/78, Ministere Public v Auer
  [1979] ECR 437   Ch: 6 N: 63
Case 139/78, Coccioli v Bundesanstalt fur Arbeit
  [1979] ECR 991   Ch: 6 N: 89
Case 175/78, R v Saunders
  [1979] ECR 1129   Ch: 6 N: 36, 38
Cases 41/79, 121/79, 796/79, Testa Maggio and Vitale v Bundesanstalt
fur Arbeit
  [1980] ECR 1979   Ch: 6 N: 89
Case 52/79, Debauve
  [1980] ECR 833   Ch: 6 N: 64
Case 57/79, Videl Martins, Sophie v Uruguay
  UNGAOR 37th Sess. Supp. No. 40 (A/37/40) 1982   Ch: 3 N: 219
Case 98/79, Pecastaing v Belgium
  [1980] ECR 691   Ch: 6 N: 75
Case 131/79, Santillo
  [1980] ECR 1585   Ch: 6 N: 74
Case 149/79, Commission v Belgium
  [1980] ECR 3881   Ch: 6 N: 17
                                                     Ch: 7 N: 73

Goffar v ECO, Dacca
  [1975] Imm. A.R. 142   Ch: 10 N: 91
Goldman and Van Zyl
  18 February 1983, TH/97569/82 (2616) and TH/97524/80   Ch: 12 N: 227
Gonzales v Williams
  192 U.S. 1 (1903)   Ch: 4 N: 74, 99
Gonzalez, In Re
  217 F. Supp. 717 (1963)   Ch: 7 N: 108
Goods of Shiphris, Re
  3 Pe. M. (1950–51) 272; 17 ILR (1950) 110   Ch: 7 N: 245
Gopalan, A.K. v The State
  [1950] A.I.R. (SC) 27   Ch: 2 N: 203
Greek National
  B. Verw. G. 4 August 1983, Inf. Ausl. R. 1983, 308   Ch: 11 N: 30
Grewal v Home Secretary
  [1979–80] Imm. A.R. 119   Ch: 6 N: 43
Grundul v Bryner
  83 A.T.F.S. (1951-I) 16   Ch: 12 N: 310
Guarneri v Kessler
  98 F. 2d. 580 (1938)   Ch: 13 N: 85
Guerre v Gutersohn
  1954, D. 539   Ch: 12 N: 297
Guinn v Beal
  238 U.S. 1 (1915)   Ch: 13 N: 200
Gungere v Falk
  16 A.D. (1949) 224 (No. 68)   Ch: 4 N: 35
Gupta v Home Secretary
  [1979–80] Imm. A.R. 52   Ch: 5 N: 35
H., In the matter of
  9 I.N. 640 (1962)   Ch: 11 N: 135
H. v H.
  [1953] 2 All ER 1232   Ch: 11 N: 110, 127
H.H., In the matter of
  6 I.N. 278 (1954)   Ch: 11 N: 130
Habtu Kahsai Haitu v Home Secretary
  1 December 1977, TH/3926/76   Ch: 12 N: 174
Haitian Refugee Center v Civiletti
  503 F. Supp. 442 (S.D. Fla 1980) aff'd as modified 676 F. 2d. 1023
  (1982)   Ch: 12 N: 188
Haitian Refugee Center v Smith
  676 F. 2d. 1023 (1982)   Ch: 12 N: 143
Haj-Ismail v Minister for Immigration and Ethnic Affairs
  36 ALR 516, (1981)   Ch: 10 N: 115
Haji and Others v Home Secretary
  [1978] Imm. A.R. 26   Ch: 9 N: 100
Hallet and Browne v Jenks
  3 Cranch 210, 219, (1805)   Ch: 5 N: 142
Harmail Singh v Immigration Appeal Tribunal
  [1978] Imm. A.R. 140 (C.A.)   Ch: 11 N: 74
Hashim v Home Secretary
  [1982] Imm. A.R. 113   Ch: 10 N: 88

Manan, Abdul, In Re
[1971] 1 W.LR. 859   Ch: 5 N: 8
Mandla v Lee
[1983] 1 All ER 1062   Ch: 12 N: 200
Maneka Gandhi v Union
[1978] A.I.R. (SC) 597   Ch: 3 N: 213
Marantan v I.N.S.
425 F. 2d. 693 (1970)   Ch; 13 N: 78
Margetson v Attorney General
12 W.I.R. (1968) 469   Ch: 1 N: 114
Markwald v Attorney General
[1920] 1 Ch. 348   Ch: 1 N: 74
Martens v Marten
[1952] 3 S.A. 771, 776   Ch: 11 N: 110, 127
Martin v Home Secretary
[1972] Imm. A.R. 7   Ch: 11 N: 72
Martinez-Romero v Immigration and Naturalization Service
692 F. 2d. 592 (1982)   Ch: 12 N: 181
Martonelli Case, The
63 F. 437 (1894)   Ch: 4 N: 73
Matkov v Home Secretary
24 May 1984, TH/106300/83 (3331)   Ch: 12 N: 228
Matrimonial Home (Germany) Case
[1953] E.B. 58   Ch: 7 N: 40
Mavrommatis Palestine Concessions Case
PCIJ Ser A, No. 2 (1924)   Ch: 1 N: 263
May v May and Lehmann
[1946] 2 All ER 146   Ch: 12 N: 303
Mazel v Home Secretary
7 January 1985, TH/120591/84   Ch: 12 N: 228
McGillivray v Home Secretary
[1972] Imm. A.R. 63   Ch: 11 N: 72
McMullen, Re v Immigration and Naturalization Service
658 F. 2d. 1312 (1981)   Ch: 12 N: 231
Melloch v Aberdeen Corporation
[1971] 1 W.L.R. 1578   Ch: 13 N: 156
Merge Claim   20 or 22 ILR?
20 ILR (1955) 443   Ch:1 N: 266
                                                                 Ch; 4 N: 182

Mesina v Rosenberg
278 F. 2d. 291 (1960)   Ch: 13 N: 78
Messih v Minister of the Interior
28 ILR (1950) 291   Ch: 1 N: 239
Meunier, Re
[1894] 2 Q.B. 415   Ch: 7 N: 107
Miller v Home Secretary
4 November 1985, TH/120585/84   Ch: 12 N: 228
Minister of the Interior v Montcho
11 July 1980, Rec. Cons. d'Et. 1980, p. 315   Ch: 11 N: 149
Ministere Public v Triandafilou
11 A.D. (Supplementary Volume, 1919–1942) 165 (No. 86)   Ch: 5 N: 114

Sidhu v M.E.I.
  14 June 1978, C.L.I.C. No. 1.31 — Ch: 11 N: 148
Silva v Bell
  605 F. 2d. 978 (1979) — Ch: 11 N: 62
Silver v Silver
  [1955] 2 All ER 614 — Ch: 11 N: 110, 127
Simon v Phillips
  (1916) 85 LJKB 656 — Ch: 3 N: 121
Simsek v Minister for Immigration
  (1982) 40 ALR 61 — Ch: 12 N: 292
Sloley v ECO, Kingston, Jamaica
  [1973] Imm. A.R. 54 — Ch: 11 N: 72
Smith v Peters
  (1875) L.R. 20 Eq. 511 — Ch: 3 N: 143
Smith v Turner (Passenger Cases)
  48 U.S. 282; 7 How 283 (1849) — Ch: 2 N: 49
Society for the Propagation of the Gospel in Foreign Parts v New Haven
  8 Wheat 464 (1823) — Ch: 5 N: 23
Sovich v Esperdy
  206 F. Supp. 558 (1963) — Ch: 12 N: 190
Spaulding Claim, The
  24 ILR (1956) 452 — Ch: 4 N: 182
Stacher v Rosenberg
  216 F. Supp. 511 (1963) — Ch: 5 N: 15
Stansbury and Arkwright
  5 C and P (1833) 575 — Ch: 1 N: 251
State v Czardas
  Norsk Retstidende (1955) 953 — Ch: 13 N: 155
State, The (Duggan) v Tapley
  [1952] I.R. 62; 18 I.L.R. (1951) 336 — Ch: 12 N: 280
Sultanow v Minister of Foreign Affairs
  SWNTA V (1927) No. 1183; 4 A.D. (1927–8) 328 (No. 221) — Ch: 2 N: 148
Sutton v Sutton
  (1830) 1 R and M 163 — Ch: 1 N: 251
Swedish Engine Drivers Case
  ECHR Series A, No. 20 (1976) — Ch: 7 N: 233
Swick v Home Secretary
  2 September 1983, TH/98626/82 (2892) — Ch: 12 N: 228
T. Michael Peter
  Decision of Senate 18 January 1979, 57 B. Verw. G. 229 (No. 31) — Ch: 11 N: 31
Talma, George et al. v Minister of the Interior
  8 A.D. (1935–1937) 313 (No. 142) — Ch: 12 N: 282
Tekle v Visa Officer, Prague
  [1986] Imm. A.R. 71 — Ch: 12 N: 8
Terhoch v Daudin et Assitance Publique
  14 A.D. (1947) 121 (No. 54) — Ch: 4 N: 170
Thackrah, Re
  [1939] 2 All ER 4 — Ch: 12 N: 206

516

U.S. v Rubenstein	
151 F. 2d. 915 (1945)	Ch: 11 N: 115
U.S. v Tod	
285 F. 523 (1922); 26 A.L.R. 1316	Ch: 4 N: 76
U.S. v Travis	
241 F. Supp 468 (1963)	Ch: 3 N: 102
U.S. v Villato	
2 U.S. 370 (1797)	Ch: 1 N: 58
U.S. v Walus	
453 F. Supp. 699 (1978)	Ch: 13 N: 107
U.S. v Williams	
184 F. 322 (1911); 106 C.C.A. 464	Ch: 4 N: 75
U.S. v Wong Kim Ark	
169 U.S. 649 (1897)	Ch: 1 N: 36, 64
U.S. ex rel Carrollo v Bode	
204 F. 2d. 220 (1953)	Ch: 13 N: 89
U.S. ex rel. Guarino v Uhl	
107 F. 2d. 399 (1939)	Ch: 13 N: 98
U.S. ex rel. Huber v Sibray	
178 F. 144 (1910)	Ch: 13 N: 95
U.S. ex rel. Karpay v Uhl	
70 F. 2d 792 (1934)	Ch: 13 N: 87
U.S. ex rel. Manzella v Zimmerman	
71 F. Supp. 534 (1947)	Ch: 13 N: 82
U.S. ex rel. Robinson v Day	
51 F. 2d. 1022 (1931)	Ch: 13 N: 91
U.S. ex rel. Schladzien v Warden of Eastern State Penitentiary	
45 F. 2d. 204 (1930)	Ch: 13 N: 84
U.S. ex rel. Steinworth v Watkins	
14 A.D. (1947) 107 (No. 41)	Ch: 4 N: 157
U.S. ex rel. Lacas v Curran	
297 F. 219 (1924)	Ch: 1 N: 36
U.S. ex rel. Polymeris v Tindell	
284 U.S. 279 (1931)	Ch: 2 N: 148
U.S. ex rel. Schwarzkopf v Uhl	
137 F. 2d 878; 12 A.D. (1943–45) 188 (No. 54)	Ch: 1 N: 259
Ullman v Ministere Public	
(1915–16) RDIP 67	Ch: 1 N: 260
Union of India v H. Mohmed	
[1954] A.I.R. 505 (Bom.)	Ch: 13 N: 155
Union of India v Ghaus Mohammed	
[1961] A.I.R. 1526	Ch: 3 N: 204
Vagrancy Cases	
ECHR Series A No. 12 (1971)	Ch: 7 N: 233
van Andel, Jonkers, van Rattingen and van de Loo	
8 August 1977, N.J. (1977) No. 567 Court of Appeal Arnheim	Ch: 3 N: 167
Van Duyn v Home Office: see Case 41/74, Van Duyn v Home Office	
Van Rensburg v Ballinger	
[1950] 4 S.A. 427	Ch: 5 N: 17
Vincent, Re v M.E.I.	
[1983] 148 DLR (3d) 385 (F.C.A.)	Ch: 12 N: 293

Table of Statutes
(including European Community Legislation)

| 1967 | Entry Control (Ascension) Ordinance (No. 1) | | |
| 1979 | Entry Control (Ascension) Ordinance (No. 1) | Ch: 4 | N: 128 |

AUSTRALIA

1881	(State of Victoria) Chinese Act	Ch: 2	N: 78
1901	Pacific Island Labourer Act (No. 16)	Ch: 2	N: 12
1901	Immigration Restriction Bill	Ch: 1	N: 102
		Ch: 2	N: 61
1901	Immigration Restriction Act (No. 17)	Ch: 2	N: 61
1905	Immigration Restriction (Amendment) Act (No. 17)		
1908	Immigration Restriction Act (No. 25)	Ch: 2	N: 61
1910	Immigration Restriction Act (No. 10)	Ch: 2	N: 61
1912	Immigration Act (No. 38)	Ch: 1	N: 81
		Ch: 2	N: 61
1920	Immigration Act (No. 31)	Ch: 1	N: 81
		Ch: 2	N: 61
1924	Immigration Act (No. 47)	Ch: 1	N: 81
1925	Immigration Act (No. 7)	Ch: 1	N: 81
		Ch: 2	N: 61
1930	Immigration Act (No. 56)	Ch: 1	N: 81
		Ch: 2	N: 61
1930	Immigration Act (No. 56)	Ch: 1	N: 81
		Ch: 2	N: 61
1932	Immigration Act (No. 26)	Ch: 1	N: 81
		Ch: 2	N: 61
1933	Immigration Act (No. 37)	Ch: 1	N: 81
		Ch: 2	N: 61
1935	Immigration Act (No. 13)	Ch: 1	N: 81
		Ch: 2	N: 61
1940	Immigration Act (No. 36)	Ch: 1	N: 81
		Ch: 2	N: 61
1946	Immigration Act (No. 31)	Ch: 1	N: 81
		Ch: 2	N: 61
1948	Immigration Act (No. 86)	Ch: 1	N: 81
		Ch: 2	N: 61
1948	Nationality and Citizenship Act (No. 83)	Ch: 1	N: 102
1950	Nationality and Citizenship Act (No. 58)	Ch: 1	N: 102
1952	Nationality and Citizenship Act (No. 70)	Ch: 1	N: 102
1953	Nationality and Citizenship Act (No. 58)	Ch: 1	N: 102
1955	Nationality and Citizenship Act (No. 1)	Ch: 1	N: 102
1958	Nationality and Citizenship Act (No. 63)	Ch: 1	N: 102
1959	Nationality and Citizenship Act (No. 79)	Ch: 1	B: 102
1960	Nationality and Citizenship Act (No. 82)	Ch: 1	N: 102
1966	Nationality and Citizenship Act (No. 11)	Ch: 1	N: 102
1967	Nationality and Citizenship Act (No. 11)	Ch: 1	N: 102
1969	Nationality and Citizenship Act (No. 22)	Ch: 1	N: 102
1948–69	Citizenship Act	Ch: 1	N: 81

1958	Migration Act 1958 (No. 62)	Ch: 2	N: 179
		Ch: 5	N: 13
		Ch: 5	N: 42
		Ch: 8	N: 180
		Ch: 8	N: 180
		Ch: 10	N: 113
		Ch: 13	N: 117
1958	Nationality and Citizenship Act (No. 85)	Ch: 2	N: 102
1959	Migration Regulations (No. 35)	Ch: 9	N: 162
		Ch: 10	N: 114
1959	Migration Regulations (No. 89)	Ch: 9	N: 162
		Ch: 10	N: 114
1964	Migration Regulation (No. 158)	Ch: 9	N: 162
		Ch: 10	N: 114
1966	Migration Regulation (No. 86)	Ch: 9	N: 162
		Ch: 10	N: 114
1966	Migration Act (No. 19)	Ch: 5	N: 42
		Ch: 9	N: 164
1970	Migration Regulations (No. 41)	Ch: 9	N: 162
		Ch: 10	N: 114
1976	Migration Regulations (No. 225)	Ch: 9	N: 162
		Ch: 10	N: 114
1979	Migration Regulations (No. 234)	Ch: 9	N: 162
		Ch: 10	N: 114
1979	Migration Amendment Act (No. 117)	Ch: 9	N: 160
1980	Migration Amendment (No. 2) Act (No. 175)	Ch: 9	N: 160
1983	Migration Amendment Act (No. 112)	Ch: 9	N: 160
1983	Migration Law (No. 117)	Ch: 5	N: 13
1984	Taxation Laws Amendment Act (No. 123)	Ch: 9	N: 164

AUSTRIA

1867	Basic Law of State of 21 December RGBl No. 142 as amended 1 January 1975	Ch: 3	N: 14
1954	Fremdenpolizeigesetz of 17 March BGBl 1954/75	Ch: 5	N: 2
1974	Fremdenpolizeigesetz Amendment of 11 July BGBl 1974/422	Ch: –	N: –

BAHAMAS

1973	Constitution of 10 July	Ch: 3	N: 15
		Ch: 4	N: 20

BAHRAIN

1973	Constitution of June	Ch: 3	N: 56

BARBADOS

1927	Expulsion of Undesirables Act	Ch: 2	N: 169

1939	Aliens Restriction Act	Ch: 2	N: 169
1952	Immigration Act	Ch: 2	N: 169
		Ch: 11	N: 104
1066	Constitution of 13 December	Ch: 3	N: 16
1976	Immigration Act	Ch: 10	N: 96
		Ch: 10	N: 97

BELGIUM

1856	Extradition Law of 22 March	Ch: 7	N: 103
1930	Royal Order of 15 December	Ch: 2	N: 152
1963	Extradition Law of 1 October	Ch: 7	N: 103
1971	Law of 30 July	Ch: 2	N: 187
1976	Law of 22 July	Ch: 2	N: 187
1979	Royal Decree of 5 October	Ch: 2	N: 185
1980	Law of 15 December	Ch: 11	N: 123
		Ch: 13	N: 117
		Ch: 5	N: 7
1981	Royal Decree of 8 October	Ch: 12	N: 285
		Ch: 5	N: 7

BELIZE

| 1981 | Constitution of 28 July | Ch: 3 | N: 17 |

BENIN

| 1979 | Constitution | Ch: 3 | N: 56 |

BOLIVIA

1880	Constitution	Ch: 2	N: 96
1887	Consular Regulations of 4 July	Ch: 5	N: 64
1967	Constitution of 2 February	Ch: 3	N: 18
		Ch: 11	N: 18

BOTSWANA

| 1966 | Constitution of 30 September | Ch: 3 | N: 56 |
| 1981 | Employment of Non-Citizens Act (No. 11) | Ch: 9 | N: 88 |

BRAZIL

1891	Constitution	Ch: 2	N: 95
1969	Constitution of 17 October	Ch: 3	N: 19
		Ch: 11	N: 18

BRITISH INDIAN OCEAN TERRITORY

| 1971 | Immigration Ordinance (No. 1) | Ch: 4 | N: 128 |

| 1981 | Law Revision (Miscellaneous Amendments) Ordinance | Ch: 4 | N: 128 |

BRITISH VIRGIN ISLANDS

| 1977 | Immigration and Passport Ordinance (No. 9) | Ch: 4 | N: 132) |

BULGARIA

| 1971 | Constitution of 18 May | Ch: 11 | N: 18 |
| | | Ch: 12 | N: 83 |

BURKINA FASO

| 1984 | Ordonnance No. 84–049/CNR/Res of 4 August | Ch: 3 | N: 200 |

BURMA

| 1974 | Constitution of 3 January | Ch: 4 | N: 21 |
| | | Ch: 11 | N: 18 |

BURUNDI

| 1981 | Constitution of 20 November | Ch: 3 | N: 56 |

BYELORUSSION S.S.R.

| 1937 | Constitution of 19 February | Ch: 11 | N: 18 |

CAMEROONS

| 1972 | Constitution of 20 May | Ch: 11 | N: 18 |

CANADA

1794	Nova Scotia Act 38 Geo. III, c.1	Ch: 2	N: 32
1828	Naturalization Act (Upper Canada) 9 Geo. IV, c. 21	Ch: 1	N: 70
1831	Naturalization Act (Lower Canada) I Will IV, c. 53	Ch: 1	N: 70
1841	Naturalization Act 4 & 5 Vict c. 7	Ch: 1	N: 70
1849	Naturalization Act 12 Vict c. 197	Ch: 1	N: 70
1851	(Nova Scotia) Aliens Act	Ch: 2	N: 47
1854	Naturalization Act 18 Vict c. 6	Ch: 1	N: 70
1858	Naturalization Act 22 Vict c. 1	Ch: 1	N: 70
1864	(Nova Scotia) Aliens Act	Ch: 2	N: 47
1869	Immigration Act 32–33 Vict c. 10	Ch: 2	N: 64
1872	Immigration Act 35 Vict c. 23	Ch: 2	N: 65
1872	Dominion Lands Act 35 Vict c. 23	Ch: 2	N: 67
1878	Homestead Exemption Act 41 Vict c. 15	Ch: 2	N: 66
1883	Dominion Lands Act 46 Vict c. 17	Ch: 2	N: 67
1885	Chinese Immigration Act 48–49 Vict c. 71	Ch: 2	N: 68
1892	Chinese Immigration (Amendment) Act 55–56 Vict c. 25	Ch: 2	N: 69

524

1897	Alien Labour Act 60–61 Vict c. 11	Ch: 2	N: 81
1902	Immigration Act 2 Ed VII, c. 14	Ch: 2	N: 108
1905	Immigration Act 4–5 Ed VII, c.14	Ch: 2	N: 108
1906	Immigration Act 6 Ed VII, c.19	Ch: 2	N: 108
1907	Immigration Act 6–7 Ed VII, c. 19	Ch: 2	N: 108
1908	Immigration Act 7–8 Ed VII, c. 33	Ch: 2	N: 108
1908	P.C. 2037 of 11 September	Ch: 2	N: 109
1910	Immigration Act 9–10 Ed VII, c. 17	Ch: 2	N: 108
1910	Order in Council P.C. 485 of 15 March	Ch: 2	N: 109
1911	Immigration Act 1–2 Geo. V, c. 2	Ch: 2	N: 108
1919	P.C. 1204 of 9 June	Ch: 2	N: 70
1922	P.C. 1206 of 7 June	Ch: 2	N: 152
1923	P.C. 182 of 31 January	Ch: 2	N: 71
1927	Immigration Act 18–19 Geo. V, c. 29	Ch: 2	N: 71
1930	P.C. 1966 of 14 August	Ch: 2	N: 71
1930	P.C. 2115 of 16 September	Ch: 1	N: 80
		Ch: 2	N: 71
1947	Immigration Act, 11 Geo. VI, c. 19	Ch: 2	N: 163
1950	An Act to Amend the Canadian Citizenship Act 14 Geo. VI, c. 29	Ch: 1	N: 101
1952	Immigration Act 1 Eliz 11 c. 42	Ch: 2	N: 164
		Ch: 5	N: 11
1976–77	Immigration Act s.c. 1976–77 c. 52	Ch: 5	N: 10
		Ch: 5	N: 41
		Ch: 9	N: 157
		Ch: 10	N: 109
		Ch: 11	N: 78
		Ch: 13	N: 118
1978	Immigration Regulations S.O.R/78–172 (1978)112	Ch: 11	N: 80, 81, 82, 83, 84, 87, 124, 155
1982	Canada Act c. 11	Ch: 3	N: 20
1982	Constitution Act (Schedule B to Canada Act 1982 c. 11)	Ch: 3	N: 20

CAPE VERDE

| 1980 | Constitution of 7 October | Ch: 4 | N: 22 |

CAYMAN ISLANDS

1971	Caymananian Protection Law (No. 23)	Ch: 4	N: 135
1977	Caymananian Protection (Amendment) Laws (No. 7); (No. 22) and (No. 32)	Ch: 4	N: 135
1979	Caymananian Protection (Amendment) Laws (No. 13) and (No. 3)	Ch: 4	N: 135
1982	Caymananian Protection (Amendment) Law (No. 3)	Ch: 4	N: 135
1983	Caymananian Protection (Amendment) Law (No. 13)	Ch: 4	N: 135
1984	Caymananian Protection (Amendment) Law (No. 24)	Ch: 4	N: 135
1984	Cayman Islands (Constitution) (Amendment) Order S.I. No. 126	Ch: 4	N: 135

526

1949	Constitution of November 1949	Ch: 3	N: 23
		Ch: 11	N: 18
		Ch: 12	N: 94
1971	Law of 28 July (No. 4812)	Ch: 4	N: 183
1977	Constitutional Amendment of 15 June	Ch: 12	N: 94
1981	Regulations of 18 December	Ch: 4	N: 183

CUBA

1932	Presidential Decree of 19 April	Ch: 2	N: 152
1976	Constitution of 24 February	Ch: 11	N: 18
		Ch: 12	N: 100

CYPRUS

1952	Aliens and Immigration Regulations	Ch: 5	N: 7
1960	Constitution	Ch: 3	N: 24
1967	Republic of Cyprus Citizenship Law	Ch: 1	N: 109

CZECHOSLOVAKIA

1928	Law No. 39 of 13 March	Ch: 2	N: 152
1960	Constitution of 11 July	Ch: 11	N: 18
		Ch: 12	N: 85

DENMARK

1926	Law of 31 March	Ch: 2	N: 152
1983	Aliens Act of 8 June (No. 226)	Ch: 3	N: 117
		Ch: 5	N: 3
		Ch: 11	N: 99

DOMINICA

1978	Constitution of 25 July	Ch: 4	N: 25
		Ch: 11	N: 18

ECUADOR

1916	Presidential Decree of 27 October	Ch: 5	N: 64
1939	Aliens Law of February 1938	Ch: 12	N: 121
1967	Constitution of 25 May	Ch: 11	N: 18
1971	Ley de Migracion 30 December Decreto No. 1899	Ch: 8	N: 92
1971	Reglamento para Ley de Migracion 30 December Decreto No. 1900	Ch: 8	N: 92

EGYPT

1980	Constitution of 22 May	Ch: 4	N: 26
		Ch: 11	N: 18
		Ch: 12	N: 101

EL SALVADOR

1962	Constitution	Ch: 12	N: 92
1983	Constitution of 15 December	Ch: 4	N: 27
		Ch: 11	N: 18
		Ch: 12	N: 93

EQUATORIAL GUINEA

1982	Constitution of 15 August	Ch: 4	N: 28

EUROPEAN COMMUNITIES

1954	European Coal and Steel Community Decision of 8 December	Ch: 6	N: 5
1958	Council Regulation 3/58 of 15 December on Social Security of Migrant Workers, O.J. 1958, 561	Ch: 6	N: 83
1958	Council Regulation 4/58 of 15 December on Social Security of Migrant Workers, O.J. 1958, 597	Ch: 6	N: 83
1961	European Coal and Steel Community Decision of 16 May	Ch: 6	N: 5
1962	Euratom Council Directive of 5 March	Ch: 6	N: 5
1963	E.C. Council Directives 63/261 of 2 April concerning Agriculture, J.O. 1963 1323, O.J. Sp. Ed 1963–64 19	Ch: 6	N: 57
1963	E.C. Council Directives 63/262 of 2 April concerning Agriculture, J.O. 1963 1326, O.J. Sp. Ed 1963–64 22	Ch: 6	N: 57
1964	E.C. Council Directive 64/221 15 February on Coordinations of Special Measures concerning the Movement and Residence of Foreign Nationals O.J. Sp. Ed. 1963–64 117	Ch: Int	N: 33
		Ch: 6	N: 20, 67
		Ch: 7	N: 21
1964	E.C. Council Directive 64/223 of 25 February concerning Wholesale Trade J.O. 1964 863 O.J. Sp. Ed 1963–64, 123	Ch: 6	N: 57
1964	E.C. Council Directive 64/224 of 25 February concerning Activities of Intermediaries in Commerce, Industry and Small Craft Industries J.O. 1964 869 O.J. Sp. Ed. 1963–64 125	Ch: 6	N: 57
1964	E.C. Council Declaration 64/305 of 25 March on Refugees, J.O. 22 May 1964, No. 78	Ch: 6	N: 40
1964	E.C. Council Directive 64/427 of 7 July concerning Self-Employed Persons in Manufacturing Industries, O.J. Sp. Ed. 1963–64 148	Ch: 6	N: 34
1965	E.C. Council Directive 65/264 of 13 May concerning the Film Industry J.O. 1965 1437 O.J. Sp. Ed. 1965–66 62	Ch: 6	N: 57
1967	E.C. Council Directive 67/43 of 12 January concerning Activities of self-emploed persons concerned with Real Esatate J.O. 1967 140 O.J. Sp. Ed. 1967 3	Ch: 6	N: 57
1967	E.C. Council Directive 67/530 of 25 July concerning Agriculture J.O. 1967 190/1, O.J. Sp. Ed 1967 228	Ch: 6	N: 57

528

1967	E.C. Council Directive 67/531 of 25 July concerning Agriculture, J.O. 1967 190/3, O.J. Sp. Ed 1967 230	Ch: 6	N: 57
1967	E.C. Council Directive 67/532 of 25 July concerning Agriculture J.O. 1967 190/5, O.J. Sp. Ed 1967 232	Ch: 6	N: 57
1968	E.C. Council Directive 68/360 of 15 October on the Abolition of Restrictions on Movement & Residence O.J. Sp. Ed. 1968 485	Ch: Int	N: 33
		Ch: 3	N: 9, 126, 208
		Ch: 6	N: 14, 21
		Ch: 7	N: 168
		Ch: 10	N: 16, 51
1968	E.C. Council Regulation 1612/68 of 15 October on Freedom of Movement O.J. Sp. Ed 1968 475	Ch: Int	N: 33
		Ch: 6	N: 14
		Ch: 7	N: 191
		Ch: 11	N: 32, 96
1968	E.C. Council Directive 68/369 of 15 October concerning the Film Industry J.O. 1968 L 260/22 O.J. Sp. Ed 1968 520	Ch: 6	N: 57
1968	E.C. Council Directive 68/363 of 15 October concerning Self-Employed Persons in Retail Trade J.O 1968 L 260/1 O.J. Sp. Ed 1968 476	Ch: 6	N: 57
1968	E.C. Council Directive 68/365 of 15 October concerning Self-Employed Persons in Food Manufacturing & Beverage Industries J.O 1968 L 260/9 O.J. Sp. Ed 1968 505	Ch: 6	N: 57
1968	E.C. Council Directive 68/415 of 20 December concerning Agriculture, J.O 1968 L 308/17 O.J. Sp. Ed 1968 589	Ch: 6	N: 57
1970	E.C. Council Regulation 1251/70 of 29 June on the Right of Workers to Remain in the Territory of Member States, J.O. 1970 L 142/24; O.J. Sp. Ed. 1970, 402	Ch: 6	N: 14
1970	E.C. Council Directive 71/18 of 16 December concerning Agriculture J.O 1971 L 8/24 O.J. Sp. Ed 1971, 23	Ch: 6	N: 57
1971	E.C. Council Regulation 1408/71 on the application of social security schemes, O.J. Sp. Ed. 1971, 416.	Ch: 6	N: 84–104
		Ch: 7	N: 161, 163
1972	E.C. Council Directive 72/194 of 18 May	Ch: Int	N: 33
1972	E.C. Council Regulation 574/72 of 21 March 1972, O.J. Ed. 1972, 159	Ch: 6	N: 84
1973	E.C. Council Directive 73/148 of 21 May on Abolition of Restrictions on Movement and Residence with Regard to Establishment and the Provision of Services O.J. 1973 L 172/10	Ch: 6	N: 46
1974	E.C. Council Directive 75/34 of 17 December on the Right to Remain after Pursuing a Self-Employed Activity, O.J. 1975 L 14/10	Ch: Int	N: 42
1974	E.C. Council Directive 75/35 of 17 December extending the Scope of Directive 64/221, O.J. 1975 L 14/14	Ch: –	N: –
1975	E.C. Council Directive 75/117 of 10 February on the Principle of Equal Pay for Men and Women O.J. 1975 45/19	Ch: 9	N: 55

1975	E.C. Council Directive 75/362 of 16 June concerning the Mutual Recognition of Diplomas in Medicine O.J. 1975 L 167/1	Ch: 6	N: 58
1975	E.C. Council Directive 75/363 of 16 June concerning the coordination of Provisions in Respect of Activities of Doctors O.J. 1975 L 169/14	Ch: 6	N: 58
1975	E.C. Court Directives 75/368 of 16 June on Various Activities O.J. 1975 L 167/22	Ch: 6	N: 57
1975	E.C. Council Directives 75/369 of 16 June on Various Activities O.J. 1975 L. 167/29	Ch: 6	N: 57
1976	E.C. Council Regulation 311/76 on Compilation of Statistics on Migrant Workers, O.J. 1976 L 39/1	Ch: 6	N: 105
1976	E.C. Council Regulation 312/76 of 9 February O.J 1976 L 38/2	Ch: 6	N: 14
1977	E.C. Council Directive 77/249 of 22 March to Facilitate the Effective Exercise by Lawyers of Freedom to Provide Services O.J. 1977 L 78/17	Ch: 6	N: 59
1977	E.C. Council Directive 77/452 of 27 June concerning the Mutual Recognition of Diplomas of Nurses O.J. 1977 L 176/1	Ch: 6	N: 58
1977	E.C. Council Directive 77/486 of 25 July on Provision of Free Education to Children of Migrant Workers, O.J. 1977 L 199/32	Ch: 6	N: 54
1978	E.C. Council Directive 78/686 of 25 July concerning the Mutual Recognition of Diplomas in Dentistry O.J. 1978 L 233/1	Ch: 6	N: 58
1978	E.C. Council Directive 78/1028 of 18 December concerning the Mutual Recognition of Diplomas in Veterinary Medicine O.J. 1978 L 362/1	Ch: 6	N: 58
1979	E.C. Council Directive 80/154 of 18 December concerning the Mutual Recognition of Diplomas in Midwifery O.J. 1980 L 33/1	Ch: 6	N: 58
1980	Decision 1/80 (Council Doc. 8795/1/80) of Council Association	Ch: 3	N: 7
1982	E.C. Council Regulation 1390/81 of 1 July	Ch: 6	N: 92
1983	E.C. Council Regulation 2001/83 of 2 June amending and updating Regulation 1408/71 O.J. 1983 L 230/6	Ch: 6	N: 88
		Ch: 7	N: 161

FALKLAND ISLANDS

1965	Immigration Ordinance (No. 10)	Ch: 4	N: 140, 144
1967	Immigration (Amendment) Ordinance (No. 12)	Ch: 4	N: 140
1968	Immigration (Amendment) Ordinance (No. 10)	Ch: 4	N: 140
1974	Immigration (Amendment) Ordinance (No. 10)	Ch: 4	N: 140

FIJI

1970	Constitution of 30 September	Ch: 4	N: 29

530

1981	Decree No. 81–891 of 1 October J.O.R.F. 2 October 1981 p. 2687 D (L) 1981 345	Ch: 9	N: 148
1981	Administrative Circular of 22 October D 1981 (L) 384, J.O.R.F. 28 November 1981 p. 10396	Ch: 9	N: 147
1981	Law No. 81–973 of 29 October J.O.R.F. 30 October 1981 p. 2970 D 1981 (L) 361	Ch: 2	N: 185
		Ch: 9	N: 150
		Ch: 11	N: 94
		Ch: 13	N: 34
1984	Law No. 84–622 of 17 July J.O.R.F. 19 July 1984 p. 2324 D 1984 (L) 458	Ch: 5	N: 3
		Ch: 9	N: 139, 151
		Ch: 11	N: 91
1986	Law No. 86–1025 of 9 September 1986, D 1986 (L) 474	Ch: 5	N: 3

GABON

1975	Constitution of May 1975	Ch: 11	N: 18
		Ch: 12	N: 102

GAMBIA

1970	Constitution of 24 April	Ch: 4	N: 30

GERMANY (DEMOCRATIC REPUBLIC)

1979	Constitution of 7 October	Ch: 3	N: 56
		Ch: 11	N: 18
		Ch: 12	N: 87
1979	Aliens Act of 28 June	Ch: 3	N: 192
1979	Decree on Passport and Visa Matters of 28 June	Ch: 3	N: 183, 192
1982	Order Governing Travel of Citizens of the DDR of 15 February	Ch: 3	N: 192
1983	Ordinance on Matters of Family Reunification of 15 September	Ch: 3	N: 192

GERMANY (FEDERAL REPUBLIC)

1935	Reichburgergesetz (State Citizenship Law) of 9 May, RGBl 1938 I 1053	Ch: 4	N: 169
1937	Gesetz uber das Pass-, das Auslanderpolizei- und das Meldewesen sowie uber das Ausweisweren (Law on Passports, Aliens Control, Reporting of Changes of Adress and Identity Cards) of 11 May, RGBl 1937 I, 589	Ch: 2	N: 158
1938	Auslanderpolizeiverordnung (Aliens Control Decree) of 22 August, RGBl 1938 I, 593	Ch: 4	N: 169
1949	Grundgesetz (Basic Law)	Ch: 6	N: 116
		Ch: 11	N: 18
		Ch: 12	N: 77
1952	Gesetz uber das Passwesen (Passport Law) of 4 March, BGBl 1952 I, 290	Ch: 3	N: 183

532

1982	Auslandergesetz (Aliens Law of 21 October (Bremen)	Ch: 7	N: 236
1983	Wehrpflichtgesetz (Conscription Law) of 6 May, BGBl 1983 I, 529	Ch: 3	N: 185
1983	Gesetz uber der Zivildienst der Kriegsdienstverweiger (Civilian Service Act) of 29 September, BGBl 1983 I, 1221	Ch: 3	N: 186
1983	Gesetz zur forderung der Rukketirbereitschaft von Auslander (Act to Promote the Preparation of Foreign Workers to Return) of 28 November, BGBl 1983 i, 1377	Ch: 9	N: 136
1985	Gesetz zur Regelung der gewerbsmassiger Arbeitnehmeruberlassung (Law on the Protection of Subcontracted Labour) of 25 June, BGBl 1985 I, 1069	Ch: 9	N: 134
1985	Auslandergesetz (Aliens Law) of 28 April, BGBl 1985 I, 353	Ch: 2	N: 187
1986	Wehrpflichtgesetz (Conscription Law) of 13 June, BGBl 1986 I, 879	Ch: 3	N: 185

GHANA

1933	Aliens Act	Ch: 13	N: 117
1963	Aliens Act (No. 160)	Ch: 9	N: 178
1963	Aliens Regulations L 1 265	Ch: 9	N: 179
1965	Aliens (Amendment) Act (No. 265)	Ch: 9	N: 178
1973	Selective Alien Employment Tax Decree N.R.C.D. No. 201	Ch: 9	N: 180
1974	Aliens (Registration) Amendment Regulations L.I. 883	Ch: 11	N: 101
1975	Aliens Registration (Amendment No. 2) Regulations L.I. 1052	Ch: 11	N: 102
1985	Investment Code PNDCL 116	Ch: 9	Ch: 180

GIBRALTAR

1962	Immigration Control Ordinance No. 12	Ch: 4	N: 137
1962	Gibraltarian Status Ordinance (No. 13)	Ch: 4	N: 138
1962	Immigration Control (Amendment) Ordinance (No. 19)	Ch: 4	N: 137
1963	Gibraltarian Status (Amendment) Ordinance (No. 13)	Ch: 4	N: 138
1963	Immigration Control (Amendment) Ordinance (No. 20)	Ch: 4	N: 137
1967	Immigration Control (Amendment) Ordinance (No. 11)	Ch: 4	N: 137
1972	Immigration Control (Amendment) Ordinance (No. 19)	Ch: 4	N: 137
		Ch: 4	N: 142
1976	Immigration Control (Amendment) (No. 2) Ordinance (No. 17)	Ch: 4	N: 137
1983	Immigration Control (Amendment) Ordinance (No. 7)	Ch: 4	N: 137
		Ch: 4	N: 142
1983	Administration of Justice Ordinance (No. 12)	Ch: 4	N: 137
1985	European Communities (Spanish and Portuguese Accession Ordinance) (No. 21)	Ch: 4	N: 142
1985	European Communities (Amendment) Ordinance (No. 2)	Ch: 4	N: 142

534

GREECE

1926	Royal Decree of 10 March	Ch: 2	N: 152
1927	Royal Decree of 17 June	Ch: 2	N: 152
1975	Constitution of 7 June	Ch: 4	N: 31

GUATEMALA

1982	Fundamental Statute of Government, Decree Law No. 24	Ch: 12	N: 96
1982	Decree Law No. 36	Ch: 3	N: 25
		Ch: 4	N: 32
		Ch: 12	N: 96
1985	Constitution of 31 May	Ch: 11	N: 18

GUINEA (POPULAR REVOLUTIONARY REPUBLIC)

1982	Constitution of 14 May	Ch: 12	N: 92

GUYANA

1980	Constitution of 20 February	Ch: 3	N: 26

HAITI

1864	Aliens Immigration Law of 21 September	Ch: 2	N: 130
1903	Immigration Law of 13 August	Ch: 2	N: 96
1983	Constitution of 31 August	Ch: 12	N: 98

HONDURAS

1929	Decree No. 101	Ch: 2	N: 152
1982	Constitution of 11 January	Ch: 11	N: 18

HONG KONG

1971	Immigration Ordinance (No. 55)	Ch: 4	N: 129
		Ch: 4	N: 141
1971	Immigration Ordinance (No. 75)	Ch: 4	N: 129
		Ch: 4	N: 141
1972	Legal Notice No. 183/172	Ch: 4	N: 129
1972	Immigration Ordinance (No. 57)	Ch: 4	N: 129
1976	Immigration Ordinance (No. 52)	Ch: 4	N: 129
1977	Immigration Ordinance (No. 47)	Ch: 4	N: 129
1979	Immigration Ordinance (No. 3)	Ch: 4	N: 129
1979	Immigration Ordinance (No. 42)	Ch: 4	N: 129
1979	Immigration Ordinance (No. 61)	Ch: 4	N: 129
1980	Legal Notice No. 302/80	Ch: 4	N: 129
1980	Legal Notice No. 315/80	Ch: 4	N: 129
1980	Immigration Ordinance (No. 15)	Ch: 4	N: 129
1980	Immigration Ordinance (No. 62)	Ch: 4	N: 129

1981	Immigration Ordinance (No. 35)	Ch: 4	N: 129
1981	Immigration Ordinance (No. 64)	Ch: 4	N: 129
1981	Immigration Ordinance (No. 66)	Ch: 4	N: 129
1982	Legal Notice No. 346/82	Ch: 4	N: 129
1982	Legal Notice No. 392/82	Ch: 4	N: 129
1982	Immigration Ordinance (No. 42)	Ch: 4	N: 129
1982	Immigration Ordinance (No. 78)	Ch: 4	N: 129
1982	Immigration Ordinance (No. 79)	Ch: 4	N: 129
1983	Legal Notice No. 87/83	Ch: 4	N: 129
1983	Immigration Ordinance (No. 55)	Ch: 4	N: 129
1984	Legal Notice No. 382/84	Ch: 4	N: 129
1984	Immigration Ordinance (No. 24)	Ch: 4	N: 129
1984	Immigration Ordinance (No. 31)	Ch: 4	N: 129
1985	Immigration Ordinance (No. 40)	Ch: 4	N: 129
1985	Hong Kong Act	Ch: 1	N: 147
1986	Hong Kong (British Nationality) Order (Cmnd 9637) of 17 October	Ch: 1	N: 147

HUNGARY

1929	Law 1929/IV	Ch: 2	N: 152
1930	Decree No. 100 000	Ch: 2	N: 152
1949	Constitution of 20 August	Ch: 11	N: 18
		Ch: 12	N: 86

ICELAND

1951	Law No. 39 of 15 March 1951	Ch: 5	N: 7
1952	Law. No. 100 of 23 December 1952	Ch: 5	N: 7

INDIA

1926	Indian Naturalisation Act	Ch: 2	N: 142
1935	Government of India Act	Ch: 2	N: 142
1943	Reciprocity Act (No. 9)	Ch: 2	N: 142
1944	Reciprocity (South Africa) Rules	Ch: 2	N: 142
1944	Reciprocity (Natal and the Transvaal) Rules	Ch: 2	N: 142
1944	Reciprocity (South Africa) (Local Franchise) Rules	Ch: 2	N: 142
1946	Foreigners Act	Ch: 13	N: 117
1948	Foreigners Order	Ch: 10	N: 108
1949	Constitution of 26 November	Ch: 11	N: 18
1950	Passport (Entry into India) Rules	Ch: 10	N: 106
1955	Indian Citizenship Act (No. 57)	Ch: 1	N: 106
1967	Passport Act (No. 15)	Ch: 3	N: 211
1968	Passport (Entry into India) Agreement Rules G.S.R.	Ch: 4	N: 80
1973	Foreign Exchange Regulation act (No. 46)	Ch: 9	N: 190
1979	Inter-State Migrant Workmen (Regulation of Employment and Conditions of Service) Act (No. 30)	Ch: 10	N: 43

1962	Jamaican Nationality Act (No. 8)	Ch: 2	N: 166, 168
1964	Foreign Nationals and Commonwealth Citizens (Employment) Act 1964 (No. 48)	Ch: 2	N: 166, 168
1964	Foreign Nationals and Commonwealth Citizens (Employment) Act (Appointed Day) Notice	Ch: 4	N: 122
1964	Foreign Nationals and Commonwealth Citizens (Employment) Act	Ch: 5	N: 52
1964	Foreign Nationals and Commonwealth Citizens (Employment) Exemption Regulations	Ch: 5 Ch: 11	N: 52 N: 107

JAPAN

1947	Constitution of 3 May	Ch: 3	N: 29
1951	Immigration Control and Refugee Recognition Act (Cabinet Order 319)	Ch: 3 Ch: 10	N: 175 N: 116
1952	Imperial Ordinance concerning Orders to be issued in Consequence of the Acceptance of the Potsdam Declaration (No. 126)	Ch: 10	N: 121
1953	Surrender of a Fugitive from Justice Law of 21 July (No. 68)	Ch: 13 Ch: 3	N: 136 N: 178
1965	Special Immigration Laws for the Enforcement of the Agreement on the Legal Status and Treatment of the Nationals of the People's Republic of Korea Residing in Japan (No. 146)	Ch: 10	N: 121

JORDAN

1952	Constitution of 1 January	Ch: 3 Ch: 4	N: 30 N: 35
1984	Constitution of 1 August	Ch: 12	N: 101

KENYA

1965	Constitution of Kenya (Amendment) Act (No. 14)	Ch: 4	N: 77
1967	Immigration Act (No. 25)	Ch: 4 Ch: 5 Ch: 9	N: 77 N: 42 N: 185
1967	Immigration Regulations	Ch: 4 Ch: 11	N: 77 N: 103
1967	Trade Licensing Act (No. 33)	Ch: 4 Ch: 9	N: 77 N: 185
1968	Trade Licensing (General Business Areas) Order	Ch: 4	N: 77
1968	Trade Licensing (Specific Goods) Order	Ch: 4	N: 71
1969	Constitution of Kenya Act (No. 5)	Ch: 3	N: 31
1969	Trade Licensing (Amendment) Act (No. 17)	Ch: 4	N: 77
1968–69	Immigration Amendment Regulations	Ch: 4	N: 77

538

KIRIBATI

1969	Constitution of 12 July	Ch: 3	N: 32
		Ch: 4	N: 36

KOREA (DEMOCRATIC PEOPLE'S REPUBLIC OF SOUTH KOREA)

1967	Law (No. 1900 on Control of Exit and Entry) of 3 March	Ch: 5	N: 146
		Ch: 5	N: 147
1972	Republic of Korea Constitution of 5th Republic of 27 December	Ch: 3	N: 33
		Ch: 4	N: 37
		Ch: 11	N: 18
		Ch: 12	N: 88

KUWAIT

1969	Constitution of 11 November	Ch: 3	N: 34
		Ch: 4	N: 38
		Ch: 11	N: 18
		Ch: 12	N: 101

LATVIA

1929	Regulation of 15 April	Ch: 2	N: 152

LIBERIA

1983	Draft Constitution of 28 January	Ch: 3	N: 35
1984	Constitution of 3 July	Ch: 4	N: 39

LIBYA

1970	Revolutionary Decree of 26 March	Ch: Int	N: 36
1972	Law No. 113 of 28 August	Ch: Int	N: 36
1974	Constitution of 18 January	Ch: 11	N: 18

LIECHTENSTEIN

1921	Constitution of 5 October (as amended)	Ch: 4	N: 40

LITHUANIA

1919	Lithuanian Citizenship of Law of 9 January	Ch: 2	N: 152
1924	Regulations for Residence of Aliens in Lithuania of 15 February	Ch: 2	N: 152
1925	Law of 27 February		
1929	Law of 25 June	Ch: 2	N: 152
1930	Employment Law of 1 January	Ch: 2	N: 152
1931	Emigration Law of 1 January	Ch: 2	N: 152

LUXEMBOURG

| 1972 | Law of 28 March | Ch: 5 | N: 7 |
| | | Ch: 13 | N: 118 |

MADAGASCAR

| 1959 | Constitution f 29 April | Ch: 11 | N: 18 |

MALAYSIA

1957	Constitution of 31 August (as amended)	Ch: 4	N: 41
1957	Federal Constitution of 11 December	Ch: 4	N: 112
1959	Immigration Act (Consolidating Ordiance No. 12)	Ch: 4	N: 113
1963	Immigration Act (No. 27)	Ch: 4	N: 113
1963	Immigration (Transitional Provisions) Order LN 226	Ch: 4	N: 113
1963	Immigration Exemption Order	Ch: 5	N: 42
1964	Constitution (Amendment) Act	Ch: 4	N: 112
1964	Citizenship Rules LN 82	Ch: 4	N: 114
1965	Constitution and Malaysia (Singapore Amendment) Act	Ch: 4	N: 112

MALI

| 1974 | Constitution of 2 June | Ch: 12 | N: 102 |

MALTA

| 1964 | Constitution of 21 September (as amended) | Ch: 3 | N: 36 |
| | | Ch: 4 | N: 42 |

MAURITANIA

| 1978 | Constitution of 10 July | Ch: 4 | N: 43 |

MAURITIUS

1968	Constitution of 4 March	Ch: 3	N: 37
		Ch: 4	N: 44
1973	Immigration Act	Ch: 10	N: 104

MEXICO

| 1931 | Decree of 13 august | Ch: 2 | N: 152 |

MONGOLIA (PEOPLE'S REPUBLIC)

| 1960 | Constitution of 6 July | Ch: 12 | N: 82 |

540

1945	Immigration and Passport Ordinance (No. 7)	Ch: 4	N: 133
1954	Immigration and Passport (Amendment) Ordinance (No. 13)	Ch: 4	N: 133
1956	Immigration and Passport (Amendment) Ordinance (No. 15)	Ch: 4	N: 133
1959	Immigration and Passport (Amendment) Ordinance (No. 10)	Ch: 4	N: 133
1970	Immigration and Passport (Amendment) Ordinance (No. 18)	Ch: 4	N: 133
1973	Immigration and Passport (Amendment) Ordinance (No. 3)	Ch: 4	N: 133
1975	Immigration and Passport (Amendment) Ordinance (No. 25)	Ch: 4	N: 133
1975	Immigration and Passport (Amendment) Ordinance (No. 29)	Ch: 4	N: 133
1979	Immigration and Passport (Amendment) Ordinance (No. 21)	Ch: 4	N: 133
1982	Immigration and Passport (Amendment) Ordinance (No. 24)	Ch: 4	N: 133
1984	Immigration and Passport (Amendment) Ordinance (No. 6)	Ch: 4	N: 133

NEPAL

1962	Constitution of 16 December (as amended)	Ch: 4	N: 45

NETHERLANDS

1858	Act of 4 June	Ch: 2	N: 152
1887	Royal Decree of 27 July	Ch: 2	N: 152
1920	Royal Decree of 11 August	Ch: 2	N: 152
1922	Royal Decree of 31 March	Ch: 2	N: 152
1922	Royal Decree of 12 December	Ch: 2	N: 152
1964	Act on Aliens Work Permits of 22 February	Ch: 9	N: 152
1965	Aliens Act (Vreemdelingenwet) of 13 January	Ch: 3	N: 168
		Ch: 5	N: 4
		Ch: 11	N: 98
		Ch: 12	N: 111
		Ch: 13	N: 117
		Ch: 13	N: 155
1966	Aliens Decree (Vreemdelingenbesluit) of 19 September	Ch: 3	N: 168
		Ch: 11	N: 98
		Ch: 12	N: 111
1966	Aliens Regulation (Voorschrift Vreemdelingen) of 22 September	Ch: 3	N: 168
		Ch: 11	N: 95
1972	Royal Decree of 9 August	Ch: 12	N: 185
1974	Ministry of Justice Aliens Circular of 21 February	Ch: 12	N: 111

1974	Royal Decree of 1 October	Ch: 12	N: 157
1976	Act Concerning the Status of Moluccans	Ch: –	N: –
1978	Administrative Law Review Act	Ch: 12	N: 111
1978	Act of 9 November	Ch: 2	N: 185
		Ch: 9	N: 152
1979	Royal Decree of 26 October (stb. 1979 No. 567)	Ch: 2	N: 185
		Ch: 9	N: 152
1982	Aliens Circular	Ch: 11	N: 95
1983	Revised Constitution	Ch: 12	N: 111

NEW HEBRIDES

1979	Immigration Regulation (No. 18)	Ch: 4	N: 136

NEW ZEALAND

1908	Immigration Restriction Act (No. 78)	Ch: 2	N: 63
		Ch: 4	N: 107
1910	Immigration Restriction Act	Ch: 4	N: 107
1919	Undesirable Immigrants Exclusion Act	Ch: 4	N: 110
1920	Immigration Restriction (Amendment) Act (No. 23)	Ch: 2	N: 63
1923	Immigration Restriction (Amendment) Act	Ch: 4	N: 110
1944	Finance Act (No. 3)	Ch: 2	N: 63
1948	British Nationality and New Zealand Citizenship Act		
	(No. 15)	Ch: 1	N: 103
		Ch: 4	N: 107
1950	Western Samoa Protected Persons Order	Ch: 4	N: 107
1957	Diplomatic Immunities and Privileges Act (No. 21)	Ch: 5	N: 96
1961	Western Samoa Act	Ch: 4	N: 108
1964	Immigration Restriction Act (No. 43)	Ch: 4	N: 110
		Ch: 5	N: 42
		Ch: 5	N: 96
1965	Immigration (Amendment) Act	Ch: 4	N: 110
1968	Immigration (Amendment) Act	Ch: 4	N: 110
1969	Immigration (Amendment) Act	Ch: 4	N: 110
1976	Immigration (Amendment) Act	Ch: 4	N: 110
1977	Immigration (Amendment) Act	Ch: 4	N: 110
1978	Immigration (Amendment) Act	Ch: 4	N: 110
1978	Immigration (Amendment) Act (No. 2)	Ch: 4	N: 110
1979	Immigration (Amendment) Act	Ch: 4	N: 110
1980	Immigration (Amendment) Act	Ch: 4	N: 110
1968	Diplomatic Privileges and Immunities Act (No. 36)	Ch: 5	N: 96
1969	Immigration Amendment Act (No. 83)	Ch: 5	N: 96
1977	Commonwealth Counties Act	Ch: 4	N: 108
1977	Citizenship Act	Ch: 4	N: 108
1980	Passports Act	Ch: 4	N: 110
1983	Foreign Affairs and Overseas Service Act	Ch: 4	N: 108

542

543

PAPUA NEW GUINEA

| 1975 | Constitution of 15 August | Ch: 4 | N: 49 |

PARAGUAY

| 1967 | Constitution of 25 August | Ch: 3 | N: 40 |
| | | Ch: 11 | N: 18 |

PERU

| 1983 | Circular of 21 October | Ch: 8 | N: 91 |

PHILIPPINES

1940	Immigration Act	Ch: 5	N: 40
1950	Aliens Registration Act of 21 June (Rep Act No. 502)	Ch: 5	N: 54
1950	Rules and Regulations Governing Issuance of Certificates of Residence of 13 January	Ch: 5	N: 55
1950	Act to Require the Registration and Fingerprinting of Aliens	Ch: 5	N: 54
1973	Constitution of 10 January	Ch: 3	N: 41
		Ch: 5	N: 153

POLAND

1927	Basic Decree of 4 June	Ch: 2	N: 152
1931	Ministerial Decree of 20 February	Ch: 2	N: 152
1952	Constitution of 22 July	Ch: 11	N: 18
		Ch: 12	N: 80
1963	Aliens Law of 29 March	Ch: 13	N: 117

PORTUGAL

1930	Decree No. 18415 of 3 June	Ch: 2	N: 152
1976	Constitution of 2 April	Ch: 3	N: 42
		Ch: 4	N: 42
		Ch: 11	N: 18
1980	Law No. 38/80 of 1 August	Ch: 11	N: 60–63
1981	Law No. 37/81 of 3 October	Ch: 1	N: 234
1981	Decree Law 264–B181	Ch: 5	N: 7
		Ch: 13	N: 117

ROUMANIA

1930	Royal Decree No. 118 of 1 April	Ch: 2	N: 152
1953	Law of 25 January	Ch: 12	N: 304
1965	Constitution of 21 August	Ch: 11	N: 18
		Ch: 12	N: 81

544

RWANDA

1978	Constitution of 20 December	Ch: 3	N: 43
		Ch: 4	N: 51
		Ch: 11	N: 18

ST CHRISTOPHER, NEVIS AND ANGUILLA

1968	Immigration and Passport (Amendment) Act No. 20	Ch: 4	N: 131
1983	Constitution of 23 June	Ch: 3	N: 44
		Ch: 4	N: 52

ST HELENA

1969	Immigration Land Holding (Restriction) Ordinance (No. 8)	Ch: 4	N: 134
1972	Immigration Ordinance (No. 6)	Ch: 4	N: 134
1985	Immigration (Amendment) Ordinance (No. 13)	Ch: 4	N: 134

ST LUCIA

| 1979 | Constitution of 22 February | Ch: 3 | N: 45 |
| | | Ch: 4 | N: 53 |

ST VINCENT

| 1979 | Constitution 27 October | Ch: 3 | N: 46 |

SENEGAL

1963	Constitution of 8 March	Ch: 3	N: 55
		Ch: 11	N: 18
		Ch: 12	N: 102

SEYCHELLES

1979	Immigration Decree (No. 18)	Ch: 10	N: 105
1982	Immigration (Amendment) Act (No. 17)	Ch: 10	N: 105
1985	Immigration (Amendment) Act (No. 6)	Ch: 10	N: 105

SIERRA LEONE

| 1978 | Constitution of 14 June (No. 12) | Ch: 3 | N: 47 |
| | | Ch: 4 | N: 55 |

SINGAPORE

| 1963 | Constitution of 5 September | Ch: 4 | N: 56 |

SOLOMON ISLANDS

| 1978 | Constitution of 7 July | Ch: 4 | N: 57 |

SOMALIA

| 1979 | Constitution of August | Ch: 11 | N: 18 |

SOUTH AFRICA

1896	(Transvaal) Act of 25 December	Ch: 2	N: 131
1939	Asiatic (Transvaal Land and Trading) Act (No. 28)	Ch: 2	N: 142
1955	Departure from the Union Regulation Act (No. 34)	Ch: 3	N: 197
1972	Admission of Persons to the Republic Regulation Act (No. 59)	Ch: 10	N: 37
1978	Admission of Persons to the Republic Regulation Act (No. 42)	Ch: 10	N: 37
1979	Admission of Persons to the Republic Regulation Act (No. 6)	Ch: 10	N: 37
1980	Admission of Persons to the Republic Regulation Act (No. 29)	Ch: 10	N: 37
1981	Republic of South Africa Constitution Second Amendment Act (No. 101)	Ch: 10	N: 37
1984	Aliens and Immigration Laws Amendment Act (No. 49)	Ch: 10	N: 37

SPAIN

1923	Royal Decree of 6 July	Ch: 2	N: 152
1930	Law of 5 April	Ch: 2	N: 152
1931	Law of 16 January	Ch: 2	N: 152
1978	Constitution of 29 December	Ch: 3	N: 48
		Ch: 4	N: 58
		Ch: 11	N: 18
1985	Aliens Law of 1 June	Ch: 11	N: 161

SRI LANKA

1948	Citizenship Act (No. 18)	Ch: 1	N: 108
1967	India-Ceylon Agreement Implementation Act (No. 14)	Ch: 13	N: 174
1971	India-Ceylon Agreement Implementation (Amendment) Act (No. 43)	Ch: 13	N: 174

SUDAN

| 1973 | Constitution of 8 May | Ch: 4 | N: 59 |
| 1974 | Regulation of Asylum Act (No. 45) | Ch: 12 | N: 125 |

SWEDEN

| 1894 | Law of 6 August | Ch: 2 | N: 152 |

546

1927	Law of 2 August	Ch: 2	N: 152
1957	Aliens Regulations of 25 January	Ch: 11	N: 100
1974	Instrument of Government	Ch: 4	N: 60
1975	Aliens Act	Ch: 12	N: 112
1980	Utlanningslagen	Ch: 12	N: 114
1980	Aliens Order (No. 377)	Ch: 2	N: 185
1985	Rikspolisstryrelsens Cirkular C.M. 1/85 p. 3	Ch: 12	N: 115

SWITZERLAND

1798	Law of 25 July	Ch: 2	N: 32
1799	Law of 13 February on the Rights of Citizenship and Freedom of Establishment	Ch: 2	N: 32
1874	Constitution of 31 January	Ch: 11	N: 18
1931	Federal Law on the Sojourn and Establishment of Aliens of 26 March	Ch: 2	N: 152
		Ch: 5	N: 7
1968	Decree of 28 February	Ch: 5	N: 18
1969	Decree of 26 March	Ch: 5	N: 18
1979	Loi sur l'asile of 5 October	Ch: 12	N: 183
1983	Ordinance of 20 April	Ch: 2	N: 185

SYRIA (ARAB REPUBLIC)

| 1975 | Constitution of 13 March | Ch: 11 | N: 18 |
| | | Ch: 12 | N: 101 |

TANZANIA

| 1972 | Immigration Act (No. 8) | Ch: 4 | N: 182 |

THAILAND

| 1978 | Constitution of 22 December | Ch: 4 | N: 61 |

TOGO

| 1979 | Constitution of 30 December | Ch: 12 | N; 102 |

TRINIDAD AND TOBAGO

| 1974 | Constitution of 22 January | Ch: 3 | N: 49 |

TRISTAN DA CUNHA

| 1967 | Entry Control (Triastan da Cunha) Ordinance (No. 1) | Ch: 4 | N: 134 |

TUNISIA

1959	Constitution of 1 June	Ch: 3	N: 50
		Ch: 4	N: 62
		Ch: 12	N: 103

TURKEY

1980	Act of Residence and Travel of Aliens No. 5683 of 15 July	Ch: 13	N: 116
1982	Constitution of 9 November	Ch: 3	N: 51
		Ch: 4	N: 63
		Ch: 11	N: 18

TURKS AND CAICOS ISLANDS

1971	Immigration Ordinance No. 4	Ch: 4	N: 129
1974	Immigration Ordinance (Amendment) No. 2	Ch: 4	N: 129
1975	Immigration Ordinance (Amendment) No. 8	Ch: 4	N: 129
1979	Immigration Ordinance (Amendment) No. 9	Ch: 4	N: 129
1979	Banking (Special Provisions) Ordinance (No. 4)	Ch: 4	N: 145

TUVALU

| 1978 | Constitution of 25 July | Ch: 3 | N: 52 |
| | | Ch: 4 | N: 64 |

UGANDA

1967	Constitution of 8 September	Ch: 4	N: 65
1975	Properties and Business (Acquisition) Decree (No. 11)	Ch: 13	N: 193
1975	Assets of Deported Asians (Amendment) Decree (No. 12)	Ch: 13	N: 193
1969	Immigration Act (No. 19)	Ch: 4	N: 77
		Ch: 9	N: 184
		Ch: 13	N: 192
1969	Immigration Regulations (No. 165)	Ch: 4	N: 77
		Ch: 13	N: 192
1969	Trade (Licensing) Act (No. 14)	Ch: 4	N: 77
		Ch: 9	N: 184
1969	Trade (Licensing) (Amendment of Schedule) Instrument	Ch: 4	N: 77
1969	Trade (LIcensing) (Prescription of Forms) Regulation	Ch: 4	N: 77
1969	Trade (Licensing) (Appointment of Licensing Authority) Instrument	Ch: 4	N: 77
1972	Declaration of Assets (Non Citizen Asians) Decree (No. 27) 4–5 October 1972	Ch: 4	N: 86
		Ch: 13	N: 192
1972	(Cancellation of Entry Permits and Certificates of Residence) Decree No. 17	Ch: 4	N: 86
		Ch: 13	N: 192
1982	Expropriated Properties Act	Ch: 13	N: 194

UKRAINIAN S.S.R.

| 1937 | Constitution of 30 January | Ch: 11 | N: 18 |

UNION OF SOVIET SOCIALIST REPUBLICS

–	Criminal Code of the RSFSR	Ch: 3	N: 150
1931	Soviet Citizenship Act No. 22 of 22 April	Ch: 1	N: 186
1933	Decree on Considering the Appeals of Working People and Taking the Necessary Measures in Regard to Them of 14 December	Ch: 3	N: 152
1936	Constitution of 5 December	Ch: 1	N: 179
1938	Soviet Citizenship Act No. 198 of 19 August	Ch: 1	N: 179
1968	Edict of the Praesidium of USSR Supreme Soviet of 12 April	Ch: 3	N: 152
1970	Statute on Entry and Exit Confirmed by Decree of USSR Council of Ministers of 22 September	Ch: 3	N: 146
1970	Regulations of 22 September	Ch: 10	N: 65
1972	Statute of the Ministry of Justice confirmed by Decree of the USSR Council of Ministers of 21 March (No. 194)	Ch: 3	N: 151
1972	Laws 572 and 573 of 3 August	Ch: 3	N: 154
1974	Statute on the Passport System confirmed by Decree of the USSR Council of Ministers of 28 August	Ch: 3	N: 145
1977	Constitution of 7 October	Ch: 1	N: 187
		Ch: 10	N: 64
		Ch: 12	N: 78
1978	Law on Citizenship of 1 December	Ch: 1	N: 188
1981	Law of 24 June on Legal Status of Foreign Citizens in the Ussr	Ch: 10	N: 64
		Ch: 13	N: 121
1986	Regulations on Entry into the USSR and Exit from the USSR of 23 August	Ch: 3	N: 147

UNITED ARAB EMIRATES

| 1971 | Provisional Constitution of 18 July | Ch: 4 | N: 66 |

UNITED KINGDOM OF GREAT BRITAIN AND NORTHERN IRELAND

930 AD	(Circa) – Statute of Aethelstan II, 2	Ch: 1	N: 22
1066	1066–1086 Ten Articles of William I	Ch: 1	N: 32
1215	Magna Carta	Ch: 2	N: 12
		Ch: 3	N: 57
1335	9 Ed III Stat. 1, c.I.	Ch: 2	N: 14
1351	Statute De Natis Ultra Mare 25 Ed III Stat. 1	Ch: 1	N: 29
1382	6 R 11 c.8	Ch: 2	N: 14
1387	11 R 11 c.7	Ch: 2	N; 14
1389	13 R 11 Stat. 1 c/20	Ch: 2	N: 14
1390	14 R 11 c.6	Ch: 2	N: 14
1391	16 R 11 c.3	Ch: 2	N: 14

1415	2 Hen V c.6	Ch: 2	N: 14
1436	15 Hen VI c.7	Ch: 2	N: 14
1708	Act of Anne 7 Ann c.5	Ch: 1	N: 442
1711	10 Ann. c.5	Ch: 1	N: 39
1730	British Nationality Act 4 Geo 11 c.21	Ch: 1	N: 82
1740	Act for the Naturalisation of Foreign Protestants Settled in the Colonies of America 13 Geo 11 c.7	Ch: 1	N: 56
1772	British Nationality Act 18 Geo 111 c.21	Ch: 1	N: 52
1773	Naturalisation Act 14 Geo 111 c.84	Ch: 1	N: 56
1792	Aliens Bill	Ch: 2	N: 12
1793	Aliens Bill	Ch: 2	N: 26
1793	Aliens Act 33 Geo 111 c.4	Ch: 2	N: 46
1794	Traiterous Correspondence Bill	Ch: 2	N: 28
1794	Libel Bill	Ch: 2	N: 28
1802	42 Geo 111 c.92	Ch: 2	N: 33
1802	43 Geo 111 c.155	Ch: 2	N: 33
1813	East India Company Act 58 Geo 111 c.155	Ch: 1	N: 50
1814	54 Geo. 111 c.155	Ch: 2	N: 33
1816	Aliens Act 56 Geo. 111 c.86	Ch: 2	N: 41
1818	Aliens Bill	Ch: 2	N: 33
1818	Aliens Act 56 Geo. 111 c.97	Ch: 2	N: 33
1822	Aliens Bill	Ch: 2	N: 33
1823	Lascars Act 4 Geo IV c.80	Ch: 2	N: 72
		Ch: 2	N: 73
1824	Aliens Act 5 Geo IV c.37	Ch: 2	N: 40
1826	Aliens Registration Act 7 Geo IV c.54	Ch: 2	N: 41
1836	Aliens Restriction Act (6 and 7 Will IV c.11)	Ch: 2	N: 42
1844	Aliens Act 10 and 11 Vict c.83	Ch: 2	N: 37
1848	Aliens Removal Act 11 and 12 Vict c.20	Ch: 2	N: 41
1867	British North America Act 30 and 31 Vict c.3	Ch: 1	N: 83
1870	Naturalisation Act 33 and 34 Vict c.14	Ch: 1	N: 68
		Ch: 1	N: 70
1882	Prevention of Crime (Ireland) Act 45 and 46 Vict c.25	Ch: 2	N: 42
1894	Merchant Shipping Act 57 and 58Vict c.60	Ch: 2	N: 73
1984	Aliens Bill	Ch: 2	N: 111
1878	Aliens Bill	Ch: 2	N: 111
1904	Aliens Bill	Ch: 2	N: 112
1905	Aliens Bill	Ch: 2	N: 114
1905	Aliens Act 5 Ed VII c.13	Ch: 2	N: 43
1914	British Nationality and Status of Aliens Act 4 and 5 Geo IV c.17 to 6 and 7 Geo IV c.14	Ch: 1	N: 54
1914	Aliens Restriction Act 4 and 5 Geo V c.12	Ch: 2	N: 118
		Ch: 3	N: 121
1914	Aliens Restriction (Belgian Refugees) Order S.I. 1478	Ch: 2	N: 121
1914	Aliens Restriction (Consolidation) Order S.I. 1374	Ch: 2	N: 121
1918	British Nationality and Status of Aliens act 8 and 9 Geo V c.38	Ch: 1	N: 75
1919	Aliens Order S.I. 1077	Ch: 2	N: 133
1919	Aliens Restriction (Amendment) Act 9 and 10 Geo V c.92	Ch: 2	N: 119
		Ch: 5	N: 51

550

UNITED STATES OF AMERICA

554

1945	War Brides Act of 28 December 59 Stat. 659	Ch: 2	N: 170
1946	G.I Fiancees Act of 29 June 60 Stat. 339	Ch: 2	N: 171
1946	Act of 2 July 60 Stat. 416	Ch: 2	N: 162
1946	Presidential Proclamation of 4 July 60 Stat. 1353	Ch: 2	N: 162
1947	UN-US Headquarters Agreement Accepted 4 August 61 Stat. 756	Ch: 5	N: 105
1948	Displaced Persons Act of 25 June 62 Stat. 1009	Ch: 2	N: 172
1950	Act of 16 June 64 Stat. 219	Ch: 2	N: 173
1952	Immigration and Nationality Act (Walter McCarren Act) of 27 June 66 Stat. 163	Ch: Int	N: 40
		Ch: 1	N: 148
		Ch: 3	N: 102, 112, 212
		Ch: 5	N: 14, 39, 77, 99, 122
		Ch: 9	N: 73, 165
		Ch: 10	N: 59, 62
		Ch: 11	N: 19, 20, 21, 61, 62, 118, 119, 158
		Ch: 12	N: 126
		Ch: 13	N: 75
1957	Immigration and Nationality Act 11 September (P.L 85–316) 71 Stat. 63	Ch: 1	N: 164
		Ch: 5	N: 48
		Ch: 9	N: 165
1959	Immigration and Nationality Act 22 September (P.L 86–363)	Ch: 4	N: 166
1959	Departmental Regulation 108.411, 24 F.R. 6682 of 18 August	Ch: 5	N: 106
1965	Immigration and Nationality Act of 3 October 79 Stat. 911	Ch: 2	N: 179
		Ch: 9	N: 165
1966	Cuban Adjustment Act	Ch: 11	N: 62
1980	Refugee Act P.L. No. 96–212 94 Stat. 102	Ch: 12	N: 126
		Ch: 12	N: 289
1981	Temporary Mexican Workers Act under title VI of Omnibus Immigration Act 97th Cong. 1st Session, S.601	Ch: 9	N: 88
1981	Migrant and Seasonal Agricultural Workers Protection Act 96 Stat. 2583	Ch: 9	N: 89
		Ch: 10	N: 62
1983	Immigration Reform and Control Act (Simpson-Mazzoli Bill)	Ch: 9	N: 88
		Ch: 12	N: 135
1983	Aliens Act	Ch: 11	N: 159
1986	Immigration Reform Control Act of 14 October	Ch: 9	N: 89

URUGUAY

| 1976 | Constitution of 27 June | Ch: 11 | N: 18 |

VANUATU

1971	Immigration Regulation (No. 18)	Ch: 4	N: 143
1980	Joint Regulation 21	Ch: 4	N: 143
1984	Immigration Regulation (Amendment) Act (No. 8)	Ch: 4	N: 143

VENEZUELA

1919	Immigration Law of 24 June	Ch: 2	N: 99
1961	Constitution of 23 January (as amended)	Ch: 4	N: 67
		Ch: 3	N: 53
		Ch: 11	N: 18
1973	Constitution of May 1973	Ch: 12	N: 95

VIETNAM (DEMOCRATIC REPUBLIC)

1960	Constitution of 1 January	Ch: 12	N: 91
1980	Constitution of 18 December	Ch: 11	N: 18

YEMEN (DEMOCRATIC REPUBLIC)

1978	Constitution of 31 October	Ch: 11	N: 18
		Ch: 12	N: 101

YUGOSLAVIA

1974	Constitution of 21 February	Ch: 12	N: 88
1974	Aliens Act	Ch: 11	N: 156

ZAIRE

1967	Constitution of 25 June (as amended)	Ch: 4	N: 68
		Ch: 12	N: 102
1978	Amended Constitution of 15 February	Ch: 12	N: 102

ZAMBIA

1965	Immigration and Deportation Regulations	Ch: 4	N: 77
1965	Immigration and Deportation Act (No. 29)	Ch: 4	N: 77
		Ch: 9	N: 186
1967	Immigration and Deportation Regulations (Commencement) Order	Ch: 4	N: 77
1967	Immigration and Deportation (Amendment) Act (No. 20)	Ch: 4	N: 77
1967	Immigration and Deportation Amendment (No. 3) Regulations	Ch: 4	N: 77
1968	Trades Licensing Act (No. 41)	Ch: 4	N: 77
		Ch: 9	N: 186
1969	Trades Licensing (Amendment) Act (No. 41)	Ch: 4	N: 77
1973	Constitution of 25 August	Ch: 4	N: 69
		Ch:3	N: 5

556

Table of Treaties and Other International Instruments

1921	Convention and Statute on Freedom of Transit, Barcelona, 20 April; 7 LNTS 11	Ch: 10	N: 58
1922	Arrangement with Regard to the Issue of Identity Certificates to Russian Refugees, Geneva, 5 July; 13 LNTS 237	Ch: 12	N: 53
1923	Treaty of Peace, Lausanne, 30 January; 32 LNTS 75	Ch: 13	N: 170
1923	Central American Convention on Extradition, Washington, 7 February; 2 Hudson 954	Ch: 7	N: 88
1923	Treaty between South Africa and Portugal, Lisbon, 31 March; 18 LNTS 30	Ch: 10	N: 24
1923	Convention on the International Regime of Maritime Ports, Geneva, 9 December; 58 LNTS 285	Ch: 5 Ch: 10	N: 158 N: 58
1925	Convention on the Status of Aliens, Havana, 20 February; 4 USTS 4722	Ch: 4	N: 18
1925	Treaty of Friendship, Commerce and Consular Rights between the United States and Estonia, Washington, 23 December; 7 Bevans 820	Ch: 10	N: 60
1926	Arrangement Relating to the Issue of Identity Certificates to Russian and Armenian Refugees, Geneva, 12 May: 89 LNTS 47	Ch: 12	N: 53, 163
1926	Convention concerning the Simplification of the Inspection of Emigrants on Board Ship, ILO Convention No. 21, Geneva, 5 June 1926; 38 UNTS 281	Ch: 9	N: 3
1926	Convention concerning Seamens' Articles of Agreement, ILO Convention No. 22, Geneva, 24 June; 38 UNTS 295	Ch: 9	N: 5
1926	Convention concerning the Repatriation of Seamen, ILO Convention No. 23, Geneva, 23 June; 38 UNTS 315	Ch: 9	N: 6
1926	Agreement on Implementation of Treaty of Lausanne, 1 December; 68 LNTS 11	Ch: 13	N: 170
1927	Treaty of Friendship, Commerce and Consular Rights between the United States and Honduras, Tegucigalpa, 7 December; 8 Bevans 905	Ch: 10	N: 60
1928	Convention concerning the Status of Aliens, Havana, 20 February; 132 LNTS 301	Int Ch: 2	N: 46 N: 149
1928	Convention on Asylum, Havana, 20 February; 132 LNTS 323	Ch: 12	N: 257
1928	Pan American Convention on Diplomatic Officers, Havana, 20 February; 155 LNTS 259	Ch: 5	N: 63
1928	'Bustamante' Code on Asylum, Havana, 20 February; 4 Hudson 2412	Ch: 7	N: 89
1928	Treaty of Friendship, Commerce and Consular Rights between the United States and Latvia, Riga, 20 April; 80 LNTS 35	Ch: 10	N: 60
1928	Arrangement Facilitating the Admission of Student Employees between Great Britain and France, Paris, 16 May; 80 LNTS 257	Ch: 10	N: 45
1928	Treaty of Friendship, Commerce and Consular Rights between the United States and Norway, Washington, 5		

	June; 134 LNTS 81	Ch: 10	N: 60
1928	Treaty of Friendship, Commerce and Consular Rights between the United States and Austria, Vienna, 18 June; 5 Bevans 341	Ch: 10	N: 60
1928	Arrangement Concerning the Extension to Other Categories of Refugees of Certain Measures in Favour of Russian and Armenian Refugees, Geneva, 30 June; 93 LNTS 377	Ch: 12	N: 53, 163
1928	Convention relating to the Introduction of Native Labour from Mozambique into the Province of the Transvaal, Railway Matters and the Commercial Intercourse between South Africa and Mozambique (Portugal), Pretoria, 11 September; 197 LNTS 306	Ch: 10	N: 25
1929	Draft Convention adopted at the International Conference on the Treatment of Foreigners, Paris, 5 March; L.N. Doc. C 36 M 21 (1929–II) 421; L.N. Publication 1929 II 5	Ch: 2	N: 150
1929	International Convention for the Safety of Life at Sea, London, 31 May; 136 LNTS 81	Ch: 5	N: 156
1930	Convention concerning Certain Questions relating to the Conflict of Nationality Laws, The Hague, 12 April; 179 LNTS 89	Ch: 1	N: 222, 283
1930	Protocol relating to a Certain Case of Statelessness, The Hague, 12 April; 179 LNTS 116	Ch: 1	N: 283
1930	Special Protocol on Statelessness, The Hague, 12 April; UKTS No. 112	Ch: 4	N: 154
1930	Protocol relating to Military Obligations in Certain Cases of Double Nationality, The Hague, 12 April; 178 LNTS 227	Ch: 1	N: 88, 285
1930	Convention concerning Forced or Compulsory Labour, ILO Convention No. 29, Geneva, 28 June; 39 UNTS 55	Ch: 9	N: 7
1930	Exchange of Notes Facilitating the Admission of Student Employees into France and the Netherlands, Paris 16 and 29 October; 125 LNTS 29	Ch: 10	N: 45
1931	Exchange of Notes Regarding the Admission into the United Kingdom of Student Employees from the Netherlands, London, 12 January, 23 March and 9 April; 125 LNTS 41	Ch: 10	N: 45
1931	Treaty of Establishment and Sojourn between the United States and Turkey, Ankara, 28 October; 138 LNTS 345	Ch: 10	N: 60
1933	Treaty on Labour Establishment between the Netherlands and Belgium, Protocol and Exchange of Notes, Geneva, 20 February, and Brussels, 7 January 1936; 165 LNTS 383	Ch: 8	N: 20
1933	Convention concerning Establishment and Labour between Luxembourg and the Netherlands, The Hague, 1 April; 179 LNTS 11	Ch: 8	N: 20
1933	Convention relating to the International Status of Refugees, Geneva, 28 October; 159 LNTS 199	Ch: 1 Ch: 12	N: 289 N: 28, 163, 258
1933	Convention on Political Asylum: Montevideo, 3–26 December; 28 AJIL (1934) Supp. 70	Ch: 12	N: 38, 257

562

1950	Agreement concerning the Free Movement of Persons between Belgium and Luxembourg, Luxembourg, 6 April; 65 UNTS 147	Ch: 8	N: 7
1950	Minorities Treaty. Agreement between Pakistan and India, New Delhi, 8 April; 131 UNTS 4	Ch: 1	N: 276
1950	Convention concerning Student Employees, Brussels, 17 April; UKTS 1951 (No. 8)	Ch: 10	N: 47
1950	Convention on Frontier Workers, Brussels, 17 April; 131 UNTS 99	Ch: 10	N: 16
1950	Agreement concerning the Free Movement of Persons between Belgium and Luxembourg, Luxembourg, 13 and 19 September; 79 UNTS 328	Ch: 8	N: 8
1950	European Convention on Human Rights, Rome, 4 November; 213 Unts 223	Ch: 7 Ch: 10 Ch: 11 Ch: 13	N: 22, 177 N: 201 N: 5 N: 127
1950	Statute of the UNHCR, UNGA Res. 428 (v) of 14 December	Ch: 12	N: 39
1950	Agreement concerning the Exchange of Student Employees between France and Turkey, Paris, 22 December; 98 UNTS 11	Ch: 10	N: 46
1951	Agreement for Assisted Migration between Australia and the Netherlands, Canberra, 22 February; 128 UNTS 115	Ch: 9	N: 79
1951	Arrangement concerning the Admission of Student Employees between Belgium and Finland, Brussels, 20 March; 110 UNTS 27	Ch: 10	NL 45
1951	Agreement between the Federal Republic of Germany and Italy on the Admission of Workers, Rome, 21 March; G.U. 1953 No. 22	Ch: 9	N: 140
1951	Agreement on Assisted Migration between Australia and Italy, Melbourne, 29 March; 131 UNTS 187	Ch: 9	N: 79
1951	European Coal and Steel Community Treaty, Paris, 18 April; 261 UNTS 140	Ch: 6	N: 5
1951	NATO Status of Forces Agreement, London, 19 June; 199 UNTS 67	Ch: 5	N: 116
1951	Convention relating to the Status of Refugees, Geneva, 28 July; 189 UNTS 150	Ch: 1 Ch: 1 Ch: 6 Ch: 11 Ch: 12 Ch: 13	N: 114 N: 290 N: 91 N: 55, 56 N: 10 N: 128
1951	Treaty of Friendship, Commerce and Navigation between the United States and Greece, Athens, 3 August; 224 UNTS 279	Ch: 10	N: 60
1951	Treaty of Friendship, Commerce and Navigation between the United States and Israel, Washington, 23 August; 219 UNTS 237	Ch: 10	N: 60
1951	Treaty of Amity and Economic Relations between the		

	United States and Ethiopia, Addis Ababa, 7 September; 205 UNTS 41	Ch: 10	N: 60
1951	Agreement between Canada and Italy for the Settlement of Certain Canadian War Claims and the Release of Italian Assets in Canada, Ottawa, 20 September, 236 UNTS 252	Ch: 1	N: 272
1951	Treaty of Friendship, Commerce and Navigation between the United States and Denmark, Copenhagen, 1 October; 421 UNTS 105	Ch: 10	N: 60
1951	Agreement on the Status of NATO National Representatives and International Staff, Ottawa, 12 December; 5 UST 1087	Ch: 5	N: 117
1952	Agreement on the Recruitment of Workers between the Federal Republic of Germany and Spain, Bonn, 25 January; Boletin Oficial 1953, 1616	Ch: 9	N: 127
1952	Treaty of Friendship, Establishment and Navigation between the United States and Luxembourg, Luxembourg, 23 February; 474 UNTS 3	Ch: 10	N: 60
1952	Convention concerning Social Security (Minimum Standards), ILO Convention No. 102, Geneva, 28 June; 210 UNTS 131	Ch: 8	N: 74
1952	Protocol on the Status of the International Military Headquarters, Paris, 28 August; 5 UST 870	Ch: 5	N: 118
1952	Agreement on Assisted Migration between Australia and the Federal Republic of Germany, Bonn, 29 August; 184 UNTS 147	Ch: 9	N: 79
1952	First Protocol on the Universal Copyright Convention concerning the Application of that Convention to the Works of Stateless Persons and Refugees, Geneva, 6 October; 216 UNTS 176	Ch: 1	N: 290
1952	Exchange of Notes concerning Exchange of Student Employees between the Netherlands and Switzerland, Berne, 20 November; 163 UNTS 121	Ch: 10	N: 46
1953	Agreement for the Liberalization of Minor Frontier Traffic between Belgium and the Netherlands, Brussels, 26 March; 165 UNTS 297	Ch: 8	N: 9
1953	Treaty of Friendship, Commerce and Navigation between the United States and Japan, Tokyo, 2 April; 206 UNTS 143	Ch: 10	N: 60
1953	Agreement on the Recruitment of Workers between the Federal Republic of Germany and Italy, Bonn, 5 May; BGBl 1969, 134	Ch: 9	N: 126
1953	Agreement concerning Exchange of Student Employees between Sweden and Germany, Bonn, 15 May; 227 UNTS 195	Ch: 10	N: 46
1953	ILO Constitution, Instrument of Amendment, Geneva, 25 June; 191 UNTS 143	Ch: 9	N: 14
1953	European Interim Agreement on Social Security Schemes relating to Old Age, Invalidity and Survivors (with Protocol), Paris, 11 December; 218 UNTS 211	Ch: 7	N: 56, 158
1954	Agreement regarding the Status of the UN Forces in		

568

between France and Tunisia, Paris, 6 March; J.O. (1955)
609   Ch: 1   N: 200

1955	Agreement to Improve the Condition of Refugees Settled in Belgium and Luxembourg and to Facilitate their Movement between the Two Countries, Luxembourg, 4 April; 211 UNTS 57	Ch: 8	N: 11
1955	Agreement concerning the Movement of Refugees between the Netherlands and Luxembourg, Luxembroug, 4 May; 292 UNTS 17	Ch: 8	N: 11
1955	Treaty of Amity, Economic Relations and Consular Rights between the United States and Iran, Tehran, 15 August; 284 UNTS 93	Ch: 10	N: 60
1955	Convention on Citizenship between France and Vietnam, Paris, 16 August; Recueil (1959) 7	Ch: 1	N: 200
1955	Exchange of Notes between the United States and the Philippines implementing Provisions of the Act of 18 June 1954, 6 September; 238 UNTS 109	Ch: 10	N: 60
1955	Exchange of Notes concerning Exchange of Student Employees between Sweden and Austria, Vienna, 3 November; 262 UNTS 289	Ch: 10	N: 46
1955	Protocol of Accession to the Nordic Labour Agreement, Stockholm, 3 November 1955, 199 UNTS 29	Ch: 8	N: 29
1955	European Convention on Establishment, Paris, 13 December; 529 UNTS 141	Ch: 7	N: 6, 57, 126, 178
		Ch: 10	N: 5
		Ch: 13	N: 161, 182
1956	Exchange of Letters concerning Exchange of Student Employees between Belgium and Austria, Brussels, 20 January; 248 UNTS 3	Ch: 10	N: 46
1956	Agreement on the Recruitment of Migrant Workers between France and Spain, 17 March; 1 Censo de Tratados Internacionales 228	Ch: 9	N: 140
1956	Treaty of Friendship, Commerce and Navigation between the United States and Surinam, The Hague, 27 March; 285 UNTS 231		
1956	Treaty of Friendship, Commerce and Navigation between the United States and the Netherlands, The Hague, 27 March; 285 UNTS 231	Ch: 10	N: 60
1956	Hague Labour Treaty, The Hague, 7 June; 381 UNTS 158	Ch: 8	N: 13
1956	Netherlands Assisted Migration Agreement, The Hague, 1 August; 280 UNTS 3	Ch: 9	N: 82
1956	Treaty of Friendship, Commerce and Navigation between the United States and the Republic of Korea, Seoul, 28 November; 301 UNTS 281	Ch: 10	N: 60
1956	Convention respecting Emigration between Belgium and Spain, Brussels, 28 November; 308 UNTS 285	Ch: 9	N: 80
		Ch: 11	N: 47
1957	Exchange of Letters Constituting an Agreement between the United Nations and Egypt in respect of the UN		

	Expeditionary Force, New York, 8 February; 260 UNTS 61	Ch: 5	N: 84
1957	Convention on the Nationality of Married Women, New York, 20 February; 309 UNTS 65	Ch: 1	N: 297
1957	Provisional Labour Agreement, Brussels, 20 March; Bulletin Trimestriel Benelux No. 1, June 1957 p. 31	Ch: 8	N: 14
1957	Agreement on the Time Limits and Procedure of Further Repatriation from the USSR of Persons of Polish Nationality, Moscow, 25 March; 281 UNTS 121	Ch: 3	N: 159
1957	Treaty establishing the European Economic Community, Rome, 25 March; 298 UNTS 11	Int:	N: 40
		Ch: 4	N: 94
		Ch: 6	N: 6
		Ch: 7	N: 70, 171
		Ch: 8	N: 36
1957	Treaty Establishing the European Atomic Energy Community, Rome, 25 March; 298 UNTS 169	Ch: 6	N: 5
1957	Agreement on the Recruitment of Migrant Workers between France and Spain, 27 March; Boletin Oficial 1957 1409	Ch: 9	N: 140
1957	Convention concerning the Waiver of Passport Control at the Intra-Nordic Frontiers, Copenhagen, 12 July; 322 UNTS 245	Ch: 8	N: 96
		Ch: 12	N: 115
1957	Agreement relating to Refugee Seamen, The Hague, 23 November; 506 UNTS 125	Ch: 12	N: 46
1957	European Convention on Extradition, Paris, 13 December; 359 UNTS 276	Ch: 7	N: 7, 83
1957	European Agreement on Regulations governing the Movement of Persons between Member States of the Council of Europe, Paris, 13 December; 315 UNTS 139	Ch: 10	N: 50
1958	Exchange of Notes constituting an Agreement relative to the Removal of Undesirable Persons between the Netherlands and Belgium, Brussels, 14 January and 4 February; 330 UNTS 83	Ch: 8	N: 12
1958	Cultural Agreement relating to the Admission of Foreign Students between the German Democratic Republic and the USSR, Berlin, 21 February; 6 DARDDR 425	Ch: 10	N: 44
1958	Treaty of Peace, Friendship, Commerce and Navigation between the United States and Bolivia, La Paz, 13 May; 5 Bevans 721	Ch: 10	N: 60
1958	Convention concerning Discrimination (Employment and Occupation), ILO Convention No. 111, Geneva, 25 June; 362 UNTS 31	Ch: 8	N: 74
1958	Workmen's Compensation Agreement between Rhodesia/ Nyasaland and South Africa, Salisbury, 11 October; 373 UNTS 75	Ch: 10	N: 36
1958	Agreement on the Recruitment of Migrant Workers between France and Portugal, 30 October; Recueil des traites et accords de la France 1956, 16	Ch: 9	N: 140

572

1962	Convention on Consent to Marriage, Minimum Age for Marriage and Registration of Marriages, New York, 10 December 1962; 521 UNTS 231	Ch: 11	N: 13
1963	Convention on the Reduction of Cases of Multiple Nationality, Strasbourg, 6 May; 634 UNTS 221	Ch: 1	N: 299
1963	Agreement on the Recruitment of Migrant Workers between the Federal Republic of Germany and Morocco, Bonn, 21 May; BGBl 1971 11 1365	Ch: 9	N: 130
1963	Agreement on the Recruitment of Migrant Workers between France and Morocco, Paris, 1 June; J.O.R.F. 2 August 1963 p. 7161	Ch: 9 Ch: 11	N: 141 N: 49
1963	Agreement on the Recruitment of Migrant Workers between France and Italy. Exchange of Notes, 2 August; 18 Diritto Internazionale (1964) 254	Ch: 9	N: 140
1963	Agreement on the Recruitment of Migrant Workers between France and Tunisia, Paris, 9 August; Recueil des traites et accords de la France, 1963, No. 70	Ch: 9	N: 141
1963	European Convention on Human Rights, Fourth Protocol. Strasbourg, 16 September; 58 AJIL (1964) 334, ETS No. 46	Ch: 3 Ch: 4 Ch: 4 Ch: 7 Ch: 13	N: 5, 66 N: 17 N: 93 N: 3 N: 180
1963	Agreement between the Netherlands and Portugal concerning Migration, Recruitment and Employment of Portuguese Workers, Lisbon, 22 November; 492 UNTS 31	Ch: 9	N: 81
1963	European Agreement on the Abolition of Visas for Refugees, Strasbourg, 4 December; ETS No. 31	Ch: 10	N: 55
1964	Exhange of Letters constituting an Agreement concerning the Status of the United Nations Peacekeeping Force in Cyprus, New York, 31 March; 492 UNTS 57	Ch: 5	N: 133
1964	European Code on Social Security, Strasbourg, 16 April; 648 UNTS 235	Ch: 7	N: 156
1964	Cultural Agreement relating to the Adsmission of Foreign Students between the German Democratic Republic and Ghana, Berlin, 14 May; 12 DARDDR 746	Ch: 10	N: 44
1964	Agreement between Austria and Turkey concerning the Recruitment and Employment of Turkish Workers, Vienna, 15 May; 515 UNTS 108	Ch: 9	N: 81
1964	Cultural Agreement relating to the Admission of Foreign Students between the German Democratic Republic and Guinea, Conakry, 29 May; 12 DARDDR 759	Ch: 10	N: 44
1964	Consular Convention between the USSR and the United States of America, Moscow, 1 June; 655 UNTS 213	Ch: 5	N: 72
1964	Cultural Agreement relating to the Admission of Foreign Students between the German Democratic Republic and Mali, Bemako, 3 June; 12 DARDDR 849	Ch: 10	N: 44
1964	Workmen's Compensation Agreement between Southern		

	Rhodesia and South Africa, Salisbury, 3 June; SATS 1964 No. 3	Ch: 10	N: 36
1964	Convention concerning Employment Injury Benefits, ILO Convention No. 121, Geneva, 8 July; 602 UNTS 259	Ch: 9	N: 75
1964	Convention concerning Employment Policy, ILO Convention No. 122 Geneva, 9 July; 569 UNTS 65	Ch: 8	N: 74
1964	ILO Recommendation No. 122 concerning Employment Policy	Ch: 9	N: 42, 73
1964	Exchange of Notes on the Regulation of Migration between France and Canada, 22 July; 1 Recueil general des traites de la France, Ser. II. Accords bilateraux non-publies	Ch: 9	N: 144
1964	Accarda tra l'Italia e la Svizzera relativo all'emigrazione dei lavoratori italiani in Svizzera, Rome, 10 August; G.U. No. 54, 2 March 1965, p. 988	Ch: 11	N: 45
1964	Agreement on the Recruitment of Migrant Workers between France and Spain, San Sebastian, 29 August; J.O.R.F. 7 January 1965, 171	Ch: 9	N: 140
1964	Convention on the Exchange of Information concerning Acquisition of Nationality, Paris, 10 September; 932 UNTS 81	Ch: 1	N: 300
1964	Agreement on the Recruitment of Migrant Workers between the Federal Republic of Germany and Turkey, Bonn, 30 September; BAnz 1968, 22	Ch: 9	N: 129
1964	Agreement concerning Mozambican Migrant Workers between the Government of South Africa and Portugal, 13 October 1964 and 1 January 1965; SATS 1964 No. 11	Ch: 10	N: 25
1964	Shasti-Banderanayake Pact on the Transfer of Populations between India and Sri Lanka, 30 October	Ch: 13	N: 174
1964	Treaty Establishing a Central African Economic and Customs Union, Geneva, 8 December; 4 ILM 699	Ch: 8	N: 47
1965	Council of Europe Recommendation 434 (1965) on the Right of Asylum	Ch: 7	N: 209, 223
1965	Protocol on the Privileges and Immunities of the European Communities, Brussels, 8 April; 1 Ybk (1965) 429	Ch: 5	N: 83
1965	L'echange de lettres entre la France et Saint Marin, destine a permettre aux travaillerus San-Marinais en France de beneficier des avantages accordes aux ressortissants italiens en matiere d'allocations familiales, Paris, 21 May; J.O.R.F. 21 and 22 June, p. 5155	Ch: 11	N: 50
1965	Cultural Agreement relating to the Admission of Foreign Students between the German Democratic Republic and Mongolia, Berlin, 28 May 1965; 336 D.Z 51	Ch: 10	N: 44
1965	Cultural Agreement relating to the Admission of Foreign Students between the German Democratic Republic and China, Beijing, 15 July; 1965 Agreements of the People's Republic of China 94	Ch: 10	N: 44
1965	General Convention on the Privileges and Immunities of the Organization of African Unity, Accra, 25 october; 1 Sohn 117	Ch: 5	N: 83

1969	Organization of African Unity Convention governing the Specific Aspects of Refugee Problems in Africa, Addis Ababa, 10 September; 1001 UNTS 46	Ch: 10	N: 27
		Ch: 12	N: 52
1969	American Convention on Human Rights, San Jose, 22 November; 9 ILM (1970) 673	Ch: 3	N: 6
		Ch: 4	N: 15, 93
		Ch: 11	N: 6
		Ch: 12	N: 50
		Ch: 13	N: 181
1969	European Agreement on Au Pair Placement, Strasbourg, 24 November; ETS No. 68	Ch: 10	N: 56
1970	Council of Europe Resolution 70 (2) on the Acquisition by Refugees of Nationality	Ch: 7	N: 243
1970	Exchange of Notes concerning Mozambican Migrant Labour between the Governments of South Africa and Portugal, Pretoria, 1 January and 26 March; SATS 1970 No. 3	Ch: 10	N: 25
1970	Convention concerning the Employment and Residence in Belgium of Algerian Workers and their Families, Algiers, 8 January; 717 UNTS 321	Ch: 9	N: 80
		Ch: 11	N: 44
1970	Agreement on the Residence and Employment of Yugoslav Citizens in Australia, Canberra, 12 February; 742 UNTS 299		
1970	Protocol d'Accord of C.E.A.O., Bamako, 21 May;	Ch: 8	N: 29
1970	Agreement of the Resettlement of Vietnamese Refugees between Japan and South Vietnam, Tokyo, 20 May; O van Kien Ngoai-Giao	Ch: 11	N: 59
1970	Convention concerning Minimum Wage Fixing with Special Reference to Developing Countries, ILO Convention No. 131, Geneva, 22 June; 825 UNTS 77	Ch: 8	N: 74
1970	Convention concerning the Employment and Residence in Belgium of Yugoslav Workers, Belgrade, 23 July; 784 UNTS 223	Ch: 9	N: 80
1970	Statute of the World Tourism Organization, Mexico City, 27 September; 27 UST 2213	Ch: 10	N: 10, 48
1970	Convention on the Unlawful Seizure of Aircraft, The Hague, 16 December; 860 UNTS 105	Ch: 7	N: 117
1971	Council of Europe Regulation 1408/71 of 14 June on the Application of Social Security Schemes, O.J. Sp. Ed. 1971 416	Ch: 6	N: 84, 95, 103
		Ch: 7	N: 161, 186
1971	Agreement on the Recruitment of Migrant Workers between the Federal Republic of Germany and Turkey, Bonn, 15 June; Resmi Gazete 1971, 2409	Ch: 9	N: 129
1971	Convention for the Suppression of Unlawful Acts against the Safety of Civil Aviation, Monttreal, 23 September; 10 ILM (1971) 1151	Ch: 7	N: 118
1972	Constitution of the International Labour Organization,		

	Instrument of Amendment, Geneva, 22 June; UKTS 110 (1975)	Ch: 9	N: 14
1972	Agreement on the Recruitment of Migrant Workers between the Federal republic of Germany and Turkey, Bonn, 7 December; BGBl 1973 11 747	Ch: 9	N: 129
1972	European Convention on Social Security, Paris, 14 December; ETS No. 78	Ch: 7	N: 9, 155
1973	General Convention on Social Security between France and Algeria, Paris, 23 January; 964 UNTS 248	Ch: 9	N: 143
1973	Decision 70 de la Comision del Acuerdo de Cartagena contenido las condiciones para la adhesion de Venezuela al Acuerdo y Acta final de las negociaciones entre la Comision del Acuerdo de Cartagena y el Gobierno de Venezuela para la adhesion de dicha pais la Acuerdo, Lima, 13 February;	Ch: 8	N: 69
1973	Treaty Establishing the Economic Community of West Africa (Communaute economique de l'Afrique de l'Ouest), Abidjan, 17 April;	Ch: 8	N; 29
1973	Protocol relating to Refugee Seamen, The Hague, 12 June; 965 UNTS 445	Ch: 12	N: 46
1973	Treaty Establishing the Caribbean Community, Chaguaranas, 4 July; 947 UNTS 17	Ch: 8	N: 64
1973	Labour Agreement between South Africa and Lesotho, Pretoria and Maseru, 24 August; SATS 1973 No. 1	Ch: 10	N: 33
1973	Agreement on the Resettlement of Vietnamese Refugees between Japan and South Vietnam, Tokyo, 3 October; Joyakushu 759	Ch: 11	N: 59
1973	EEC Association Agreement with Turkey, Ankara, 12 September; O.J.C. 113 24 December 1973, p. 2	Ch: 6	N: 7
1973	Convention on the Prevention and Punishment of Crimes against Internationally Protected Persons, Including Diplomatic Agents, New York, 14 December; 28 UST 1975; 13 ILM (1974) 41	Ch: 7 Ch: 12	N: 119 N: 284
1973	Labour Agreement between South Africa and Botswana, Pretoria and Gabarone, 24 December; SATS 1973 No. 3	Ch: 10	N: 32
1974	Agreement between India and Sri Lanka concerning the Status and Future of 150,000 Persons of Indian Origin, New Delhi, 27 January; Indian Ministry of External Affairs Report (1975) 162	Ch: 13	N: 174
1974	Agreement on the Resettlement of Vietnamese Refugees between Japan and South Vietnam, Tokyo, 30 March; Joyakushu 1055	Ch: 11	N: 59
1974	Cooperation Agreement on Manpower between the Gabonese Republic and the United Republic of Cameroon, Yaounde, 9 August; Official Gazette of the United Republic of Cameroon, 15 May 1977, No. 10, p. 999	Ch: 11	N: 48
1974	Memorandum of Understanding between Australia and Tonga, October	Ch: 10	N: 42

580

	25 February; Cmnd. 9096	Ch: 1	N: 279
1982	Convention on the Elimination of Mercenarism in Africa. Benin, 3 May	Ch: 12	N: 164
1982	Convention concerning Rights in Social Security, ILO Convention No. 157, Geneva, 21 June; ILO Official Bulletin (1982) Ser. A. No. 2, p. 61	Ch: 9	N: 68, 191
1982	Double Taxation Agreement between the United Kingdom and Tunisia, London, 15 December; Cmnd. 9345	Ch: 1	N: 279
1982	Exchange of Notes between the Government of the United Kingdom and the Government of the Italian Republic replacing the Declaration on the Definition of the Term Nationality made at the Time of Signature of the Treaty of Accession of 22 January 1972 by the United Kingdom to the European Community, Rome, 31 December; UKTS 67 (1983); O.J. (1983) C 23 1	Ch: Int Ch: 3	N: 34 N: 128
1983	Promotion of Investments Agreement between the United Kingdom and St Lucia, Castries, 18 January; Cmnd. 8872	Ch: 1	N: 279
1983	Double Taxation Agreement between the United Kingdom and Sweden, Stockholm, 30 August; Cmnd. 9330	Ch: 1	N: 279
1983	Concluding Document of the Madrid Session of the Conference on Security and Cooperation in Europe, 11 November 1980; 22 I.L.M. 1395	Ch: 3 Ch: 11	N: 4 N: 4
1983	Promotion of Investments Agreement between the United Kingdom and Panama, Panama City, 7 October; Cmnd. 9736	Ch: 1	N: 279
1983	Economic Community of Central African States, treaty, Libreville, 19 October; 23 ILM (1984) 945	Ch: 8	N: 51
1983	Double Taxation Agreement between the United Kingdom and New Zealand, London, 22 December; Cmnd. 9264	Ch: 1	N: 279
1984	Recommendation R(84) 1 on the Protection of Persons not Formally Recognized as Refugees	Ch: 7	N: 228
1984	Draft Declaration of Principles of International Law on Mass Expulsion. American Society of International Law; 78 Proc. A.S.I.L. (1984) 342	Ch: 13	N: 167
1984	The Employment Policy (Supplementary Provisions) Convention, ILO Convention No. 168 and 169	Ch: 9	N: 75
1984	Double Taxation Agreement between the United Kingdom and Togo, London, 9 February, Cmnd. 9229	Ch: 1	N: 279
1984	Accord between South Africa and Mozambique, Nkomati, 16 March	Ch: 10	N: 30
1984	Double Taxation Agreement between the United Kingdom and China, Beijing, 26 July; Cmnd. 9439	Ch: 1	N: 279
1984	European Convention on Human Rights, Seventh Protocol 27 November; Council of Europe No. 117	Ch: 7	N: 4
1984	Third Treaty of Lome, 8 December; 24 ILM (1985) 571	Ch: 6	N: 8
1985	Act concerning the Conditions of Accession of the Kingdom of Spain and the Portuguese Republic to the European Community, Articles 55–60, annexed to Treaty		

	of Accession, 12 June; O.J. 1985 L 302/9 at 35	Ch: 6	N: 3
1985	Treaty of Schengen, 14 June; J.O.R.F. 5 August 1986	Ch: 8	N: 2
1985	Double Taxation Agreement between the United Kingdom and Norway, Oslo, 3 October; Cmnd. 9730	Ch: 1	N: 279
1985	Joint Declaration on the Status of Hong Kong, Beijing, 19 December; UKTS No. 26 (1985)	Ch: 1	N: 146
1986	Single European Act. The Hague. 17 and 28 February; 25 I.L.M. (1986) 506	Ch: 6	N: 4, 105, 106, 107, 108, 109
		Ch: 8	N: 3
1986	South Africa-Swaziland Labour Agreement, Pretoria, 22 August; SATS 1986 No.3	Ch: 10	N: 34

Index

586